SOLDIERS OF CHRIST

SOLDIERS OF CHRIST

Preaching in Late Medieval and Reformation France

LARISSA TAYLOR

New York   Oxford
OXFORD UNIVERSITY PRESS
1992

Oxford University Press

Oxford   New York   Toronto
Delhi   Bombay   Calcutta   Madras   Karachi
Petaling Jaya   Singapore   Hong Kong   Tokyo
Nairobi   Dar es Salaam   Cape Town
Melbourne   Auckland

and associated companies in
Berlin   Ibadan

Copyright © 1992 by Oxford University Press, Inc.

Published by Oxford University Press, Inc.,
200 Madison Avenue, New York, New York 10016

Oxford is a registered trademark of Oxford University Press

Library of Congress Cataloging-in-Publication Data
Taylor, Larissa.
Soldiers of Christ : preaching in late medieval
and reformation France / Larissa Taylor.
p. cm.   Includes bibliographical references and index.
ISBN 0-19-506993-5
1. Preaching—France—History.
2. France—Religious life and customs.   I. Title.
BV4208.F8T38   1992
251'.00944'09024—dc20
91-26715

1 3 5 7 9 8 3 4 2

Printed in the United States of America
on acid-free paper

To Jim and Brian Mahoney

Preface

This book was conceived in a 1982 graduate reading course at Brown University on the nature of late medieval piety in which we began by trying to define piety. Going beyond a dictionary definition proved unexpectedly difficult, for while one might say "devoutness," "spirituality," or "orthodox behavior," the term inevitably provoked subjective responses. The attempt to define piety was useful because it sensitized us to a larger problem: By whose standards can piety be measured? Although it is impossible to eliminate bias altogether, what I have striven for in this book is an approach that sets such terms (and there are many) within the context of the times. So "What is piety?" becomes "What did pious behavior mean to a medieval man?" Similarly, concepts such as Christianity have different meanings at different times. To a medieval woman, proper Christian behavior would undoubtedly mean something quite different than it would for a contemporary woman. Medieval values, must, therefore, be approached with sensitivity and without judgmental attitudes that can only interfere with our understanding of the past.

As we began reading secondary sources on religious history and *mentalités* for the period 1450–1550, it soon became apparent that there was a relative lack of works in English on French religious history in the late medieval and Reformation era. Although this is not a problem for most scholars and graduate students, it posed the prospect of future difficulties in teaching this subject to undergraduates. Despite major recent contributions by D. Catherine Brown, Natalie Zemon Davis, Jean Delumeau, Carlos Eire, James Farge, A. N. Galpern, Mark Greengrass, and others, I still found it necessary seven years later to make French a course requirement when I taught a seminar at Wellesley College on the French Renaissance. By contrast, there is a great deal of material in English for Germany and Italy in the same period. Does fascination with the "German Reformation" and the "Italian Renaissance" discourage scholars from studying the fifteenth and sixteenth centuries in other countries? This may be part of the problem, but there is another reason as well. In both teaching and research, there has been a tendency to bracket time periods, such as "The Middle Ages, 500–1500," or "Early Modern Europe, 1500–1789." In both cases, the years around 1500 are ignored in regions of Europe where they were not as "eventful" as in Italy and

Germany. I came out of the reading course at Brown hoping to one day make a contribution to this missing but very important period of religious change in France.

To do so required a comprehensive study of France during this period. In the past few decades, numerous regional studies have appeared (mostly in French) that have added tremendously to our knowledge of the beliefs and behaviors of ordinary men and women. The value of these works cannot be overstated, but at the risk of generalization, I chose not to limit my study to a particular city or region. The topic of sermons provided an ideal subject for a synthetic study, although my original plan to study early Protestant sermons proved impossible because of lack of sources. Fortunately, the large number of extant Catholic sermons offered an ideal opportunity to study *mentalités* using a source that had, for the most part, been neglected. The subject was a stimulating one, for it revived questions about late medieval piety that had been explored in the reading course. To my delight, the sermons provided a much broader picture of religious life at the end of the Middle Ages than one might expect from such a study, and challenged many of my beliefs about the late medieval church. Replete with zeal, outrage, frustration, gentleness, and humor, the sermons were never dull. They offered a panoramic view of contemporary religion and society at this critical juncture in French history and society.

I have incurred many scholarly debts during the research and writing of this book. Phil Benedict devised the reading course at Brown, and was the first to suggest the possibility of working on sermons. In the ensuing ten years, he has guided and criticized my work, making this a much better book than it would otherwise have been. Nancy Roelker and Tony Molho read it in a number of versions, and offered very useful advice and support. James Smither, D. Catherine Brown, and R. Po-chia Hsia all read the manuscript and offered suggestions that have improved the book immeasurably.

As an undergraduate I was fortunate to have had the opportunity to work with a leading Reformation scholar, Steven Ozment, who inspired me with a love of sixteenth-century religious history. His ideas and his friendship have been a spur to me throughout the years. I would also like to thank Alice Robinson, my first history adviser, and more recently a friend and colleague, for her continuous support. Encouragement and help also came from my seminar students at Wellesley College, especially my research assistants, Donna Padar and Elizabeth Putnam.

I was introduced to the world of French historical scholarship by Christiane Klapisch-Zuber, André Godin, and Denis Crouzet. Christiane Klapisch-Zuber, in particular, is a dear friend to whom I owe a great deal. Although Hervé Martin and I have never met, we have corresponded regularly, sharing our sometimes different perspectives on an overlapping group of preachers. Without his work, my own would be much less complete. The helpfulness of the staff at the Bibliothèque Nationale, especially Bernard Blot, Bernard Riester, and Michel Bourdon, made my task much easier. I would also like to extend my gratitude to the library staffs of the Bibliothèque Sainte-

Geneviève and the Société de l'histoire du protestantisme français, as well as the archivists at the Archives Départementales de la Seine-Maritime in Rouen and the Archives municipales in Dijon.

I owe a debt of gratitude to Burr Litchfield, who allowed me to use the History Department computer at Brown, making typing of the manuscript much easier. At Oxford University Press, special thanks must go to Paul Schlotthauer and Stephen Wagley, whose expertise was evident throughout the editing process. I would also like to thank Nancy Lane, my editor, and David Roll.

Wellesley, Massachusetts   L. T.
October 1991

AUTHOR'S NOTE

When translating from medieval Latin, I have made every attempt to render the original flavor of the language rather than giving a completely literal translation. Scripture texts are taken from The New American Bible with Revised New Testament copyright © 1970 by the Confraternity of Christian Doctrine, Washington, D.C., and are used by permission of the copyright owner. All rights reserved.

Contents

List of Tables

SOLDIERS OF CHRIST

1

Introduction

In the century between 1400 and 1500, the countries and people of western Europe experienced enormous changes in almost every facet of life. The demographic catastrophes of the fourteenth century had seriously weakened the feudal system, and in the long term led to a significant improvement in the standard of living for most peasants. For some, growing cities offered greater personal freedom and opportunities for social mobility, but such gains were offset by urban crime, poverty, and the pressing need for poor relief. At the top of the social pyramid, kings began to gather ever more power for the central government, in the process creating large bureaucracies to carry out their will. Royal subsidies for voyages of discovery began to open new worlds, offering limitless possibilities for exploration, settlement, missionary work, and economic exploitation.

At the same time, the printing revolution profoundly altered the life of the mind and changed the habits of centuries. The printing press opened up new worlds in much the same way as the explorers had. Before the development of movable type, books had been the work of the monastic scribe, and the long and laborious process of copying had chiefly benefited those within the religious community. Now—for a cost—books could be owned by anyone. The increasing importance of a "middle" class, broadly defined to include both skilled artisans and professionals, provided the perfect outlet for these new products. Although it should not be exaggerated, the impact of the printing press on literacy, linguistic standardization, and even thought processes was beginning to be felt by 1500.[1] The printing industry helped expand the passion for classical antiquity beyond the Alps to northern Europe, and led to new ways of thinking about the world and all God's creation, including man.

The great monolith of the Catholic Church, which had challenged the powers of kings in earlier times, was beginning to recover from the shocks of schism and corruption that had shaken it in the fourteenth and early fifteenth centuries. After the Council of Constance, churchmen at all levels began to make efforts to reform the church from within. Leaders of the Observantine movement sought to bring monastic life into line with monastic vows, while reforming bishops breathed new life into the church by exercising their pastoral functions, holding synods, and repairing the physical damage

3

done to churches by decades of warfare. But in terms of belief, the cracks in the edifice had opened into fissures where individual heterodoxy flourished. In the universities, humanist and Platonist currents competed with philological and Pauline studies for the attention of the great scholars of the era, providing a volatile mix of new elements. The emergence of Christian humanism and the *devotio moderna,* both of which encouraged a life based on personal devotion and simplicity, paradoxically had the effect of introducing a certain amount of "freethinking" among lay men and women.

Many of these changes would have gone unnoticed by the average man or woman of 1500. Intellectual debate, church policy, and reading were, for the most part, the preserve of the leisured class. Although literacy was increasing in response to the development of printing, urbanization, and vocational demands, books were not the primary source of information for the peasant, artisan, wife, or mother. News and information were imparted in other ways—through word of mouth, at the local tavern, in church, and at sermons. In this sense, the world of 1500 was not so different from earlier times.

Until recently, investigations of late medieval religion focused on the history of the institutional church and scholastic theology. Under the influence of the *Annales* school and the methods of religious sociology pioneered by Gabriel Le Bras,[2] historians have begun to look at the beliefs and behaviors of ordinary Christians. The sources for this kind of social history include not only correspondence and chronicles, but also communal records, criminal investigations, inquisitorial proceedings, *répertoire des visitations,* wills, and inventories after death. Surprisingly, most French scholars have paid very little attention to one of the richest sources for the history of popular religion: sermons. In an age when the printed book was still in its infancy, the pulpit was the mass medium of the era. Cities competed with one another to attract the leading preachers, nearly all of whom were university-trained theologians, to their pulpits. Their sermons were the chief occasion for attempting to bridge the gap between high theology and popular culture. Chronicles tell us that thousands of people thronged to hear these learned doctors speak.

Despite the centrality of sermons for an understanding of popular *mentalités,* the student of five years ago eager to learn about what was being preached in France just prior to and during the early Reformation era would have found very little in the way of secondary literature to satisfy his or her curiosity. Studies of sermon literature in the late Middle Ages and Reformation period in Germany, Switzerland, Italy, and England have proliferated, but until very recently, the only works on French preaching from 1300 to 1600 dated to the nineteenth century. This book is an attempt to fill the gap.

This study is limited to the hundred-year period from 1460 to 1560 for a number of reasons. Most important was my desire to focus on late medieval and Reformation spirituality. Previous studies of French sermons have concentrated either on the High Middle Ages or the classical age of the seventeenth century, ignoring or glossing over the most critical period of change in religious ideology. By looking at sermons given both before and after the

Reformation, we are able to observe the process of change in both the preacher's formulation of his craft and conditions in society at large. The year 1460 is a convenient starting date because the printing press had just been developed, and preachers were quick to grasp its potential value. My own tabulation of the printing of sermons in France in the sixteenth century, based on available summaries of printed works, suggests that it attained a peak between 1500 and 1520 that was not surpassed at any time later in the century (See figure). These findings are significant because they indicate just how important preaching was *before* the Reformation. Other studies have shown that in Europe as a whole, over five thousand volumes of sermons and related preaching aids appeared in print between 1460 and 1500.[3] In Strasbourg, Miriam Chrisman found that sermons made up 25 percent of all religious books published by 1500, and constituted a substantial part of the total works printed.[4] The greatest demand for these works came from scholars and clerics who hoped to gain greater insights into the art of preaching, for all preachers were advised to consult the sermons of the great preachers, especially contemporary or nearly contemporary ones, as models for their own work.

The terminal date for the study was equally convenient, because it coincides with the beginning of the religious wars that would convulse France for the remainder of the sixteenth century. A comprehensive study of preaching during the Wars of Religion would be fascinating,[5] but would introduce issues that are substantially different from those that I will pose here. A brief glance at some of the sermons from the last four decades of the sixteenth century confirms this view. Personal themes of penitence and reformation remain important, but the tension and conflicts between Catholics and Protestants, soon to erupt into open warfare, lend an increasingly polemical and militant tone that often overshadows the spiritual content of the sermons.

It would have been desirable to study all sermons—printed and manuscript, Protestant and Catholic—given in France during this period, but limitations of sources and recent additions to scholarship have made certain choices necessary. There are virtually no extant Protestant sermons until after the beginning of the Wars of Religion, so we must rely on other sources for information about Protestant preaching. On the other hand, Catholic sermons are plentiful. It is a measure of how central the study of sermons is to current concerns in religious history that scholars have recently devoted considerable attention to Catholic manuscript sermons. In *Le métier du prédicateur à la fin du Moyen Age, 1350–1520,*[6] a revised version of his thesis on the ministry of the Word,[7] Hervé Martin has compiled information on thousands of mostly anonymous preachers who left behind few traces. His study of 770 sermons (80 percent of them unpublished) preached in northern France from 1350 to 1520 concentrates on the first three-quarters of the fifteenth century, examining the training of preachers, the dynamic between the preacher and his listeners, and the preachers' use of metaphors from daily life. His earlier study of the mendicant orders in Brittany also provides some significant information on the social history of preaching.[8] Two other important contributions include André Godin's monograph on Jean Glapion and Jean Vitrier, which examines

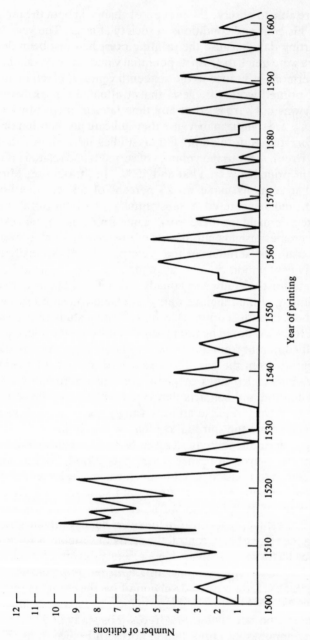

Figure 1. The Printing of Sermons in France, 1500–1599. (Based on J. Baudrier, *Bibliographie lyonnaise* [reprinted Paris: F. de Noble, 1964]; Louis Desgraves, *Répertoire bibliographique des livres imprimés en France au seizième siècle* [Bordeaux: Heitz, 1968–1980]; Philippe Renouard, *Imprimeurs & libraires parisiens du XVIe siècle* [Paris: Baaleu-Banville, 1969].)

the theology of two famous preachers of the so-called *préréforme*,[9] and Olivia Holloway McIntyre's study of the manuscript sermons of two Celestine monks, Pierre Bard and Antoine Pocquet, which traces the changes in monastic preaching between the fifteenth and mid sixteenth centuries.[10]

Manuscript sermons in the period from 1460 to 1560 are essential for an understanding of less well-known and even anonymous preachers, and the works by Martin, Godin, and McIntyre have filled an important gap in our knowledge. But the availability of the printing press led to a differentiation among preachers based on quality and content. When manuscripts were the only means of preserving a sermon, there was little distinction between the work of a great preacher and that of a poor one. The publishing business introduced new criteria for judging the value of a sermon collection, and sermons that remained in manuscript form once publication was an option were often not of comparable quality or of generalizable interest. That is not to say that all manuscript sermons after 1460 were of inferior quality—a number of factors would have influenced the decision to publish a sermon. But, in general, the sermons that were printed between 1460 and 1560 were those considered worthy to serve as models for the use of less talented preachers.

One recent study of published sermons, D. Catherine Brown's analysis of the popular sermons of Jean Gerson, combines sensitivity with a positive and perceptive understanding of the medieval religious experience. Brown devotes only limited space to the social history of preaching, but does an excellent job of presenting Gerson's pastoral theology within the context of his times.[11] Throughout this book, I will rely on Brown's characterizations of popular preaching and theology at the beginning of the fifteenth century as both a control and a standard for later preachers.

Despite the importance of these recent additions to the history of late medieval preaching, there is still much work to be done, and I believe that this book offers an important contribution to our understanding of this subject. As Brown points out, "there is still considerable obscurity and this is likely to remain until the sermons, tracts and other works, many still in manuscript, of more theologians of the period are edited and examined."[12]

The material presented here is taken from twenty-three preachers and 1,657 sermons in forty-three collections, most of which have never before been analyzed in detail. These are the works of all preachers active in France between 1460 and 1560 who have left even small collections of printed sermons. The sermons represent a large and diverse corpus in terms of form, style, interpretation, and use of allusion. For purposes of comparison, and to fill the gap created when sermons virtually ceased to be printed after the 1530s, I also looked at sixty-eight manuscript sermons in the Bibliothèque Nationale, Paris.

There are some significant differences between the research undertaken here and that of both Martin and Brown. Although this book offers some comparisons between printed and manuscript sources, Martin's book remains the most complete examination of manuscript sermons for all of France in the late Middle Ages. The slight difference in time period between this book and Martin's provides the rationale for this concentration on printed sermons. His emphasis on the early fifteenth century mandated the use of manuscript sources, while my starting date of 1460, *after* the invention of the printing press, is the beginning of a period that saw widespread dissemination of sermons by the most educated, competent, and popular preachers. More important, even though both books discuss the sermons of Jean Cleree and Michel Menot, our approaches to the material differ substantially. Martin's primary interest in social history is obvious from his masterful discussions of the preachers in their chosen milieu. He brings to light considerable archival material that helps to clarify the relationship between a preacher and his audience, and offers good statistical estimates that go a long way toward proving how important preaching was at the end of the Middle Ages. Although he does not neglect popular theology, this is not his focus. Finally, his cutoff point of 1520, the year in which Lutheran doctrines began to spread throughout France, makes impossible an examination of the impact of the new ideas on Catholic popular theology. This is one of the most interesting questions of this period, for by looking at the "before" and "after" we can ascertain a great deal about late-medieval Catholicism.

In orientation, this book is similar to Brown's study of Gerson, and centers on popular theology. Although we share many of the same conclusions, they were derived from a significantly different base of sources. Gerson was one of the greatest of medieval theologians, admired even by some Protestants. He was actively involved in some of the great challenges of his time, including the conciliar movement, attempts to end the Great Schism, and efforts to eradicate the heresy of Jan Hus. While less than a century separates Gerson and some of the earliest preachers studied here, conditions by the end of the fifteenth century were considerably different from those at the beginning, when economic disaster, social dysfunction, and almost continuous warfare were the norm. My hope is to build on Brown's work, offering a base for comparison between preachers of somewhat lower stature than Gerson who were active between fifty and one hundred and fifty years after his death.

The challenge of a study of this kind—to penetrate the late medieval mind—is complicated by the nature of the source. The printed sermon may well differ from the spoken original, making a study of late medieval preaching based on printed sermons rely partially on the subjective impressions of the reader. Reading one sermon gives little appreciation for the force of the preached Word, but after reading hundreds of sermons, one starts to "hear" the preacher. The reader also becomes aware of significant differences between preachers, each of whom assumes a distinct personality. Commonplaces abound, but they do not obscure the originality and uniqueness of each preacher's contribution.

While it is not possible to state categorically that every sermon examined here was actually preached, the evidence strongly suggests that the great majority of them were. The many "shorthand" sermons, which were compiled by auditors, were certainly preached. In a few cases, we can directly connect a specific sermon to a particular date, place, and event. Some printed sermons include this information on the title page; in other cases, chronicles mention the preaching of one of the men in this study at a particular event such as a procession, the burning of a heretic, or the funeral of a great noble or clergyman.

We can also use information about the audience to determine how accurately the printed sermon reflects the preached Word. Large numbers of people—often thousands—came to hear a famed preacher. Every type of source, including physical evidence, confirms this fact. Internal evidence from the sermons as well as statements in chronicles and even criminal proceedings all point to significant audience participation in the event. Within the sermons, simulated dialogues convey some feeling for audience reactions. Although the preachers invented these dialogues, they were chosen because of their relevance to the auditors, who would hardly have responded to examples and situations that bore little resemblance to their daily life. Archival records, chronicles, and memoirs supplement these details, providing picturesque examples of crowd reactions, which not surprisingly became more vociferous and violent after the Reformation. Indignant rejoinders, sacred bonfires, mass conversions of prostitutes, iconoclasm—all of these signal that, in one way or another, people responded to the preachers' message. Do these reactions, as well as the more mundane responses of boredom, napping, and flirting, fit the message of the sermons? We must each judge according to the evidence.

The works of many historians have influenced my research, including several who specialize in the German Reformation but who have put forward ideas that could be equally important for the study of late medieval religiosity and reformation in France. No one has been more influential than Steven Ozment, whose provocative study, *The Reformation in the Cities,* inspired this book. In this study, based on confessional manuals, Ozment contends that late medieval Catholicism imposed heavy psychological burdens on the laity because of its insistence on fulfilling the Law, something that no human being, had it in his power to do. The result, in Ozment's view, was a generalized sense of impotence and despair, perhaps best epitomized by Luther's personal struggle with belief. Luther's theology of justification by faith alone provided the appeal of Protestantism by freeing man from this intolerable burden of helplessness and guilt.[13]

The dark side of medieval piety has fascinated scholars over the years. Although characterizations—that follow Johan Huizinga—of the later Middle Ages as an era of catastrophe and decline have largely been refuted,[14] the idea of a more generalized religious *Angst* persists. Jean Delumeau describes the whole of the later Middle Ages as a time pervaded by psychological and eschatological fear,[15] but does not examine how changed social and economic conditions after the Black Death may have influenced the collective psyche. Étienne Delaruelle characterizes the period as one imbued with religious sentiments that were often morbid and expressed in aberrant ways in a climate of nightmares, everyday horrors, and incredible violence.[16] In his recent study on iconoclasm, Carlos Eire claims "that the intensification of external religious ritual and devotion failed to quiet the inner anguish that drove the laity to seek grace and salvation through an ever-increasing multitude of intercessors and material objects. . . . Religious anxiety must have increased proportionately to the distancing of God through materialism and 'parapolytheism.' Paradoxically, in seeking divinity through more immediate means, late medieval religion only succeeded in making it even more distant."[17] By contrast, Jacques Toussaert speaks of religion in this period as little more than a framework of formalities,[18] a view that has attracted adherents. While not resolving this dilemma, Delaruelle concludes that "the man or woman of the year 1500 was a paradox: indifferent to doctrine, but sensitive to problems of morality; reassured despite everything by his lax priests and his accumulation of indulgences, but shaken sometimes by scruples; faithful to works, whether they were pilgrimages, alms to hospitals or confraternal prayers, yet believing in salvation by faith and Christ the Redeemer."[19]

The paradox of late medieval religiosity as expressed in the historical literature was another inspiration for this study. Bernd Moeller asserts that outward displays of piety and "churchliness" were never higher in Germany than in the years preceding the Reformation.[20] This is confirmed by A. N. Galpern's study of popular religion in Champagne, in which he describes an "Indian summer" of late medieval piety around 1500.[21] Preaching had become so important in religious and civic life that Martin speaks of its widespread institutionalization by the fifteenth century.[22] "The century preceding the Reformation experienced an incredible growth in preaching: never before had there been so much preaching, never before had sacred orators enjoyed such popular success."[23]

How can these seeming contradictions be resolved? Or is there a contradiction at all? What is the relationship between outward display and internal belief? Delumeau offers a possible explanation for some of these questions in *Catholicism between Luther and Voltaire*. He contends that the people of Europe were not properly Christianized until the full implementation of the Catholic reform in the seventeenth century, and asks, "if everything in the Christianity of the *ancien régime* that was constraint, conformism, and official worship, everything that was rejection of the world despite the fact that it was the only world men had, everything that was magic, Manichaeism and fear, had been excised, what, for many people, would have remained?"[24] In one of the most blatant examples of judging medieval religion by modern standards, Delumeau fails to recognize that religion before the Council of Trent was far less conformist than after; in medieval times, the marriage of popular religion and official church teaching was not always a happy one, but for many it provided a vital and sustaining framework for daily existence.

This book will not resolve the contradictions in late medieval religious life, because they were very real. In times of profound change, contradictions, even in one person's beliefs and behaviors, may have been the rule rather than the exception. What I hope this book will do is offer an understanding of popular *mentalités* in the light of medieval, rather than modern, sensibilities.

The chapters that make up Part I will examine the social dynamics of the preaching event, the life and training of a preacher, and the construction of sermons. Part II will deal with content—the popular theology of the sermons and the preachers' reflections on contemporary society. Part III will concentrate on the problem of heresy in late medieval and early Reformation France.

I

The Art of Preaching

1

The Art of Preaching

2

The Sermon as Event

He began to reproach the towns where most of his miracles had been worked, with their failure to reform: "It will go ill with you, Chorazin! And just as ill with you, Bethsaida. If the miracles worked in you had taken place in Tyre and Sidon, they would have reformed in sackcloth and ashes long ago. . . . If the miracles worked in you had taken place in Sodom, it would be standing today. I assure you, it will go easier for Sodom than for you on the day of judgment."

Matthew 11:20–21,23–24

Preaching was predominantly an urban phenomenon, although by the late Middle Ages all but the most desolate of rural or mountainous areas usually had access to regular preaching.[1] Hervé Martin has convincingly shown that the number of actual and potential preachers throughout northern France was well into the thousands.[2] But to reach the largest number of people, it was clearly expedient to concentrate on cities. As Michel Menot points out, the Bible provided strong support for the urban mission—Isaiah and Jeremiah were sent by the Lord to Jerusalem, Jonah to Nineveh, Daniel to Babylon, and Paul to Rome.[3] While the large cities typically attracted the great itinerant preachers for Lenten and Advent series, numerous smaller towns and large rural parishes were able to draw on preachers from their local convents.

It was a generally accepted view among preachers that the sins committed in large cities greatly outnumbered those in rural areas, and the preachers did not spare city dwellers. As one preacher assured his listeners, "Why does the Lord say that preachers ought to work in large cities rather than small towns and rural villages? . . . Is it because there are great and wise doctors there? Do they get paid better there? No, no! . . . This is the real reason: there are more sins committed in big cities than in little villages."[4] Olivier Maillard says of Paris: "it was once said to be the fount of all wisdom, justice, and morality. But now it is the fount of iniquity, injustice, and deceitfulness."[5] Jean Cleree claims that there are many in Paris who have more sins than they have hairs on their head.[6] While Maillard considers the capital to be a cesspool,[7] Menot singles out Tours for special blame: "I have preached and I have labored, but I do not know how much I have accomplished: I ask God to bring forth the fruit. Either all scripture is wrong, or the city of Tours will

15

not long endure in this state. . . . If you go to Paris you will find a good deal of evil, but you will not find so many public ills, so many pimps, so many bathhouses as here."[8] Echoing the theme of Matthew 11:20–24, Maillard argues that there are certainly many cities in the world where the people would reform if they had the quantity and quality of preaching that the people of France do.[9]

People living far from a town did not hear the Word of God preached as often as city dwellers, yet Guillaume Pepin marvels that "we see more evil men, who are especially stubborn and hardened in sin, in large cities, where they have preaching all the time, than in the countryside where they scarcely have one sermon a year."[10] It would be wrong to conclude, however, that rural areas were totally untouched by preaching. Rumors of the impending visit of a famous preacher to the nearest town regularly reached the surrounding areas. When Vincent Ferrier preached in the Breton towns of Vannes and Josselin in 1418, peasants traveled from as far away as fifty kilometers to hear him speak.[11] In chronicles and archival listings, the arrival of a great preacher in town is usually accompanied by a note that people came from great distances to hear him.[12] Preachers also ventured into the countryside to preach at the behest of the local nobility.[13]

Still, preaching was above all an affair of the cities, and the material presented here is primarily a study of urban religious *mentalités,* for few written records of preaching in rural areas have survived. This chapter will delve into the logistics of town-preacher relations: the occasions for preaching; the selection, engagement, contractual obligations, and payment of the preacher; the physical aspects of preaching and sermon attendance; and reactions and behavior of members of the audience.

Occasions for Sermons

> Go up onto a high mountain, Zion, herald of glad tidings; Cry out at the top of your voice, Jerusalem, herald of good news! Fear not to cry out and say to the cities of Judah: Here is your God!   Isaiah 40:9

As early as the High Middle Ages, there was a tendency for the sermon to disappear from the mass. Preaching by the mendicant orders began in the early thirteenth century partially as a response to the decay of the missal sermon (*prône*) and, in effect, sealed its fate in most places. Later complaints that the parish clergy were not fulfilling their duties as preachers must be put in their proper perspective, for the enormous success of this "extraordinary" preaching obviated the need for preaching during church services in most urban parishes.

The evangelical movement at the beginning of the sixteenth century brought about a resurgence of the *prône* among Catholic reformers. Guillaume Briçonnet, bishop of Meaux, whose diocese seems to have suffered far more than usual from irregular preaching, not only encouraged preaching in a more strictly biblical manner during extraordinary preaching, but also insisted that parish priests exercise their preaching function during mass. In 1523, he wrote to the clergy of his diocese, "in your *prônes,* engage your congregation to pray for the souls of the dead, to believe in the existence of purgatory, and to invoke the aid of the Virgin Mary and the saints. Repeat these litanies often."[14]

Preaching was a regular occurrence on Sundays and feast days. An examination of the payment records of various towns indicates that in most urban areas there were regular Sunday sermons being preached concurrently in several different parishes.[15] The great thirteenth-century preacher, Jacques de Vitry, had divided the liturgical year into four preaching seasons corresponding to the life and death of Jesus Christ, a convention followed by many of the preachers studied here: (1) *tempus deviationis* (Advent to Septuagesima); (2) *tempus revocationis* (Septuagesima to Easter); (3) *tempus reconciliationis* (Easter to Pentecost); and (4) *tempus peregrinationis* (Pentecost to Advent). A great number of extant series for Sundays and feast days provide sermons under the heading of *sermones de tempore* or *sermones dominicales.* Normally, such a series comprises sixty to seventy sermons,[16] with each sermon taking as its theme the gospel or epistle of the day. Of the sermons in this study 28 percent (458) were "ordinary" sermons for the subdivisions of the church year.

The preaching cycle at Lent, which was very popular, first caught on in the fourteenth century. The largest selection dealt with here (506 sermons or 31 percent) comes from the many tomes of extant *quadragesimales.* During Lent, sermons were given daily; therefore, the number still in existence is correspondingly greater. The change in themes during Menot's Lenten series at Tours in 1508 conveys the penitential mood of these sermons. Until Easter Sunday, he had daily repeated the theme: "Be not so very angry, Lord, keep not our guilt forever in mind; look upon us, who are all your people" (Isaiah 64:8). The dominant themes of sin, repentance, and hope were used with varying emphasis according to his purpose and the nearness to Good Friday and Easter Sunday. Eventually, the trials of Jesus' last days and the sorrows of the Crucifixion gave way to a spirit of rejoicing in the Resurrection, which Menot elucidates in his Easter theme: "This is the day the Lord has made; let us be glad and rejoice in it" (Psalm 118:24). The *triduum* of sermons for Holy Thursday, Good Friday, and the Saturday before Easter were distinct from and yet inextricably linked to the *quadragesimale.* The *expositio passionis Iesu Christi* was a special sermon given on Good Friday, based on the Crucifixion and stressing more than usual the literal, historical sense of the gospels. It was a moving, emotive account that personalized and dramatized the actors and scenes from the Passion.

The four Sundays of Advent marked the season of anticipation for the coming of Christ in the flesh, and were, like Lent, a time of almost continuous preaching. Of the sermons studied here, 11 percent (177) were prepared for Advent. *Sermones de adventu domini* were also given on a daily basis, and often expressed two distinct themes—some preachers spoke of the truly joyous expectation of the season, while others drew parallels between the First Coming and the Second. In this way, Advent sermons could alternate between announcements of glad tidings and descriptions of frightful horrors. Themes from some of the Advent sermons speak of hope and faith soon to be fulfilled: "It is now the hour for you to wake from sleep, for our salvation is closer than when we first accepted the faith" (Romans 13:11);[17] "Strip away all that is filthy, every vicious excess. Humbly welcome the word that has taken root in you, with its power to save you" (James 1:21).[18] Others inspire dread: "There will be signs in the sun, the moon and the stars. On the earth, nations will be anguish, distraught at the roaring of the sea and the waves. Men will die of fright in anticipation of what is coming upon the earth" (Luke 21:25–26).[19]

Sermones de sanctis were given to celebrate the feast day of a particular saint. Two saints' day series have been examined in this study, those by Pepin (eighty-eight sermons), which cover a full range of saints as well as special occasions, such as the feasts of the Annunciation and the Circumcision (the New Year's sermon), and the more limited collection by Maillard (thirty-one). There are also *sermones de sanctis* included in the general collection of Josse Clichtove's sermons. These hagiographical expositions deal primarily with the major saints of the early church, such as Paul, Peter, and Mary Magdalene, but the Church Fathers and recently canonized saints such as Catherine of Siena were also included. "Specialized" saints were rarely the subjects of sermons, perhaps, as Martin suggests, because the church was trying to discourage the popular canonization of saints.[20] A book of saint's day sermons often concludes with a sermon on the *commune sanctorum,* that is, all the saints of a particular category, such as virgins or martyrs. Pepin's collection ends with common sermons for martyrs, virgins, and confessors. In some cases, biographical detail predominates in the sermon, making it less valuable for historical study, but in other cases, the discussion of the saint is little more than a pretext for introducing another subject of the preacher's choosing. Related to sermons on the saints are sermons in praise of the Virgin Mary or in celebration of her special feast days. Another sixty-two of Pepin's sermons celebrate the feast days of the Virgin.

Funeral obsequies for the great also provided an occasion for preaching, but these sermons were not printed as frequently because of their specificity. As the classical influences of the Renaissance began to reach France, preachers became more interested in publishing their gems of oratorical skill, and some funeral sermons were included in larger collections by the mid sixteenth century. This study includes eulogies by Claude Guilliaud, François LePicart, and Étienne Paris. The form was variable, with few set rules,[21] but the panegyric element was pronounced. The existential themes of a funeral sermon were frequently used to promote moral reformation. In a slightly less edifying manner, the preachers might use names to trace genealogies in the manner of the Bible, which would always redound to the great credit of the subject. Deducing from his theme, "Peter, do you love me?" (John 21:15) the similarity of merit between the apostle and his subject, Pierre, duke of Bourbon,

Laurent Bureau traced the deceased's ancestry far back into the royal house of France.[22] With its emphasis on rhetorical talent and classical knowledge, this type of preaching was often reserved for royal or aristocratic audiences.

The indulgence preacher was a much-vilified character, despised by serious preachers as a self-important, greedy individual who preyed on the credulity and meagre resources of the poor and helpless. As early as 1410, synodal statutes and bishops in Normandy had denounced the *indulgence sermon,* but it continued to be a familiar aspect of urban life in the late fifteenth and early sixteenth centuries. Indulgences often were used to support the papal curia or to raise funds for a projected crusade against the Turks, who posed a very real threat to Europe in the 1520s. Proceeds might also go to the poor or aid in the construction of hospitals, schools, sanctuaries, bridges, and dams.[23] The possibilities for abuse were recognized by the authorities, who limited the access of indulgence preachers to churches to keep them well within the purview of local officials.[24] Two Paris doctors of theology, Nicolas Cappelly and Nicolas Payen, were censured by the faculty in 1518 for preaching that "whoever puts a *teston* or something of equal value into this chest for the crusade, will deliver a soul from Purgatory, and that soul will go directly to paradise. By giving ten *testons* for a thousand years, these souls will all go to paradise."[25]

Many sermons had no liturgical basis, and were given to celebrate special events. The *sermo casualis* often brought news of peace, announced a marriage treaty, proclaimed victory in battle, or asked God's aid for the safe return of the king from captivity.[26] In 1468, Louis XI sent a preacher into Lower Normandy for the express purpose of exhorting his subjects to remain faithful in the face of a conspiracy by the dukes of Brittany and Burgundy to put Louis's brother Charles on the throne as a puppet king.[27] *Missionary sermons* were given not only to attract new converts to the faith, but also to fight heretics, who had often responded to the lack of preaching in their dioceses by learning the New Testament and preaching themselves. This type of preaching remained important in the four centuries after the fourth Lateran Council (1215) approved the foundation of the mendicant orders. Preaching to Catholics whose zeal was flagging or to sinners (such as prostitutes) in need of conversion was one type of missionary sermon. Thomas Illyricus's preaching in Bordeaux in 1519 was of this type.[28] Not surprisingly, the growth of Protestantism unleashed a new wave of missionary preaching in the 1520s,[29] which provoked a response in kind from the court. Louise of Savoy sent twelve doctors of theology into the provinces to preach the Catholic faith and combat the new heresy.[30] Later, in 1544, Brother Germain Lamy was dispatched to Normandy "to preach the faith, stop the progress of heresy, and pacify tempers."[31]

Procession sermons and those given at the condemnation of a heretic were also common. But another "occasion" for preaching had largely disappeared by the end of the Middle Ages—that of charismatic, prophetical preaching during times of catastrophe.[32] A few preachers, such as Illyricus, continued to preach in this manner, but conditions were no longer as conducive to this

kind of preaching. *Pest sermons* were still used to invoke heavenly aid, especially in times of epidemic, against such creatures as rats or insects that
endangered human life or work.[33] In short, almost any occasion could provide
the pretext for a sermon.

The Selection and Engagement of a Preacher

> I am sure you have heard of the ministry which God in his goodness gave
> me in your regard. That is why to me, Paul, a prisoner for Christ Jesus
> on behalf of the Gentiles, God's secret plan as I have briefly described it
> was revealed.   Ephesians 3:1–3

The engagement of a popular preacher before the Reformation was normally
the responsibility of the city magistrates, who paid his fees.[34] Although most
large towns were fortunate enough to be favored with the visit of a great
itinerant preacher at some time or other, and when possible attracted advanced theology students to preach the Lenten or Advent series, it was most
common to employ preachers from local convents. The Grenoble archives of
1488 inform us that the religious of the Dominican and Franciscan convents
furnished a preacher in alternate years, evidently chosen by the religious
themselves. The candidate for this year was to be "an excellent preacher,
learned and well-spoken, who throughout Lent will preach in the city as
follows: one week he will preach in the Dominicans' church, the next in the
Franciscans', except on Tuesday, Thursday, Saturday, and Sunday mornings,
on which days and times he will preach in the cathedral of Notre-Dame. After
dinner on Sundays he will preach in his own convent church."[35] This selection
pattern for preachers at the most important church or cathedral continued
the rule, for in 1554, Claude Haton relates that the Franciscans and Dominicans of Provins each alternated years preaching at Advent and Lent. Sometimes the order specified would bring in outsiders, so great was the desire
between the sons of Francis and Dominic to outdo one another. In 1560,
when it was the Dominicans' turn to preach, they offered the position to an
arch-Catholic, Brother Ivollé of the Auxerre convent, for in previous years
their local appointees had shown marked heretical tendencies.[36]

The desire for high-quality preaching often led to lively competition between the local orders. In the 1450s, the city of Lyon invited the local Dominicans and Carmelites to submit nominations and qualifications for the
selection of a preacher "to pronounce the sermon for the third Sunday of
Lent, which is to take place beyond the Pont-du-Rhône." The Dominicans
carried the day.[37]

In her study of the clergy in Aix-en-Provence during the sixteenth century,
Claire Dolan describes the rotation of preaching assignments to particular
stations or churches, although sometimes the rotation would take place within
an Advent or Lenten series. This had the advantage of giving parishioners
some variety, which was especially important when a preacher did not measure

up to expectations. At the cathedral of Saint-Sauveur, the first Sunday was reserved for the Dominicans, the second for the Franciscans, the third for the Augustinians, and the fourth for the Carmelites. More often, each major church would have one preacher throughout Advent or Lent, with the city's most prestigious church being honored with the most outstanding candidate. Dolan contends that the rotation system had fallen into disuse in Aix, with an individual preacher's talent and renown being of greater importance than the order to which he belonged.[38]

A city sometimes had to negotiate well in advance for the services of a great itinerant preacher. The bourgeoisie of Abbéville were so pleased with the preaching of Jean Standonck during his travels through Picardy in 1496, that they asked him to come back for the next year's Lenten series, but it took some months for all the details to be worked out.[39] When the citizens of Montauban heard that Illyricus was preaching nearby at Verdun-sur-Garonne, they immediately sent a delegation to him, asking him to come to their town to preach and offering to pay all expenses and construct a special outdoor pulpit to accommodate the anticipated crowds.[40]

Although the mendicant orders were chiefly responsible for preaching in the later Middle Ages, secular priests could and sometimes did preach. Martin argues that at all times there was a veritable army of "potential" preachers among the seculars, and the great rivalry between priests and mendicants over use of the parish church for preaching testifies to at least some activity by seculars.[41]

Sometimes the desire to appoint a regular preacher led a community to offer a contract. Because of its permanent nature, this position often went to a secular. Although we are poorly informed on this subject for France, it is well known that many cities in the Holy Roman Empire established permanent municipal preacherships funded by the town or private patrons. In 1478, Johan Geiler von Kaysersberg was hired under a contract between him and the city of Strasbourg that stipulated the following: each year he was to have four weeks' vacation, but otherwise he was not to leave the town for even a single night without the permission of the dean, and never during the important seasons of the liturgical year. He was required to preach every day of Lent, every Sunday and feast day during the rest of the year, and on extraordinary occasions such as times of plague, war, or bad weather. Except in cases of illness, he could not dispense with any element of his preaching without the dean's permission and only then if he found a secular (*never* a mendicant) to replace him in the pulpit. He was not to engage in disputes with the cathedral canons or the curé of the chapel. Furthermore, he could not publish any bulls without the dean's authorization and had to promise formally that he would obey the cathedral chapter in all matters.[42]

Many of the same provisions appear in a late-fifteenth-century contract for a preacher at Augsburg: four weeks of vacation and prohibition from spending even one night outside the town, unless the bishop ordered him to visit his diocese or reform a convent. In addition to carefully specified preaching duties, he was to offer a weekly class in theology if there was enough interest, and a special discourse to the clergy of the diocese at Christmas and one other time to be determined by the chapter. If he became ill, he was to be replaced by the *penitencier* or other secular priest designated by the chapter.[43]

At Avignon, admittedly not a typical French city, Nicolas Peitel was hired in 1545 as the city's permanent preacher, with the charge to preach every Sunday and to teach the Pauline epistles on the other days of the week.[44] Similarly, in 1517, two Grenoble magistrates engaged the services of Pierre de Sebiville as their regular preacher and eased his change from the Cistercian to the Franciscan order to regularize his position in the town.[45] When the Observants purged the Franciscan convent in Grenoble, Sebiville was offered perpetual lodging by the town.[46]

Concern about careful selection of both temporary and permanent preachers shows up clearly after the Reformation. Hoffman notes that by 1542, the church vestries in Lyon were making the decisions, with increasing consultation between parishioners and canons by the 1550s.[47] Once the diversity of religions had become an established fact, popular participation often led to direct conflict with the city or ecclesiastical authorities. In 1530–1531, the parlement of Rouen issued an *arrêt* forbidding the townspeople of Caudebec from taking the choice of a Lenten preacher into their own hands. Instead, it was left to the archbishop or his vicars to choose a suitable preacher. Before Lent in 1553, the Augustinians of Bourges were prohibited from preaching outside of their own convent because of past improprieties, and no amount of popular pressure could lift the ban.[48] When the canons of Saint-Nizier in Lyon rejected the popular choice for preacher, the laity threatened to withhold funds they had promised for church repairs.[49]

Increasingly, the bishop or other high church official was charged with the task of finding (and often paying) a preacher, especially if he was not prepared to preach himself.[50] This was especially necessary in troubled times. In 1561, the bishop of Grenoble was urged to select a good preacher capable of "ending seditions and daily assemblies [of Protestants]."[51]

Remuneration

> Could I have done wrong when I preached the gospel of God to you free
> of charge?   2 Corinthians 11:7

Once a preacher was selected, he (or his convent) and the town had to discuss financial arrangements.[52] Payments to preachers were quite variable, depending on a number of factors, such as mendicant or secular status, whether the preacher was local or extraregional, the occasion(s) on which he preached, his skill, the town's wealth and importance, and current economic conditions. While renowned preachers from outside the region received large stipends, local preachers often received only nominal payments. Yet despite the nominal fee, there seems to have been a genuine hierarchy of values placed on the different occasions for preaching and the preacher's skill. In some areas, payments to preachers were variable and intermittent, as in Brittany before 1500, where they ranged from 50 sous to 40 livres. In the first half of the sixteenth century, the mendicant orders there were usually accorded a fixed sum in silver (usually 10 l. per preacher), but payments by chapters and local parishes were often less.[53] While most archival fiscal records note occasional grants to preachers, few have consistent entries throughout the period under study, and even the famous do not always appear in town records. Although Maillard preached his sermon in Nantes around 1470, there is no mention of this fact in the fairly complete city records.

The records from Amiens are the most complete we have, listing payments to preachers from 1444 to 1566 (Table 2-1). It is clear that the average payment for a Lenten series at Amiens was 60 s., although by the mid-sixteenth century 100 s. had become common. At Nantes in the 1480s, the going rate fluctuated between 10 l. and 20 l.,[54] while the single payment listings we have for the Gironde and Agen in the same period are for the very disparate sums of 25 s. and 40 l. respectively.[55] The payment records at Dijon are reasonably complete from 1521 to 1562 (Table 2-2), showing the average payment there to have been 40 to 50 s. Except for the years 1539, 1545, 1547, 1552, and 1559, the stipend went down as time passed, in spite of rising inflation. Both in Normandy in the 1530s and Boulogne in the 1560s, preachers were regularly paid 100 s.[56] In the early fifteenth century, payments were typically 13 to 15 florins in Grenoble;[57] by 1488, 20 fl. was usual,[58] and by 1517, 25 fl. was given to the preacher.[59]

A preacher was usually paid more for Lent than for any other occasion, because of the number of sermons required and the cycle's popularity.[60] Martin found Advent preachers typically received 25 percent to 50 percent less than Lenten preachers.[61] Some cities expected to be furnished with an Advent preacher free if they paid for the services of a Lenten preacher. While Advent sermons sometimes earned 60 or 100 s., payments for them were much less fixed. In 1499, each of the Advent preachers was paid only 10 s.,[62] and two years later the preachers were paid 32 and 35 sous parisiens respectively.[63] In 1562, the city received a bill from the preachers which broke down their costs as 100 s. per man for Lent and 40 s. for Advent.[64] Several preachers who are not identified in the Amiens records as Advent or Lenten preachers, but are mentioned for unspecified preaching—"preaching in parishes," "seven weeks of preaching," or "one month of preaching"[65]—were paid the standard rate of 60 s. Extraordinary sermons were paid at a much lower rate, for they required much less time and preparation. The preacher who announced the peace in Grenoble in 1514 received only 6 s.[66]

Some of the discrepancies in payment may relate to the quality of preaching or the town's fiscal circumstances in a given year. The 100 s. each allotted to the Dominican and Augustinian friars who preached the Lenten series in 1444 carries with it the notation that "they worked very hard."[67] However, Jean Sarrasin, one of the two preachers thus rewarded, was accorded only

Table 2-1. Payments to Preachers in Amiens, 1444–1556.

Year	Amount	Period	Preacher
1444	100 s.	Lent	Jehan Sarrasin (D)
1444	100 s.	Lent	Jehan Loir (A)
1446	60 s.	Lent	Jehan Sarrasin (D)
1447	60 s.	Lent	Jehan Desgardins (D)
1447	60 s.	Lent	Masse Lecarpentier (A)
1449	4 l.	Lent	Rémont Pascal (D)
1449	4 l.	Lent	Jehan Marcille (U)
1452	60 s.	Lent	Rémont Pascal (D)
1454	6 l.	Lent	(Unnamed A,F,D)
1458	0	Lent	M. Enguerran (D)
1458	60 s.	Lent	Laurent Perrier (A)
1459	60 s.	Lent	Andrieu Bellet (A)
1460	60 s.	Lent	Robert Clément (A)
1461	60 s.	Lent	Guillaume de Villenoeuve (A)
1463	60 s.	Lent	Jean Pillory (D)
1463	60 s.	Lent	Frère Ambroise (A)
1463	60 s.	Lent	Thibaut Blondet (F)
1465	60 s.	Lent	(Unnamed D,F,A)
1465	60 s.	One month	Hervé Guynot (A)
1466	60 s.	Lent	(Unnamed D,F,A)
1467	60 s.	Lent	Jean Trouvé (D)
1467	60 s.	Lent	Jean Darie (F)
1471	40 s.	Lent	Henry de Fourière (F)
1472	60 s.	Lent	(Unnamed, three)
1473	1 écu d'or	Advent	Nicole Ducastel (C)
1473	60 s.	Lent	Thomas Hairon (D)
1473	60 s.	Lent	Guillaume Cotart (F)
1473	60 s.	Lent	Pierre Ligier (A)
1474	9 l.	Lent	Georges Delays (D)
			Jean Puchot (A)
			Guillaume Bourdin (F)
1475	60 s.	Lent	Nicole Ducastel (C)
1475	60 s.	Lent	Jean Poyade (D)
			Jean Donnon (F)
1476	60 s.	Lent	Jean Cossart (D)
1476	60 s.	Lent	Guillaume Dufour (A)
1476	60 s.	Lent	Nicole Paillart (F)
1476	60 s.	seven weeks	Jean Mengart (D)
1477	60 s.	Lent	Hervé Guynant (*sic*) (A)
1477	60 s.	Lent	Raoul Desmarques (D)
1477	60 s.	Lent	Frère Alexandre (F)
1478	60 s.	Lent	Pierre Legrant (A)
1478	60 s.	Lent	Pierre Dauphlin (D)
1478	60 s.	Lent	Thibaut (F)
1479	60 s.	Lent	Pierre Legris (U)
1479	60 s.	Lent	Guerart Rodachy (U)
1479	60 s.	Lent	Thibaut (F)
1480	60 s.	Lent	Eustache de la Court (F)
1480	60 s.	Lent	Jean Cappellier (A)
1480	60 s.	Lent	Jean Masselin (D)
1482	60 s.t.	Parishes	Jean Mengart (D)
1486	60 s.t.	Many sermons	Jean Mengart (D)
1497	60 s.	Lent	(Unnamed D,F,A)
1497	60 s.	Lent	Toussaint Fabry

Table 2–1 (continued)

Year	Amount	Period	Preacher
1498	60 s.	(Unspecified)	
1499	4li. 10 s.	Lent	Gratien de Tours (A)
1499	4li. 10 s.	Lent	Robert de Boude (D)
1499	4li. 10 s.	Lent	Nicole de Voisins (M)
1499	10 s.	Advent	(Unnamed)
1501	32 s.p.	Advent	Pierre Hérouart (D)
1501	35 s.p.	Advent	Jacques Cappellot (U)
1505	20 s.t.	Lent	Beau père (D)
1506	60 s.	Lent	(Unnamed)
1508	60 s.	Preaching	(Unnamed Fs)
1541	60 s.	Advent	Robert Lemaistre (F)
1541	100 s.	Lent	(Unnamed)
1543	100 s.	Lent	(Unnamed)
1544	100 s.	Preaching	Gilles Monier (A)
1544	50 s.	Preaching	(Unnamed C)
1547	100 s.	Lent	(Unnamed)
1549	60 s.	Advent	(Unnamed)
1550	1 écu "tip"	Preaching	(Unnamed)
1554	100 s.	Lent	(Unnamed, four)
1557	100 s.t.	Lent	(Unnamed D,F,A)
1560	100 s.t.	Lent	Jean Mabille (F)
1563	100 s.	Lent	(Unnamed, four)
1566	100 s.	Lent	(Unnamed, four)

ABBREVIATIONS: A, Augustinian; C, Carmelite; D, Dominican; F, Franciscan; M, Minime; U, Unknown.

60 s. two years later despite his "great and noteworthy sermons."[68] This may simply reflect hard times for the town, because in 1505 the prior of the Dominican convent received only 20 sous tournois for his Lenten sermons.[69]

Recognition of unusual talent was not rare. The city of Nantes gave Hervé Guynot 20 l. in the same year that the other preachers received only 10 l.[70] Guynot was a doctor of theology, born and raised in Amiens, whose fame and the rigors of travel no doubt procured him a larger honorarium. Also,

Table 2-2. Payments to Preachers in Dijon, 1518–1562.

Year	Amount	Year	Amount
1518	50 s.	1548	50 s.
1521	60 s.	1550	50 s.
1527	60 s.	1550	40 s.
152?	3 fr.	1552	100 s.
1530	50 s.	1553	40 s.
1535	3 fr.	1554	40 s.
1539	60 s.	155x	40 s.
1540	10 l.t.	1559	60 s.
1545	60 s.	1560	10 l.t.
1547	60 s.	1562	25 l.t.

as the memoirist Claude Haton remarks very perceptively, "it is a truism that
we esteem more highly and pay more attention to a preacher whom we have
never seen before than one whom we see every day."[71] Sometimes a town
would also add a sum of money to the customary payment if the preacher's
convent was in great need of funds,[72] assuming always that the preacher had
performed in a satisfactory manner. In some localities, the city council would
add a gratuity "for the love of God" and "without prejudice for the future."[73]
In 1463, one of the friars, Jean Pillory, received the same 60 s. as two other
preachers, but was also given a "tip" of 20 s.[74] Nevertheless, most towns were
wary of setting expensive precedents for the future.

  While a preacher's excellent performance sometimes earned a gratuity,
an unsatisfactory sermon was equally likely to leave him without a sou. In
1538, the city of Grenoble requested a replacement for brother Valentine
Gauthier, whose preaching had proved unacceptable, and later refused his
request for a stipend, for "he had preached badly and the city had always
considered the honoraria as alms which they were at liberty to accord or
refuse."[75] In other cases, personal promises made by a city's representatives
were not honored by the council as a whole, despite excellent preaching.
This led some preachers to seek legal remedies to obtain monies owed
them. Sebiville had been promised the considerable sum of 50 écus by two
of the town's magistrates if he came to Grenoble to preach, plus a gratuity
of 14 écus, 6 s. if his preaching pleased them.[76] He demanded payment,
but the city council, horrified at the promises made by their representatives,
had to take up a collection.[77] When very little was produced and Sebiville
threatened to sue, the two magistrates had to make up much of the difference out of their own pockets.[78]

  A town would sometimes pay a preacher's legal fees if his preaching got
him into trouble. When the Augustinian *prescheur ordinaire* of Nîmes was
arrested because of his preaching in 1532 (apparently not for heresy), the city
did everything in its power to secure his release, and debated over and agreed
to a raise in salary to help pay his expenses.[79]

  Preachers who were hired permanently also received gratuities. Nicolas
Peitel's salary at Avignon was fixed at 50 écus, which the vice-legate feared
was not enough to retain the services of so distinguished a preacher, so he
set himself to obtain a bonus or benefice for the preacher. In 1548, he succeeded in getting Peitel a deaconate at Saint-Agricol.[80] In Nîmes, the city
assessor judged that the preacher mentioned above was worthy of the considerable sum of 40 l., which he donated from his own funds.[81]

  The city council did not always pay a preacher's expenses. Guillaume
Briçonnet's ambitious effort to ensure preaching throughout all the parishes
in his cure cost the diocese 900 l. during the first year, and 700 l. and 600 l.
in succeeding years.[82] As Protestantism grew in strength, even orthodox Catholics began to fret over paying preaching expenses when it was, after all, one
of the theoretical duties of a bishop to preach. In the 1560s, Master Alesti,
an archdeacon, was asked by his bishop to engage for one of the churches in

the Gard a preacher for the year, to be paid either in advance or rewarded with a sum equal to that of a canon's prebend.[83] In 1540 in Agen, the bishop was held "to feed, provide for, and pay the Lenten and Advent preacher,"[84] while in Aix, the cost of the preacher was split between the archbishop and the council.[85] Where the city council was composed primarily of Protestants, this took on politicoreligious overtones when the magistrates forced a bishop to pay the costs of Catholic preaching for the previous year. The town of Amiens, with a substantially Protestant council membership, refused the mendicant's petition to be paid in 1562 "because it is the business of Monseigneur, the bishop of Amiens, to pay them. In addition, the ordonnance put forward by M. du Mont prohibited the mendicants from asking alms of the city, so the request by the preachers is denied, and this time nothing will be given to them."[86]

Preachers were sometimes paid partially or wholly in kind or offered gifts in lieu of monetary payments. Sometimes cities specified that the money was to be used for a new robe or habit,[87] probably intending the rewards to go directly to the preacher rather than to his convent. During Standonck's Lenten series at Saint-Georges in Abbéville, his lodging, fish, and wine were provided, and his acclaim was so great that the city awarded him "36 l., 5 s., which seemed extraordinary, for the year before they had paid the Lenten preacher 10 l., and his predecessor had recieved only 6 l."[88] Standonck, a secular, refused the money, saying he had done nothing to deserve it, but added that he would not object if the money was used for charitable purposes. The merchants, after taking counsel among themselves, bought several lengths of gray and black fabric, which they sent to Paris for the clothing of the poor. They also paid for a new costume for the "poor cleric who accompanied the preacher."[89]

Partial payments with gifts of food were common. The records of Grenoble indicate at least two "gifts of fish" to the Lenten and ordinary preachers, worth 19 s. and 20 s. respectively.[90] At Aix, the preacher received an allotment for bread and wine,[91] while in the Gard region, the preacher was given a quarter of mutton weighing nine pounds, worth 7 s., 6 d.[92]

In most cases, the preacher was treated as an honored guest by the city's elite. After preaching in 1520 in his home convent of Évreux, Guillaume Pepin was feted by the assembled company. Besides the 10 l. in alms his preaching had earned for the convent, fiscal records indicate that he was treated to a special feast: "Also to Pierre Madeleine, fishmonger, for the fish that he prepared and delivered during Lent of last year to the Dominican convent of this town of Evreux for Master Pepin, who preached the entire Lenten series. The officials of the town and several other officers gathered here, as was their custom. . . . For almonds, grapes, figs, spices, and other delicacies, brought to the convent of Saint-Louis at the dinner for the preacher. . . ."[93] Exotic fruits and nuts were regularly provided to celebrate the preacher's accomplishments at the end of the Lenten fast. The honorarium for the Lenten preacher in Toulouse was 80 l. in 1540. He was also given a barrel of white wine, apples, prunes, almonds, sugar, walnuts, raisins, herring, and oranges.[94] A feast to celebrate the end of Lent would also give the locals a chance to show off their hospitality and culinary specialties.[95]

Accommodations could also be part of the arrangement. The sieur de Gouberville records several instances in which arrangements were made for housing and feeding a preacher brought in from the outside. The town notables would sometimes take their evening meal with the preacher, who would either sleep in his home convent if preaching locally, among his confreres if in another town, or with a member of the local ruling elite. In January, 1558, Gouberville notes that he had invited the young preacher to dine with him, but that he had refused, preferring to make his way to Gonneville, where he was next scheduled to preach.[96] On other occasions, Gouberville was luckier, as was the case when Raoul Tiercelin accepted his invitation for bed and board at the squire's country estate.[97] Even a holy hermit might get such a reception. In 1539, the hermit Charles de Parente preached and enjoyed the bourgeois hospitality of the town of Carpentras, along with his rather surprising retinue of four brothers and three mounts.[98]

The Event: Physical Aspects

> Such great crowds gathered around him that he went and took his seat in a boat while the crowd stood along the shore. He addressed them at length in parables.   Matthew 13:2–3

When a great preacher came to town, representatives of all classes and occupations would often turn out to greet him at the city gates.[99] Vincent Ferrier was greeted with all manner of honors when he took his mission to a town. "Nobles, bourgeoisie, and clerics made a cortege around him, humbling themselves in the most ostentatious manner."[100] It was usually the great prophetic preachers who received this kind of welcome, but all great preachers could expect some sort of civic greeting when they entered a town to preach an Advent or Lenten series. Much less ceremonial naturally attended the preaching of a local mendicant.

It is not entirely clear whether people sat or stood during the sermon. Ecclesiastical injunctions specified that people were to sit during the sermon, normally on the floor,[101] although some women brought their taborets, and wooden benches were reserved for local magistrates and possibly pregnant women.[102] Others might lean against the piers and walls of the church.[103] Pepin comments that "modern Christians balk at having to stand one hour in church to hear a sermon,"[104] and contemporary drawings and frontispieces sometimes show people sitting, and at other times standing. The sexes were separated most of the time, with men on the north side of the nave and women on the south.[105]

Despite the large capacity of many churches, preachers were often confronted by such large audiences that the churches could not contain them. Illyricus had planned to preach in churches during his mission to Guyenne, but the press of the crowd made this impossible.[106] Contemporary chroniclers estimate that as many as thirty thousand people came to hear him.[107] In 1495, Maillard preached to over four thousand in Toulouse.[108] Even allowing for medieval exaggeration, it is obvious from chronicles and the inadequacy of the churches that the great preachers attracted thousands of listeners.

The only alternative was preaching in the open air, which Martin argues was standard practice, weather permitting.[109] Sometimes a pulpit or raised platform was built onto the exterior wall of the church,[110] as was done in Saint-Lô and Vitré.[111] The central marketplace, cathedral square, or open fields[112] all were possible sites for a sermon. In these cases, a portable pulpit was used. Kiessling describes a typical scene: "After determining the quarter from which the wind came, the preacher would erect a small movable pulpit, call the people together by ringing the church bells, and proceed to deliver his sermon."[113] Outdoors, a rope would divide the men from the women.[114]

Even more popular as a site for outdoor preaching was the cemetery, usually adjacent to a church. The cemetery had many advantages—proximity to the church, its large capacity, and not least its effectiveness in conjuring up lugubrious mental images, especially the *ubi sunt* ("where are they now?") themes. The preachers spoke of the transitory glories of the world, which were but passing moments compared to God's eternity. Imagine the scene evoked by Menot if he were speaking in a cemetery:

> I believe that there is not one wretched sinner here today, who if he knew he were to die in the next twenty-four hours, would not put his house in order, that is, his conscience. So surely this king, when he heard the messenger of God, began to tremble all over and could not stand up, fearing that voice just as some wretch who, when he is up on a ladder, trembles for fear that he will fall. O, you worldly ones who are here, do you not recognize your predecessors, your parents, your friends? Are they not dead and rotting in the ground? . . . You ladies, who are full of vanity, I ask that when you visit the tombs of your parents and friends, you ask them this, and cry aloud: "O my father, you were a surgeon, so hard and cruel and inhuman, who cut with his knife down to the bone. Where are you now?" . . . They will respond with the Psalm: "I am a worm, not a man; the scorn of men, despised by the people." (Psalm 22:7)[115]

The practice of open-air preaching had become so ubiquitous by 1448 that the Council of Angers "prohibited all clerics and laymen from erecting 'wooden platforms, commonly known as *chaufiers,* for the usage of preachers.'"[116] Ecclesiastical authorities preferred the greater control that use of the church gave them, for mendicants had to obtain permission from the bishop or curé to preach in a church other their own. Nevertheless, open-air preaching continued throughout France, at least in times of good weather, for it was the most practical means of reaching the greatest number of people.[117]

The sermon was always signaled by the ringing of church bells,[118] but the time of day when the sermon was delivered was very variable. We find references to almost all times of the day, ranging from early morning until evening. As we have seen, mendicants could preach in parish churches only with the permission of the curé and when regular services or preaching were not going on.[119] Sermons were usually delivered before or after mass, which was usually held at nine or ten in the morning.[120] With the disappearance of the lengthy mass sermon, the early morning hours, noontime, or late afternoon were free for preaching. Preachers sometimes continued their sermons in the evening after Vespers.[121] Many of the great preachers gave several sermons a day.

The preacher's philosophy and style could affect the starting time of sermons. Jean Vitrier, who sometimes preached as often as seven times a day,[122] naturally had to start very early. The occasion also determined the length of the sermon, which in turn affected the starting time. Lenten and Advent sermons were always longer than ordinary Sunday sermons, and were sometimes split into two parts: *in mane* and *post prandium*.

The length of the average sermon was as variable as the starting time. The manuals of Surgant and Dungersheim urged slow and careful speaking, warning that "a physician cannot cure his patient in transit."[123] The typical length seems to have been one hour, according to internal evidence from the sermons as well as firsthand reports from the chronicles. Antoine Farinier complained that his listeners were so dead in spirit that they found a one-hour sermon too much to take, with some saying that the sermons after Easter, which were shorter, were preferable.[124] LePicart carefully adhered to the hour length, although he often wished he had more time: "I am running a little late, and wish the hour was longer so I could speak of the honor and dignity of the priesthood, but that will be enough for now."[125] He realized that it was all relative—if the listener enjoyed the sermon, an hour would seem short; if he was bored or uncomfortable, it would seem too long.[126]

Not all preachers followed this rule of thumb. In England, Cox found an instance from the fourteenth century in which the listeners thought the quality of the sermon was fine, but that it was too brief.[127] But many preachers seemed to have erred on the side of too great length. Illyricus often spoke for four or five hours.[128] In Strasbourg, Geiler von Kaysersberg rigidly followed the hour rule, for the sake of his listeners as well as himself: "These long sermons have no other effect than to put people to sleep, make the ladies wet their pants, and tire the preacher himself."[129] While the audience was expected to behave in a reasonable manner during the sermon, the preacher would often stop at the end of main sections to give the listeners a chance to cough or shift their positions.[130]

Read aloud, the extant sermons vary considerably in time required for delivery, due to the abbreviated state of many of them. Menot's sermon for the Sunday after Easter takes half an hour; as much as half the material has been omitted by the copyist. LePicart's sermons take a little over half an hour, while some of Pepin's more complete and lengthy sermons would have taken at least two and one-half hours to deliver.

The Audience

> Jesus finished this discourse and left the crowds spellbound at his teaching. The reason was that he taught with authority and not like their scribes.   Matthew 7:28–29

All classes and groups of society attended sermons; the internal evidence from the preacher's sermons is indisputable on this point, although Martin suggests that the merchant and artisan classes were overrepresented.[131] Pepin tells us that "not only the simple people, but also the great, including kings, are invited to sermons, but they would rather not come. . . . The nobles rarely or never want to hear the Word of God."[132] At the top of the social pyramid, sermons might be given to small, select groups. Well-disposed toward the reformers, Francis I was determined to hear François Landry, curé of Sainte-Croix in Paris, whose outspoken sermons had attracted large crowds throughout the city. According to Theodore Beza, Landry was presented to the king at Saint-Germain-en-Laye, but "unaccustomed to preaching before the great, he stood entirely mute in front of the king." Although disappointed, the king suggested with considerable irony that *if* at other times the preacher made heretical pronouncements, then his errors should be brought to the king's notice.[133] In the group of preachers studied here, Maillard, Pepin, Jean de Gaigny, Cleree, and Jean Tisserand regularly gave sermons to royalty.

The strong presence of the bourgeoisie can be deduced from the sermons. The very frequent references to lawyers and merchants would have served little purpose if few were in attendance. Particular references to clothing styles mark out the merchants in the audience: "A merchant will come [to church], his head held high, wearing his high shoes, but will turn his ankle and fall in the mud."[134] Maillard draws analogies that the merchants can understand: "My lord burgesses, when you go to the rue Saint-Jacques, you dine with your wife and your friends. Similarly, Christ dined with his disciples."[135]

The poor are seldom mentioned in regard to sermon attendance, possibly because their interests ran more in the direction of mystery plays and performances.[136] The preachers also were less likely to single them out for rebuke, since they felt considerable sympathy for them as a group, contrasting sharply with their feelings about the nobility and the bourgeoisie.

According to Menot, women outnumbered men at sermons by at least four to one:

> We see by experience that at every sermon you will find four women for every man. I think there were probably also a lot of children [present at Christ's sermons], if the women of that time were like those in this city, where they do not come to a sermon without babies hanging from their breasts and a great multitude of small children trailing behind them who yell throughout the sermon. They make it very difficult for the preacher and those in attendance.[137]

Although some preachers complained about the distractions caused by small children, the medieval theologian Guillaume de Tournai had dedicated one chapter of his *De modo docendi pueros* to the problem of preaching to children, and Dominican councils repeatedly urged the practice.[138] Ferrier's mission to Brittany was at least partially directed at children, and some of the priests in his retinue taught the children prayers and the more physical aspects of devotion during the mass.[139]

Pepin exhorts even excommunicates to attend sermons, for in that way they will learn how to heal their souls.[140] But not all residents of a given town turned out to hear even the most famous preachers. "There are many who do not want to go to sermons, so that they will not have to worry. They believe that their ignorance will excuse them, but in fact they sin even more grievously,"[141] charged LePicart, while Jean de Monluc denounced the behavior of those who preferred other forms of Sunday entertainment:

> Others rise early and hear mass, then eat breakfast and pass the rest of the day eating, going to taverns, drinking, gossiping, singing silly and bawdy songs. . . . It's on this day that the prostitutes, as they themselves say, reap their harvests, more so than during the rest of the week. . . . Jugglers, tambourine players, and others who all live off the people's folly are listened to and received more willingly than a preacher of the Word of God.[142]

Pepin tells of a particular instance that aroused his anger:

> It happened that one Sunday during Lent, I was preaching in a particular town, but the important men of the town did not attend my four o'clock sermon. I was surprised at this, and when I brought my sermon to a close, I decided to find out the cause . . . because other days the sermons were well attended. And behold! When I entered the house, I found my lords seated at the table, playing cards. This amazed me greatly. They were confused and worried, and asked that I not mention this in my sermons. You see how the leaders of the Christian people act iniquitously, playing such games. These gamesters, who have so much time to play, neglect the divine services, the mass, vespers, preaching, and prayers. Except, of course, they pray fervently that God will not end their rule.[143]

Sermons were obviously popular events, judging from the estimates of the number of people in attendance that we possess. Undoubtedly some people did not attend sermons regularly, but the preachers' distress in this regard must be understood against their desire to reach everyone.

Behavior and Reactions

> Some in the crowd who heard these words began to say, "This must be the Prophet." Others were claiming, "He is the Messiah." But an objection was raised: "Surely the Messiah is not to come from Galilee. . . ."
> In this fashion the crowd was sharply divided over him. Some of them even wanted to apprehend him.   John 7:40–41, 43–44

If the preachers were very disturbed by those who failed to attend their sermons, they were often no more pleased by the behavior of those who did.

Not everyone who attended a sermon did so out of unambiguously pious motives, and it was a staple of pulpit rhetoric to denounce those who came out of curiosity.[144] Some went simply out of a desire to find fault with the preacher or to see who else was there,[145] while others "amused themselves by mocking the preacher and twisting his words around."[146] Menot remarks, "It is certain that today many come to sermons out of curiosity. After they eat supper and their stomachs are full, they say, 'Let's go hear this preacher, so that we can hear something that will amuse us.' Other wretches go to see if the preacher will say anything they can argue with and thereby better him. . . . Others, more studious, go to learn . . . while some hope to profit for the salvation of their souls."[147] Many succumbed to the allure of a new arrival. LePicart tells how "when a new preacher comes to town, everyone runs after him."[148]

Some people went to sermons out of a spirit of contentiousness, to argue rather than to be edified. The root of the problem, according to Pepin, lay originally with preachers who insisted on making *sic et non* arguments from the pulpits, a practice that belonged in the schools.[149] Monluc agrees: "There are many who are moved to study and to go to sermons out of a contentious spirit, to be able to speak about the diversity of opinions. We find churchmen who never open a Bible, but who have dozens of arguments at their disposal to back up their opinions. For their part, some people attempt to learn how to contradict their priests, to dispute with their curés, and others who come to preach to them."[150]

Disturbances were common. Farinier mentions dogs wandering in and out of the church as well as nobles bringing their pet falcons along with them.[151] Instead of praying, Pepin railed, some "look now at the ceiling of the church, now in front of them, now in back, now to their right, now to their left, now talking and laughing with this one or that one."[152] Similarly, Menot fulminates against people who laugh loudly throughout the mass and walk around doing whatever they please.[153] This latter situation was serious enough in Poitiers for the *présidial* to prohibit people, under pain of a 10 l. fine, from "walking about inside the cathedral and other churches during the offices and sermons."[154] It goes without saying that auditors occasionally fell asleep during sermons. For those who remained awake, girl-watching was a regular pastime.[155] Merlin accuses men of going to see the pretty women,[156] a complaint echoed by Maillard, who denounces those who attend in order to be with their lovers.[157] Pepin reprimands those who leave church just before the sermon begins.[158]

Some historians have argued that late medieval society was imbued with a sense of religious Angst,[159] but there is very little in the sermons to support such a contention. It is difficult to determine whether the preachers were too demanding or their audiences too lax, but it appears likely that the preachers' frustration was at least partially a reaction to the latter. Menot reminds the crowd that "you have in sacred memory Antoine Farinier, [Jean] Tisserand, Jean Bourgeois, and so many others who told you how to act so that you would not incur the wrath of God, yet what correction have you made in your lives? You only get worse and worse."[160] Looking out over his audience, Maillard does not see men and women overly fearful about their salvation, but rather people who already think they are good enough—after all, they have come to the sermons of their own free will![161] Usually when a preacher reproved them too sternly, members of the audience would begin to murmur or answer back. "If a preacher of the truth touches on a sore point, the weak sinner shakes his head and says: 'This preacher talks too deeply about this matter; he is too rigorous.'"[162] Pepin admits that some people stay away from sermons because the preacher sharply reproves their vices.[163] Others recognized a preacher's eloquence and erudition, but did not necessarily think that they should act upon his advice.[164] John Calvin echoed this theme to a much different audience decades later: "No matter how much the gospel is preached and the voice of God resonates everywhere, still many people remain exactly as they were, and do not change at all."[165]

The congregation was particularly obdurate when the preacher dwelt on one of his favorite themes—penitence. Menot laments that "when a preacher talks of penitence, many people deride him, or simply do not care."[166] There was a general feeling among the preachers that the world was against good and zealous preachers.[167] Messier denounces those who claim they want to hear the truth, but start to murmur when he touches them personally.[168] Other members of the audience, less apathetic, might be moved to tears by the words of a preacher, but after exiting the church, they "leave behind all compunction, devotion, and resolutions for a better life. . . . It is not enough to hear the Word of God unless it is retained in memory and implemented in one's life."[169]

Although most preachers complained of the spiritual malaise of their listeners, they recognized genuine piety as well. Some of the preachers lauded the laity, whose behavior was especially praiseworthy when compared to the less-than-pious behavior of many priests and monks. When Ferrier preached in Toulouse, the faithful would often prostrate themselves on the ground, shouting, "Pity! Pity! Pity!" and as he finished, the crowd would swarm around him, trying to kiss his hands and touch his robes.[170] Occasionally, there were spectacular instances of conversion, which might culminate in a "sacred bonfire." This could take many forms. One of the preachers studied by Martin, Thomas Cornette, would set bands of children on women's trains, which once detached would be set afire, as a dire warning against the vanities of the world.[171] Illyricus made a specialty of provoking bonfires of playing cards,[172] and even François Lambert, one of the apostles of the French Reformation, was known for the *bûchers de vanités* that accompanied his sermons.[173]

Prostitutes were often the subject of special solicitude by the preachers, frequently with impressive results. Menot invokes the memory of Tisserand, who had founded a monastery dedicated to the rehabilitation of ex-prostitutes and abandoned women:[174] "Alas, now God has taken the soul of Brother Jean Tisserand. When he preached in Paris, with the bishop in attendance, he converted many young women and made them repent. It is wonderful to see such good in a holy father."[175] At Lyon, conversions were so numerous after an "Italian named brother Thomas" (probably Illyricus) preached that the town fathers did not know how they were going to be able to care for the women.[176]

Because preachers saw themselves as the conscience of the Christian community, they often attracted the attention of the authorities, frequently with unpleasant results. Benefit of clergy availed them very little. Farinier, Maillard, LePicart, Jacques Merlin, and Standonck all suffered for their outspoken or antiroyalist preaching, and records from Amiens indicate that banishment or imprisonment was not an uncommon punishment. In 1485, an Augustinian from the local convent had preached of the dissension between the town's nobility and its ecclesiastical authorities. Several representatives of both groups were in attendance, and began to murmur. After the sermon was completed, the preacher was dragged away to the hôtel de ville by the town leaders, subjected to rigorous questioning, and ultimately imprisoned, apparently because he had angered too many influential people.[177] Ten years later, the Dominican Jean Masselin, who had preached in the town earlier without repercussions, spoke out against several married women of the town. His words were "evil sounding and dishonorable to the said women," so he too was led away to the city hall. Here, perhaps under duress, Masselin named those who had advised him to speak out, and was required to give another sermon retracting his statements. He was then banned from the city for three to four years.[178] Surprisingly, such strong reprisals did not deter other preachers. Just two years later, a Franciscan preaching in the church of Saint-Frémin-en-Castillon claimed in his sermon that the rich hardly paid any taxes, leaving the full burden to fall on the shoulders of the poor. As a result of his words, which singled out "fourteen or sixteen" individuals, "sedition, commotions, and danger followed." The Franciscan was taken to the échevinage (magistrates court), where he excused himself, saying that "certain persons of the town, whom he would not be able to identify, came to him and said that because of the taxes and subsidies required of them, they could no longer afford to live or eat... and so he should exhort the town's leaders to help the poor. He said he certainly had not intended to cause riots." The outcome of the case is not known.[179] After Maillard lashed out at royal policies, Louis XI sent one of his officers to threaten the preacher that, if he did not desist, he would be tied up in a sack and thrown into the river. Maillard quipped in response that he would then arrive in paradise sooner than the king.[180] Ironically, this same threat was made to the preacher Panigarole a century later by members of the Seize; (the Sixteen, that is, opponents of Henry III in Paris), who complained that he had spoken against preachers who were slandering the king.[181]

Drastic actions against preachers whose words were *mal sonnantes* were naturally not confined to Amiens. In 1518, Francis I sent one of his maître des requêtes throughout the city of Paris to inform him about preachers who were speaking out against the Concordat of Bologna, even though they were doing so with the knowledge and authorization of the Faculty of Theology.[182] Eight Franciscan brothers, a doctor of theology, and several members of parlement were summoned to appear before the authorities because of their preaching against the king and pope.[183] During Lent in 1524, a Cluniac monk named Guillaume Josse was taken in hand by Captain Fédéric on the orders of the king because he had spoken "against the honor of the king and the bad administration of the realm" during his sermons at Saint-Séverin.[184] The chronicler Versoris claims that the people were outraged,[185] but this did not spare the preacher an indefinite term of imprisonment in the Conciergerie. When Antoine Farinier was exiled in perpetuity by Louis XI in 1478, "there was great dismay among the crowds who had been coming to hear him, and they could be heard to say that this was great folly, for the king knew nothing of these matters and should not interfere."[186] As he was escorted out of Paris, the people followed him, sighing and shrieking. Large, weeping crowds also followed LePicart to the gates of Paris when he was exiled to Rheims in 1533.[187]

The relationship between town and preacher was surprisingly businesslike, based on oral agreements, contracts, and sometimes accompanied by legal proceedings. This was the result of the growing "institutionalization of the Word" observed by Martin to be one of the crucial religious developments of the later Middle Ages.[188]

The sermon was in every way an event for the people—an opportunity to dress up, exchange gossip, flirt, make assignations and, of course, listen to and perhaps profit from the words of the preacher. If held in the open air during fine weather, it could be an enjoyable outing. For some, the sermon offered intellectual stimulation, humorous interludes, and possibilities for debate. Others clearly had less mundane preoccupations in mind when attending a sermon. In this religious age, the dramatic evocation of sin and glory could reduce numbers of people to tears. This heightened emotion, manifested before the Reformation in sacred bonfires, mass conversions, or flagellant processions, needed only a spark to become something more.

While preaching may have been institutionalized by the fifteenth century, this does not mean that the leaders of church and society controlled what was being preached. The nineteenth-century historian Antony Méray designated as *libres prêcheurs* those preachers who "thundered against tyrannical excesses, certain insupportable practices, and pillaging done with the complicity of the civil and ecclesiastical authorities."[189] There was a real concern for the poor and the helpless that invariably led to problems with authorities who were chiefly concerned with the preservation of social order. Even so, the preachers were not always truculent in their attitudes toward those in control. They often used diplomacy, exercising their influence to bring about social justice and social reconciliation.[190]

At this point it is appropriate to turn to the preachers themselves. What kind of men chose to devote their lives to spreading the Christian gospel, and what kind of preparation was required for this sacred ministry?

3

The Life of a Preacher

You saw brother Antoine, brother Richard, brother Jean Tisserand, who
saved poor penitent girls, brother Jean Bourgeoys, brother Olivier Maillard, who worked miracles, whose life and doctrine was approved by
all.   Michel Menot[1]

Since preaching was the specialty of the mendicant orders, it is not surprising
that the majority of the preachers studied here were friars, including all but
four of the pre-Reformation preachers.[2] Benedictines and other cloistered
monks whose vocations were centered inside the monastery provided far fewer
preachers than the orders of friars. While specially trained preachers, especially from the Franciscan, Dominican, Carmelite, and Augustinian orders,
were the mainstay of medieval preaching, all mendicants and many seculars
were at least in theory expected to be able to preach. Despite the large number
of potential preachers among seculars,[3] their numbers were still far inferior
to the mendicants. Pepin laments that "it is a very rare thing today to see
seculars preach."[4] Largely because of the Protestant challenge, significantly
more seculars began to preach after the Reformation.[5]

Preaching was part of the office of bishop, and occasionally in the later
Middle Ages, bishops and archbishops carried out this pastoral function. In
Bourges, later to become a hotbed of reform, the mid-fifteenth-century archbishop, Jean Coeur, not only promulgated synodal statutes requiring preaching in his diocese, but preached frequently himself.[6] But his case was unusual,
and many bishops rarely preached, or only on great occasions, a fact that
amazed Pepin since "Christ, the true son of God, did not think himself too
good to preach."[7] Martin points out that in Chartres, the bishop was expected
to preach a dozen times a year, but usually farmed the obligation out to
others.[8] The problem was sufficiently serious that on the rare occasions when
a bishop did preach, the people were astounded. The orthodoxy of Antoine
Carraciole, created bishop of Troyes in 1550, was suspect at an early date
largely because he preached regularly.[9]

The preachers in this study were the best and the brightest practitioners
of their art in France during the one-hundred-year period between 1460 and
1560. Short biographical sketches appear in the Appendix, but here it is

appropriate to introduce the preachers and to point out the chronological differences among them. Two of them, Antoine Farinier and Jean Tisserand, died before 1500. Their sermons reflect some of the prevalent themes of preaching during their youth, and differ in many ways from those of sixteenth-century preachers. Étienne Brulefer, Jean Cleree, Nicolas Denisse, Thomas Illyricus, Olivier Maillard, and Jean Raulin all died before 1517, while another, Michel Menot, died in 1518, probably aware of Luther's challenge to the church. Still another group was significantly active in the decades both before and after the Reformation, including Josse Clichtove, Artus Fillon, Jacques Merlin, Robert Messier, and Guillaume Pepin. This group is particularly important both as an index of change and a measure of continuity with the preachers of the pre-Reformation era. For the sake of convenience, all these preachers have been referred to throughout the book as "pre-Reformation Catholic preachers" or "late medieval Catholic preachers." Another group consists of Catholic preachers who were not active before the Reformation, but whose preaching careers matured in the years between 1520 and 1560: Jean de Gaigny, Claude Guilliaud, Jean Lansperge, François LePicart, Jean de Monluc, and Etienne Paris. Two other groups of sermons are identifiable as the work of six post-1550 Catholic preachers, Jean Scoepperus, and an anonymous author. These eight preachers have been termed "post-Reformation Catholic preachers." Finally, although their beliefs were often substantially different one from the other, Aimé Meigret, John Calvin, Pierre Viret, and other "heretics" have been designated "Protestant preachers." If not taken too literally, these labels can serve a useful function for purposes of generalization.

Doctors of theology predominate among these preachers. Fifteen can definitely be identified as such, and only two definitely were not. Although Martin speaks of a certain "vulgarization" of advanced degrees in theology by the end of the Middle Ages,[10] advanced studies appear to have been one of the qualifications of a successful preacher. In Aix, degrees in theology were more common among Dominicans than among Carmelites or Augustinians, possibly as a result of the stronger intellectual tradition of the Friars Preachers. The general preponderance of doctors of theology among itinerant preachers is confirmed by the town records, where payments to preachers indicate that doctors are second only to "brothers," some of whom may also have been doctors, but whose titles are unspecified. Bachelors, masters, and licensees were also regularly listed as popular preachers.

Interestingly, these preachers, in spite of their fame, have left behind few details of their life histories. The famed Franciscan preacher Jean Glapion is typical. His date of birth, educational attainment, and even nationality are obscure.[11] Almost nothing is known about less famous preachers. Because of these limitations, this chapter will focus on the life of one of the great preachers in our study, Guillaume Pepin, with supplemental material drawn from the lives of the other preachers. We will look at Pepin's social origins, training and education, nonpredicatory positions, and literary production. Although this may not provide us with the biography of an "average" preacher, many of those who did not attain such heights followed a similar course.

Early Life and Education

> On the third day, they came upon him in the temple sitting in the midst
> of the teachers, listening to them and asking them questions.
>
> Luke 2:46

Based on the date when he received his doctorate in theology, Guillaume Pepin was probably born around 1465 near the town of Évreux in Normandy. Normandy, Champagne, and the Île-de-France were the cradle of many of the best-known preachers because of the importance of these areas in court life, their large population bases, and their proximity to the University of Paris graduate school of theology. Not surprisingly, the dioceses of Sens, Rouen, and Rheims produced 65.4 percent of all doctors of theology during the years 1500 to 1536.[12] While seven of the preachers studied here came from Normandy or the Île-de-France, almost every corner of France is represented, as well as the Holy Roman Empire and Dalmatia.

Although the Hundred Years' War had finally come to an end, Normandy in the early years of Pepin's life was wracked by the intrigues of princes against the young king, Louis XI. At the end of 1465, the duke of Bourbon had taken possession of Évreux, and the ensuing years saw continued troop movements through the province as the king and his adversaries alternated control of the duchy.[13] This state of affairs weighed most heavily on those least able to bear it, the peasants, from whose ranks Pepin came. The son of a *laboureur,* a small cultivator, his records at the University of Paris simply designate him as "poor." Pepin's early life would have been very different indeed from that of François LePicart, who came from an ancient noble family, and whose importance is attested by his baptism at the hands of François de Rohan, archbishop of Lyon, and his confirmation by Étienne Poncher, bishop of Paris.[14] In this, LePicart was more typical of well-known preachers. Of Pepin's family, nothing is known. How is it that the son of a poor cultivator was able to enter the local Dominican convent of Saint-Louis in Évreux? Did his parents give of their meagre resources to educate their son? Was he orphaned and taken in out of charity by the local Order of Preachers? The answers to these questions are elusive—we know only that as an adolescent he arrived at the *porte Saint Louis* of the convent and asked for admittance.[15] Although the founders of the various mendicant orders had not envisioned exclusive societies, and made some provision for scholarships, noble or bourgeois blood (or money) was a de facto entrance requirement by the fifteenth century. Property qualifications to dower a novice typically excluded the lower classes, while vows of voluntary poverty would have held little attraction for the poor, who "lived the material circumstances of the *vita apostolica* by necessity, not by choice."[16] Nevertheless, once an adolescent[17] had enrolled in a convent school, social distinctions became less sharply defined, and Guillaume's talents and intelligence soon became evident to his superiors. It may be that Jean Balue or Raoul du Fou, successively bishops of Évreux in these years and intimates of the king, took a personal interest in his career, for influential patrons could virtually guarantee a successful course of studies.[18]

Life in a mendicant convent centered on preparation for preaching, since brothers who preferred the contemplative life usually took their vows in Benedictine or Cistercian monasteries. A glance at the communal records of several towns (Amiens, Dijon, Grenoble, and Nantes) makes it clear that both preachers and their sponsors took very seriously Johann Ulrich Surgant's advice that they be learned in theology.[19] A student in mendicant orders was not permitted to study at an arts college because of secular-mendicant rivalries and fear that the friars would unfairly dominate their secular confreres. Instead, the young friar received his general education in logic and philosophy within the confines of his convent, followed sometimes by attendance at a local *studium naturalium,* where he studied natural philosophy and Aristotle, and then a *studium bibliae et sententiarum.*[20] Convent schools had their own libraries, and brothers were permitted to take books to their room for study.[21] There was also a sort of interlibrary loan service available.[22] A student who showed particular talent might then be nominated to matriculate at the University of Paris or another theological faculty. Those who entered the university were clearly the best from the provinces and local convent schools, for the mendicant orders were allowed relatively few appointments per year.[23]

LePicart and others studying for the priesthood would have begun the arts curriculum at approximately age fifteen, and continued for three and a half years. There were many arts colleges attached to the University of Paris, but those whose students were most likely to go on to advanced degrees were the famed Collège de Montaigu, the stature of which had risen considerably after the reforms of Standonck, the relatively new Collège de Sainte-Barbe, and finally the illustrious Collège de Navarre. The largest theological colleges, which took on these arts graduates, were Navarre and the Sorbonne. The *quinquennium* was complete after another year and a half spent in a trial regency, usually in grammar. Although the rule was occasionally relaxed, the regent master was required to be twenty-one years of age.[24] Aristotle's works formed the core of the arts curriculum, and students were expected to be able to lecture on all of them.[25] A contemporary list of the required readings at Oxford, the curriculum of which was similar to that of Paris throughout the Middle Ages, lists these requirements:

1. Grammar: Priscian *Major* or *Minor;*
2. Rhetoric: Aristotle's *Rhetoric* or Book IV of Boethius' *Topics* or Cicero or Ovid's *Metamorphoses* or Virgil;
3. Logic: *Peri Hermeneias,* or Books I–III of Boethius' *Topics* or Aristotle's *Prior Analytics* or *Topics;*

4. Arithmetic and Music: Boethius;
5. Science: Aristotle's *Physics, On the Heavens, On the Properties of the Elements, Meteorologics, On Vegetables and Plants, On the Soul,* or *On Animals;*
6. Moral Philosophy: Aristotle's *Ethics, Economics,* or *Politics;* and
7. Metaphysics: Aristotle's *Metaphysics.*

In addition, students were expected to be familiar with the New Testament commentaries and trinitarian doctrines in Gilbert de la Porrée's *Six Principles.*[26] Although the curriculum had changed little over the centuries, other works were occasionally added. In 1452, Cardinal d'Estouteville put forth a reading list that included not only the old favorites, but also grammatical works such as Alexandre de Villedieu's *Doctrinal,* Evrard de Béthune's *Grecisme,* and the treatises of John of Halifax and Pierre d'Ailly's *De sphaera.* After 1474, prohibitions on certain works, especially by the Nominalists and Aquinas, were lifted, and these authors provided lively matter for study and debate.[27]

Whether secular or mendicant, the student then spent another thirteen to fifteen years studying and lecturing for the doctorate in theology, beginning as a "student in theology" and working up to the position of *cursor* for the seculars and *biblicus ordinarius* for the mendicants. The great variety of books read during the previous years of study was now replaced by in-depth study of two works. The student devoted two full years to lecturing on the Bible under the guidance of a master chosen by him or assigned by his college or convent.[28] After passing the *tentativa,* the student spent a further year lecturing on Peter Lombard's *Sentences.*[29] Naturally, study of the Bible required reading commentaries on it by Church Fathers such as Augustine, Jerome, and Ambrose, and scholastic thinkers such as Alexander of Hales, William of Auxerre, and Duns Scotus. The exegetical works of Hugh of Saint-Cher and the famed fourteenth-century Hebraist Nicolas of Lyra, who stressed the importance of the literal sense of the Bible, were also very popular.[30]

In 1494, Pepin was named professor by the general chapter held at Le Mans,[31] and sent to the Dominican convent of Saint-Jacques in Paris to begin his advanced studies under the tutelage of another of the preachers studied here, Jean Cleree. Although the reputation of the convent had suffered during years of relaxed discipline, former instructors at Saint-Jacques, founded in 1221, had included Thomas Aquinas and Albert the Great, and it was still widely reputed to be the best conventual school in Paris.[32]

Although the entire course of study could be prohibitively expensive,[33] Pepin's fees and living expenses would have been paid by his order or convent. He attended classes and lectured at the university, but the young friar was required to eat and sleep in his convent. In order to ensure that the friars would not frequent the many Parisian taverns, the *procureur* of Saint-Jacques ran a canteen where wine was sold.[34] At this stage, most of Pepin's efforts would have gone into working on the *Sentences,* the method of which was "to propose a doctrinal thesis or question, to bring forward authorities for and against this thesis from Scripture, the Councils, the Canons and the Fathers, and then give judgment on the issue."[35] At the end of these studies, the student was considered a *baccalarius formatus*. Mendicants were not required to spend the full three years in residence; instead, they could undertake a further disputation, the *disputatio de quodlibet*.[36] Held during Advent or Lent, the *quodlibetales* were open questions on subjects that were "in the air" at a given time.[37] Although their purpose was to train a theology student in the principles of argumentation, in practice *quodlibeta* were often used to get even with a difficult master by attacking his opinions.[38] With his initiation now complete, the bachelor would begin to spend a substantial portion of his time preaching, a requirement of the faculty.[39]

The *baccalarius formatus* then spent another four years in which he had to participate in three academic disputations of varying degrees of difficulty, which would culminate in the licentiate in theology. This gave the candidate the right to teach anywhere in the world. A student who survived this rigorous endurance test usually completed a final year, including two further disputations, the *vesperia* and the *magisterium,* which ended with the awarding of the doctorate.[40] Pepin received his license on January 3, 1500, with a rank of ten in a class of twenty. He received his doctorate a year later.[41]

The advance of humanistic and philological studies at the University of Paris had begun to make itself felt even before 1500. The years between 1474 and 1494 were stimulating ones at the university, not simply because of esoteric theological debates over nominalism or realism, but because of the first stirrings of Italian humanist ideas in France. In 1495, the Collège de Montaigu opened its doors to Erasmus who, despite his short stay, delivered a series of well-attended sermons on the saints. The next year saw the first printings in France of Terence, Ovid, Sallust, and Virgil.[42] Although nominalist thought still reigned supreme in the arts faculties, new influences could be seen in Dominican scholarship at this time. Under the influence of Jean Mair, Pieter Crockaert, and Robert Ceneau, Occamist thought gradually gave way to revised Thomist studies.[43] The humanist Jacques Lefèvre d'Étaples was teaching Boethius's Vulgate with corrections according to the Greek originals.[44]

> Lefèvre wanted his students to go beyond Aristotelianism and the prudent exploration of the world of appearances. He anxiously searched the mystics to see if they had had a glimpse of supreme realities. He tried the Neoplatonism of Ficino and Pico, the hermetic books, and the works of Raymond Lulle, Denys, Richard of Saint-Victor, Saint Hildegarde, and Saint Mechtilde. From Nicolas of Cusa he learned how to distinguish the rational from the intellectual order in the processes of reasoning, and metaphysical thought.[45]

Although Paris would eventually retrench in the face of Luther's threat, the forces that had been unleashed, along with the reforming zeal of Standonck, Raulin, Maillard, and Pepin, inevitably had a strong impact on even the most orthodox of students. This is evident from a perusal of the list of 450 books that have been located and catalogued from Claude Guilliaud's fifteen-hundred-volume library. Guilliaud received his doctorate in theology from the University of Paris in 1532, and used some of his later appointments to amass his great collection. The library shows the strong influence of humanistic thought. Eighty-five of these books (19%) were biblical texts and commentaries, by far the largest category of books in the collection. The list also mentions thirty-eight works on grammar or dictionaries, thirty-four classical texts, thirty-three patristic authors, twenty-one Catholic polemical works, sixteen sermon books, twelve pietistic or devotional works, eleven titles of Erasmus, and ten liturgical books. Scholastic theological books, commentaries on the *Sentences,* and books of canon law account for only a fraction of the list.[46] Guilliaud owned tomes by Aristotle, Albert the Great, and Aquinas, but these were definitely in the minority. He also had a copy of the *Genealogia deorum* of Boccaccio as well as the works of Piccolomini, Ficino, and Budé. His library included such classics as Cato, Cicero, Herodotus, Hippocrates, Martial, Plato, Plutarch, Sallust, Seneca, Livy, Xenophon, and Virgil. He had no less than thirteen works by Clichtove, as well as Lefèvre's *Psalterium quincuplex, Commentarii in epistolas catholicas,* and *Commentarius in epistolas Pauli.* Guilliaud also exhibited great interest in the contemporary religious dialogue, with copies of Erasmus's *Annotationes in novum testamentum* and the *Elenchus in censuras erroneas Natalis Beda,* as well as many of Johann Eck's sermons and writings against the Lutherans. He owned multiple copies of Pepin's sermons, Raulin's *Sermones quadragesimales,* and two of Illyricus's works against the Lutherans. The library also included the works of many of his contemporaries from the University of Paris, including Noël Beda, Jérôme Hangest, and Nicolas Maillard. Interestingly, Guilliaud had a copy of Philip Melanchthon's *Grammatica.*[47]

The Apprentice Preacher

> Jesus next went to his native place and spent his time teaching them in their synagogue. They were filled with amazement, and said to one another, "Where did this man get such wisdom and miraculous powers? Isn't this the carpenter's son?"   Matthew 13:54

It is hard to be sure of the age at which preachers first climbed into a pulpit. Concern for the great dignity and importance of the preacher's task and a desire to emulate Jesus, who had begun his ministry in Galilee at the age of thirty (Luke 3:23), had inspired Saint Bonaventure to insist that the preacher should be "of the right age, not far from 30; he must not be boyish in appearance or in habits."[48] Olivier Maillard was born in 1430 and died in 1502. The lengthy title at the head of one of his series of Advent sermons states that "he began speaking to assembled crowds around the year 1460" and his epitaph confirms this: "Alas! The great fruit he achieved and perfected in the space of forty-two years."[49] Mendicants were permitted to preach outside of their convents at the age of twenty-five,[50] and Illyricus did begin preaching at this age.[51] This was possible only because he was not following a course in theology, for most preachers who were enrolled in advanced theology programs did not have the free time required for full-time preaching until they were further along in their studies.

As preaching was such an integral part of their function in society, mendicants started to preach while still at the university.[52] School officials frequently complained that so many *baccalarii sententiarii* were off preaching Lenten sermons that they were not able to lecture adequately on the *Sentences*.[53] In 1465, the town of Amiens gave "60 s. to brother Hervé Guynot, bachelor in theology and Augustinian monk, who preached during one month in several churches in the town, where he acquitted himself well, delivering fine and noteworthy sermons, in order to help him to become a master of theology."[54] The town's support was evidently very helpful to Guynot, for twelve years later he returned, by then a doctor of theology.[55] His renown was so great that by 1482 he was preaching as far afield as Brittany.[56]

While this book concentrates on the best preachers of the era, most of them doctors of theology, there were hundreds of other preachers who did not have the aptitude or means for advanced study. These men could nonetheless become good preachers by using the many preaching resources that were widely available, including printed sermons. They could begin with Surgant's (d. 1503) *Manuale curatorum,* which contained a list of recommended books for preachers. This was kind of a "correspondence course" for preachers in convents who were unable to obtain university degrees. Surgant first presented a list of those authors who, in his opinion, were indispensable: (1) William of Paris; (2) the fourteenth-century Dominican theologian Peter of La Palu; (3) Peter Lombard; (4) the canonist and liturgical writer William Durand; (5) Albert the Great or Hugh of Argenteuil; and (6) Johann Busch, a specialist in ecclesiology, or Aegidius Aurifaber. Other highly recommended authors included a famous archbishop of Florence, Antoninus Florentinus (d. 1459), Johann Herolt, and Vincent Ferrier. Surgant also suggested works of contemporary preachers, including one of the collections by Étienne Brulefer. These sermons had the advantage of being readily adaptable to the needs of the time. The manual and suggested syllabus show an awareness that not all would-be preachers would have the intellectual skills to expound the difficult passages of Augustine or Aquinas, although these writers, along with Jerome, Ambrose, Gregory, and others, were on the list for those with greater ambition. Surgant informed his readers that most of the recommended books would be available in monastic libraries.[57]

Prior of Évreux and Regent Doctor at Paris

Come after me and I will make you fishers of men.   Matthew 4:19

Even in the last stages of his formal education, Pepin remained concerned with the affairs of his home convent in Évreux. In 1498, he was instrumental in convincing the brothers to join the reformed Congregation of Holland,[58] which emphasized a totally communal life and the importance of preaching.[59] Like all mendicants, he was accorded the privilege of hearing confession, a task Pepin considered very important for ordinary people "who blush to confess their sins to their priest. Besides, many priests are ignorant and feeble-minded, not knowing how to discern between one leper and another."[60] This "privilege," however, took so much time and caused so many conflicts with parish priests that the Congregation of Holland prohibited penitents—mostly devout women and female religious—from coming to them for this purpose more than once a week.[61]

In his early forties, after receiving the doctorate, Pepin became prior of Évreux (November 1504), a position that he held until September 1506.[62] He probably resided in his own priory house on the convent grounds, or if such a house did not exist, he would have been accorded private chambers.[63] In this post, he was responsible for the conduct of daily activities and supervision of the convent schools.[64] According to Humbert of Romans, the prior should "willingly be present . . . at spiritual exercises within the cloister, such as lectures, conferences, sermons, the divine office, and the like."[65] It was up to Pepin to decide who might leave the house for study, preaching, or other necessary business. These administrative duties apparently interfered with his preaching, and in 1506, he ceded his post to Guillaume Petit, later confessor of Francis I.[66]

Between 1508 and 1510, Pepin returned to the University of Paris as a regent doctor.[67] While he was required to lecture only once a year on the feast of Saint Euphemia (September 16), Pepin supervised his students' courses of study, presiding over academic disputations, and ranking the students. This was a highly valued and much sought-after position.[68]

It is not possible to determine the first position held by most of these preachers, but we do know what major posts they held during their lifetimes. A number of mendicants became vicars general of their order (Cleree, Denisse, Maillard, Messier, Paris) or priors (Pepin). Illyricus served for a time as inquisitor of the faith. Prominent seculars procured stipends as directors of theological colleges (Raulin), *theologales* (Clichtove, Guilliaud), *penitenciers* (Guilliaud, Merlin), deans (LePicart), *gardiens* (Menot, Messier), or bishops (Fillon, Monluc). Some positions, such as royal confessor (Cleree, Gaigny, Tisserand) or librarian (Gaigny), depended on the patronage of the king and his entourage, although it was not uncommon for a preacher to refuse such a post. Josse Clichtove rejected the dauphin's invitation to become his confessor in 1517, preferring a more contemplative life away from court.[69] Several preachers served as part-time diplomats and negotiators for the court. Maillard became embroiled in controversy during the reign of Charles VIII by successfully insisting on the restitution of Roussillon and Cerdagne to Aragon, in his mind unjustly acquired by Louis XI.[70] Some sixty years later, Jean de Monluc spent so much time on diplomatic missions for Catherine de Médicis in the courts of Europe that he had little time left for preaching. Appointments to bishoprics and other prestigious posts were tied more to social rank than to preaching or scholarly ability, although LePicart's selection as dean of the two very important churches of Notre-Dame and Saint-Germain l'Auxerrois in Paris showed that influence and merit could go hand in hand. But while court life provided many preachers with the opportunity to influence royal policies and attitudes, it was also fraught with danger, even before the Reformation, for few preachers tempered their views out of deference to royalty. Maillard's vehement opposition to Louis XII's divorce, and his subsequent fall from grace, is but one example.

Mendicant friars often traveled far and wide to proclaim the message of Christ, especially those who were famed preachers. Pepin preached many times before Francis I,[71] and his studies at the university and position as regent doctor all made him well-known to the people of the capital. But his home and priory were in Évreux, and he spent a good part of his life preaching there. Menot's numerous homely references to the Beauce suggest that this was his native region. He studied law at Orléans, probably in the 1460s, and his description of the funeral obsequies of Charles VII places him in Paris in 1461. In his 1508 *Carême de Tours,* he mentions that twelve years earlier he had passed through Amiens, Montdidier, Senlis, and Tours. Internal evidence from the sermons also suggests that he may also have preached in Savoy, the Alps, and even Italy.[72] Similarly, there is evidence that Maillard, both in his capacity as vicar general of the Franciscan Observants and royal negotiator, preached almost everywhere in France,[73] as well as in the Low Countries, Germany, Hungary, and England.[74] After his banishment in perpetuity by Louis XI, Farinier took his preaching to the Holy Land, and participated in the defense of Rhodes against a Moslem siege.[75] But it was Illyricus whose travels were the most extensive, for France was only one of many stops on a European preaching tour by this native of Dalmatia. He retired to a convent in Monaco, were he established close ties with the ruling Grimaldi family.[76]

The Preacher at Work

> Tell the daughter of Zion,
> Your king comes to you without display
> astride an ass, astride a colt,
> the foal of a beast of burden.
> Matthew 21:5

The mendicants had mastered the art of drama during the fifteenth century, displaying considerable talent for making scenes come alive, much in the manner of the mystery plays.[77] Nowhere is this more apparent than in some of the sermons given during Holy Week, the time of Christ's Crucifixion. Menot's Passion sermon revolves around a vibrant tableau of biblical characters, "medievalized" in the style of fifteenth-century art.[78] The use of theatrical techniques was enhanced by appearance. The reformer François Lambert, writing after his conversion, told the people of Wittenberg how as a youth, he had admired "the propriety of [the monks'] habits, their lowered eyes, bent heads . . . and bare feet covered by sandals. I was enraptured by the dignity of their appearance, their serious bearing, their arms crossed on their chest, the gestures full of elegance that accompanied their preaching."[79] Illyricus, tall, emaciated, with a pale complexion, long nose, and beard[80] would make his entrance into a town where he was to preach mounted on a broken-down mule,[81] just as Jesus had made his triumphal entry into Jerusalem. This suggests that the "poor look" was actively sought after by those in reformed orders, not only because of their vows of poverty, but also because of the visual impact it would have on the audience. An austere appearance would have been a reproach to those whose love of worldly goods and pleasures had debilitated the church. All the same, Bonaventure had argued that the preacher "should have no bodily deformities,"[82] although there could be exceptions. The fiscal records of Amiens for 1497 list payments to the three regular Lenten preachers, plus "the same amount to M. Toussaint Fabry, blind man, who preached during Lent at Saint-Germain and elsewhere."[83]

If the preacher was well-known, his arrival in town was marked by an elaborate ritual. Prophetic preachers, such as Vincent Ferrier, were often escorted by throngs of wandering penitents. This strange retinue would be greeted at the city gates by a procession of regulars, seculars, town notables, guild representatives, members of confraternities, and, of course, common people. The next day, Ferrier would speak to a huge crowd, describing with frightful realism the pains of the Last Judgment. Then, in the same sermon, he would gently evoke the delights of heaven awaiting the elect.[84] Aware that other less talented preachers might try to mimic Ferrier's style, the Council of Nantes in 1431 decreed that "preachers should avoid making terrible outcries, waving their hands about wildly, posturing excessively, and gesticulating outrageously."[85] As we saw in Chapter 2, the choice of a cemetery for the sermon could add to the drama, providing an ideally macabre setting which the preachers were not ashamed to exploit. It seems likely, given Pepin's attitudes toward preaching and his deprecation of frivolity and excess among his collegues, that he was more than usually restrained in his presentation.[86] Yet in an age in which passions ran high, and tastes for the dramatic, the humorous, and the terrifying dominated, all preachers had to satisfy popular appetites to some extent.

The Writer

> I am writing to you in this way not to shame you but to admonish you as
> my beloved children.   Corinthians 4:14

Pepin was not only a renowned preacher, but also a prolific writer. Fourteen collections of his sermons were printed, a number considerably higher than that of most of his colleagues. Even more impressive was the number of later editions of his works, which went through eighty-eight printings and were in demand by printers not only in France, but also in Venice, Antwerp, and Cologne. Some continued to be reprinted as late as 1656.[87] With an average edition comprising between two hundred and one thousand books,[88] it is likely that about fifty thousand books of his sermons were in circulation. Of contemporary Paris doctors of theology who were also popular preachers, only Clichtove surpassed him in total number of published works, with over fifty.

Most, but not all, of Pepin's publications were sermons. As one of the great popularizers of devotion to the rosary, he produced such works as the *Rosareum aureum B. Mariae Virginis,* which doubled as sermons and combined the practical aspects of Marian devotion with earlier theological formulations. Some of his Mariologies display a certain theological creativity,[89] although Pepin never breached the limits of orthodoxy. He published one work on the imitation of the saints,[90] works on confession that could also serve as sermons, commentaries on Genesis, Exodus, and the Gospels,[91] and a discussion of moral decretals.[92]

Pepin must have been gathering together his sermons in the decade after receiving his doctorate, with an eye toward their publication. The convent in Évreux (since destroyed) possessed an eight-volume manuscript set of his work written in the gothic hand of one of his Dominican brothers, possibly his copyist.[93] His first work, the sermons on the penitential Psalms, appeared in Paris in 1510.[94] Most of the sermon collections had been printed by 1528, including the 1520 edition of his Advent sermons dedicated to his mentor, Jean Cleree, and the *Sermones dominicales totius anni,* his best-seller in terms of later editions (eleven).

The written works of the other preachers display the same versatility. Despite his lack of formal training, Illyricus produced a series of epistles directed at various groups such as soldiers, judges, and married people.[95] In addition, he authored a confessional manual and a treatise on marriage.[96] Besides his many volumes of sermons, Jean Raulin wrote a short treatise on death.[97] A lesser-known Dominican preacher of the mid-fifteenth century, Esprit Rodier, not only published a sermon, but also a tract against astrology.[98]

The Last Days

> Not immortal is any son of man.
> Is anything brighter than the sun?
>   Yet it can be eclipsed.
> How obscure then the thoughts of flesh and blood!
> God watches over the hosts of highest heaven,
>   while all men are dust and ashes.
>
>   Sirach 17:25–27

The last years of Pepin's life must have been much like the early decades of his preaching career, with continuing efforts to find new ways to communicate the Christian message and to come to grips with the new and pressing problem of "Lutheranism." These were also years spent grappling with a problem that had occupied him since his student days in the 1490s: the need for reformation within the church. Many convents had been reformed, but others proved recalcitrant, and in the 1520s, the issue took on new urgency, for the less-than-exemplary lives of certain clerics and the illiteracy and apathy of others presented the many Catholic preachers and priests who led good lives with a seemingly insurmountable problem: how to convince others of the righteousness of Catholicism when so many individual cases of abuse could be pointed out.

As far as we can tell, Pepin and most of his reformed brothers practiced what they preached. There is no hint of scandal in the lives of any of the pre-Reformation preachers examined in this study. The regulars and their secular counterparts who lived after the first years of the Reformation were in the spotlight; had Pepin, Messier, LePicart, or Merlin lived other than blameless lives, we would have heard about it. Later in the century, however, there was a preacher who did not live up to his own high standards. Monluc, perhaps the least typical preacher in our study, preached to the clergy of his diocese against "priests and other clerics who publicly maintain concubines and who live with or spend much time with suspect women, especially those who are not relatives or of an age that puts them beyond suspicion,"[99] yet he was living with his mistress of many years, who had borne him a son.[100]

Guillaume Pepin died on January 18, 1533, in Evreux.[101] The epitaph on his tomb reads: "Here lie the very brilliant theologians, brothers Robert Bignon and Guillaume Pepin, who, excelling in purity and great erudition, had the cure of souls in this reformed convent, where they lived until the end of their lives, bequeathing to posterity their numerous books."[102] As a mendicant who had no right to personal property, Pepin naturally did not leave a will, nor did any of the other mendicant friars studied here, but we are fortunate to have the testaments of three seculars of the period, Josse Clichtove, Artus Fillon, and Jean de Gaigny.

Clichtove's will, made in Chartres, where he had lived for the better part of two decades until his death in 1543, betrays a traditional concern for the state of his soul after death. All the clerics of his church of Saint-André were to attend services in Chartres cathedral, after which they were to bear his coffin down the winding roads to their church. In the choir, solemn masses were to be sung and the church bells rung. Finally, the canons were to inter his body beneath the choir, to the accompaniment of singing and prayer. The canons of Saint-André, his colleagues at the colleges of Navarre and the Sorbonne, the Franciscans and Dominicans of Chartres, and the town poor, were all given alms to sing masses for his soul. Clichtove's library, with the exception of several of his own books reserved for the cathedral chapter at Chartres and ten to be selected by the director of the Collège de Navarre, were to be sold along with his furniture and clothing to pay for the masses as well as wages for his servants. He also left a parcel of land and the remainder of his monetary estate to the cathedral chapter.[103]

Unlike Clichtove, Artus Fillon (d. 1526) expressly prohibited all pomp at his *funerailles*.[104] During his lifetime, he had shown great interest in architectural projects,[105] but on his deathbed, he left behind the secular world. He did not even specify where in the cathedral of Senlis he was to be buried and the stone above his tomb bears no inscription.[106] Moreover, he did not order any masses to be said for his soul. The largest part of his estate, 1200 l.t., was given to the cathedral chapter at Senlis, with gifts of furniture, silver, and money allotted to his successor and to the churches in which he had served during his early years. He funded four scholarships to his alma mater, the Collège de Harcourt, two to be given to students from Senlis and two to students from Verneuil, his birthplace. The schools of Senlis benefited from the remainder of his estate.[107]

Jean de Gaigny's (d. 1549) testament differs significantly from the other two. Although he requested burial at the Collège de Navarre, his will shows little concern for his soul after death. Instead, it proclaims his passion for printing, which he had developed during his tenure as the king's librarian. His will shows how far this obsession had driven him. The loans he took out for paper, matrices, punches, and the "augmentation of his house . . . to make room for the printing press" led to insolvency, and most of his press had to be dismantled and sold after his death to repay loans and pay for the services and medications he had required during his last illness.[108]

Of the other seculars in this study, we know only that LePicart left an annual rente of 60 l. to the church of Saint-Germain, of which he was dean,[109] and Merlin left his library to the cathedral chapter and the Collège de Navarre.[110] Another preacher, Martial Mazurier (d. 1551), whose allegedly heretical preaching will be examined briefly in a later chapter, died in the Catholic faith, and specified in his will that his house should be sold to finance Lenten sermons, probably at Notre-Dame, with a proviso specifying that the preacher ask the congregation to pray for his soul.[111] Finally, Jean Bertoul, a noted preacher who left no sermons, gave a substantial monetary bequest, his house, his gardens, and other lands to the Collège de Laon to establish a scholarship.[112]

These wills and inventories are testimony to the different effects of evangelism, humanism, and Lutheranism on churchmen. Most showed a sincere desire to promote learning, leaving scholarships, libraries, and bequests to colleges and chapters with which they had been associated. Clichtove, one of the leading early players in the Catholic evangelical movement, showed himself the most spiritually conservative, while Fillon, also noble-born, insisted upon the simplest of funerals. Gaigny worried more about his debts and printing press than the welcome awaiting him in heaven. Their eclectic tastes in devotional practice bear striking witness to the age in which they lived.

The life of Pepin was remarkable in many ways. At a time when it had become increasingly difficult for the poor to enter convents, he went on to complete successfully the lengthy course of study that culminated in the doctorate in theology. His skills were so great that he became one of the most noted preachers in France and one of the most prolific authors of sermon books and other religious treatises of his time. His biography shows that there was still a place for merit in religious advancement.

At the other end of the social scale was LePicart, born with every advantage, and destined to become one of the great secular preachers of sixteenth-century France. Many of the other preachers, secular or regular, fell between these two extremes, although at least upper-middle-class status seems to have been the norm. Despite differences in social background, or status as mendicant or secular, most men who became preachers had remarkably similar educational training. Although they were well versed in medieval scholastic thought, the Bible and commentaries on it were the focus of their curriculum. These facts go a long way toward explaining the surprisingly strong biblical content of pre-Reformation sermons as well as the uniformity of theological doctrine we find among all Catholic preachers in this period.

Once a friar had obtained his theological degrees, his duties took him beyond the walls of the convent or university. Many preachers examined here were seriously involved in efforts to reform their orders, and all recognized their pastoral mission. They knew that to preach effectively, they had to use all the tools at their disposal to retain the interest of the already converted, renew the zeal of those whose faith had wavered, and attract converts to the Christian faith.

4

The Study of Sermons

In Iconium likewise, they entered the Jewish synagogue and spoke in such
a way as to convince a good number of Jews and Greeks.

Acts 14:1

Although sermons in late medieval and early Reformation France have been
largely overlooked as a historical source, the general study of sermons has
been an active field of research since the nineteenth century. In his seminal
work *La chaire française au moyen âge,* Albert Lecoy de la Marche recognized
the value of preaching for a study of social history and popular piety. His
tripartite division of material into studies of the preachers, their sermons,
and the social context of preaching continues to serve as a model for historians.
Some scholars have chosen to emphasize the literary components of the sermon, stressing form, style, use of rhetorical devices, and classical and scriptural allusion. Writers such as J. W. Blench have built on solid historical
foundations,[1] but others have focused exclusively on the sermon as a literary
genre, without reference to the social, political, and religious context of the
times.[2] While sermons throughout the ages deserve literary recognition according to the talents of individual preachers, to see sermons *only* as examples
of oratory and style is to distort their original purpose and meaning. The
sermon was intended as the living Word of God, expressed in the symbolic
language, meanings, and gestures of a particular time and place. Reading the
sermons textually, without reference to their oral nature and the shared meanings and bonds between preacher and audience, is a pitfall that scholars must
try to avoid.[3] Donald Kelley argues that even after the invention of printing,
"oral modes of discourse continued to be essential. . . . [I]ndeed it is impossible
to understand the explosion of religious enthusiasm without appreciating the
force of the spoken word, especially in the collective experience of the
sermon."[4]

Manuscripts

The preaching of sermons is speaking to a few of mankind, printing books
is talking to the whole world.

Daniel Defoe[5]

Over 80 percent of the sermons in this study (1,336) come from the period 1460 to 1533, which quite possibly was the high point in history for the printing of sermons. Nevertheless, many sermons from this period were not published. Martin's work indirectly shows the problem of studying manuscript sermons after the mid fifteenth century. Prior to this date, highly acclaimed popular preachers would have had no choice but to circulate their sermons in manuscript form; afterwards, they could avail themselves of the printing press. After 1450, it was the more obscure preachers whose works remained in manuscript form. Significantly, Martin chose the printed sermons of Jean Cleree and Michel Menot as representative of the latest part of his study.

In addition, the manuscripts of this period present the researcher with significant problems of identification. As McIntyre remarks, "among the manuscripts collections of the great Paris libraries... only 20 volumes of sermons from the fourteenth to the sixteenth centuries can be identified by the preacher and the place of preaching."[6] An example given by Hirsch illustrates how difficult it can be to identify sermons by author: "The title *Sermones Bonaventurae* in a medieval codex might have any one of the following meanings: a) sermons *composed* by St. Bonaventure of Fidenza; b) sermons composed by some other writer called Bonaventure; c) sermons copied by a friar called Bonaventure; d) sermons copied by an unnamed friar who belonged to a house called after St. Bonaventure; e) sermons preached by some friar called Bonaventure (but not composed by him); f) a volume of sermons which once belonged to a friar called Bonaventure; g) a volume of sermons which once belonged to a house called Bonaventure; and h) a volume of sermons by various authors of which the first (or deemed most important) was by some Bonaventure and which was consequently shelved in a library under Bonaventure."[7]

The manuscript sermons of Jean de Gaigny, Jacques Merlin, and Jean Lansperge have been studied in detail in order to compare them to the printed sermons of the same period. Although the basic theological content is similar to that found in printed sermons, there are some structural differences. Manuscript sermons are usually shorter than their printed counterparts, and the divisions within them are less complicated. These sixty-eight sermons contain fewer than six citations per sermon, compared to twenty-seven in printed sermons. Here, at least some of the authorities listed in printed sermons were added later by the preacher or the printer, as an educational aid for the apprentice preacher or as a concordance for the more experienced user. The appearance of multiple citations in a sermon does not mean that the preacher rattled off all these authorities; it merely indicates to the *reader* the often multiple sources for a particular thought.

The decision to print a given series of sermons rested on its generalizable utility (the less specific the circumstances, the more desirable), the fame and reputation of the preacher, and the number of sermons available (a series being preferable to a single sermon or a small group of sermons).

Printed Sermons

He will preach without opening his mouth; without breaking silence he
will make the Lord's teaching resound in the ears of nations.

Jean Leclerc[8]

The overwhelming majority of works studied here are printed sermons (96
percent). As in later times, the decision to publish often rested on an author's
fame and previous publications, for the early costs of printing were high, and
producing the works of unknown preachers constituted a financial risk for
the printer. Fortunately for this group of preachers, most of whom were
doctors of theology, the University of Paris underwrote the printing industry
in the capital and set up the first press.

A renowned preacher sometimes personally made the decision to have his
sermons printed. The German preacher Werner Rolevinck printed his sermons in Cologne in 1470, saying, "since there is no more easy way to communicate the sermon to more people, I have had it printed in multiple
copies."[9] In post-Reformation Toulouse, the preacher Denis Peronnet explained that he published his sermon in French "so that no one can pretend
to be ignorant of the means of his salvation. I know that many find it strange
that I have written in French, alleging that henceforth women will try to
preach and simple and rustic people owning this book will content themselves
with reading it, without going to the sermon. But I would respond to my
critics that what I have written here is meant for the use of simple curés."[10]
A sermon delivered by an unspecified Franciscan around 1506, on the subject
of Saint Joseph, was "translated into French and published at the request of
several notables of Rouen who were devoted to the said saint."[11] In other
cases, a preacher might give his notes to a copyist in his home convent, who
could then ready them for publication.

More often, we find elaborations of notes taken in shorthand by clerics
hoping to profit from the material themselves. Students and other clerics
would bring notebooks to the sermon to record the preacher's words, using
an elaborate stenographic system that was based on contractions, initials,
partial words, and signs.[12] LePicart's large collection of sermons was published
after his death using notes taken by his auditors.[13]

Textual statements often provide clues as to who was responsible for producing the printed version. Revealing statements such as "sermones sua propria manu scripti aut correcti," "de novo revisi," or "per eundem
conscriptum," indicate that the work was submitted or authorized by the
preacher himself, while sermons transcribed by a fellow friar might contain
such phrases as "ex ore ipsius," "seorsum," "sub eo praedicante," "sub Dei
praecone," or "post praedicationem quotidianam factam."[14]

The level of completeness of a printed sermon also gives clues about the
preacher's role in their publication. Intermingling of French and Latin phrases
is usually a convention of the notetaker, while the absence of such phrases
suggests greater personal involvement in the publishing process by the

preacher. The use of mixed language is common, but not universal in the pre-Reformation sermons studied here. Found very frequently in the sermons of Menot and Maillard, it rarely occurs in the more complete sermons of Pepin. Finally, the length of the sermon is significant. Pepin's sermons are not in shorthand, and typically run to over thirty pages (Gothic type, two columns), whereas an average shorthand sermon of Cleree or Maillard is only three to four pages long, suggesting audience notes.

Special Sermons

> To the elders among you I, a fellow elder, a witness of Christ's sufferings and sharer in the glory that is to be revealed, make this appeal. God's flock is in your midst; give it a shepherd's care.   1 Peter 5:1–2

Most of the sermons in this study were delivered on occasions in the church year—Sundays, feast days, and seasons of the liturgical year. Even on these occasions, sermons might be devoted to such topics as sin, confession, or the penitential psalms. There were also special sermons for delivery to monks, nuns, or other clerics, which differed significantly from popular sermons in both style and content. Within the confines of schools or convents, it was acceptable to discuss esoteric subjects, mysticism, or theological subtleties. Most of the sermons in this study were intended for popular use, but sixty-three sermons were delivered to a convent of nuns, three at a synod, and one to the clergy of the diocese of Valence. Other sermon books were intended solely for the instructional use of clerics.[15]

Another specialized type was the *court sermon*. During the reign of Louis XII, the Dominican bishop of Marseilles, Antoine de Fours, preached a sermon at court in Latin honoring René de Prye, who had received a cardinal's hat from Georges, cardinal d'Amboise. In this sermon, he delineated the genealogy of the house of Amboise and went on to show how the four *cardinal* virtues must govern human (and royal) life.[16] Sermons of this kind bear a strong resemblance to those given at the papal curia.

Language

> But in all their utterances they should first of all seek to speak so they may be understood, speaking in so far as they are able with...
> clarity.   Augustine, *On Christian Doctrine*, 4.8

Of the 1,657 sermons studied here, all but 335 are in Latin. Except for five French sermons of Olivier Maillard, preached between 1460 and 1502, all the vernacular sermons come from the sixteenth century. The manuscript sermons, also from the sixteenth century, are exclusively in French, which tells us something about manuscript versus printed sources. As the lingua franca of the church, Latin could reach a far larger audience.

Few scholars today accept the claim of the influential nineteenth-century literary historian B. Haureau that the predominance of printed sermons in Latin indicates that this was the language of preaching.[17] Even in Carolingian times, the need for vernacular sermons had been recognized,[18] and later documents from the papal curia, bishops, councils, and synods continued to reflect concern that preaching be comprehensible to everyone. By Maurice de Sully's death in 1196, most preaching was done in French.[19]

Latin was the language of clerical notetakers, who lapsed into French when they did not know the Latin for a particular phrase or wanted to retain the flavor of the original language. The result was the macaronic sermon, which interspersed French with Latin. Macaronic phrases often contain an idiom that defied Latin translation. Thus the printed version of Menot's Carême de Tours reads "Hodie invenietis ung malheureux viellart a deux doitz pres d'enfer."[20] Sometimes the word *gallice* would indicate to a regional or non-French preacher the need to supply equivalently colloquial language: "Dicite mihi in veritate vos iuvenes mulieres en voz fiensailles *gallice:* sponsus vester nunquid visitavit vos aliquando?"[21]

Although French was the language of popular preaching during the fifteenth and sixteenth centuries, there was some Latin used during the sermon. The preacher read the theme and biblical quotations in Latin, followed by a loose translation. Sermons entirely in Latin remained important in nonpopular settings. At Rome, preaching before the popes was always done in classical Latin, with eloquence and rhetorical erudition the criteria for success.[22] Likewise, Latin was most commonly used by preachers in conciliar assemblies, universities, general chapters, and many monasteries of men.[23] These sermons can be identified by such phrases as "ad clericos," "ad monachos," "ad moniales," "in synodo," "ad sacerdotes," "ad scholares," and "cappelle pontificie."

The Philosophy of Preaching

> My message and my preaching had none of the persuasive force of "wise" argumentation, but the convincing power of the Spirit.
>
> 1 Corinthians 2:4

A preacher's sermons and his statements about preaching reveal a great deal not only about his personal devotion and motivation, but also about the religious sentiments of his age. Did his ideas agree with or run counter to those of his colleagues? How did he view his apostolate and his flock? Did he see his role primarily as pastoral, prophetic, pedagogical, or theatrical?

An adage of the time said that "he who does not know Pepin does not know how to preach."[24] One of Guillaume Pepin's first concerns was that "a preacher of the truth should strive to live in such a way that he can profit his listeners."[25] "The preacher should be guided by three considerations: the first is upright living . . . , the second plain and simple preaching. . . . for those of you who preach must talk plainly and clearly so that a listener, no matter how simple or uneducated, can profit from the sermon. The third consideration is proper motivation."[26] Preachers who lead irregular lives will scandalize their listeners,[27] and make them hesitate to speak out against the vices of others.[28] Pepin repeats Luke's injunction: "Physician, heal thyself."[29]

The problem, in Pepin's eyes, was that preachers had lost sight of their mission as it was originally conceived in the primitive church: "The preachers of the primitive church, the Apostles, did not seek wool [i.e., tithes], nor human praise, but the glory of God and salvation of souls. . . . In the early church preachers were few, but people were quicker to follow them and more avid to hear their sermons than in modern times, when instead we find bad preachers and irreverent listeners."[30] He laments the passing of men like John the Baptist, who are "rare birds" in his day.[31] Instead he finds Pharisees, preachers who remind him of the "ancient doctors of the Jews, who explained scripture according to their own intricate and tortuous fantasies."[32] It was the duty of a "good pastor . . . to visit his flock, and if he find them infirm or dead in their faith or morals, he ought to fortify them."[33] The preacher's task was so important that "just as the seed that falls on good earth bears fruit according to the will of God, so the word of God is spread by the mouth of good preachers, and if it touches the heart of devout listeners, brings forth much fruit."[34]

But if Pepin saw many things wrong with the preaching of his day, he did not hesitate to offer positive examples and recommendations. Besides John the Baptist, Pepin lauds the efforts of Dominic, Anthony of Padua, and Vincent Ferrier.[35] He gives many examples to help a preacher understand his role. If the models provided by the great men were not enough, the preacher might think of himself as a peacock:

> Morally, a good preacher can be compared to a peacock. For his golden plumes signify the sacred doctrine which he must have and preach to the people. His gray feathers signify the worthless clothing that he wears; the terrible voice of the peacock signifies the constancy of the preacher and his sharpness in reproaching vice; . . . incorruptibility of the flesh signifies his right intention, for he ought not to preach on account of human praise or riches or to procure benefices, as many do today to the great damnation of their souls.[36]

While a thirteenth-century manuscript from Bruges likens the good preacher to a cock, according to that bird's traits,[37] Pepin prefers the analogy of "a good dog, who senses the wolf near his master's home, coming to attack the sheep. He does not stop barking, no matter how long it takes until the wolf goes away. On the contrary, he tries to bite the wolf, and even if he is in turn bitten, does not desist from barking. In like manner, the preacher should bark out against vices and bite sinners. Such a preacher was Jonas."[38] But

alas! "Nearly all the preachers today are like dumb dogs who do not want to
bark, except perhaps against ordinary people."[39]

The preacher first should seek inspiration, "for preachers of the divine
word are unable to win over souls without the special assistance of Christ."[40]
But he must also do everything in his power to perfect his art. He should
study sacred oratory, so that he does not sow the seeds of error in the people.[41]
Scripture was his basic source:

> Can the soldiers of Christ do less than they might in the great fight? Christ
> their king provides the provisions, and the bread of doctrine, which is even
> more plentifully administered in Lent than at any other time of the year.
> In the great cities . . . there are many preachers delivering the Word of God
> at the same time, one ministering to the people the bread of the epistles,
> another the bread of the gospels, another reproving the weeds of vice,
> another exalting the virtues of the wheat of the elect, and so forth. He who
> does not eat of one loaf, at length eats of another.[42]

Preachers should not preach "subtle and curious" doctrines, but explain divine
laws and articles of faith, whenever possible contrasting the celestial rewards
prepared for those who lead good lives with the pains of hell that await evil
men.[43] "Preachers must descend to the level of simple and ordinary folk in
order to help and edify them, rather than concentrating their efforts on scholarly men of letters, who rarely pay attention to the Word of God."[44]

Preachers must also exercise restraint. Following the maxims of William
of Paris,[45] Pepin argues that while it is the duty of the preacher to reprove
vice wherever it is found, this should take the form of a general censure rather
than attacks on specific persons.[46] "The preacher should not speak all of the
truth all of the time, but should adjust his message to his audience and what
is useful for them. . . . It should not be understood by this, however, that it
is permissible for preachers to teach falsehood as opposed to truth, but rather
that certain truths should be kept quiet when it is not necessary for them to
be bruited about."[47] Constant and injudicious attacks on clerical abuses, so
commonly found in the sermons of late medieval preachers, often exacerbated
the problem. He gives the example of a town in which nearly all of the priests
keep concubines, and there is no hope of their reformation. A preacher who
publicly condemned such vices would only create further scandal among the
people, undermine their faith in the church and its sacraments, and harden
those already committed to lives of sin. Pepin also advises his fellow mendicants to temper their attacks on and rivalries with seculars, so that they do
not add scandal to scandal.[48]

The tone of a preacher should vary according to both the occasion and
the audience. Pepin tells the preacher to size up his listeners. "The preacher
must determine if his audience sins from the passions and frailty of human
nature, or out of simple obstinacy."[49] If, in the preacher's estimation, the
audience is neither particularly wicked nor obdurate, he should adopt a soft
tone toward them. "He should be as Orpheus playing the cithara, attracting
people through his sweet notes of warning and gentle invitations to peni-

tence."[50] Preachers ought to try this approach first, gently exhorting their listeners, for "a pigeon feeding on honey will attract other pigeons to his bounty; he who has this sweet honey in his mouth will wondrously attract other pigeons to him. So the preacher ought to have the sweetness of the Word in his mouth, to draw sinners to their God."[51] But at the same time, the preacher must communicate his fervor to his listeners. He must persevere in the declaration of Christ's message, giving in to neither threats, blandishments, flattery, nor bribes.[52] But lest the preacher's zeal carry him too far, Pepin adds that he should proceed reasonably, with measure, always keeping in mind what is most useful and edifying for his audience.

If, on the contrary, the preacher had in front of him a group of people who were insolent and hardened in sin despite the many warnings of preachers who had come before him, he must take a hard line.[53] "For just as John the Baptist spoke out angrily against sinners, like the Pharisees and Sadduccees, calling them the progeny of vipers, so modern preachers ought to be equally severe and chastise stubborn and inveterate sinners, so that at length, terrified, they will be brought to repentance in a way that soft and gentle warnings could not achieve."[54] In such cases, the preacher should describe the torments of hell[55] not only for the sake of the unrepentant sinner, but also to prevent others from following his example.[56]

Other preachers held strikingly similar views about how preaching should be done. All would agree with Pepin's insistence that the tone and the message must suit the needs and conditions of the audience. Menot and others argue that the zealous preacher speaking out against sin is like a trumpet that blares forth and pierces the hearts of the listeners.[57] "Never does a warhorse, hearing the trumpet to advance, tremble so much as a sinning people hearing this terrible voice."[58] For Menot, Saint Paul perfectly personified this trumpet: "I believe that Christ never had a more faithful servant and soldier than Paul."[59] There were two factors in the conversion of a sinner. "The first is to move sinners through fear of divine judgment and grief over their sins. The second is to heal the soul through the infusion of grace. . . . The first can be induced by the preacher, but not the second. Whence William of Paris: The conversion of sinners is not the work of the preacher, but of God."[60]

Raulin and LePicart agree with Pepin that the preacher must not tell all the truth all the time.[61] Menot argues that this is particularly true when discussing lofty doctrinal points: "I heard from the mouth of Master Huet, who was preaching in the Paris convent, that if it could not have been done any other way, the Virgin Mary herself would have crucified her son, for she burned with such zeal for the redemption of the human race. In chapter, such a statement would be all right. But take care, preachers, that you do not say things that will scandalize simple minds."[62] On the other hand, Maillard insists that one must preach the truth so that the audience has no excuse for not believing.[63] It was the preacher's task to find the delicate balance.

The Reformation brought about some modifications in the philosophy of preaching, with more attention to the problem of heresy and greater care in reproving the church hierarchy. But much remained the same. In Jean Lansperge's opinion, "preachers ought to teach the acts of our Lord, to inflame the hearts of their listeners to imitate him in word and deed."[64] LePicart warns that evangelical doctrines must be taught to each according to his capabilities: "If you give solid meat to a child, he will choke, so therefore you must give him milk. That is to say, for simple and carnal folk, you should only give them the doctrine and instruction that they can handle; but to more spiritual and learned people you may give more difficult and perfect doctrine."[65] He argues that it is not enough to reproach sinners and blame them for their sins—rather the preacher-confessor must also show the person how he has erred and how he may atone.[66] Irritated at the popularity and tacit royal acceptance of "Lutheran" preaching in his day, LePicart lashes out: "If during a sermon today a preacher chastises wrongdoers he is called a mutineer, a rebel."[67] "If the world says, now there is a good preacher, that is a sure sign that he is not, for he speaks to please the world."[68] For the preachers, most of the same problems remained in the mid sixteenth century, although heresy naturally presented new problems.

Form

> By means of many such parables he taught them the message in a way
> they could understand.   Mark 4:33

The Ancient Method

From the early Middle Ages until the end of the eleventh century, the homily or postil reigned supreme. The homily was "the Biblical or purely exegetical form of preaching, explaining some definite scripture tract *(pericope)* with a view to practical application."[69] It "was based ultimately on non-form or anti-theory," retaining to some extent the personal, familiar character of preaching in the earliest days of the church, when small discussion groups were typical.[70] It was a simple method of exposition, without division or subdivision.[71] Variations on the homily, which have been examined in depth by Rudolf Cruel,[72] are not particularly important for our study. Related to the homily was the so-called "ancient method" of sermon preparation. This could be either the explication of a text or topical discussion of any subject, based on reason and scripture, and using the techniques of classical oratory: (1) *exordium;* (2) *narratio;* (3) *partitio;* (4) *confirmatio;* (5) *reprehensio* or *refutatio;* and (6) *conclusio.*[73] Most pre-Reformation preachers used the modern method, but those who preferred a simpler style continued to use the ancient method. Vitrier, the great Flemish preacher who died the year before the publication of the Ninety-Five Theses, was praised by his admirer, Erasmus, for breaking with medieval tradition:

> His sermons hardly had any divisions. . . . By a sort of continuous discourse,
> binding the epistle of the day to the gospel, he allowed the listener to enter
> into it with him. He did not gesticulate wildly nor give himself over to showy

display; on the contrary, he kept himself in full control at all times. One felt that the Word proceeded from a simple and ardent heart. He never drew things out to inordinate length so that everyone got bored nor did he try to vaunt himself by citing huge numbers of authorities. Each homily that he pronounced was filled with Holy Scripture; he could preach nothing else.[74]

The Modern Method

The rediscovery of Aristotelian logic and the techniques of scholastic argumentation led to the development of the "modern method." Its use was originally confined to the schools, for popular preaching was not widespread before the founding of mendicant orders after 1215. In a modified form, the modern or thematic sermon was adopted by itinerant preachers and remained in vogue until the middle of the sixteenth century. Over three-quarters (1,307) of the sermons studied here utilize to a greater or lesser degree the modern method. In this method, the sermon is composed of four parts: the theme, *prothema,* division, and subdivision. Jacob de Fusignano, the thirteenth-century author of a preaching manual, first compared the sermon to a tree.[75] "The theme develops into the protheme or prelocution as root into trunk. Then the prelocution or protheme grows into the principal divisions of theme as the trunk into the main branches."[76]

According to the *Aquinas Tract,*[77] one of the preaching manuals (*artes praedicandi*) in regular use during the later Middle Ages, the theme had to be "taken from the Bible, be well-quoted; have quantity; have quality; be not too short; be not too long; have complete meaning; be fit for oral delivery; and be adorned with homiletical terms."[78] In the more elaborate university sermons, the theme could be a grouping of texts around the central idea.[79] Most daily and saint's day sermons drew their themes from the liturgy, normally the gospel or epistle of the day. During Advent and Lent, the preachers would often use the same theme throughout the preaching cycle. Pepin's forty-sermon series, *De destructione Ninive,* takes its name from the theme that was repeated daily: "Adhuc quadraginta dies & Ninive subvertetur" (Jonah 3).

The *prothema* was first introduced by Humbert de Romans in the thirteenth century and served a function similar to that of the preface in a book.[80] It was supposed to be short and draw the listener's attention back to the theme. The protheme could be deduced either through sound (the use of a homiletic term found originally in the theme) or through meaning, where there was an obvious connection between theme and protheme in a spiritual sense or by synonym.[81] Ideally, the preacher would look for scriptural or patristic texts that would echo the sound or meaning of the theme. By the later Middle Ages, however, changes had crept into this part of the thematic sermon. There was often little correlation between the theme and protheme, and the latter became in effect a "miniature sermon" distinct from the theme and the later divisions.[82] It would often include oratorical disclaimers, such as the preacher's unworthiness to treat such great matters. In his sermon

before Francis I, Jean de Gaigny expressed "great hope that in answer to
your prayers, the grace of God will enlighten the sterility of my understanding."[83] An Ave Maria followed the supplication for divine help. The
protheme of the sermon never became obligatory and was often omitted.

Following the angelic salutation and invocatory prayer, the preacher proceeded to the main body of his sermon, which began with a question based
on theology or canon law. A two- or threefold division into a simple literal
explication or a theological argument and a moral application followed. Each
preacher had his own formulaic way of introducing the body of the sermon.
Menot's is typical: "In the present sermon there will be two parts. In the first
a theological question will be set forth. In the second, the exposition of the
theme will be carried out."[84]

By the late medieval period, differences in sermon style between Franciscans and Dominicans had diminished, although the Dominicans still tended
to use more elaborate divisions than the Friars Minor.[85] In the beginning, the
Franciscans had relied on emotional appeal, especially when preaching to the
humblest members of society, while the Dominicans had geared their intellectual approach to the literate, upwardly mobile classes.[86] This was all part
of the preacher's challenge to find the "right argument communicable to the
right audience in the right circumstances,"[87] although the two orders went
about it in different ways.

The divisions themselves were often very elaborate. A diagram of Sermon
19 from Pepin's *De destructione Ninive,* "The Destruction of the Abbeys of
the City of Nineveh," shows three main parts: *causa, forma,* and *resistentia.*
But from these three major divisions, there are no less than thirty subdivisions
(Table 4-1). In many cases, there is a simple division into examples which
help to establish a given point. In others, the division is based on connected
adverbs or nouns. A shorthand sermon, such as Maillard's Christmas Day
sermon, naturally contained far fewer divisions (Table 4-2). In all cases, there
is a logical progression through the series of divisions, and if one "listens"
to the preacher rather than simply reading his words, the structural complexity
becomes less evident. At the same time, repetitive divisions serve to imprint
the material on the listener's mind.

There were many ways in which a preacher, using the manuals, could
"enrich" his sermon. One of the most common medieval techniques was the
use of a fourfold interpretation of scripture: (1) historical or literal; (2) tro-
pological or morally edifying; (3) allegorical; and (4) anagogical, the mystical
or spiritual interpretation. The preachers analyzed here used all the senses
liberally.

Concordance of authorities, used very frequently in university sermons,
was somewhat less common in popular preaching, although it was retained
in printed sermons. In addition, words could be defined either through their
contraries or through a moral signification shown in etymologies.[88] "Et pour
vous donner a entendre l'ethmologie de ces noms, convient noter que *pascha,*
ou *pasque:* nom hebreu, ne signifie autre chose que une *passée.*"[89] Similarly,

Table 4-1. Outline of *De Destructione Abbatiarum Civitatis Ninive* (Pepin).

THEME: Adhuc quadraginta dies et Ninive subvertetur (Jonah 3)
PROTHEME
  I. CAUSA
   A. EXTRINSECA
     1. laicalis
     2. ecclesiasticalis
   B. INTRINSECA
     1. essentialis
       a. transgressio voti obedientie
         1. generalis
           a. filii
             1. dei auctoritatem
             2. precepti equitatem
               a. esse
               b. nutrimentum
               c. documentum
             3. transgressionis penitalitem
               a. generalis
               b. rationalis
               c. cordialis
           b. servis
             1. velociter
             2. hilariter
             3. libenter
           c. uxoribus
         2. specialis (ad prelatos et superiores)
           a. curatos
           b. episcopos
           c. pontifex summus
             1. precepti
             2. exempli
             3. periculi
         3. specialissima (obedientia religiosorum)
           a. inductionis
             1. angeli
             2. patriarche
               a. Noe
               b. Abraham
               c. Joseph
             3. prophetie
               a. verbo
               b. signo
               c. facto
             4. christus
               a. in principio
               b. in medio
               c. in fine
             5. apostoli
             6. demones
               a. exemplum 1
               b. exemplum 2
               c. exemplum 3

Table 4-1 (continued)

       7. sanctes patres
         a. exemplum 1
         b. exemplum 2
         c. exemplum 3
       8. bruta
         a. exemplum 1
         b. exemplum 2
         c. exemplum 3
       9. insensibilia
    b. conditionis
      1. libenter
      2. simpliciter
      3. hilariter
      4. velociter
      5. viriliter
      6. humiliter
      7. perseveranter
      8. prudenter (sapienter)
      9. amicabiliter
    c. utilitatis
      1. perficit
      2. claudit
      3. aperit
  b. transgressio voti continentia
    1. generalis
      a. institutionis
      b. significationis
      c. fructificationis
        1. procreatio populis
         a. multiplicatio & conservatio generis humani
         b. subventio parentum
         c. restauratio & reparatio ruinarum celestium
        2. vitatio fornicationis
         a. amor inordinatus
         b. omnis turis actus
         c. Thorus violatus
        3. dilatatio charitatis & amicitie, atque procuratio pacis
    2. specialis
      a. vita distractionis
      b. sancte operationis
      c. divine acceptationis
    3. specialissima
      a. auctoritate
      b. ratione
      c. figura
      d. similitudinem
      e. exemplo
        1. vitatio distractionis
        2. dignitas ministrationis
        3. sublimitas conditionis
  c. transgressio voti paupertatis
    1. simulata
    2. coacta

Table 4-1 (continued)

---

            3. voluntaria
                a. exemplaritatem
                    1. christi
                        a. in nativitate
                        b. in vita
                        c. in morte
                    2. apostolorum
                    3. sanctorum patrum
                b. utilitatem
                    1. ad sequendum
                    2. ad emendum
                    3. ad luctandum
                c. premiabilitatem
                    1. ascendendo
                    2. benedicendo
                    3. usurando
        2. accidentalis
II. FORMA
    A. INOBEDIENTIE
        1. grossam
        2. mediocrem
        3. parvam
    B. INCONTINENTIE
        1. grossam
        2. mediocrem
        3. parvam
    C. PROPRIETATIS
        1. grossam
        2. mediocrem
        3. parvam
III. RESISTENTIA
CLOSING PRAYER

---

the properties of things, such as the attributes of the Virgin, could be enumerated.[90]

Preachers could also resort to analogies and natural truths, comparisons, use of synonyms, marking of opposites, and interpretation of names. The preachers used the latter category quite frequently. In his sermon for the celebration of the feast of Saint Barbara, Pepin makes each major point by using a letter of her name. Despite the artificiality of the technique, the sermon itself is an effective and morally edifying presentation of the saint's life.[91] On quite another level, Messier uses such a technique to comment on the papal curia:[92]

R		Radix
O		Omnium
M	id est	Malorum
A		Avaritia.

While these were the recommended ways of constructing and amplifying an argument, preachers were capable of originality. Maillard was straight-

Table 4-2. Outline of *In Die Nativitatis Domine* (Maillard).

THEME: Abiicientes omnes immundiciam et abundantiam malicie. (James 1)
PROTHEME
 I. Fluvius egrediebatur de loco voluptatis
   A. Primo dignitas precedentis
   B. Secundo sublimitas parentis
   C. Tertio utilitas recipientis minam
 II. Jesus est fluvius que exivit de loco voluptatis
   A. Primo gratie ad mundandum peccatum
   B. Secundo Sapientie ad tenebras depellendum
   C. Tertio glorie ad appetitum totaliter satiandum
AVE MARIA
REITERATION OF THEME
MAIN SERMON
 I. A. Movetur questio terminata in doctrina magistrorum
     1. Ritus imaginum introductus est in ecclesia
       a. Primo propter simplicium ruditatem
       b. Secundo propter effectum tarditatem
       c. Tertio propter memoria facilitatem
   B. Movetur questio notabilis
 II. PART I: De incarnationis sacratissime profunda dignitate
   A. Quid dixit angelus pastoribus
     1. Primo annunciavit eis pacem . . . inter deum et hominem
     2. Secundo dixit eos . . . ad visitandum puerum natum
   B. Oportet ire in Bethleem per meditationem
     1. Primo singularitatem ex parte parentis & prolis
       a. eternitas capit novitatem
       b. immensitas brevitatem
       c. claritas obscuritatem
       d. sapientia infantiam
       e. opulentia indigentiam
     2. Secundo humilitatem utriusque
     3. Tertio veritate ratione manifestationis
 III. PART II: De devotione circa verbum incarnatum
   A. Ad bene nutriendum pueros
     1. Prima puer est involuendus
       a. primo levat puerum
       b. secunda cingit eum
     2. Secundo puer est lavandus
       a. confessio
       b. contritio
     3. Tertia puer est custodiendus
       a. intus – tranquillitas
       b. exterius – religiositas
CLOSING PRAYER

---

forward about his use of mnemonic devices: "I ask you who come to my sermons to study the alphabet. I will repeat twenty letters of the alphabet and each letter will signify one sin. A signifies adulation; B blasphemy; C conspiracy; etc."[93] In another sermon, he uses the medieval passion for numerology to develop and ornament his thought: "Secondly, there is the mode of preaching on the cross, saying those seven words which are the seven most beautiful leaves against the seven deadly sins. A place is to be loved on account of the trees that blossom there."[94]

The preachers used stories as both parables and entertainment. The exemplum was "a short narrative used to illustrate or confirm a general statement,"[95] but could be as long as the rest of the sermon.[96] Exempla normally were given at the end of the sermon, following the divisions, but could appear anywhere in a sermon. Used only in popular preaching, the exemplum was first introduced at the end of the twelfth century by Maurice de Sully, and was further developed during the following century by Jacques de Vitry and Étienne de Bourbon, whose *Sermones vulgares* (Vitry) and *Tractatus de diversis materiis predicabilibus* (Bourbon) furnished countless generations of preachers with instructive and amusing anecdotes. By the early fifteenth century, exempla were used so freely that ecclesiastical authorities made attempts to limit their employment. In 1528, the Council of Sens "forbade under the pain of interdict 'those ridiculous recitals, those stories of good wives, having for their end laughter only.'"[97] These injunctions may have worked, for Martin found that the exemplum in its original form was rarely used by the early sixteenth century, replaced by other anecdotes and histories.[98]

Collections of exempla sometimes appeared under the titles of *sermones ad status,* which should not be confused with sermons actually delivered to an audience. These groupings of exempla were collated according to subject or status, as in Arnold de Liège's encyclopedic *Alphabet des récits,* which contains 555 rubrics on such topics as women.[99] A study by F. C. Tubach lists six thousand exempla, but even this figure is incomplete.[100] Besides the works already noted, preachers could turn to Aesop, Nicolaus Pergamenus' *Dialogus creaturarum,* John Herolt's *Promptuarium exemplorum,* John Bromyard's *Summa praedicantium,* Jacobus de Voragine's *Legenda aurea,* Gulielmus Peraldus's *Summa virtutum ac vitiorum,* Robert Holcot's *Opus super sapientiam Solomonis,* Pelbartus de Themeswar's *Pomerium,* Anthony Rampegolus's *Biblia aurea vel figurae bibliorum,* and many others for appropriate stories. Herolt, Pelbartus, Voragine, and Bromyard all figure prominently in the lists of sermons printed throughout France during the late fifteenth and sixteenth centuries.

The stories told as exempla often transmitted oral and folkloric memories, helping to bridge the intellectual gap between the leaders of the church and its humblest members.[101] Preachers used them to retain (or regain) the interest and attention of their auditors—an exemplum near the end of the sermon would serve to awaken those who had dozed off. Its didactic purpose was preeminent, for a good example made difficult moral or theological points comprehensible and meaningful for an audience. Menot makes this point forcefully when he says to his listeners, "If you won't believe the scriptures, you will believe through examples."[102]

The source of the exemplum can often be deduced from the preacher's introduction to the story. Phrases such as "memini," "vidi," "je me souviens," or "j'ai vu" indicate the personal experience or reminiscences of the preacher;

the impersonal "audivi" or "j'ai entendu" suggest knowledge through a second party, while an example borrowed from a book or collection of exempla is indicated by "legitur in" or "lit dans," followed by the citation. A fable was usually introduced by "dicitur."[103]

Examples are often missing from the sermons, replaced only by the instruction "da exemplum" or a more specific reference such as "exemplum de david qui captus fuit aspectui Bersabee,"[104] which indicated to another preacher that he would have to insert an example at this point. Although most preachers used exempla, Pepin, following the line taken by Alain de Lille,[105] argues that "preachers should not preach vain and curious things, or fables, or tragedies, or human laws or poetry, as do so many modern preachers, who care only to please the ears of their listeners."[106]

Broadly defined, exempla can be divided into four main categories: (1) histories and legends; (2) contemporary events and reminiscences of the preacher; (3) fables; and (4) descriptions taken from bestiaries.[107] The first two categories are most commonly used in pre-Reformation sermons, which signals a shift from earlier medieval usage, when fables and animal stories were more prominent. Menot borrows the *ubi sunt* theme from François Villon's *Ballade des seigneurs du temps jadis:* "King Charles [VIII], in the flower of his youth, made all of Italy tremble before him, but now he lies rotting in the ground."[108] In another example, Menot relates an episode from Valerius Maximus, in which a young matron of ancient Rome, hearing that her mother had been condemned to death by starvation, went to the emperor to ask for mercy. The emperor would not relent, but allowed the woman to visit her mother daily. She was forced to make these visits naked so that she could not conceal food under her garments. "Without blushing, the woman said to her mother, 'Mother, I came nude from your belly. I am not allowed to bring you bread or meat, but just as you gave suck to me, so now you will suck me.'" When her ruse was discovered, the young woman was dragged nude from the prison and taken into the emperor's presence. The latter, "beholding such charity and compassion of a daughter for her mother, said 'My daughter, I give you your mother. You have earned her freedom.'"[109] Here Menot used the prurient instincts of some members of the audience to bring home the message of the commandment, "Honor your father and your mother."

The preachers also favored stories about contemporary life. Menot tells of the dangers facing a contemporary businessman:

> When a merchant carrying a lot of money goes to Rome, he must pass through the city of Lyon, where he proceeds along a road full of robbers and murderers, of which the earth is full. If a wise man were with him, he would say, "Why do you go along a road where so many snares are laid for you? You put yourself in the valley of death. I would go by another road if I were you, for yesterday two merchants were robbed along this road; this morning, two more were flayed, and no one crosses here without losing his money pouch."[110]

This simple story illustrates the dangers of the world and makes clear that people must choose the right path carefully, by placing their trust in the Lord.

Examples of animal behavior were easy for the audience to understand. Messier tells the tale of the monkey and the fox:

> Seeing his own ugliness, which he could not cover, the monkey sent a messenger to the fox, asking for part of his tail, since he had more than he needed. The servants of the fox responded: "Certainly not. Our lord will not dismantle his tail; he will not part with a single hair of it." And so the monkey always had a very short tail. Morally, the monkey being without a tail is like a priest without a benefice, the man who makes a long speech without a title. The fox, however, having such a large tail, is like one with many benefices—four or five—who does not share his wealth with the poor, because he has to feed his dogs and birds and groom his horses.[111]

Pepin takes a poke at officials and others who get to the top quickly, but whose inexperience makes them like a "monkey who, when he climbs a tree, exposes his backside."[112] Comparing man unfavorably to insects, Raulin says: "Bees and even ants, which are very wise little animals, are very strict about what they eat."[113] Other material for exempla came from parables, jests, satirical anecdotes, and excerpts from fabliaux and romances.[114]

Finally, the sermon would end with a peroration, or reiteration of the themes and elements of the sermon. Then came another prayer, such as "we pray to God that he will give us grace in the present and glory in the future. Amen."[115] In some sermons, a preacher's desire to observe time limitations could lead to very abrupt endings. The Strasbourg preacher Geiler von Kaysersberg felt so strongly that preachers should never exceed an hour in length that when his hour was up, he would simply stop speaking.[116]

The Post-Reformation Catholic Sermon

Many early post-Reformation Catholic preachers also utilized the modern method. Pepin and Messier both lived and preached well after the advent of Protestantism in France, and did not change their format. The use of division continued after the Reformation, but was not as elaborate. In a combined ancient-modern format sometimes called the substitute method, Jean Lansperge delivered fifty-five sermons to a congregation of nuns. These closely follow the gospel texts, but contain a threefold division into the text of the gospel, the exposition or narrative, and "eruditions" or doctrines, which explain the moral significance of the words and deeds of Christ. Catholic reformers, especially those associated with the Circle of Meaux, preferred a simple exegetical format, often in the form of commentaries on the epistles of Paul.[117] In his popular preaching, Gérard Roussel would explain first the gospels and then the epistles of Paul; to the learned he would explicate the Psalms.[118] Although Clichtove's sermons follow a basic, formal division, they are much simpler and plainer than typical late medieval sermons. Evangelical Catholics such as Clichtove and Lefèvre d'Étaples recognized the sovereignty,

but not the exclusivity, of scripture. Basing their understanding on a "pro-
longed revelation" which included not only the Fathers but the living faith
of the church, they combined the old and the new. Yet in the end, patristic
tradition, church authority, and questions of piety all continued to play significant roles in reformed Catholic exegesis.[119]

Criticisms by Catholic and Protestant reformers about the elaborate
medieval style encouraged even the most orthodox to simplify the format
of their sermons. LePicart's homiletic style is not significantly different
from that of many Protestants, except in content. His sermon for the second Sunday after Easter is typical, taking as its theme: "I am the good
shepherd; the good shepherd lays down his life for the sheep" (John
10:11). This theme is carefully explored throughout his exposition, with
the terms *vray pasteur* and *bon pasteur* appearing no less than thirty-six
times. The theme is used to delineate the difference between the good and
the bad pastor, with the goal of teaching his listeners how to differentiate
between orthodox and heretical sermons.

At mid century, the Council of Trent discussed popular preaching but left
all specifics to synods and bishops. The council stressed that sermons were
to be based on scripture, but said nothing about form.[120] Later Counter-
Reformation writers, however, warned that too great a reliance on the literal,
historical sense would lead to frigidity.[121] Sermons preached at the papal court
at this time followed the form of exordium, enumeration of topics, and peroration,[122] and most of the later examples mentioned here follow this pattern.
The ornate Platonic sermons of the humanist Catholic Étienne Paris resemble
the modern method only in their theme and closing prayer. The latest preacher
in this study, Jean de Monluc, composed sermons in an austere homiletic
format, with "no false windows for symmetry's sake."[123] But Monluc was no
ordinary Catholic. The bishop of Valence and Die, diplomat and confidante
of Catherine de Médicis, Monluc was formally accused of heresy by the
Inquisition in 1563,[124] but later cleared.

Style

For the One whom God has sent speaks the words of God; he does not
ration his gift of the Spirit.   John 3:34

Christ's preaching served as a model for the church and was closely followed
during the Middle Ages. Murphy describes Jesus' practice: "he confirmed
and reinforced the Judaic practice of using Scripture as proof; he distinguished
carefully between parables and 'direct' discourse; he distinguished evangeliz-
ing [announcement] and teaching [exposition of doctrine]; and finally he made
constant comparison of earthly and divine through use of analogy and metaphor."[125] In his Ciceronian-based discourse on sacred eloquence, Augustine
counseled the preacher "to spurn . . . none of these three things, that is, to

teach, to delight, and to persuade."[126] In order to reveal what was "hidden," to make known God's truth, it was both acceptable and necessary to use the art of eloquence, although this was never to be an end in itself, nor a means of displaying the preacher's learning.

Most rhetoricians divide sermons into three basic styles: (1) the colloquial, or racy, style; (2) the plain, unadorned style; and (3) the elaborate, or ornate, style. Although there is considerable overlap, certain basic characteristics pertain to each. The colloquial style is distinguished by its familiar, often picaresque idioms, the general avoidance of rhetorical schemata, and the plentiful use of exempla. The plain style often uses narrative unadorned by exempla or schemata, except where they are necessary to clarify meaning. Finally, the ornate style employs rhetorical schemata or figures and exempla freely, and is sometimes characterized by euphuistic oratory. Within each style, there were three levels to be used according to subject matter and place in the sermon: the grand, the middle, and the plain.[127] These styles were fluid, crossing time periods and religious affiliations.

Most of the late medieval and early post-Reformation Catholic preachers included here used either the colloquial or the modified ornate style.[128] Facetiae, witty or coarsely humorous sayings, abound in the sermons of Maillard and Menot. Menot says, "A brothel is a place where there are whores. If there is a whore in the house of a canon, then it is a bordello. Where the king is, there is his court."[129] The language is that of the people, complete with ribaldry, slang, and irreverence. Menot's sermons are full of homely anecdotes and proverbs that reflect popular preoccupation with animals, food, and sex: "nud comme ung ver"; "maigre comme un hareng soret"; "qui m'ayme, il ayme mon chien." Preachers who used the colloquial style were more likely than others to intermingle poetry with their prose. Menot's *Sermon on the Passion*, unlike most of his other sermons, was liberally laced with poetry. While he uses prose to tell the gospel story, he presents the stages of Christ's passion poetically in an overt attempt to evoke an emotional response from his listeners. Menot ends the sermon with this simple but moving stanza:

> Hé, doulx Jesus, comment peult estre fait
> Qu'amour te fist ung si tresdur hostage,
> Que en sepulchre t'a enclos et attraict,
> Pour repos prandre de ton pelerinaige?
> Hé, doulx Jesus, trop dur fut le voyage
> Qu'amour te fist en ce monde tenir.
> Ce fust pour moy, bien m'en doyt souvenir.[130]

Maillard's French poetry explaining the Ten Commandments shows the possibilities inherent in this genre as a mnemonic device for the listener:

> LE PREMIER
> Ung seul Dieu, de tout Créateur,
> Tu serviras et aymeras,

Et en luy l'amour de ton cueur
Sur toutes choses tu mettras.

LE SECOND
Le nom de Dieu et de ses sainctz
Sans grant necessité ne iures.
Tu te damnes, soyes certains,
Si en iurant tu te pariures.

LE TIERS
De labeur tu dois reposer
Toy et ta famille et tes bestes,
Et à Dieu servir disposer,
Tous les dimenches et les festes.

LE QUART
Pour amour et pour charité,
Père et mère honoreras
S'ilz ont de toy necessité
Ou du tien, tu les secourras,
etc.[131]

This simple poetry shows only one of the ways late medieval preachers chose
to impart the Christian message to their listeners. But by the end of the
sixteenth and the early seventeenth century, the increasing emphasis on classical oratory blurred the distinction between poetry and prose.[132]

Other late medieval preachers combined a less racy version of the colloquial style with some of the rhetorical schemata associated with the ornate
style. While translation into Latin may have diluted the power of the original
figures, the results show that translators made conscientious efforts to capture
the intent of the original. Those preachers who doubled as monastic preachers
or who were famed for their preaching style often displayed considerable
rhetorical ingenuity. Pepin attacked the Pragmatic Sanction in one sermon
with a full volley of anaphora, the deliberate repetition of words at the beginning of successive phrases:

> *Nonne* saepe interveniunt preces armatae? *Nonne* rogatur, interdum pro
> personis erubesco dicere infamibus magis arma, quam leges scientibus?
> *Nonne* plus favetur ab electoribus literis commendatitiis principium & mag-
> natum, quam iustitiae aequitati utilitati ecclesiasticarum & saluti animarum?
> *Nonne* curiae parlamentorum plenae sunt quaerelis contendentium ad idem
> beneficium electivum, sive regulare, sive episcopale? . . . *Nonne* haec omnia
> & similia iram Dei provocant, cum videt sponsam suam ecclesiam *sic* con-
> culcari, *sic* deprimi, *sic* opprimi ad iniustus hominibus. Quod si pragmatica
> *sanctio sancta est,* si concilium Basiliensis sanctum, *cur non* conceditur, *cur
> non* permittitur electionis libera facultas eligendi idoneum pastorem eccle-
> siae suae, *cur non* omnis violentia rescinditur, *cur* favetur *malis bonis* op-
> pressis? *Cur* praesides & iudices causas & lites inde ortas non cito absolvunt,
> claudunt & extinguunt?[133]

In the same text, he puns on the words *sanctio* (the Pragmatic Sanction) and
sancta (holy), to drive home his point. Brulefer uses paronomasia, the more

formal use of punning, in his three extant sermons, delivered at synod. In one case, he correlates the priest's ordination with his privilege of dispensing the sacrament of the mass: "Inde denique sacerdotes quasi sacris dotati: vel sacerdotes quasi sacra dantes."[134] This type of rhetorical play is very common.

The racy, colloquial style, a subject of ridicule by both Protestant and Catholic reformers, was a victim of the Reformation. Mid-century Catholic preaching tended toward either the plain or ornate styles. Clichtove would begin with a simple gospel text, such as "Our Father, who art in heaven" (Matthew 6) and proceed to show how the faithful must understand this prayer: "the faithful ought to sanctify the name of God, in word and deed, insisting on observation of the laws of God, and all good works, alms, fasting, prayer, and other things of this kind."[135] Monluc's "eloquence was inspired by scripture alone. He excluded all profane reminiscences and tasteless displays of knowledge from the fabric of his discourse. He chose a sacred text, commented on it, developed it, and drew conclusions appropriate to the spiritual needs of the audience."[136] But he embellished his commentaries with sophisticated use of such schemata as anaphora, isocolon (use of phrases of equal length), homoioteleuton (use of a series of similar word endings), and parison/antithesis (use of balanced phrases to draw a contrast). The humanist preacher Étienne Paris uses a highly ornate style, in which rhetorical devices overwhelm content. His sermon for Christmas day, a commentary on the gospel of John, begins:

> Sainct Iehan, de plume bien taillee, en stile profond, & grave, fidelement descript la genealogie de Iesuchrist, selon la deité, qu'il n'a pas devinee ou inventee de son cerveau, & ne la tient de luy: mais dormant sus la poictrine de son maistre, souef, & mol oreillier, son esprit a veu un huys au ciel ouvert, ou est entré iusques en la chambre de monsieur, de là en son contoir, sa guarderobe, & son cabinet, & de tels lieux a emprunté ce hault scavoir. Ce grand aigle avec ses aefles legeres & mobiles, a volé iusques au plus haut cedre du mont de Liban, & ne s'est attaché à l'escorce de l'arbre, ains l'a vivement enfoncé, succé, & tiré la movelle du dedans, qu'il nous presente pour nourriture & engressement, quand il dict, in principio erat verbum.[137]

Obviously, there were some significant changes in Catholic sermon style by the mid sixteenth century as a result of the influence of humanism and criticism by Protestants.

Biblical and Literary Allusion

> Never did he [Vitrier] adopt the style of citing huge quantities of authors, as is so popular, stringing from end to end sterile extracts, sometimes from Scotus, Thomas, Durand; sometimes from canon and civil law; sometimes from poets, in order to appear to ignore nothing in the eyes of the people. Each homily that he delivered was filled with holy scripture, for he knew how to preach nothing else. André Godin[138]

Table 4-3. Citation of Old Testament Books by Pre-Reformation Preachers.

Book	Number of Citations	Percentage of quotations
Psalms	4,405	21
Isaiah	2,023	10
Sirach	1,624	8
Genesis	1,386	7
Proverbs	1,363	7
Samuel/Kings	1,271	6
Job	984	5
Wisdom	898	4
Exodus	864	4
Jeremiah	719	3
Other	5,035	25

The myth that biblical-based preaching began with Luther remains surprisingly strong. The reformers decried preaching that, in their view, rested on authorities other than scripture, and in particular on medieval scholastic theologians. A detailed examination of the citations used in Catholic sermons both before and after the Reformation reveals that, on the contrary, the Bible was the overwhelming first choice as a source for all preachers.

Pre-Reformation Catholic Preachers

In the 1,337 sermons that fall into this category, there are 49,117 citations, or an average of about 37 citations per sermon. This mean does not reflect the number of citations in a particular sermon, however, for a skewed distribution results from different levels of completeness among the sermons. Pepin's sermons, which are not abridged, may be considered fairly typical of complete sermons, with an average of more than forty citations per sermon.

Seventy-six percent (37,244) of all citations by the fifteen pre-Reformation preachers come from the Bible. Citations from the Old Testament (20,572) outnumber texts from the New Testament (16,672). Psalms is the most frequently quoted book of the Old Testament (Table 4-3), and almost half of all Old Testament citations come from the wisdom books, partially as a result of the heavy reliance on Psalms (Table 4-4). The relative unimportance of the historical books (except for Kings and Samuel) is borne out by comparison with preachers in England during this same time period. Blench finds regular use of the prophetic and wisdom books by Fisher, Longland, and others, but the historical books were rarely cited.[139] While the number of references to

Table 4-4. Citation of Sections of the Old Testament by Pre-Reformation Preachers.

Section	Number of Citations	Percentage of quotations
Wisdom Books	10,103	49
Prophetic Books	4,815	23
Pentateuch	3,539	17
Historical Books	2,115	11

Table 4-5. Citation of New Testament Books by Pre-Reformation Preachers.

Book	Number of Citations	Percentage of quotations
Matthew	3,849	23
John	2,894	17
Luke	2,818	17
Corinthians	1,337	8
Romans	941	6
Revelation	869	5
Acts	622	4
Hebrews	597	4
Ephesians	404	2
James	397	2
Other	1,944	12

the historical books is small, they were a common source for exempla, which were rarely supplied in printed sermons.

In the New Testament, the gospels of Matthew, John, and Luke are the most popular sources (Table 4-5). Despite the predominance of the gospels (other than Mark, which is rarely cited), the Pauline epistles, especially Romans and Corinthians, are heavily used by the preachers (Table 4-6), reflecting the increasing popularity of Pauline studies during the late fifteenth and early sixteenth centuries.[140]

Almost one-quarter of references (11,873) do not come from the Bible. The preachers took material from the original sources, preaching manuals, and books of exempla. Twenty-two percent of all "other" references were to Augustine, and another 10 percent to Gregory the Great (Table 4-7). As a group, the Church Fathers, both Latin and Greek, constitute a substantial majority (Table 4-8). The only other significant group can loosely be termed "medieval theologians." Pagan authors do not figure as prominently as we might expect, although many single references, sometimes to obscure scientists or philosophers, add up to 10 percent of all "other" authors (1,175). The historians Livy, Suetonius, and Valerius Maximus all figure prominently because of the interesting anecdotes that they contain, while Cicero's works on rhetoric and Plato's philosophy had begun to exercise a considerable fascination in the fifteenth century. More surprisingly, we find references to and citations from various pre-Socratic philosophers (Anaximenes, Empedocles,

Table 4-6. Citation of Sections of the New Testament by Pre-Reformation Preachers.

Section	Number of Citations	Percentage of quotations
Gospels	9,889	60
Pauline epistles	4,541	27
Revelation	869	5
Acts	622	4
Other epistles	751	4

Table 4-7. Citation of Nonbiblical Authors by Pre-Reformation Preachers.

Name	Number of Citations	Percentage of quotations
Augustine	2,642	22
Gregory the Great	1,202	10
Bernard	946	8
Aquinas	830	7
Jerome	820	7
Chrysostom	645	5
Ambrose	570	5
Aristotle	426	4
Bonaventure	404	3
Seneca	245	2
Antoninus Florentinus	241	2
Duns Scotus	217	2
Isidore	193	2
Nicolas of Lyra	181	2
Hugh of Saint Victor	163	1
Other	2,148	18

Democritus, Crates, and Pythagoras) as well as occasional borrowings from the noted Islamic speculative theologians, Avicenna, Averroës, and Mohammed himself. Contemporary or recently dead French preachers occupy only an insignificant place in the citations, but include Pepin, Maillard, and Raulin.

Post-Reformation Catholic Preachers

In the 267 post-Reformation Catholic sermons examined, there are 6,944 citations, 91 percent of which are taken from the Bible. This produces an average of 26 per sermon, a figure considerably more representative of an individual sermon because of the small number of preachers (seven) in this

Table 4-8. Citation of Nonbiblical Authors by Pre-Reformation Preachers by Type of Literature.*

Type of Source	Number of Citations	Percentage of quotations
Patristic	6,681	56
Medieval Theologians	3,211	27
Pagan Philosophers	697	6
Pagan Historians	277	2
Archbishops	245	2
Pagan Poets	148	1
Preachers	130	1
Popes	124	1
Jurists	115	1
Manual authors	97	1
Other	148	1

*Sources are classified according to the category in which they are most noted.

Table 4-9. Citation of O. T. Books by Post-Reformation Catholic Preachers.

Book	Number of Citations	Percentage of quotations
Psalms	654	35
Genesis	234	12
Isaiah	216	12
Kings	105	6
Exodus	97	5
Proverbs	71	4
Ecclesiastes	66	4
Job	46	2
Jeremiah	44	2
Sirach	34	2
Others	302	16

group. One major change is in the predominance of New Testament texts, which are used two and one-half times more frequently than verses from the Old Testament. Of the Old Testament citations, Psalms is still the most frequently cited, representing over one-third of all Old Testament references (Table 4-9). Overall, there is very little change in the degree of frequency with which certain books or parts of the Old Testament are used (Table 4-10), although the preachers quote the Pentateuch slightly more often.

Citations from the New Testament total 64 percent of all citations and once again reveal the preachers' predilection for the three gospels of Matthew, John, and Luke (Table 4-11). While the gospels remain the most popular

Table 4-10. Citation of Sections of the O. T. by Post-Reformation Catholic Preachers.

Section	Number of Citations	Percentage of quotations
Wisdom Books	919	49
Pentateuch	418	23
Prophetic Books	395	21
Historical Books	137	7

Table 4-11. Citation of N. T. Books by Post-Reformation Catholic Preachers.

Book	Number of Citations	Percentage of quotations
Matthew	776	18
John	752	17
Luke	542	12
Romans	507	11
Corinthians	480	11
Hebrews	232	5
Acts	216	5
Timothy	130	3
Mark	123	3
Peter	112	3
Other	552	12

Table 4-12. Citation of Sections of the N. T. by Post-Reformation Catholic Preachers.

Section	Number of Citations	Percentage of quotations
Gospels	2,193	50
Pauline epistles	1,718	39
Acts	216	5
Revelation	92	2
Other epistles	203	4

New Testament books, the preachers refer to the Pauline epistles significantly more often. The decreasing reliance on Revelation may be due to the smaller sample or may indicate a decline in mystical or apocalyptic tendencies (Table 4-12).

Interestingly, only 9 percent of all citations by post-Reformation Catholic preachers were taken from patristic, classical, or literary sources. Because of LePicart's special interest in John Chrysostom, the Greek father places first on this list, although Augustine remains the preferred source for all other preachers in this group (Tables 4-13 and 4-14).

It is clear that Catholic preachers in the fifteenth and sixteenth centuries

Table 4-13. Citation of Nonbiblical Authors by Post-Reformation Catholic Preachers.

Author	Number of Citations	Percentage of quotations
Chrysostom	187	29
Augustine	99	15
Jerome	77	12
Bernard	39	6
Ambrose	34	5
Rupert	31	5
Cyprian	26	4
Aristotle	21	3
Aquinas	21	3
Origen	18	3
Gregory the Great	18	3
Other	82	12

Table 4-14. Citation of Nonbiblical Authors by Post-Reformation Catholic Preachers by Type of Literature.

Type of Source	Number of Citations	Percentage of quotations
Patristic	501	77
Medieval Theologians	101	16
Pagan Philosophers	21	3
Church Historians	12	2
Popes	5	1
Pagan Poets	4	1
Pagan Rhetoricians	3	—
Pagan Historians	2	—
Moslems	1	—
Roman de la Rose	1	—
Unknown	2	—

both knew and used the Bible. Depending on time period, between 76 percent and 91 percent of all citations were biblical. But to Protestants who believed in *sola scriptura* and simple biblical commentary, the medieval preaching style was an adulteration of the Word.

Themes

> This is what we proclaim to you:
> what was from the beginning,
> what we have heard,
> what we have seen with our eyes,
> what we have looked upon
> and our hands have touched—
> we speak the word of life.
>
> 1 John 1:1

The *Aquinas Tract* suggested that all the material needed for sermons could be found in ten topics: God, the Devil, the heavenly city, the inferno, the world, the soul, the body, sin, penitence, and virtue,[141] while Surgant advised preaching all that was to be believed, done, avoided, feared, and desired.[142] In the critical religious climate of the sixteenth century, preachers added two additional topics: the church and heresy.

The facts about pre-Reformation sermons have too often been distorted by the claims of later Protestants, as well as by men who were trying to improve the Catholic Church from within. Erasmus, in the end a loyal Catholic, was able to find some positive elements in pre-Reformation preaching, but others found little good to say. Henri Estienne commented of late medieval preachers that "they were not content simply to add to stories of the Bible, just like those who, when retelling a story, are accustomed to enrich their tale to make it the more interesting; they are given license to abuse Scripture in all ways, indeed to the point of inventing passages to confirm their false doctrines."[143] While this may have been true of some preachers, most notably the purveyors of indulgences, it was not true of the group of preachers studied here. In fact, the last decades of the fifteenth century were remarkable for the amount of reforming zeal in the air—a situation that resulted in the appellation prereformer being applied to many religious leaders and preachers of the time. On the whole, even the most avid of the so-called prereformers did not consider the "modern method" of elaborate sermon construction to be an abuse. Why should they? People came in the thousands to hear them. While some spoke out against the use of "trivial" nonbiblical material, especially jokes and fables, most seemed to realize that this was a useful way to attract listeners to their sermons, retain the attention of the audience, and make their message more accessible. Jesus Christ had spoken in different ways to different people; the medieval preacher followed Jesus' example, using everything at his disposal to teach his listeners about Christianity. Most of the fables, historical examples, and other nonbiblical references were designed to clarify the central biblical or moral teaching that was the core of the sermon. This was the tool of the teacher who would stop at nothing to make his students learn. The centrality of scripture was never challenged; other authorities were cited either to clarify meaning, support an argument, or demonstrate the historical position of the church on a given issue.

The reformers' emphasis on preaching was nothing new, but their "back-to-basics" approach profoundly influenced the nature and style of preaching. Increasing literacy among the laity and the intellectual curiosity that it so often provoked created a group of listeners who were less in need of examples and parables for clarification. This in turn affected Catholic homiletics. A glance at the sermons of Catholics at mid century shows that the process of simplification had gone quite far. While basic divisions were still used to some extent, they were less artificial and more obviously connected to the biblical text. The new simplicity permitted Catholic preachers to respond more easily to the Protestant challenge.

A less desirable aspect of the simplification of the sermon and the revival of classical rhetoric was ironically a tendency to fashion sermons that were linguistically elegant, but devoid of the popular elements of earlier sermons. Simplification may in the long run have contributed to a greater knowledge of the Bible by lay men and women, but in the early years after the Reformation it may have made the Bible more confusing to some. The esoteric protobaroque sermons of Étienne Paris were more appropriate for the courts of kings and popes than for popular preaching.

Presentation was obviously very important, for a good speaker could convey the message of Christianity and move his listeners to act upon his words. But for these preachers, the literary and rhetorical aspects of sermons were means, not ends. Their goal was Christian instruction.

II

The Preached Word
at the End of the Middle Ages

5

The Quest for Salvation

Here are questions worthy of the great and (as some call them) illuminated theologians, questions to make them prick up their ears—if they ever chance upon them. Whether divine generation took place at a particular time? Whether there are several sonships in Christ? Whether this is a possible proposition: God the Father hates the Son? Whether God could have taken upon himself the likeness of a woman? Or of a devil? Or an ass? Or a gourd? Or a piece of flint? Then how would a gourd have preached, performed miracles, or been crucified. . . . These finespun trifles are beyond number, with others even more subtle, having to do with instants of time, notions, relations, accidents, quiddities, entities, etc.

Erasmus, *The Praise of Folly*

Paul Kristeller has remarked that "modern scholarship has been far too much influenced by all kinds of prejudices, against the use of Latin, against scholasticism, [and] against the medieval church."[1] This has been particularly true of sermons. If popular preachers had indeed spent their time asking their listeners to consider whether God could have taken on the form of a gourd, they would have deserved the opprobrium that has been their fate. But we must make a very clear distinction between theologians and preachers trained in theology. Scholastic debates did not, for the most part, furnish material for popular preaching. A preacher might quote Aristotle or Aquinas, but would rarely enter the realms of speculative philosophy. On the contrary, a preacher who brought up subjects that belonged in the schools would be roundly condemned by his peers.[2] Illyricus tells his listeners: "I preach to you for the health of your souls. Whoever wants to hear philosophy preached will have to seek it from someone else."[3] Because the preacher had to teach ordinary people, many of whom were illiterate, he would frame his discussion of theology and doctrine in terms that people could understand.

Despite individual differences over certain matters, the theological formulations of all the pre-Tridentine Catholic preachers treated here are very similar, differing only in emphasis. Issues raised by the Protestants inevitably provoked discussion and response, but seldom caused a preacher to deviate from the accepted tenets of Catholic theology. Beginning with the Fall, the preachers described a religion based on sin and atonement that offered the possibility of salvation to everyone willing to do what was in him (*facere quod in se est*).

Original Sin

> You are free to eat from any of the trees of the garden except the tree of knowledge of good and bad. From that tree you shall not eat....
>
> Genesis 2:16–17

The whole of medieval theology proceeded from the fact of original sin—the disobedience of Adam and Eve to God in the Garden of Eden. The preachers' view of postlapsarian human nature was ultimately pessimistic, for the rupture was caused by man's disobedience to God. While the immediate cause of damnation was the eating of the apple, the apple was only the object through which God tested man's obedience: "O, how many greater sins we see committed daily than the eating of an apple. . . . But Adam would not have sinned if this one act had not been prohibited, for in itself the eating of an apple is good."[4] The moment Adam chose to disobey God, he gave up all claim to the blessed state in which he had been created, and as the first member of the human race, passed on this sin to his heirs. "We should not be surprised if the first parents transmitted this deadly legacy to succeeding generations, for in a similar way the leper infects all those around him with the disease."[5] Recognizing that this pessimistic anthropology created anxiety or desperation in some, the preachers offered some consolation to men and women about the human condition, based on man's creation in God's image.[6] Raulin posits a Platonic view: "What is man? Man is memory. So man is nothing, but memory of God."[7] Menot assures his listeners that Christ's sacrifice on the cross erased the stain of original sin, although an inextinguishable inclination toward actual sin (*fomes peccati*) remained.[8]

The preachers explained to their listeners the differences between mortal and venial sins. Pepin defines sin in the Neoplatonic-Augustinian sense of that "which turns man from the way that leads to paradise; it is separation from all that is good."[9] Suggestion and opportunity were the roots of sin. A mortal sin was the commission of an act prohibited by God or the omission of one that was commanded,[10] and even one mortal sin, unexpiated, would lead to spiritual death.[11] By contrast, a venial sin diminished man's inclination toward goodness and charity, and disposed him more readily to mortal sin, but did not preclude the possibility of grace.[12] Venial sins also increased the distance between God and man.[13] On his deathbed, a man who had not confessed his venial sins could not feel the same assurance about his salvation as one who had unburdened his conscience.

The preachers made it very clear that no one should despair, not even the most hardened sinner, for God's love for his human creation outweighed their sins.[14] They realized that life in the world might be conducive to despair, especially among sensitive individuals, but warned that it was the sin of Cain to believe that God's malice exceeded his bounty, for God was the perfect embodiment of compassion.[15] Despair was a sign that the sinner did not know his God.[16] The preachers provided numerous examples to support their contention that no one should despair. Paris exhorts his audience, "People, cry no more! Do not torment yourselves, rejoice and take heart!"[17] David earned God's forgiveness when he poured out his heart and uttered the three words, "I have sinned."[18] The same was true of Mary Magdalene, who was a great sinner, but did not despair.[19] "The poor sinner should never despair of God's indulgence, but consider the present as a mystery, and wait, because God will have mercy on his creation. . . . "[20] Cleree tells his listeners that "even if you deny Christ along with Peter, persecute him like Paul, sin publicly like Magdalene, still if you repent and change your ways you will obtain God's mercy."[21] "Do we not read of the thief who had done no good during his life, yet who at its end found great mercy with Christ?"[22] Ironically, these examples were sometimes used against the preachers by listeners who not surprisingly came to the conclusion that they, too, could leave penitence to the very end. One listener might quip, "David, Peter, Paul, and Magdalene were all sinners, but look where they are now,"[23] while another would draw a more dangerous conclusion: "If David committed adultery, why can't I?"[24] Pepin responds to these people: "You must not presume on God's goodwill, like those who say, "God is good, God is merciful, he will remit my sins without my doing anything, for we read that even Paul persecuted the church of God." The preachers insisted that such miracles were rare, and no sinner could hope to attain grace if he was not willing to do everything possible.[25]

Happily, it was possible to overcome sin, for unlike the body, the soul could not be mortally wounded.[26] An attempt to conquer the impulse to sin was the first step, but if one sinned, the appropriate response was repentance. Cleree explains that when a statue is broken, it must be restored to its original state; so when the soul is deformed by sins, it must be repaired through penitence.[27] The medieval theology of salvation juxtaposed the damaged human condition against God's largesse, making every man's salvation not only possible, but truly desired by God.

Free Will

> My brothers, count it pure joy when you are involved in every sort of trial.
>
> James 1:2

The problem of the freedom or bondage of the will first manifested itself in the events of the Garden, for it was the free choice of Adam and Eve to disobey God. The compatibility of God's foreknowledge and man's free will first advanced by Augustine influenced all later theologians to one degree or another:

> It is with justice that rewards are appointed for good actions and punishment
> for sins. The fact that God foreknew that a man would sin does not make
> a man sin; on the contrary, it cannot be doubted that it is the man himself
> who sins just because he whose prescience cannot be mistaken has foreseen
> that the man himself would sin. A man does not sin unless he wills to sin;
> and if he had willed not to sin, then God would have foreseen that refusal.[28]

Augustine further explains that since God cannot cause evil, in "the evil of
the soul, its own will takes the initiative; but for its good, the will of its
Creator makes the first move."[29]

Augustine's influence is immediately apparent in the preachers' discussion
of the will. Menot uses the analogy of a mother and her wayward child to
show that God could never be the cause of sin: "A woman sees her son
leading an evil life. Some say of this woman, 'You are evil.' Why? 'Because
seeing your bad son, you do not correct him.' Behold, we see people suffer
for their prince, father for son. . . . I say to you that God is neither the ac-
cidental nor the active cause of the commission of sins; rather they proceed
from unchecked will."[30] Maillard insists that from the time of Adam there
has not been a man alive who could not have had the grace of God if he had
chosen, by doing what was in him.[31] Menot presents the case of a sinner who
repented late in life: "There was in this city a man of evil life, who denied
God. Late in the day he began to do good and in the morning he was found
dead. So was he damned or predestined to glory? We learn from Scotus that
if anyone is eternally predestined, it is through the grace of God. No one,
however, is damned by God without bringing it about through his own efforts."[32] He answers this with the parable of the laborers in the vineyard
(Matthew 20), in which those who were hired at the end of the day received
the same wages as those hired first.[33] Cleree stresses the element of personal
responsibility, remarking that "we should not try to excuse ourselves by
attributing our sins to God or saying that the Devil made us do it. Nor do
the stars incline us toward such acts."[34] Coming full circle, Pepin insists that
man should not despair at this freedom, for it allows him the opportunity to
choose good.[35]

As the basis of the preachers' theology of salvation, free will gave men
and women the opportunity to make the right choices. A pessimistic anthropology was therefore balanced by an optimistic soteriology in which, thanks
to God, everything was possible for the repentant sinner. Through the Commandments and the new law of Jesus Christ, God offered the sinner the
means by which he could find the right path.

The Law

> Do not think that I have come to abolish the law and the prophets: I have
> come, not to abolish them, but to fulfill them.   Matthew 5:17

After the Fall, the power of the human will was debilitated, making divine
assistance necessary to restore humanity to the right way.[36] The Law was

given to Moses by God as a guideline for behavior and observance among men and between man and his Creator. Its purpose was not to constrain the just, but to instruct the sinner.[37] In their discussion of the Law, the preachers emphasized different aspects, some stressing specific precepts of the Decalogue: "You say that you are Christians. But look how you serve the Law. Has God not commanded that you love and honor him? That you observe his holy days? That you not take his name in vain? That you not bear false witness? That you not commit adultery? That you not steal or lust after another's possessions? That you not commit usury or rapine?"[38] In a comparison the merchants in his audience would understand, Maillard warns that it is not sufficient to observe *some* of the Commandments: "We buy the heritage of paradise. The Seller [God] puts down certain conditions for us. These are his commandments. If we neglect even one, the deal is off."[39]

Intentions were very important in the observance of the Law. Raulin points to the historical breaking of the tablets by Moses (Exodus 32:19) in response to the people's idolatry as an example that sin not only proceeds from malice, but also from preoccupation, negligence, and ignorance.[40] Pepin tells his listeners that man accepted the Law when he realized he could not do enough to save himself, but goes on to argue that this soon led to rigid observance: "The Jews believed that only outwardly bad actions were condemned by God, that is, theft, adultery, and murder. They did not, however, pay any attention to inward actions, such as bad will."[41] The spirit of the Law was more important than the letter.

One problem with using the Law as a religious standard was that it restrained man's free will to choose good or evil. It was an instrument of servitude and fear, based on the worst in human nature. "The Old Testament given by Moses, the servant of God, could not endure forever, because in it God menaced people and made them serve him through fear."[42] A certain amount of fear made the sinner aware of the need for atonement,[43] but God preferred a loving obedience.[44] Christ's fulfillment of the Law (Matthew 5:17) had the effect of internalizing righteousness and divided those who "followed" the Law from those who lived the new law:

> You have not received the Spirit in slavery and fear like before. Rather it is the spirit of adoption of children, which is why we can confidently call him our Father. . . . On this feast of Pentecost [in ancient times] there came a great sound from the sky, like a strong gust of wind. This caused the Jews great fear, but gave consolation to the Apostles. This was done to show that the law of fear and rigor has been superseded by a new law of love and gentleness.[45]

The Bible was like a fabric torn in two, signifying that the power of the Law had ceased.[46] Messier explains that "the sacrificial animals of the old law were not sufficient to pacify God's ire. They were in fact a dead sacrifice."[47] With the Law a dead letter, God had recourse to a new "law"—the reign of Christ. But Lansperge draws an analogy between the blood of the sacrificial animals and the New Testament, which was confirmed by the blood of Jesus Christ.

Before his sacrifice, the truth had been hidden as if behind clouds.[48] Paris continues this theme: "The Word was hidden from men, written on paper by God the Father in a hand so tiny and subtle that no one could read it. It was a muted wisdom, an unknown treasure, and, as the Prophets say, God was truly hidden."[49]

Grace

> God has saved us and has called us to a holy life, not because of any merit of ourselves but according to his own design—the grace held out to us in Christ Jesus before the world began but now made manifest through the appearance of our Savior.
>
> 2 Timothy 1:9–10

The preachers' theology of justification centered on the relative importance of grace, faith, and good works. The preachers explained that man did not merit God's grace but that it was freely given. Without God's grace, man would be entirely helpless. God softened the hearts of sinners to prepare them to receive his grace,[50] inducing a state in which they were free to co-operate with it. The sinner should presume nothing of himself, but ask God's assistance to do what is in him. Then God will take pity on him.[51] "Christians, Christ offers his grace to you.... You must hope with all your might to gain paradise: for God's grace will extinguish your evil desires."[52] Pepin continues this theme: "By ourselves we can do no good, nor can we resist even the smallest temptation, for as our Savior said: 'No more than a branch can bear fruit of itself apart from the vine can you bear fruit apart from me" (John 15:4).[53] Menot makes it clear that it is up to man to respond to God's call:

> If you see two people bathing in the river, you would say: "These two are great fools. We are scarcely able to keep warm in our house, and here are two people bathing nude in the water."... One of them approaches a deep hole, where he will be in great danger of going under. A person standing on the bridge yells to him not to go there, but he goes on heedlessly and is submerged. The other avoids the hole and goes back. I ask you, does the man on the bridge make the first bather go under or put him in danger? Certainly not.[54]

Maillard asks the rhetorical question: "Brother, what must we do to regain this grace so that we can be reunited with God?" He responds: "I say that you must have much love, goodwill, and works; then you will be with God."[55] Christ's sacrifice was the sine qua non of salvation, but it did not save all men, for while his act was *sufficient* to save all, it was only *efficacious* for those who chose to follow him.[56] "Why is the whole world not saved? Because not everyone obeys him, not everyone obeys the gospel or the Word of our Lord Jesus Christ. Because the fruit and efficacy of his grace only comes to those who obey him and keep his commandments."[57]

The preachers presented the Augustinian view of cooperating with God's grace, combined with the notion of *facere quod in se est.* "There are many good seeds that a man ought to sow in the field of his conscience, and by so doing he cooperates with the principal sower, that is, God. He prepares himself by doing what is in him in order that God will infuse him with grace. This man then spreads the seed through his good works."[58] Although God is depicted as the principal cause of all good, the reciprocal nature of the relationship is emphasized. Jesus Christ died for the human race, so men and women must reach out to him for salvation. Menot advises his listeners not to wait, for "now is the right time, when God is truly disposed to give his grace to all those who are truly penitent."[59] Hope for the future depended on this combination, "for if the flowers do not come first, the fruit will not follow. So if grace and virtue do not come first, glory and happiness will not follow."[60]

Faith

There was a woman in the area who had been afflicted with a hemorrhage for a dozen years. . . . She had heard about Jesus and came up behind him in the crowd and put her hand to his cloak. "If I just touch his clothing," she thought, "I shall get well. . . . " He said to her, "Daughter, it is your faith that has cured you." Mark 5:25,27–28, 34

Faith followed from grace. Maillard defines faith as "believing in that which you do not see."[61] It was like the moon, casting light on the darkness of the night[62]; it was like the true light that illuminated man in this world.[63] For Pepin, faith means believing that "Christ was the Son of God, the Creator of the world, the maker and remaker of man. Without this faith, we will die in our sins."[64] The matters grasped by faith usually could not be comprehended by the human intellect, as Claude Despence explains: "We must not ask why he was sent into this world, because God's plans cannot be grasped by our small understanding."[65]

Faith was the first of the three theological virtues[66] and the base of the whole spiritual edifice. However, while faith had to come first, it was not more important than hope and charity.

There are three chief miseries that would fill the hearts of all men in this present life without the aid of God. The first is ignorance of the one truth, God. The second is depression over earthly matters. The third is inordinate love of the self, which leads man to act contemptuously toward God. But if a man wishes to cooperate in his own salvation, he will be helped by God with the aid of the three theological virtues, faith, hope, and charity, which will remedy these three miseries. Man is illuminated by faith against ignorance. Hope elevates his heart above earthly depression. Charity inflames the heart with contempt for the self and love of God above all other things.[67]

Pepin describes faith as "good gold. Hope is better gold, for it uplifts the soul. Charity is the best gold, for it joins us with God."[68] The preachers offered several illustrations of true faith. God gave the ultimate test to Abraham, demanding that he sacrifice his son.[69] Likewise, the Samaritan woman's belief that she was truly speaking with the Lord showed her superior faith.[70] But the most perfect example of faith in the gospels, regularly presented by all the preachers, was the Canaanite woman, who followed after Jesus in the hope that he would cure her daughter. LePicart explains: "For all that Jesus pretended to take no notice of this poor Canaanite woman, even when she cried after him and begged his pity, in fact he held her in high esteem, which we see when he spoke with her publicly. But he only feigned lack of interest and pushed her away, as if he did not want to hear her, in order to find out how strong her faith was. She did indeed have great faith in our Lord Jesus Christ."[71] Despite her initial reception, the woman's faith was so great that LePicart compares Saint Peter unfavorably to her: "We find in Holy Scripture that our Lord Jesus Christ speaks of little faith and great faith. He speaks of little faith, when he says to St. Peter: 'What kind of faith is this, that you doubt?' And here, to this woman, he speaks of great faith: 'Great is your faith.'"[72] Tribulations or temptations were God's means of testing one's faith, and should be considered a sign of election.[73] Susanna's ordeal with the elders of the temple was brought to a happy conclusion because of her unwavering faith in God.[74]

At the end of life, a strong faith in the merits of Christ through his Passion would bring the greatest of all rewards: "A person who on his deathbed recommends himself to God, believing in the merits of the passion of Christ, will go securely to paradise. No matter how saintly a person is, even if he is another John the Baptist, he will not gain paradise without the merits of Christ's sacrifice."[75]

Facere Quod in Se Est

> My brothers, what good is it to profess faith without practicing it? Such faith has no power to save one, has it? . . . Show me your faith without works, and I will show you the faith that underlies my works.
>
> James 2:14, 18

Faith alone was not enough. LePicart expresses the delicate balance between faith and works: "Turks have fidelity, justice and other virtues, but for all that they are not pleasing to God, because they do not have faith in Jesus Christ. . . . Works alone and of themselves are not at all agreeable to God. But the Christian who has faith and preaches and does miracles and the like is not pleasing to God if he lacks charity. . . . Faith without charity is dead, but charity cannot exist without faith.[76] The preachers expressed man's relation to God in the covenantal terms of nominalist theology. The words "promise" and "pact" figure prominently. Pepin tells his listeners that "God is faithful to his promises, and he is not able to lie or deceive, but carries out what he has promised."[77] Even the promises of princes may be forgotten tomorrow, but God is true to his Word.[78] "God never deserts those who put their whole hope and faith in him, because he is faithful and has promised that he will carry out his end."[79] The divine pact is comprised of God's gift and our merits.[80]

As we have seen, man's part of the pact was to do what was in him, *facere quod in se est,* and around this concept the whole late medieval theology of justification revolved. One could be sure that God would do his part, infusing grace into the sinner, who then must act on his faith by doing what was in him. This did not detract from Christ's sacrifice on the cross, but rather allowed the penitent to enter into that sacrifice by doing his small part. LePicart explains how it works: "You will say that you don't know if your work is satisfactory considering your sins. It is true that your work, coming totally from you, is not satisfactory in itself. . . . But your work is based on the merits of Jesus Christ, so however much your work is nothing of itself, when added to the work of Jesus Christ it is sufficient for the remission of your sins. And it is as agreeable to God as if Jesus Christ had himself done it."[81] Over and over again, the preachers emphasized the text of James 2:26: "It does not suffice for salvation to have faith in your heart if good works do not follow. For [as James 2 says], faith without works is dead."[82] Raulin compares man to a tree, whose flowers are good thoughts and whose fruits are good deeds: "The fruit shows the quality of the tree."[83] Good works are the *necessary* fruit of true faith: "If the Holy Spirit lives in us, reviving us through grace, we show such an interior life by good exterior works, which come from the Holy Spirit. For good works are signs that we are alive spiritually and that the Holy Spirit lives in us."[84] The preachers used examples to prove that there could be no faith apart from charity: "Woman, your sins are pardoned. . . . We see here . . . that our Lord Jesus Christ attributed her justification to charity and love of God, which do not exist without good works."[85] Only very young children were exempt from this requirement, for they had neither the maturity nor the necessary understanding to act according to the gospels. For them, the merits of Jesus Christ alone sufficed.[86]

"Good works" to a late medieval Catholic preacher meant the act of faith, a proper inward disposition, the commission of good, and the omission of evil. They were a necessary part of the imitation of Christ, to complete his work in man. "From good works and in the joy of the life of the Spirit proceed hope, which . . . is a certain expectation of future happiness."[87] Works also provided a remedy against despair, "for [they] generate hope in the compassion of God. . . . Among all the things that help a man who has fallen into despair, the best is almsgiving."[88] The preachers believed that laziness was at the heart of people's disinclination to do good: "All men desire to be saved, but few want to do anything to earn their salvation."[89] The first step was to change one's attitude: "What does it mean to repent? First, you must change your will from bad to good. Get rid of your evil desires and give your heart to God. Be ashamed that you have offended him."[90] But then, the sinner must follow through on his promises; if he returned to his sins, the deal was off.[91]

The attitude with which one carried out good works was of fundamental importance. Fasting, crying, flagellation, pilgrimages, and giving to the poor were all useful and necessary when done in the proper spirit. The preachers demanded inward devotion, for without it Christians were no different than the Pharisees condemned by Jesus.[92] Menot likens penitence to a race, in which paradise is the final goal: "It is not sufficient to fast or do other good works of this sort, unless we do them with the proper spirit."[93] Works must be performed for the honor of God, and not to gain the praise of men.[94] "O how grievous! There are many in all classes, to whom justice is only a word, and not something on which they base their actions. This is true of many prelates and preachers who say many good things, but do not do them themselves."[95] One must be a Christian in more than name.[96]

Knowledge of Salvation

I will come to you like a thief, at a time you cannot know.

Revelation 3:3

Stressing the essential role of God in the process of salvation, the preachers warned that there was no way to be absolutely certain of salvation: "We can do works of penitence, but we cannot gain absolute security. I will never say, 'He is damned.' Neither will I say, 'He is saved.'"[97] There was not a man or woman alive, no matter how just, who could be absolutely secure in matters of salvation, for all things were uncertain "in a world that is like the ocean, where there is not security but only danger."[98] Even the Apostle Paul, who was called by God, and should have felt quite sure of his status, knew that he had to do all in his power to merit God's grace.[99] Some listeners would retort that God did not put them in this world in order to damn them, which Maillard admits is true, but he warns that this is not all there is to the issue.[100]

Although salvation is uncertain, there are certain providential signs. Goodness and hope suggest an inclination toward God.[101] Menot says that if at the hour of death, a person recommends himself to God, he can die securely.[102] Here we come full circle, to the notion of *facere quod in se est*.[103] "If a good and devout Catholic is asked what will happen to him after death, he will say with confidence in divine pity: I go to my heavenly Father and will dwell with him for all eternity."[104] LePicart reiterates that while we cannot know, we must hope.[105]

Unwillingness to heed the promptings of the Holy Spirit was a likely sign of damnation:

> There is no one so just in this world that he can know of his election or reprobation. But, just as the death of the body can be foreseen in the state of a sick person, so can the damnation of an individual be seen by his perseverance in sin. I say that when a sick person does not want to take medicine or food and his body is diseased and his pulse weak, this is a sign

that he will die. So he who treads on the inspirations of the Holy Spirit will likely be damned.[106]

Contrition and penitence were essential, but the preachers demanded that change be permanent, enduring till the end of life.[107] Unfortunately, too many people did not take seriously the danger facing them, saying, "We will think of our salvation when we grow old."[108] To counter this attitude, the preachers called for immediate remorse and atonement, evoking the spectre of death.[109] "Today you are healthy, laughing, and playing. Tomorrow you will be dead. As Seneca says, our life is only a race toward death."[110] *Ubi sunt* themes kept death before the audience's eyes to make them think about their mortal state and help them avoid temptation.[111] "You who live voluptuously, I invite you to the funeral of one of your fellows, who will be interred tomorrow."[112]

The Last Things

The background of all life in the world seems black. Everywhere the flames of hatred arise and injustice reigns. Satan covers a gloomy earth with sombre wings. In vain the militant church battles, the preachers deliver their sermons; the world remains unconverted.

Johan Huizinga[113]

Although Huizinga's view of the late Middle Ages has been challenged by many scholars, some historians continue to describe the fourteenth through sixteenth centuries as an era imbued with eschatological fears. Delumeau speaks of the "unanimity among historians who judge that from the Great Schism onwards, there was a greater diffusion of fear and apocalyptic expectation, which reached its height in Vincent Ferrier, Manfred de Vercelli, Savonarola, Sebastian Brant, and Thomas Münzer. The last great diabolical offensive had begun."[114] In another work, Delumeau continues the Huizingian tradition by stressing an atmosphere of fear that, in his opinion, pervaded life from the Black Death to the Wars of Religion, creating conditions of psychological maladaptation and dysfunction among large groups of people.[115] He suggests that "the Protestant Reformation was the result of profound eschatological ferment that in turn augmented the diffusion of apocalyptic expectations."[116] While there were certainly periods in the Middle Ages and the sixteenth century that conformed to Delumeau's vision, his hypothesis is too simplistic, assuming conditions in one century or one decade to have been static. He does not take into account changing economic and social factors that inevitably influenced the collective psyche.

Although eschatological prophecy had waned after the failure of Christ to return in glory in the first century A.D., the apocalyptic visions of Joachim of Fiore (d. 1201) signaled a return of these hopes and fears, especially among marginal or heretical groups. After the devastations of the plague, flagellant processions and prophetic, charismatic preachers became fairly common sights.[117] Joachim's belief that the end would be heralded by a second Charles led in the later Middle Ages to speculation that the French king Charles VIII or the Holy Roman Emperor Charles V might be the long-awaited successor to Charlemagne. For the years after 1550, Denis Crouzet has been able to trace the dissemination of eschatological prophecy in astrological predictions and almanachs, which grew until the French Catholic League's demise. He believes that the 1580s marked a crisis in apocalyptic forboding that conditioned the ideology of the League.[118]

The "anti-Huizingian" viewpoint has been advanced in recent years by both Étienne Delaruelle and Jacques Chiffoleau. In Delaruelle's analysis, the doctrine of the Antichrist in the later Middle Ages was far more ethical in content than dogmatic. "We are very far from Joachim of Fiore and his successors: in Vincent [Ferrier] there is no philosophy of history. . . . As with Vincent, the preaching of Manfred [de Vercelli] is essentially the preaching of penitence."[119] Going even further, Chiffoleau interprets the two centuries between 1340 and 1530 as "neither the Middle Ages in crisis nor the Renaissance in gestation, but rather an original, creative, and modern period . . . that we must study rather than content ourselves with the vague colors of autumn painted by Huizinga."[120] Martin remarks that preachers (and people) in the mid-fifteenth century had not yet noticed many of the (positive) changes resulting from the Black Death, but argues that by the time of Cleree and Menot, "one can see signs that the anger of God has been appeased."[121]

These opposing viewpoints recall the paradox of late medieval religiosity posed in the Introduction. How do the preachers' views of the unfolding of sacred history agree with these different historical analyses? Was the world in a state of crisis around the year 1500, with almost daily expectation of the coming of the Antichrist and then Christ in his glory? Were the Second Coming and the Last Judgment expressed in tones and language of joyful expectation or terrible dread? Did the appearance of Protestantism alter the ideology of the end of the world?

Purgatory

> That day will make its appearance with fire, and fire will test the quality
> of each man's work.   1 Corinthians 3:13

The concept of purgatory is inextricably bound to both soteriological and eschatological thought, "for it dramatized the end of earthly existence and charged it with an intensity compounded of mingled fear and hope."[122] Although the notion of an "intermediate place" had existed as early as the fourth century A.D., it was not until the twelfth century that the church began to use the noun *purgatorium* and belief began to be systematized.[123] The concept reached the more remote areas of France as late as the beginning of the fourteenth century.[124] According to Jacques LeGoff, what began as scholastic speculation achieved popularity through the preaching of the friars.[125]

Surprisingly, the sermons contain far fewer references to purgatory than one would expect; compared with other penitential themes, mentions of purgatory are infrequent. There are vague comments that could apply equally well to purgatory or hell, such as Cleree's statement that "God does not always punish great sinners in this world because he wants to punish them more in the next,"[126] and references to limbo and the nebulous soteriological status of the great patriarchs and unbaptized infants.[127] Pepin offers some clearer definitions. Telling his listeners that venial sins delay the soul's progress toward celestial glory if not expunged before death, he adds that sinning souls have to spend time in purgatory before ascending to heaven.[128] He specifies the gradation of sins that lead to a stay in purgatory: (1) mortal sins that have not been confessed, except in a general confession; (2) mortal sins that have been confessed but not completely expiated; and (3) venial sins that have not been confessed. The first will spend more time in purgatory than the second, the second more than the third. "But we can never be certain how long a soul will spend in purgatory, for we cannot be sure of the seriousness of our own guilt."[129] Prayers for the souls in purgatory could lessen their suffering or the length of their stay,[130] but it was better to avoid purgatory altogether by making satisfaction for sin and doing good on earth.[131] Confession was the best way to do this: "The . . . effect of confession is to commute one sort of penalty into another, that is, eternal into temporal, for those who desire to avoid the pains of purgatory must bear their punishments in this life."[132] The pains of purgatory are rarely specified. Instead, they are compared to suffering on earth: "In purgatory there are many evils of a sort that the pains of this world cannot possibly compare; yet all the same these souls endure their troubles with hope, for they know they will be delivered in the end."[133]

Why this relative lack of interest in purgatory, particularly in light of its alleged popularization through preaching? The answer is that most people probably learned of it through other channels—mystery plays,[134] artistic representations in frescoes and altarpieces,[135] and the less reputable indulgence preachers who made purgatory their special domain. Through vivid descriptions of torments and suffering, these preachers were able to beg alms and fill their chests with silver. The more respectable preachers chose to distance themselves from the notorious claims of the pardoners.

Hell

Here sighs and cries and wails
  coiled and recoiled on the starless air,
    spilling my soul to tears. A confusion of tongues and monstrous accents
  toiled in pain and anger.
  Voices hoarse and shrill and sounds of blows,
    all intermingled, raised tumult and pandemonium that still
  whirls on the air forever dirty with it.

Dante, *Inferno,* Canto 3:22–28

The concept of hell was much older than that of purgatory, and appears in various incarnations in the Hindu, Iranian, Egyptian, Babylonian, and Greek religions, among others.[136] The Hebrew *sheol,* or infernal underworld, and *gehenna,* hell proper, were both important for later Christian representations, but LeGoff has convincingly shown that Book VI of the *Aeneid* was a closer typology for the medieval hell in its "mixture of pleasure and pain, the dim perception of heaven's light, the references to imprisonment, the detailing of penalties, the combination of expiation and purification, and the idea of purification by fire."[137] It was no coincidence that Virgil served as Dante's guide in Inferno.

Hell, like purgatory, should have provided preachers with an arsenal of vivid and terrifying images with which to stir their listeners to repentance. Was hell depicted to greater effect than purgatory by the preachers? The answer is a qualified yes, for there are more specific descriptions, and a closer connection with penitential themes. Although hell is not mentioned with any great regularity in discussions of penitence, there is often an implicit assumption that does not require elaboration.

Questions about the geography of the underworld first arose in the early centuries of the Christian era.[138] In the Middle Ages, some theologians speculated about specific celestial or earthly locations for hell, with Bonaventure vaguely designating hell as being "in the north,"[139] and others suggesting precise spots such as Mount Etna in Sicily or the caverns of Ireland.[140] Borrowing from certain statements made in the thirteenth century by Étienne de Bourbon, who had described nocturnal sabbath gatherings in the area, Menot asks: "Have you gone to the mountains of Savoy, in the Vau Pute, which is very near to the suburbs of hell? It is said that there are many sorceresses there."[141] Pepin describes the "three provinces" of the afterlife:

> The first is above us, in heaven. The second is below us, in hell. The third is this present world. In the first, we find the elect. In the second there are evil men and women. In the first province, the ruler, who is none other than the omnipotent God, at one time purged his place of Lucifer and his ilk, sending them all into the abyss of hell. . . . The second province is totally the opposite of the first—it will never be purged of nor let go of evildoers. For in hell we find murderers, the sacrilegious, thieves, adulterers, blasphemers, lechers, the envious, gluttons, snobs, violent men, and the like.[142]

Hell was a negation of heaven, devoid of God's presence. Maillard describes it as "a lake without measure, deep, without bottom, filled with fire and intolerable stench, a place of unquenchable and innumerable griefs. Here we find misery, shadows, lack of order, eternal horror, with no hope for goodness nor even despair for evil."[143] Allegorically, he depicts "the four porters who carry the cadaver into the tomb as the porters who lead the soul into hell, that is, the charms of the present life, the blindness of the spirit, presumption about the future, and neglect of one's salvation."[144] Pepin stresses the eternity of hell for those listeners who might confuse it with purgatory,[145] saying that there is no way out, not for a thousand, nay two thousand, years, for punishment lasts forever.[146] Tragically, thousands were damned who would not have been had they known the hour of their death. It was therefore best to act immediately: "My friend, just as in prison one goes from the upper levels to the lower, so I say that no one descends into the inferno all at once, but by many stages. The first is the greatness of the sin, the second the number of sins, the third the infamy of the sin."[147] The preachers' motivation was ethical, not apocalyptic—they described hell in the hope that people would change their ways.

As is familiar to readers of Dante, the punishment in hell was designed to match the crime. "The whore will be bound in one bundle with her pimp as food for the fire, in the manner that we see snakes intertwined."[148] Those who "eat" the poor down to the bone in this world will drink the dregs of wine in the next and be eaten themselves by the wrath of God.[149]

As we might expect, people did not particularly care to hear these things. Maillard laments, "Do you know what many of them say?—'O, those preachers talk about hell to make us fearful.'"[150] Pepin agrees with Maillard, saying that "many do not really believe in what is to come, as we see by the words and deeds of those who mock preachers who speak of these things, and say that those who preach about the Last Judgment do not tell us this because it is true, but rather to terrify us, and call us to penitence."[151] Others saw the truth in the preachers' words, but responded that to do what they called for was hard.[152]

The Coming of the Eschaton?

> During that period after trials of every sort the sun will be darkened, the moon will not shed its light, stars will fall out of the skies, and the heavenly hosts will be shaken. Then men will see the Son of Man coming in the clouds with great power and glory.... I assure you, this generation will not pass away until all these things take place.   Mark 13:24–26, 30

The greatest preacher of the early fifteenth century in France was unquestionably Vincent Ferrier, a native of Valencia in Spain. Martin describes his practice:

> Vincent's sermon on the end of the world was absolutely terrifying. After a lengthy preamble, the sermon took on a cosmic character. As at twilight, we see the light of Christ dimming in all parts of the earth and the world returning to its former state of darkness. Is this not the time to do penance and to beg pardon? With a consummate artistry, Vincent knew how to take the faithful from a state of induced terror to one of calm, by then evoking the joys of the elect in the afterlife.[153]

Delumeau depicts this constant state of psychological tension between terrible fear and great hope as a necessary element in producing fear-ridden individuals.[154] How does Delumeau's view fit the picture of preaching at the end of the fifteenth and beginning of the sixteenth century presented here? While it is particularly difficult to interpret written versions of sermons with regard to fear, it is possible to discern a change in tone. Although some preachers continued to use apocalyptic language, they did not do so with the same frequency or literalism as in earlier times. Men and women buoyed by economic revival and a significantly improved standard of living by the end of the fifteenth century were not prepared to listen without objection to or believe unquestioningly in dire prophecies. Pepin tells of those who "make fun of preachers who talk about the pains of the inferno, the severity of the Last Judgment, or the pitiful works of piety they display."[155] While disease and intermittent warfare still took their toll, the great epidemic plagues and the Hundred Years' War were over and the world was still intact. References to the nearness of the end testify less to eschatological awareness than to a continuing need to use a theme so obviously valuable for inspiring penitence. Taken as a whole, the sermons do not present too dire a picture.

Maillard compares the ages of a man's life to stages through which the world has passed:

> Just as there are seven stages in the life of men, so there are seven stages through which the world has passed. The first stage is infancy, the second childhood, the third adolescence, the fourth youth, the fifth manhood, the sixth old age, and the seventh senility. . . . So from the beginning to the end of the world there are seven stages: The first began with Adam. . . . the second with Noah. . . . the third Abraham. . . . the fourth Moses. . . . the fifth David. . . . the sixth the end of the patriarchal age. . . . and the seventh the advent of Christ, which will last until the end of the world.[156]

Maillard's description differs from Joachim of Fiore's vision, for he concentrates on what has already come to pass rather than what is yet to come. Joachimite prophecy described history as a succession of three stages. The first stage, the age of the Father, comprises Maillard's first six stages; the second stage, the age of the Son or of the Gospel, is equivalent to Maillard's seventh stage. But Maillard does not delineate the third age, which Joachim had described as the age of the Spirit, the culmination of human history.[157] Very few of the preachers offered a philosophy of last things that went beyond a description of the signs. Instead they made mundane comparisons between the end of individual human lives and the end of the world, analogies that drew on ordinary fears of death for their inspiration.[158] Menot argues ambiguously that "on the last day, the day of the ultimate battle, all the artillery of the Devil will be brought to bear. . . . Behold in what manner the soul is assailed at the hour of death."[159]

The most common eschatological themes are the signs that will precede the Last Judgment. Tisserand and Raulin, two of the earliest preachers in our study, are notable exceptions for their apparently serious concern with eschatological issues. Only in their sermons does a sense of apocalyptic pessimism assume significant proportions. Raulin bases his sermon for the second Sunday of Advent on passages in Mark 13. He describes the eight signs that will herald the Judgment: (1) divisions within the (Holy) Roman Empire; (2) great wars and sedition; (3) a horrendous storm; (4) earthquakes; (5) plagues; (6) famines; (7) the appearance of false prophets; and (8) the coming of the Antichrist. Examining these signs in greater detail, he finds a number of them present in his own time: "We can see clearly now that hardly anyone obeys the Holy Roman Emperor, but in the time of the apostles the empire flourished. . . . Second, we find divisions in the church itself, and little obedience to the Roman pontiff. This is true at present. Third, we find divisions within the Catholic faith, not everywhere, but in many places such as Asia and Africa, where they have turned against Christ."[160] As with most of the later preachers studied here, discussions of the end take on ethical and moralistic, rather than eschatological, overtones, for Raulin mentions in the same text bad judges, bishops, and learned doctors who currently hold sway in the church. However terrifying this sermon may have been, its purpose was to provoke reformation. Tisserand, on the other hand, talks of the signs of the end in a less ethical context. He, too, believes that pestilence and sedition will signal the advent of the Antichrist, and many will come in the Lord's name to seduce the people.[161] In a horrifying passage, Tisserand blends direct borrowing from the Vulgate, paraphrase, and his own poetic interpretation.

> But it is sufficient for now to take the signs that are mentioned in our theme. Whence it is said that the nations of the earth will be in anguish; distress will be such that people will hide in the caves of the earth. And this because of the confusion that arises with the roaring of the seas and rivers. The seas will rise wondrously over all of the hills, and then they will subside. So with the rivers, and they will make a thunderous noise. . . . The rivers will bring forth great waves, and the voices of all of the waters will lift themselves on high to our Lord. And then the rivers will strike against the lands, according to the gospel, so that men will die of fright in the face of them.[162]

His imagery is laden with apocalyptic symbolism, the caves being accepted images for the mouths of hell and purgatory.[163] In another sermon, Tisserand warns the damned that they will have the signs of demons upon them, and will drink of the sulfurous ire of God.[164] For the third week of Advent, Tisserand unveiled his most terrifying sermons of the *dies irae,* in which he begins by describing the purifying fire that will engulf the earth: "Fire will come down from the sky when Christ comes. . . . The fire will descend against its elemental nature, for fire normally leaps upward."[165] This was a sure sign of the times, for natural laws have been suspended. Mountains will be leveled and the waters of the earth will freeze over. He describes the work of the purificatory fire:

> O, wretched sinners, who take your gain in this or that: the fire will consume you along with your wealth. . . . It will cleanse the elect who were biding their time in purgatory . . . for after the Judgment there will be no more purgatory. And after the Judgment the fire will descend with the damned into hell, for the earth will open up, and the greatest of horrors will rush to greet the damned. The damned and the fire will descend at the same moment into this pit of filth and sulfur. Immediately after the descent of

the damned, the purifying fire will return to renew the earth. After the Judgment, the fire will return to its original state.[166]

The damned will see cadavers and be struck by horrible fear.[167]

The very considerable emphasis on eschatology in Tisserand's relatively few extant sermons finds little echo in the sermons of most of the other preachers, including those for whom we have hundreds of complete sermons. Pepin warns the oppressors of the poor "that at the end of the world a huge boulder will plunge down the mountainside, that is, Christ will come down from the heavens, and bit by bit he will tear apart the arms and torsos of sinners, and throw them into hell because of their treatment of the poor."[168] He, too, evokes a fiery scenario: "Once outside, if they look back, they will see the whole world ablaze in the fire of the great conflagration."[169] It will be a time of wailing, beating of breasts and begging for divine mercy.[170] The end will be signaled by an eclipse of the sun and the appearance of a moon bathed in blood.[171] Despite the terrifying imagery, these references are overwhelmingly outweighed by other themes, such as the need for penitence and the imitation of Christ.

References to the Judgment are not entirely horrific. Most of the preachers used the carrot-and-stick technique, giving equal time to the joys awaiting the elect. Like Vincent Ferrier before him, Menot combines the two themes:

> Here is the imperial throne of Heaven in which Our Lord is seated along with the saints and the Virgin Mary. But then the earth will open and the mouth of hell will lie agape and all the devils and the masses of the damned will be shrieking and letting out great sighs. They will put themselves on the earth near the mouth of the inferno, hoping that in the divine judgment they will be taken from the mouth of hell and eternity without end. But the blessed will be raised to heaven.[172]

Raulin contrasts the angels who will come down to lead the elect into heaven with those who will come to confront evildoers.[173] In another passage, he promises those who have lived good and decent lives that after the Resurrection they will be glorified just as Jesus Christ had been.[174] The preachers promised that in the next world, men would be incorruptible,[175] existing in a state of great and overflowing love, without fear.[176]

The preachers occasionally discussed the timing of the Last Days. Pepin tells his listeners that "through our reason we are not able to know when the Day of Judgment will come, for this transcends human powers of investigation."[177] Many used the concept of the "thief in the night" to great effect, telling their listeners that they must be in a constant state of preparedness.[178] Others suggested the Judgment was very near. Raulin explicitly states that "the world will come to an end in our times."[179] LePicart sees the challenge to the Catholic church as an indication that the end is near, for "Saint Paul says that when one deserts the faith of Jesus Christ, and no longer recognizes the papacy and the Roman Catholic Church, it is a sign that the Judgment is approaching."[180] It is surprising only that he does not push this theme further.

The preachers were extremely concerned with the need for penitence, and referred to the eschatological event in this context. Tisserand's concern is the exception that proves the rule. He was one of the earliest-born in the group of preachers, and grew up under the influence of prophetic preaching. The fact that references to purgatory, hell, and the Last Judgment do not seem to have increased dramatically with the coming of the Reformation is noteworthy, for we would have expected Luther's appearance to spark off a new wave of prophecy. LePicart did make the connection. But the occasional reference does not suggest a sense of eschatological imminence; on the contrary, it appears that such expectations had decreased considerably during the fifteenth century.

The preachers presented the quest for salvation in nominalist covenantal terms, but in a familiar, down-to-earth language that even the simplest of their listeners could have understood. They explained theological doctrines using analogies with family life, human relations, and nature that were readily comprehensible. The central theme of late medieval Catholic theology was that God gave man the ability to cooperate with grace, to do what was in him. The preachers did not demand the impossible, but insisted that man's creation in God's image allowed him to participate in the business of his own salvation. As Brown found in Gerson's pastoral theology, gentleness was the dominant note, a desire to console rather than to condemn.[181] It would have been an unusually educated and psychologically introspective man or woman who turned that message into an intolerable burden.

The surprising infrequency of eschatological themes in the sermons studied here, especially after the third quarter of the fifteenth century, points to a world view that had changed significantly since the pessimistic and melancholy years that followed the first onset of the Black Death. The more practical approach adopted by most of the preachers stands in stark contrast to the abstract and mystical notions presented by Tisserand. More concerned with moral reformation and penitence than dire predictions of the end of the world or the millenium, the preachers used these ideas metaphorically to elicit the desired responses. They were very far indeed from the preachers of the early fifteenth century who spoke of little but the *malheur du temps*. Pierre-aux-Boeufs, confessor to Isabelle of Bavaria in 1418, had preached constantly of "schism, war, dissension, adversity, tribulations, scarcity, high prices, poverty, plagues, and death."[182] His was a universe in full disarray.[183] While some of the same themes appear in the sermons, the dominant mood is not one of a world on the brink of disaster, but a world that was likely to continue. The preachers' experience in some ways paralleled that of the early Christians active in the generations after the Crucifixion, when it became clear that the world was going to continue indefinitely. Their world was occupied by complacent and reasonably well-off individuals who should have been spending their time reflecting on their lives and doing good for their less well-off neighbors. That was the real meaning of *facere quod in se est*.

6

The Religious Cosmos

[U]nlike the saints of sterner times, the corpus of God's human friendship
in the last medieval century or so does not seem to be characterised, in
a primary way, by the possession of power.... It was easier, by concentrating on the individual saints and their everyday traffic between heaven
and earth, to get a glimpse of what would remain a familiar social universe,
but transfigured into friendship with God and with man.

John Bossy[1]

For most medieval people, religion was not an abstract system of beliefs, but
a vital part of daily existence that included a familiar cast of characters—God
the Father, Jesus Christ, the Holy Spirit, the Virgin Mary, the saints, and
the Devil. In the animistic universe of the man or woman of 1500, these beings
mirrored human and community relations on earth and illustrated in a way
that concepts alone could not the ideals of Christian love and brotherhood.
Although Protestants and Catholics disagreed about the importance of the
saints, for *le menu peuple* there can be no doubt that these quasi-divine
characters provided an important link to God.

God the Creator

Then the Lord said to Moses, "Go to Pharaoh, for I have made him
obdurate in order that I may perform these signs of mine among them
and that you may recount to your son and grandson how ruthlessly I dealt
with the Egyptians and what signs I wrought among them, so that you
may know that I am the Lord. Exodus 10:1–2

Beloved, let us love one another because love is of God; everyone who
loves is begotten of God and has knowledge of God. The man without
love has known nothing of God, for God is love. God's love was revealed
in our midst in this way: he sent his only Son to the world.

1 John 4:7–9

In the sermons studied in this book, God the Creator has two faces—the
angry, righteous God of the Old Testament, and the merciful, compassionate

102

Father who sent his only Son to redeem the human race. A number of factors influenced the preachers' choice of which aspect to highlight, including the season of the church year and the type of audience. The preachers rendered a popular version of God's absolute versus his ordained power in this rather simplistic dichotomy:

Old Testament = Wrathful God, the Law = *potestas absoluta*
New Testament = Merciful God (Jesus Christ), Love = *potestas ordinata*

The relationship of loving obedience envisioned in the new covenant was a formulation that suited the improved material conditions in France by the late fifteenth and early sixteenth centuries. Although images of the wrathful God are not absent from the sermons, they rarely approach the intensity of the earlier fifteenth-century preacher Pierre-aux-Boeufs who described a God who "afflicts us with evils in this life, sends us plagues, death, wars, and tribulations. He takes food from us, he separates us from the goods of the earth, and he makes few grapes on the vines and little wheat in the fields. He sends us scarcity."[2]

Most of the preachers in this study emphasized God's goodness and love for humanity,[3] although some of the earliest preachers in the group retained more of the formulations typified by Pierre-aux-Boeufs. This presentation was consistent with a preaching philosophy that taught that men and women were more easily won by kindness and persuasion than by threats. As the height of all goodness, God knew that charity and love won hearts, not terror and menace, so he was more willing to show mercy than to wreak vengeance.[4] Liberation, not torture, was his aim.[5] When God saw a man on the road to perdition, he did everything in his power to deflect him from such a course.[6] "For our most holy Creator God does not want the death of sinners, but for them to convert and live; he wants no one to perish, but all to walk the way of truth."[7] "Our holy mother church says: O, poor children, revert to your Lord God, who is so loving, kind, and caring, who waits for your penitence and desires nothing but your salvation."[8]

In the religious cosmos, the Virgin Mary assumed the role of mother, with all the appropriate maternal qualities with regard to "her" human children. In a similar manner, God the Creator acted the role of father—a father who expected respect and obedience, and who was willing to use discipline when necessary, but who truly loved his human offspring in spite of their faults. In the French sermons of the late fifteenth and early sixteenth centuries, God was more paternal than patriarchal. He was the father who welcomed back the Prodigal Son, forgiving the latter's transgressions out of joy at having him back.[9] Cleree uses the parable of the vineyard owner to show that God is the height of all that is good: "Certainly the head of the family, who here is called a man, is God the Father who is like this man. Man is indeed the gentlest and most benign of all creatures. So God the Father is the summit of all goodness. He is the father of mercy, the God of all consolation."[10] The proof of God's love and compassion was the Incarnation and Resurrection. "After the Fall, God wanted to sustain men, promote peace, and restrain rebels,"[11] and although he was free to choose many ways to remit men's sins *(potestas absoluta)*, he felt that the sacrifice of his Son for all men *(potestas ordinata)* was both appropriate and necessary.[12] The knowledge that God *could* punish with all the force of his power proved his goodwill.[13] To doubters, LePicart points out that man's sense of judgment and justice is far more severe than God's.[14]

God's compassion was no excuse for spiritual malaise. When Calvin claimed, "Today, if one always preaches pleasant and delightful things, the people will only scoff, and will want to make friends with God, to play with him as if he were a mere mortal,"[15] he was voicing a complaint familiar to pre-Reformation preachers. Raulin argues that "it is no wonder that God gets angry with us, for daily he expects us to repent, yet we do not."[16] But Cleree contrasts the Old Testament God with the God who sent Christ. He tells his listeners that before the Incarnation, God reigned more with severe justice than with compassion. "When God is angry, he sends plagues, wars, and other evils that make life very difficult. But people! Now Christ places himself before the divine judge and stands up for us, saying, My Father."[17] The age in which an angry God ruled the universe was past, but should not be forgotten.

The preachers did not stop at such one-dimensional views of God. To explain the problem of evil and human suffering, the preachers called on medieval theologians and scholastic argumentation, but translated it into everyday parlance: "My lady, you will understand this better if I give you an example. You have a son who has gallstones. They must be removed. You cry, of course; nevertheless it is necessary to put him in danger of death at the hands of the surgeon if he is to be cured."[18] God is portrayed as the surgeon, who may have to give pain for the long-term good of the patient. Not only does God not cause evil, but he will not withdraw his help unless one knowingly commits evil deeds or perseveres in sin.[19] A logical corollary might be to blame God for one's own guilt, "saying that if God so desired, no one would sin."[20] But God gave man the power to choose through free will: "It is not a defect in the sun if eyes cannot see; so with men, it is their defects that make them unwilling to open their eyes and receive the sunlight."[21]

The Trinity as a concept was discussed less often than its individual members. Using Aristotle's argument of a prime mover as developed in the *Physics* and the *Metaphysics,* Pepin makes a hierarchical argument:

> By natural reason we are able to know and conclude that God is one.... We see in all the heavens that one is supreme, who is called the first mover, just as among the seven planets only one has primacy. In addition, we see that in politics there is only one supreme monarch, who gives all the orders, and this is the most perfect form of rule. We find the same in the church, in which one pope alone rules. And from all of these examples we can conclude that God is one.[22]

As long as people understood the basic concept of the Trinity, the preachers were generally content to discuss separately God's three Persons.[23]

The Holy Spirit

> The Spirit too helps us in our weakness, for we do not know how to pray
> as we ought; but the Spirit himself makes intercession for us with groanings
> that cannot be expressed in speech. He who searches hearts knows what
> the Spirit means, for the Spirit intercedes for the saints as God himself
> wills. Romans 8:26–27

The Holy Spirit, like the Trinity, could not be presented in the same manner
as the other characters in the religious cosmos because of his ineffability. One
of the most detailed discussions can be found in Gaigny's "Homily on the
Advent of the Holy Spirit and the Feast of Pentecost," preached in 1521 in
the presence of Francis I. The feast required that Gaigny attempt to explain
at length this most intangible Person of the Trinity, a task made easier by
the intellectual level of the audience.

> God the Father, considering in himself his Being, engenders a consciousness
> and intelligence of himself. And this understanding that the Father has of
> himself is necessarily other than the Father. . . . It is other than the Father
> and the Son in the same manner as love is distinct from the lover. This love
> is Christian virtue, the third person of the Trinity, who because of our own
> lack of understanding cannot be expressed sufficiently in one name.[24]

The preachers presented the Holy Spirit as a force whose objective was to
burn away sins and cleanse the conscience of carnal desire in order to make
one wholly spiritual.[25] The Spirit, which lives in the church, making possible
continuing revelation, embodies the "new" face of God—the new life of love
that has come about through the Incarnation and Resurrection of Jesus
Christ.[26] "The Lord did not want to tell everything that must be done or
believed to his apostles, but chose to leave some part of it to be explained
to their successors through the inspiration of the Holy Spirit."[27]

More popular sermons also dealt with the subject of the Holy Spirit,
emphasizing his properties of love, faith, and consolation. The Spirit looks
into the heart, soul, and thoughts of man, moving him to prayer, and inviting
him to accept God's grace. Citing Sirach 25:1—"With three things I am
delighted, for they are pleasing to the Lord and to men: Harmony among
brethren, friendship among neighbors, and the mutual love of husband and
wife"—Menot infers that these keep love of the soul and the Holy Spirit in
one's memories. In sexually suggestive language, he says: "The Holy Spirit
comes to your bed by day and night and says: 'Open yourself to me, my wife,
my sister,' giving inspiration."[28] In striking contrast to his regular use of
zoological examples, Messier describes in moving terms the essential role of
the Holy Spirit in awakening man to God:

> Most loving and holy is he who is the giver of all grace, which is love
> proceeding from the Father and the Son. But however much the Father acts
> and the Son suffers, nothing could be accomplished without the Holy Spirit.

For this is the manner in which it acts—through the preached Word. It will sing of the Incarnation of the Word, and by this greeting will bring forth your grateful response. Consent in you is given by this inspiration, by which you will be saved.[29]

One who "shows contempt for the divine word drives the Spirit from him."[30]

As in their treatment of God, our preachers emphasized the loving, consolatory face of the Holy Spirit rather than the unforgiving Spirit or the Spirit who drove Jesus into the desert to suffer the temptations of the Devil. Love was also the primary characteristic of the final, and for our preachers, the most personally relevant member of the Trinity, Jesus Christ.

Jesus Christ

[The Pharisee] asked him, "Teacher which commandment of the law is the greatest?" Jesus said to him:

"'You shall love the Lord your God
with your whole heart,
and your whole soul,
and with all your mind.'

This is the greatest and first commandment. The second is like it;

'You shall love your neighbor as yourself.'"

Matthew 22:35–39

Who was this man Jesus Christ, and why did he take on human form? The answer to this question formed the crux of medieval Catholic Christology. Christ was so important in medieval preaching that Lansperge remarks, "it is truly very rare for a sermon to make no mention of the death, passion, and work of redemption of our Lord."[31]

Why would God send his Son to earth, knowing in advance his fate at the hands of men? The answer was simple—it was the only way to pay the outstanding debt for the transgressions of the first parents,[32] which man alone, no matter how good, could never satisfy.[33] Christ "had to take on flesh to be above flesh, and against flesh, and because only by taking on flesh could he achieve his mission."[34] The death on the cross overcame death itself, and made peace between God and man.

The preachers discussed Christ's abstract nature symbolically. Often using marital and sexual analogies, the preachers described his mystical body as the body of all Christian believers gathered together in God's church.[35] But it was primarily the historical Jesus who interested the preachers. While the Holy Spirit and even God were intangible entities difficult for simple minds to grasp, Jesus Christ had been a living, breathing human being. But it was the delicate task of the preacher to explain to his listeners that Christ was not *just* like them, which of course involved some theological interpretation. Illyricus uses a botanical example to explain Christ's natures: "Just as with a tree, when one branch is grafted onto another kind of tree, we obtain different kinds of fruit; so in the unity of Christ's person the properties of his divine nature and his human nature came together."[36]

The sermons concentrate on Christ's earthly ministry, including his preaching, his manner of living, and the example he set for mortal men and women. When discussing Christ's birth, the preachers relied most heavily on the account in Luke 2:1–20. Maillard begins his Christmas sermon by repeating in part Jesus' parable of the wedding banquet (Matthew 22:2), although it is taken out of context. "This king was God the Father who sent his Son into the womb of the Blessed Virgin; Christ assumed human nature so that all human infants would be made legitimate."[37] The details, down to the actual birth and nursing of the infant, are given in order to enhance the identification of Christ with human babies and to evoke sympathetic and maternal feelings in his listeners.[38] Maillard then asks his listeners briefly to forget the world, leaving aside their Pater Nosters and Ave Marias, and go with him spiritually into Bethlehem to think about this special child.[39] Menot explains how the circumstances of Christ's birth set the tone for his life: "He had a most humble birth, being born in a poor dwelling and surrounded by the poorest of furnishings. He experienced the same sort of poverty during his life, without riches or earthly possessions."[40] LePicart adds that Jesus wanted to be conceived in Nazareth rather than Jerusalem in order to show men that they must not look for greatness in the eyes of men or the world, but before God.[41]

The imitation of Christ was a central theme, and the sermons reflect many of the ideas found in Thomas à Kempis's masterpiece. "We must hold to the road of paradise, as Paul teaches us. . . . Be imitators of Christ."[42] A primary concern of the preachers was the fulfillment of the great commandment, by which man was ordered to love God and his neighbors as himself. "We ought to truly love our neighbors in imitation of Christ, and not because they love us, or can do something for us."[43] One must meditate on Christ's sacrifice,[44] then try to become as like him as possible—one of his soldiers, carrying the cross of penitence.[45] The imitation of Christ meant embodying his qualities of humility, piety, compassion, and justice in one's own life.[46] Jesus had made clear to his disciples and would-be followers that this would not be easy. "The first thing our Lord Jesus Christ preached when he came into this world was the need for penitence. . . . It is impossible for us to be saved if we are not penitent."[47] Imitation of Christ meant identification with the poor. One must willingly choose the life of poverty, and give to the poor, who are all brothers in Christ.[48] The true poor were already with Christ: "If you see poor women with five or six children laboring every day in the fields, with nothing to eat but grass and salt, and ask them, 'What will you dine on?' They will answer, 'Christ.'"[49] It was up to the true follower of Christ to become like these women.[50]

The image of Christ shedding his blood was a favorite medieval theme that linked divinity to the ordinary person,[51] and Christ's last days on earth were described in great detail in Passion sermons. Menot laments that "Christ came, speaking softly to sinners, by whom he was received with harsh words, then harsher blows, and finally the most severe of torments."[52] Lansperge tells us that Jesus would neither eat nor drink until the realm of God had come to pass, and the new law had replaced the old.[53] The suffering Christ provided the preachers and people with the purest display of God's great love. In the manner of a late medieval artist, Maillard paints the scene of the Crucifixion for his listeners: "All people who desire to live virtuously and love God must put themselves at the foot of the cross, and gaze at the blood that flows from it; they must present themselves to God the Creator, weeping and sighing, begging his pardon, asking his grace, which they will surely receive if they persevere."[54] He asks his listeners to raise their eyes to Christ, nailed to the cross, and to think of all he had suffered for them.[55] Menot invests his Passion sermon with a strong sense of emotional drama. He opens the sermon with the comment that when the head of a family dies, the whole family is afflicted and puts on mourning: "The wife grieves for she has lost her good husband, the children because they have lost a father who would have helped them through life, the servants because they have lost their good master. So must we all grieve when we see Christ preparing to meet his death."[56] He then announces his intention of tracing Jesus' steps from the moment he was taken in the garden through his examination by Pontius Pilate and the road to the cross. Christ's doubts in the garden showed his particularly human side:

> The passion of Our Lord was a marvelous pilgrimage, one during which he rested six times. . . . When he first walked into the Garden, he was greatly afraid and troubled. . . . And then, lifting up his eyes to Heaven, his hands joined together, his poor heart struck with terror, he cried in a piteous voice: "O, Father, the death that I must suffer today is hard to bear. O, Father, is there no other way? Must I die such a death? I am your only child. Nevertheless, Father, I will do your will."[57]

Menot is surprisingly tolerant of Pilate:

> Pilate, hearing our Lord speak, knew that he was a wise man and was astonished by his responses, so he went over to the Jews who were waiting at the door and said: "You brought this man to me. But I find nothing in him that calls for the death sentence. But I say to you, it is your choice to save one man." Pilate tried three times to save Christ from death, knowing that he did not deserve it.[58]

Other preachers were less tolerant of Pilate, some describing him as a "crafty fox."[59]

Menot's embroidery on the gospel account made the Passion a living event for his listeners. We can see this clearly in his description of the burial scene. The gospel of Mark (15:45–47) describes the scene thus: "Learning from [the centurion] that [Jesus] was dead, Pilate released the corpse to Joseph. Then, having bought a linen shroud, Joseph took [Jesus] down, wrapped him in the linen, and laid him in a tomb which had been cut out of rock. Finally he rolled a stone across the entrance of the tomb. Meanwhile, Mary Magdalene and Mary the mother of Jesus observed where he had been laid." Menot dramatizes the scene as follows:

Joseph asked for the body from Pilate and anointed it with an ointment of myrrh and aloes worth 100 l. and covered him with a costly cloth. With the centurion, he climbed up the mount, ready with a hammer and pincers to take Christ down off the cross. Seeing the blessed Mary and her companions coming from afar, he said to his friends: "They think we are going to do him some further harm." The women approached with hands joined, and contented themselves that he was dead. Joseph and his companion said to Mary: "My Lady, we do not come to make you unhappy, or to harm your dear child. We come to take him down and bury him as is his right." And she thanked them humbly. Setting to work, therefore, they first detached one arm, then the other, then his feet.[60]

Late medieval French preachers portrayed the death and resurrection of Jesus Christ as the culmination of his incarnation and earthly mission. The two natures of Christ and his corporal-spiritual mission were truly joined at this moment: "We understand that Christ's suffering and dying on the cross confirms in us the truth of faith that comes from his humanity. The signs he showed us in his Resurrection from death confirm our faith in his divinity. We believe him to be both the true God and perfect man."[61] LePicart refers to the Resurrection as the sum total of the Christian's faith.[62] For those who might identify too greatly with the human Christ, Menot warns that the Resurrection is not to be thought of as simply bodily resurrection, but spiritual as well.[63] It was done to fortify man's faith, for if Christ had not risen from the dead, no one would have believed he was the true God.[64] The Resurrection gave man hope for his own rebirth.[65] "He died that we would be redeemed, and we are mortified in order to learn spiritually. He rose from the dead in order to give us hope in the Resurrection and to teach us how to pull ourselves out of a life of sin."[66] Belief in Christ's resurrection brought light after the darkness. "All of our sadness will be turned into joy."[67] This is the heart of the Resurrection message: "He was taken up to the sky . . . to offer remission continually to sinners. O what confidence! O what hope! What consolation! Our judge is our advocate and continual intercessor."[68]

In summary, the Catholic interpretation of Jesus Christ in the late medieval and early Reformation era stressed the unity of Christ in both his human and divine natures. The Christocentrism of late medieval Catholicism has been remarked upon by Delaruelle who, speaking of Bernardino of Siena, said that for him, "salvation was defined by Jesus Christ; the moral life was Christocentric."[69] Even the evangelical reformer, Jacques Lefèvre d'Étaples, believed in such a Christocentric interpretation. In this he was typical of his generation, for the late medieval preachers all emphasized the words and deeds of the historical Jesus. Although they dramatized the scenes of Jesus' human life in order to make the gospels more meaningful to ordinary people, they did not lose sight of the saving work of the risen Christ. The medieval Catholic view is well expressed by a modern theologian, who suggests that "the cross cannot be understood apart from the life which it ended."[70] Medieval Catholic theologians generally understood the Resurrection as the culmination of a specific life, a divine intervention in historical time and place, which gave them the unique opportunity to study God's message as voiced by Jesus.

By contrast, Protestants, especially Luther, focused on the post-Resurrection Christ witnessed to by Paul. Here, too, modern scholarship is helpful. The fact that Paul never knew the historical Jesus is of critical importance in understanding why Catholics and Protestants differed so significantly. "Quite decisively Paul says ... that the earthly Jesus, the human personality Jesus, has no meaning whatever for his religious life, for him as one who is 'in Christ' and thereby belongs to a higher reality than the earth."[71] William Wrede argues that Pauline Christology tends to "crush out the man Jesus."[72] The fundamental divergence between Catholics and Protestants on the issue of "Jesus versus Paul" was at the heart of the reformers' complaints about Catholic preaching. Protestants accused Catholics of being too concerned about ethics, while Catholics felt Protestants overlooked Jesus' teachings on earth. Criticism by either side about "faith alone" or "works salvation" was a simplification of this important theological difference.

The inherent value of late medieval theology cannot be easily understood apart from this distinction. The preachers used allegory, fables, and even a mediatory mother to promote a real understanding of Jesus' mission and, thereby, of the Resurrection. Protestants, more concerned with the risen Christ, saw no need for such elaboration, for all one had to do was heed the words of Paul and have faith. The relative understanding of the human and the divine, and its meaning for Christianity, inexorably shaped how a preacher went about his work.

The Virgin Mary

Blest is she who trusted that the Lord's words to her would be fulfilled.

Luke 1:45

The Virgin Mary filled a role similar to that of Christ in the minds of many late medieval people. Heiko Oberman points to the theological closeness between Mary and the ordinary sinner that preachers actively fostered:

> By her humility Mary attracted and preserved the grace of God; the sinner attracts God's grace by doing his very best. Mary earned her eternal glory; still this reward exceeds her merits and is a gift of divine liberality. The sinner must also earn his salvation, but this is still subject to God's acceptance. Since even before the reception of the first grace Mary had more humility than any other creature, she has been elected above all other creatures. But her way to glory is essentially the same as that of any other creature.[73]

For some people, Mary's intercessory and helping powers were superior even to those of Christ, for she had been only human and could sympathize more easily with the human plight. She was important to medieval Christians pre-

cisely because of Christ's humanity—Jesus was conceived, born of, and nur-
tured by his human mother Mary.[74] Throughout the Middle Ages, two images
of Mary coexisted, one that endowed her with quasi-divine status and another
that emphasized her motherly role. The former was more prominent in the
High Middle Ages, with the latter predominant by the fourteenth and fifteenth
centuries.[75]

Discussion of the Immaculate Conception of the Virgin was widespread
in thirteenth-century scholastic circles, and ranged from Richard of Saint
Laurent's (d. post 1245) divinization of Mary[76] to Thomas Aquinas's utter
rejection of Mary's exemption from original sin.[77] In the beginning, Franciscans supported the Immaculate Conception of the Virgin and Dominicans
denied it, but by the fifteenth century Dominicans were often equally enthu-
siastic: "The conception of Christ could not be other than holy, pure, and
immaculate. The conception of the Virgin Mary came through the special
grace of God, and was both prevenient and preservative from the corruption,
inchastity, and pollution that is present in the conception of other human
beings. And this was in order to recognize the special privilege and beneficence
shown to her."[78] Illyricus explains that "Mary was truly infused with all grace.
For the angel said to Mary, 'Hail, Mary, full of grace.' By these words he
made clear that the blessed Virgin was conceived without any stain and was
adorned with the purity of her original innocence."[79] Tisserand compares
Mary to Adam before the Fall.[80] Brulefer logically extends the doctrine to
show that not only was the Virgin exempt from original sin, but actual sin as
well.[81] Its importance clearly related to Christ's own purity as well as a desire
to honor the Virgin. Some, like Lefèvre d'Étaples, "argued that through
scriptural witness and animated by the spirit of piety, one could prove the
Immaculate Conception. If we are to honor our parents, how better could
we honor the Virgin Mary than by recognizing her Immaculate Conception?"[82]
In 1438, the Council of Basel, later disavowed by the Pope, officially proclaimed that Mary had been conceived without original sin,[83] and this position
was accepted by the Paris Faculty of Theology in 1498.[84] None of the preachers
exhibited any heterodox leanings on this issue, possibly, as Maillard suggests,
because it was very dangerous to assert that Mary was conceived in original
sin after the Council of Basel.[85]

The doctrines of purity and perpetual virginity needed some explaining to
convince people who were quite aware of reproductive processes. Pepin expressed concern at the possibility of misunderstanding: "The Virgin Mary
was not conceived simply through a kiss between Joachim and Anne, as many
simple people believe who see representations of Joachim and Anne kissing
each other in churches and paintings."[86] Speaking of Mary's marriage, Menot
explains that she and Joseph were joined together in Christian virtue rather
than in flesh. "The marriage of Mary and Joseph was one more true and
honest than can ever be found in this world between two people. Understanding Mary's initial doubts, the Holy Spirit revealed to her: 'Mary, you
will not have any problem entering this marriage because your fiancé shares
your desire [for virginity] and will never ask you to do that which you do not

desire.'"[87] Mary was compared to the burning bush of Exodus 3:2, which should have been consumed but was preserved through grace, just as her virginity was preserved in spite of her motherhood.[88] Because the flesh of the mother and the Son were of one nature, Mary was not only a human mother, but also the Mother of God, just as Christ was one person with two natures.[89]

Like the artists of the time, most preachers stressed Mary's human and maternal qualities, but the latter expressed concern that this not be taken to extremes. According to Maillard, Mary bore Jesus without any of the normal labor pains that beset ordinary women.[90] But LePicart complains that artists depict her just like other women: "Painters paint the glorious Virgin Mary laying down in her bed, as if she was having labor pains, and in need of a midwife. This is a great abuse! For without any pain she gave birth to our Lord Jesus Christ, and she did this alone, thus preserving her bodily integrity."[91]

Some scholars have asserted that Mary's "freedom from sex, painful delivery, age, death, and all sin exalted her ipso facto above ordinary women."[92] The paradox of virginity and motherhood set her off from other women: "The Blessed Virgin was like a closed door in her virginity, but she was an open door to allow all to enter the heavens through her great love, as she assiduously prays for this end. . . . Just as the sun shines through a window without breaking it, so Christ went through the womb of the Virgin."[93] Mary did not suffer from the normal feminine drawbacks of fragility, inconstancy, or lack of judgment,[94] nor did she flaunt her beauty through makeup or extravagant clothing. Instead she chose to hide it.[95] As the helpmate of the Lord in man's redemption and justification,[96] she was not only wiser than all other women, but more so than all other creatures.[97] Mary's perfection could undoubtedly reflect badly on mortal women, but, as Marina Warner remarks, "[any] goddess is better than no goddess at all."[98]

The preachers vividly depicted Mary's grief over Christ's suffering and death on the cross. Pepin describes the scene between mother and son: "Turning to her female companions who were crying, and also to John and Magdalene, she said: 'O, O, help me, for I see my son will die in this way, nor will it do any good for me to touch him. . . .' Then turning to her son, she said to him, 'O, my sweet son, how will I survive?'"[99] Her suffering was multiplied when the disciples refused to believe in Christ's resurrection.[100]

Mary held a particularly important role as an intermediary between God and man and a refuge for sinners.[101] "First, acting as our advocate, she wisely starts to make our case to Christ. She plays on his benevolence. . . . Next, she makes known to him our misery. Finally, she asks for his pity."[102] She was the medium through whom human beings could be reunited with God through love, the intercessor for man's justification and reconciliation, and the means through which men and women communicated with God.[103] To obtain grace through the Holy Spirit, the preachers suggested that their listeners approach Mary first, saying, "Hail, Mary," for prayer was the best way to gain her goodwill: "Christians, I know very well, and it is the truth, that the Virgin Mary can and does do miracles . . . for God has given her the power to do things that he himself has done. . . . It is therefore a very good thing to get on one's knees before an image of the glorious Virgin . . . and to pray for her child."[104] To those who challenged this reverence for the Virgin, LePicart remarks that even Mohammed bore witness to Mary's sanctity—how then could good Christians do less?[105]

Not everyone took the cult of the Virgin quite so far. Quoting Duns Scotus, Tisserand says that however glorious Mary was, if she had died before her Son, she would not have gone to heaven immediately.[106]

Although medieval belief in a soteriological role for the Virgin Mary had no scriptural foundation, her growing popularity testified to the need for a truly human figure in the divine brotherhood who could act as a mother to all men and women. Nurturing images of Christ as mother were plentiful in the Middle Ages,[107] but theologians and laymen alike seem to have felt a real need for a female mother with whom they could positively identify. The growing devotion to the Holy Family likewise attests to the needs of people to understand their God in human terms, a need that many of the reformers failed to recognize.

The Saints

Then the Lamb appeared in my vision. He was standing on Mount Zion, and with him were the hundred and forty-four thousand who had his name and the name of his Father written on their foreheads.

Revelation 14:1

Saint's day sermons deal with the actual or legendary histories of individuals and groups of saints, and typically provide less information than other sermons about contemporary life. Discussion of the saints follows the standard hagiographic format of *imitanda* and *admiranda* found in books of saints' lives.[108] As Weinstein and Bell have pointed out, "the saint's life demonstrated the highly personal nature of piety and the demands made upon individual religious conscience, [but] the cult was a collective enterprise in which the community joined in supplication and celebration of a holy person who consented to share hard-won spiritual graces with ordinary sinners."[109]

For those who could not read, visual aids and oral transmission were the main sources for knowledge of the saints, although this knowledge did not always come from sermons. Local tradition often supplemented the recognized saints with popular local choices. One example of popular devotion was the cult of Saint Guinefort, the dog martyr who saved his master's baby from a snake and then was mistakenly killed by his master.[110] In his important study of ecclesiastical control over sainthood, André Vauchez argues that in the later Middle Ages there were competing notions of what constituted saintliness,[111] and from the fourteenth century on, the church increasingly began to stress that "official sainthood" was the only acceptable outlet for popular devotion.[112] To some degree, the selection of "established" saints as

Table 6-1. Guillaume Pepin, *Conciones de sanctis sive de imitatione sanctorum.*

Andrew	Mary Magdalene
Barbara	James
Nicolas	Christopher
Conception of the Blessed Virgin	Anne (2)
Thomas	Peter in Chains
Nativity of the Lord	Feast of the Lord [Transfiguration]
Stephen	Lawrence
John (2)	Assumption of the Virgin (3)
Holy Innocents	Bartholomew
Circumcision of the Lord	Saint Louis (2)
Day of the Kings [Epiphany] (2)	Augustine
Sebastian	Decollation of John the Baptist
Vincent Martyr	Nativity of the Virgin
Paul	Feast of the Exaltation of the Cross (2)
Purification of the Virgin	Matthew
Blaise	Michael
Peter	Jerome
Matthew (2)	Francis of Assisi
Thomas Aquinas	Saint Denis
Gregory	Luke
Barbara	Simon and Judas
Annunciation Sunday	All Saints (2)
Ambrose	Feast of the Dead [All Souls]
Vincent the Confessor	Martin
George the Martyr	Clement
Mark	Catherine the Martyr
Peter Martyr	First Sunday of Advent
Catharine of Siena	First Sunday of Septuagesima
Philip and James	Easter
The True Cross	Ascension of the Lord
The Lord's Crown	Pentecost (2)
Barnabas	Holy Trinity
Anthony of Padua	Corpus Christi (2)
John the Baptist	Dedication of a Church (2)
Peter	Common Sermon for Martyrs (2)
Paul	Common Sermon for Bishop Confessors
Visitation of the Virgin	Common Sermon for Nonbishop Confessors
	Common Sermon for Virgins

subjects for sermons was an effort by the preachers to control popular piety and to channel the people's devotion in ways acceptable to the church hierarchy. But a more important consideration was the church calendar, which often dictated a preacher's subject matter. A preacher who chose to discuss a subject not found in his sermon book could adapt the basic form, changing the specifics by referring to the *Legenda aurea* or other hagiographical materials.

Sermons were not always devoted to individual saints. Events in the life of Christ and the Virgin or groups of saints, such as the Holy Innocents, were regular subjects. Tables 6-1 and 6-2 list the subjects in two saints' day collections. Of Pepin's eighty-eight saints' sermons, only fifty-five were devoted

Table 6-2. Olivier Maillard, *Sermones de sanctis*.

Andrew	Mark and Other Post-Easter Saints
Nicolas	Saint Mark's Processional [Major Rogation]
Conception of the Virgin	Philip and James
Thomas	The True Cross
Nativity of the Lord	Ascension of the Lord
Stephen the Martyr	Sunday within the Octave of Ascension
John	Pentecost (2)
Circumcision of the Lord	Holy Trinity
Epiphany	John the Baptist (2)
Conversion of Paul	Peter and Paul
Purification of the Virgin	Assumption of the Virgin (2)
Peter	Nativity of the Virgin
Matthew	Sermon of the Angels
Annunciation of the Virgin	All Saints

to individual saints other than the Virgin Mary, while thirteen of Maillard's thirty-one saint's day sermons dealt with individuals. Saints closely involved with Christ were featured most prominently, especially the evangelists, the apostles, John the Baptist, and Stephen. The Church Fathers and the founders of the mendicant orders all had sermons dedicated to them. A glance at the contents of Maillard's *Sermones de sanctis* confirms that saints from the apostolic era appear more frequently than recently canonized men or women, although there is an occasional sermon devoted to someone such as Catherine of Siena. The preachers stressed that sanctity was available to women as well as men.[113] Most of the sermons for "ordinary saints" were for males, although when the sermons for Mary Magdalene, Barbara, Catherine, and Anne are added to those for the Virgin, the gap narrows considerably. Although Kieckhefer has found an increase in the canonization of lay men & women after the fourteenth century,[114] there is little evidence that this change affected preaching.

In many cases, the saint's day sermon was only a pretext for showing how contemporary men and women failed to live up to the standards of a particular saint. In a sermon for the feast of Saint Ambrose, Pepin exclaims: "There are very few Ambroses in the world today. For when one bishop dies, two, three, or even more men endeavor to take his place. . . . And we see few or no bishops in these times who do miracles either in their life or after their death."[115] The preachers hoped that the story of a saint's life would inspire reformation of life in their hearers.

With a concern seldom seen in discussions of the Virgin Mary, the preachers expressed fear that people might attach superstitious beliefs to either the image or the saint himself. Pepin differentiates between the proper and improper use of saints' images: "The faithful of Christ do not believe that divinity resides in these images as idolators do. The images are put in the church not to be adored, but to imprint the excellence and glory of the saints more effectively and simply on the minds of the faithful."[116] For the illiterate, statues and paintings were like picture books that told biblical and ecclesiastical stories. Maillard explains that images exist for three reasons: (1) to provide physical representations to help the simple folk believe; (2) to help people remember the image later and use it to assist them in their prayers and devotions; and (3) to help people remember the teachings of the church more easily.[117] But Menot warns his listeners not to worship pieces of stone.[118] Illyricus makes the dangers of idolatry abundantly clear:

> Many run about to different places to visit the relics of the saints and delight in hearing about their exploits. They poke around in the large buildings of the sanctuaries and kiss the locks and gold of the reliquaries that contain the bones of the saints. And yet when they are present at the altar of God, the saint of saints, the Creator of all things, the Lord over the angels, they show only a small amount of reverence. O how grievous! Look how many people there are wandering all over the place. In many locales where there are many relics of the saints, they hold processions in honor of them, carrying torches and candles. Yet for the honor of the most precious body of our Lord they scarcely carry one torch. . . . O, great is the insanity of men! With the relics we find much curiosity and secret innovations. But these people hardly ever improve their lives based on such an experience.[119]

Tisserand also develops this theme, arguing that it is fine to pray to the saints if one has mended one's ways, but not if one plans to persevere in sin.[120]

Proper reverence toward the saints involved the understanding that Jesus Christ was working in them.[121] LePicart explains, "it is through Jesus Christ alone that we are saved, but the good lady his mother, and all of the saints in heaven, make us participants in his work. In this way, they are our intercessors with God."[122] The saints were neither better nor more compassionate than God, but merely another channel through which a sinner could expiate his sins.[123] Maillard suggests that "the sinner should pray to the saints, if he does not dare go directly to God. It is appropriate to beg God's forgiveness through his friends."[124] Like Illyricus, LePicart chastises people who forget the true meaning of the saints and engage in purely external rites:

> If you make a pilgrimage in faith and devotion out of the love you have for God and his saints, for the grace and virtue God has given them and the suffering they have endured for him, and if you do all of this in good faith you will gain eternal life. But if you abuse God's grace you will anger rather than appease him, for many show irreverence on such pilgrimages. . . . "Let us take a day," you will say, "and go visit Saint Fiacre. It will be so pleasant in such good weather, and we can play in the fields."[125]

Angels were also sometimes the subject of sermons, as in Maillard's *Sermo de angelis,* but more commonly these ethereal beings were referred to in biblical context. Maillard describes an angel as an "incorporeal intellectual substance,"[126] a helper of God who fights the Devil for the souls of the penitent. Angels would have been most familiar to medieval listeners through their intervention in human affairs as messengers of God.

The preachers treated the Virgin Mary and the saints in much the same way, although the Virgin's status was naturally higher than that of the saints.

The preachers' universe, like that of their listeners, was peopled with individuals who had a special relationship with God. But the preachers showed great concern that people understand the proper role of the saints and not make them excuses for their own misbehavior or irreverence. In their sharp criticism of abuses connected with veneration of the saints and pilgrimages, late medieval preachers agreed with the criticisms of Erasmus and some of the early reformers. But unlike the latter, they believed that statues, paintings, and reliquaries served to educate the illiterate.

The Devil and His Minions

The huge dragon, the ancient serpent known as the devil or Satan, the seducer of the whole world, was driven out; he was hurled down to earth and his minions with him.   Revelation 12:9

Jeffrey Burton Russell contends that at the end of the Middle Ages, "none of the main intellectual currents of the period was conducive to diabology."[127] Scholasticism, nominalism, mysticism, and humanism all downplayed the Devil, but according to Russell, belief in the Devil was kept alive by the popular theology of sermons and mystery plays, in which he was portrayed either as a terrifying figure or a laughingstock.[128]

The Devil does not figure prominently in the sermons of most of the preachers. But there was a consciousness of Satan as a specific being, the personification of evil and rebellion against God, which can be seen in this poem by Maillard:

Cursed Satan, inventor of war.
leader of a damned sect,
took to the field of battle as a warrior,
instigator of a deadly plot,
who has by his diabolical arts drawn
all his old soldiers from the Plutonic abyss
whom he judged to be bold, powerful and strong.
And to manifest his terrible plans,
to gain victory
he believed that by arms or sorcery
he would take the spoils for himself and his confederates:
the Lily ever growing in triumph and victory.[129]

More commonly, however, the Devil and demons were metaphors for evil.[130] The Devil posited by the preachers was not a Manichaean embodiment of evil that ruled the universe along with the good, but rather God's own creation, expelled from heaven for his arrogance and presumption.[131] After the expulsion, God decided to use the Devil as an instrument to tempt man and to make him aware of his need for divine assistance.[132]

In imagery the Devil took many forms. He was variously described as a murderer, a thief, or a dragon.[133] "Daily we see the dragon appearing before us, with his mouth open ready to devour us. Yet we sleep, and we play, and feel so secure in our laziness before he who desires nothing but our damnation."[134] He was a snake who changed colors in order to deceive,[135] ready to entrap man by mixing honey with poison.[136] At other times he was synonymous with the obstinate sinner.[137] According to Denisse, "the Devil shows himself here now, then there; now a lamb, then a wolf; now light, then darkness. He is there at all times and places in various forms to offer temptations to man."[138]

Adam was the first to respond to the temptations of Satan, but all men and women are subject to his blandishments.[139] The very good were the Devil's favorite targets.[140] Menot admits that there are many who do not succumb to Satan's charms, although he claims few of them could be found in Tours.[141] The Devil and his minions were particularly active at the hour of death. "When a man is on his deathbed, the Devil calls his soldiers together, not allowing the poor soul to go to heaven, but snatching it away by his army of demons."[142] If one demon did not suffice to capture a soul, then Lucifer would send more, sometimes a whole host of them.[143] The air was full of hundreds of thousands of demons.[144]

The preachers considered men and women in their day so hardened to sin that they were often unaware of the Devil's machinations.[145] Once the Devil took over, not all the power of the saints and the Virgin Mary could prevent him from capturing a man's soul.[146] The miseries of the present life led some to give themselves over to the Devil, thinking that once they were dead they would suffer no more.[147] The only way to avoid him was "to arm oneself with virtues, grace, merits, and holy works."[148] But although the Devil actively tried to win souls from God, one should not blame him for human weakness: "At this response, the Devil will give him a box on the ear, saying: 'You lie, saying the Devil made you do it! I am the Devil, who appeared to you in a certain place, with whom you chose to walk, and I prevailed upon you. You did not want to change, even when the dangers were preached to you.'"[149]

Although two Dominicans first published the bible of witch-hunting, *Malleus Maleficarum,* which set forth the accepted doctrine of witchcraft, in the 1480s, incidents of witch persecutions were rare in the fifteenth and early sixteenth centuries, and the concept of the diabolic pact lay in the future. A famous witchcraft case of 1460–1461 in Arras illustrates some credulity on the part of the leaders of society, especially the Dominican Jacques du Boys, who began the proceedings. But in the same year in which several people were condemned as witches, a trial began in the Parlement of Paris that was to last for the next thirty years. At its end, the inquisitor's actions were condemned and his aides, as well as the duke of Burgundy, were ordered to make restitution for their wrongful activities. A two-and-one-half hour sermon condemning the procedures and rehabilitating its victims was delivered to some eight thousand people. The contemporary chronicler Jacques du Clercq recounts that not one person in a thousand had believed in the truth of the witchcraft charges.[150]

Sorcery was widely condemned by preachers, but largely because its practitioners bypassed the rites of the church and promoted alternative beliefs. Raulin explains the rationale for the church's injunctions against sorcery: "The magical arts are prohibited under pain of death, not only because in them demons are worshiped, but also because these arts impugn the value of true faith, by their apparent truths."[151] Cleree contends that many in France practice the diabolic arts.[152] Sometimes this was no more serious than an effort to find a lost object, but the preachers were concerned that this encouraged superstition and even heresy.[153] The preachers considered sorcerers and their clients an abomination to the true faith, but not, for the most part, witches.

A historian critical of the "materialism" of religion in the late Middle Ages comments that "late medieval religion sought to grasp the transcendent by making it immanent: It was a religion that sought to embody itself in images, reduce the infinite to the finite, blend the holy and the profane."[154] The truth of this assertion cannot be denied, but the implicit assumption that there was something terribly wrong with such a religion can be challenged. As Augustine had realized many centuries before, the city of God was very different from the city of the world. Christian theology, both Catholic and Protestant, recognized man's fallen nature, and neither ascribed to humans the ability to achieve perfection in the world. The humanization of the divine permitted preachers to impart an understanding of God, Christ, the Virgin, the saints, and the Devil, that made religion come to life in a way that discussions of theological concepts could not.

The social milieu of the heavens mirrored the ideal of community on earth. As Weinstein and Bell remark, "the community joined in supplication and celebration of a holy person who consented to share hard-won spiritual graces with ordinary sinners. They were fathomable whereas God was not."[155] The preachers' purpose was to impress their listeners with the events, historic and divine, that made up the Bible and to set these as models for human behavior. Their interpretation of scripture was more than a mere commentary—it was often a dramatization that brought to life the characters of the Bible. At the center of the great drama was Jesus Christ, man and God, whose life on earth was a model for every Christian. Mary's special role in the religious universe reflected the interplay between high and low culture, for while theologians might debate such problems as her Immaculate Conception, ordinary people could think of her as a motherly figure, someone who could successfully gain favors from God for those who honored her. By portraying God, Christ, the Virgin, and the saints as real and knowable characters, the preachers were able to draw moral lessons for men and women in much the same way as Jesus had done by teaching in parables.

7

Practical Theology:
The Life of the Christian Believer

Now forgive my sin, and return with me, that I may worship the LORD.
1 Samuel 15:25

The presentation of theology to ordinary people was intended to foster not only belief, but practice as well. The structure of the church, its hierarchy, and the sacraments all provided a formal framework for worship in which people acted upon their understanding of the religious cosmos. In discussing the sacraments, the preachers described ideal conditions, and then commented on how ordinary Christians performed their religious duties. At the same time, they did their best to refute another aspect of "religious" practice—magic and folk beliefs.

Ecclesiology

I for my part declare to you, you are "Rock," and on this rock I will build my church, and the jaws of death shall not prevail against it. I will entrust to you the keys of the kingdom of heaven. Whatever you declare bound on earth shall be bound in heaven; whatever you declare loosed on earth shall be loosed in heaven.   Matthew 16:18–19

It is in the areas of ecclesiology and sacramental theology that we might expect to find the greatest differences between pre- and post-Reformation Catholic preachers, but surprisingly only questions of emphasis separate them. Before the Reformation, ecclesiology was not a major issue. Struggles for hegemony between conciliarists and ultramontanes and the question of Gallican liberties had been and continued to be important issues for clerics and theologians, but they found little place in the popular theology of sermons. For the most part, Gallicanism appeared in popular sermons only at times of heightened interest—with the promulgation of the Pragmatic Sanction of Bourges (1438) and, in this period, the Concordat of Bologna (1516). It was

also expressed in tempered antipapal statements. But the idea of a real challenge to a church structure that had grown up over 1500 years did not occur
to most preachers in France before 1518. Instead they focused on conditions
in the contemporary church and how it compared with the early Christian
church, a discussion that had been going on for at least two centuries among
"radicals" in the church and was to a great extent tied to antipapalism.[1]
Primitivism—the desire to return to some pristine apostolic model—was directly linked to concerns that pastoral duties were not being properly fulfilled
in the contemporary church. The preachers' critical comments and their attempts to reform their secular and regular confrères must therefore be understood within the context of their zeal to make the church conform to the early
apostolic ideal.

A standard lament was that the church had never been in a worse state.
"I say that never has the church descended so low as now; never were churchmen so irreverent as now; never were religious so imperfect as now. Things
were better even in the time of Saint Francis than now. . . . We are indeed a
long way from the primitive institution."[2] The opposition between the early
Christian era and the modern church was a constant refrain. "In the beginning
the church produced many true sons—martyrs and confessors. But all that
has ended now."[3] Pepin remarks that "seeing the state of the church today,
Christ weeps, [for] . . . the church militant has been deserted."[4]

Menot traces the problems of the church of his day to the Donation of
Constantine, which, authentic or not, introduced temporal concerns into the
church: "The temporal fruits were first given to the church by Constantine,
who transferred the imperium to the church. The popes who came after,
especially Sylvester, were quite content with this state of affairs. Just as the
soul cannot live without the body, neither can churchmen live without temporal goods. We read that after hearing that this donation was made, an angel
in the sky proclaimed: 'Today poison has infected the church.'"[5] The preachers unanimously voiced concern that the church had become alienated from
the ideals of the early Christians, with the desire for worldly goods and power
stronger than the desire to benefit one's fellow man.

Menot defines the church militant as the congregation of the faithful—
the bad as well as the good.[6] "[T]he church does not only exist for those who
are already Christians: on Good Friday the church prays for Christians, and
also for pagans, Jews, and all people, excepting only those who have been
excluded through excommunication."[7] If Jews or Moslems requested baptism,
then they too would become full members of the church.[8] Being a member
of the congregation of the faithful obligated one to support other members
who were simpler or who wavered in their faith:[9] "There are many simple
people whose faith is not whole, who do not know the articles of the faith,
and who vacillate about what is to be believed. They are nevertheless quite
willing to believe what is necessary. So, therefore, those who are infirm in
their faith must be supported by discreet confessors and instructed with all
kindness. They should not be reproached or frightened, as is the way with
so many modern confessors."[10] The mission of the church and its ministers,

even before the foundation of the Jesuit order, was to take the message to all ends of the earth, to India and to Africa.[11]

Even excommunicates were not necessarily excluded from fellowship in the church, if they had been unjustly censured. In this case, although they could not partake of the external ceremonies of the church, they remained "invisible" members.[12] Unjust excommunication was not a baseless worry, for according to several of our preachers, many people were wrongly excommunicated for temporal matters. "There are many canon lawyers and bishops who are quick to fulminate sentences and anathemas against members of their flocks, even for the slightest of reasons. Sentences of this kind ought to be condemned, just as the churchmen are ready to condemn others. Besides, these ecclesiastical lords show themselves very ready to absolve from excommunication those who have great power, for they fear them or hope to gain some temporal reward."[13] In addition to creating injustice, the misuse of excommunication and interdict undermined their ability to inspire dread in church members. But excommunication wisely used was a scalpel through which evil was excised from the church.[14] A man justly excommunicated suffered the worst of all penalties, for he was anathematized by Jesus Christ, separated from him through sin, and separated equally from the body of the faithful in the church militant, to whom he had been joined in Christian love.[15] Excommunication was a far more awesome weapon than any secular punishment, for it affected the welfare of the soul.[16]

The aspect of ecclesiology that most concerned Catholic churchmen and preachers after the Reformation was the function of the priesthood and the hierarchy. This issue had been hotly debated during the conciliar epoch because of the Western Schism, but had subsided somewhat after the rapprochement of 1417. After 1520, it was revived by Luther's arguments for the priesthood of all believers. In the sermons of LePicart, in particular, we find a growing discussion of the role of the priesthood. There is, however, very little change in substance between pre- and post-Reformation Catholic preachers.

The priesthood was instituted by God to make an offering for the Passion and death of Christ.[17] As mediator between God and his people, the priest's role was to pacify God, to offer prayers that God's anger would not fall on his people, and to ask for the grace and compassion of Jesus Christ.[18] LePicart explains that "Our Lord took three of his disciples with him up the mountain in order to show that no one can come to God and the knowledge of his salvation unless he too climbs this mountain."[19] This implies not only that the believer must follow the path of Christ, but that certain men were called to lead.

In view of the great importance of the priesthood, it was important for the preachers to deal with the issue of the sinning priest. The fundamental point was the priest's role as lieutenant, or channel, through which God's love was relayed to his people. "The priest remits sins as a minister, *tenant le lieu de Dieu,* standing in the place of God, through the power and authority he has received from God."[20] The man and his office were two distinct entities, and a priest should not be considered as a private person, but through the office he holds as God's representative.[21] LePicart tells his listeners that "even if I am a bad priest and lead an evil life, I am still a priest, because my dignity and my authority come not from my goodness or charity, but from the Word of God."[22] A bad pope was still a pope, and a bad-living bishop was as much a bishop as the best in the world. A priest who administered the sacraments in a state of mortal sin, sinned each time and would be damned, but the recipient of the sacrament did not receive it any the less, for the sacerdotal authority was not based on the priest's merits or good life, but on Jesus Christ.[23] The preachers insisted that the laity respect and obey the sacerdotal office, even if the man filling it was a great sinner.[24]

The priest's fundamental role as intermediary did not exclude another, nonsacerdotal, ministry of all Christians. Pepin tells the faithful that they should "minister to each other according to the gifts given them by the Lord,"[25] a statement that LePicart qualifies: "It is true that we are all religious, and we are all held to keep the Christian religion and the commandments of God and our Holy Mother Church. But some are held to a more strict observance."[26]

The preachers relied heavily on church tradition, portraying the the hierarchy as successors to the apostles.[27] The argument of the sinning priest was now extended. While individuals were fallible, the church was not, as was shown through the long centuries of tradition. LePicart explains that "the church cannot make mistakes or do wrong, but I in my person can err."[28] He claims that "the church was before scripture. We must therefore believe in the tradition and interpretation of the church. The spirit is present in it."[29] The unity of the church since the time of the Apostles proved that it was the one true church. "Why should we not believe the combined witness of prophets, evangelists, apostles, doctors of theology, and preachers of the truth?"[30] But the unity and infallibility of the church did not preclude criticism—the lack of devotion in the contemporary church was a sign to Raulin that the church had in a sense grown old, "for now it seems almost decrepit, and tends toward corruption."[31]

The papacy was, in the opinion of many, all too fallible, at least in its individual representatives. The preachers accepted that Jesus' statement to Peter was intended to convey the supreme apostolic dignity to his successors in Rome,[32] but emphasized the failings of individual popes and the corruption of the Roman curia.[33] Illyricus admits that the pope has a plenitude of power in this world, but denies that this carries over to the next,[34] a clear reference to the sale of indulgences. Popes too often exceeded their power:

> This is shown by the example of the son of the king of Aragon, who had entered a religious order. When his father died and he was recognized as successor, the pope dispensed him from his vows, and he married for the sake of the realm. When he had begotten a son, he reentered the cloister, leaving the kingdom to his son. He had had continuous scruples about

violating his vows of chastity. The pope had dispensed him, but in this case
the pope had exceeded his power. It is not improper to say that the pope
can err.[35]

Papal misuse of power was even a subject for mockery: "O, brother, don't
you know the magic word? The lord pope has dispensed us."[36]

Because the structure of the church was essentially unchallenged before
the Reformation, the preachers felt free to attack both specific and general
abuses committed by the church's servants. Their primary concern was to
reform a church that had lost sight of its original mission. But they never
suggested that there was an intrinsic defect in the church itself, unless it was
the church's pretensions in temporal matters and acquisition of worldly goods,
a problem that was ultimately correctable. Rather it was the all-too-human
people who led the church who were in need of reform. After the Reformation, those areas that Luther had attacked, including the mediatory role
of the clergy and the papacy as successor to Saint Peter, were treated more
carefully, although Catholic preachers continued to criticize those who abused
their authority. Ignoring the deficiences of the church would only add fuel to
the fire.

The Sacraments

> He for his part confirmed the message with his grace and caused signs
> and wonders to be done at their hands.   Acts 14:3

In the Catholic church, religious life centers on the sacraments. Through the
significant life stages marked by the sacraments, the Christian believer becomes a participant not only in his religion, but also in his salvation. The
sacraments were the means of rebirth,[37] instruments God used to humble,
teach, and excite men.[38] They were visible signs, akin to the miracles Christ
had performed, given as representations of the higher gifts that await men
and women in the future.[39] Bossy argues persuasively that the infrequency of
the sacraments in the medieval church served an important social function
by intensifying communal sharing and commensality at the times when the
eucharist was celebrated.[40]

Participation in the sacraments was essential, not simply to receive the
benefits they conferred but also because good Christians had to believe inwardly and testify outwardly through participation in church rituals. The
preachers stressed the strong reciprocal interdependence between outward
expressions of sacramental piety and their internalization, warning against
purely mechanical piety. Referring to the Pharisees' preoccupation with outward observance (Luke 18:11–14; Matthew 23:1–39), Menot warns his audience that this is not the road to salvation.[41] Raulin explains the correct
balance between inward and outward devotion:

> Inner devotion pleases God much more than outward, for God is spirit. It is necessary to adore him in spirit and truth. The external ritual is as much a sign as the internal. The gestures and sacrifices are symbols of internal devotion. But it is a false sign to stand on outward ceremonies, without feeling true devotion.... God hates this false sign, but the Devil loves it, so he approaches the house empty of love, with its ornate ceremonies, as we find in so many religions. But nevertheless, ceremonies should not be eliminated, because from them people learn devotion.[42]

The sacraments were rarely mentioned all together at the same time. When they were, the context was more general than when they were discussed individually. For example, Pepin asks, "Why does the Lord get so angry at men and women singing and dancing? It is because they sin against the seven sacraments of the church."[43] Occasionally, a preacher would group several of the sacraments together to show how each individually responded to a specific theological virtue: "This is the order of their effects. Baptism is the sacrament of faith; confirmation of hope; and the eucharist of love. This is because baptism enlightens, confirmation fortifies, and the eucharist arouses our passion."[44] Confirmation and extreme unction receive considerably less attention than the other sacraments, although Clichtove devotes sermons to each in a series of sermons on all the sacraments. When discussing extreme unction, the preachers continually urged their listeners not to wait until the last minute to reconcile themselves with God:

> When your husband is ill, do you send for a priest to confess him? No, because we fear the priest will upset him or make him sad, so we send for a doctor instead and give him medicine to make him feel better. But when he is no longer able to talk, we send for the priest and have him administer extreme unction, holding the cross before him and sprinkling him with holy water. And we all shout loudly, 'Jesus!' But when Christ is present with his mother and all the angels, this is not the time to be penitent and to convert to God. For earlier you had a chance to do so voluntarily, but now it is involuntary.[45]

The most detailed treatments were reserved for discussions of baptism, penance, and the eucharist, and were often tied to particular liturgical occasions, such as the feast of Corpus Christi.

Baptism

> They asked Peter and the other apostles, "What are we to do, brothers?" Peter answered: "You must reform and be baptized, each one of you, in the name of Jesus Christ, that your sins may be forgiven; then you will receive the gift of the Holy Spirit."   Acts 2:37–38

Infant baptism, as a symbol of the new covenant, was a doctrine accepted by all but the most extreme sectarians during the pre-Reformation period. Christ had had himself baptized not because he was in need of purification, but to indicate that all men and women, no matter how saintly, had to be reborn in the same manner,[46] "for we are all born in original sin, which is removed through baptism as a symbol of the reception of Jesus Christ."[47] A person who had not been baptized retained more of the tinder of sin,[48] but once baptized, men and women became sons and daughters of God and "lived in his house."[49] Maillard explains that "it was not enough for Christ to redeem us. He wanted to open his heart. And from it flowed blood and water miraculously in signification of the two sacraments of baptism and the eucharist."[50] Aside from its soteriological value, baptism had great social significance in making the individual part of the community of believers.

The preachers also dealt with practical situations, such as the acceptability of lay baptism in cases of dire necessity.[51] After the Reformation, the sacrament of baptism became the focus of special attention. LePicart, aware of the sectarian doctrine of adult baptism, charges that "when a man dies once through baptism, if he is rebaptized, that says that Jesus Christ has died more than once. It is the Anabaptists who hold this, and they are in error."[52]

Confession

> Then I acknowledged my sin to you,
>   my guilt I covered not.
> I said, "I confess my faults to the Lord,"
> and you took away the guilt of my sin.
>   Psalm 32:5

More than any other sacrament, penance played a continuing role in the life of the believer. Few aspects of late medieval religion have generated so much interest in recent years as the social history of the sacrament of penance and the practical business of confession. In his study of the appeal of early Protestantism in Germany and Switzerland, Ozment argues forcefully that confession "could be a very tough inquisitorial process," for "the confessor was manifestly not the penitent's friend but his judge and jury."[53] In his opinion, the system made late medieval religion both "psychologically and socially burdensome."[54] Thomas Tentler describes penance as a system of social control, based on sacerdotal dominance, obedience not only to men but to morality and law, and the conscientious fulfillment of Christian duties. Although founded on personal guilt, it provided the penitent with real consolation.[55] But Lawrence Duggan challenges the view that the late medieval confessional system was repressive, concluding that "just as in modern Catholicism, people knew who the 'tough' priests were and could avoid them in favor of more lenient ones, so too could men and women in the late Middle Ages."[56] He concludes that even "if severity had been the aim of the late medieval penitential system, it did not work that way."[57] Bossy argues for the socially beneficial elements of a system that "expressed the positive conviction that sin was a state of offence inhering in communities rather than in individuals."[58]

The sacrament of penance reconciled the sinner to God, and to the church of which he was a member, helping to minimize social hostility within the community at large.[59] This beneficial aspect of confession was lost to Catholicism by the Council of Trent's new emphasis on the personal nature of atonement.[60]

The preachers discussed confession at some length, not only in their roles as preachers, but also in their capacities as sometime confessors and authors of manuals. They offered both theoretical formulations and practical observations. The preachers continued to invoke the imagery of water and cleansing. Just as baptism washed away the stain of original sin at birth, the sacrament of penance purified adults whose lives of sin had caused them to lose the effects of baptism. "A man confessing his sin is washed inwardly in his conscience, and is made new in the sight of God."[61]

There were three components to the sacrament of penance—contrition, confession, and satisfaction—that exemplified the collective and individual values of the sacrament.[62] In response to these three actions on the part of the sinner, God remits his sins, gives him grace, and promises future glory.[63] A good confession offered solace and comfort to the penitent. "Neither the greatness nor the magnitude of one's sins, nor the multitude of turpitude and vice, nor the lateness of penitence, even including perseverance in sin, can keep one from the possibility of remission, pardon, and divine compassion if the sinner repents of his sins and corrects them according to the will of God."[64]

Contrition was the sine qua non of penance. The penitent must believe in his mind what he says with his mouth.[65] "Be truly contrite, repent, and make your confession to a priest, lieutenant and vicar of God."[66] In the absence of true repentance, confession served no purpose: "Why confess if I am not able to abstain from such and such a sin? By so doing, I increase God's wrath rather than earning his clemency and compassion. That does an injury to the sacrament, for no one ought to go to confession unless he proposes to mend his ways."[67] In his typically down-to-earth manner, Messier compares penitence to the motion of the sea, adding that "the movement of penitence provokes vomiting in confession."[68] Using a similar analogy, Menot complains of those who get down on their knees and confess only to return to their vomit.[69] In a curious adage, Maillard explains that "confession washes with tears. True contrition dries them with a linen cloth and puts a hood on the head [*luy met ung beguyn sur la teste*]."[70]

Contrition was incomplete without confession and satisfaction.[71] The preachers presented confession as an absolute necessity, although they were aware of the dangers of the too-scrupulous conscience. Maillard explains that "whatever serious sins you commit, if you confess them completely and under appropriate conditions, you will not be damned. But if you commit even one mortal sin, and do as much good as is possible, you will be damned if you do not confess."[72] No criminal act was so heinous that it could not be forgiven through proper confession.[73]

The preachers devoted considerable space to advising men and women on the practical aspects of confession. The first requirement was that confession should be made to a properly constituted authority—the parish priest, bishop, bishop's vicar, or friar. Under certain conditions, when no suitable confessor could be found and the sinner was in danger of imminent death or severely troubled in his conscience, it was acceptable to confess to a lay person.[74] While this was useful and comforting, the layman could not give absolution, and such a confession did not confer the automatic benefits of the sacrament of penance.

The sinner must speak clearly and plainly, avoiding long disgressions that served no other purpose than to hide sins, and to "break the priest's head."[75] He must search his conscience with diligence and honesty:[76] "For confession is nothing other than when the sinner humbly and sincerely recognizes that he has offended God and from that moment on seeks his indulgence, with the intention of reforming, and with the willingness to do whatever is required of him."[77] The sinner should not leave it up to the confessor to ask all the questions, in the hope that he can avoid uncomfortable subjects.[78] Nor should he confess minor sins, but hide major ones.[79] Specifically, he should mention anger, vindictiveness, lust for his neighbor's wife, or other adulterous relationships, in thought as well as deed.[80] It was not enough to confess in general what would be a greater sin if confessed specifically. "A woman who has committed incest with her brother should not simply confess that she slept with a man. She must say, 'I slept with my brother,' even though such a statement implicates someone else."[81] All the circumstances of the sin had to be detailed as to person, place, time, manner, and number.

The purpose of going to confession was to accuse oneself, not to tell the confessor how righteous one was.[82] Pepin lists some of the defenses used by ordinary people: "One will blame someone else, or say, I did not do it. Others say they did it and did it well. Or if it was bad, it was not very bad. Or if it was very bad, it was not done with evil intent."[83] Rationalizing one's actions, or blaming others, only angered God: "So today there are many Ninivites, that is, sinners, who do not confess their own sins, but accuse their neighbors, and others. For example, some say they have the worst sort of neighbors, with whom it is impossible to live in peace. The same is true of women who complain incessantly about their hard-hearted husbands. And also women who after committing adultery say that they were seduced against their will."[84] One should not say, "I was angry and beat up my neighbor," then add, "but he started it."[85]

The sinner must not confess the same thing over and over again.[86] Following Gerson, LePicart warns that such repetition only leads to further anguish:

> It is a dangerous thing to repeat your sins frequently at confession, which sometimes happens when your soul is disturbed. . . . If you confess one thing two or three times, this only leads to greater trepidation. You repeat them in order to achieve some peace of mind, but instead you become more upset. So don't do this, but rather confide in Jesus Christ, who is your support, and believe the good advice that is given to you. Believe that God is good. Do you think he wants to damn you when you have done your

duties as well as you can? Do you think the justice of God is more cruel than that of men?[87]

This is one of many examples that demonstrates the preachers' great concern for the consolatory and reconciliatory aspects of confession.

Works of compassion and piety inevitably followed a good confession,[88] and gave a sense of consolation and hope in times of tribulation.[89] LePicart asks his listeners, "Do you not feel consolation, repose, and spiritual joy in your heart after having discharged your conscience?"[90] At this point, the devout Catholic should beg God to preserve him from future evildoing by saying a prayer: "O, Lord God, I thank you, for although I am worthy of eternal punishment, you have through your goodness and compassion re-mitted my sins. Since I am not able to stop myself from sinning without your help, I pray to you to give me this aid."[91]

Despite these elaborate instructions, the preachers believed that most men or women did not make good or even adequate confessions.[92] Cleree tries to specify the number of these people, suggesting that in Paris there were at least ten thousand people who had never made a good confession.[93] The sure sign of a bad confession was unwillingness to do good afterwards.[94]

Church law required penitents to confess at least once a year, in prepa-ration for receiving the host at Easter.[95] Although many recent studies suggest that infrequent confession was the norm at the end of the Middle Ages,[96] the sermons indicate a dichotomy between those who confessed as infrequently as possible and those who confessed so frequently that they exasperated their confessors.[97] Most late medieval theologians, including Gerson, advocated more frequent confession.[98] The preachers agreed.[99] Many expressed doubts that people would ever go to confession if Easter did not come, while others complained that people only confessed at Easter and on their deathbeds, when they had no choice.[100] Procrastination was the main problem: "One person will say, 'Shouldn't we go to confession?' But the other will respond, 'O, there's plenty of time.'"[101]

One of the most serious problems with infrequent confession was that it made remembering all of one's sins difficult. In this situation, the sinner must diligently search his memory for all of the sins he has committed since his last confession.[102] Menot dramatizes the situation in a dialogue between pen-itent and confessor: "'Father, I have confessed all of my sins except for those I have forgotten.'—'Why have you forgotten them?' 'Father, I confessed last year, but now I am not able to remember half of my sins.'—O, what a great abuse! The Lord gives you a full year to take care of your obligations and remember what you have done!"[103] He also recounts the case of a man who had waited a year to confess, and then during four hours with his confessor, was not able to remember all he had done, and so could not be effectively purged of his sins.[104] Fillon warns that "if you wait too long, you will have doubts, even if the priest absolves you."[105] But if the penitent has done everything in his power to remember and still comes up with a blank, then a general confession will suffice,[106] although he will have to pay a penalty in purgatory. This was a practical solution, based on expediency and the inference that the sinner had not committed the sin again. Maillard shows that the clergy was not trying to make this task impossible by explaining that God only asked the sinner to do his best: "But you say, 'Father, I do not remember one of my sins.' Or, 'I am not exactly sure whether this is a sin, but in a sermon I heard a preacher say so. Should I go back to the same confessor and tell him this? Or should I repeat all of my sins?'—'No! Not if you have done everything in your power.'"[107]

Nevertheless, there were some, especially devout women, who went to confession too often. Maillard mentions some women who came to him. One says, "'Father, I confess regularly. But I do not fully understand mortal sins.' Another woman will say, 'Father, I confessed to a learned doctor. But my soul is still not at peace.'"[108] He tells her that if she has a good confessor and she is sincere, then she should believe him and rest easy in her conscience.

At first glance, the sermons seem to support the view that infrequent confession had its roots in unwillingness on the part of the penitent. It is possible that fear or shame lay behind this reluctance. Some might worry that what was told to the priest or friar under the "seal of the confessional" would become public knowledge and lead to disgrace,[109] a not unreasonable concern since truly private confession was not yet universally practiced.[110] Other sins, such as sodomy and bestiality, were so shocking that people were ashamed to confess them to a priest: "Desperation is caused by a sense of horror and abomination that accompanies the crime. . . . There are several sins [of a sexual nature] that are so horrible that poor sinners do not dare to confess them, nor do they believe that God can possibly forgive them. These include sins against nature like those committed with beasts, etc."[111] But Pepin goes on to say that such thinking is a trick of the Devil, designed to make sinners believe that their sins are unforgivable. The sinner must recognize the deception and trust that God is capable of forgiving all manner of sins, for it is very foolish to forego a doctor out of disgust at one's wounds.[112] Others worried about the financial aspects—confessors expected a "donation," but LePicart tells his listeners that lack of means should not deter anyone from going to confession.[113] Many avoided confession because they worried about restitution: "A great usurer does not want to go to a sermon or hear the truth, for he fears to be ensnared by the preacher. Others do not want to confess to a learned doctor, nor show themselves to be great sinners."[114]

Despite the preachers' frequent admonitions, some people displayed devil-may-care attitudes. Menot mentions a soldier who, confronted by the comment, "'You are not fasting! You ought to confess!' responds, 'Oh? And what do I have to confess? What have I done?' Such is his incredulity. There is no fear of God before his eyes."[115] Some sinners claimed that there was little harm in sin, for they did not feel evil![116] Others voiced similar feelings, laying this partially at the doorstep of unfit priests, commenting, "Why should I give my money to a priest? By God, I would much rather take it to a tavern or spend it on a pretty girl than give it to such a priest."[117]

Confessors were regular targets of advice from the preachers. Carrying out confessional duties well was extremely important, for many laymen found it difficult to make a good confession and receive absolution without the guidance of a good confessor.[118] Gerson, the author of numerous confessional manuals, warned his colleagues of the need for empathy and sensitivity in hearing confessions.[119] The preachers required a confessor to be discreet and knowledgeable, authoritative, and holy.[120] Illiterate confessors were likely to absolve all indifferently, without any attention to the gravity of the sin.[121] A good confessor was like a doctor: "When you are sick and the doctor comes to visit you, you only tell him what is wrong with you. . . . You do not tell him what medicine to prescribe for you, but leave it to his goodwill and discretion, and you take what he prescribes for you. The doctor of your soul is our Lord Jesus Christ. Tell him your malady, your sins, by saying them aloud to the priest, who is his lieutenant."[122] The priest must be ready at all times to listen to a contrite sinner and grant him absolution.[123] He must try to win over the penitent through love, making him believe in God's compassion.[124] He should not be hard and judgmental, nor offer a separate justice to rich men.[125] Nor should he absolve anyone whom he does not truly believe to have been forgiven by God. Too many confessors wanted to get things over with as quickly as possible, saying, "'I absolve you from all of your sins, for you have a contrite heart and you have confessed.' By so doing they act wrongly."[126] This attitude was frequently shared by penitents: "The priest is negligent and only asks that you hurry along. You ask nothing but to speed things up and say, 'O, I have found a master priest. If I told him everything, we wouldn't get it over with so quickly.'"[127] Another person says, "I have my Monsieur Jean, to whom I say: 'I will give you a good *teston* if you will grant me absolution.'"[128]

The preachers offered special advice for confessors and women: "Young women in particular ought to fix their eyes on the ground. That way their confessors can hear them and vice versa, but they cannot see each other. This is to avoid the temptations of the flesh. Woman and confessor, both of you should avert your eyes. Many discreet confessors regularly put a sheet between themselves and female penitents."[129]

The confessor had to weigh all factors when imposing satisfaction—place, time, perseverance in sin, who was involved, and how it was done.[130] The idea of satisfaction was to restore a previously existing condition, whether by giving alms to the poor[131] or paying back the ill-gotten gains of usury. Maillard explains the operation of restitution in detail:

> We must make restitution because justice wishes it, charity demands it, and God commands it. Justice desires it for . . . the commandments of justice are to live honestly, harm no one, and give each his due. Charity requires . . . it because you must not do unto others what you would not want done to yourself. The divine law commands it . . . for if you want to make your offering to God, first make peace with your brother. Otherwise your offering will not please God.[132]

Pepin warns his congregation that they must not go to confession if they are not prepared to make satisfaction, for if they have been guilty of theft, the confessor will impose restitution.[133] Satisfaction was to be imposed according to the condition of the penitent and the nature of his sin. If the sinner was young and strong, fasting or a long pilgrimage would be appropriate; if he was rich, he should give alms.[134] Some restitution always had to be imposed, even though Jesus had pardoned the adulterous woman without ordering any satisfaction. That was a special case, not to be considered an example for confessors.[135]

The sale of indulgences to remit the *poena* imposed by priests was widespread in the later Middle Ages, and Luther was far from the first to complain about the proliferation and misuse of indulgences. In January, 1518, Guillaume Petit informed Francis I of "the great scandals and abuses of those preachers who are exacting money for a crusade, and who oppress the people much more with their demands than do those who collect Peter's pence or the *gabelle* [salt tax]."[136] He advised the Faculty of Theology to have bishops warn their flocks against "these false, ridiculous, scandalous, and dangerous preachers who extort from the poor." The preachers accused indulgence preachers of speaking in riddles in order to deceive.[137] Their complaints centered on the indulgence preachers themselves, the superstitious practices they encouraged, and the inefficacy of indulgences. Maillard, one of the most outspoken opponents of the practice, cites the medieval theologian, William Durand, to show that there is no mention of indulgences in the Bible, and charges that those who sell them are little more than thieves.[138] Messier believes that indulgence preachers make a mockery of religion, adulterating the Word of God and putting a price tag on the miracles of the saints.[139] Pepin describes them as "ruffians who go about on horseback carrying the relics of the saints, deceiving simple people with their many lies, and extorting money from the poor."[140] The popes and the church hierarchy were responsible for this state of affairs:

> I do not want to revoke the keys of the church, but I will say that when the pope and cardinals know that there is no necessity or just and reasonable cause, then they ought not to permit the sale of indulgences. The proceeds of indulgences are given to rich convents where there are fools and religious who already have too much gold and silver, a fact about which the pope does not appear to be sufficiently informed. Do you really believe that a great usurer, full of vices and having thousands of sins on his conscience, will gain remission by throwing six silver coins into a chest? Certainly this is hard for me to believe and even harder to preach.[141]

Pepin accuses church leaders who support these practices of innovation based on greed.[142] Similarly, Messier compares them to the Pharisees, because of their avarice and their emphasis on outward acts.[143]

Menot argues against the validity of indulgences, for the *quêteurs* go about telling the people that they are absolved from vows and pilgrimages that have been imposed by their confessors.[144] Besides, they were useless if unaccompanied by the proper feelings of contrition.[145] Cleree describes it metaphorically: "In a jubilee year sins are remitted for those who go on pilgrimage to Rome. Certainly if you want to walk the way of penitence during Lent you will do this. But he who does not go to Rome does not merit the indulgence. Therefore he who does not walk the way of penitence will not gain remission of his sins."[146] If you want to go to Rome and receive an indulgence, that is fine, says Maillard, but you must make restitution all the same.[147] Indulgences were therefore a waste of money.

While the reports of the preachers confirm a general reluctance among the population to avoid more than minimal confessional requirements, this is not to say that people felt an intolerable Angst about the status of their salvation. There is very little in the sermons to support the idea that a majority of people felt that, despite their best efforts, they could not do what God— and the Catholic church—required of them. Fear there may have been, but it was of a more mundane sort.

The Mass

> Thereupon Jesus said to them:
> "Let me solemnly assure you,
> if you do not eat the flesh of the Son of Man
> and drink his blood,
> you have no life in you.
> He who feeds on my flesh
> and drinks my blood
> has life eternal
> and I will raise him up on the last day.
> For my flesh is real food
> and my blood real drink.
> The man who feeds on my flesh
> and drinks my blood
> remains in me, and I in him."
>
> John 6:53–56

While the social history of confession has sparked the greatest interest among historians in recent years, it was the meaning of the mass that most excited contemporaries.[148] Even before the Reformation, whole collections of sermons were devoted to the eucharist, although they were printed with greater frequency after the Reformation. The preachers discussed the nature of Christ in the eucharist, who should and should not take communion, the spirit of reception, the results a true believer might expect, and the priest's role in the celebration. For Catholics, the sacrament had a particular value that set it above the other sacraments—when celebrated, it conferred benefits not only on the person receiving it, but also on all the faithful, whether living or dead.[149]

Age was an important consideration in reception of the eucharist. It was the firm belief of the Catholic church that a proper understanding of the mass was essential for its efficacy. Illyricus explains: "The eucharist must not be given to children below the age of discretion and devotion. For before a child receives holy communion, he should have fulfilled three conditions. He should be eleven or twelve years old. He should be able to recognize the differences between the sacrament and ordinary bread. Finally, he should show a spirit of devotion."[150] The recipient must be mature, faithful, well disposed of mind, properly prepared, and devout.[151] Lansperge advises his listeners that it is not necessary for them to *know* that they are worthy as long as they confide in God's grace, for no one could be completely sure of his status. Men and women should proceed to the altar with the knowledge that they have committed no illicit acts since confession and without thoughts of worldly matters.[152] The appropriate demeanor was important if the sacrament was to bring about spiritual regeneration in Christ. One should kneel, inclining the head reverently.[153] A man should not think about women or the things of this world, for this will alienate him from Christ.[154] Nor should he receive in a spirit of doubt or curiosity;[155] rather, he must believe wholly, with a spiritual understanding, adoring the host with sincerity and faith.[156] The recipient should reflect on the events of Holy Thursday: "As we read in Luke 22, Christ said to his disciples: 'I want to eat with you this Passover before I suffer.' And so he ate with them, which shows us that Christ does not want to send anyone away from his table. He wants all men to be saved."[157] Gaigny exclaims: "There is no sinner so miserable that he cannot have hope for the future through the regeneration he receives at Easter."[158] LePicart warns that sickness, plague, wars, sudden death, and other evils reign when little reverence is shown to the blessed sacrament.[159] The idea of *facere quod in se est* is implicit, for contrition and confession prepared the way for this ceremony. Frequent communion, like confession, was encouraged.[160]

On the other hand, there were certain factors or conditions that disqualified one from receiving communion or made its reception inappropriate. Those who rejected Jesus' ethical teachings in the Sermon on the Mount and hated their neighbors were unworthy,[161] as were women whose clothing and excessive ornamentation suggested wordly preoccupations.[162] So too were usurers, prostitutes and pimps, and men who engaged in tournaments or duels.[163] If such people took communion, they would put themselves in further danger of mortal sin, for "God does not love those who are unworthy and ungrateful to him."[164] An unworthy recipient risked everlasting death for himself, and negated the effects of the Crucifixion and Resurrection.[165]

> Note that the sacrament is effective for many, but not for all. This is seen in the case of the traitor Judas, who received the sacrament from Christ's hands. Peter and Judas ate of the same bread; but Peter did so for life, Judas for death. Against this, some would point out that Christ said, "All who drink of my blood will gain the kingdom of God." But that would be true if Judas had eaten spiritually.... But no, he ate sacramentally, not spiritually. If you want to receive the body of our Lord spiritually along with his disciples, then first cleanse and prepare yourself through confession.[166]

However, if the sinner was not ready for the mass, he must bear the full consequences, for this was one of his Christian duties.[167]

The role of the priest as God's lieutenant has already been discussed, but it was his power to consecrate the host and perform the sacrifice of the mass that set him apart from the laity as well as many regulars and nonordained clergymen. As we might expect, the preachers studied here, most of whom were regulars, constantly inveighed against a priesthood that did not measure up to this lofty task. But the mediatorial role itself ensured that the personal character and sinfulness of the priest did not damage the salvific effects of the eucharist. In some detail, Brulefer explains that "the mass does not simply depend on the personal merits of the priest making the offering, but also on Christ's sacrifice and the performance of the rite as well as the general merits of the church."[168] The automatic effects depended not on the priest as an individual, but on Christ's work, so that even a notorious sinner could celebrate the mass with a salutary result for the recipient. However, because of his state of sin, the bad priest *added* nothing to the mass, so that it was better to take communion from a good priest than a bad one.[169]

As the initiate who understood better than the layman God's purpose, the priest was to stand between Christ and the sinner in order to effect a reconciliation.[170] Cleree urges the priest holding the precious body and blood of Christ in his hands to elevate his mind because of the great responsibility he bears.[171] The priest must explain that the celebration of the eucharist is an offering to God for his own sins and for those of the people in his care, in memory of the sacrifice made on the cross.[172] It was not a repetition, but rather a continuation of that sacrifice made once and for all.[173]

Attacks on transubstantiation predated the Reformation by hundreds of years. Despite its doctrinal formalization at the Fourth Lateran Council in 1215, a long line of heretics had questioned it. The eleventh-century churchman Berengarius posed the first serious challenge on theological grounds, although he recanted when shown his errors.[174] John Wyclif and Jan Hus, despite their differences on this issue, were grouped together by Catholic preachers for "speaking ill of the sacrament of the altar."[175] Reciting a lengthy list of those who had challenged the church's eucharistic teaching had the advantage of not giving its latest foes, the Protestants, too much attention. Pepin describes at length the many variations put forward by both living and dead heretics:

> The first are those who are scandalized at the idea of his existence in the sacrament of the altar. There are three sorts. The first are those who do not consider it possible that his whole body and blood could be contained in a small, round wafer. The second are those who consider it inhuman and cruel for the faithful to eat the body of Christ and drink his blood. . . . The third group are those who consider it impossible that Christ's body could be contained each time in every church in Christendom without being diminished. But Christ answers these people, for he says, "Blessed is he who is not scandalized in me." First, therefore, they ought not to be scandalized . . . for divinity was also contained in the womb of the Virgin. . . . Second, they must not be scandalized because the body and blood of Christ is not eaten carnally and visibly in this sacrament, nor similarly is his blood drunk. It is done sacramentally and invisibly, so that the senses cannot taste or

smell it, but only the bread and wine. . . . This is not cruelty, therefore, but great love. Third, they must not be scandalized because the body of Christ in this sacrament is not consumed in a corporal manner like other foods, but sacramentally, so it is not diminished as other foods are.[176]

The preachers explained that just as Jesus Christ was able to multiply the loaves to feed the five thousand, the faithful miraculously feed on him at each reception of the host.[177] Although LePicart admits that the word transubstantiation is not expressly contained in scripture, he asserts that the doctrine is implicit in Jesus' words.[178] Both LePicart and Maillard use the analogy of iron and fire to show how one substance can be entirely transmuted into another.[179] "In this holy sacrament, we participate in divinity and are transformed into God. Just as iron is by nature cold, when it is put in the fire, it participates in the fire until there is nothing but fire left. So the man who receives Jesus Christ worthily loses his terrestrial nature and is deified, a divine man."[180] The words of the institution effect this miraculous transformation.[181] The result of the transformation could only be appreciated through faith,[182] and the appearance of bread and wine that remained was only an accident,[183] not to be confused with Christ himself: "He is not to be measured according to qualities like color, roundness, or size,"[184] for the "things that are seen, touched, tasted, or broken are only accidents of the substance that before consecration was bread."[185] At the same time, listeners were advised not to adore the bread and wine, for that would be idolatry in the worst sense.[186]

The preachers emphasized the memorial quality of the sacrament, but not apart from the sustaining idea of the real presence. Menot describes the symbolic action of the priest in imitation and memory of Christ:

> O! How much the memory of the Passion of Christ will keep you from harm. For in the sacrament of the altar, we hear Christ's words, "Do this in remembrance of me" (I Corinthians 11:24), that is, commit to memory his Passion. There are certain signs that help us remember more easily. After the consecration, the priest first elevates the host, then the cup, which signals to us that we must be mindful of Christ's suffering and death.[187]

Menot, responding to threats that had been posed by Hussites and others, discusses in some detail the administration of the sacrament in both kinds. Basing his argument on biblical miracle stories, he explains that God's body and blood are *both* contained in the host: "The priest does not give you the cup, but the host for your salvation, which is both food and drink."[188] The sacramental grace was what mattered, and although LePicart admits some may receive more grace than others because of their faith and devotion, that has nothing to do with whether they receive the eucharist in one or two kinds.[189] Raulin describes the heretics' thinking: "They will say: 'If the blood of Christ is contained in the bread, then the priest consecrates the wine to no purpose. If Christ is wholly contained in the bread, then the sacrament is perfect, which makes the cup superfluous.'"[190] In response, he explains that the cup is reserved for the priesthood in recognition of the dignity of their calling and to honor them above all other men. If the laity were given the cup, Raulin fears that it would result in increasing temerity in both men and women, who might be inclined to drink it all.[191]

For the person who worthily took communion, wondrous results followed. It confirmed one's faith and hope, inspiring one to perform charitable acts. The sinner was consoled and strengthened against temptation.[192] Raulin enumerates the benefits: "Here God is truly hidden under the elements, and by virtue of his presence, idolatry ceases. . . . First, in sorrow, we become contrite. . . . Second, we feel shame at our sins and go to confession. . . . Third, we make satisfaction for our sins. . . . We find a refuge from desperation."[193]

Prayer

> So I say to you, "Ask and you shall receive; seek and you shall find; knock and it shall be opened to you." For whoever asks, receives; whoever seeks, finds; whoever knocks, is admitted. Luke 11:9–10

For the most part, churchmen and preachers wrote separate devotional works addressing the issue of prayer, but did not neglect the subject in their sermons. In her study of popular prayer in France, Virginia Reinburg concludes, not surprisingly, that lay people appropriated the prayers taught to them by the church and adapted them to suit their particular devotional needs.[194]

> Personal prayer ranged all the way from very elaborate series of Latin or French prayers read from a book, to short devotional phrases or Pater Nosters uttered at important moments like the Elevation, to "devout thoughts," to using rosary beads. Totally unlettered people prayed in ways both devotionally and psychologically complex: addressing images, employing memorized formulas, contemplating the Passion in response to gestural and ceremonial acts.[195]

Reinburg argues for an individual devotional dynamic between the Christian believer and the prayer or prayer book that was to some degree lost with increasing literacy, the printing revolution, and linguistic standardization.[196]

In prayer, simplicity was highly desirable. Pepin tells his listeners that "it is helpful to repeat the Lord's Prayer often as a symbol of one's faith: 'I believe in God. . . .'"[197] In his prayers, the penitent should confide lovingly in God, seeking God's honor, his neighbor's edification, and his own spiritual well-being.[198] "Christians should pray during the reading of the gospels at mass. Some people, especially those who understand Latin, often approach the altar at this point. After the reading is over, they return to their seats. . . . Even those who do not know Latin sometimes do so out of special devotion and reverence for the gospels, for it is written, 'Blessed are they who hear the Word of God.'"[199] This confirms Reinburg's contention that some of the Latin regularly used during mass and prayers was familiar to the people, or that its meaning was evident.[200] Pepin teaches his listeners how to pray correctly, warning against asking for material rewards or things that would be harmful to them or their neighbors.[201] The preachers reproached those who prayed with the mouth, but not the heart, for one's inward disposition was at least as important as the repetition of certain words.[202] Emotional affect was crucial: "You must direct yourself to God with all your soul, for it is better to sing five psalms with devotion, than to sing the whole Psalter without interest or with anxiety."[203] Even if God did not grant one's requests, that was no reason to give up, for God knew better than man what was good for him.[204]

The Magical Arts

> Let there not be found among you anyone who immolates his son or daughter in the fire, nor a fortuneteller, soothsayer, charmer, diviner, or caster of spells, nor one who consults ghosts or spirits or seeks oracles from the dead. Anyone who does such things is an abomination to the Lord.   Deuteronomy 18:10–12

While the teachings and activities of the church and its sacramental system were intended fully to encompass the religious life of the believer, some people distorted these practices or added beliefs of their own. Some historians have portrayed the late medieval era as an age when "superstition" flourished, often with the implicit approval of the church. Robert Mandrou describes reliance on astrology, the multiplication of cults, and the proliferation of pilgrimages as a response to the existential anguish of the times.[205] According to Delumeau, "the mental structures and the sluggishness of a still-archaic civilization encouraged the folklorization not only of ceremonies and feast days but also of beliefs, and thereby brought about a species of relapse into paganism."[206] Keith Thomas attributes the encouragement of such practices to a church that had abandoned resistance, preferring instead to accommodate magic within the cult of the church. Churchmen were "condoning a situation in which a belief in the potency of church magic was often fundamental to popular devotion."[207]

The sermons do not support the view that the church had turned a blind eye to magical practices. Gerson was only one of many preachers who had expressed a strong interest in combating such practices early in the fifteenth century.[208] While not all preachers discussed the problem of "superstitious" accretions, those who did made it clear that magical practices were neither an adjunct to the church's ritual nor acceptable within the framework of Christian belief. Where possible, the church attempted to channel such beliefs into acceptable outlets. For example, Martin finds that in the early fifteenth century, rural cults associated with the Rogation Day ritual were tamed by such preachers as Pierre-aux-Boeufs, who used agrarian metaphors to strip such beliefs of reality, replacing them with an interiorized Christocentric understanding.[209]

The people of the late Middle Ages did not see a necessary connection between simple magic and diabolic witchcraft involving the Devil and his minions (discussed in chapter 6). Taking his cue from the *City of God,* Raulin describes superstition as all "rituals of whatever sort which are superfluous, as well as those who perform such rituals."[210] One who used magic violated the First Commandment by denying God and worshiping Satan.[211] Maillard divides "superstitious" practioners into five categories: (1) sorcerers who employed herbs or other substances to cause maladies, prevent conception, or win the love or favor of another; (2) charmers who pretended to cure wounds with signs or words; (3) clairvoyants who claimed the power to discover thieves, reveal secrets, and predict the future; (4) palm readers; and (5) those who interpreted dreams or prescribed talismans.[212] Pepin ridicules those who put their faith in cunning men or women who say they can find lost articles or discover ancient treasures in the ground.[213] He also condemns the wearing of phylacteries, strips of cloth with mysterious words or symbols on them: "People go about believing that as long as they wear these faithfully, no harm can come to them, nor will they be killed in battle."[214] Nor should people repeat over and over again the Lord's Prayer or a Hail Mary, thinking thereby to increase its efficacy. The source of these misconceptions was improper religious instruction.[215]

The preachers, while not especially interested in refuting the "science" of astrology, expressed concern that belief in astrological phenomena undermined faith in God and his working in the universe. They used essentially rationalistic arguments to discredit predictions. To refute those who believed that the zodiac influenced human lives, Pepin points out that

> many are conceived in the same place and born under the same constellation, yet we often see that twins have entirely different dispositions. The case of Jacob and Esau is typical, for they were conceived and born at the same time, but while one was truly good and predestined for glory, the other was truly bad and reprobate. The role of the stars is merely contingent, for they do not necessarily influence man's rational will. A prudent man can overcome these influences, and thus he should not excuse his sins by blaming them on astral configurations.[216]

He admits that astrologers frequently seem to predict the truth concerning wars and other human events, but attributes this to chance, for an inexorable flow of predetermined events would negate man's free will.[217] The astrologers' apparent success could be explained by the variety of opposing qualities found in the planets, which allowed them to pick and choose according to the situation.[218]

While the problem of superstition was not discussed at great length, the preachers took a strong line against those who, in their opinion, undermined belief in God and his church by their activities.[219] Belief in astrology endowed inanimate bodies with too much power, and denied free will and God's causality. The wearing of amulets or belief in incantations was specifically contrary to God's will as expressed in scripture, and led to a reliance on the Devil, although most preachers of the late Middle Ages ascribed such practices to ignorance rather than malevolence.

In the period from 1460 to 1560, Catholic preachers taught a theology aimed at helping the ordinary person conform to God's will and the church's teaching. Both in its theoretical and practical formulations, popular theology was, on balance, comforting and consolatory, stressing that if a man did everything in his power he would be saved. Despite a pessimistic anthropology, the preachers put forward a hopeful and optimistic soteriology, which stressed God's goodness and omnipotence. The man or woman who turned to God for solace could confidently expect forgiveness and eternal glory. God was realistic in his expectations, and would not even turn away at failure, for as Jesus promised in the gospel of Matthew (9:13), "I have come to call, not the self-righteous, but sinners."[220]

For the most part, the preachers described worship within the sacramental system. Penance and communion were the ideal framework for forgiveness and reconciliation, which incorporated the human being into God's community and promoted peace within the community on earth. In practice, confession was subject to the failings of those who carried out their sacerdotal duties in a harsh or unforgiving manner, a serious problem that should not be minimized. Such confessors may have led some men and women to fear both the physical act and its soteriological sequelae. Yet the evidence suggests that sympathetic confessors, as well as men such as Monsieur Jean (who would grant absolution for a monetary consideration), more than made up for these men.

The lack of detailed attention to modes of nonsacramental piety may indicate a desire positively to emphasize the religious and social value of the sacraments and an attempt negatively to discourage individual avenues of religiosity. The preachers acknowledged the value of meditation, prayer, and pilgrimage, but were primarily interested in informing their listeners about the proper inward spirit that must accompany any manifestation of piety.

8

The Orders of Society

Just then the disciples came up to Jesus with the question, "Who is of
greatest importance in the kingdom of God?" He called a little child over
and stood him in their midst and said: "I assure you, unless you change
and become like little children, you will not enter the kingdom of God.
Whoever makes himself lowly, becoming like this child, is of greatest
importance in that heavenly reign."   Matthew 18:1–4

Preachers were advised by the manuals to tailor their message to the needs
of their particular audience, and a reading of the sermons makes it clear that
they took this dictum seriously. Collections with subdivisions such as
"women" or "the nobility" had been popular in the High Middle Ages, but
these were becoming rare by the fifteenth century.[1] It was understood, of
course, that preachers who used these works were not to deliver a given
sermon verbatim, for seldom would the audience be composed of only one
class or group. Instead, they were to pick and choose, adapting parts of each
to suit the special needs of their audience. Most sermons, even when not so
specific, make frequent references to the different orders of society. Although
many of the statements about each particular group are stereotypes that can
be found in sermon collections throughout the Middle Ages, they nevertheless
provide some insight into what the preachers thought of these different groups.

The Church Hierarchy

The bishop as God's steward must be blameless. He may not be self-
willed or arrogant, a drunkard, a violent or greedy man. He should, on
the contrary, be hospitable and a lover of goodness, steady, just, holy
and self-controlled.   Titus 1:7–8

Although recent studies have cast doubt on the extent of the problem, the
belief persists that abuses were rampant in the late medieval church. The
reformers of the early sixteenth century naturally exaggerated both the nature
and extent of the irregularities found among monks, nuns, and priests in order

141

to promote their own cause, and until recent decades, historians have accepted these charges at face value. As Lawrence Duggan remarks, "historians inclined toward a more strictly religious interpretation speak broadly of 'the decline of the medieval church' in this period. On this view intractable abuses abounded at all levels."[2] Delumeau perpetuates this notion, claiming that "the church met the people's religious expectations . . . inadequately, distanced the sacraments, [and] said mass and prayed incompetently."[3] However, many recent studies, using monastic and diocesan records in England and Europe from the later Middle Ages, have demonstrated that while abuses did exist, they were neither so widespread nor of such great magnitude as was originally believed. Nicole LeMaître's recent study of the diocese of Rodez depicts a church and community well on the way to reformation even before the events of the 1520s. The bishops in Rodez were the leaders in a pragmatic and even visionary program of reform for both clergy and laity.[4] "Clerical abuses" in the diocese consisted more often of apathy, relaxation of the rule, and the accumulation of wealth than of sexual misconduct of felonious behavior.

While problems and abuses have been exaggerated, there is no question that complaints were being voiced in the late medieval period as never before. Concern within the ecclesiastical establishment as well as greater lay expectations and involvement in religious life make it appear on the surface that conditions had deteriorated. But rather than proving de facto deterioration, these complaints signal a recognition of problems and a willingness to correct them, which suggest revival more than decadence. Many of the preachers in this study, including Maillard, Raulin, Cleree, and Pepin, played leading roles in the Observantine movement; it is not surprising, therefore, to find considerable discussion of clerical and monastic conditions in their sermons. There is considerable evidence that despite initial resistance, their work had substantial effect.[5]

One of the most famous critics of the late medieval church in France was Jacques Lefèvre d'Étaples. Eire states that "Lefèvre's critique of contemporary religion shared one essential concept with humanism and Erasmianism: the desire to return to the 'pristine' sources of the early church. Lefèvre's primitivism and biblicism combined to create a powerful reform ideology."[6] Interestingly, this comment applies equally well to many of the preachers studied here, who harked back to a semimythical primitive church that closely followed the precepts of Jesus Christ, scorned the accumulation of wealth, and was more concerned with missionary work than worldly splendor. In contrast to this ideal, the preachers described at great length specific problems within the the the church, ranging from the failings of the ecclesiastical establishment to excessive wealth, simony, pluralism, absenteeism, nepotism, concubinage, and inadequate performance of religious duties.

The evidence from sermons alone would suggest that the church was in a worse state than ever before. The theme of "then" and "now" is ubiquitous. In fact, the words *nunc* (now) and *hodie* (today) usually signal a complaint about contemporary society. Compared to the holy men of the early church, modern clerics are "adulterous offshoots," completely unlike their forebears in habits, deeds, knowledge, and conscience.[7] The preachers compared priests and monks unfavorably to laymen who "run after Christ," attending sermons more frequently than their clerical brothers, and reforming more quickly when they have sinned.[8] Menot claims, "Although you have as much preaching nowadays as you could possibly desire, I say to you that the church has never descended so low as now; never were churchmen so lacking in devotion as now; never were religious so imperfect as now."[9] Messier agrees: "Today the church is practically in ruins. . . . Behold the bishop's see—today it seems more like a cathedral of pestilence."[10] LePicart states simply that "today we are in bad times."[11] "We are so lazy and negligent in terms of doing good that we are worse today than we were yesterday."[12] Pepin maintains that if you are looking for lechers, simoniacs, killers or thieves, the place to find them is the church of Christ.[13]

In a frankly Gallican spirit, the preachers charged that many of the problems of the contemporary church could be traced directly to Rome. "Our great doctors in France do not speak the truth. Daily we see the great and enormous abuses that exist throughout the realm, which come from the Roman curia."[14] Menot specifies some of the problems: "Alas, today it boggles a poor mind to see the false contracts and dispensations which come from Rome, which are directly contrary to God's will, divine law, and the rule of the church."[15]

The pope as an individual did not escape the preachers' censure. Menot traces the problems of simony and nepotism to the rule of Sixtus IV, who "opened the doors."[16] The preachers used zoological examples to make the point. Messier charges that the office of cardinal is like an ass, that is, a sinning soul to lead men to Christ. "The pope himself is just such an ass."[17] This theme is echoed by Menot, who complains that the church of Jesus is in ruins because in the place of the apostles and saints one now finds crowned asses.[18] Instead of spirituality, gold was the ruling force in Rome, oiling the wheels of dispensation, even when the Pope had no right to dispense.[19] The effect on the laity was chilling; men and women scoffed at preachers, saying, "What is this, brother, won't the pope remit our sins?"[20] The pope was also blamed for the condition of the monasteries, because he allowed their exemption from ordinary jurisdiction and visitation.[21] When attempts were made to reform such monasteries, their representatives went to Rome to plead for the pope's intervention, saying that they could not possibly follow such an onerous rule.[22]

Cleree warns churchmen that the state of the souls in their care directly reflects upon them: "Take one prelate who has charge of one hundred monks, few of whom are good men. This is certainly no honor to him. It is the same in a city under a bishop's jurisdiction. On the contrary, it is said of good princes and prelates that the Holy Spirit is their glory and is shown by the multitude of good people in their care."[23]

Monastic wealth was one of the key problems facing those attempting to reform the orders. According to Menot, too many who became priests, monks, or nuns sought not to save their souls, but to amass wealth and live lives of ease.[24] Pepin complains that there are many convents, both male and female, in which vows of poverty are no longer observed,[25] tracing this to the laxness shown by those in charge: "There are many rich and negligent prelates who are remiss in the care of their subordinates, permitting what ought not to be permitted, even allowing their charges to ignore the rule of poverty. In one instance, I heard that the abbot conceded to his monks the right to keep for themselves money in the amount of 5 s."[26] Even though there were many convents in Paris in which the monks and nuns led holy lives, Menot laments that their example is not enough to change the others.[27] He complains that while some mendicant convents have been reformed, there are still abbeys in which "abominations of wealth" remain.[28]

A common complaint was that the church enriched itself at the expense of the poor. Menot admonishes his colleagues not to waste the goods of the church on buildings or prostitutes, but to use them for church necessities and almsgiving.[29] "Today few or no bishops attain the kingdom of heaven. . . . While they spend prodigally on women and sin through gluttony, they make no efforts at restitution and take away what rightfully belongs to the poor."[30] Great prelates enjoyed fantastic dinner parties and banquets, while the poor starved on their very doorsteps.[31] Such men and women were worse than wolves—they were precursors of the Antichrist.[32] "If a churchman retains food and clothing from the church beyond his needs, then he is a thief, not a minister or servant of God."[33] Those who engaged in price-gouging were even worse, for instead of giving to the poor, they take from them.[34]

One of the most striking and common laments is that churchmen spend the church's money on dogs and horses. Some ornamented their steeds with golden trappings,[35] while others gloried in the size of their retinues and the beauty of their horses.[36] Pepin reminds his colleagues that beasts of burden should be just that: "If from necessity a monk must ride a horse or mule, he should choose a humble beast as his companion. However, we see that many abbots, priors, and even mendicants do just the reverse. You will often see mendicants going on visitations with retinues of thirteen or more mounts."[37] Many were accompanied by so many dogs that they constituted a veritable army.[38] Pets had a deleterious effect on the monasteries themselves, turning retreats of quiet solitude and contemplation into kennels for barking dogs of all sizes and shapes. If some poor naive monk desired quiet and complained about the noise or chased the dogs out, he would be chastised by the abbot.[39]

Still others wasted church wealth on women and gambling. Our preachers believed that vice among churchmen was one of the reasons the church was in such a sorry state. Pepin asks, "Why have you vowed chastity if you do not want to observe this state?"[40] Churchmen are warned not to give in to libidinous urges, even if they know that they can get away with it.[41] The reasons were at least partially practical: "We find that those who have concubines have to provide for them even more than if they were lawfully married. These women are often greedy, unfaithful, insatiable, and tenacious. This is one of the reasons that priests and religious must live chastely."[42] Gambling away church money was another great sin, but if the gambler won, he was advised to return the profits to the church.[43] Maillard chastises burghers for playing card games with members of orders, since the money monks bet is not their own.[44]

Nepotism was another serious issue confronting the church. The problem often resulted directly from concubinage, for clerics had to provide for the children they had begotten in illicit relationships.[45] When favors or lineage determined the choice, the candidate was often incapable of carrying out his duties.[46] Sometimes even young boys were given bishoprics and parish churches.[47]

Related to the accumulation and improper use of wealth was the problem of simony, the buying and selling of church offices. LePicart charges that in his day the wealth of the church is marketed just like temporal goods.[48] At the merest rumor that a benefice is to become vacant through death, the vultures gather to negotiate for its acquisition.[49] Many obtain their positions in the hierarchy not through a vocation, but by means of bribery or the favors of a prince.[50] "Simony is a sacrilege, and he who commits such a sacrilege takes the property of others"[51] Monluc tells those who accumulate benefice after benefice to come out into the open and greet their leader, Simon Magus.[52]

The associated problem of pluralism was also of great concern. Part of the problem was the mercenary spirit of a church in which men did anything to obtain benefices; the more they had, the more they desired.[53] Raulin feels that nothing is tearing the church apart more in his day than the accumulation of benefices, which is the result of cupidity, ambition, and lust.[54] The responsibility of a good pastor is to reside with his flock so that he can help them,[55] something obviously impossible for a pluralist. A man without benefices murmurs hypocritically against those in possession of them, but when he begins to accumulate benefices himself, he forgets his qualms.[56] Once elevated, men who were simple and devout become creatures of their new-found wealth.[57]

The preachers offered some recommendations for correcting these abuses. The church's very survival depended on reformation from within, starting at the top, for "a ship without a captain is lost."[58] Lower in the hierarchy, priests and monks were reminded of the proverb, "the habit does not make the monk."[59] The preachers offered the positive example of the reformed monasteries in Germany.[60] In short, their advice to regulars was, "Get thee to a reformed nunnery or monastery."[61]

During many of the preachers' lifetimes, substantial progress was made in reforming convents. But that was only half of the problem, the other being unqualified or incompetent priests. To correct this situation, the preachers urged more frequent visitations of both seculars and regulars by those charged with this duty. They insisted that bishops visit their dioceses in person, rather than committing this essential task to subordinates.[62] Men who might have good motives but lack the education or fitness for a post in the church should be removed.[63] Church leaders were urged to set a personal example and preach regularly, perhaps even on a daily basis.[64] On a lower level, priests must interest themselves in the daily lives of those in their care.[65] Finally, the ecclesiastical establishment had to put an end to the endless quarrels and bickering that had almost torn the church apart.

Kingship

> So they went to Samaria, where they buried the king. When the chariot was washed at the pool of Samaria, the dogs licked up his blood and harlots bathed there, as the LORD had prophesied.   I Kings 22:37–38

Unlike the other orders of lay society, royalty sometimes heard sermons privately. Gaigny's homilies were preached before Francis I and the dauphin, possibly during one of the king's military campaigns. More frequently, the royal family was part of a wider, if still select, audience. In one of Maillard's sermons for Epiphany, we find the notation that the sermon was preached publicly with the king and queen of Spain in attendance.[66] The presence of royalty did not intimidate most preachers, nor did it cause them to alter their message, for obsequiousness was rarely a fault of late medieval preachers.

God's attitude toward kingship as expressed in the historical books of Samuel and Kings provided the preachers with their basic model. In this respect there are some significant differences between the group studied here and that studied by Martin. He found "a fervent celebration of the royal power," which he believes went along with increasing centralization of the monarchy.[67] Possibly as a result of the strengthening of the royal power in the late fifteenth century, the group studied here had little good to say about kings. Even so, there were certain qualities that the preachers felt the ideal prince should have. As God's highest representative in temporal society, he should unite in his person certain divine attributes. He must be wise, just, and merciful,[68] showing magnanimity and striving for stability.[69] Pepin describes the ideal:

> The king's justice is too often unjust through its power to oppress. The good prince should judge fairly between a man and his neighbor, defend widows and children, punish theft and adultery, banish evil men from his court, expel the impious, execute parricides, defend the church, give alms to the poor, raise just men to positions of authority, make old and wise men his counselors, banish superstition, defer his wrath, make his country strong against its adversaries, and make sure that his family and sons set a good example for their people.[70]

The king should begin by leading a blameless life.

> Kings and princes of this world ought to love justice, rendering punishment to evildoers, truth to the good, and defense for the oppressed. It is said that the Holy Spirit instructs kings and princes who judge the earth and men (but not souls) to live soberly, to be good to their neighbors, and to

speak with God. They must, of course, begin with themselves, correcting their own faults. Once they have done that, they will be better able to render justice to others. For as our Savior said to the Scribes and Pharisees about the adulterous woman: "Let the man among you who has no sin be the first to cast a stone at her." Sinners will be punished, but not by other sinners.[71]

As God's representative in the secular world, the king had to be more than a good man—he had to take a paternal interest in the well-being of his subjects.[72]

Not everyone believed that monarchy was the most desirable form of government. Pepin speaks of some distant past time, a virtual state of nature, "when there were no kings or princes, but rather each person lived in freedom. . . . When kings took power, tyranny truly began, for they took the property and possessions of their subjects."[73] Pepin claims that many princes refuse to hear or implement the Word of God in their realms,[74] and wage unjust wars and despoil their people like King Ahab.[75] They want only to be flattered by preachers.[76] Unbridled ambition leads them to extend their dominion by whatever means, good or ill, in order to enhance their reputations.[77] Instead of oppressing the church, as many kings had done, they should emulate leaders such as Constantine and Charlemagne in their faith.[78] Occasionally one of the preachers referred positively to the reigns of contemporary kings such as Louis XI and Charles VIII, although the former in particular was no great favorite of preachers.

If preachers did not hesitate to speak their minds about royal policies, this is because they claimed for the sacerdotal office a status surpassing that of a monarch. Maillard asserts that a simple priest is more worthy than a king, for the priest receives this dignity directly from God.[79] LePicart, the target of royal wrath in the 1530s, takes a direct jab at Francis I: "O, Lord, you are the sovereign king of the sky and of the earth, but me, even if I am the king of France, I am only an inconsequential servant compared to you. Can I be a king before you? Certainly not! I am only your servant and official. The king should consider this and say: I am the leader of the people of God. He gave me this office. But compared to my master, I am nothing more than a dead dog."[80] The preachers complained that the people honored kings and princes more than God. "In the city of Paris . . . if the king passes by, everyone goes outside to see him. But when the body of our Lord is carried aloft in procession, we do not budge from our houses or even look outside."[81]

Although obedience to God was the first obligation of all Christians, the preachers insisted that loyalty was owed to the king, for the relationship was similar. "You merchants know that it is a good thing to obey the king. . . . Just so it is necessary to obey God."[82] "A king has to have an army to defend his subjects. If a king is besieging a city and one of his captains turns his back as he enters the city, and goes over to the king's enemies with all of his subordinates, what would you men of parlement do with him?" Maillard answers that whoever incites a city, province, or country against its ruler should be put to death.[83]

Horse Sellers, Liars, Pimps, Courtiers, and Soldiers

The Pharisees and the lawyers, on the other hand, by failing to receive
his baptism defeated God's plan in their regard.   Luke 7:30

The fifteenth and sixteenth centuries witnessed a substantial expansion of the
royal bureaucracy and from roughly 1485 onward, appointments were made
to offices in return for monetary payments.[84] This practice was roundly condemned by the preachers. "Today many princes sell public offices for gold
and silver, which is a very dangerous thing. These officeholders, wanting to
recoup their investments, commonly commit numerous frauds, for they are
not content with their own salaries."[85] The possibilities for social advancement
which this practice opened up for the crown's subjects also exposed them to
new dangers of ambition, which put their souls in great jeopardy.[86] The
preachers advised officials to base their actions on God's law, not merely on
the king's bidding. "Officeholders, do you ever serve on the basis of justice
and right? Do you owe more to the king than God?" Maillard queries.[87]
Parents who bought offices for their offspring expected them to advance the
interests of the family rather than to serve the common good.[88] They were
often mistaken. "When a man takes possession of an office, he no longer
knows any of his former associates. He is as arrogant as a great devil, often
turning his back on his parents and others who made his success possible."[89]
According to the preachers, most officials did not fulfill their obligations.
Menot refers to these men as *gros godons,* oppressors of the poor and helpless
in whom no more sincerity and concern for the public weal could be found
than in apes.[90]

For the preachers, an honest lawyer was a contradiction in terms. Although
this was certainly not a new lament in the fifteenth and early sixteenth centuries, it is almost as common a theme as female vanity. Maillard describes
law as the single most dangerous profession from the point of view of personal
salvation.[91] Quoting Gregory the Great, Menot classes lawyers with horse
sellers, liars, pimps, courtiers, and soldiers, saying that "there are few professions so damaging to the soul."[92] Judges in parlement, whose responsibility
was to provide impartial justice, were so concerned with personal glory and
worldly honor that they hesitated to speak the truth if it might hurt their
careers.[93] But Menot warns that the judgment of men is a far different thing
from that of God: "There are two courts—that of parlement and that of
paradise, and they are very different. . . . The judgment of this world is based
on hatred, favors, and poor prosecution of cases. Ignorance, love, fraud, and
bribes all pervert human justice."[94] In contemporary France, justice was the
preserve of the well-to-do—the poor and the powerless, especially widows
and orphans, could expect nothing from judges and lawyers but further
oppression.[95] The preachers considered notaries as bad as lawyers for fraud-
ulently changing numbers in contracts for self-gain.[96]

Merchants rarely found favor with the preachers, who felt that commercial activity was inconsistent with Christian life.[97] Pepin is categorical: "Today, no matter where you look, you will not find fidelity in men of middling status."[98] The suspicion of mercantile activity derived from the view that it was based on cupidity and self-interest.[99] One of the most regular complaints was that merchants made their money by working very little—either through usury, fraud, or overvaluation of their goods. Raulin complains that "even prudent and wise merchants make a lot of money, yet they work very little and lead delicate lives. Meanwhile, poor men carry all the burdens on their backs, working harder and making less."[100] Negative attitudes toward merchants were reinforced by the biblical story of the money changers in the Temple.[101] Menot claims that in his day, merchants set themselves up in the church precincts near the cemeteries on Sundays, hoping to profit from the crowds of people attending services or sermons. But unlike lawyers, merchants received occasional approbation from the preachers. Raulin admits that some merchants perform a valuable service, especially when they sell the country's surplus goods abroad where they are needed.[102] Still, the implicit assumption was that a merchant should do this out of Christian compassion, not for personal gain.

Soldiers were also unpopular with the preachers, who were concerned not so much with the issue of warmaking, but with the depredations soldiers wrought upon innocent people. Menot complains that "soldiers in villages commit many wrongs at the expense of the poor people, eating their food and taking their money."[103] If the poor die of hunger as a result, the soldiers return to pillage their belongings without ever saying a single *Pater Noster* over their corpses.[104] Farinier complains that a soldier will "borrow" the cow of a poor widow; if she seeks restitution, he arrogantly announces his intention to keep it.[105] Even the church was not safe.[106]

The preachers' comments about all these "professional" groups are remarkably similar, and can be reduced to the fact that they lived at the expense of those less fortunate than themselves. There was little recognition that any of these people made positive contributions to society in their professional capacities.

Rich Man, Poor Man

How hard it will be for the rich to go into the kingdom of God! Indeed, it is easier for a camel to go through a needle's eye than for a rich man to enter the kingdom of heaven.   Luke 18:24–25

Sell all you have and give to the poor. You will have treasure in heaven. Then come and follow me.   Luke 18:22

The social contrast between the rich and the poor and the deeper spiritual meaning of the two conditions is one of the dominant themes in the preachers' sermons. The poor were the special concern of preachers who often spoke out so vehemently on behalf of the downtrodden that they incurred the wrath of the well-to-do and government officials. Not surprisingly, the preachers spent considerable time trying to convince the haves that it was their Christian duty to share with the have-nots. Although the lack of charity was a stock theme in medieval and early modern preaching, the abundance of such references in the sermons suggests that this problem may have begun to reach critical proportions during this period.

The preachers explained that God's gifts to the human race were not material rewards. More than most of his colleagues, Pepin was aware of the vagaries of a life in which the few were rich and the many poor, and knew this was one of the questions about God that would bother his listeners:

> Why does God want some in this world to be rich and others poor? It would seem better if the wealth were equally divided. God endowed all men equally with souls, with the great and the small made in his image. His Son shed his blood to save all equally, so it will be said that all ought to share equally in the riches of the world. I say that God has till now ordained that some are rich and others poor, so that each one has the material at hand to merit the kingdom of God. The rich by giving alms to the poor, the poor by patiently doing their work, and praying that the rich will sustain them.[107]

The rich and poor depended on each other for their salvation, as Pepin argues in another sermon:

> If the kingdom of heaven belongs to the poor, according to the words of Christ, it follows that if rich men want to attain it, they must ask this favor of the poor, and in effect buy it from them by giving alms. Then the poor will arrange for their admittance into heaven through their special prayers and the rich man's vicarious "participation" in their poverty. The rich can place their money in no place as safe as in the hands of the poor.[108]

The preachers anticipated protests from the audience. Although "each of you will say in your heart that it is better to be rich than poor, it is not so, for the poor are truly better off."[109] Too much prosperity was the primary cause of damnation, as could be seen in the case of the rich man who sadly walked away from Christ after hearing that he must give up all that he had (Luke 18:22–23; Matthew 19:16–22; Mark 10:17–22). Menot tells those gathered before him that if it were a simple matter for a rich man to be saved, then God would have made the apostles rich.[110] He adds that the prophets Elijah and Enoch were sent to preach the truth and comfort the poor, not the rich, and uses the theme of *memento mori* to drive home the point that riches will avail naught when the Devil comes to seize a man's soul:[111] "O sinners, go to the cemetery of the Holy Innocents and look at their bones. Can you tell the difference between the bones of a poor man and those of a rich man? In one sense you can, for on earth the rich men ate delicate foods, so now their bodies stink in the ground more than do those of the poor."[112] Messier compares rich men to pigs,[113] a simile that Menot describes as fatal for the soul: "In his *Moralibus,* Gregory says: 'An obvious sign of eternal damnation is continual success and prosperity in this world. A pig will be killed with his riches.'"[114] The truly wise man should imitate Christ's poverty, which will lead him directly to the portals of Heaven.[115]

The preachers often contrasted the ostentatious luxury of the rich with the sight of poor men and women dying of hunger.[116] "I say to you that the blood of Christ calls out for pity for the poor, despoiled of their livelihood and unjustly afflicted. Your shroud calls out for vengeance, because this is the blood of the poor."[117] They expressed outrage that a rich man could ignore scraps of food that fall from his table, while a poor man may have to subsist on the flesh of a dog.[118] Contemporary society had no place for the poor. "If you look in the house of a lord, you will find that each cat and dog, each rooster and hen, has its special place—but we find no mention of the poor."[119] It troubled the preachers greatly that the rich spent extravagantly and wastefully on clothes while the poor went without: "'My pompous lady, Madame *la bragarde,* you have six or seven blouses in your wardrobe which you scarcely wear three times a year.' . . . I cannot imagine what excuse this lady will come up with when she sees a naked pauper crying out because of the cold."[120]

Hunger and cold were not the only problems facing the poor. Pepin decries the fact that there are so few people willing to care for the poor, the sick, and the handicapped.[121] People despised the poor and sick on account of their infirmity, and were unwilling to visit them or receive pilgrims, just as the rich man had not wanted to allow Lazarus into his home.[122] Maillard works on the consciences of his listeners: "I see that you have many evils in this town. . . . Do you go to hospitals to see the poor who are dying of starvation and without confession? Do you go in person?"[123]

The problem was not limited to a lack of charity, for the powerlessness of the poor put them at the mercy of the rich:

> You afflict the poor in two ways. First, temporally, you rob them of their skin, that is, their worldly goods, even to the point of taking away their clothes, which are then put on public sale to pay their debts. Secondly, you afflict them bodily, making them go hungry and die of starvation because you have taken all of their necessities; or you put them in prison because they don't have the wherewithal to pay you, as we see more and more every day.[124]

According to Pepin, violence against the poor is worse in his modern Nineveh than in ancient times.[125] He compares powerful men who take the possessions of the poor to pirates.[126] They extend their own fields by taking those of their neighbors,[127] thinking nothing of perverting justice if it will enhance their own wealth or prestige.[128] Menot claims that the whole city of Paris is awash in the blood of the poor.[129] Price gouging, especially of basic foodstuffs, was the most flagrant violation of the Christian ethic. Menot complains that in times of scarcity, the well-to-do sell wheat for twice what they have paid for it, even though their barns and storehouses are full.[130] Rich men would rather watch the grain rot than fill the mouths of the poor.[131]

Besides the physical suffering they must endure, the poor were often dragged along the road to damnation by rich men: "The rich man gives alms to the poor man so that the latter will testify against his [the rich man's] enemies. The poor man does this either because of threats or fear, or out of lack of concern for his own salvation. So he says what the rich man tells him to. As a result, his stomach is filled, but these alms will carry him straight to hell, as Augustine teaches us."[132]

With the medieval love of oppositions and changes in the wheel of fortune, the preachers insisted that those who have abundance in this world will have nothing in the next, while those who are humble and abject will appear on high in all their glory.[133] Menot urges the rich man to ponder the future: "O lords, when the poor clamor at your doors, your servants say to them, 'Be quiet! You'll disturb my master.' O wretched sinners, when you are at death's door, you too will seek mercy, but your prayers will not be heard. Instead you will be cast away from the doors of paradise, just as you turn the poor away from your household."[134] The taxes and exactions the rich had placed on their poor subjects would provide the salt and spices to season their roasted flesh in hell.[135]

Lack of charity and depredations against the poor were, for the preachers, the most basic violation of the Great Commandment. Their condemnations of the different orders of society inexorably led back to this problem, for the gain of one was the loss of another.

The Non-Christian World

It is actually reported that there is lewd conduct among you of a kind not even found among the pagans.   I Corinthians 5:1

The people of the later Middle Ages were in general less tolerant of Jews and Moslems than people in earlier times. The period witnessed the wholesale expulsion of Jews and Moors from the Iberian Peninsula as well as forced conversions. The contemporary Italian preacher Bernardino da Feltre regularly used his sermons to incite pogroms against the Jews, even though such behavior was condemned by the papacy. In the sermons of the fourteenth and early fifteenth centuries, the Jews were often considered synonymous with the Devil.[136] But somewhat surprisingly, overt anti-Semitism is rare in the sermons. Although references to the Jews are fairly common, most allusions to non-Christians were used in a scripturally based effort to shame Christians into reforming their lives.

We have already noted that pre-Reformation preachers borrowed heavily from the Old Testament, and displayed a true reverence for the great leaders of Israel before the coming of Christ. Moses, Abraham, David, Solomon, Judith, and many others figure prominently in the sermons as examples of righteousness. However, the preachers contrasted the patriarchs, kings, and queens of earlier ages with the Jews who refused to recognize Christ as the promised Messiah. They emphasized that the Jews had been God's chosen people: "At one time the light shone only on the Jews, who were the only ones to have real faith, spiritual grace and true doctrine. All the Gentiles lived in the shadow of unfaith, guilt, and ignorance. But after the Resurrection of Christ, it was the Gentiles who converted and who were effused with true faith, grace, and doctrine."[137] "The leaders of the Jews were idolators in the desert, but Moses extirpated their heresy, and chased away the demon. Now [at the time of Crucifixion] we see that they have returned to their idolatry, for they urged the Romans to put Christ to death."[138] As a result, the Jews lost the true faith,[139] leading to their diaspora through all the lands of the earth.[140]

Although Christ had come to save the Jews,[141] the early church soon comprised people of all nations and races.[142] The preachers stressed that Jews and pagans must never be compelled to believe,[143] but if they converted to Christianity, they would become full members of the church.[144] Every Christian was obliged to pray for this end:

> The church prays for all men who are *viators*, except for the damned, for *viators* are capable of receiving divine grace and pity, but the damned are not. Whence Augustine, Sermon [71]: No one must despair for the patience of God will bring him to penitence. A man may be a pagan today, but do you realize that tomorrow he might become a Christian? A man may be a Jew today: but what if tomorrow he comes to believe in Christ? A man may be a heretic today, but tomorrow he may become a true Catholic believer. A man may be a schismatic today, but tomorrow he may live in Catholic peace.[145]

Negative references to the Jews center on two themes: their part in the crucifixion of Christ and the hypocrisy of the Pharisees (Matthew 15:1–20). In discussing the Crucifixion, the preachers closely followed the accounts in the gospels. In his emotive portrayal of the Crucifixion, Menot reproaches the Jews for having treated so badly one who desired their salvation: "He preached to you, he brought you back to life. It seems to me that if he did no wrong and spoke no ill of you, he certainly was very severely punished. But they averted their faces, saying, 'Crucify him.'"[146] Pepin reminds his listeners that the Jews would suffer in the end for their unbelief—as Christ was pierced during the Passion, so would the Jews be in hell.[147] The preachers also attacked the hypocrisy of the Pharisees, who were so concerned with outward acts that they forgot the true meaning of religion and cared only for the praise of men.[148]

Occasionally, the preachers described Jewish history and beliefs, usually in relation to Old Testament stories or Christ's interactions with the Jews. They often quoted the Jewish historian Josephus. Most comments revolved around the events or practices of the early first century, such as Herod's attempt to exterminate all male children in response to a prophecy,[149] and the exchange between Pilate and the Jewish leaders. Menot even gives a description of the Temple:

There were three parts to the Temple of Solomon. The first was called the
Holy of Holies, in which the high priest entered once a year, and here they
kept the tables of Moses on the ark. They maintained these with respect,
just as we Christians do with the body of our Lord. The second part was
the sanctuary, and this was the place in which the priests offered the sacrifices
for the people. It compares to the nave of our church. The third was called
the atrium, at the front of the temple, just like the part before the aisle in
our churches. It was here that the doctors gathered and the people heard
the Word of God. The merchants also gathered there.[150]

The preachers were more interested in shocking their Christian listeners
into penitence with unfavorable comparisons than in fomenting anti-Jewish
sentiment. Jews and infidels might be the natural enemies of Christ and his
church, but they were not nearly as bad as those Christians who did not live
as they should. The latter had received the light of faith and turned their
back on it, which was much worse than having never seen it at all.[151] Maillard
tells of a situation during the reign of Louis VIII: "In the city of Tours there
were some Jews who, hearing Christians blaspheme the name of God, said,
'You say that Christ died for you, yet we are amazed that you do such injuries
to him.' I dare say that many are more insolent in the church of Christ than
in the temple of the Jews."[152] Menot makes the important point that despite
the fact that they are outside the faith, many Jews (and pagans) lead more
perfect moral lives than Christians,[153] while Farinier claims that more peace
and love can be found among these groups.[154] The preachers gave specific
examples to support their position. Menot says that "there were Jews and
Lombards expelled from the realm because the whole world detested usury,
but now we put up with worse usurers than the Jews or Lombards ever
were."[155] Many of the preachers argued with chagrin that modern churchmen
outdo the ancient Jews in the practice of simony and their desire for human
glory.[156]

The preachers discussed pagans less frequently, but in exactly the same
context. The ancient philosophers were revered in the same way as the great
patriarchs. Although the ancients had not had the benefit of the sacraments,
their search for virtue made them better than many Christians.[157] Citing one
of Christ's regular laments (Matthew 11:20–24), Cleree asserts that if the
Saracens had had as many preachers among them as do modern Christians,
they would have repented more quickly,[158] for like the Jews, the Muslims
keep their own laws better than do Christians.[159]

Pre-Reformation preachers made few references to atheists, although there
was the definite feeling that people did not believe as they should. Pepin
mentions that "few miracles are seen among Christians because of general
incredulity. For today many are Christians in name only."[160] Menot goes
further, deducing from the unholy lives of many, that "some believe that
there is neither heaven nor hell, neither God nor the Devil, and that nothing
can harm them."[161] Post-Reformation Catholics referred to atheists more
frequently, but their targets were usually Protestants or sectarians. Paris
claims that "there is no nation so barbarous, no people so strange and savage

that they have no natural sentiment of divinity,"[162] but others were less sure. LePicart complains simply that "today God is unknown."[163] Guilliaud comes closest to a modern definition of atheism, telling his listeners that atheists believe that everything dies at the moment of death, the soul as well as the body.[164]

The underlying ethos of love for God and one's neighbor was at the heart of many sermons, and influenced the preachers' discussions of the orders of society. Not surprisingly, the preachers had little good to say about any particular group. Their main attacks were directed at those who had the greatest means and the greatest opportunity to sin—the rich, because their wealth and worldly power blinded them to their Christian responsibilities, and merchants, soldiers, and members of other professions whose positions gave them so many opportunities to defraud or mistreat the lower classes. They reserved some of the strongest condemnations for kings and churchmen who, as God's representatives on earth, were expected to set a spiritual example for the rest of society. The strong emphasis on the church and its problems suggests that this was one of the key issues of the day. But rather than indicating that things had deteriorated since the days of the Babylonian Captivity and Western Schism, this kind of criticism shows that a spirit of regeneration could be found in all levels of the clergy. Reform was in the air.

9

The Preachers and Women

> On their journey Jesus entered a village where a woman named Martha
> welcomed him to her home. She had a sister named Mary, who seated
> herself at the Lord's feet and listened to his words.   Luke 10:38–39

The effects of the Reformation on women and the more general issue of
women's role in religion have recently received considerable attention, largely
because of interest provoked by social history and gender studies. A great
deal of debate centers on how women's roles changed during the Renaissance
and Reformation.[1] There may never be general agreement on this matter,
but what has emerged is a shift in focus from male attitudes and perceptions
of women to women's views of themselves, with Caroline Walker Bynum's
work being of particular importance.[2]

A study of preaching is necessarily limited to looking at male attitudes
toward women. Still, within these limitations, it is useful to understand precisely what male preachers were saying to and about women. Even if women
did not internalize such attitudes, as Bynum suggests,[3] the attitudes of men
toward women in male-dominated societies are quite important. We can also
compare and contrast the different preachers' beliefs and also see how attitudes changed during the one-hundred-year period from 1460 to 1560.

Eve and Mary

> The serpent said to the woman: "You certainly will not die! No, God
> knows well that the moment you eat of it your eyes will be opened and
> you will be like gods who know what is good and what is bad." The woman
> saw that the tree was good for food, pleasing to the eyes, and desirable
> for gaining wisdom. So she took some of its fruit and ate it; and she also
> gave some to her husband, who was with her, and he ate it.
>
> Genesis 3:4–6

Most scholars generally accept that preachers throughout the ages have
condemned women as the cause of, or at least the occasion for, sin. In his

study of Franciscan preaching in the late Middle Ages, A. J. Krailsheimer asserts that "to say that the preachers are antifeminist is almost like saying that they are against sin,"[4] while Delumeau remarks that "the antifeminist litanies recited by the preachers vary only in form."[5] In a study of the portrayal of marriage in literature, Katharine Rogers claims that "the baneful effects of women's influence were reinforced by every possible example from the Bible. . . . [C]lerical feeling in the Middle Ages definitely inclined toward anti-feminism."[6] Other scholars have suggested a striking ambivalence in the church about women. Eileen Power argues that people "went to their churches on Sundays and listened while preachers told them in one breath that woman was the gate of hell and that Mary was the Queen of Heaven."[7] Even this last argument is too simplistic, for it takes no account of the enormous differences that could exist among preachers. While some preachers saw a little (or a lot) of Eve in every woman, a surprising number of late medieval preachers stressed the dignity of woman and her equal role in Christian life.

The lines from the creation story have in many ways shaped Western attitudes to the female sex. Although the gospels present women in a very positive light, the same cannot be said of the Pauline epistles.[8] For most of the early Church Fathers, Eve was the symbol of woman, the embodiment of evil and carnal desire. For Tertullian, Eve was the eternal temptress.[9] Using the typology of Eve, Augustine preached that in women "the good Christian . . . likes what is human [quod homo est], loathes what is feminine [quod uxor est]."[10] The language is significant, predicating humanity as an attribute of maleness. Yet while most early Church Fathers favored this view, Ambrose and and a few others pointed out that the greater fault lay with Adam, "[f]or we know that Adam, and not Eve, had received the commandment from God. Woman had not yet been made."[11]

The influence of Paul and the Church Fathers continued to be of great importance throughout the medieval and early modern period. While the church often portrayed woman as a serpent[12] or even the Devil incarnate,[13] more wholesome evaluations continued as well. Delaruelle speaks of a veritable *"promotion de la femme"*[14] in the later Middle Ages, largely as a result of Marian devotion. Although the relative importance of Mariology in elevating the status of women is debatable, Mary's symbolic importance was essential to balance more negative views.

Following Tertullian and Jerome, Farinier states that "women takes the precious soul of man."[15] His use of the present tense is significant, for it links contemporary women with Eve. Surprisingly, Farinier's position finds relatively little support among other Catholic preachers. Most of the preachers offered the standard argument that the sin of Eve was removed because Christ was born of woman.[16] Illyricus stresses the honor that Mary's status as the Mother of God gave to women: "the hand of woman wounded us, and the hand of woman healed us."[17] George Tavard explains the background and context of this more positive, or at least more balanced, view of women in an egalitarian scheme of downfall and redemption:

> With Irenaeus, this contrasting parallel between Eve and Mary obtains a
> new setting. . . . As Adam is the type of Christ, so is Eve the type of Mary.
> Between type and antitype relation exists by similarity and contrast. Adam
> sinned and Christ redeemed; Eve disobeyed and Mary obeyed. These two
> couples, Adam-Eve, Christ-Mary, are not isolated and separated from each
> other, but actively interrelated. The second couple "recapitulates" and re-
> stores the work of the first.[18]

Relying on Augustine,[19] Pepin and Menot go even further than many of their
contemporaries in making Adam bear most of the blame for original sin.
Menot shows surprisingly little sympathy with Adam: "After sinning, Adam
excused himself by blaming his wife, saying: it was the woman who gave it
to me, etc. So by this ruse he thought to escape; but instead he made things
worse."[20] In view of the Adam-Eve/Christ-Mary relationship, Pepin finds it
annoying that men place all the blame on women, without attributing part
of their salvation to a woman.[21] He makes the two sexes equally culpable,
drawing a moral lesson for husbands and wives in his own day: "There was
extraordinary discord between men and women, who reproached each other
for the transgressions of the first parents, with the men saying that the woman
had seduced the man. For their part, the women claimed Adam was stupid
to have behaved in such a way, wanting to please his wife more than God.
Therefore to end this strife, Christ was sent into the world."[22] Here the women
not only had the last word, but also the more sophisticated argument.

Woman as Eve

> Women must deport themselves properly. They should dress modestly
> and quietly, and not be decked out in fancy hair styles, gold ornaments,
> pearls, or costly clothing.   1 Timothy 2:9–19

The sinful lure of woman was a common theme among preachers, although
its importance has been exaggerated by historians. The vanity theme appears
with some regularity in the sermons, but even Maillard, who harps on these
themes, frames his attacks on women's clothing with denunciations of the
failings of other groups, such as lawyers or merchants. Attacks on vanity were
simply one of the more obvious ways to reproach women as a group and urge
them to reform.

Female beauty, and its capacity for inspiring lust, lay at the heart of the
problem. Illyricus puts it quite simply: "The beauty of women is a great
occasion for evil."[23] But what could be done? Illyricus suggests that it is best
to hide one's beauty.[24] Speaking to a group of nuns, Lansperge echoes this
theme: "Here you should teach girls and women to cover themselves, and to
hide those things that inspire lust."[25] Menot uses the imagery of death and
decay to convey this message: "Nothing comes from a beautiful woman but
fetor. . . . Alas, that which is pleasing in this world, is nothing but stench!"[26]

Besides provoking sinful desire in others, a woman's beauty could pose a very real danger to her through the sin of pride. "There are very few pretty girls or women in the world today who do not revel in their beauty."[27]

The preachers vigorously denounced vanity in both men and women, but believed that vanity was more common among females. They felt the time spent in enhancing one's beauty could be better spent in less mundane occupations. Pepin talks of women who waste so much time on dress and makeup, especially on feast days, that they miss mass.[28] Using *memento mori* themes, Maillard warns women where such behavior will inexorably lead: "when you are at the hour of death and see a thousand devils at your side who want to take your soul, then you will wish that you had never led such a life of pomp and excess! Take care!"[29] Although preaching formulas called for general rather than individual censure, the early fifteenth-century preacher Jacques Legrand turned his fury on Queen Isabelle of Bavaria, whose horned headdresses and décolletage had provoked his outrage. This was a symbolic attack on the queen's sexual proclivities, as well as her vanity, by a preacher who felt that the queen was setting a bad example for the people of Paris.[30]

Certain parts of feminine attire attracted more fire than others. Besides the headdresses, which were symbols of cuckoldry analogous to the devil's horns, the style of long trains and sleeves provoked the preachers' indignation. The preachers compared women (and sometimes men) to peacocks, because of the ornateness and color of their finery and the arrogance and pride that accompanied such display. "Look at those vain and curious women, who on feast days dress up and walk around the streets and neighborhoods, to see and be seen. In this they imitate the peacock, who glories in the beauty of its feathers and rejoices when it is secretly admired by men, and who haughtily turns about and fans its tail, and is roused by the loveliness of its feathers."[31] Maillard vents his fury against women who wear revealing clothes: "You young women who bare your breasts, it would be better for you to have leprosy."[32] Of even greater concern were female religious, who not only mimicked their secular sisters, but often exceeded them in vanity.[33] A somewhat more unusual complaint centered on women dressing as men. Menot implies that cross-dressing by women was a subtle attempt to contravene social norms: "It is an abominable and extraordinary thing that women today go about in the guise of a man to games of dice and masquerades, with masks covering their faces."[34] Such disguises could be a subterfuge for women to visit churchmen,[35] or to allow men to infiltrate the section of the church normally reserved for women.[36]

Makeup was also a subject for serious reproof.[37] Since beauty was the tool of the prostitute,[38] it was wrong for decent women to enhance their appearance through artificial means.[39] Raulin argues against it from a more practical point of view: "After a while, so many wrinkles appear that a woman forty years of age will appear to be sixty or seventy."[40]

Attacks on vanity were commonplaces that women often chose to ignore.

Ha, my ladies! You should not wear long-sleeved gowns or a lot of accessories. —Ha, brother! We wear them without wrongdoing; we can wear them honestly. —Certainly, this is true, but if a woman is good and honest, it will be said that she has cast her virtue aside. —Ha, brother! Sometimes we see gentlemen and greater clerics than you wearing them and they say there is no harm in it. —Surely, my lady, no cleric should wear such things. And anyone who says so is lying.[41]

In a slightly bizarre twist, LePicart complains of sacrilege by the artists of his day who paint holy figures in contemporary dress: "The painters depict the blessed saints in ways other than they should. They do wrong in the way they paint the pious Magdalene at the foot of the cross. If I were to preach that she, the Virgin Mary, and others were dressed in such a worldly and pompous manner, I would be corrected, and with good cause. Why do we permit such abuses? Why don't we reprove them."[42]

But beyond the lure of sin that surrounded extravagant or revealing display, why did the preachers take such offense at such seemingly insignificant issues? It was because vanity had a price. Menot complains that women even stoop to prostitution in order to have beautiful clothing.[43] Their husbands often had to work harder or engage in unfair business practices to pay for their extravagance.[44] Maillard insists that "if this is the price of lust, which comes as a result of theft and dishonest contracts, then these clothes are soiled with leprosy and must be burned."[45] Menot points out that such money could be put to better use feeding and clothing the poor. "Oh, how grievous! It is with a sorrowful heart that I say: The long trains of our young ladies, and other such excesses serve no purpose but to please the world, and are completely unnecessary! At the same time, orphans, widows, and the needy go without and die of exposure."[46]

Closely related to the danger of vanity was the problem of behavior in church. Maillard complains of "women who make amorous signals to their lovers, while saying their hours,"[47] and Merlin insists that beautiful women distract others from their religious duties, for "a lot of people come to sermons to see the pretty ladies rather than to be instructed."[48] Pepin presents a gloomy picture:

> There are many loose-living women who wander about the church and other sacred places with no other purpose but to see and be seen. Such women pollute the holy temple of God. They enter God's church in a spirit of drunkenness and gluttony. This is also true among rural people who attend their confraternities (out of respect, they say), and on certain days they gather and celebrate their feasts in the church, for they say there is no room in their houses. And so they profane and pollute God's sanctuary with their gluttony, drunkenness, filth, and shouting.[49]

Here Pepin includes some men among the malefactors, but in other passages insists that alcohol abuse is a serious problem among women. He advises women to abstain from alcohol, for "they do not commonly have such a head for wine as men."[50]

Envy was another flaw in the female character. In a mocking tone, Cleree mimics women: "A woman like that shouldn't put herself ahead of me in church; for I come of a better house than she."[51] Some women were jealous of rivals more beautiful than they,[52] while others resented those who preceded them at the offertory.[53] A final trait outside of the marital relation that the preachers found reprehensible was garrulousness. Using a zoological analogy, Pepin reprimands his female listeners: "When he was preaching in a certain place, there were so many magpies whose chattering kept those in attendance from hearing the sermon, that the preacher said to them: 'My sisters, magpies, now is my time to talk, for you have talked enough up till now.'"[54]

In the preachers' view women were far from flawless creatures. But what originally appear to be obscure attacks on petty faults were aimed primarily at countering the deadly sins of pride and lust, and encouraging love of one's neighbor. The preachers were concerned not only with the moral effects of certain behaviors, but also with what they considered to be a shocking disregard of the truly important things in life.

Marriage

> To those not married and to widows I have this to say: It would be well
> if they remain as they are, even as I do myself; but if they cannot exercise
> self-control, they should marry. It is better to marry than to be on fire.
>
> 1 Corinthians 7:8–9

In his study of thirteenth-century French preaching, Lecoy de la Marche asserts that "the preachers always honored woman by exalting marriage, presenting it not only as a sacrament, but almost as a religious order, with its own rule and special sort of sanctity."[55] This was still true in the late fifteenth and early sixteenth centuries.

Marriage in the Catholic Church is a sacrament, matrimony, the joining together of a man and a woman in a relationship analogous to the union of Christ with his church. Pepin positively rejoices at the gift of love which could join together men and women of very different circumstances: "It is indeed a special gift of God that a man and a woman of different parents, often from different regions, and of quite different appearances, can love each other mutually in the Lord when they are united in holy matrimony."[56] He continues, "marriage stands for all that is most excellent, worthy, and lofty, that is, the joining of Christ with his church."[57] Raulin compares the union of man and woman to the intermingling of body and soul.[58] On a practical level, Clichtove warns parents not to force their children to marry someone they do not love.[59]

Despite its symbolic beauty and sacramental character, marriage was not considered more desirable than virginity or widowhood.[60] The preachers took Paul very literally. However holy and filled with Christological symbolism, marriage was an imperfect institution in an imperfect world, but the preachers were fully aware that for the majority of their listeners, lifelong celibacy was not possible. For these people, they held up the chaste Saint Louis as a model for the ideal state of matrimony.[61] Therefore they tried to emphasize the positive possibilities of marriage.

The ennobling love between a man and a woman, which at its best mirrored divine love, was one of the main purposes of marriage. Another goal of marriage was "the procreation of children to honor God, multiply the human race, and renew and refill the celestial mansion."[62] Marriage was also a vital social institution:

> There are many nobles today who marry late and consecrate their youth to all sorts of wanton behavior. After they defile young maidens, they hand over these girls in marriage to their attendants or subjects, so they can more easily have their will with them. There are others who get married, but after their wives die, they choose to remain widowed rather than remarry and thus diminish the inheritance of their children. But saying that they cannot remain continent, they lead shameful lives, producing many bastards.[63]

The topic of sex appears frequently in the sermons. While sensual pleasure should never be of overriding importance,[64] the preachers accepted the Augustinian notion of rendering the marital debt. They warn, however, that "the time is not always right for playing or taking one's pleasure in matrimony. It is sometimes necessary to curb one's desires."[65] Maillard has harsh words for women who use sex to gain specific ends,[66] while Cleree accuses women of "taking all manner of vows to avoid rendering the marital debt."[67]

When the preachers expressed approval for marital intercourse, it was for what they considered *normal* sex.[68] Menot speaks gravely of some of the sins perpetrated within matrimony: "Marriage is truly worthy, but under its cover many foul, dishonest, and execrable acts are perpetrated, which would make animals blush. Many husbands and wives are damned on account of shameful acts in marriage more quickly than they would be by adultery or whoring."[69] To the imagined objection, "But brother, what can we do? My lord teaches me that I live by his largesse; unless I do what he wants, he will throw me out of the house with two great blows from his cane,"[70] Menot responds by citing Duns Scotus, making it plain that where conflicting demands are made, one must obey God first.

The preachers recognized a certain egalitarianism within the marital relationship that went beyond sexual rights. Relying on a commonly used argument first enunciated by Ambrose and Augustine, and later by Peter Lombard and Hugh of Saint Victor,[71] Maillard admonishes his listeners to remember that in the act of creation, Eve was not taken from Adam's head or his feet, but from his side; therefore husband and wife are meant to be companions.[72] Using the same rationale, Pepin insists that while the man is the head of the family, his wife is neither his slave nor his servant, a theme that appears repeatedly in his sermons.[73] To soften Paul's harsh words on the subordination of women, he follows Aquinas to show that this is not a subjection of slavish fear, but one of love and guidance.

What precisely were the roles of husband and wife in marriage? First, they owed one another fidelity and equal access to sexual intercourse.[74] A husband was expected to provide love and guidance, and to protect his wife's reputation.[75] To women, Cleree emphasizes both the naturalness of the married state and the theological theme of *facere quod in se est:* "The Lord calls you to this state of matrimony, to which you are appointed; if you do all that is in you, you will be parishioners of Christ and receive your reward tenfold."[76] It was a wife's responsibility to love her husband, bear his children, educate them (and the servants, if any), and take good care of the house. She should listen to her husband, and avoid giving offense. Interestingly, it was also her duty to help him earn his living,[77] which was often the case among the lower and middle classes during the Middle Ages. Very importantly, it was the wife's obligation to work for her husband's salvation.[78] Quoting from the life of Saint Elzear, Menot reminds his listeners that "an evil-living man was saved by a good woman."[79] Pepin agrees, for "a woman can be a spiritual advocate in those things concerning the salvation of the soul."[80]

In the preachers' opinion, this idyllic conception of what marriage should be was rarely found in practice. Reminiscing of times past when women did not presume so much, an earlier French preacher, Guillaume de Montreuil, then turned to contemporary men: "Today [their husbands] call them vile strumpets, whores; they bite and hit them for no reason, and sometimes kill them. Husbands and wives today are like cats and dogs."[81] The home, which should be a haven of peace and security, was instead a place of discord. "How can peace be found in the home, with a bad wife and five chattering children who are never satisfied?"[82] Pepin sadly relates that some women "honor their dogs more than their husbands. For when the husband returns from out of doors with his dog, his wife makes much of the dog, and applauds it, but she turns her face away from her husband."[83] The preachers did not single out women for this evil state of affairs. Menot says that one should look to the men as the cause of such behavior: "I say to you that often, when wives see their husbands' regimen as so wretched and unhappy, with no rewards, then for their part they give themselves over to dissipation and infamy. Thus man is often the cause of the evil his wife does, which nevertheless she ought not to do for all the world."[84]

On the subject of adultery, most late medieval preachers apportioned the blame equally between men and women. Adultery violated the (mutual) promise of good faith, so the sin was the same if committed by a man or a woman.[85] "What is not allowed to women, is not allowed to men."[86] Practically speaking, the problem was considerably more complicated. Marital status, attempting to kill one's spouse, or adulterous relations with kinsfolk, all added to the gravity of the sin on an individual basis. In certain cases, however, a man or woman could be held more responsible. Medieval stereotypes considered women more lustful than men,[87] although Pepin argues that women are more modest by nature.[88] This natural modesty should help them avoid the sin of fornication, so they err all the more grievously if they engage in proscribed sexual behavior.[89] When discussing female sexuality, the preachers were most concerned with problems of legitimacy and inheritance. There was little sympathy for a woman who became pregnant as a result of an adulterous union: "If a woman produces a child from adultery, she sins much more gravely than a man, because she gives birth to an heir and deprives the others of their rightful inheritance, admitting into the family one whom she knows to be illegitimate."[90] While natural modesty and the possibility of pregnancy should deter women from adulterous liaisons, their "weakness" relative to men excused them to some degree, for men were supposed to be stronger and more virtuous than women.[91] Menot decries the adulterous male who despises his good and honest wife, and who is willing to destroy his home in order to satisfy his lust.[92] Despite Old Testament precedents, the preachers would not allow a man to commit adultery, even if his wife was sterile or permanently infirm.[93] But there was one condition under which adultery was sinless, although not without tragic consequences—the case of a woman who remarries after her husband has not returned from war after seven years.[94]

When dealing with individuals, the preachers could be extremely compassionate. The story of the adulterous woman in the gospel of John proved that no sin was too great for God to forgive in the presence of true contrition. Menot tells of a notorious young woman who despaired because of the magnitude of her sins:

> A newly married young woman, who often committed adultery to the damnation of her poor soul, the confusion of all her relatives, the displeasure of God and the injury and the distress of her husband, said to me: O, Father, I am the unhappiest woman on earth; I should never have been born. I wish the earth would swallow me up, for I have sinned greatly against my husband and I know I have acted badly. —O, my friend, do not despair, because nothing is so bad that it cannot be remitted through penitence. . . . —O, Father, I would willingly do what you say, but my husband is strict, and rough; he will not receive me with compassion. —Listen, my daughter, to Jeremiah 3: You fornicated with many lovers; but if you turn to me I will sustain you. —O, Father, what I would give for him to take me back, but he does not want me, though I would be his servant or his cook. I am not worthy to be looked upon by him. —No, my daughter, it will not be like that. . . . —O, Father, it is true, he will smite and torture me until I die. — No, he will not, because as it is said in Ezechiel XVIII[XXXIII]: I do not want the death of the sinner, but rather for him to convert and live. —O, Father let me be, do not stay with me. —No, no daughter. Zechariah 1: Return to me and I will return to you, says the Lord. Certainly never so gently and lovingly does a mother comfort her little one who has fallen to the ground, raising him up and embracing him. Just so the Lord does with the soul of a sinner who has returned to him through penitence.[95]

The allegorical purpose of the anecdote was to show that even if her earthly husband would not forgive her (a fact not conceded by the preacher), her heavenly Father would.

Although the preachers did not discuss birth control frequently, it was evidently a common practice in the Middle Ages. Using theological sources, P. P. A. Biller argues for "appreciable contraceptive practice in the middle ages . . . which had become quite widespread in some areas by the early fourteenth century."[96] Because contraception circumvented one of the basic reasons for marriage, Pepin and others considered it a great sin.[97] Except for the preachers who have left large collections of sermons, there are few lengthy discussions of abortion, but most at least mention the practice. This suggests that it, too, may have been more common in the fifteenth and sixteenth centuries than has been generally supposed.[98] Whether done to protect the reputation of the woman,[99] or to prevent adulterous offspring,[100] abortion was morally wrong. Maillard warns women that should they die in an abortion attempt, the Devil will take their souls.[101] Pepin, who spends a good deal of time on the problem, suggests that one should sympathize with the plight of a pregnant woman:

> We must seriously consider this question, for occasion should not be given to a pregnant woman [to lose her baby or procure an abortion] just because she is not used to her condition or taking care of a fetus. Some illustrious men preach falsely, insisting that such little ones seek vengeance from the lord against their mothers. I would not universally excuse mothers from blame, but I would like to exempt these little ones generally from all sadness and perpetual pain.[102]

Pepin goes on to clarify the soteriological status of the unborn child, which seems to be the rationale behind most antiabortion statements. Medieval theology was ambivalent on the subject of an unbaptized child's share in original sin. A millenium earlier, Augustine had admitted: "As for abortions, . . . I cannot bring myself either to affirm or deny that they will share in the resurrection,"[103] although his later positions left little hope for the salvation of unbaptized infants.[104] Because of this concern, Raulin urges pregnant women not to fast, so that they will not endanger the fetus.[105] Abortion was one sinful response to an unwanted pregnancy, and infanticide was another. The preachers feared the latter would appeal to nuns seeking to avoid scandal.[106]

In discussing childrearing, the preachers made little differentiation between the roles of the father and the mother, although there was often the implicit assumption that this was the primary concern of women. As parents, men and women were advised not to be afraid to provide both correction and instruction to their children.[107] Lamenting that there are too few Monicas in his world,[108] Pepin finds instead "many foolish mothers who cannot tolerate the correction of their children."[109] This theme of "coddling," which is ubiquitous in the preachers' discussions of family life, further weakens Lawrence Stone's assessment of parent-child relations in the premodern era as psychologically distant.[110] Because they believed that strictness was necessary for the ultimate well-being of the child, the preachers felt that mother-child relations were entirely *too* affective. Cleree warns mothers of the consequences of their soft-heartedness: "Women, if you have daughters or sons eight years old who look in your purse, you must cure them of this habit now, or they will learn later with their blood."[111] Besides seeing that they attend church and go to sermons, Clichtove tells parents to teach their children to love their neighbors and care for the poor.[112] They should be taught how to care for their bodies, in terms of both hygiene and morality. Finally, parents should see to it that their children do not associate with the wrong sort of friends.[113] Ambition for their offspring was another parental failing. The upper classes would send their sons to schools or universities at too young an age, before their moral formation was complete,[114] or place their children with ladies of the court, noblemen, or bishops in order for them to learn the arts of society. LePicart challenges such thinking: "What will they learn there? Is your son who lives with the nobleman or bishop there to seek Jesus Christ? No, he is there to forget Christ, and he will surely lose whatever good doctrine he may have had."[115] Others hoped to marry their daughters "well," even if this compromised their spiritual health: "It is all the same to you if you give her to some great robbing usurer. You do not consider her soul, for you only care about giving her body to a man of high status."[116] The preachers also rebuked parents who put their children into religious orders without a vocation.[117]

Late-medieval French preachers stressed spiritual equality, but never implied that women were not subject to men in temporal matters. That was the "natural" order of things. Within this limitation, the preachers strove to honor women in their capacities as wives and mothers. But when they discussed states other than marriage, the preachers often expressed views that were quite the opposite of the antifeminism of which they are so often accused.

Widowhood

> If her husband dies she is free to marry, but on one condition, that it be in the Lord. She will be happier, though, in my opinion, if she stays unmarried.
>   1 Corinthians 7:39–40

Widowhood was held in high esteem by the preachers, perhaps because of the existence of the order of widows in the early Christian church.[118] The widow's exalted position derived primarily from the chaste style of living that the preachers envisioned: "The state of widowhood well-observed is by far more perfect and more wholesome than the state of marriage."[119] While second marriages were by no means condemned, it was considered better (and closer to virginity) for a woman to know only one man during her lifetime.[120] Menot tells the story of a young woman considering remarriage: "'I was married to a man of good name, but he died. Then along came a young man, good enough, who would take care of me. I want your opinion.' 'If it seems good to you, my friend, marry him.' 'Ha,' she says, 'Father, I fear things would be bad.' 'If you are worried, then do not marry him.'"[121] Obviously this was not an easy situation in which to provide guidance. Widows who did not remarry were often at the mercy of unscrupulous suitors and lawyers, and would find few to champion their cause.[122] Menot laments that "no one is more greatly despised [than the widow]."[123]

The sermons contain some intriguing arguments against remarriage. Menot speaks of the unpleasantness of married life for some women: "A married woman has to concern herself with things of the world and how to please her husband. She does not dare make a will, give her goods away, or go to confession whenever she wants. She has a husband who is *ung diable enchaîné*, who after spending all day in the tavern comes home and beats her. She has no choice but to endure all this."[124] Pepin argues that by remaining a widow, a woman can preserve her independence: "When a woman does not remarry, but remains a widow, she has much greater freedom. She is mistress of herself, her family, and her home. However, if she marries a powerful man, she will not afterwards be able to dispose of herself or her possessions, except perhaps a few personal belongings."[125] The belief that widows had both the right and ability to control their lives and property was not an unusual position among preachers, for in 1501, Geiler von Kaysersberg fought against the city government of Strasbourg, which had been trying to appoint "guardians" for widows.[126]

What are we to make of such statements? These arguments may simply have been an attempt to convince women of the better Christian way by appealing to their selfish instincts. But whatever their reasons, the preachers recognized in women a legitimate desire for independence, as well as a genuine religiosity that was often deflected by the demands of family life. By remaining a widow, a woman could regain control of her person and goods, play the role of matriarch, and express her devotion without restraint.

Woman as Victim

As soon as the maids had left, the two old men got up and hurried to her. "Look," they said, "the garden doors are shut, and no one can see us; give in to our desire, and lie with us. If you refuse, we will testify against you. . . . " But Susanna cried aloud: "O eternal God . . . you know that they have testified falsely against me. . . . "

Daniel 13:19–21, 42–43

If we were to accept the stereotyped view of medieval preachers as essentially antifeminist, it would be difficult indeed to explain their lengthy discussions of women as victims. Menot devotes the better part of one sermon to the story of Susanna, in which he presents her reactions to the men's blackmail: "Then this good lady, seeing herself thus entangled, groaned and was greatly terrified."[127] He is making the moral point that one must not consent to evil, yet his choice of this example to illustrate the point is interesting. Susanna was the innocent victim of male lust. The sermons present a litany of examples in which men were the active cause of sin, thus inverting the Adam and Eve relationship.

Sexual misconduct was the most common form of victimization of women by men. Maillard castigates men who "take women in 'marriage' by night, without the solemnification of the church."[128] Likewise, he argues that anyone who deflowers a virgin ought to marry her himself or provide her with a husband.[129] Pepin complains that "smooth-talking men try to deceive modest virgins by talking about betrothal. Certainly we find many rich and notable men, including churchmen, who promise much to these girls, saying that they will marry well and have many fine things, but who leave them as soon as they have had their way with them."[130] Menot cautions widows: "You will make the acquaintance of a young *calamistratus, souffleurs de plume,* who does nothing but abuse women."[131] In another sermon, he denounces in the strongest possible terms men who molest virgins, leading them into a life of infamy and prostitution.[132]

Lawyers, never popular with preachers, were described as especially unethical in their dealings with female clients: "Behold, a widow is alone. If she has a legal case, no one will defend her. She goes to a lawyer for a legal document. If she wants his services, she must use her body as payment. O, what a pitiful message to send to young women today! And we see a thousand such deceptions."[133] Similarly, parents who do not properly look out for their daughters' welfare leave them at the mercy of evil men's wiles: "A churchman or lawyer, under the pretense of going eating or drinking, follows his lust, for here at the tavern he will find a brothel. You would be better off sending your daughter to beg than putting her to work serving in a tavern. There you make a whore of her."[134]

Examples of incest were not uncommon. Farinier tells the lurid story of a woman so moved by a preacher's words that she stood up in the midst of the congregation and proclaimed her tragic tale of sin:

> I was a girl in my father's house, talkative, always wandering about and singing, and in every way spoiled, yet still a virgin. Then, one day, my father gave in to the temptations of the devil, and raped me. When we persevered in sin, my mother began to notice it and reproached me. Not wanting to let go, I visited a witch and got some poison which I gave to my mother and she died. With no one left to expose us, I sinned ever more freely with my father, who after several years realized his sin and wanted to break it off. He showed me how much he was grieving at the magnitude and baseness of such a sin. This displeased me, so I went back to the witch, and did the same thing to my father as I had to my mother. Yes, I did all this. But if there is a place for penitence, I will deal with whatever is thought of me.[135]

At the end of the sermon, still not believing such forgiveness was possible, the woman approached the preacher and fell to her knees. "Then calling on the people, he said, 'You have heard the confession of this sinner. If she repents as sincerely in her heart as her words suggest, I have faith in God that her sins will be forgiven her. But this is a difficult question, for her sin is great, and she has suffered no serious punishment. Let us all pray that her punishment be removed, or at least lessened, so that she may be found worthy.'"[136] But in a dramatic ending, Farinier relates that as the congregation prayed for the woman, a voice from above interceded: "Preacher, do not pray for her, but ask her to pray for you, for now she is with God."[137] As

Farinier is rarely sympathetic to women, it is not surprising that the woman in question was made an accomplice to the crime. But in another case, an innocent girl was seduced by a male relative. Menot, borrowing from Herolt's book of exempla, makes it quite clear that her only real crime lay in not confessing it.[138] He adds, in his preface to the story, that such vices are common, especially in the homes of the nobility.[139]

Incest was not restricted to blood relationships. Farinier considers sexual intercourse between a woman and a father figure in the church especially reprehensible and suggests that it should lead to the deposition of the cleric.[140]

Medieval law clearly recognized a husband's right to beat his wife, as long as he neither killed nor maimed her.[141] The preachers frequently discussed the problem of wife-beating and almost unilaterally took the side of the woman. The connection with male drunkenness is striking. Menot tells of such a situation in Lyon: "Near Lyon there was one of those gallants who haunted the tavern. And his wife said to the preachers: "By the love of God, you hear my husband's confessions. It is a wondrous thing to hear him complain about his life. He goes to the tavern; later he beats me, and breaks everything.'"[142] Cleree takes a dim view of those who call on men to beat women who will not consent to their sexual demands.[143] Maillard offers the qualification that beating one's wife could not be permitted except for the most serious transgressions.[144] LePicart goes further. Citing the moral consequences for family life, he says: "It is simply too indecent a thing to beat one's wife. What kind of life do children have when they see their parents fighting?"[145]

Although one or two of our preachers provided occasional justification for male behavior in such cases, most spoke out clearly agains the social and individual problems of rape, harassment, incest, and wife-beating. In a society that complacently accepted ill treatment of women,[146] the preachers' voices rang out as a cry for the Christian dignity of woman.

Prostitution

> Turning then to the woman, he said to Simon, "You see this woman? I came to your home and you provided me with no water for my feet. She has washed my feet with her tears and wiped them with her hair. You gave me no kiss, but she has not ceased kissing my feet since I entered. You did not anoint my head with oil, but she has anointed my feet with perfume. I tell you, that is why her many sins are forgiven—because of her great love."
>
> Luke 7:44–47

The medieval church held surprisingly tolerant views of prostitution.[147] The Church Fathers felt that prostitution was a necessary evil, arguing that without it "everything would be polluted by lust."[148] By the fourteenth and fifteenth centuries, partially in response to the demographic and psychological consequences of the Black Death, prostitution had become so accepted that it was not unusual for town governments to run brothels.

For the preachers, prostitution was a very loose term, denoting *"filles de joie,"* women who consorted with churchmen, and straying wives. Simple fornication was a venial sin, but one which the preachers regarded as serious, because it often led to greater sins. Farinier suggests that it is better by far not to touch women.[149] Taking a more egalitarian approach, Pepin warns that "nothing is more dangerous to a man than a woman, and to a woman than a man."[150] Menot admonishes young girls that they must not allow themselves to be kissed or touched, for this could lead to incest or seduction. "For what other reason does a boy want to touch you, if not to make you his concubine?"[151] Maillard asks the girls in his audience if their fiancés make improper advances to them. If so, he maintains that this will lead to postmarital problems: "When your fiancés come to visit you before the wedding, do not agree to do whatever they want, for after the wedding they will reproach you, saying that you will do the same thing with someone else."[152] But women themselves were sometimes guilty of leading girls into prostitution: "You hostesses, do you not have good and honest girls in your houses whom you make serve in the tavern? And under the guise of waiting on tables, they are soon dragged down and made into prostitutes."[153] Here and elsewhere, the preachers stressed that creating the opportunity for sin was at the root of the problem.[154] Maillard cannot understand mothers who "take their daughters to places where there are men and lead them into a room and shut the door behind them."[155] Referring to legendary stories of Mary Magdalene's life, Menot argues like a behavioral psychologist that if she had been brought up properly in honest surroundings, she would not have become a prostitute.[156] This unexpectedly implies that it is life and the opportunity for evil that leads to corruption, not human nature per se.

While prostitution was abhorrent to the preachers, the prostitute herself was not. Besides Mary Magdalene, stories of prostitutes-become-saints abounded in the Middle Ages. The legends of Saint Mary the Harlot, Saint Afra, Saint Pelagia, and Saint Thaïs all "inculcated a different attitude toward the prostitute, as a woman to be pitied more than condemned, and as an ever present possibility for conversion."[157] Maillard asks his audience, "in what quarter of town do prostitutes not abound?"[158] In another sermon, he suggests the cause: "Why are so many virgins and married women in Paris led into such a life? It is because of the pimps, for we do not punish them."[159]

Although Leah Otis argues that by the fifteenth century a new rigorism had come to prevail in sexual mores, society still did not view prostitutes as beyond redemption. A prostitute's reintegration into society was quite commonplace, especially after she turned thirty, when her services were less in demand.[160] Taking his cue from the gospels, Menot argues that "prostitutes are converted by preaching."[161] The preachers were not satisfied with mere words, but looked for active repentance and reformation. During the reign of Louis XI, Farinier customarily preached with such fervor that "several condemned, lost women left their evil lives and most of them retired to monasteries."[162] The Franciscan Tisserand was so interested in the conversion of prostitutes that in 1495 he founded the Society of Penitent Women at Paris, later to become the Magdalenes.[163] A flamboyant preacher often produced startling chain reaction conversions among prostitutes.[164] In 1517, after the stirring sermons of a certain brother Thomas in Lyon,[165] so many prostitutes were converted that it was "difficult to feed and shelter so many repentant women."[166] Interestingly, the process of conversion through preaching could be a dialogue. LePicart tells of a married woman who retorted: "'Why should I mend my ways—me? Everyone points their finger at me.'—'Listen to me: The Magdalene was also a public woman who was pointed out. Nevertheless, God forgave her.'"[167] The mendicants were so successful in attracting latter-day Magdalenes to their sermons that the charge was made against them that "only whores follow you."[168]

Not surprisingly, the preachers considered sexual liaisons between women and churchmen completely untenable. When the Faculty of Theology censured Friar Jean Angeli in the 1480s for arguing that "those who cause mass to be celebrated by a priest keeping a suspect woman, sin mortally,"[169] their concern was theological and not moral. But the church was very disturbed at sexual misconduct by its clerical members, and while some argued from an Eve typology,[170] most held the ecclesiastic responsible for initiating the affair.

The Piety of Late Medieval Women

> I assure you, this poor widow has put in more than all the rest. They make contributions out of their surplus, but she from her want has given what she could not afford—every penny she had to live on.
>
> Luke 21:3–4

That the preachers should consider women more compassionate than men is not terribly surprising—both biblical exempla and medieval thought were in agreement on this point. The cultic role of the Virgin Mary as a loving, motherly intercessor helped to foster such a belief. Somewhat more surprising is the general view that women were more devout than men, a view that seems to have been shared by many women.[171]

Female compassion could ultimately be traced to inborn maternal feelings. Maillard compares a mother grieving over her dying son to Christ's lament for the death of sinners.[172] Because of their greater compassion, women's role in healing the sick was commonly recognized: "It is revealed from this story that women are more compassionate to the sick and infirm than men, about whom we do not read such things. On account of this you find kindly nuns ministering to the needs of the sick in the great hospitals, such as the Hôtel Dieu in Paris, and the hospital called Magdalene in Rouen."[173] Women were also more pacific by nature, and Menot suggests that they could be looked to for settling disputes.[174]

A favorite theme was the tenacity of the women at the cross, who had followed Jesus to Jerusalem and who stayed during the dark days when even the disciples had fled.[175] Pepin contrasts the men who insulted Christ with the women who bewailed his misery.[176] But this was simply a manifestation of women's greater piety. What was its cause? Pepin answers that men presume too much in their own faculties: "Women are more easily drawn to faith and the correction of morals than men. For we often see women who have sinned gravely stung by the words of a preacher. But it is only rarely and always late in the day that we see evil men change their lives. And this is at least partially because men presume too much in their abilities and trust in their reason. It is not that way with women. So we find they are commonly more devout than men."[177]

The preachers regularly observed the devotion of women in formal worship. A reading of large numbers of sermons makes it clear that in the late fifteenth and early sixteenth centuries, women outnumbered men at sermons. Menot claims that four times more women than men come to sermons. Alluding to Biblical precedent, Maillard comments that "it is not just in modern times that women attend sermons in such numbers, for in the time of Christ many also attended."[178] Pepin compares his female auditors to the queen of Sheba: "The queen of Sheba, who came from the ends of the earth to hear the wisdom of Solomon, signifies that in many things women are more avid to hear the word of God than men. For men trust in their reason, and often do not care to go to sermons."[179] Bitter that his audience had been depleted by evangelical preaching at the Louvre, LePicart complained that only old women attended his sermons.[180]

Similarly, women were more constant in church attendance than men.[181] While men talked or napped during services, women piously said their rosaries,[182] which caused some to mock them as church hens.[183] This charge was especially serious when made by churchmen attempting to dissuade women from frequent displays of devotion: "Among churchmen, we often speak ill of a woman who goes to confession every Sunday, saying it is not the proper business of a woman to go so often. This is wrong, and I counsel all those who are able to go every day to do so."[184] Although annual confession was the norm, Pepin mentions women who confessed their sins once a month or more.[185] Some women were more scrupulous than their confessors: "A good woman will say: 'Father, my conscience bothers me about something I did in my marriage, but the confessor never asked me about it. I do not know if it was a venial or mortal sin.'"[186] Despite having confided her sins to a competent confessor, one woman still had qualms that she discussed with the preacher. He advised her to trust her confessor rather than giving in to her own fantasies.[187]

The sermons indicate that women took the sacraments, prayed, and went on pilgrimage more than their male counterparts: "There are indeed women who in many things are more devout than men, whether it be praying, visiting holy places, or taking the sacraments. Many confess often and take communion on the principal feast days, while few men do so."[188] Maillard comforts a woman who obtained an indulgence in good faith: "An honest woman will say: 'Father, I cannot judge of such great things. If I obtain an indulgence in good faith, do I thereby do wrong?' I say that if you obtain an indulgence in the name of God and you cast away your sins, they will be forgiven you. Nor do I wish to suggest that indulgences are not good if they are collected for charity."[189] The woman's faith was the crucial point. While men found it difficult to fast even occasionally, women not only fasted on feast days of the Virgin, but extended this practice to every Sunday. This may have had an anorectic component,[190] but Pepin argues that such behavior verges on heterodoxy: "There are others who, believing it a great service to do this for their child and husband, want to cease all manual work on the Sabbath, especially after noon, and who judge others who continue to work to be sinners. . . . Preachers must constantly inveigh against such indiscreet and dangerous devotion, for under the pretext of piety, superstition and heresy creep in."[191] The preachers warned women not to carry devotion beyond reasonable limits, for this could lead to domestic strife.[192]

Women were passionate about religious issues. Everywhere in Europe, women were actively involved with preaching. In Nuremberg, Johannes Nider printed his book of sermons at the express request of townswomen,[193] while in Strasbourg it was at the behest of Suzanne de Coëlle, a leading citizen, that a search was made for a permanent preacher, resulting in the hiring of Geiler von Kaysersberg.[194] In France, women resorted to violence in defense of their beliefs or as partisans in religious disputes. In 1478, when Louis XI attempted to silence Farinier for criticizing the well-to-do, the townswomen threw rocks at the king's emissaries.[195]

That women had pretensions in theological matters is evident from even the most cursory reading of late medieval sermons. Brown indicates that Gerson found this highly distasteful: "They wish to speak and dispute about theology more than many a great theologian, and wishing to judge sermons and reprove preachers, they say of one that he has told a story from the Bible badly, and of another that he is teaching heresy; and when they have an opinion fixed in their heads, nothing will get rid of it."[196] Yet many preachers seemed to accept this and use it to their advantage, referring to their listeners as *mesdames les theologiennes, semi-theologales,* and *bone theologiane.* Despite the mocking tone, the preachers tried to involve their female listeners in their arguments and channel their interests into love of God and Christian behavior. Maillard asks the ladies in his audience: "Do you not study theology? O, that you would be good theologians and love God."[197]

Upper- and middle-class women had greater educational opportunities open to them than ever before,[198] and evidence of female literacy appears in these sermons. Many women brought their books of hours to church with them, although Pepin questions their motivation: "There are women who bring their devotional books, called books of hours, to church with them. Inside, we find various stories illuminated in gold which they kiss with great devotion. But this is only to be seen by the people around them. They cannot do it without arrogance or hypocrisy."[199] Reading devotional works was not objectionable as long as the motive was sincere. By contrast, romances were soundly condemned, for they provoked desire and led to sin.[200]

Menot and Maillard both mention women owning vernacular Bibles. In an attempt to make the women understand his arguments, Maillard asks: "My ladies, do you not have your French Bibles in your bedchambers?"[201] Menot is not happy with the practice, and groups vernacular Bibles with novels: "My ladies, do you not have French Bibles and novels? Do you think you will find anyone in paradise who, like yourselves, persists in such pompousness?"[202] Possibly these "Bibles" were other religious books (such as books of hours or saints' lives), or even popularized versions of Bible stories.[203] Krailsheimer speculates that allusions to Bible translations might simply refer to parodies of scripture that were popular in the Middle Ages,[204] yet the context suggests more than that. In her masterful study of the vernacular Bible in the Middle Ages, Margaret Deanesley points out that biblical translations were freely used in women's convents throughout Europe during the fifteenth century,[205] and Susan Groag Bell has demonstrated that as early as the twelfth century, women were commissioning vernacular Bibles.[206]

The Question of Mary Magdalene

> He first appeared to Mary Magdalene, out of whom he had cast seven demons. She went to announce the good news to his followers, who were now grieving and weeping. But when they heard that he was alive and had been seen by her, they refused to believe it.   Mark 16:9–11

The theological question of why the risen Christ first appeared to Mary Magdalene and chose her to announce the Resurrection to his disciples was an issue of considerable importance for fifteenth- and sixteenth-century preachers, and one that seemed to challenge male superiority. It is also an issue that allows us to investigate differences among the preachers.

Illyricus presents an already familiar argument. Relying on Augustine, he says: "But some may ask why Christ first appeared to Mary Magdalene rather than Peter or one of the other disciples. The resurrection of Christ was announced to men by a woman so that the serpent would be soundly defeated, for he first announced death through a woman. So life is given to man by woman."[207] Illyricus goes on to congratulate Mary for "before the Apostles, you saw Jesus Christ; you addressed him; . . . you were called by your name by Christ."[208] Despite his bantering tone and allusions to contemporary attitudes, Messier insists that women first announced the Resurrection because they had studied well in the school of Christ, and because women were so much better at talking.[209] Maillard simply announces the fact of Christ's appearance to Mary Magdalene without any attempt at explication.[210] But Menot is less circumspect. Drawing his listeners into the Resurrection drama, he exclaims: "There were many women crying.... And on ascending the mount, Christ looked around to see if any of the disciples had remained. Alas, no."[211] Pepin elaborates on this idea:

> It is proven that women are more devout than men, and this through the example of those learned women who were so devoted to Christ. Although during his time on earth, Christ found certain men agreeable, never did he find such perseverance and constancy among his disciples as he found in these women. These were the women who followed him as he traveled through the countryside preaching, and who ministered to his needs according to their abilities. These were the women who followed him to the cross although his disciples had fled. And these were women who upon his death prepared the aromatic ointments for his body in the tomb. Others were neither terrified of the shadows and darkness of night nor the ferocity of the armed soldiers.... And so women announced the triumph of the resurrection, for Christ knew that above all grace was the grace of a woman.[212]

This is not an isolated statement in Pepin's sermons; taken with other remarks it forms a significant corpus on the importance of women in religion. In another sermon, Pepin argues that while women's testimony is not generally accepted in civil law, a woman has the right to testify in spiritual matters; hence Mary's announcement to the disciples.[213]

While many pre-Reformation preachers presented a surprisingly enlightened viewpoint on women, attitudes hardened during the sixteenth century. Bynum argues that in the Middle Ages the notion of "weak women" could express some positive ideal because of New Testament precedents and the implicit connotation of rejection of the world,[214] but the explicit emphasis on the connection between Christ's appearance to Mary Magdalene and the fact that she was a "weak woman" is first seen in LePicart. He says that Christ first appeared to a woman because choosing the weak as his instruments was Christ's modus operandi: "You have heard why he first wanted to declare and manifest his resurrection to women.... When our Lord wanted to do great things, he always chose simple people, or poor sinners. And so he chose to manifest his resurrection to women, who are the weak sex, and of little virtue."[215] LePicart continues, pointing out that Mary wanted to hold and embrace Christ, "so that she would not lose him again. She did this because of her imbecility."[216] What has happened to the dignity of woman? Even the noblest acts are disparaged. Although the "weakness" issue may have been implicit in medieval exegeses of the relevant passages in the New Testament, it was the preachers of the mid sixteenth century, both Catholic and Protestant,[217] who fully developed it in a manner that supported patriarchal attitudes. When the weakness of women was explicitly underlined by men like LePicart, it was with a new cynicism that was not present in the sermons of late medieval preachers like Pepin.

Preaching by Women

> It is a disgrace when a women speaks in the assembly. Did the preaching
> of God's word originate with you? Are you the only ones to whom it has
> come?   1 Corinthians 14:35–36

Mary Magdalene's announcement of the "good news" to the disciples has
sometimes been interpreted as a sanction for female preaching. Women in
the early church had the right to prophesy (Acts 21:9; 1 Corinthians 11:15),
but the council of Carthage in 398 denied the ministry of the Word to
women.[218] Nevertheless, throughout the Middle Ages, women occasionally
preached, especially to other women in convents. This did not violate biblical
injunctions against women teaching men. But in the early thirteenth century,
Pope Honorius III had to warn the bishops of Valence and Burgos to stop
certain abbesses from preaching publicly.[219] A few decades later, Rose of
Viterbo, a Franciscan tertiary, was given papal permission to preach from
church pulpits, where she is said to have converted many sinners.[220] Various
saints, particularly Clare of Montefalco and Margaret of Cortona, regularly
went on preaching tours,[221] and Vauchez describes a *prise de parole généralisée
de la part des femmes* between 1378 and 1430.[222] Among the Waldensian
heretics, women had always had the same right to preach as men, and the
practice continued in the fifteenth century, although with less frequency than
had characterized the earlier movement.[223] In the sixteenth century, a Spanish
Franciscan tertiary, Joanna a Cruce, (died 1534) preached seventy-one sermons for feast days and other occasions under the title of *El Conorte.*[224]

Practice notwithstanding, theory remained rigid. In his preaching manual,
the thirteenth-century preacher Humbert of Romans set the tone for why
women must not be allowed to preach: "First is lack of judgment, for a woman
has less than a man. Second is the condition of servitude that was inflicted
on her. . . . Third, if she were to preach, her appearance would provoke las-
civious thoughts. . . . Fourth, in remembrance of the foolishness of the first
woman."[225]

After relating the tale of the Samaritan woman, Raulin simply restates the
standard Pauline prohibition.[226] Pepin does not agree. Beginning with the
issue of prophecy, he warns men not to scorn the gift in women, as many
such cases are attested by sacred scripture. He notes the specific example of
the prophetess Anna, wife of Tobit,[227] but does not stop there: "There are
those who object that the office of preaching does not belong to women, for
this was prohibited by the Apostle, saying: It is not permitted for women to
preach. This is conceded regularly, and in common law. However, in certain
cases, through the action of the Holy Spirit, this can be done."[228] Referring
to the legend that Mary Magdalene and some of the disciples had ended their
life proselytizing in Provence,[229] he adds: "Then in Marseilles and afterwards
in Aix, [Mary Magdalene] proclaimed the Word and attracted people to the
faith by her preaching. And if it is said by some that a woman should not
preach publicly, as with the Apostle's statement in 1 Timothy 2 . . . , it must

be answered that this is normally the case. But God is not bound by human laws, and can make women, just like men, assume the office of preaching."[230]

But by the 1540s, possibly in response to perceived threats from Lutherans and a misunderstanding of Luther's conception of the priesthood of all believers, LePicart adopts a very defensive attitude toward the Samaritan woman:

> She went into the city to announce to all what Jesus Christ had told her, saying: 'Is this one not the Christ? Is he not the son of God, the true Messiah promised in the law? He told me everything I had done in my life.' By this example, the Lutherans want us to believe that women can preach and that the Samaritan woman preached. The Samaritan woman did not speak in the manner of preaching, but spoke rather through the admiration she felt for the Lord, who had declared her whole life to her."[231]

Sometimes LePicart protests a bit too much, which suggests that contemporary women may have occasionally used these arguments as a license to preach. "It is prohibited for women to preach and teach in public places; but privately a mother may teach her children and others in her household, like servants. The abbess can teach her nuns. But in public and in full congregation, it is not a woman's place to teach, and it is repugnant for them to preach. And the reason is that to preach is to have authority, and the natural and proper condition of woman is one of subjection."[232] Étienne Paris advances an argument based on the "natural" order: "Public doctrine belongs only to the perfect sex, which has more solid reason, better judgment, and greater erudition. Their charge was not to preach in public, because that would put them above male listeners in subversion of the order of nature, which does not allow woman to dominate man."[233]

Of late medieval preachers who discussed the issue of preaching by women, opinions were quite varied. Raulin adopts the standard position based on Paul, but without invective. On the other hand, both Pepin and Clichtove maintain that through the working of God's grace, women have prophesied and preached in the past, and will no doubt do so in the future. They base their argument on the spiritual equality between men and women, and on the omnipotence of God. But by the mid-sixteenth century, there was an increasing rigidity of attitudes among both Catholics and Protestants that precluded such openmindedness.

Many of the positions expressed in the sermons can be found in the works of the Church Fathers and medieval theologians, but even the choice of commonplaces can be revealing, especially for changes in content and tone over time. The findings here support Bynum, who shows that men held increasingly positive images of women in the later Middle Ages, an ironic development because of a new appreciation of the merits of weakness and rejection of the world. "In revering female saints, worshiping the Virgin Mary, attracting female followers, holding up saintly women as a reproach to worldly prelates, and describing themselves as women and fools, medieval men were in one sense ignoring the negative side of the earlier medieval image."[234] The fluidity of gender language regarding sacred characters in the Middle Ages[235] may have allowed women a greater part in the mental world of their religion than was possible in a later, more patriarchal age.

Late medieval preachers took women very seriously, at least in part because women appear to have participated so much more frequently and fervently than men in the rites and activities of the church, including attendance at sermons. While women as a group were regularly accused of vanity, arrogance, and envy, these charges were countered by positive biblical models. The Virgin Mary may have been too perfect to have provided a satisfactory role model for ordinary women, but Mary Magdalene, the Samaritan woman, the Canaanite woman, Judith, and the female saints of the early church were more accessible. The increasing feminization of sainthood in the later Middle Ages[236] presented to women the idea that something close to perfection could be achieved by a woman.[237] Relying heavily on scripture, the pre-Reformation preachers emphasized many of women's strong points, such as devoutness and tenacity, to a degree seldom recognized by historians. They dealt with problems of women in everyday life, and gave counsel on appropriate religious observance, usually with compassion and sensitivity. Pepin and others regularly turned the tables on those who traced the problems of the human race to Eve—and all women—by countering with images of faith and salvation offered by women.

The decline in monastic vitality during the sixteenth century and the uncertainty of the times removed an alternative vocation for many women, while the Protestant lessening of emphasis on the Virgin Mary and the saints in practice eliminated the most positive female images from religion, leaving only the negative. Eire describes this increasing masculinization of piety: "The removal of these feminine representations marks a definite shift away from a gender-balanced, feminized piety to a more strictly masculine one. . . . The richly symbolic feminine aspects represented by the Virgin Mary as 'Mother of God' and by other female saints, were suddenly replaced by those of a transcendent, but overtly masculine piety."[238] Even among Catholics, the age of reform witnessed a significant drop in the percentage of women saints, from 27.7 percent to 18.1 percent, a decline that continued throughout the seventeenth century.[239] Correspondingly, a decrease in male desire to emulate the image of "weak woman" may have widened the gulf between men and women in the real world.

At this point, we must turn our attention to a problem that concerned a minority of men and women very directly—the problem of heresy. At the end of the Middle Ages, the church had stood as the bulwark of Christendom for fifteen hundred years. Although there had been numerous challenges, both great and small, to its tradition and beliefs during these centuries, no individual or group had ever succeeded in undermining the basic edifice. But in the volatile atmosphere of the late fifteenth century, the combination of strong reforming currents and greater individuality in religious expression set the stage for a major split within the Western Christian community.

III

Heresy:
Challenge and
Response

10

Heterodoxy and Heresy before 1520

*There may even have to be factions among you for the tried and true to
stand out clearly.* 1 Corinthians 11:19

Heresy in France in the late Middle Ages took one of two forms: individual
cases of dissidence unrelated to mass movements, and group heresy, which
had become increasingly uncommon as a result of the combined effects of
the Inquisition and the more aggressive approach to religious instruction that
the mendicant orders provided. While the only significant remaining group
heresy, the Waldensians, still existed, its adherents were not the threat to the
church that they had once been.[1] In 1487, the church mounted a crusade
against them in the south of France, but by 1500, it felt confident enough to
adopt a more tolerant policy. In an investigation into the Waldensian heresy
in 1501, Laurent Bureau, confessor to Louis XII and himself a renowned
preacher, proved sympathetic to the people's plight, remarking, "the clergy
ought to send competent preachers, and see that their flocks are not seduced,
rather than neglect them and punish them when they go astray."[2] Because
of the significant amount of scholarly attention paid to the Waldensians in
recent years, and the diminishing threat they posed to the church, we will
focus on individual cases of heresy before the Reformation.

The definition of heresy was not static; it changed according to the times
and to the individuals who led the church. The fluidity of the idea of heresy
is obvious from many scholars' attempts to define it. Bossy describes the
individual heresies of the later Middle Ages as "effervescences of orthodoxy
defined into exclusion by an unimaginative establishment."[3] M. D. Lambert,
who has studied the full range of medieval heresies, defines heresy as "whatever the papacy explicitly or implicitly condemned during the period."[4] It
"differed from orthodoxy and mere heterodoxy less in assumptions than emphasis and conclusions. It became heresy from pressing these too far."[5] Heresy
was extremism *within* an existing set of beliefs and the term was not applied
to the beliefs of non-Christians. A set of characteristics that had been developed during the early centuries of the church continued to be used in the
late Middle Ages to distinguish heretics from the rest of the Christian community. A heretic who persisted in his false beliefs, even when shown the

error of his ways, set himself up as an enemy of the church and the community at large.[6] The heretic differed from the orthodox believer in his isolation, pride, restlessness, fickleness, and intellectual dependence upon uncanonical sources. Earlier Church Fathers had developed a psychology of the heretic: "The heretic was a certain *kind* of person, not merely an honest, if misled, dissenter. Against the *consensus ecclesiae*, the common opinion of the Church, the heretic proudly posited a personal vision which threatened ecclesiastical unity, wholly ignoring scripture, tradition and creed."[7] Additional characteristics included: (1) a superficial appearance of piety, intended to deceive; (2) secrecy; and (3) obduracy or recidivism—"error became heresy when, shown his deviation, the obstinate one refused to obey and retract."[8] As such, he was a serious threat to society.

In a provocative article on deviant preaching in northern France between 1400 and 1500, Hervé Martin concludes that "this was a time of great intellectual ferment, a time of theological experimentation, of risk, of improvisation. It is impossible to formulate a model of deviance and to draw a portrait of the 'marginal' preacher. Rare are the themes on which there was general agreement."[9] Nevertheless, Martin identifies certain *thèmes-hantises,* obsessions, that occupied a number of preachers, with deviant or heterodox preaching occasionally found on both sides of a question. Martin lists the rivalry between mendicants and seculars, the issue of indulgences, the immaculate conception of the Virgin Mary, and the cult of the saints as some of the key issues that sparked extremist opinions.[10] This diversity of opinions continued in the preaching of the first reformers.

None of the pre-Reformation preachers in this study got into serious trouble for preaching heretical ideas; obviously if they had, their sermons would not have been printed. Therefore, we will examine a few of the most notorious examples in the registers of the Faculty of Theology: the cases of Jean Vitrier, Claude Cousin, Jean Laillier, and Jean Angeli.

We have already encountered Vitrier, the ardent and prolific preacher praised by Erasmus for his simple homiletic style and his zeal for preaching the gospels. In a series of sermons delivered in 1498 at Tournai, Vitrier denounced unreformed convents, concubinage among priests, and the cult of the saints.[11] Alarmed by such statements from a preacher of renown, the town council and the bishop joined to bring the case before the Faculty at Paris. Among Vitrier's propositions that were censured were the following:

(I) It would be better to cut the throat of your child than to place him in an unreformed monastery.

(V) If your curé or other priest has women in his house, you should go there yourself and drag them out.

(VI) Music during church services is nothing but lechery and provocation to lechery.

(X) Pardons [indulgences] come straight from hell.

(XI) When you hear the mass, you must not speak, and when the priest elevates the host, you should look at the ground and not at the sacrament.

(XII) You should not pray to the saints.

(XIV) There are some who say prayers to the Virgin Mary so that they can see her when they die. You will see the Devil, not the Blessed Virgin.

(XVI) I would rather be the cause of a man's death than go to bed with a woman.[12]

Although the exact disposition of the case is unknown, Godin believes that Vitrier was either able to justify his remarks or that he recanted in submission to the faculty's findings. In 1500, preaching in his home convent of Saint-Omer, Vitrier again became embroiled in controversy by "reproaching the stupid confidence people had that their sins would be remitted simply by throwing money into a chest."[13] It was not the wisest course to take considering his recent problems, for 1500 was a jubilee year, and the papacy was encouraging people to obtain indulgences. When he refused a bribe to keep silent, he was called before the bishop, who denounced several of his propositions. Once again, he appears to have emerged unscathed, but his biting invective and refusal to play by the rules finally took its toll in 1503 when he was relieved of his position as *gardien* of Saint-Omer, relegated to a convent of nuns in Courtrai, and forbidden to preach.[14]

The tradition of heretical preaching at Tournai was established even before Vitrier preached there. In 1482, the Franciscan Jean Angeli had been sent by the guardian of the Paris convent to preach in Tournai.[15] The result was a serious scandal. His remarks betray a special concern over the respective powers of mendicants and seculars:

(I) Franciscans approved by the bishop are true curés and have better title to this than the seculars, because the friars receive their power directly from the pope, while the seculars receive it at the hands of the bishop.

(II) A parishioner can make his annual confession to a Franciscan, even without the authorization of his curé.

(III) If a curé refuses to administer the sacrament of the altar to a parishioner who has confessed to a Franciscan, then the Franciscan can administer it himself.

(V) A curé who teaches his parishioners that they must confess to him is excommunicated.

(VI) Anyone who has the mass celebrated by a priest who has a concubine sins mortally.

(VIII) The pope can do away with canon law and replace it with a new law.

(IX) Certain saints are *enragés*. [The meaning of this statement is not entirely clear. It was, however, sufficiently unorthodox to warrant condemnation by the Paris theologians.]

(X) The pope has jurisdiction over the souls in purgatory, and if he wants to, he can release them all.[16]

(XI) The pope can take away half of the revenues of a churchman and give them to another without giving any reason.

(XII) Anyone who opposes the will of the pope acts like a pagan, and can be excommunicated. No one can reprove the pope, except in matters of heresy.[17]

The cathedral chapter immediately reacted to this challenge to the powers of the secular clergy. They summoned Angeli to appear before them, demanding that he retract his statements. He refused to comply, and went on to deliver a sermon the following Sunday that touched on many of the same issues. The royal *bailli* intervened, and at this point Angeli saw the wisdom of taking his message elsewhere. The controversy did not end with Angeli's removal; the Franciscans and the chapter engaged in heated legal disputes over their respective rights, particularly the right of "free preaching." Both the Parlement of Paris and the Faculty of Theology interceded, and an agreement was finally reached whereby the friars agreed to retract Angeli's statements and respect the rights of the chapter, while the chapter agreed to allow the Franciscans jurisdiction over their own affairs and preaching.[18]

On the eve of the Reformation, in 1516, Claude Cousin, a Dominican bachelor of theology from Champagne got into trouble for his preaching in Beauvais. A number of the doctrines he preached bear a strong resemblance to Angeli's articles.

(I) Anyone who marries the son or daughter of a priest, and receives dower money from the priest, must restore that money under pain of damnation.

(III) The Franciscans and the Dominicans are the real priests and are to be preferred to parish priests, because they are given their power by the pope while the curés have it from the bishop alone.

(IV) The said friars can absolve sins that curés cannot.

(V) If a parishioner confesses to a mendicant, he does not have to make confession to or present himself to his parish priest.

(VI) If a curé refuses to administer the sacrament of the altar to a parishioner who has confessed to a friar, the friar shall administer the sacrament.

(VII) A parish priest who preaches that his parishioners must confess to him once a year is excommunicated.

(IX) A parish priest is not permitted to take anything from his parishioners for hearing confession or administering the sacraments; if he does, he is a simoniac.

(X) Parishioners who pay their curés or vicars for the administration of the sacraments sin.

(XI) People, I counsel you not to give anything to them for the sacraments, so that they will no longer be so anxious to confess you out of their avarice; nor will they try to stop you from confessing to the Dominicans or Franciscans.

(XII) I have preached before more important people than those at Beauvais without being reproached.

> (XIII) I have a *teston* from Champagne, which is worth more than a *teston* or a *teston* and a half from Picardy.[19]

Sometimes the arrogance of a particular assertion (XII), or its very oddness (XIII) seems to have led to its condemnation. When the bishop brought the case before the Faculty of Theology, Cousin protested that he had not intended to say anything that was contrary to sacred scripture, the councils, or the learned doctors of Paris. Evidently his meekness satisfied the faculty, for on October 1, 1516, they decided to permit Cousin to continue his theological studies over the protests of the bishop of Beauvais.[20]

Another late fifteenth-century preacher, Jean Laillier, a priest and master of arts, licensed in theology, and later a staunch opponent of Standonck's reforming measures,[21] put forward several heretical statements in his public Sorbonica, which he was ordered to retract by the Faculty of Theology. These display a real hostility toward Rome:

> (I) Peter was not given power or primacy by Christ over the other apostles.

> (II) All members of the church hierarchy have equal power as given by Christ.

> (III) The pope is not able to remit all the punishments given out to sinners, even when his indulgences are just.

> (IV) Confession is not part of the divine law.

> (V) If you want me to speak about the supreme pontiff, I will completely demolish the whole edifice.

> (VI) Simple priests are useless.

> (IX) Decretals of the pope are nothing more than meaningless trifles.

> (X) The Roman church is not the head of all other churches.[22]

During his examination, Laillier expressed serious reservations about sainthood, asserting that in his day and age only the rich were canonized, and that for his part he did not believe in their sanctity. Consistent with his other statements, Laillier traced this problem to the pope, who "will canonize anyone if given a certain amount of ducats."[23] He went on to advise his audience that they, too, should refuse to believe in saints of this sort. Laillier pointed out that Eastern Orthodox priests did not sin by marrying[24] and argued that "from the time of our Lord up until the days of Gregory VII, [priests] were married."[25] Laillier was forced to retract his statements publicly, and while absolved by the faculty, remained under threat of excommunication if he ever again took up these propositions.[26]

There are strong similarities in the condemned articles of these preachers. The sermons of Cousin and Angeli show the degree to which quarrels between mendicants and seculars had intruded on popular preaching, with Angeli's preaching being the result of an unusually bitter conflict between local factions. The dispute over rights to confer the sacraments not only centered on the origins of their power, but on the mendicants' ability to collect alms. Laillier's bias against Rome may also have been due to mendicant-secular rivalry, but some of his statements were so extreme that a censure for heresy seems to have been warranted. Vitrier's assertions, on the other hand, display no particular special concern or anxiety, but show strong tendencies toward reformation and asceticism to which all his biographers attest.

Other pre-Reformation heretical preaching included debates over Mary's immaculate conception, clerical celibacy, and exegetical issues. Intending to employ the scholastic debating technique of first presenting one side of an issue and then refuting it, Jean Grillot preached a morning sermon at Saint-Germain l'Auxerrois in Paris in which he expressed the tenet that Mary was conceived in original sin, a subject which in earlier times had set Dominicans against Franciscans.[27] Unfortunately, his listeners were not aware that he was planning to tell the other side in the afternoon session, and the crowd began to murmur against the preacher, leading to his examination by the Faculty of Theology. Sometimes a preacher was called before the Faculty for preaching theologically controversial issues, as in 1507, when Johan Berger preached in La Rochelle that "God began to be at a certain instant of time and in some future instant will no longer be."[28] Here the theologians simply warned Berger not to preach such doctrines to the people, although he could continue to discuss them within the confines of the schools or monasteries.

If we look at some of the same issues in the sermons of the preachers, we can get a better idea of what constituted heresy in the decades before the Reformation. Vitrier had argued that one should not pray to the saints. Early in the fifteenth century, Pierre d'Ailly had argued against the growing "cult" of the saints in *De reformatione* (1416), a position also held by Jean Gerson.[29] The preachers studied in this book, following the official church position set forth by Basil of Caesarea (ca. 329–379), condemned idol worship, insisting that people understand the meaning behind the representations. They stressed proper motivation toward and understanding of the saints and their images, but did not attack sainthood as such.

Clerical avarice and immorality were some of the most commonly sounded themes in the sermons. But on questions of priestly morality and the conferral of the sacraments, the preachers were generally more circumspect than the preachers censured for heresy. The preachers in this study condemned clerical concubinage and avarice, pointing out that such men jeopardized the souls in their care. Menot questions the value of absolution obtained from "a priest who asks for nothing more than that you hurry along your confession and cross his palm with silver. He then gives you absolution and says: 'Go, friend.' I ask you, where does such absolution lead? Straight to the devil."[30] But on the right to confer the sacraments, Maillard introduces a cautionary note: "If from devotion you go to one of the mendicant's churches, you still must not take the sacraments from the hands of anyone but your parish priest without his permission, except for the sacrament of penance, which you are permitted to receive from a mendicant."[31] In statements about priests and their sacramental duties, there is a distinct difference between the kind of comments made by the preachers included in this study and those censured for heresy.

The remarks made by the former were both censorious and abusive, but fairly general. More important, none of them challenged the authority of sinful priests to carry out their sacerdotal duties, nor did they speak of inefficacy or damnation for the recipient of sacraments conferred by a sinning priest. They condemned the priests and relates as individual sinners, but did not question the ecclesiastical order or encourage the laity to disobey their priests.

The hotly debated issue of indulgences sparked heterodox opinion on both sides, but in this case even the orthodox position was not clear. The preachers studied here were of one mind, feeling that the sale of indulgences was neither theologically sound nor efficacious. Only the inward act of piety that inspired the purchase would contribute to salvation. Similarly, the question of ecclesiastical compulsion could be expressed in both an orthodox and heterodox manner. As we will see in the next chapter, the heretic Aimé Meigret argued vehemently against laws that were coercive, giving as examples the church's rules on celibacy and fasting. Menot expressed virtually the same thoughts, but *without* the examples: "I say that the law binds, and he who is bound is not able to do things voluntarily, with free will."[32] The context of the statement is important. Meigret was attacking some of the basic tenets of the church, while Menot was discussing the Law and free will.

One other issue exercised the religious imagination of the late Middle Ages. The debate over the uniqueness or plurality of Magdalenes occupied the Faculty of Theology from 1517 to 1520, ending in its formal condemnation of the notion of three distinct Marys. Mary Magdalene, Mary of Bethany, and the unidentified sinner who washed Jesus' feet were henceforth to be considered one, a decision that called into question the philosophical and critical methods that had arrived at the plurality.[33] The issue had exercised the great minds of the era, with Clichtove and Lefèvre d'Étaples both arguing that this was more a historical question than one of faith.[34] However, Clichtove quickly retracted his belief in the plurality after the faculty's action. In one of Pepin's sermons in the *Conciones domini totius anni* (according to one unverified source, first published in 1520, although Farge's exhaustive survey found no editions before 1526), he says: "the appearance of three Mary gathered together in one signifies that God appears through his grace to all true believers to be three and one."[35] The statement is ambiguous, perhaps by design, but it shows a certain temerity in view of the faculty's finding. On the other hand, Aimé Meigret's outspoken adherence to the idea of three Marys even after the faculty's decision alerted the authorities that he was someone to be watched carefully.

Except for isolated outbreaks of Waldensianism, heresy before Luther was an individual and usually not terribly serious affair. A statement in isolation, provided it was not too extreme, was not taken too seriously, but several unorthodox assertions made a preacher suspect. Apart from Meigret, we seldom find two questionable statements in one sermon by any of the preachers who are the central concern of this book, but the same cannot be said for Vitrier, Laillier, Angeli, and Cousin.[36] Laillier's sermon, in particular, challenged the church hierarchy and its practices. The ecclesiastical establishment, including the preachers studied in this book, felt that preaching of this sort would lead to confusion, scandals, and irreverence among the people.

In the years before the Reformation, heterodoxy flourished, as churchmen began to question some of the church's teachings in the process of trying to correct the problems that had led to the Avignonese residence and the Western Schism. A preacher's heterodoxy rarely posed a serious threat to the church, and the taint of heresy adhered only in particularly outrageous or persistent cases. But at the end of the Middle Ages, the gray area between heterodoxy and heresy was narrowing, to be closed almost completely by the words and actions of Martin Luther.

11

Heretical Preaching
after the Reformation

> In times past there were false prophets among God's people, and among
> you also there will be false teachers who will smuggle in pernicious her-
> esies. They will go so far as to deny the Master who acquired them for
> his own, thereby bringing on themselves swift disaster. Their lustful ways
> will lure many away. Through them, the true way will be made subject
> to contempt.
> 2 Peter 2:1–2

Although heresy had been a recurring problem for the Christian church during
the fifteen hundred years of its existence, the combination of advances in
scholarship and technology, increasing literacy and expectations among the
laity, and Luther's distinctive new theology provided the most serious challenge the Western Christian community had ever faced. The years around
1520 produced some of the most interesting preaching in the history of the
Western church, but unfortunately in France, almost no "Protestant" sermons
have survived. Many of the reformers did not share the Catholics preachers'
enthusiasm for preserving their sermons,[1] nor did they wish to endanger their
lives and work unnecessarily. In some cases, publication of a questionable
sermon was approved, but for unknown reasons it was never printed.[2] In
another case, three volumes of manuscript sermons by the heretic Pierre
Alexandre were burned by the Inquisition in Brussels.[3] The one sermon that
did survive, published by the Dominican Aimé Meigret in 1524, must be
supplemented with material from the Faculty of Theology registers and the
chronicles and memoirs of the period. In addition, I have used some sermons
by Calvin and Viret. Although they were delivered and printed in Switzerland,
both men had preached in France, and their sermons would have been as
important to French Protestant preachers as were the sermons of the great
late medieval preachers to lesser clerics.

The history and spread of early Protestantism in France has been well
documented.[4] In its very earliest phases, French Protestantism is difficult to
distinguish from the evangelical Catholicism epitomized by Bishop Guillaume
Briçonnet and the circle of Meaux. Evangelism, primitivism, Platonism, and
Christocentrism, which reached their highest expression in the works of Le-

189

fèvre,[5] were an outgrowth of the strong tendencies toward reformation in the late fifteenth century, and without Luther's challenge to the Catholic Church, it is unlikely that these ideas would have incurred censure. But Luther's actions had a revolutionary effect on the church and its hierarchy, forcing an unspoken change in the definition of heresy and an unwillingness to tolerate the kind of heterodoxy that had flourished at the end of the fifteenth century.

Under Francis I, reformers and evangelical Catholics had reason to hope for the progress of new ideas in France. Although not himself a scholar, this Renaissance prince was a patron of learning and the arts, often willing to intercede on behalf of reformers who had incurred the wrath of the Catholic establishment. With the encouragement of his reform-minded sister, Marguerite of Navarre, he extended royal protection to scholars, printers, and even to young reformers such as Calvin. The end of the first phase of reform coincided with two major developments—growing repression after the Affair of the Placards (17–18 October 1534) and especially during the reign of Henry II (1547–1559), and the evolution of French Protestantism away from the evangelical reformism of men such as Gérard Roussel and even the Lutheranism of François Lambert toward the more militant and activist religion of Guillaume Farel and John Calvin.

Recruitment during the first phase of reform had come primarily from preachers already ordained or in religious orders. By contrast, the second phase was marked by a concerted effort to form leaders specially trained in the new theology and preaching methods. Calvin's academy in Geneva was the place of formation for men in this latter category.[6] The selection of a minister was a difficult matter for members of the Reformed Church, because of the seriousness of the post and the secrecy required. Often a local boy would be sent to Geneva with the understanding that upon completing his course of study, he would return to become pastor of his community. The town of Aubénas made a typical arrangement: "M. Claude de Cabanes, inhabitant of Aubénas in the Vivarais, a man of learning and honest conversation, with the goodness to profit from the church and the Lord; having these ends in mind we have given him money according to our small ability to go to Geneva, where he will stay for two or three months to study for the ministry."[7] The inhabitants of Uzès had done likewise, but when their candidate did not return within a reasonable amount of time, they wrote to Geneva pleading for his immediate dispatch.[8] Individual citizens often sought Calvin's help in procuring a pastor for them.[9] At Angoulême, the inhabitants asked for someone who could "not only preach, but also give lessons in theology to young people to prepare them for the ministry."[10] If a town did not send anyone for training, the selection and assignment process was left up to the Genevan Company.[11] Although a town could indicate special needs or requirements, there were simply not enough Calvinist pastors to go around.[12] In such uncertain times, even a "Catholic" preacher might work out well for Protestant sympathizers. At Marseilles and Courthézon in 1543, the city notables had hired Raphaël de Podio, who, despite his claim to be the king's ambassador to the Ottoman Empire, turned out to be a notorious heretic. But so satisfied were the officials with his preaching that when the prior of Notre-Dame-des-Doms sent his notary and vice-procurer to investigate, they were met by an armed crowd and forced to retreat without the suspect.[13]

"Protestant" preachers often began their careers at a significantly younger age than their Catholic counterparts. While some of the earliest reformers had begun theology programs in Catholic universities, many abandoned them either to go to Geneva to study, or to begin preaching immediately. Having come from the Pays de Vaud to study for the priesthood at the Collège de Montaigu in 1527, Pierre Viret followed this course when the situation in Paris became uncomfortable. By 1530, his outspokenness forced him to return to his native Switzerland, where on May 5, 1531, at the age of twenty, he was ordained by Farel and began to preach in Orbe.[14]

Although Catholics misinterpreted Luther's understanding of the "priesthood of all believers" to include a ministry by women, there is evidence that some women were spreading the Protestant message at mid century. In 1556, two Genevan women named Marguerite and Jacqueline conducted nocturnal *prêches* (Protestant services) in the cellars of Montélimar.[15]

A Protestant preacher had numerous obstacles in the way of his ministry, most notably the need for discretion and sometimes secrecy. In the beginning, when some mendicants espoused the new faith but had not yet discarded their habits, it was possible to preach in churches. Jean Michel regularly preached in Bourges at Notre-Dame-du-Fourchaud from the mid 1530s until his eventual condemnation and execution in 1539. But as the breach widened between the two faiths, this practice became more difficult.

Not surprisingly, many of the early reformers chose the same places for preaching as did their Catholic counterparts. Farel preached in the cemetery when the pulpits of the two churches in Payerne were closed to him,[16] saying that he was willing to take his message anywhere—"to the city gates, into the parishes, to open fields, and into private homes."[17] The preacher at the fair of Guibray in Normandy in 1561 spoke in a walled enclosure, protected by forty men and half a dozen halberdiers.[18] But the dangers attendant on these *prêches* made private homes the primary meeting places for Protestants. Claude Haton, a Catholic observer, gives this account of the meetings:

> The Lutherans hold secret assemblies day and night at which they preach to each other, inside and outside of the city, in the home of one of the members. Here they hold the service of the Lord and sing his praises. One of them reads a chapter of the Old or New Testament from a printed French Bible, which pleases the assembly greatly. Then they read another chapter, from the books of Exodus or Deuteronomy, which tells of the laws God gave to Moses on stone tablets. These Lutherans claim to be the true observers of the Law. To move the hearts of each other and especially the new adherents, they sing some of the Psalms of David, which were translated into French by Clément Marot, two or three times. These praises are sung

at the beginning, middle, and end of the ceremony, which they call a *prêche*.
Then they all embrace one another and the preacher talks of the love they
must have for each other.[19]

Although the account degenerates into a salacious description of what forms
their love took, the recital up to that point seems fairly accurate. In a well-
known painting of a Protestant *prêche* at the Temple of Lyon,[20] the preacher
speaks from a central pulpit and the people (and a dog) stand or sit on benches
scattered throughout the room and on the balcony above. The informality of
the gathering is one of its most striking features.

In the beginning, French Protestants often preached at the hours that had
been normal in the pre-Reformation period, although they began preaching
at other times because of their desire to reach as many people as possible.
In 1525 Gérard Roussel wrote excitedly to Briçonnet about what he had
observed in Strasbourg: "From five to six in the morning there are sermons
in several churches and common prayers are said. Then at seven the same is
done, and at eight or thereabouts a sermon is delivered in the cathedral. . . .
In the same church a sermon is given again at four o'clock in the afternoon."[21]
The chronicler Glaumeau relates that on Sundays in Bourges the people were
accustomed to hearing a sermon between eight and nine.[22] In that same city,
Jean Michel regularly preached at noon,[23] which was not a time his parishioners normally came to hear the Word preached. But this time soon proved
amenable to Catholics as well, and the archbishop of Bourges mandated the
preaching of a noon sermon in 1561.[24] In Provins, Haton mentions regular
sermons at eight, nine, ten, and twelve[25] while at Guibray, a heretical Franciscan from the local convent preached at four in the afternoon.[26] In private
homes *prêches* were often held in the evening,[27] for the cloak of darkness
offered Protestants some protection from their Catholic enemies. Unfortunately for the Protestants, it also led to rumors of indecent behavior.

Where sermons could be given publicly, the size of the crowd seems to
have equalled the large numbers attracted by Catholic preachers. Most of the
figures come from the 1560s, but there is no reason to suppose that large
attendance at Protestant sermons was a new phenomenon. Viret is said to
have preached to eight thousand people in Nîmes,[28] while the elderly pastor
Godard may have spoken to as many as thirteen thousand people in one day
in different areas of the Pays de Caux.[29] Despite civic prohibitions, some three
thousand men and women assembled in Saint-Maixent to hear the preaching
of the heretic Pivet,[30] and Beza spoke to crowds of more than twenty thousand
in Paris after the Colloquy of Poissy in 1561.[31] Even allowing for the customary
inflation of figures, there can be little doubt that Protestant preachers drew
very large crowds, often rivaling or surpassing their Catholic counterparts.

As with Catholic sermons, and in some cases even more so because of the
now charged atmosphere, public Protestant preaching often evoked strong
crowd reactions. If people came to sermons out of curiosity before the Reformation, this was even more true after the Reformation began. Haton relates
the scene that occurred when the Dominicans appointed Jean Nynost as their
Lenten preacher in 1554. The townspeople looked at one another and began

muttering: "Who is this? Is this the preacher the Jacobins are providing us with? No one will come." On Ash Wednesday, the listeners and those who came to "see the preacher but not to listen to him" were unhappy, exchanging glances, and saying, "'It is not who we thought it would be.' The others answered, 'Yes, it is, it is he.' Others commented, 'No, he does not preach as well as the other one'; yet others, 'It is he.' But in the end, all agreed, saying, 'He preached well, we should come back tomorrow'."[32] While Calvin was often unhappy at the lethargic response he received, complaining of "so many stupid people, who are not touched at all, and who are moved no more than stones,"[33] less passive reactions were quite common. Women were often involved in such confrontations, as was the case when various noblewomen in Bourges menaced a Catholic preacher with their taborets.[34] In Metz in 1525, a group of *évangeliennes* got into trouble for meeting regularly to discuss Lutheran ideas, read scripture, and even add glosses of their own to their Bibles.[35] After receiving instruction in scripture from her master in La Rochelle, a Poitevin servant girl, Marie Bécaudelle, returned to her native Essars, where she vociferously remonstrated with "a friar who did not preach the Word of God, which she demonstrated to him by quoting passages of scripture."[36] She suffered martyrdom for her efforts. In 1555, the duchess of Guise, Anna d'Este, dabbled in heresy by publicly supporting a preacher named Boturnus, prior of the Hôtel-Dieu of Provins, who had been recommended by her mother, Renée of France, duchess of Ferrara.[37] Two years later, the duchess made Boturnus her almoner, stretching her husband's patience to its limit. After hearing from the pope that this preacher "was one of the most contemptible and greatest heretics in Christianity,"[38] the duke threatened his wife that if she did not remove Boturnus from her household, she would be sorry. This had the desired effect, but not before the duchess had urged the preacher to flee the realm to save his life. In the same year, thirty-five women were among the 130 people prosecuted after the forcible interruption of a Calvinist service in the rue Saint-Jacques.[39] On the eve of the religious wars, women comprised one-third of an armed escort leading a Genevan minister into the town of Gignac.[40]

Women were not the only ones to react strongly to religious controversy. When Michel began to deliver one of his sermons at Bourges, a local official in the audience stood up and interrupted him, beginning to intone the omitted Ave Maria himself. Heckled by men and women in the audience, the official had to desist.[41] When an inquisitor of the faith, Mathieu Ory, later tried to undo the damage he felt Michel had done, he only made matters worse. Reporters of the scene, no doubt with Protestant sympathies, claimed that he began his sermon in a low and effeminate voice, then suddenly began raging like a bull, so that his speech became known as the "sermon of the trumpet." Witnesses deplored the fact that he knew nothing of doctrine.[42] One of the more picturesque incidents occurred during Farel's preaching in Montbéliard in 1524. A Franciscan *gardien* arose in church to castigate the reformer, arousing the anger of both Frenchmen and Germans in the congregation. Ulrich, duke of Württemburg, suzerain of the region, appeared personally in the church, where he threatened the Franciscan that he would return with his harquebusiers and halberdiers if he did not desist. Unintimidated by these threats, the *gardien* mounted the pulpit of another church and denounced Farel, resulting in his own imprisonment by the duke.[43]

Actual violence was not uncommon. When the Faculty of Theology substituted Jean Corion for the reputed heretic Michel Mazurier, a riot ensued in which the preacher was struck by one of his listeners.[44] In 1560, a congregation went on a rampage in Caen after a sermon, throwing stones and breaking windows,[45] while the peasants of the Limousin drove the preachers away with stones and pitchforks, "as if they were werewolves."[46] Although both Luther and Calvin deplored religious violence and advised their followers not to engage in iconoclasm, many felt the issues too keenly to refrain. Some preachers argued against the practice of placing candles in front of images, and seemed unwilling or unable to foresee the possible consequences of their remarks.[47] Farel's hot-tempered preaching often resulted in idol smashing, leading to many of his problems with local authorities.[48] The diarist Leriche details certain iconoclastic incidents that occurred in Poitiers. Interestingly, in Poitiers it was not the preaching of a Protestant that led to an iconoclastic outbreak, but rather the Easter sermon of a Dominican preaching in his own convent. "There was a great riot against the preacher and his convent, where the people broke down the doors, smashed the images and broke the windows."[49] When the Calvinist preacher Guy de Morange arrived in Anduze, a huge crowd greeted him, and after his sermon, "they began wandering about the village at night, breaking crucifixes and smashing statues of the Virgin, afterwards receiving the approval of their minister."[50]

The king's officials sometimes came to the aid of a preacher whose sermons had gotten him into trouble. This was the case in Provins after Charles Privé preached certain "scandalous doctrines." M. Nicolle Barengeon, *élu* for the king in Provins, admitted that he had been at Privé's sermons, and "after conferring with his wife, who had also been in attendance, he announced to his interrogators that he thought Privé had preached very well, and that he had spoken the truth without disguising it, unlike so many others." Even though Barengeon and his brothers were "secret Lutheran heretics,"[51] it is interesting to note that when the statements were not directed against the king or other elected officials, action was often deferred.

Various measures were employed to try to prevent the preacher of one or the other faith from proceeding with his sermon. The mendicants of Bourges would sing masses for the dead when Jean Michel preached, but this backfired when Michel's adherents began to cry out against them, knocking over their books, and chasing them out of the church.[52] The ringing of church bells was used to silence Claude Dieudonné and Farel during their mission to Aigle.[53] In Amiens in 1558, the Dominican preacher could not be heard "because of the great noise that many people made while wandering about the church."[54] This was clearly intended to disrupt the sermon, unlike the ordinary movement about which preachers regularly complained, for a provision was made that in the future the town's *huissier* and two dozen night patrolmen would guard the church doors, closing them after all of the faithful had left. In Pézenas, the house where the preachers had lodged was burned to the ground,[55] while at Grandson the Franciscans broke the Protestant preacher's pulpit.[56] Gérard Roussel's preaching was ended forever at Mauléon when an ardent Catholic took a hatchet to his pulpit while he was preaching. Pinned under the collapsed structure, Roussel was dragged free by his supporters, but died en route to Oléron.[57]

The structure of a sermon was one area in which Protestants and Catholics differed significantly. When Luther first unleashed his attack on certain practices of the Roman Catholic Church, his method of sermon construction still contained significant medieval elements, even if the literal text of the Bible always guided him. His sermon style has been described as "heroic disorder," a not always happy mélange of medieval scholasticism and simple scriptural exegesis.[58] As one commentator states, "the contents of Luther's sermons determined their form. Filled with a zeal to convey his evangelical theology to his audience, he showed little or no concern for composition and style." His sermons, as well as those of most reformers, could be classified as "kerygmatic, didactic, paracletic, and polemic."[59] Like medieval Catholic preachers, Luther realized that the same message and form was not appropriate for all listeners, for the gospel could only be addressed to "those who are trying seriously to embody the law in their lives."[60]

In much the same way as Counter-Reformation writers had done, later sixteenth-century Protestant theorists realized the problems inherent in a too-literal interpretation. While biblical texts had to remain the basis for all preaching, the *De formandis concionibus sacris seu de interpretatione Scripturarum populari* of Andreas Hyperius prescribed five categories that must be dealt with in preaching: (1) doctrine; (2) refutation of error; (3) morals; (4) correction; and (5) consolation.[61] As Protestantism came to enjoy a more settled status, form and style began to emerge as important considerations. The sermons of both Calvin and Viret are more centrally unified and stylistically conceived than those of the earliest Protestants. Calvin's sermons perfectly embody the plain style (see Chapter 4). When choosing his text for a day, he would comment on Old Testament verses during working days, New Testament texts on Sunday mornings, and Psalms and the New Testament on Sunday afternoons.[62] He usually followed the texts sequentially from day to day, or Sunday to Sunday, a practiced copied by many other reformers.

But in some ways, the reformers did not differ as much as they would have liked to believe from their pre-Reformation counterparts. While it is true that most of the reformers adopted the plain style because of its suitability for simple biblical commentary and exegesis, the earliest reformers retained some of the rhetorical schemata, probably in an effort to persuade people by proven methods and because many had been trained in this form of preaching. Viret continued the scholastic tradition of using a protheme to introduce the main body of the sermon, and even resorted to zoological analogies: "Today savage beasts, ravenous wolves, and tyrants have all banded together against the poor church of God."[63] Robert Scribner has shown that "by the later part

Table 11-1. Citation of Old Testament Books by Protestant Preachers.

Book	Number of citations	Percentage of quotations
Psalms	52	25
Isaiah	44	21
Genesis	19	9
Exodus	13	6
Jeremiah	12	6
Deuteronomy	10	5
Numbers	9	4
Samuel	8	4
Kings	6	3
Proverbs	5	2
Other	29	14

of the sixteenth century, animal allegories were a stock part of the Protestant propaganda repertoire."[64] Many of the themes prevalent before 1517 reappear in the sermons of Calvin, who was more interested in problems of earthly morality than the more literal and theologically minded Luther.[65] In spite of their desire to convey a purely scriptural message, many Protestants realized the need to amuse and delight their audience while at the same time attacking their opponents.

If we briefly examine usage of biblical books in a small sample of sermons (fifty-three) given by Calvin, Viret, and Meigret, we find some significant differences between Protestants and Catholics, but the similarities are also striking. Protestants, no doubt because of their desire to simplify their sermons, used significantly fewer references, with an average of twelve per sermon. Of 611 citations, 99.5 percent (607) are biblical, the four "other" references being used by Meigret.

In this small sample, we find that Calvin and Viret used the New Testament twice as much as the Old, which was also true of post-Reformation Catholic preachers. Significantly, while the gospel of Matthew was the most quoted of New Testament books (Table 11-1), the Pauline epistles as a group provided the bulk of the quotations (Table 11-2). Romans and Corinthians were used with approximately the same frequency as had been done by the Catholic preachers examined in this study, but the use of other Pauline epistles makes Paul dominant in Protestant New Testament usage. The emphasis on the Pauline epistles reflects not only the concept of faith alone, but also a theology that gave primary emphasis to the Resurrection and only secondary attention to the events of Jesus' life. The mystical and allegorical aspects of the books

Table 11-2. Citation of Sections of the Old Testament by Protestant Preachers.

Section	Number of citations	Percentage of quotations
Prophetic Books	81	39
Wisdom Books	60	29
Pentateuch	51	25
Historical Books	15	7

Table 11-3. Citation of New Testament Books by Protestant Preachers.

Book	Number of citations	Percentage of quotations
Matthew	67	17
Corinthians	53	13
Romans	51	13
Luke	36	9
Acts	27	7
Hebrews	27	7
John	26	7
Colossians	18	5
Ephesians	17	4
Timothy	16	4
Other	62	15

of John and Revelation were obviously less amenable to Protestants, who used them less frequently.

One-third of all citations come from the Old Testament, with Psalms quoted most often (Table 11-3). There is, however, a significant change in emphasis on sections of the Old Testament, with the prophetic books providing the greatest number of texts (Table 11-4). The Protestants in this sample used the historical books to the same degree as the post-Reformation Catholics, but less often than the pre-Reformation preachers. While the historical books were used freely by both Protestant and Catholic pamphleteers by the second half of the sixteenth century,[66] this is not true of the sermons, despite the utility of Old Testament historical lessons for propagandistic purposes. The books of Isaiah and Genesis remained important, while an increase in the use of Numbers and Deuteronomy by the Protestants reflects the legalistic bent of Calvinism and the Protestant concern with the Law and grace. Most significantly, Protestants discarded the Apocrypha, reducing the importance of the sapiential books as a whole. Wisdom and Sirach were heavily utilized by Catholics, and their absence from Protestant sermons increased the importance of the prophetic books as a group. Similarly, the greater antiquity of the prophetic books, already demonstrated by Hebraïsts, naturally appealed to Protestants, whose interest in biblical philology led them to place a higher value on the older texts.

The most dramatic and obvious change made by the Reformation was the omission of secondary authorities, although Meigret referred to Augustine, Ambrose, and Gerson. In their sermons, the Protestants adhered rigidly to

Table 11-4. Citation of Sections of the New Testament by Protestant Preachers.

Section	Number of citations	Percentage of quotations
Pauline epistles	209	52
Gospels	139	35
Acts	27	7
Revelations	1	—
Other epistles	24	6

the tenet of *sola scriptura,* although they freely admitted the value of patristic and other authorities when these were in harmony with scripture. But aside from the use of nonbiblical authors, the differences between Protestants and Catholics were not as great as we might expect.

Early "Heretics"

> It is obvious what proceeds from the flesh: lewd conduct, impurity, licentiousness, idolatry, sorcery, hostilities, bickering, jealousy, outbursts of rage, selfish rivalries, dissensions, factions.   Galatians 5:19–20

Thanks to the attention given to "Lutheran" heresy in France in the 1520s by the Paris Faculty of theology, we are well informed about the doctrines that were preached. While the registers of determinations are not an unbiased source, they seem to provide a reasonably accurate summary of what was being preached, and often include responses by the accused to various points. The plurality of Marys was a regular topic brought up by the reforming circle at Meaux, reflecting their interest in biblical philology and exegesis, and Mazurier expounded this belief to his congregation in Meaux cathedral. One of his colleagues, Pierre Caroli, later a professor at Viret's academy in Lausanne, was also brought before the faculty in 1524. Caroli argued against ecclesiastical compulsion, praying to the saints, and the requirements of fasting and abstinence. Not surprisingly, considering his connections, Caroli displayed particular concern for scriptural primacy and preaching. According to him, "holy scripture is now understood better than ever before, and was not well-interpreted in the past." He argued that preaching was not the sole preserve of theologians, "for God can illuminate the heart of a woman with the true sense of scripture, if she has a simple goodness in her."[67] Another doctor of theology, Jean Bernard, jailed with Meigret in 1526,[68] questioned the role of the church and its hierarchy: "I doubt that the church has the power to obligate under pain of damnation." He further insisted that one must pray to God before addressing one's prayers to the saints, and added that he had never read in scripture that one saint could pray to God for another.[69]

On the issue of faith and grace, Étienne Lecourt argued that a man without grace could do nothing for his salvation; he could not be saved by his own merits. In this case, it was not so much what a reformer said as how he said it. Lecourt did not explicitly challenge the existence of purgatory, but made the unusual assertion that if the pope could liberate souls from purgatory, it would be evil to do so, for people needed to be purged. Although these statements were closely examined, it was his propositions concerning the saints, vernacular translations of the Bible, and the mass that attracted the most attention. His third proposition, which stated that the "saints have no power, and it is pure folly to go on pilgrimages and offer candles to their images," was censured as Lutheran. Another statement could have been considered an incitement to iconoclasm: "If the bones of Saint Peter were in my church, I would bury them honorably in the ground; but if my parishioners went to venerate them, I would myself take the bones and put them in a sack and throw them into the river."[70] In his fifth proposition, Lecourt insisted that everyone should have the Bible in French, while his eighth proposition argued that merchants would be better off keeping their children at home than sending them to mass. In the last (ninth) proposition extracted from his preaching, he insisted that scripture had been too long hidden in the Latin tongue, and that women were capable of interpreting it as well as bishops. For this statement, he was condemned for Waldensianism.

In 1523, Arnold de Bronosse preached certain doctrines at Saint-Médard in the Paris suburbs that challenged papal power, and argued that "it is stupid to believe that it is a more serious sin to eat meat on Good Friday or any other Friday than to lie or deceive your neighbor."[71] Despite his own lack of orthodoxy, Bronosse had turned in Jean Finet for scandalous preaching a few months earlier.[72]

The propositions advanced by Jacques Pavannes, one of Briçonnet's collaborators, were clearly heretical. Pavannes spent considerable time refuting the doctrines of purgatory and confession, and along with Mathieu Saunier, preached that candles and other offerings to the saints were idolatrous. He supported iconoclasm, and attacked the mass, which "does nothing to aid in the remission of sins." Saunier qualified this by saying that Christ instituted the sacrament for the living, not the dead, adding that it was better to hear one good sermon than one hundred masses. This statement was similar to one made by one of the preachers included in this study, Jacques Merlin, but it was seen as dangerous in the context of so many other heretical propositions. Finally, Saunier attacked baptism and holy water.[73]

Farel also attacked ecclesiastical compulsion:

> Christ prescribed a very definite rule of life for us, and it is permitted to no one to add or subtract from this rule. This rule is the basis of Christian liberty and annuls the tyranny of human constitutions, but leaves intact the civil power, of which no one is free. One must not put one's faith for salvation in oneself, but rather in God; as a consequence, one must not attach oneself to an order or a habit, to continence or abstinence, or to ceremonies and prayers other than those in scripture. Jesus Christ alone is to be honored.[74]

Farel's violent and abusive style, which earned him the nickname of "Phallicus" from Erasmus,[75] first marked him as a heretic in the eyes of the church. He thundered from the pulpit that "all those who say mass are evil men, murderers, thieves, deniers of the passion of Jesus Christ, and seducers of the people."[76] Despite an initial disclaimer, Farel worked himself into a righteous passion in his personal account of his preaching in a missive to the Council of Bern:

> I have exhorted, invited, and instructed my brethren to live fraternally as pious Christians; to wrong no one, but to respect each other's interests; to give heart and soul to God in true faith, honor, praise, and obedience to

him to whom these things are due, to acquire a true love and knowledge of God by the renunciation of their worldliness and arrogance. I have also taught that our works do not conform to the commandments of God. . . . I have blasted false oaths. . . . I have also preached that the religious observation of feast days has become for too many people the occasion for debauchery, drunkenness, quarrels, lewdness, and other violations of the divine law. I have condemned the lack of respect shown toward parents. I have also denounced the irascibility and the hatred that people show toward their neighbors, for he who hates his brother is a murderer. . . . Then I preached vigorously against adultery, for there are many men with chaste and pious wives who bring courtesans into their homes, to the great detriment of their fortunes, their health, and their souls. Finally, I condemned theft, and the possession of goods unjustly acquired.[77]

Early reformed preaching in France was not only the province of the trained or the educated. In 1523, *ung povre homme ignorant, soy dissant hermite* was burned in front of Notre-Dame of Paris for having preached that Jesus was conceived during carnal intercourse between Mary and Joseph.[78] Several of those censured by the Sorbonne, including Augustin Marlorat and Jacques Pavannes, were followed about by hermits who themselves began interpreting what they had heard to assembled crowds.[79]

The Sermon of Aimé Meigret

We have found that this man is a troublemaker who stirs up sedition among the Jews all over the world. He is a ringleader of the sect of Nazoreans.

Acts 24:5

Aimé Meigret, a Dominican friar, received his doctorate in theology in 1520 from the University of Paris, where he had studied under the renowned Thomist Pieter Crockaert and come under the influence of Lefèvre's circle.[80] By this time, he was already the author of commentaries on Aristotle's *De coelo et mundo* (1514) and *De generatione et corruptione* (1519). In 1515, some of his verses, addressed to his fellow students, were published in Crockaert's *Questiones super opusculum Sanctae Thomae de ente et essentia.*[81]

Until he was summoned before the faculty in 1522 for preaching the plurality of Magdalenes, Meigret does not seem to have strayed too far from orthodoxy in his preaching. It was undoubtedly a combination of Meigret's noble status, his parlementary connections, his advanced degree in theology, and his geographical distance from Paris that allowed him to publish a sermon he delivered in Grenoble on April 25, 1524, in Lyon in November 1524 although the arrival of the king's reform-minded sister in Lyon in August 1524 was probably the single most important factor.[82] In 1890, Nathanaël Weiss excerpted portions of the sermon in a short article,[83] but did not analyze it in any depth. The sermon was first reprinted in its entirety in the *Annales de l'Université de Grenoble* in 1928 by Henri Guy, who offered a brief analysis.

In 1857 Henri Hours had published the texts of the depositions taken from witnesses in attendance at the Lyon sermon, and offered a comparison between the printed text of the Grenoble sermon and these depositions.[84] This sermon is of singular importance because its author gives details of the events that led to its publication, and internal comments give some appreciation of the crowd reaction. Meigret knew he was facing a largely hostile audience, and his words were chosen with care and for effect.

Meigret's sermon bears very little resemblance to the orderly, structured sermons typical of pre-Reformation preachers, which is somewhat surprising considering his training as a Dominican doctor of theology. Guy insists that the division into five points is an artificial construction, with the first two parts connected to the last three by only a thread.[85] Yet to see this sermon as five separate minisermons, each with its own theme and argument, would be incorrect. When examined closely, the parts of the text betray a well-prepared and concerted plan by the preacher.

The day before he preached in Grenoble, the scene had been set for Meigret's sermon, when one of his adversaries, Claude Rollin, read his works and preached in a wholly orthodox manner on the subjects Meigret was to touch upon. When Meigret preached the next day, "the cathedral was overflowing with men and women, magistrates and councilors, and many priests interested in the controversy. But the most notable presence was that of the preacher and reformer Pierre de Sebiville."[86] Rollin was also in attendance. One of the deponents who was later interviewed during the heresy proceedings, Pierre Hérvard, prior of the Dominican convent of Montfleury, mentioned that he could not hear what was being said because the commotion was so great. Not everyone, however, was displeased by Meigret's sermon— so aroused by the preacher's words was Sebiville that he rather imprudently nudged his neighbor, the orthodox Dominican preacher Jean Audry, and said, "Just wait till the end, and you'll see that he will say great things and sustain the opinions of Luther."[87]

Given on the feast of Saint Mark (April 25), Meigret's sermon begins with a discussion of God, whom he interprets through his working in King David. He begins: "In many ways and in several different passages, the prophet and king David, inspired by the grace of the Holy Spirit, manifests to us the glory of God in order to make us understand that all goodness and perfection proceeds from him, and that he is never the cause of evil."[88] From this standard scholastic argument, he explains why God is sometimes unjustly accused of causing evil. However, when he quotes Psalm 3:2: "O Lord, how many are my adversaries! Many rise up against me!" Meigret probably had more in mind than simply scriptural support for the argument at hand. After the absence of a theme and protheme, this is one of the first indications that his sermon would be no ordinary one. By tracing David's growing despair through the passages: "How long, O Lord? Will you utterly forget me? How long will you hide your face from me? How long shall I harbor sorrow in my soul, grief in my heart day after day? How long will my enemy triumph over me?"[89] Meigret shows how some people, when faced with calamities and tribulations, despair to the point of denying God's existence.[90] "The fool says in his heart, 'There is no God.'"[91] The results of despair and atheism are that the sinner "goes from bad to worse, from vice to greater vice, from fragility to iniquity, from ignorance to malice, from inconstancy to obduracy, from venial to mortal sin."[92] There could be no hope, no order in the world, without belief in God. "All alike have gone astray; they have become perverse; there is not one who does good, not even one."[93] Although Guy suggests that the sermon is completely orthodox until Meigret's citation of John 16:8 ("When the Paraclete comes"[94]), we find an earlier indication of the direction his sermon will take: "Who is responsible (in your opinion) that for so long human beings (excepting the Jewish people) were in such great darkness, reprobate, alienated, doing (as Saint Paul says) works that were not fit, but contrary to their nature. Is not that why they said, 'There is no God.'"[95] But Meigret is not yet ready to plunge fully into the matter of faith and works. Instead, he goes on to prove, again in scholastic fashion, that saying God is the cause of evil is equivalent to saying there is no God.[96] The results of such thinking are "sudden death, sacking of villages, perils on the sea, wars on land, plagues, oppression of the poor, and other inhuman and irrational evils."[97] Along with the prophet Jeremiah, Meigret questions why the evil seem to prosper on earth.[98] Unlike Jeremiah, however, Meigret does not wish to dispute with God, "but against you and your ilk, whoever of you are calumniators of God, quicker to blame God for the evils that you justly endure for your sins than to praise him for the good which he gives to you solely from his great bounty."[99] After this repartee, Meigret finishes the section with a scholastic proof of God's goodness, but then goes on to quote the epistle of James: "If any of you is without wisdom, let him ask it from the God who gives generously and ungrudgingly to all, and it will be given him. Yet he must ask in faith, never doubting."[100] The selection of this passage is significant, and shows us why Meigret has spent the first ten or fifteen minutes of his sermon discussing a topic for the schools. Although this part of the sermon is on the surface completely orthodox, Meigret has used proofs for the existence of God and the problem of evil to present the issue of faith and subtly to introduce the question of who has and who does not have faith.

The second part of the sermon seems to form a real break with the first, and may have lulled some of his listeners from their fears: "In recognition that all our good comes from divine grace, we celebrate the feasts of the saints, first in order to praise and honor God for the grace he has chosen to give them and others; and second, so that we will be encouraged to follow their example and thus become more agreeable to God."[101] But once again, relying on orthodox sources, Meigret hints at the direction his sermon will take. He relates the legendary story of Saint Mark, whose feast day they were celebrating, "whose great humility led him to cut off his thumb . . . for he felt he was unworthy of the priesthood or prelacy, unless it was that of him from whom all goodness comes."[102] It seems to be Meigret's point that if Mark felt himself unworthy, who then could be worthy? He goes on to point out that God has given us life "not by constraint, not by some necessity of his nature, not moved by our merits, but from his grace alone."[103] This is a preparatory phrase in a preparatory section; Meigret is not yet ready to discuss the subject fully, but is introducing the concepts of constraint and grace *alone*. Drawing on his Aristotelian training, he admits that there is a constituted order in all worldly things that governs our life on earth and pertains to exterior works.[104] But there are limits to this power, "for the heart of a king is in the hands of God, who can do what he wants with him according to his pleasure."[105] While he has just admitted that there is a need for peace and order in this world, Meigret now demonstrates that in some respects the opposite is indicated. He provides several examples, two of which involved Moses: God's order to avenge the Israelites on the Midianites and Moses' arming of the Levites to punish the idolatry of his people, "even though he was one of the most gentle men on earth."[106] From these examples, Meigret concludes that "you see that wrath and reasonable anger often is the minister of good and just works."[107] This brings him to his leading question: What is the great sin against the Holy Spirit, that incurs such wrath?[108]

Part II is linked to the next part with the answer to this question: "Because they did not believe in me."[109] While "theologians" have variously responded that the one unforgivable sin against the Holy Spirit is blasphemy, rebellion, or lack of penitence, Meigret disagrees, feeling that learned men have looked beyond the original sin, which is infidelity, or unfaith.[110] In one crucial passage, he presents his Christology, in which he defines faith:

> What does it mean to believe in Jesus Christ? Is it to believe that he is God and man, crucified and dead for us, that he descended into hell, ascended to the heavens, is seated at the right hand of God, and will come to judge the world. I say (with Saint James), no. What then should our faith be? The faith that you must have, is to believe firmly and hope that because the Son of God was made man, that you, a poor creature, of no esteem compared to God, will have divine perfections imparted to you. Because Jesus Christ suffered a painful death, your sins will be pardoned. Because he descended into hell, the devil no longer has power over you. Because he was resurrected, one day we too will be like him, participants in his immortality, splendor, impassivity, and other such glories. Because he ascended into the heavens, paradise is open to us, and we will enter after him. Briefly, faith in Jesus Christ means to believe that we will never gain paradise except by the virtue of the faith or confidence—they are the same thing—that we have in him.[111]

Interestingly, the last sentence is almost identical to one of Menot's.[112] Meigret contrasts his own simple definition of faith with that of the "theologians," who argue that faith is an act of assent or hope in obtaining celestial happiness through merits and grace.[113] Meigret responds acerbically that this is to put the "cart before the horse."[114] He then presents a standard Lutheran argument to support his position, based on Galatians 2:21: "If justification proceeds from the virtue of our works, then Jesus Christ died to no avail."[115] Here he interrupts the flow of his argument to respond to his audience, who were muttering loudly by this point.

> I know that this doctrine is new to you and that some of you will find it
> disagreeable. What do you want me to do? . . . To what state of affairs have
> we come that when someone preaches and declares the gospel to you, you
> call him a heretic or a Lutheran, but someone who glorifies human traditions
> and inventions is in your opinion a preacher of the gospel? Now if this
> sermon, which is the first one I have preached in your presence, displeases
> you, content yourselves with the fact that it will be the last. Already I see
> you murmuring and disputing among yourselves, and saying that if faith is
> sufficient for justification, we have no more need of good works.[116]

The admission that he was preaching something "new" is a telling argument
against his orthodoxy. However, sensing that his audience was worried about
the antinomian implications of such a doctrine, Meigret explains in a wholly
Lutheran manner his understanding based on James 2:18, that if one has faith,
good works will necessarily follow.[117] "We are justified by faith. Good works
agreeable to God are the fruit of our justification."[118]

The discussion of justification by faith alone inexorably leads to the opposition of Law and gospel. "The Law was our pedagogue, that led us to the
faith in Jesus Christ that justifies."[119] He compares the Law to a schoolmaster,
whose task is to introduce his students to the principles of morality, but who
has little control over their subsequent behavior.[120] If we are no longer under
the tutelage of the Law, but rather subjects of the Holy Spirit through God's
freely given grace, then human laws that constrain are not only useless but
damnable:

> No matter how reasonable, instructive, and salutary are the rules of Saint
> Francis, Saint Benedict, Saint Dominic, and others, if they constrain, they
> are pedagogic. And if such laws are coercive, but not justificative, they are
> pedagogic. Do you want me to accord greater dignity to the laws of man
> than to those of God? To the rule of Saint Francis or Saint Augustine rather
> than the law given to Moses? Now I am not saying that it is a bad thing to
> wear a long gray habit, a corded rope instead of a belt, a woolen tunic
> instead of a shirt, sandals, a hood, a shaven head and to have no money in
> one's purse. I do not say it is a sin to wear a white robe, and to complete
> the outfit with a black cape and scapular, or not to eat meat, or to drink
> only with both hands, and many other such external observances. But I
> want to say that if coercive power is used to force you to such actions, these
> things are damnable.[121]

Meigret firmly adheres to this point throughout the sermon. He considers
such practices *adiaphora,* things indifferent, some of which are intrinsically
good, but which become damnable when commanded. "What affair do we
have with such petty teachers, who in most cases do not know how to govern
themselves?"[122] Finally, as proof of his argument that faith in Jesus Christ
alone justifies, Meigret points to Moses and the other patriarchs, who for all
of their virtues, were prisoners in hell until the coming of Christ.[123] He now
returns to his beginning, reiterating that the real sin against the Holy Spirit
is not believing in the grace of God and in the atoning power of Jesus Christ.[124]

Meigret begins Part IV with a precept of Jesus: "Because I go to my

Father, you will not see me for a while."[125] After feigning confusion over this statement, Meigret explains it by another line from Scripture: "It is much better for you that I go. If I did not go, the Paraclete would never come to you, whereas if I go, I will send him to you."[126] Did this mean that the corporal presence of Jesus Christ was displeasing to the Holy Spirit?[127] Of course not, says Meigret, it means simply that if you do not leave that which you love, you will never have that which you truly desire.[128] The Apostles themselves were more attached to Christ's bodily than to his spiritual presence, which Meigret uses to make the Pauline (and Protestant) point that the Resurrection (and one's faith in it) are more important than even the historical acts and words of Jesus.[129] But it is his concern with the worldly spirit that plagues the church and spirituality that is the heart of this discourse. Since worldly materialism and desire can lead only to dissatisfaction and heartbreak, God is the answer, for "if we persevere and have confidence in God, he will say to us like the Apostles: 'Your sadness will be turned into joy'."[130]

Part V begins with John 16:11: "The prince of this world is already judged." Meigret stresses the consequences of inordinate attachment to the things of this world: "Now is the time for the judgment of the world; now will the prince of this world be chased from his kingdom. By these words we are to understand that our Lord has lifted the power of Satan from upon us. And because the world has reconstituted Satan in his primal authority and put itself in his thrall, it will be judged by the Holy Spirit: for the prince of this world is already judged."[131] Now Meigret begins to make the equation of the world with Satan and the Catholic Church.

> Someone will ask what diabolic laws the world has approved as good? What statutes are observed by Christians as necessary for their salvation, which have been invented and supported by the devil? . . . It is necessary for us to look beyond [the commandments of God] to those laws which carry the superficial appearance of goodness and justice, as Saint Paul says, which appear to have a certain sort of wisdom for the observance of religion and humility, yet are all the same diabolical.[132]

He then returns to the theme first explicitly discussed in Part III—the question of ecclesiastical compulsion. Meigret now attacks the church directly. Using 1 Timothy 4:1-3 as his starting point, he goes on: "The Spirit distinctly says that in later times some will turn away from the faith and will heed deceitful spirits and things taught by demons through plausible liars—men with seared consciences who forbid marriage and require abstinence from foods which God created to be received with thanksgiving by believers who know the truth."[133] Meigret intends us to understand the "plausible liars" to be the church hierarchy. Once again, he hastens to assure his listeners that fasting and continence are not evil in themselves, but condemns as hypocrites those who command them.[134] The problem, as Meigret sees it, is not only the principle of the matter, but the fact that such human prohibitions take no account of human frailty, another Lutheran tenet: "They do not consider human fragility, so however excellent the work may be, few people will be able to accomplish it. Those who command do not see (as Saint Paul testifies) that the multiplication of laws simply leads to the multiplication of sins. . . . Many, many Christians would be in paradise instead of hell, had there not been commandments to fast and observe other ceremonies and abstinence."[135] Curiously, he does not reconcile the problem of why human beings go to hell for not obeying laws unjustly promulgated by the church. Does this mean that God cannot correct the faults of a sinning church? Or is the church, no matter how evil, still the arbiter of human affairs even when it trespasses against the laws of God? Meigret never resolves this paradox.

While admitting that other sections of Paul are less clear-cut, Meigret insists that Paul never argued for coercion.[136] Anticipating what his listeners and others will say, he adds that he is not telling churchmen to marry or ordinary people not to fast.[137] "While the work is just and praiseworthy, the commandment of it is iniquitous and diabolical,"[138] for no human creature is permitted to add to the laws of God. Meigret fears that some in his audience will now maintain that the road to paradise is too wide, but says that this is nothing more than blasphemy against the Son of God.[139] After saying Amen, Meigret concluded his sermon to a tumultuous and, on the whole, negative reaction from the crowd.

When Meigret had his sermon printed, he added a Latin preamble directed at members of parlement. The epistle is high polemic at its best, addressed to the judges and directed against his enemies, particularly his special adversaries, Jean Faisan, the vicar of the bishop of Grenoble, and Rollin, the Dominican preacher. Meigret begins with an angry reference to the "cleansing fire, which [he wishes] would purify all of the Dauphiné, so that no errors, no Satanic laws, no hypocritical cermonies, and no foolish old wives' tales would remain."[140] Meigret had, he said, undertaken to kindle this fire, a fire that he likens to the one that consumed the Babylonians who put to death God's true servants.[141] The preamble supports the view that early statements in Parts I and II of the sermon were directed against his enemies and a church that had betrayed its mission. The reference to the Babylonians is surely not fortuitous.[142] Meigret informs the judges that he had offered to dispute Faisan or Rollin, in Latin or French, but that neither would agree; moreover, they insulted him and were themselves responsible for the tumult in the city.[143] Most of the remainder of the epistle need not detain us, although Meigret uses one particularly interesting argument to refute his enemies. He points out that the primary argument of his sermon, that ecclesiastical authorities have no right to compel obedience to rules under pain of damnation, comes from none other than Jean Gerson, the famous fifteenth-century theologian. "However, if his divine witness is not enough, one can look to Ambrose, Augustine, and others."[144] So if his opponents judge his utterances to be false and heretical, then they must also condemn the statements of Augustine and Gerson.[145] He ends the letter with a virulent attack on those pastors who are in reality nothing but wolves (Faisan and Rollin?), who neglect their flocks, and neither comfort the infirm, nor rectify errors of faith. "Nay, rather they flay, smite, and lose their sheep."[146]

It is obvious from a comparison of the two sources that the doctors of the Faculty of Theology extracted the propositions from the printed sermon, for the statements are extraordinarily accurate. Not surprisingly, the theologians of Paris objected to many of Meigret's points. His arguments that the church could not obligate under pain of damnation (propositions I, VI, VII, VIII), those about putting the cart before the horse (II), the Law as pedagogue (III, IV, V), and his assertion that no one may add to the commandments of God (X) were all deemed heretical by the Faculty of Theology.[147] Although propositions extracted from the unprinted Lyon sermon may not be quite so reliable, they add some other doctrinal points to help us formulate a more complete picture of Meigret as theologian and preacher. He is alleged to have denied the necessity of confession, which is consistent with his attitude to ecclesiastical compulsion in the Grenoble sermon. Proposition VIII denounces those who condemn Luther, while Proposition XII gives parish priests the same power to remit sins as that held by bishops and the pope. Meigret also reiterates the plurality of Marys.[148] The testimony of the deponents who were present at the Lyon sermon reinforces the themes found in the Grenoble sermon. The preacher Pierre Chambert felt that Meigret was surely a Lutheran, for he expressed the same opinions, "though Meigret claimed he was not a follower of Martin Luther,"[149] a statement confirmed by many others.[150] Many of the deponents expressed their disapproval of Meigret's sermon, although two, Antoine Chappuys, a thirty-three-year-old presbyter of the cathedral, and Bernardine de Tavannes, a medical doctor, recounted the events but expressed no judgments.[151] Meigret personally responded to some of the articles put before him by the inquisitors in Lyon. He did not touch on all the propositions, which suggests that some were reasonably accurate. Most of his answers were simply clarifications of what he had said with regard to fasting and abstinence. From his responses, it is obvious that he did not consider the theological understanding of the eucharist, baptism, or even *sola scriptura* to be the most important problem facing the church, but rather the ecclesiological issue of the church's power over the community of believers.

How are these sermons to be judged? Are they the work of an evangelical Catholic criticizing the abuses of the church? Or of one newly convinced of the righteousness of Luther's attack on the church? While Farge claims there is little in the depositions that suggest offensive doctrines,[152] Hours argues that Meigret's doctrine of faith shows a sentimental and intellectual break with the church.[153] The examination of the sermon, the prefatory epistle, the propositions, and the depositions here make it clear that Meigret was preaching heresy. Far from being simple extempore preaching, the Grenoble sermon displays elements of careful preparation. The first two sections are careful attempts to seduce his listeners through a presentation that, if not strictly orthodox, did not deviate in any major way from the teachings of the church and contemporary Catholic preaching. They set the groundwork for the major attack on the doctrine of justification by works and ecclesiastical compulsion that rises to a crescendo by the end of the work. Many of the individual statements made by Meigret might be found in the sermons of any late-

medieval preacher, but according to our definition of heresy, it is the mul-
tiplicity of doctrines, plus the manner of their presentation, that determines
whether or not a given work or sermon was heretical. Meigret knew that
many of these doctrines had already been condemned by the papacy. From
beginning to end, he showed himself comfortable with Lutheran and Swiss
ideas. His omission of the eucharist proves little, for this issue was not as
important in France as elsewhere. The emphasis on justification, Pauline
interpretations, and the limits on ecclesiastical power all point to a man
who had drunk the new wine offered by Luther. That is not to say he
was a Lutheran. He was a French reformer interested in Luther's ideas
and intrigued by the new possibilities opening up in scriptural interpretation.

The Bourgeois of Paris claims that Meigret made an *amende honorable* at
Lyon,[154] but this is probably incorrect, for the faculty records state that he
was imprisoned.[155] Meigret's probable death in the Empire, possibly in Strasbourg,[156] suggests that both he and the church authorities recognized that no
reconciliation was possible, and that only his high connections saved him from
a worse fate.

Early reformed preaching in France was very much in the tradition of the
Catholic *préréforme* in France, and many of the doctrines preached in the
initial stages were not significantly different from those preached by late-
medieval orthodox preachers. The intellectual vigor and heterodoxical traditions of the late fifteenth century led naturally to a desire to spread the
Word with whatever new tools and methods could be found. Therefore, in
the beginning, Luther was simply an interesting new "contribution" to preexisting French evangelical and mystical tendencies.

But once it became clear that Luther's beliefs could not be contained within
the Catholic Church and that his theology represented a challenge unlike any
the church had faced, even simple heterodoxy became suspect. At a time
when the church was under siege, one had to close ranks and conform scru-
pulously to the church's doctrine, lest it be assumed that one had joined the
reformers. And so heterodoxy and heresy became virtually synonymous.

That many evangelical reformers had no intention of disavowing the Catholic Church is obvious in retrospect, but was not so clear at the time. Briçonnet, Lefèvre, and Roussel all believed ardently in reform, but within a
Catholic framework. When they were forced to choose, they chose Catholicism. For them, evangelism, humanism, and biblicism were not inconsistent
with the church's living tradition, and they were uninterested in a new theology. For others, like Caroli and Mazurier, the attractions of Lutheranism
were strong, yet they too died more or less reconciled with the Roman Catholic
Church. Finally, there were those who preached doctrines both implicitly and
explicitly condemned by the papacy. Although some of Meigret's statements
taken alone could be interpreted within the evangelical framework of the
Circle of Meaux, the number of suspect statements, their polemical tone, and

his persistence in preaching condemned doctrines all testify to his rejection of the Roman Catholic Church.

Heresy after the death of Francis I was a much more serious matter. The repressive policies of Henry II, including the *chambre ardente* (the popular name for the section of the Parlement of Paris that heard cases involving heresy) drew sharp lines between the adherents of the two faiths. Although the number of suspects convicted and burned was never very large, even in Paris and Toulouse,[157] royal policy was no longer ambivalent. At the same time, Calvinist preachers had begun to spread the new gospel systematically throughout France in the 1550s and 1560s. But even earlier than this, Catholic preachers had recognized the dangers of the new heresy and had begun a counteroffensive.

12

The Catholic Response to
Early Protestant Heresy

Why do you glory in evil,
  you champion of infamy? All the day you plot harm;
  your tongue is like a sharpened razor, you practiced deceiver!
You love evil rather than good,
  falsehood rather than honest speech.
You love all that means ruin,
  you of the deceitful tongue!   Psalm 52:3–6

David Nicholls argues that among the Catholic hierarchy and preachers in France there was a "seeming inability to recognise the dynamism of Protestantism, leading to the threat not being taken sufficiently seriously at an early enough stage." He characterizes Catholic preaching against the Protestants as "ineffectual," with "special sermons against the Protestant threat . . . few and far between."[1] Nicholls bases his argument partially on the lack of anti-Protestant literature published in Rouen during the first two decades of the Reformation, and suggests that it was not until 1542 that a systematic preaching effort was used to combat heresy.[2] Similarly, Philip Hoffman speaks of a "revival" of Catholic preaching in Lyon in the 1550s as a result of the Counter-Reformation,[3] and Marc Venard agrees that by 1540 it was widely felt that preaching must be used to confound the heretics.[4]

Are these descriptions accurate? The impression that Catholics were slow to respond to heresy through preaching may derive from the drastic decline in the number of sermons printed in the decades after 1535. It is unlikely that this decline in printing was correlated with an actual decline in preaching, since archival records make it clear that Catholic preaching continued unabated throughout France. Rather than indicating a decrease in preaching, the lack of published sermons relates to changes in the printing industry and those who controlled the presses. By the late 1530s, large numbers of sermon books were already in circulation, perhaps limiting the need or desire for newer works. In some cities, printers had overestimated the demand for certain books and flooded the market.[5] In addition, both censorship and caution had an inhibiting effect on the printing of sermons.

Besides the wide availability of sermon collections by leading contemporary preachers (including sermons against the "Lutheran" heresy), a major factor in the decline of printed sermons was the attack on printing after the Placards (17–18 October 1534), and the even more repressive surveillance and censorship of "questionable" works which was fully instituted by 1542.[6] Although books in French were censored much more rigorously than those in Latin, 43 percent of all Latin works examined by the Faculty of Theology of Paris between 1520 and 1542 were censored.[7] All religious works, even by reputable Catholic authors, were checked for heterodoxy. While this was certainly not an attempt to stifle orthodox Catholic sermon production, the sheer bulk of the works to be examined would have led to serious delays. Printed works and sermons that had passed unnoticed before the Reformation were not always approved after. In 1512, Merlin wrote his *Apologia pro Origène,* which defended Origen against charges of heresy.[8] In 1522, the work was attacked by Christian Masseus, who was soon joined by that inveterate foe of the reformers, Noël Beda.[9] They saw the work as particularly dangerous in light of the growing Lutheran threat, for Origen had been condemned by the sixth-century Council of Constantinople and the Church Father Jerome. The case dragged on for six years, and ended only when Merlin and the faculty's lawyer (for the other side) were both imprisoned for complaining about the regent Louise of Savoy's plan to tax the Parisian population.[10] In 1525, when Claude Chevallon tried to reissue Menot's *Carême de Tours,* first published in 1519, he met an immediate roadblock: Pierre Ramaille, one of the faculty's representatives, allowed the printing only on the condition that Menot's disapproval of excommunication for temporal matters be deleted.[11] The censorship was evidently not very successful, for the 1525 Chevallon edition carries the unexpurgated statement: "In my opinion, fulminations and excommunications should not be made on account of temporal matters."[12] While the Faculty of Theology was concerned even at this early date about what appeared in printed sermons, the extent and difficulty of the task was already apparent. There can be little doubt that the machinery of censorship inhibited printing to some extent. If James Farge is correct in his assertion that the "Articles of Faith [of 1543] emerged less from censorship of books . . . than from censorship of preaching,"[13] then a conclusion that sermons suffered even more than other religious books from the faculty's activities seems warranted.

Another factor that would have dampened the enthusiasm of many would-be authors was the changing definition of heresy and heterodoxy, and the fear of unwittingly voicing a questionable opinion. This very real possibility was demonstrated in the case of Antoine Heyraud, provincial of the Dominicans in Provence and assistant to Jacopo Sadoleto, bishop of Carpentras. Heyraud was specially assigned to preach against heresy, but made statements on justification and predestination that Sadoleto felt personally compelled to refute.[14] Correction and rebuttal were fairly simple matters for preached sermons, but not so easy with printed sermons. If large numbers of provincial preachers began using suspect sermons with little or no alteration, heresy could spread dramatically.

Even for the most orthodox preachers, the climate in the capital was enough to give them pause. Before and to some degree after the Placards, the king and his sister Marguerite stood for a policy of tolerance and clemency toward heretics. This so infuriated many orthodox Catholic preachers, including LePicart, that in their their attacks on Protestants from the pulpit, they openly ridiculed the queen of Navarre, leading to their imprisonment and exile. The lack of a concerted royal policy against heresy did not stifle Catholic preaching, but it undoubtedly had an effect on the printing of sermons. LePicart's sermons, delivered from the 1530s to the 1550s, were published only posthumously.

These three factors—censorship, caution, and a glut on the market—make it difficult to assess the strength of the Catholic response. Sermons that deal with heresy must be supplemented with information from chronicles and journals, as well as from the Faculty of Theology registers. There are numerous references in these sources to sermons that deal specifically with heresy. Whenever a heretic was condemned to death by the secular authorities, a sermon was delivered for the edification of the victim as well as for those who had come to watch the spectacle. Merlin, then *penitencier* of Paris, preached at the Place de la Grève in August, 1524, when a young Picard student was burned for saying that the Virgin had no more power than any other saint.[15] Similarly, when several inhabitants of Meaux were condemned to death in 1546, LePicart addressed the accused as well as the large crowd of spectators, choosing as his subject the holy eucharist.[16] A probable identification of this sermon with one of several appended to his series from Easter to Trinity Sunday makes it clear that another purpose of this type of sermon was to serve as a warning to others not to imitate the heretics. In a bitter attack on his adversaries, LePicart complains: "And his [Luther's] disciples are worse than he, for many of them claim there is nothing to the sacrament of the altar, and many have been burned for sustaining such malicious and damnable thoughts—I've seen it myself."[17] A "burning sermon" could at times become a dialogue or even provoke another sermon in response. When LePicart, instead of raging at the heretics as was his wont, exhorted one of the condemned to patience, the man responded, "Praise be to God that you have changed your language. But if you were in my place, would you dare boast of having the good patience that God gave you?"[18] On his way to death at the Place Maubert, Alexandre Canus turned to his captors and begged their permission to speak a few words. Out of pity for a man who had suffered unspeakable torments, the *lieutenant criminel* of the Châtelet prison and the precentor of the Sainte-Chapelle unwisely assented. Taking one of his enemies' favorite themes as his subject, Canus elaborated on his understanding of the eucharist, preaching with such "vehemence and spirit that many of the faithful who were there and who had heard him preach before, said that they had never heard him speak with such eloquence."[19]

Processions provided another opportunity for preachers to attack heretics. The *theologus* of Paris, Jean Bertoul, whose position required weekly preaching, was called upon by Cardinal Jean Du Bellay to preach an expiatory sermon after the affair of the Placards in 1534.[20] Some years later, Claude Guilliaud delivered a sermon during a procession after the desecration of the host.[21]

Discussion of the "Lutheran" heresy can be found in sermons by almost all preachers who were active after the Reformation, but there was no general consensus among the preachers as to the best way to handle the problem. Most relied on one of the two methods regularly employed by the Catholic Church against heresy: the way of *caritas,* attempting to convince heretics through teaching, exhortation, preaching, and propaganda; or the way of *potestas,* legal coercion.[22]

The Early Response

> O how grievous! This is not a guess, but the most certain of prophecies, for the present is shown to us by the past, and we must remember the beginnings and causes of things just as if we had seen them with our own eyes. I do not know what will come out of this great tempest. But daily we see it increasing in strength, which confirms my fears. Kings, princes, and bishops, who should stand guard against those who attack the church, have lost the true faith. Now it is as if all the church's friends have turned against her, and instead they have become her enemies.   Illyricus[23]

Illyricus's prophecy of July 9, 1521, decisively connects the present threat to the church's well-being with past (heretical) attacks, yet exudes a pessimism that suggests the danger was never before so great. He was not alone in perceiving the importance of the threat of heresy at a very early date. An examination of Menot's printed sermons is interesting. The *Carême de Tours* was published in 1508, the *Premier Carême de Paris* in 1517, and the *Second Carême de Paris* in 1518. Although there is no specific reference to Lutheranism or any discussion of contemporary heresy, there is a subtle but perceptible shift in tone toward a more dogmatic insistence on certain church practices such as fasting,[24] and a more overt discussion of justification, in the *Second Carême.*[25] But if Menot's knowledge of Lutheran doctrines at this point is conjectural, Pepin's is not. His *Sermones quadraginta de destructione Ninive* first appeared in 1518, the same year as Menot's *Second Carême.* When we consider the time necessary for printing, the conclusion is inescapable that Pepin was aware of events in the Empire as they were happening. In Sermon 13, he uses the same language as Illyricus, alluding briefly to "this Lutheran tempest."[26] Sermon 33, entitled "De destructione vici Lutherianorum, i. hereticorum civitatis Ninive" is completely devoted to the problem. He describes the threat he now sees on France's borders:

> Lately the enemy has found a new and abominable instrument in one of his disciples by the name of Luther, a German, who like Judas would have done better never to have been born. He does not so much stir up new heresy as renew old heresies that have already been condemned. He has

> corrupted, polluted, and poisoned nearly all of Germany and the adjacent
> kingdoms and provinces, so that this poisonous plague reaches almost to
> France, in whose praise Jerome was once pleased to say that Gaul alone is
> spared such monstrous heretics.[27]

This passage shows that the real novelty of Luther's ideas had not yet been
realized, hardly surprising since Luther may himself not have known what
their impact would be. But what did Pepin really know of Luther at this early
date? In response to Luther's doctrine of justification by faith alone, Pepin
says: "God compels no one to believe in the true faith, but leaves each to
his free will. . . . Faith is the first fundament of the spiritual edifice and it is
first among the three theological virtues of faith, hope and love."[28] He correctly asserts that Lutherans attach less importance than Catholics to the issue
of free will, concluding that they are antinomian.[29] He complains that the
Lutherans show particular animosity toward the saints, for they say "that we
are not to pray to them and they do not pray for us."[30] In response to the
heretics' insistence on scriptural primacy, Pepin complains that they consider
"everything false that cannot be proven through the authority of sacred scripture."[31] He suggests strongly that they stop "bombarding" the Apostle Paul
and return to their mother, the church.[32]

Pepin felt that the danger of the new heresy was exacerbated by the stature
of many of its adherents.

> Truly this tempest is seen to grow and to be passed on by those who lead
> the people in temporal and spiritual affairs, which is the greatest sort of
> iniquity. Many nobles and powerful men, many churchmen, many who are
> esteemed for their learning, finally many commoners, do not fear or blush
> to favor, encourage, protect, and defend, now openly, now covertly, those
> pestiferous errors sustained by that son of perdition named Luther. And
> they do this to the damnation of their souls, and in spite of the recent
> censures from the holy apostolic see.[33]

He characterizes the heretics as cruel and arrogant in their belief that they
know better than the church what is right.[34] Although this particular heresy
originated in Germany, Pepin does not lay all the blame on the German
nation: "Germany is indeed a very cold country, owing to its distance from
the sun. However, I do not want to put the fault on the glory of this nation,
which once produced great men and for a long time deserved the imperial
majesty. Rather I blame this very evil man Luther and his confederates.
Would that Germany had never produced them!"[35]

Understanding the nature of the threat was the first step, but Catholic
preachers also had to decide how to deal with the problem. Pepin looks to
Francis I for help:

> Why does the Lord allow these heretics so much time to carry out their evil
> deeds? It seems to devout Catholics that he ought to quickly exterminate
> them. Whence lately I heard of our great and generous prince of this realm
> of France, who said with the fervency and zeal of his great faith, that if
> some day word of Lutherans in his realm comes to him, "I will with my
> own hand willingly put to death all Lutherans, and be their great torment."[36]

Pepin details a multifaceted program for dealing with heretics. First, one must determine accurately if a person is a heretic or not. Those willing to correct their opinions and amend their lives when shown the truth should not be punished. If, however, a person persistently adheres to heretical propositions and will not assent to the truths of the Catholic Church when they are presented to him, then he should be punished.[37] The obstinate heretic should "lose his offices, benefices, dignities, and all his temporal goods."[38] These goods would not revert to the heretic or his family even if he recanted, for that would set a bad example for others.[39] Excommunication was the spiritual penalty for heresy, and death the temporal. This was only reasonable, Pepin argues, since others were punished capitally for less serious offenses:

> [H]eretics are to suffer corporal punishment, not of any sort whatever, but the punishment of death. . . . It is a much worse thing to falsify the faith, than to falsify money, which is the support of life on this earth. But counterfeiters and other malefactors are immediately put to death by secular princes. Therefore a fortiori convicted heretics are not only to be separated from the church and the faithful, but justly put to death. Yet we see that the church shows great compassion toward them. They are not turned over to the secular branch for execution after the first lapse, but are given a warning. Afterwards, if they want to return to the faith and they abjure their heresy, they are given penance, and are spared the death penalty. But if they relapse later, they will not be spared, but turned over to the secular arm for punishment by death.[40]

Finally, heretics will suffer eternal punishment, for their sins are worse than all others.[41] "O! How these wretched Lutherans will be struck senseless when after this life they see themselves separated from all the joys of the elect, and sent down in confusion into the company of demons and all of the damned."[42] Pepin's primary concern is not the punishment of the heretic—that could be left to God—but rather to prevent the infection from spreading to the faithful. He uses the example of Arius to show that when unchecked, a heretic could lead many good Catholics astray.[43] When heretics mixed with the community of the faithful, wars, discord, and dissension were the result, "leading to the damnation of many Catholics where the heretics prevail."[44] Urging his listeners to take seriously the dangers facing them, he paints a picture of the cruelty and inhumanity of the heretics.[45]

Pepin draws a distinction between secret and open heresy, which he relates to the dangers the heretic poses to the Christian community:

> There are two sorts of heretics. The first are the secret heretics, the second the open ones. The first sort are not immediately to be expelled from the church, and perhaps will come around through popular preaching. This is because the church does not judge hidden beliefs, but only open ones. The first group is able to return to the fold of mother church and become good and devout Catholics. The second group must be eradicated, extirpated, and killed as soon as possible, especially if they are entirely incorrigible, obdurate, pertinacious, and convicted of such beliefs.[46]

Pepin considers secret heretics to be less dangerous than outspoken ones, for their opinions are more nebulous and unformed.

Besides the social and financial deterrents to heresy, Pepin looks to bishops and curés as the first line of defense, a suggestion that could be traced to Augustine and Ambrose.[47]

> Whenever heretics invade the flock, the pastors are held personally to protect and defend them even under peril of death. The truth of the matter is that prelates and especially bishops are under the obligation to exercise their pastoral functions in order to save the souls of the people in their care. Therefore, as the salvation of his people requires his actual presence, the good pastor must not desert his flock, whether it be for temporal gain or because of the threat of personal danger, for he must be willing to lay down his life for his sheep. The salvation of his people requires that a pastor reside with them so that whenever they are invaded by heretics, he can repel them, with devout prayers, holy preaching, healthy doctrine, and the use of reason.[48]

Although his ideas on heresy were never again so fully developed as in the destruction of Nineveh series, Pepin held to the tenets expressed there. He did not simply apply preexisting medieval classifications of heresy, but informed himself of the particular ideas and activities of the Lutherans.

If we turn to other preachers in the early post-Reformation era, we find proportionately fewer references, primarily because far fewer sermons have survived for each man. Clichtove, perhaps somewhat defensively in view of his earlier interest in reform, became involved in the Faculty of Theology's debates over Lutheranism. In his sermons, he talks about heresy fairly often, but only occasionally mentions Luther by name.[49] But it is obvious in his other discussions of heresy that he has Luther in mind, for he mentions specific Lutheran tenets such as justification by faith alone.[50] He warns that the heretics "mix honey and wine with their poison" in order to lure good Catholics to the new religion.[51] Preaching in 1521, Jean de Gaigny alluded to Luther, but did not seem to share the pessimism of Pepin and Illyricus or the awareness of the dangers the new heresy posed: "Inasmuch as France remains in the integrity of the faith, we will have no reason to fear our enemies. But we must not stop at faith alone. We must go to the Mount of Olives, for the eminent virtue of charity. . . . Works are necessary, and love for God and one's neighbors, as well as faith."[52] Gaigny chooses to refute the heretics on a more subtle, doctrinal level, giving them no publicity. Messier prefers to ridicule them.

> Let us take the case of the foxes who destroy the vineyards. For foxes have sharp tongues. So our Lutherans have sharp tongues as well, as we see by their eloquence and their rhetoric. Foxes have pretty fur—that is, their knowledge that seems so admirable. According to them, priests should marry, and similar things. But such knowledge is worth nothing. Foxes have long tails. So there are many who follow the heretics. Foxes have fetid breath when they pant; so the heretics' knowledge stinks and avails nothing.[53]

Messier also complains that through their "false exposition and doctrines, they attempt to extinguish the truth of scripture."[54]

Another approach to the problem of heresy can be found in a 1522 sermon by Illyricus in a collection of works entitled "A Little Book about the Power of the Supreme Pontiff." In his own words, Illyricus tells us that this is a popular sermon. He takes as his theme Matthew 16:18–19: "On this rock I will build my church," and without ever mentioning Luther by name, details a method of dealing with heresy. Despite its popular nature, this is a difficult sermon, probably intended primarily to inform clerics on how to respond when the church came under attack, without giving the heretics' views a direct airing. Relying on Augustine, he begins by defining who is *not* a heretic: "[he] who errs in matters of faith thinking that this is what the church believes, and is willing to correct his beliefs when shown the truth, is not a heretic."[55] The heretic is one who adheres to his error after being shown the truth. Illyricus proposes to deal with heresy by teaching the truth clearly so that there can be no doubt or misunderstanding. He then explains that popes, prelates, and priests are instruments of Christ, mediators between God and his people. Using the standard argument of the body, he proceeds to show that just as Peter depends on Christ for his authority, so the lower orders in the church hierarchy depend immediately on Peter's successors. After some discussion of the powers of the keys and how they are to be used, he turns to the issue of the sinning priest and heresy in a pope, admitting that "even the holy pontiff and the college of cardinals can fall from grace and deviate from the faith."[56] When this happens, the pope is separated from the church, and his plenitude of power is converted into tyranny.[57] It is not Illyricus's intent to cast doubt on the occupants of the holy apostolic see, but simply to define terms and make explicit the relations between Christ, the church's appointed ministers, and the body of the church on earth. Unlike many on both sides, he seems to have listened carefully to the church's opponents and tried to win them back through reasoned rather than inflammatory preaching.

Reform from within was thought to be one of the best ways to deal with the problem. Preaching before the Council of Lyon in 1528, Claude de Longwy, bishop of Macon, insisted on reform among both clergy and laity and a collective effort to "restore discipline, ritual, and a mores" as the best way to respond to heretics. When he became bishop of Langres in 1529 and cardinal in 1533, he used his powers to implement these proto-Tridentine reforms.[58] "Putting one's own house in order" was a goal of many preachers and churchmen well before the Reformation. It took on new urgency after 1520, and with the authority of prelates like Longwy, important progress was made.

The Next Generation

For in their mouth there is no sincerity;
their heart teems with treacheries.

> Their throat is an open grave;
>> they flatter with their tongue.
> Punish them, O God;
>> let them fall by their own devices;
> for their many sins, cast them out
>> because they have rebelled against you.
>> Psalm 5:10–11

The true second generation of French Catholic response had as its greatest exponent François LePicart. LePicart's sermons, first collected and published after his death, were delivered between 1533 and 1556; his views therefore reflect the concerns of a different time from that of Pepin, who died just as LePicart was beginning his turbulent preaching career. The dating of Le-Picart's sermons may be significant in another way as well. The first part of his collection was printed in 1560, while sermons for the full liturgical year appeared in 1562, 1563, 1565, 1566, and 1574.[59] Perhaps it was the strained religious climate of these years that prompted publication, although LePicart's invective was mild compared to the standards of preaching during the wars of Religion.[60] Nevertheless, middle-of-the-road Catholics may have hoped that LePicart's sermons would partially fill the vacuum in the publication of sermons that had existed since the 1530s. The printing of LePicart's sermons in the 1560s may also have served as a posthumous tribute to the greatest French Catholic preacher of his time.

Along with Nicolas Leclerc and Noël Beda, LePicart suffered imprisonment in 1533 for his virulent attacks on the reformers, including the king's sister, Marguerite of Navarre. He is said to have gone so far as to accuse the king of Navarre of heresy.[61] Heresy is one of the main themes in this lengthy sermon collection, and there is hardly one sermon in which the problem is not addressed. This is a significant change. Although Pepin occasionally devoted entire sermons to heresy, his primary concern was Christian instruction. In fact, a controversy had been brewing for some time with Catholic proponents on both sides—those who felt the problem needed to be addressed directly, like LePicart, and those like the Jesuit Pons Cogordan, who argued in 1555: "I would prefer that they [the preachers] spend their time instructing the people in what they must know, and inculcate virtue and correct vice. When it is absolutely necessary to speak of heresy, one should simply tell the Christian what he is to believe, without telling him what the heretics say."[62] This was a difficult and age-old problem, which ultimately was decided by each individual preacher according to his assessment of his audience's capabilities. If their understanding and intellectual capacities were limited, discussion of heretical doctrines was dangerous, as they might be mistaken for truth. A more sophisticated audience, on the other hand, could use a knowledge of heresy to refute erroneous preaching, and teach their families and neighbors. As always, a preacher had to evaluate the condition of his listeners and adapt his message to meet their needs.

Like Pepin, LePicart refers to Jerome's praise of ancient Gaul for its orthodoxy. But the situation had deteriorated since 1518: "Saint Jerome once praised this country of France, because in his time there were not any monsters, that is, heretics, here. But today there are an infinite number—you do not even have to go far from the city of Paris."[63] He feels there are more heretics in his time than ever before.[64] Like his predecessor Pepin, he connects the present heresy to those of times past:

> For about thirty years now they have spoken ill of the sacrament of the altar, ever since that contemptible and unhappy man Luther, who is worse than the devil, once again put forward and renewed the heresy of those two cursed Englishmen [sic], Wyclif and Hus, and who has more disciples than Mohammed ever had. Each day more sprout up and they multiply at such a rate that it is often hard to find one person in three who is not infected with their ideas. And Luther's disciples are even worse than he is.[65]

There is a blurring of the distinction between the heresies, for the Catholics saw only one evil in many guises. It is, however, interesting to note that Luther was distinguished from "his followers"—a fairly obvious reference to the Swiss reformers.

A distinguishing mark of the heretic was his arrogance, his belief that he was right even if it meant that all previous Christian thinkers were wrong. "The spirit of the heretics is one of pride. They call the pope Antichrist and there is not a bit of meekness or humility in them."[66] LePicart defines a heretic as one "who thinks otherwise than the church says and has determined. He is a heretic because he is not ignorant of the truth, but discards it in his pertinacity."[67] Naturally, if the church had not ruled on a question, that was a different matter. Another defining trait of the heretic was his secrecy. "These heretics say nothing publicly, but are very secret about their affairs. They never talk to two people together who are not of their sect, but only to one so that that person cannot bear witness against them."[68] This is so that they cannot be accused by their enemies, according to LePicart, who describes a sort of secrecy oath among their members.[69] He does not seem to grasp the inherent paradox in his statements. If the sect was so secret, if they never shared their doctrines with more than one person not of their religion, how could a problem exist? Pepin had differentiated secret from open heretics, and did not especially fear the former. But things had changed by this point, and the extent of the danger to the church was now clear. But why then was LePicart so enraged about the "open" evangelical preaching at the Louvre in 1533? Stressing their secrecy, even in contradiction to the facts, was a clever way to single out the heretic as a sneaky, cowardly opponent who did not dare spread his ideas by the light of day.

LePicart then passes on to another recognized characteristic of the heretic—his false piety. A great portion of one Advent sermon is devoted to this particularly thorny problem. However, LePicart goes a bit too far in his description of Protestant pseudodevotion, making Protestants sound far better than Catholics:

> The heretic gives alms freely, as we see today by experience. It seems from appearances that there is much greater charity among them than among

Catholics. . . . They seem better than us, and their manner of living seems to be better than our own. . . . You see that the heretics give much to the poor, but they will get nothing out of it. . . . This is a devious trick to make us think they are not heretics. . . . They have an outward appearance of piety.[70]

"They always have Christ on their tongues," he continues, "but he is not in their hearts or their affections."[71] They have soft and pretty words that please the ears,[72] and "sometimes it seems that their preaching is excellent, but those who are accustomed to frequenting their sermons listen well and hear the secret words that are contained in them."[73] The purpose of such fine sermons and good behavior is "to deceive others and to spread their venom under the cloak of truth. . . . The heretic chooses to distort the true sense of scripture, so that others will understand it according to his manner. He is like a wolf, who seeks only to kill and destroy."[74] LePicart describes heresy as a sort of cancer, which is devastating despite its silent spread. This analogy was earlier used by Clichtove, writing the faculty's decision on Luther in 1521.[75] It was also difficult to explain why, even in the face of torture and martyrdom, the heretics displayed such constancy:

When God allows a heretic, through his obduracy, to go joyously to his death in a manner that suggests constancy, it is nothing but a temptation that God places before you, to see if you love him with your whole heart and soul, and if you are faithful and firm in your faith. Yes, you say, but look at the constancy of that one. He has no fear of death. Ah! Christians, this is not constancy, but hardness and obstinacy. He is a martyr for the devil.[76]

LePicart points to the diversity of opinions within the reformed community as evidence of heresy. "They all have different opinions, one from the other,"[77] and spread discord and division in families and throughout Christendom.[78] It is because of this division that "God allows the Turks and the infidels to take root and tear asunder the Christian peoples."[79]

LePicart was troubled by the royal response to heresy, which indeed had been less vigorously repressive under Francis I than Pepin had anticipated. "Yet we see almost everywhere that many preachers say things other than that taught by the Roman Catholic Church. Despite this, we endure it, and these people are not even punished, which in my opinion is very wrong indeed."[80] Not only were heretics left unpunished, but those who spoke the truth were openly persecuted. At one point, LePicart explains that such lax policies are the result of the heretics' influence at court. The "Lutherans and other heretics, in order to flatter princes, state that one must obey the secular power, rather than the church and its superiors, like the pope, the bishops and the curés."[81] But LePicart warns the king that this is mere subterfuge: "The heretics say today that the Christian is subject to no one, but that he must live in freedom, without obedience or subjection to anyone. For by baptism, he was made the child of God, and once he is the child of God he is free and must not be subject any more. . . . These Lutherans want to destroy the realm and the Empire if they can, for they would make everyone equal, reducing order to chaos."[82] He adds that if the heretics had been punished in the beginning, there would be no problem now.[83]

How well did LePicart understand Protestant doctrines? Even as early as 1518, some of the main points of Lutheranism were known to the intellectual elite of France; had these tenets become more clearly defined in the ensuing decades? LePicart was aware that justification by faith alone was at the core of the Lutheran teaching,[84] but he does not seem to understand the distinctions the Lutherans were making about the observance of the Law. He contends that their belief "that man can do no good work that is agreeable to God, and that in fact such works displease"[85] is incorrect, as shown by the example of the Canaanite woman, whose faith and love were good works.[86] LePicart seems to comprehend fairly well the Lutheran insistence on man's sinful nature, for after discussing their refusal to go to confession, he mockingly adds: "A Lutheran says: 'I repent, I am a great sinner, etc.' But he tells of no sins in particular."[87] Although he does not devote much attention to it, he mentions in passing that heretics ridicule the doctrine of purgatory.[88] LePicart correctly evaluates the Lutheran emphasis on *sola scriptura*. "The heretics say that it is not necessary to believe anything that is not expressly stated in the holy scriptures."[89] Defending the role of tradition, he worries that his opponents, who insist on preaching scripture alone, leave no place in their sermons for ethical discussions.[90] The heretics' denial of a role for church tradition in the development of doctrine proves to him their arrogance, for they claim that only their interpretations, based on the Bible alone, are correct.[91] In their renunciation of tradition, the reformers considered the Church Fathers little different from other men, saying that God could enlighten any man with his spirit.[92]

The issue of scripture versus tradition directly led into the ecclesiological problem posed by Luther's doctrine of the priesthood of all believers. LePicart argues against the use of the vernacular in the liturgy, "for this is not necessary. If we say it in French and you do not understand, it will profit you no more than if we say it in Hebrew, Spanish, or any other language that you do not understand."[93] He points to the unhappy consequences of such a doctrine for *le menu peuple:* "We see simple folk burned for their errors and misunderstandings because they want to discuss holy scripture, but do not understand it. Come to sermons and remember what you see. Model yourself on the sermon and put into practice what you hear."[94] It offends him to see laymen appropriating the office of priest, for "that exceeds the limits of grace that God has given you."[95] He reiterates that one must look to the priest or bishop for knowledge of God, so that one does not fall into error and contaminate others.[96] It disgusts LePicart that the heretics' priests are free to marry, though he adds that this is no true marriage, but sacrilege and incest.[97]

LePicart spends a good deal more time than Pepin discussing particular heretical doctrines, such as the attack on the sacraments of the church, the proper role of the Virgin and the saints, and practices required by the church, no doubt because Lutheran and Calvinist doctrines were better defined by this time. He uses the heretics' differences on the mass to discredit them. "It does not suffice to believe that the precious body of Jesus Christ is contained in the holy sacrament of the altar, for even Luther, who is a heretic, believes this. But it is necessary that our faith in it be full and complete."[98] He goes on: "There are some of his disciples who are worse than him, for he truly believes that our Lord Jesus Christ is present in the sacrament of the altar. But he is wrong when he says that the bread and the wine in the sacrament do not change their substance or nature."[99] He discusses at length the divisions among the "Lutherans" on the subject of the mass:

> There are many Lutherans in the world today, but they are divided. When they are speaking of the holy sacrament of the altar, we find five or six different opinions. One says that it is only bread, the other that Jesus Christ is there but the substance of the bread remains and is not transubstantiated. Another says that it is only the body of our Lord, and not a sacrifice or oblation. Yet another says that the sacrifice only profits those who receive it, and not all of the living and the dead. Another says that we must give this sacrament to the laity in both kinds. The division and variety of opinions among them is a true sign that they are not filled with the Holy Spirit, but the spirit of Satan.[100]

The heretics see only signs in the sacraments, not the grace of God.[101]

Other ecclesiastical injunctions on subjects such as fasting and abstinence were probably attacked with such regularity in the early years that the attacks had become passé by the 1560s, although LePicart occasionally mentions them: "You, a heretic, say that God does not care at all about works or whether we fast or hear mass."[102] To refute the heretics, who accuse Catholics of idolatry, he uses their favorite weapon, scripture,[103] quoting from Paul (1 Corinthians 8): "The images of saints are not idols, because they represent something."[104] LePicart tells that the Church Father John Chrysostom wished to go to Rome to touch the dust that remained from the corpse of Saint Paul.[105] In this context, he attacks the literalism of the heretics' scriptural interpretation, but raises an issue that could come back to haunt him: "There is a great danger that in trying to follow the gospel from passage to passage, we will actually do an injustice to it, if we refuse to believe everything that is not explicitly in the scriptures. Where will you find in the gospel that the glorious Virgin Mary, Mother of God, remained a perpetual virgin? Where will you find that she was conceived without original sin?"[106]

But what was to be done? LePicart championed the idea of preaching against heresy, to warn people of the dangerous ideas abroad. In a funeral oration, he presents his listeners with the edifying Catholic example of Pierre de Cornibus, who always taught the milk of pure doctrine.[107] He urges good churchmen to study Protestant doctrines in order to refute their errors,[108] for only by understanding them could clerics and laymen stop those who would spread error by preaching. All efforts must be made to keep heretics from preaching,[109] but if they do they must be stopped.[110] He suggests a direct approach: "If I preach any error, . . . you should not wait until the end of the sermon to tell me, because those who hear me preach will get the wrong idea of what I am saying or will be scandalized if they are not present after the sermon. So you must reprimand me publicly, in the pulpit, and tell me my mistake."[111]

The danger of infection was great. One must "flee from heretics and Lutherans more than from a man who has a thousand plagues. Neither may we converse with them, nor listen to them, for the venom of their doctrine will bring corporal and spiritual death."[112] One must on no account extend hospitality to a heretic.[113]

LePicart admits there are problems in the Catholic Church, and like those before him, proposes to silence the heretics by correcting the abuses. He insists that churchmen must lead good lives: "We write many good books, but the heretics will not be won over by them, because they can point out clerical abuses. But if we lead good lives, we will confound them, and eliminate the foundation of their errors. Then the problem will disappear like smoke. But when I see so many abuses around me, I despair that these heresies will ever cease."[114] How could heresy be stopped when bishops and archbishops lived extravagantly,[115] and priests did not reside in their parishes?[116] What kind of example did it set for the common people to see priests elevate the host in an irreverent manner, all the while thinking of other things?[117] "The dissolute and bad lives of many churchmen who do not follow the rules and ordinances of the church or their order is the occasion for the heretics to speak ill of us and to have bad feelings about religion, but for all of that, we should not abolish religion. Rather we should get rid of the abuses, and bring the heretics back into the fold through good works and ordinances."[118]

Next, measures had to be taken against the heretics. Churchmen should do their best to convert them back to Catholicism, beginning with admonitions full of kindness and love, for the hearts of men are rarely won over by rigor or constraint.[119] "God wants Martin Luther to die in a state of true repentance and contrition in his heart, because if he dies in such sin, he will lose his soul. And for all those who were damned on his account, so will his pains be increased."[120] But if a heretic would not recant, there was only one solution— he must be burned. This was not vengeance, but simply the fulfillment of God's commandment.[121]

Despite his lengthy diatribes against heretics, LePicart occasionally displays a certain optimism. He argues that "these contemptible heretics will not last much longer, but soon will be annihilated and their errors abolished."[122]

Among other preachers active between 1530 and 1560, there are relatively few references to heresy simply because of the small number of sermons left by each preacher. In his funeral sermon for Claude de Lorraine, duke of Guise, Claude Guilliaud contrasts his subject's piety with the heretics, whom he characterizes grotesquely: "The Lutherans, who believe in sexual freedom and hold all in common, are now expanding everywhere, just like the Goths, the Gepids, the Vandals, the Alans, the Ostrogoths, and other barbarians, in order to ruin Christendom."[123] Jean Lansperge exercises greater restraint than many of his colleagues, believing that it was more important to teach his listeners true Christian doctrine. He uses the heretics' own arguments to support Catholic beliefs, charging that their understanding of the mass is faulty because they cannot comprehend it by reason and their faith is lacking![124] Drawing parallels with the Jews' treatment of Christ, he argues that "he who condemns his superior or bishop, resists him, or mocks the words and warnings of holy scripture, spits in the face of Christ."[125] Lansperge's main interest is the unity of Christendom, and he argues without invective that "all Christians should be persuaded to believe that the sacrament of the altar is the true body and blood of Christ without disputation or curiosity or attempts to investigate. They must banish from their hearts all doubts and difficulties ... for the life we live is one of faith, not knowledge. ... But that is enough of this."[126]

Étienne Paris speaks of those who estrange themselves from the church and its Fathers, by their unwillingness to accept a role for tradition. He chastises the arrogant man whose "singularity is the daughter of pride, an offspring worse educated than her mother, a branch more plague-ridden than the root, engendering pertinacity, which is the mother of heresy."[127] By his time, even the saints were no longer revered, "but in certain places the bones of saints are broken up and burnt, the heretics believing by such mad tyranny to efface their memory, so ardent are they and jealous of the glory of God."[128]

As denominational conflict grew, preachers on both sides were able to preach very freely, even against royalty. During the reign of the boy-king, Francis II, the Catholic preacher Ivollé spoke heatedly of the disorders that would befall the realm if the Huguenots took over—how they would "exterminate the king and his estate." However, he ended with the cry, "Cursed is the land that has a child for king!"[129] In a later sermon, Ivollé was forced to explain himself. It is doubtful, however, that his explanation would have satisfied Francis I or Henry II:

> I know full well that there are those present who will testify against me. If they would like to meet with me afterwards, I will sign with my own hand and blood the statements I have made: That cursed is the land and the country that has a young child for its king and whose princes are disloyal and companions of thieves. Is this to speak ill of the king? Is this to say that the governors of His Majesty are thieves or companions of thieves?[130]

Seditious preaching was increasingly common after 1560. In Amiens, a Dominican had for eight consecutive days preached that "it is necessary to punish the heretics," even if this meant that "we should not obey the letters and edicts of the king."[131] So many preached along these lines that a deputation was sent to the bishop, asking him to force the preachers in question to behave more reasonably, and to eliminate invective and seditious incitement from their sermons. Instead, they were ordered to tell the people "that the king, our lord, expressly prohibits all seditious behavior and *emotions*. ... If the preachers do not cease to preach in this manner, the deputation will take steps to inform the king."[132]

Nicholls's contention that the Catholic preaching response before the 1540s was inadequate is not borne out by the sermons included here. The lack of printed sermons for this period cannot be used to measure the response to heresy, for many factors, including a glut on the market due to previous high levels of sermon printing, and increased censorship of all works after 1534, stifled publication. Caution may also have played a significant role.

The extant sermons indicate a strong concern with the "Lutheran" heresy at an early date. Pepin and others were aware of the problem even as events were occurring, and attacked heresy directly in their sermons. If we had other sermon collections as extensive as those of Pepin and LePicart, it is probable that we would find similar responses to heresy. All the preachers active after the Reformation at least mention the new heresy. If they did not spend all their time discussing Lutheranism, this was a defensible philosophical position, later reasserted by the Jesuit Cogordan, who felt that a strong frontal attack only gave heretical ideas publicity. The problem, from a Catholic point of view, was not an inadequate preaching response, but an ambivalent royal policy.

13

Conclusion

By means of many such parables he taught them the message in a way
that they could understand.   Mark 4:33

When he got home, away from the crowd, his disciples questioned him
about the proverb. "Are you, too, incapable of understanding?"
                                                                 Mark 7:17, 18

This book began with a brief overview of the many changes affecting European
society in the years around 1500. Despite these changes, oral communication
remained the most important source of news, information, and instruction
for most people. As a source, the sermon provides valuable insights into
medieval *mentalités*. Besides its spiritual and didactic value, the medieval
sermon was an event that offered people the opportunity to socialize, flirt,
debate, and catch up on the latest news and gossip. Estimates from a variety
of sources indicate that people at the end of the Middle Ages attended sermons
in great numbers.

Many more studies of preaching and piety will be necessary before we can
gain a more definitive understanding of late medieval *mentalités*. Biographies
of individual preachers and studies of their works will give us a more specific
understanding of the late medieval preacher and his work. Martin's research
on the thousands of "anonymous" preachers must be extended, perhaps with
special attention to how these men reacted to the challenges of the 1520s and
1530s. In addition, comparative studies of preaching throughout Europe will
help determine whether conclusions based on preaching in France will hold
for Germany or England. If not, then what accounts for the differences?
Finally, we must remember that preaching was only one component of late
medieval religion, and it was one that sometimes came into conflict with the
other aspects of the church. To develop a more comprehensive picture of
religion in late medieval France, we will also need synthetic studies of the
priesthood and the monastic orders. But some general conclusions can be
drawn about the preachers and the sermons examined here.

Although the invention of the printing press did not alter the fundamentally
oral nature of European culture, it did have a number of very important
effects. Preachers who spoke before thousands, but who earlier could have

preserved or transmitted their work only through the laborious process of monastic copying, now could disseminate their message throughout Latin Christendom. Printing records indicate that large numbers of preachers took advantage of this opportunity between 1450 and 1530. The sudden availability of hundreds of editions of sermon books by contemporary preachers would have had a revolutionary effect on the thousands of "anonymous" friars who may have had less talent or originality. Prior to the development of printing, a friar would have been lucky to have had access to one or two preaching manuals, often dating from a few hundred years earlier. But at the beginning of the sixteenth century there were so many printed sermon books in circulation that an interested preacher could literally choose from a variety of different types of sermons offered by the great Dominican and Franciscan preachers of the time. He could also study the classical sermons of such greats as Bernard of Clairvaux and Gregory the Great. While an uninspired preacher might simply read these sermons, a more ambitious one could adapt them to fit his audience's special interests and needs.

There is another way in which the invention of the printing press dramatically affected preaching. Although we must be wary of overstating the rise in literacy rates during this period, there were important changes between 1400 and 1600 that related not only to printing, but also to increasing urbanization and vocational demands. More and more members of the artisanal class needed to have a rudimentary ability to read and write in order to perform their duties at work. Although the interest in antiquity was originally the preserve of the well-to-do, printing exposed more and more laymen and religious to works of ancient rhetoric, philosophy, history, and literature. Classical writing had a corresponding impact on taste. The clumsiness of medieval Latin was readily apparent to humanists who could now read the elegant works of the ancient Romans. The revival of Greek and Hebrew studies directly affected religion, as scholars began to question biblical translations and challenge some of the church's long-held beliefs. Pauline studies, which grew out of these philological currents, came to enjoy great popularity in the decades *before* the Reformation.

Preaching was naturally responsive to these other developments in society. For some lay men and women, medieval Catholic preaching, with its familiar and anthropomorphic religious presentation, no longer satisfied their increasingly sophisticated understanding. Most Reformation studies have shown that those who converted to the new faith tended to be urban, mobile, and literate. That Protestantism should appeal to these people is not at all surprising; nor should it surprise us that most peasants and villagers remained tied to the beliefs of the past. For the latter, the dismantling of the religious cosmos in favor of a theology based on concepts such as faith alone threatened to shatter the entire psychology of belief. The frequency of attacks on iconoclasts may show the simplicity and naïvete of the people, but it also testifies to a continuing need for nontextual sources of religious inspiration. The church's efforts to "localize the divine power" and "make it tangible"[1] were essential to many people's understanding. That this was still a major focus of the church's teaching mission in the sixteenth century is acknowledged by Greengrass, who contends that "at the heart of the failure of the protestant church to convert the rural world to the new faith lay a failure of mission and evangelization. It could not overcome the problem of illiteracy."[2] Although less true of city dwellers, we must not exaggerate their degree of education, sophistication, and interest. Even within a city, artisans in one trade might embrace the reformed message, while their fellows in another trade would remain ardently tied to Catholic beliefs. Nevertheless, the dichotomy between rich-poor, urban-rural, and literate-illiterate is fundamental to the story of the French Reformation.

It is within this context of change that we should examine medieval sermons, so that we can begin to understand why the preachers constructed their sermons as they did and why humanists and reformers objected, often with derision and contempt. The first encounter with a late medieval printed sermon is quite daunting. Its language (Latin) is not the language in which it was delivered. The sources and authorities, overwhelmingly biblical, seem to be heaped together. The sermon is divided and subdivided, often using artificial techniques, and its main parts do not always seem to go together as well as they should. The shorthand versions in which many sermons have survived are only the barest of outlines that, lacking the development found in complete sermons, can appear overly formal and scholastic. Scripture is not expounded in a straightforward commentary, but is often "enhanced" to permit greater understanding. While use of the Bible was appropriately based on parables, miracles, and the life of Christ, often paraphrased, Martin suggests that it was also a Bible sometimes made banal, full of metaphors based on worldly existence, in short, a Bible that was reinterpreted, glossed, and liberally translated in order to make it useful.[3] To a sixteenth-century Protestant, this was nothing short of falsification, showing profound contempt, ignorance, and even malice toward the Word of God.[4]

All these impressions are based on an *educated person's reading* of the medieval sermon. In this respect, the modern reader and the sixteenth-century humanist may have more in common than the latter would have had with *le menu peuple* of his own time. To appreciate the medieval preaching technique, one must *listen* to the preacher, and try to understand his goals within the context of his audience. The preachers used allegory, humorous anecdotes, and bawdy tales to convey their message. They looked to Jesus' own example, when he realized that even his most sophisticated followers did not always understand him. Menot expressed this idea when he told his audience that if they could not grasp the meaning of scripture, they would certainly understand an example. His story of the bather heading for certain death despite the warnings of the person on the bridge was a simple and effective way to explain salvation and damnation to men and women. But it did more than that. By using a story or example, the preacher caught the attention of the audience, and explained his point in a way that people could remember once they had gone home. They could then pass it on to others who had not been in attendance. Similarly, when preachers broke down their sermons into elaborate divisions and subdivisions, or explained doctrine through the letters in a saint's name, they provided mnemonic devices for people who otherwise might have had trouble retaining what they had learned. By making the Bible familiar, medieval Catholic preachers did not feel that they were trivializing it; rather, they were attempting to make a difficult work accessible to all.

The presentation of a sermon involved far more than form and style, and in their teaching of Christian doctrine, the preachers utilized tools that any educator would recognize. Nontextual elements included the use of theater and appearance to set the stage and engage the audience. Charisma, drama, and rhetoric were adjuncts to a preacher's training in the Bible, the *Sentences*, and medieval commentaries, but very important ones. The dramatic appearance of a gaunt, robed figure riding a broken-down mule into town would certainly set the stage for a Lenten series. By playing to the audience's desire for drama and entertainment, the preacher could convey his message in an effective manner. The large crowds that went to sermons in the fifteenth and sixteenth centuries testify to the pedagogical value of these efforts.

Who were the people who complained about medieval preaching? They tended not to be poor men and women who lived in the towns or peasants from the fields. While some of these people may have become Calvinists, those who specifically denounced the medieval style of preaching were usually learned men trained in humanism and theology. They were an elite, who did not need the kind of parable that a medieval preacher offered. Protestantism "was a cerebral, learned sort of religion, one that only allowed for the Word to stand as an image of the invisible reality of the spiritual dimension. In practical terms, this meant a very concrete shift from a world brimming over with physical, visible symbols that were open to a rather wide range of interpretations—some intentionally ambiguous—to one principally with verbal symbols that were subject to the interpretation of a carefully trained and ostensibly learned ministry."[5]

Despite its didactic value, the medieval sermon fell victim to the reforming atmosphere of the sixteenth century. The changes, religious and intellectual, that were occurring in society had important effects on preaching that can be seen in both the simplified and the proto-Baroque Catholic sermons of the mid-sixteenth century. But the medieval sermon deserves respect, for its content and construction expressed the spirit of the new covenant, if not always its letter.

The sermons provide a veritable treasure trove of information about late medieval beliefs and practice as well as reflections on contemporary society. The basic theology of the sermons is immediately evident. Beginning with the Fall, the preachers taught a doctrine based on man's sinful nature. But despite the pessimistic anthropology, the preachers went on to offer everyone the possibility of salvation. Christ's incarnation, crucifixion, and resurrection paid the debt for original sin, leaving only the "tinder" of sin that could, of course be converted into actual sin. By being aware of sin, hearing the Word of God preached, having faith, and doing what was in him (*facere quod in se est*), man could effectively cooperate in his own salvation. Medieval Catholic preachers never challenged the primacy of faith and grace, but insisted that the individual who had received these God-given benefits must then exhibit hope and charity.

Consistent with their basic philosophy of preaching and their understanding of their audiences' capabilities, the preachers described an anthropomorphic cosmos peopled by the characters of the New Testament, and supplemented by "God's good friends," the saints. The central figure in the great drama was Jesus Christ, whose life and works were the fundamental basis of Catholic theology. The ethos of the Sermon on the Mount and the Great Commandment guided the preachers who, in their efforts to capture the medieval imagination and inspire men and women to follow Christ, vividly depicted his life and death, often dramatizing and elaborating on the gospel accounts. The imitation of Christ was a powerful theme, which allowed ordinary men and women to partake of divinity in their own small way. Following the way of Christ did not consist solely, or even primarily, of works, unless works were understood to mean faith, charity towards one's neighbors and the less fortunate, and proper intentions. The preachers insisted that outward manifestations of piety, both sacramental and nonsacramental, were ways of testifying to one's beliefs, but were worthless without the proper interiorized spirit.

To Protestants, the Catholic emphasis on the life of Jesus minimized the importance of the Resurrection. The Pauline corpus, by its very nature, was antithetical to such an emphasis. In their sermons, medieval Catholic preachers did not minimize the Resurrection experience; indeed, they stressed that it was the central fact of Christian *faith*. But for them, faith could not exist apart from the individual who had inspired it. Jesus' Resurrection had created the Christian religion, but it also gave greater meaning to his words and deeds on earth. Even Lefèvre d'Étaples, one of the leaders of the French evangelical movement and the inspiration for Guillaume Farel, believed that "the person of Jesus Christ [had to be] . . . the sole point of reference for the life of every Christian."[6] The doctrinal shift from Jesus to Paul carried with it enormous implications for the ordinary believer, for the change from an affective piety that embraced the notion of the imitation of Christ to a more intellectualized form of belief and observance led to physical changes on a grand scale, as representation and imagery gave way to a less materialistic, but more distant and abstract, system of beliefs. For Catholic preachers who lived into the Reformation years, the idea of faith alone, separated from the context of Jesus' life, distorted the meaning of Christianity, and had a deleterious effect on simple minds—it could too easily lead to antinomianism and a rejection of charity and brotherly love. Studies of the decline of charity and the need for social-welfare programs in the sixteenth century suggest that the preachers' fears were correct.

Because of their ethical content and the fact that they were not simple biblical commentaries, the sermons tell us a great deal about the society in which the preachers worked. The preachers discussed the problem of "superstition," the different occupational groups in society, and women's issues.

In their critique of the orders of society, they based their condemnations on Jesus' Great Commandment—the injunction to love God and one's neighbor. The preachers found too many people, both men and women, in whose lives charity had no place. They believed that certain professions, especially commerce and law, promoted the exact opposite of charity, and referred these professionals to the beatitudes and laments:

> Blest are you poor; the reign of God is yours.
> Blest are you who hunger; you shall be filled.
> Blest are you who are weeping; you shall laugh.
> But woe to you rich, for your consolation is now.
> Woe to you who are full; you shall go hungry.
> Woe to you who laugh now; you shall weep in your grief.
>
> Luke 6:20–21, 25

There was a strong connection in the preachers' minds between meekness and powerlessness in the present world and future entry into the kingdom of heaven. Just as Jesus had, the preachers stressed that it lay within everyone's power to be "poor in spirit"—by having faith, cooperating with God's grace, and loving one's neighbor. It was simply more difficult for those endowed with worldly power and riches for, as the rich would-be follower of Jesus in the New Testament had learned, it was hard to give up the good things the world had to offer.

The preachers' attitudes toward women are rather surprising. Although medieval Catholic preachers have often been accused of antifeminism, the sermons indicate that aside from issues of vanity, pre-Reformation preachers emphasized the positive traits of women. When they discussed widowhood, victimization, the piety of late medieval women, and sanctions against female preaching, the preachers showed sensitivity and compassion, often in stark contrast to the attitudes of contemporary lay society. Pre-Reformation preachers appreciated the notion of weakness much more than mid-sixteenth century Catholic and Protestant preachers, whose sermons increasingly stress woman's place in the natural order. Although not everything pre-Reformation preachers had to say about women was complimentary, the general subject of women occupied a much more significant place in their sermons than those of later preachers, who had less room for extraneous material.

We should not minimize the differences between preachers, either as individuals or over the course of time. In any study that purports to examine the works of a large number of men, generalizations must be made. In this study, the similarity of background and training of most of the preachers, their use of similar sources, and their reliance on commonplaces from earlier preachers and doctors, all lend an air of homogeneity to their sermons. In matters of theology, there are very few real differences between the preachers, except in emphasis. The one major exception appears in discussions of God and eschatology. Martin found many "doomsday" preachers in his study, and some of the earliest preachers in this group, especially Tisserand and Raulin, shared some of these concerns. But there is a noticeable change in tone between 1400 and 1500 as the times changed from pestilence, war, and famine, to greater prosperity. The angry God of 1400 was, by 1500, the compassionate father who desired nothing more than his children's salvation. This is not so much a theological difference as a change in tone and emphasis.

It is also easy to discern differences of opinion among preachers about contemporary problems, such as the Protestant threat. By the mid-sixteenth century, heresy occupied a large place in the sermons, and although all agreed that the threat to the church was serious, the preachers suggested a number of different approaches to the problem. After 1520, considerably more attention was paid to the role of the priesthood and the sacraments, issues that had been directly challenged by the reformers.

After reading so many sermons, one begins to discern major patterns, about which generalization is possible. But almost without exception, if we read a sermon by Maillard, then one by Pepin or Messier, we become very aware of them as individuals. Their style, form, language, and content differ significantly. Menot and Maillard were "people's preachers" in every sense of the word, while Pepin's style would have found wide acceptance in both popular and educated circles. On the other hand, it is difficult to imagine Paris speaking to "ordinary" people. Therefore, the generalizations made throughout this book do some injustice to these men as individuals. Yet would they have minded? As Hirsch points out, "pride in authorship existed, [but] the medieval author . . . in general looked upon himself as the representative of, and agent for, a movement or cause, and much less as an individual."[7] Everything we know about the preachers supports this conclusion, for they considered individualism to be a trait connected with proud men and heretics. The area on which the preachers most agreed, besides theology, was the philosophy of preaching. While one might adopt the colloquial style and another the plain, they shared common goals and beliefs that made such choices important only insofar as they affected the listeners.

Finally, let us return to the paradox of late medieval piety. Was this an era of existential anguish, as some scholars have claimed? There is nothing in the sermons from 1460 to 1560 to support such a view; on the contrary, a comparison of the sermons from this period with earlier ones suggests that times had changed for the better. As the traumas of the fourteenth century gave way to the relative prosperity of the late fifteenth century, the tone of the sermons changed significantly, and not even the Lutheran crisis could revive the fatalistic mentality of an earlier time. Nor is there a great deal of support for the view that people found the demands of the late medieval church to be psychologically burdensome. Not all people experienced religion in the same way as Martin Luther and Guillaume Farel; the fervor and zeal of certain men to spread the Gospel were exceptional even in an age dominated by religious passions. This group of preachers realized, sadly, that they did not have a gathering of saints before them. Although they were fully capable of unleashing fiery and even terrifying sermons, the majority of preachers chose instead to emphasize the possibilities for salvation, even if it was against the backdrop of damnation. Internal evidence from the sermons suggests that people responded cynically to preachers who pushed penitential themes too far, complaining, "This preacher is too hard," or "He is too rigorous."

It is not as easy to dismiss the view that late medieval religion was too easy, despite the preachers' best efforts to make people conform to the Christian ideal. By a contractual system that prescribed specific remedies for specific sins, people could easily ignore the requirements for inward change, although the preachers constantly pointed out the dangers of such an external, "pharisaic" religion. Audience comments that penitence could be put off for another day, or retorts about Paul or Magdalene, support this view. But even here, we must be wary of generalizations. The sermons show that many different types of people came to sermons, and for many different reasons. While some may have been cynical and apathetic, there can be no doubt that others genuinely responded to the preachers' words.

Religious reformation was an ongoing process that began not with Luther's published attack on indulgences, but early in the fifteenth century in response to a church wracked by schism, a church that many thought had lost sight of its original mission. The problems of bureaucracy, venality, anticlericalism, and related issues so preoccupied later fifteenth-century preachers that they began to make an attempt from within to correct the faults of the church and its priesthood. The faults of the church were very real, and should not be minimized. But as both Protestants and post-Tridentine Catholics discovered, it was much easier to criticize than to change.

Appendix: Biographical Sketches

BRULEFER, Étienne

Étienne Pillet, nicknamed Brulefer for his religious zeals, was born in Saint-Malo shortly before 1450. Entering the nearby Franciscan convent at Dinan with the support of Guillaume Vorilong, he was sent to Paris, where he became a leading Scotist and commentator on Bonaventure. He received his doctorate in 1482, and his reputation as a theologian soon spread to Germany and northern Italy. He left France abruptly in 1490, probably being banished for frank preaching against the king, idolatry, and papal power. Although he knew no German, he entered the convent at Mainz, where he hoped to lead an ascetic, cloistered life. However, his fame and talent led his superiors to authorize him to preach in Mainz and Metz. In 1495, according to a brief anonymous biography, he returned to the convent of Dinan in his native Brittany, where he died, probably in 1499 or 1507. (See P. Feret, *La faculté de théologie de Paris et ses docteurs les plus célèbres: Moyen Age* [Paris: Picard, 1896] 4:323; Renaudet, *Préréforme,* 95; Zawart, *Franciscan Preaching,* 304.)

CLEREE, Jean

A native of Coutances, Jean Cleree was born around 1445. Sent from the Dominican convent of Evreux to study at Saint-Jacques in Paris, he was first in his class for the licentiate in theology in 1489 and received his doctorate the following year. He preached the Lenten series at the basilica of Saint-Eustache in 1494, where his acclaim was so great that the parish clergy offered him a fine collection of printed books. In this same year he joined the reformed Dominican congregation of Holland, probably at the behest of his close friend and colleague, Jean Standonck. In 1499, the Haarlem chapter of the congregation named him their vicar general, a post he had refused to accept two years earlier; as vicar general he was responsible for reforming their convents. During these same years he acted as mentor to Guillaume Pepin, also originally from the convent of Évreux. In 1502, he became confessor to Louis XII and accompanied the king to Italy. On his return from Lombardy, he attempted to reform the convent of Troyes but met with such resistance that one religious "who had an iron mallet, threatened to break his head open." In 1507, he was named vicar general of the order by the pope in Pavia, but on his return trip he died, on August 10, 1507, some said of poison. (See Renaudet, *Préréforme,* 182, 210, 229, 313, 315, 328, 451.)

CLICHTOVE, Josse

Considered the most illustrious Paris doctor of theology in the early sixteenth century, the humanist Josse Clichtove was born in 1472 at Nieuport, in Flanders. His family, which included three brothers and one sister, was noble. He attended the Collège de Boncour, and after receiving his master's degree, taught at the Collège du Cardinal Lemoine. He pursued advanced studies at both the Sorbonne and the Collège de Navarre. He received his license in May 1506 and his doctorate in December of the same year, ranking sixth in a class of fifteen. In 1517, he refused the post of confessor to the dauphin, preferring a more contemplative life away from court. In 1522, he was made curé of Saint-Pierre de "Controvio" in Amiens and Saint-Jacques in Tournai. He lived in Chartres from 1525, serving as canon and theologus of the cathedral. Three times a week, he lectured on the Bible. In 1531, he wrote in favor of the new poor laws in Ypres. His sermons went through eighteen editions from 1534 to 1643. (See Clerval, *Judoci Clichtovei;* Farge, *Biographical Register,* 90–104; Massaut, *Critique et tradition.*)

DENISSE, Nicolas

Little is known of the life and education of Nicolas Denisse, except for his positions as *gardien* of the Franciscan convent in Rouen, vicar general of the province of France, and his status as a preacher of great renown. Although Wadding refers to him as a scholar truly adept in theology and his sermons clearly mark him as a Scotist, he evidently did not take a theology degree at Paris. He died in 1509. (see Lippens, "Glapion," 46, 48; Wadding, Scriptors *ordinis minorum,* 15:114; Zawart, *Franciscan Preaching,* 360.)

FARINIER, Antoine

Also known as Fradin, this hardy preacher left few details of his life. Born in Ville-franche-en-Beaujolais, Farinier joined the Franciscan order. His preaching so stirred up the Parisian crowd in 1478 that Louis XI banished him in perpetuity from the realm. He went on pilgrimage to the Holy Land, and was in Rhodes by 1480, where he took part in the defense against a Muslim siege. He died shortly after. (See Krailsheimer, *Rabelais,* 10; Jean de Roye, *Chroniques,* 2:71–72; Sessevalle, *Historie générale,* 2:130–31.)

FILLON, Artus

Fillon was born in 1468 in Verneuil, Normandy, the son of Jean, seigneur de la Barre. He began his studies for the priesthood at the College de Harcourt, followed by entrance into the famed Collège de Navarre. In 1504 he received his licentiate and doctorate in theology from the University of Paris. He was chosen as vicar general by Georges d'Amboise, archbishop of Rouen, in 1506. During his term he completed the *Speculum curatorum,* a small manual for the use of curés, which included particular suggestions and examples for sermon making. In 1507, he became curé of Saint-Maclou, where his stature as a preacher grew. He was chosen as a clerical representative whenever the Estates of Normandy met, and in 1514 was part of a deputation sent to Louis XII to protest against the burdens of royal taxation. He preached before Francis I in 1517. A friend of the reformer Briçonnet, he was elected bishop of Senlis in 1522. On August 27, 1526, he died, requesting that his executors bury him without pomp. (See Picot, *Fillon;* Farge, *Biographical Register,* 165.)

GAIGNY, Jean de

Although his origins are obscure, Jean de Gaigny was born in Paris around the end of the fifteenth century, possibly a relative of Jean de Ganay, *parlementaire* and chancellor of France during the reign of Louis XII. He studied Latin and Greek under the humanist Pierre Danès. In 1532, he received his licentiate in theology, but became involved in a dispute with the chancellor because he was ranked second in his class. He received the doctorate in the same year and was soon lecturing on the epistles of Paul. He had regular occasion to preach before the king and the court, and as an active member of the Faculty of Theology, he became chancellor briefly in 1546. Besides being an avid book collector, he also established his own printing press in his home. He died on November 15, 1549. Note that the three sermons examined in this book are presumed to be the work of Jean de Gaigny; their date of 1521 is problematic but not impossible. (See Farge, *Biographical Register,* 177–179; Feret, *Epoque moderne,* 2:188.)

GUILLIAUD, Claude

Born in 1493 in Villefrance-en-Beaujolais, Claude Guilliaud came from a family of modest means. A local benefcator helped him to go Paris to study theology and there he became the protégé of a well-known *parlementaire.* Jacques Merlin presided over his *vesperia* (one of the academic disputations required for the doctorate) in 1532, and he was awarded his doctorate in theology two weeks later. Jacques Hurault, bishop of Autun, became interested in Guilliaud, making him a canon at the cathedral, curé of Quarré-les-Tombes, theologal, and *penitencier.* In 1541 he delivered a sermon during the procession after a desecration of the host. He spent the years between 1540 and 1550 training the clergy of his diocese.

Guilliaud often found himself in trouble with the faculty over some of his evangelical ideas. He and Michael Servetus collaborated on a six-volume Bible, and he also showed special interest in the Pauline commentaries of Martin Bucer. He gathered together an extensive library of at least fifteen volumes, 450 of which have been located and catalogued. He died on April 13, 1551. (See Gillot and Boëll, *Supplément,* 218–21; Farge, *Biographical Register,* 213–14; Pellechet, *Catalogue.*)

ILLYRICUS, Thomas

Illyricus was born around 1485 at Vrana in Dalmatia. His family soon moved to Osimo, where he joined the Franciscan Observants. He began preaching in 1510, at the age of twenty-five. In 1515 he made a pilgrimage to the Holy Land, followed by trips to Saint-Maximin and Compostela in 1518. He attended a general chapter in Bordeaux in 1520, which began his five-year apostolate in the south of France. After returning from Guyenne and Languedoc, he retired to the convent of Carnolès in Monaco, where he became an intimate of the Grimaldi family. Returning to the convent from the oratory in 1528, he fell in the road and died. Miracles are said to have occurred on the spot. (See Mauriac, "Illyricus," 66, 68, 338; Zawart, *Franciscan Preaching,* 393.)

LANSPERGE, Jean

Except for his probable identification as a Carthusian, no information is available.

LEPICART, François

François LePicart was born the third of fifteen children on April 16, 1504, in the rue des Blancs-Manteaux in Paris. He came of an ancient noble family, and was baptized by the archbishop of Lyon, François de Rohan, and confirmed by Ètienne Poncher, bishop of Paris. At the Collège de Navarre, he studied Greek under Pierre Danès. He was ordained priest by François Poncher, bishop of Paris, in 1526.

In 1533, he preached against the teaching of Gérard Roussel and possibly also against Marguerite of Navarre, and was detained in the monastery prison of Saint-Magloire in Paris, where he continued to give lectures on positive theology. Like his friend Beda, he was sent into exile, and spent his time in Rheims with maternal relatives. In 1535, he received the licentiate and doctorate in theology. He was involved in the faculty's book censorship and helped to draw up articles of faith in 1543. In 1547, he was named dean of Notre-Dame and vicar of Jean du Bellay, bishop of Paris, and a year later dean of Saint-Germain l'Auxerrois. In 1555, Pope Paul IV asked the help of the cardinal of Lorraine in persuading LePicart to come to Rome to preach, but in poor health, LePicart refused, fearing the pope would make him a cardinal. Much beloved by the people of Paris, he died on September 17, 1556. So many people passed through Saint-Germain to pay their respects that the doors were broken. Some twenty thousand people joined the funeral procession from Saint-Germain to Notre-Dame des Blancs-Manteaux, where he was buried with his family. (See Hilarion de Coste, *Le parfait ecclésiastique.*)

MAILLARD, Olivier

Born in Yvignac, Brittany, around 1430, Maillard joined the Franciscans of the province of Aquitaine. He was sent to Paris, where he received his doctorate in theology. Out of a desire for stricter observance, he joined the Observant Franciscans at Châteauroux. He seems to have begun preaching in 1460, and his vocation took him at various times to Flanders, Germany, Hungary, England, and all parts of France. His preaching was sometimes so openly antiroyalist that Louis XI once threatened to have him tied up in a sack and thrown into the river if he did not desist. Under Charles VIII, he assumed the role of diplomat and traveled with the king to Italy. With Francis de Paul, he got into trouble for opposing the king's acquisition of Roussillon and the Cerdagne. He was vicar general of the Observants three times, in 1487, 1493, and 1499, and in this position engaged in numerous attempts to reform convents throughout France. His intemperate attacks on royalty and its privileges eventually took their toll when he opposed the divorce and remarriage of Louis XII. Having preached in public that Jeanne de Valois remained the true queen of France, he was sent into exile in Bruges. In 1501, he was recalled to Paris, and he died on June 13, 1502, in Toulouse. Wadding relates that he worked many miracles during and after his lifetime. (See Samouillan, *Maillard;* Chevalier, "Maillard," 25–39; Wadding, *Scriptoris ordinis minorum,* 15:294.)

Meigret, Aimé

Born around 1485 of an important Lyonnais family, Meigret had many close connections with the Parlement of Paris, a fact that proved to be of capital importance in his later years. He took the habit at the Dominican convent of Notre-Dame-de-Confort in Lyon around 1500, and was sent to Paris to study theology under Peter Crockaert. In 1520, he received his licentiate and doctorate in theology. His humanist background first led to problems in Rouen in 1522, when he preached the plurality of Magdalenes. In 1524, his troubles began in earnest when he preached a Lenten sermon at Lyon and a similar sermon in Grenoble a month later, with the heretic Pierre de Sebiville in attendance. Because of the local authorities' concern about its importance, the case was transferred to Paris, where things deteriorated into angry outbursts between Meigret and Noël Beda. After his temporary release, Meigret published his sermon at Lyon, leading to his rearrest on the orders of the queen mother, Louise of Savoy. What happened to him after is unclear, although it seems obvious that his parlementary connections saved him. The Bourgeois of Paris says he made an *amende honorable* at Lyon, but faculty records indicate he spent some time in prison. Farge speculates that his friends and relatives won his release, which was followed by exile in Germany. He probably died in Strasbourg in 1527. (See Farge, *Biographical Register,* 292–95; Clerval, *Registre,* 319; Hours, "Procès;" Guy, "Sermon;" Bourgeois, *Journal,* 182–83.)

Menot, Michel

Menot was probably born between 1440 and 1450 in Beauce. We do not have any information on when he entered the Franciscan order, although we may surmise that it was after he studied law at Orléans. He is often accorded the title professor of theology in records and sermons, but there is no evidence that he took a degree in theology at the University of Paris. He traveled and preached widely throughout France and probably Europe. In 1514, he became *gardien* of the convent of Chartres, and was largely responsible for successful reconstruction efforts there during the last three years of his life. He died in Chartres on December 30, 1518. (See Nève, *Sermons choisis,* "Introduction.")

Merlin, Jacques

Born in Saint-Victurnien in Limousin around 1473, Merlin probably studied under the noted humanist Girolamo Balbi during his early student days. Changing to the theology curriculum, he received his licentiate and doctorate in 1510. In 1511, he published an edition of Origen, which led to a long and bitter dispute with Noël Beda over its orthodoxy. In 1514, he became curé of Montmartre. He also held the important posts of canon and *penitencier* of Paris and curé of the Madeleine, his duties including counseling and delivering sermons to those accused of heresy. He was the last confessor of Louis de Berquin. An active opponent of heresy, he was very outspoken, which may have inclined the king's circle against him when he later spoke out against Louise of Savoy's plans to tax the Parisians and his criticism of the queen mother's slow response to threats of invasion. He was imprisoned in the Louvre for two years, from 1527 to 1529, and spent a further year of exile in Nantes. In June 1530 he was released on order of the king. From 1530 to 1532 he served as vicar general to the bishop of

Paris. He was a member of the committee that investigated the preaching of Pierre Caroli. He probably died on September 26, 1541. (See Renaudet, *Préréforme*, 123–24; Farge, *Biographical Register*, 325–29; Clerval, *Registre*, 335, 413; Feret, *Epoque moderne*, 2:186; Bourrilly, *Bourgeois*, 245.)

MESSIER, Robert

Very little is known of Messier's life. He seems to have entered the Franciscans in Amiens, and then was sent to Paris, where he earned his doctorate in theology. In 1503, he was named *gardien* of the Franciscan convent of Amiens and the next year *gardien* of Troyes, with responsibility for reforming the houses in his province. He became minister-provincial of the Province of France in 1523 and 1529 and had the same even more important position in the convent of Paris. In 1535 he was chosen as *custos* of Vermandois. He retired to Longchamps, where he acted as confessor to the Clarisses, and died in 1546. (See H. M. Feret, "Nécrologie des frères mineurs d'Auxerre," AHF 3 (1910): 535.)

MONLUC, Jean de

Monluc was born of a noble family around 1501, in Condom or Saint-Gemme in Guyenne. As a teenager, he took the Dominican habit at Condom or Agen, and soon became renowned for his learning and eloquence. He went on to study canon and civil law at the University of Toulouse, but upon his introduction to Marguerite of Navarre during one of her many stays in the Château de Nérac, he decided to abandon the monastic life in order to live in court circles. In Paris, Monluc soon came to the notice of Francis I, who confided a diplomatic mission to him in 1536. As protonotary to the bishop of Mâcon, he traveled to Rome and then to Constantinope in order to negotiate with the Turks to redirect their attacks from Austria to Naples while the French king attacked Milan. Although the mission failed, Monluc returned to Rome, where he was received by Pope Paul IV. He stayed for several years as part of the French ambassadorial staff at the Vatican. His work so pleased the king that in 1543, he was dispatched as ambassador to the doge of Venice, followed by a second mission to Constantinople in 1545. In 1548, he was sent to Scotland as Henry II's representative to Mary of Guise. In 1554, in gratitude for diplomatic services performed, he was named bishop of Valence and Saint-Dié, where he seems to have spent at least some time resident in his diocese. Monluc's orthodoxy was questioned in 1560, when the curé of Menglon denounced him as a heretic. At this point, nothing further came of the accusations, and he was sent on diplomatic missions to Queen Elizabeth of England and then on to Mary of Guise, regent of Scotland. Later in the same year he took part in the Assembly of Fontainebleau, where he openly supported Condé; he also participated in the Colloquy of Poissy (1561). At the colloquy, he joined several other bishops in refusing to attend the mass celebrated by Cardinal d'Armagnac or to take communion. Instead, along with Cardinal de Châtillon and the bishop d'Uzès, he celebrated mass, according to some, "à la mode de Genève." Although she did not like all his views or writings, Catherine de Médicis continued to support Monluc. During 1561, he also published several collections of sermons, three of which earned the censure of the Sorbonne because of his position on free will, works, the eucharist, purgatory, and the cult of the saints. In 1563, he was called before the Inquisition in Rome and charged formally with heresy, although he was eventually cleared in 1566.

From 1566 to 1572, Monluc was responsible for setting in order the financial affairs of central France, furthering royal claims wherever possible. Shortly thereafter, during a mission to Lyon, he evidently made some statements that local Huguenots found objectionable. The governor of Vienne ordered his arrest, but he was able to hide himself in the woods and escape to nearby Annonay. There, some Protestants who were not attending sermon pursued him, but again he was able to escape by climbing through a hole in the wall in one of the houses there. In 1572, he left for Poland to negotiate for the future Henry III's election as king of the Poles. Having left Paris a second time on the day before the Saint Bartholomew's Day Massacre, he fell ill with dysentery and was arrested and briefly detained in Lorraine. From 1574 to 1578, he seems to have stayed in his diocese. He died in the house of the Jesuits of Toulouse on April 12, 1579. (See Larroque, *Monluc;* Reynaud, *Monluc;* Degert, "Procès," 69; Arnaud, *Vivarais et du Velay,* 1:39.)

PARIS, Étienne

Born around 1495 in Orléans, Étienne Paris joined the Dominican order and was sent to study at the convent of Saint-Jacques in Paris. In 1530, he received his licentiate and doctorate in theology. He became vicar to Nicolas Payen in 1538, and replaced him as provincial of the order in the same year. In 1545, he preached the funeral sermon for Charles, the young son of Francis I. He was made auxiliary bishop of Rouen in 1551 and obtained the same post in his native Orléans a year later. In Rouen in 1561 he preached the foundation sermon for the Confraternity of the Blessed Sacrament. He died at Rouen in the same year. (See Farge, *Biographical Register,* 356–57; Feret, *Époque moderne,* 2:273.)

PEPIN, Guillaume

See Chapter 3.

RAULIN, Jean

Raulin was born in Toul in 1443. He studied for the priesthood and while studying for the licentiate composed an important commentary on Aristotle's *Logic*. He took his doctorate in theology from the University of Paris in 1479. A nominalist, he became head of the Collège de Navarre in 1482, which prospered under his strict and reform-minded guidance. Famed for his preaching to both the simple and the learned, he forcefully argued for reformation of the clergy from the top down. In 1497, he left the college in order to become a novice at the abbey of Cluny. He made visitations to reform the Benedictine abbeys of the Auvergne and Midi in 1499, and was named to the committee examining Reuchlin's work in 1514. He died, however, in the midst of the committee's proceedings, on February 16, 1515, in his abbey. (See Renaudet, *Préréforme,* 94, 98, 165–67, 234–36, 311, 586, 647–48.)

SCOEPPERUS, Jean

The sermon by Scoepperus is appended to a volume on the eucharist by Émond Auger, thus making his identification as a Jesuit probable. The title of the sermon refers to him as "Master," but we have no further information about him.

TISSERAND, Jean

We know relatively little of this Franciscan friar, although the frontispiece of his sermons refers to him as a doctor of theology. He was called to Paris in 1469, where he is said to have preached every day for two years, going from parish to parish each month. He became confessor and preacher to Queen Anne of Brittany and in 1495 founded the Society of Penitent Women in Paris. He died around 1497. (See Sessevalle, *Histoire générale,* 129; Zawart, *Franciscan Preaching,* 304.)

Notes

Abbreviations of Journals

AFH	*Archivum Franciscum Historicum*
AHD	*Archives d'histoire dominicaine*
AHDLMA	*Archives d'histoire doctrinale et littéraire du moyen âge*
AHR	*American Historical Review*
AM	*Annales du Midi*
ARG	*Archiv für Reformationsgeschichte*
BHR	*Bullétin d'humanisme et renaissance*
BSHPF	*Bullétin de la société de l'histoire de protestantisme français*
CCM	*Cahiers de civilisation médiévale*
CH	*Cahiers d'histoire*
CP	*Classical Philology*
JEH	*Journal of Ecclesiastical History*
JIH	*Journal of Interdisciplinary History*
JMH	*Journal of Modern History*
JRH	*Journal of Religious History*
JTS	*Journal of Theological Studies*
PMLA	*Proceedings of the Modern Language Association*
PP	*Past and Present*
RB	*Revue bourdaloue*
RH	*Revue historique*
RHEF	*Revue d'histoire de l'église de France*
RHMC	*Revue d'histoire moderne et contemporaine*
RHT	*Revue historique de Toulouse*
RN	*Revue du nord*
RNP	*Revue néoscholastique de philosophie*
RQ	*Renaissance Quarterly*
RQH	*Revue des questions historiques*
SCJ	*Sixteenth Century Journal*
TRHS	*Transactions of the Royal Historical Society*
TZ	*Theologische Zeitschrift*

Abbreviations of Sermons and Sermon Collections

Avent	François LePicart, *Les sermons . . . pour . . . l'Avent*
CA	Guillaume Pepin, *Conciones de adventu Domini*
Caresme	François LePicart, *Les sermons . . . de caresme*
CDA	Guillaume Pepin, *Concionum dominicalium . . . pars aestivalis*
CDH	Guillaume Pepin, *Conciones dominicalium . . . pars hiemalis*
CFA	Guillaume Pepin, *Conciones festorum tempore Adventus*
CPP	Guillaume Pepin, *Conciones in septem Psalmos poenitentiales*
CQ	Guillaume Pepin, *Conciones quadragesimales*
CS	Guillaume Pepin, *Conciones de sanctis*
DN	Guillaume Pepin, *Sermones . . . de destructione Ninive*
EC	Guillaume Pepin, *Elucidationem in confiteor*
Homélies	Jean de Gaigny, *Trois homélies*
Homélies	Étienne Paris, *Homélies . . . es principales festes*
Instructions	Jean de Monluc, *Deux instructions*
Libellus	Thomas Illyricus, *Libellus de potestate summi pontificis*
Oeuvres	Olivier Maillard, *Oeuvres françaises*
Paris-Alia	Michel Menot, "Carêmes de Paris," Alia Secunda Pars
Paris-1	Michel Menot, "Premier Carême de Paris"
Paris-2	Michel Menot, "Second Carême de Paris"
PS	John Calvin, *Plusieurs sermons*
QO	Olivier Maillard, *Quadragesimale opus Parisius predicatum*
QS	Robert Messier, *Super epistola et evangelia totius quadragesime sermones*
RA	Guillaume Pepin, *Rosareum aureum*
SA	Olivier Maillard, *Sermones de adventu*
SA	Jean Raulin, *Opus sermonum de adventu*
SA	Jean Tisserand, *Sermones de adventu*
SD	Olivier Maillard, *Sermones dominicales*
SE	Jean Raulin, *Sermones de eucharistia*
SA	Thomas Illyricus, *Sermones aurei ac excellentissimi*
Sermons	Jean de Monluc, *Sermons*
SP	Antoine Farinier, *Sermones . . . de peccatis*
Speculum	Artus Fillon, *Speculum curatorum*
SQ	Jean Cleree, *Sermones quadragesimale . . . sanctum Severinum*
SQ	Jean Raulin, *Sermonum quadragesimalium*
SR	Nicolas Denisse, *Sermones residui*
SS	Olivier Maillard, *Sermones de sanctis*
SSP	Olivier Maillard, *Sermones de stipendio peccati*
Tours	Michel Menot, "Carême de Tours"
Trinité	François LePicart, *Les sermons . . . depuis Pasques iusques à la Trinité*
TS	Nicolas Denisse, *Tabula sermonum*

Chapter 1

1. Rudolf Hirsch contends that "the production of early printed books in the fifteenth and early sixteenth century . . . indicates clearly that an unknown and undefinable, but steadily increasing, number of simple men and women learned how to read." Rudolf Hirsch, *Printing, Selling, and Reading, 1450–1550* (Wiesbaden: Harrassowitz, 1967), 149.

2. Gabriel Le Bras, *Etudes de sociologie religieuse* (Paris: Presses universitaires de France, 1955–56), and Le Bras, *Sociologie et religion* (Paris: Fayard, 1958).

3. Lawrence Duggan. "The Unresponsiveness of the Late Medieval Church: A Reconsideration." *SCJ* 9 (1978): 19.

4. Miriam Chrisman, *Lay Culture, Learned Culture* (New Haven: Yale University Press, 1982), 84.

5. A still useful, but somewhat outdated study, is Charles Labitte, *De la démocratie chez les prédicateurs de la Ligue* (Paris: Joubert, 1841); see also Barbara Diefendorf, "Simon Vigor: A Radical Preacher in the Sixteenth Century," *SCJ* 18 (1987): 399–410; Robert Harding, "Revolution and Reform in the Holy League: Angers, Rennes, Nantes," *JMH* 53 (1981): 379–416; G. Wylie Sypher, "Faisant ce qu'il leur vient à plaisir: The Image of Protestantism in French Catholic Polemic on the Eve of the Religious Wars," *SCJ* 11 (1980): 59–84.

6. Hervé Martin, *La métier du prédicateur à la fin du Moyen Âge, 1350–1520* (Paris: Cerf, 1988).

7. Hervé Martin, "La ministère de la parole en France septentrionale de la peste noire à la Réforme" (Dissertation for the doctorat d'état, Université de Paris IV/ Sorbonne, 1986).

8. Hervé Martin, *Les ordres mendiants en Bretagne (vers 1230–vers 1530)* (Rennes: Institut armoricain de recherches historiques, 1975).

9. André Godin, *L'homéliaire de Jean Vitrier* (Geneva: Droz, 1971).

10. Olivia Holloway McIntyre, "The Celestines of Paris: Monastic Life and Thought in the Sixteenth Century" (Ph.D. diss., Stanford University, 1984).

11. D. Catherine Brown, *Pastor and Laity in the Theology of Jean Gerson* (Cambridge: Cambridge University Press, 1987).

12. Ibid., 1.

13. Steven Ozment, *The Reformation in the Cities: The Appeal of Protestantism to Sixteenth-Century Germany and Switzerland* (New Haven: Yale University Press, 1975). John Dahmus tested Ozment's thesis in a study of German preaching, concluding that while such burdens did indeed exist, they were the result of an insufficient appreciation of the lay condition by clerics; "Preaching to the Laity in Fifteenth Century Germany: Johannes Nider's 'Harps'," *JRH* 12 (1982): 55–68.

14. See, e.g., Jacques Chiffoleau, *La comptabilité de l'au-delà* (Rome: Farnese, 1980).

15. Jean Delumeau, *La peur en occident, XIVe–XVIIIe siècles* (Paris: Fayard, 1978), pp. 15–18ff.

16. Etienne Delaruelle, *La piété populaire au moyen âge* (Turin: Bottega d'Erasmo, 1975), 455.

17. Carlos M. N. Eire, *War against the Idols: The Reformation of Worship from Erasmus to Calvin* (Cambridge: Cambridge University Press, 1986).

18. Jacques Toussaert, *Le sentiment religieux en Flandre à la fin du Moyen Âge* (Paris: Plon, 1963), 595–602.

19. Delaruelle, *Piété*, 470.

20. Bernd Moeller, "Piety in Germany around 1500," in Steven Ozment (ed.), *The Reformation in Medieval Perspective* (Chicago: Quadrangle Books, 1971), 50–75.

21. A. N. Galpern, *The Religions of the People in Sixteenth Century Champagne* (Cambridge: Cambridge University Press, 1976); cf. Eire, *War,* 24.

22. Martin, *Métier,* 29, 71.

23. Hervé Martin, "Les prédications deviantes, du début du XVᵉ siècle au début du XVIᵉ siècle, dans les provinces septentrionales de la France," in Bernard Chevalier and Robert Sauzet (eds.), *Les réformes enracinement socio-culturel: XXV colloque de Tours* (Paris: Editions de la Maisnie, 1982), 251.

24. Jean Delumeau, *Catholicism between Luther and Voltaire* (London: Burns & Oates, 1977), 230–31.

Chapter 2

1. There were some exceptions, but these were notorious. When Guillaume Briçonnet became bishop of Meaux, he found that certain parishes had not had preaching in two to ten years. Martin, *Métier,* 73, 142.

2. Ibid., 26, 49, 72, 75.

3. Michel Menot, "Premier Carême de Paris" (Paris–1) in Joseph Nève, ed., *Sermons choisis de Michel Menot* (Paris: Honoré Champion, 1924), 231.

4. "Quare dicit Dominus quod predicatores se transferant in magnas civitates plus quam ad parvas et ad villagia? . . . Diceret aliquis quia in civitatibus magnis sunt magni doctores et sapientes? Nonne ideo quod in magnis civitatibus sunt magna marsupia ad contentandum predicatores? Non, non! . . . Sed hec est ratio, quia plura peccata et plures mali habitant magnas civitates quam parva villagia" (Ibid., 230–31).

5. "Parisius olim dicebatur fons sapientie: fons iusticie: fons conscientie. Scilicet hodie est fons iniquitatis, iniusticie, & totius deceptionis" (Olivier Maillard, *Quadragesimale opus Parisius predicatum* [QO] [Lyon: Stephan Gueygnardi, 1503], fol. 175).

6. Jean Cleree, *Sermones quadragesimales declamati Parisius apud sanctum Severinum* SQ (Paris: Engleberto Marnesio, n.d.), fol. 68.

7. Olivier Maillard, *Sermones de adventu (SA)* (Paris: Jehan Petit, 1506), fol. 70.

8. "Predicavi, laboravi, nescio quid feci; rogo Deum quod sequatur fructus. Vel tota Scriptura fallit, vel villa Turonensis non longo tempore perseverabit in isto statu. . . . Eatis Parisius, ubi tot fiunt mala, sed non invenietis tot mala publica, tot macquerelles et stuphas publicas ut hic" (Menot, "Carême de Tours" [*Tours*], 214–15).

9. Maillard, *QO,* fol. 112.

10. "Et hinc est, quod videmus homines malos in magnis civitatibus, in quibus solet frequenter audiri sonus praedicationis, magis induratos, & obstinatos, quam habitantes in locis campestribus, qui vix semel in anno habent unicum sermonem" (Guillaume Pepin, *Concionum dominicalium ex epistolis et evangeliis totius anni, pars aestivalis* [*CDA*] [Antwerp: Guillelmus Lesteenius & Engelbertus Gymnicus, 1656], 183).

11. Martin, *Ordres mendiants,* 319.

12. See, e.g., Guillaume and Michel Leriche, *Le journal de Guillaume et de Michel Leriche* (*de 1534 à 1586*), ed. by A. D. de la Fantonelle de Mandoré (Saint-Maixent: Reversé, 1846), 23, 78.

13. Sire de Gouberville, *Le journal du Sire de Gouberville,* ed. by Eugène Robillard de Beaurepaire (Caen: Henri Deslesques, 1892), 210–11, 381, 397, 484, 569.

14. A. J. Herminjard, *Corréspondance des réformateurs dans les pays de langue française* (Paris: Levy, 1870), October 15, 1523, 1:157.

15. Martin, *Métier*, 24.

16. Anscar Zawart, *The History of Franciscan Preaching and of Franciscan Preachers* (New York: Wagner, 1928), 281.

17. Jean Tisserand, *Sermones de adventu* (*SA*) (Paris, 1517).

18. Maillard, *SA*.

19. Jean Raulin, *Opus sermonum de adventu* (*SA*) (Paris: Jehan Petit, 1516).

20. Martin, *Métier*, 414.

21. Peter Bayley, *French Pulpit Oratory, 1598–1650* (Cambridge: Cambridge University Press, 1980), 105.

22. Jean d'Auton, *Chroniques de Louis XII* (Paris: Renouard, 1893), 3:8.

23. Zawart, *Franciscan Preaching*, 254; Marc Venard, *"L'eglise d'Avignon au XVIème siècle"* (thesis, Université de Paris IV, 1977), 1:222.

24. J.-A. Clerval, *Régistre des procès verbaux de la faculté de théologie de Paris* (Paris, 1917), 232.

25. James Farge, *Biographical Register of Paris Doctors of Theology, 1500–1536* (Toronto: Pontifical Institute of Medieval Studies, 1980), 65.

26. See, e.g., Archives communales de Grenoble, CC600; Bourgeois de Paris, *Le journal d'un bourgeois de Paris sous le règne de François Ier, (1515–1536)*, ed. by V.-L. Bourrilly (Paris: Alphonse Picard, 1910), 8, 178, 222, 232.

27. Charles de Beaurepaire, "Quittance d'un prédicateur envoyé par Louis XI en Normandie," *Précis analytique des travaux de l'Académie des Sciences, Belles-Lettres et Arts de Rouen* (1899), 199.

28. Robert Boutruche, *Bourdeaux de 1453 à 1715* (Bordeaux: Editions Montaigne, 1966), 228–29.

29. Kelley, *The Beginning of Ideology: Consciousness and Society in the French Reformation* (Cambridge: Cambridge University Press, 1981), 110.

30. P. Imbart de la Tour, *Les origines de la réforme* (Paris: Hachette, 1909), 3:241.

31. C. Oursel, *Notes pour servir à l'histoire de la réforme en Normandie au temps de François Ier* (Caen: Henri Deslesques, 1913), 88.

32. Ibid., 79, 82.

33. Zawart, *Franciscan Preaching*, 259.

34. Ibid., 126, 157.

35. Archives Communales de Grenoble, FF5.

36. Claude Haton, *Mémoires de Claude Haton*, ed. Felix Bouquélot (Paris: Imprimérie Impériale, 1857), 1:11–12, 136–37.

37. Archives Communales de Lyon, BB8.

38. Claire Dolan, *Entre tours et clochers: Les gens d'église à Aix-en-Provence au XVIe siècle* (Sherbrooke, Que.: Centre d'études de la Renaissance, 1981), 97–98.

39. Marc Godet, *La congrégation de Montaigu (1490–1580)* (Paris: Honoré Champion, 1912), 17–18.

40. Marie-France Godfroy, "Le prédicateur franciscain Thomas Illyricus à Toulouse (novembre 1518–mai 1519)," *AM* 97 (1985): 102.

41. Martin, *Métier*, 47, 74, 114, 127, 139, 141.

42. L. Dacheux, *Un réformateur catholique à la fin du XVe siècle: Jean Geiler de Kaysersberg* (Paris: de la Grave, 1876), 31.

43. Ibid., 395–96.

44. Venard, "L'église d'Avignon," 2:547.

45. A. Prudhomme, *Simples notes sur Pierre de Sebiville* (Bourgoin: Vauvillez, 1884), 8–11.

46. Ibid., 17.

47. Philip Hoffman, *Church and Community in the Diocese of Lyon, 1500–1789* (New Haven: Yale University Press, 1984), 37.

48. Jean Glaumeau, *Journal de Jehan Glaumeau, Bourges, 1541–62* (Paris: Aubry, 1867–1868), 61.

49. Hoffman, *Church,* 37.

50. Archives Communales d'Agen, BB25, GG182. Martin, while admitting that episcopal preaching was not the norm, indicates that in Brittany at least there were several noteworthy exceptions. Martin, *Métier,* 131–32.

51. Archives Communales de Grenoble, BB18.

52. The basic unit of currency was the *livre tournois,* which was equivalent to 20 *sous tournois* or 240 *deniers;* Martin Wolfe, *The Fiscal System of Renaissance France* (New Haven: Yale University Press, 1972), 293. A *sou parisien* was worth approximately 20 percent more than a *sou tournois;* James Farge, *Orthodoxy and Reform in Early Reformation France* (Leiden: E. J. Brill, 1985), 46. The livre was only an accounting term; no such coin existed. The chief gold coin was the *écu d'or,* whose rate fluctuated according to the vagaries of royal finance and the condition of the coins themselves. The approximate value of the *écu* on specific dates was:

1456	26 s., 6 d.
1490s	36 s., 3 d.
1519	40 s.
1561	50 s.
1575	60 s.

Wolfe, *Fiscal System,* 293–94. In southern France, payments were usually made in *florins.* One *florin* was approximately equal to 13 s. 9 d; Leah L. Otis, *Prostitution in Medieval Society* (Chicago: University of Chicago Press, 1985), xvii.

53. Martin, *Ordres mendiants,* 226–27.

54. Archives Communales de Nantes, CC99.

55. Archives Départementales de la Gironde, G497; Archives Communales d'Agen, CC292.

56. Archives Départementales de la Seine-Maritime, G226–32, 234, 236, 238–42, 244–48; Archives Communales de Boulogne-sur-Mer, 1 fol. 3b, 4 fol. 6b.

57. Archives Communales de Grenoble, CC580.

58. Ibid., FF5.

59. Ibid., BB5, BB9.

60. John Bossy, *Christianity in the West, 1400–1700* (Oxford: Oxford University Press, 1987), 7.

61. Martin, *Métier,* 156.

62. Archives Communales d'Amiens, BB18, fol. 126.

63. Ibid., BB19, fol. 22.

64. Ibid., BB35, fol. 67.

65. Ibid., BB10, fol. 44; BB12, fol. 59; BB14, fol. 54; BB15, fol. 64; BB21, fol. 2.

66. Archives Communales de Grenoble, CC600.

67. Archives Communales d'Amiens, BB5, fol. 208.

68. Ibid., BB5, fol. 2.

69. Ibid., BB20, fol. 82.

70. Archives Communales de Nantes, CC99.

71. Haton, *Mémoires,* 12.

72. Archives Communales de Boulogne-sur-Mer (1564), 1 fol. 3b; Archives Communales d'Amiens, BB26, fol. 50.

73. Venard, "L'église d'Avignon," 4:1551.

74. Archives Communales d'Amiens, BB9, fol. 104.

75. Archives Communales de Grenoble, BB12.

76. Prudhomme, *Notes,* 13.

77. Archives Communales de Grenoble, BB5.

78. Prudhomme, *Notes,* 14.

79. David S. Hempsall, "The Languedoc, 1520–1540: A Study of Pre-Calvinist Heresy in France," *ARG* 62 (1971): 229–30.

80. Venard, "L'église d'Avignon," 2:548.

81. Henri Hauser, *Etudes sur la réforme française* (Paris: Picard, 1909), 189.

82. M. Mousseaux, *Aux sources françaises de la réforme: La Brie protestante* (Paris: Librairie protestante, n.d.), 25.

83. Archives Départementales du Gard, G1330.

84. Archives Communales d'Agen, GG182.

85. Archives Communales d'Aix, BB51, 54, 56, 57.

86. Archives Communales d'Amiens, BB35, fol. 67.

87. Ibid., BB5, fol. 208; BB6, fol. 91.

88. Godet, *Montaigu,* 18.

89. Ibid., 19.

90. Archives Communales de Grenoble, CC592, CC629.

91. Dolan, *Tours,* 97.

92. Archives Départementales de la Gard, G587.

93. Marie-Dominique Chapotin, "Le couvent royal de Saint-Louis d'Évreux," *Etudes historiques sur la province dominicaine de France* (Paris: Lecoffre, 1890), 42.

94. J. Contrasty, "Les prédicateurs du XVIe siècle à Sainte-Marie-de-la-Dalbade à Toulouse," *RHT,* 34:114 (1947): 20.

95. Leriche, *Journal,* 14; Venard, "L'église d'Avignon," 1:455.

96. Gouberville, *Journal,* 397.

97. Ibid., 211, 494, 569.

98. Venard, "L'église d'Avignon," 1:203.

99. Martin, *Ordres mendiants,* 319.

100. Martin, *Métier,* 54.

101. Ibid., 559.

102. Virginia Reinburg, "Popular Prayers in Late Medieval and Reformation France" (Ph.D. diss., Princeton University, 1985), 180.

103. Martin, *Métier,* 559; Jean Longère, *La prédication médiévale* (Paris: Etudes augustiniennes, 1983), 172.

104. "Et moderni christiani vix volunt stare per horam in ecclesia ad audiendum divina, sive praedicatores de divinis loquentes" (Pepin, *CDA,* 110).

105. Albert Lecoy de la Marche, *La chaire française au Moyen Age* (Geneva: Slatkine Reprints, 1974), 209; Charles Cox, *Pulpits, Lecterns and Organs in English Churches* (London: Oxford, 1915), 32.

106. Boutruche, *Bordeaux,* 229.

107. Godfroy, "Illyricus," 102.

108. Ferdinand Delorme, "Olivier Maillard et le Bx Duns Scot à Toulouse," *La France franciscaine* 17, 2d ser. (1934): 347.

109. Martin, *Métier,* 555.

110. Delaruelle, *Piété populaire*, 434.

111. Longère, *Prédication*, 174.

112. Elmer Carl Kiessling, *The Early Sermons of Luther and Their Relation to the Pre-Reformation Sermon* (Grand Rapids, MI: Zondervan, 1935), 23.

113. Kiessling, *Early Sermons*, 23.

114. Lecoy, *La chaire française*, 209n.

115. "Credo quod non est hodie tam miser peccator, qui si sciret se moriturum ante XXIIII horas, quin disponeret de domo, id est de conscientia sua, et quin sperneret omnia. Sic certe hic Rex, ut audivit nuncium Dei, cepit tremere per omnia membra et non potuit stare supra pedes suos, timens de illa voce, sicut pauper malefactor timet super scalam, nihil aliud expectans nisi ut proiiciatur inferius. O, mundani qui estis hic, nonne cognovistis vestros predecessores, parentes et amicos? Nonne sunt mortui et iam putrefacti in terra? . . . Vos, Domicelle, que estis plene vanitate, rogo, quando visitabitis sepulturas parentum vestrorum et amicorum, queratis eis et clametis ad aures eorum: O, Pater mi, quis fuit barbitonsor tam durus et crudelis ac inhumanis qui sua novacula vos rasit usque ad ossa? . . . Respondebunt vobis illud Psalmi: Ego sum vermis, et non homo; opprobrium hominum et abiectio plebis" (Menot, *Paris–1*, 228).

116. Lecoy, *La chaire française*, 232.

117. Martin, *Métier*, 555.

118. Lecoy, *La chaire française*, 205n.–206n.

119. Martin, *Métier*, 127.

120. Kiessling, *Early Sermons*, 25.

121. Contrasty, "Prédicateurs," 18.

122. Alain Derville, "Jean Vitrier et les religieuses de Ste.-Marguerite," *RN* 42 (1960): 233.

123. Quoted in Kiessling, *Early Sermons*, 24.

124. Antoine Fariniers, *Sermones viginti & unus de peccati* (SP)(Paris, 1519), fol. 20.

125. "Ie suis un petit long, mais ie voudrois que l'heure fust plus longue, pour parler de l'honneur & de la dignité des prestres, mais ce sera asses pour ceste heure" (LePicart, *Les sermons et instructions chrestiennes, pour tous les iours de l'Avent, iusques à Noël: & de tous les dimenches & festes, depuis Noël iusques à Caresme* (*Avent*) (Paris: Nicolas Chesneau, 1566], fol. 44).

126. Ibid., fol. 100.

127. Cox, *Pulpits*, 12.

128. Godfroy, "Illyricus," 102.

129. Quoted in Jean-Claude Schmitt, *Prêcher d'exemples* (Paris: Stock, 1985), 201.

130. Olivier Maillard, *Oeuvres françaises, sermons et poésies* [*Oeuvres*], ed. by Arthur de Laborderie (Geneva: Slatkine Reprints, 1968), 13, 16, 64n., 65n., 69n.

131. Martin, *Métier*, 558.

132. "Non ergo solum simplices sed & maiores, utpote reges invitantur ad sermones, sed quia non veniunt. . . . Quia ergo ipsi nobiles raro, aut nunquam volunt audire verbum Dei" (Guillaume Pepin, *Conciones in septem Psalmos poenitentiales* [*CPP*] [Antwerp: Guillelmus Lesteenius & Engelbertus Marnicus, 1656], 455).

133. Theodore Beza, *Histoire écclésiastique*, ed. G. Baum (Paris: Fischbacher, 1883), 1:47–48.

134. "Veniet enim burgensis ita elevata fronte, pantoufles haultes, pes tournera et cadet in lutum" (Menot, *Tours*, 39).

135. "Domini burgenses quando venitis ad sanctum iacobum vos cenatis cum uxore

& cum amicis vestris. Christus similiter cenavit cum discipulis suis" (Maillard, *QO*, fol. 201).

136. Martin, *Métier*, 559.

137. "Quia videmus per experientiam quod in uno sermone, pro uno homine semper quatuor mulieres. Credo etiam quod erat multitudo magna puerorum, si mulieres illius patrie erant ita instructe sicut huius civitatis, que non venirent ad sermonem nisi secum afferent puerum pendentem ad mamillam, et cum hoc magna multitudo parvorum puerorum post caudam, qui non cessabunt mugire durante sermone et impedire predicatores et assistentes" (Menot, "Second Carême de Paris" [*Paris-2*], 416. See also Menot, *Tours*, 101).

138. Lecoy, *La chaire française*, 208–9.

139. Martin, *Les ordres mendiants*, 322.

140. Pepin, *Sermones quadraginta de destructione Ninive (DN)* (Paris: Claude Chevallon, 1527), fol. 258.

141. "Plusieurs en y a qui ne veulent pas aller au sermon, afin qu'ils n'ayent des scrupules, & ils cuydent estre ignorans, mais ils pechent plus griefvement" (LePicart, *Avent*, fol. 80).

142. "Autres se levent devant iour pour ouir la messe, & desiuner le matin, & passent le demeurant de la iournee à gourmander, taverner, & yvrongner, à parler de choses oisives & inutiles, à chanter des chansons folles & scandaleuses.... C'est à ce iour-la que les femmes publiques & abandonnees sont, comme elles disent, leur moisson & leur vendanges, plus qu'en tout le reste de la sepmaine.... Basteleurs, tabourineurs, & autres qui vivent de la folie du peuple, sont plus volontiers escoutez & receus que ne seroit un bon predicateur de la parole de Dieu" (Monluc, *Sermons de l'evesque de Valence, sur certains poincts de la religion, recueillis fidelement, ainsi qu'ilz ont esté prononcez* [*Sermons*] [Paris: Vascosan, 1558], fol. 114).

143. "Unde accidit, quod me semel praedicante per quadragesimam in quodam oppido, maiores dicti oppido non interfuerunt concioni postmeridianae Dominicae quartae. Super quo admiratus, statim finita concione declinavi ad quandam domum, mihi satis familiarem sciscitaturus de causa . . . qui aliis diebus satis bene frequentaverat conciones nostras. Et ecce me ingrediente domum inveni Dominos meos ad mensam sedentes & libros regum revoluentes. Super quo excessu valde obstupui. Similiter, & illi non minus obstupuerunt prae confusione sua, rogantes, ut non scandalizarem eos in sermone. Ecce ergo quomodo dominatores populi christiani inique agunt, tam in ordine ad alios lusores, quam in ordine ad christiani inique agunt, ut habeant maius tempus ad ludendum, in die festo negligunt divina, utpote missas, vesperas, praedicationes & orationes, nisi forte orent, ut Deus faciat eos vincere" (Guillaume Pepin, *Elucidationem in confiteor* [*EC*] [Antwerp: Guillelmus Lesteenius & Engelbertus Gymnicus, 1656], 230–31).

144. See, e.g., Thomas Illyricus, *Sermones aurei ac excellentissimi (SA)* (Toulouse, 1521), fol. 56.

145. Maillard, *Oeuvres*, 15.

146. "Aucuns . . . vont au sermon pour ce mocquer, & mesdire de celuy qui la leur presche & declare" (Jean de Monluc, *Deux instructions, et deux épistres, faictes, & envoyees au clergé & peuple de Valence, & de Dye, par leur évesque* [*Instructions*] [Paris: Vascosan, 1557], fol. 19).

147. "Sic certe multi hodie veniunt ad sermonem tantum curiose. Postquam fecerunt prandium et quod sunt saturati et repleti, dicunt: Eamus ad audiendum illum predicatorem, ut audiamus aliquid quod nos letificet. Alii malitiose, ut viderent si diceret dominus aliquid quod possent arguere et caperent eum in sermone.... —

Alii, studiose, ut aliquid discant. . . . Alii fructuose, ut audiant aliquid pro salute anime sue" (Menot, *Paris-2,* 421).

148. "Quand il vient en la ville un nouveau predicateur, on va apres" (LePicart, *Avent,* fol. 93).

149. Pepin, *EC,* 149.

150. "Il y en a plusieurs qui se meuvent à estudier & escouter les predications par un esprit contentieux, pour pouvoir parler de la diversité des opinions. Tellement qu'il y a des gens d'Eglise qui sont contens de ne voir iamais la Bible, mais qu'ilz puissent avoir une vingtaine d'argumens pour authoriser leur opinion. Le peuple de l'autre costé, au moins quelques uns, estudient volontiers pour apprendre de mesdire des prestres, & de disputer contre leur curé, & autres qui viennent prescher en leur parole" (Monluc, *Sermons,* 61).

151. Farinier, *SP,* fol. 3.

152. "Et hodie multi orantes in ecclesia vertunt oculos nunc sursum respicientes tectum ecclesiae, nunc ante, nunc retro, nunc a dextris, nunc a sinistris, nunc ridendo, & colloquendo cum isto, nunc cum illo" (Pepin, *Conciones dominicalium ex epistolis et evangeliis totius anni, pars hiemalis* [*CDH*] [Antwerp: Guillelmus Lesteenius & Engelbertus Gymnicus, 1656], 194).

153. Menot, *Paris-Alia,* 483.

154. Archives Départementales de la Vienne, G505.

155. Pepin, *EC,* 288.

156. Jacques Merlin, *Sermons,* BN Ms. fr. 13319, fol. 61.

157. Maillard, *Oeuvres,* 104; cf. Maillard, *QO,* fol. 153.

158. Guillaume Pepin, *Conciones quadragesimales ad sacros evangeliorum sensus pro feriis quadragesimae mystice et moraliter explicandos* (*CQ*) [Antwerp: Guillelmus Lesteenius & Engelbertus Gymnicus, 1656], 497.

159. See, e.g., Ozment, *Reformation in the Cities,* 50.

160. "Habetis bene memoriam sanctorum virorum, scilicet fratris Antonii Farmier [sic], Tisserandi, fratris Ioannis Burgensis et tantorum qui dixerunt vobis modum quomodo potuissetis evadere offensam Dei. Ubi est correctio propter omnes predicationes quas habuistis. Vous allez de pis en pis" (Menot, *Tours,* 55–56).

161. Maillard, *QO,* fol. 116.

162. "Sic predicator veritatis, si percutit ubi scit esse vulnus, tunc fricat se infirmus et dicit: Iste predicator nimis profunde loquitur de hac materia: est nimis rigorosus. (Menot, *Paris-1,* 267).

163. Pepin, *CDH,* 341.

164. Pepin, *CQ,* 233.

165. ". . . [C]ombien que l'Evangile se presche, & que la voix de Dieu resonne & retentisse par tout, neantmoins que beaucoup de gens demeureront tels qu'ils estoyent, & ne changeront point" (John Calvin, *Plusieurs sermons* [*PS*] [Geneva: Conrad Badius, 1558], fol. 509).

166. "Quia si sit hodie predicator predicans penitentiam, videtur multis quod sit irrisio, nec curant" (Menot, "Premier Carême de Paris," 246; cf. LePicart, *Les sermons et instructions chrestiennes pour tous les dimenches & toutes les festes des saincts, depuis Pasques iusques à la Trinité* [*Trinité*] [Paris: Nicolas Chesneau, 1566], fol. 57).

167. Pepin, *CQ,* 313.

168. Robert Messier, *Super epistola et evangelia totius quadragesime sermones* (*QS*) (Paris: Jehan Petit, 1531), fol. 8.

169. "Sunt enim plerique, qui cum magna suavitate gustant, & audiunt verbum

Dei, ita ut quandoque resolvatur in lachrymas, sed quamprimum inde recedunt, recedit pariter ab eis omnis compunctio, & devotio, & propositum vitae melioris.... Non ergo sufficit ad salutem verbum Dei audire nisi etiam memoriter retineatur, & efficaciter tempore, & loco impleatur" (Pepin, *EC,* 288).

170. Contrasty, "Prédicateur," 3.

171. Martin, *Métier,* 57.

172. Antoine de Serent, *Les frères mineurs français en face du protestantisme au XVIe siècle* (Paris: Société et Librairie St. François d'Assise, 1930), 12.

173. Venard, "L'église d'Avignon," 1:114.

174. François de Sessevalle, *Histoire générale de l'ordre de Saint François: Le Moyen Age (1209–1517)* (LePuy-en-Velay: La Haute-Loire, 1937), 129.

175. "Heu, Deus habeat animam fratris Ioannis Tisserand. Dum predicaret Parisius coram episcopo parisiensi, ad Deum convertit plures filias et ad statum penitentie induxit. Erat pulchrum videre tantum meritum in isto sancto patre" (Menot, *Paris-2,* 350–51).

176. Archives Communales de Lyon, BB36.

177. Archives Communales d'Amiens, BB14, fol. 190.

178. Ibid., BB17., fol. 47

179. Ibid., BB18, fol. 76.

180. Alexandre Samouillan, *Olivier Maillard: Sa prédication et son temps* (Toulouse: Privat, 1891), 26.

181. Labitte, *Démocratie,* 87.

182. Farge, *Orthodoxy,* 226.

183. Bourgeois, *Journal,* 56–61; Farge, *Biographical Register,* 21.

184. Bourgeois, *Journal,* 156.

185. Nicolas de Versoris, *Livre de raison* (Paris: G. Fagniez, 1885), 43.

186. Jean de Roye, *Journal de Jean de Roye connu sous le nom de chronique scandaleuse, 1460–1483,* ed. by Bernard Mandrot (Paris: Renouard, 1896), 2:72–73.

187. F. Hilarion de Coste, *Le parfait ecclésiastique ou l'histoire de la vie et de la mort de François LePicart, Seigneur d'Attily & de Villeron, docteur en théologie de Paris & doyen de Saint-Germain l'Auxerrois* (Paris: Sebastian Cramoisy, 1658), 76.

188. Martin, *Métier,* 71.

189. Antony Méray, *La vie au temps des libres prêcheurs* (Paris: Claudin, 1878), 2:274.

190. Martin, *Métier,* 609.

Chapter 3

1. "Vidistis fratrem Antonium, fratrem Richardum, fratrem Ioannem Tisserant qui reduxit pauperes filias penitentes, fratrem Ioannem Bourgoys, fratrem Oliverium Maillard, qui clarent miraculis, quorum vita et doctrina ab omnibus approbatur" (Menot, *Paris-2,* 329).

2. The group includes five seculars (Fillon, Gaigny, Guilliaud, LePicart, and Merlin), eight Franciscans (Brulefer, Denisse, Farinier, Illyricus, Maillard, Menot, Messier and Tisserand), five Dominicans (Cleree, Meigret, Monluc, Paris and Pepin), one Carthusian (Lansperge), one Cluniac (Raulin), one Jesuit (Scoepperus), one canon (Clichtove), and one about whom nothing is known. It should be noted that Raulin was a secular until he joined the Cluniacs late in life. Other preachers, such

as Vitrier, Glapion, Standonck, Despence, and Ivollé, who have not left printed sermons or who were active after 1560, have been referred to in this study.

3. Martin, *Métier*, 47, 74, 114, 139, 141. Synodal statutes, especially after 1450, regularly enjoined seculars to preach at least the basics to their flocks, if for no other reason than to counter the threat they saw in the mendicant orders. Ibid., 141–42.

4. "Quod autem domini seculares interdum predicent, hoc est de contingenti raro." (Pepin, *DN,* fol. 245.)

5. Of the seven seculars in this study, none died before the Reformation. Most began their preaching careers after 1520.

6. G. Godineau, "Statuts synodaux inédits du diocèse de Bourges promulgés par Jean Coeur en 1451," *RHEF* 72 (1986): 59.

7. "Et istud est contra quosdam mundanos clericos, & praelatos, qui erubescunt praedicare, cum tamen christus, qui erat verus Dei Patris naturalis filius, non erubuerit praedicare" *CDA,* 160; cf. *CDA,* 159).

8. Martin, *Métier*, 132.

9. Beza, *Histoire ecclésiastique,* 1:102.

10. Martin, *Métier*, 113.

11. Hugolin Lippens, "Jean Glapion, défenseur de la réforme de l'Observance," *AFH* 44 (1951): 3–70.

12. Farge, *Orthodoxy,* 58.

13. Paul Kendall, *Louis XI* (New York: Norton, 1971), 191.

14. Farge, *Biographical Register,* 161.

15. Chapotin, "Couvent royal," 41.

16. Donald Weinstein and Rudolph M. Bell, *Saints and Society* (Chicago: University of Chicago Press, 1982), 216; C. H. Lawrence, *Medieval Monasticism: Forms of Religious Life in Western Europe in the Middle Ages* (London: Longman, 1984), 110, 200; Dolan, *Tours,* 91–92; Martin, *Ordres mendiants,* 133.

17. Child oblates had been phased out during the Middle Ages in the belief that an informed decision should be made by the postulant himself; Lawrence, *Monasticism,* 222. Although novices could enter the Dominican and Augustinian orders in Aix at the age of seven, they could not make profession until they had attained the ages of sixteen and eighteen respectively; Dolan, *Tours,* 91. See also Weinstein and Bell, *Saints and Society,* 217.

18. Martin, *Métier*, 109–10.

19. Dorothea Roth, *Die mittelalterliche Predigttheorie und das Manuale curatorum des Johann Ulrich Surgant* (Basel & Stuttgart: Helbing & Lichtenhahn, 1956), 152.

20. R. F. Bennett, *The Early Dominicans* (New York: Russell and Russell, 1971), 55.

21. Dolan, *Tours,* 93.

22. Martin, *Métier*, 123.

23. Farge, *Orthodoxy,* 18.

24. Ibid., 11–12, 73–76, 86.

25. Gordon Leff, *Paris and Oxford Universities in the Thirteenth and Fourteenth Centuries: An Institutional and Intellectual History* (New York: John Wiley, 1968), 140.

26. Ibid., 146, 149.

27. Augustin Renaudet, *Préréforme et humanisme à Paris pendant les premières guerres d'Italie* (Paris: Honoré Champion, 1916), 28–29.

28. David Knowles, *The Evolution of Medieval Thought* (New York: Vintage Books, 1962), 174.

29. Farge, *Orthodoxy*, 21.

30. Renaudet, *Préréforme*, 55–56; Leff, *Oxford and Paris*, 162–63.

31. Chapotin, "Couvent royal," 41.

32. Renaudet, *Préréforme*, 36.

33. Martin, *Métier*, 111.

34. Renaudet, *Préréforme*, 37.

35. Knowles, *Medieval Thought*, 180.

36. Farge, *Orthodoxy*, 22.

37. Knowles, *Medieval Thought*, 175.

38. Leff, *Paris and Oxford*, 171–72.

39. Renaudet, *Préréforme*, 27.

40. Farge, *Orthodoxy*, 26–27.

41. Farge, *Biographical Register*, 364.

42. Renaudet, *Préréforme*, 90, 267–68, 273.

43. Ibid., 404; Farge, *Biographical Register*, 126.

44. Renaudet, *Préréforme*, 416.

45. Ibid., 699–700.

46. Farge, *Biographical Register*, 185.

47. Marie Pellechet, *Catalogue des livres de la bibliothèque d'un chanoine d'Autun: Claude Guilliaud, 1493–1551* (Autun: Mémoires de la société Eduenne, new ser., 1890); A. Gillot and Charles Boëll, *Supplément au catalogue des livres de la bibliothèque d'un chanoine d'Autun: Claude Guilliaud, 1493–1551* (Autun: Mémoires de la société Eduenne, new ser., 1910).

48. Quoted in Harry Caplan, "Classical Rhetoric and the Mediaeval Theory of Preaching," *CP* 28, no.2 (1933): 91–92.

49. "Helas le grant fruit/quil a fait/Et parfait./L'espace de quarante et deux ans" (Olivier Maillard, *L'épitaphe de frère Olivier Maillard*, Lyon, 1502, n.p.).

50. Bennett, *Dominicans*, 80.

51. R.M. Mauriac, "Un réformateur catholique: Thomas Illyricus, frère mineur de l'Observance," *Etudes franciscaines* 23 (1934): 332.

52. Martin, *Métier*, 115–16.

53. Farge, *Orthodoxy*, 22.

54. Archives Communales d'Amiens, BB10, fol. 44; see also BB8, fol. 111; BB9, fol. 104; BB33, fol. 95.

55. Ibid., BB12, fol. 90.

56. Archives Communales de Nantes, CC99.

57. Rudolf Hirsch, "Surgant's List of Recommended Books for Preachers (1502–1503)," *RQ* 20, no.2 (1967): 204–10.

58. Chapotin, "Couvent royal," 41.

59. Albert de Meyer, *La congrégation de Hollande ou la réforme dominicaine en territoire bourguignon, 1465–1515* (Liège: Imprimérie Soledi, 1946), cx, cxvi.

60. "Unde postmodum suo ordini, pariter & ordini fratrum Minorum datum est privilegium Apostolicum, quoad administrationem sacramenti poenitentiae, ut patet in clemen. de Sepulturis.c.dudum. Nunc autem eodem privilegio gaudent Augustinienses & Carmelitae, praedictum autem privilegium datum est huiusmodi fratribus, non solum in favorem eorum, verum in favorem christi fidelium, inter quos nonnulli erubescunt confiteri suis ordinariis. Insuper inter ordinarios multi sunt imbecilles, & ignari, nescientes discernere inter lepram, & lepram" (Pepin, *Conciones de sanctis sive de imitatione sanctorum* [*CS*] [Antwerp: Guillelmus Lesteenius & Engelbertus Gymnicus, 1656], 347).

61. Meyer, *Congrégation,* cix.

62. J. Quétif and J. Echard, *Scriptores ordinis praedicatorum* (New York: Franklin, 1959), 2:1:87.

63. William A. Hinnebusch, *The Early English Friars Preacher* (Vatican City: Institutum Historicum FF. Praedicatorum, 1951), 197.

64. William A. Hinnebusch, *The History of the Dominican Order: Intellectual and Cultural Life to 1500* (New York: Alba House, 1973), 2:8.

65. Quoted in Hinnebusch, *Dominican Order 2,* 4.

66. Chapotin, "Couvent royal," 41–43.

67. Farge, *Biographical Register,* 364.

68. Farge, *Orthodoxy,* 34–35, 51.

69. Farge, *Biographical Register,* 92.

70. Bernard Chevalier, "Olivier Maillard et la réforme des Cordeliers (1482–1502)," *RHEF* 65, no. 174 (1979): 32.

71. Quétif and Echard, *Scriptores,* 2:1:87.

72. Nève, *Sermons choisis,* x.

73. Sermons from Paris, Nantes, Poitiers, Laval, Tours, Toulouse, Albi, and Cahors are extant.

74. Samouillan, *Maillard,* 17.

75. Sessevalle, *Histoire générale,* 130–31.

76. Mauriac, "Illyricus," 66.

77. Martin, *Métier,* 583.

78. See Menot, "Exposition passionis Iesu christi," *Tours,* 177–94.

79. Herminjard, *Corréspondence,* February 1523, 1:118.

80. Mauriac, "Un réformateur catholique," 337. One of Maillard's hagiographers also describes him as pale and emaciated; André Mabille de Poncheville, *Bienheureux Olivier Maillard* (Paris: Éditions franciscaines, 1946), 28.

81. Boutruche, *Bordeaux,* 229.

82. Caplan, "Classical Rhetoric," 92.

83. Archives Communales d'Amiens, BB17, fol. 159.

84. Martin, *Ordres mendiants,* 318–20.

85. Ibid., 324.

86. This was also true of Vitrier, who earned the admiration of Erasmus for his simple style of presentation; André Godin, *Érasme: Vies de Jean Vitrier et de John Colet* (Angers: Éditions Moreana, 1982), 31.

87. Farge, *Biographical Register,* 364.

88. Eisenstein, *Printing Press,* 11.

89. P. Feret, *La faculté de théologie et ses docteurs les plus célèbres: Époque moderne* (Paris: Picard. 1896), 2:261.

90. Guillaume Pepin, *De imitatione sanctorum* (Paris: Claude Chevallon, 1528).

91. Guillaume Pepin, *Expositio in Genesim* (Paris: Claude Chevallon, 1528); Pepin, *Expositio in Exodum* (Paris: Claude Chevallon, 1534); Pepin, *Expositio evangeliorum quadragesimalium* (Paris: A. Girault, 1540).

92. Guillaume Pepin, *Decretales moralizate* (Caen: Angier, 1523).

93. Chapotin, "Couvent royal," 42.

94. Farge, *Biographical Register,* 365.

95. Thomas Illyricus, *Epistola ad milites sub rege Francorum* (Toulouse: Jean Febvre, 1519); Illyricus, *Epistola pro defensione nominis Ihesu directa ad sacrum Senatum Tholosarum* (Toulouse: Jean Febvre, 1519); Illyricus, *Epistola de ordine*

servando in matrimonio: ac de laudibus matrimonii ad omnes Christi fideles directa (Toulouse: Jean Febvre, 1519).

96.Thomas Illyricus, *Modus confitendi* (Toulouse: Jean Febvre, 1519); Illyricus, *Regule et laudes matrimonii cum invectivus feminarum in viros et virorum in feminas ac remedio contra concubinas* (Toulouse: Jean Febvre, 1519).

97. Jean Raulin, *Doctrinale mortis* (Caen: Laurent Hostingue, 1521).

98. Esprit Rodier, *Praeconium ac defensio quadragesime; cui pluribus requiren-tibus, adjunctus est sermo de ratione institutionis divinissimi Eucharistiae sacramenti* (Toulouse: Boudeville, 1552); Rodier, *Contra astrologos et divinatricem astrologiam* (Toulouse: Boudeville, 1549).

99. "Les prebstres & autres personnes ecclesiastiques qui entretiennent publique-ment les concubines, & habitent & hantent librement, sans aucun respect, avec femmes suspectes, & qui ne sont leurs proches parentes, ou en tel aage qu'il n'y ait lieu de soupeçonner" (Monluc, *Sermons,* fol. 127).

100. Pierre Chevalier, *Henri III* (Paris: Fayard, 1985), 187.

101. Chapotin, "Couvent royal," 43.

102. "Hic jacent clarissimi in theologia magistri Fratres Robertus Bignonis et Guillelmus Pepin, qui morum integritate et multa eruditione praestantes, hunc con-ventum reformate [*sic*], in eodem usque ad vitae terminum religiose vivendo, tandem mortem obierunt, primus anno MDXXX aprilis XXII, secundus anno MDXXXII januarii XVIII libros multos a se editos relinquentes" (Ibid.).

103. J.-A. Clerval, *De Judoci Clichtovei: Vita et Operibus (1472–1543)* (Paris: Picard, 1894), 113–18.

104. Emile Picot, *Artus Fillon: Chanoine d'Évreux et de Rouen puis évêque de Senlis* (Evreux: Hérissey, 1911), 45.

105. Farge, *Biographical Register,* 165.

106. Picot, *Fillon,* 16.

107. Ibid., 44–45.

108. Ernest Coyecque, *Recueils d'actes notariés relatifs à l'histoire de Paris et de ses environs (1532–55)* (Paris: Imprimerie Nationale, 1924), 2:369–71.

109. Farge, *Biographical Register,* 264.

110. Ibid., 329.

111. Ibid., 322.

112. Ibid., 45.

Chapter 4

1. J. W. Blench, *Preaching in England in the Late Fifteenth and Sixteenth Centuries: A Study of English Sermons, 1450–1600* (New York: Barnes & Noble, 1964).

2. L. Petit de Julleville, *Histoire de la langue et de la littérature français: Moyen Âge* (Paris: Armand Colin, 1896), vol. 2.

3. Brian Stock, *The Implications of Literacy: Written Language and Models of Interpretation in the Eleventh and Twelfth Centuries* (Princeton: Princeton University Press, 1983).

4. Donald Kelley, *Beginning,* 104.

5. Daniel Defoe, quoted in Elizabeth L. Eisenstein, *The Printing Press as an Agent of Change* (Cambridge: Cambridge University Press, 1979), 316.

6. McIntyre, "Celestines," 164

7. Hirsch, *Printing, 8.*

8. *Jean Leclercq, quoted in Eisenstein, Printing Press, 316–17.*

9. Hirsch, *Printing, 8.*

10. Contrasty, "Prédicateurs," 14.

11. Anonymous, *Ung notable sermon contenant l'excellence et saincteté du pur et saint vierge ioseph espoux a la tres digne mere de Dieu la vierge honoree* (Rouen: Martin Morin, n.d.).

12. R. Havette, "La notation des sermons à l'audition et la sténographie," *RB* (1903):325.

13. Farge, *Biographical Register,* 265.

14. Samouillan, *Maillard,* 63–64.

15. See Artus Fillon, *Speculum curatorum una cum confessionale ac tractatu de misterio misse & his que concernunt eum, de videlicet: de sacramenti altaris dignitate: utilitate: & processione. Necnon de sacerdotalibus vestimentis, ad dei laudem statusque ecclesiastici decorem (Speculum)* (Paris, 1503) (two sermons).

16. Auton, *Chroniques,* 4, 385–86.

17. B. Haureau, *Histoire littéraire de la France* (Paris, 1873), 26:388–90.

18. Longère, *Prédication,* 236.

19. Ibid., 247; Lecoy, *La chaire française,* 235; Michael Zink, *La prédication en langue roman avant 1300* (Paris: Honoré Champion, 1976).

20. Menot, *Tours,* 111.

21. Maillard, *SA,* fol. 99.

22. John O'Malley, *Praise and Blame in Renaissance Rome* (Durham, NC: Duke University Press, 1979), 28

23. Longère, *Prédication,* 164

24. "Nescit praedicare qui nescit Pepin" (A. Vacant, E. Mangenot, and E. Amman, eds., *Dictionnaire de théologie catholique* [Paris, 1899–1950], 12:1186).

25. "Studeat ergo praedicator veritatis taliter vivere: ut possit populo proficere, & dicere" (Pepin, *CPP,* 332).

26. "Mystice in verbis praedictis dicuntur tria praedicatori expedientia. Primum est sublimis conversatio ... Secundum est facilis, & plana praedicatio ... Quasi diceret, vos praedicatores plane, & clare loquamini, ut quilibet etiam quantumcunque simplex, & indoctus possit in sermone vestro proficere. Tertium est recta intentio" (Pepin, *CDA, 82*).

27. Guillaume Pepin, *Rosareum aureum B. Mariae virginis (RA)* (Antwerp: Guillelmus Lesteenius & Engelbertus Gymnicus, 1656), 86.

28. Pepin, *CPP,* 453.

29. "Medice, cura teipsum" (Ibid.).

30. "Nam praedicatores primitivae ecclesiae, quales erant Apostoli, non quaerebant lanam, nec humanam laudem, sed Dei gloriam, & animarum salutem.... Nam in primitiva ecclesia cum essent valde rari praedicatores, populus erat promptior ad sequendum, & devote audiendum sermones, quam modernis temporibus, sed vae malis praedicatoribus, & indevotis auditoribus" (Pepin, *CS,* 270; cf. Pepin, *CDA,* 81).

31. Pepin, *CDH,* 344.

32. "Et nota, quod hodie aliqui praedicatores sunt similes antiquis doctoribus Iudaeorum, sicut, qui volunt exponere sacram scripturam ad fantasiam suam, & quandoque multum tortuose" (Pepin, *CQ,* 19).

33. "Bonus ergo pastor debet visitare gregem suum, & si quem viderit infirmum, & debilem in fide, aut moribus, debet ipsum consolidare" (Ibid., 46).

34. "Nam sicut semen quod cadit in terram bonam fructificat secundum Domini sententiam: ita verbum Dei decisum ab ore boni praedicatoris, si cadit in terram devoti cordis, multum fructum affert" (*CPP*, 487).

35. Pepin, *CS*, 248, 346; cf. Pepin, *RA*, 165.

36. "Moraliter praedicator recte comparari potest pavoni. Nam plumae aureae pavonis significant sacram doctrinam quam debet habere, & populo praedicare: plumae vero griseae significant vestis vilitatem, quam debet interius, & exterius gerere: vox terribilis pavonis significat praedicatoris constantiam, & acrimoniam in reprehensione vitiorum;... carnium incorruptio designat rectam intentionem, quia non debet praedicare propter humanam laudem aut propter divitias congregandas, seu beneficia procuranda, sicut plerique faciunt in damnationem animarum suarum" (Pepin, *Conciones de adventu Domini* [*CA*] [Antwerp: Guillelmus Lesteenius & Englebertus Marnicus, 1656], 146).

37. Caplan, "Classical Rhetoric," 83.

38. "Debet itaque praedicator tenere conditionem boni canis, qui si senserit lupum prope domum magistri sui tempore nocturno rapere volentem oves illius, non cessat latrare quousque abierit: immo quandoque studet eum mordere, quod si ediverso mordeatur a lupo non tamen cessat a latratu, sic, & praedicator debet severe latrare contra vitia & mordere peccatores.... Tales praedicator fuit Jonas" (Pepin, *CPP*, 453). In fact, Dominican preachers were nicknamed *domini canes*, hounds of the Lord (Weinstein and Bell, *Saints and Society*, 23).

39. "Ferme enim hodie omnes praedicatores sunt velut canes muti non volentes latrare, nisi forsitan contra communem populum" (Pepin, *EC*, 305).

40. "[P]raedicatores divini verbi sine christi speciali assistentia nihil proficiunt in lucrandis animabus" (Pepin, *CQ*, 497).

41. Pepin, *CS*, 248.

42. "Sed ne milites Christi deficiant in tali pugna providet eis rex suus christus de annona, & de pane doctrinae, qui peramplius, & copiosus ministratur christi fidelibus in Quadragesime. Nec quidem dat eis tantum unum panem manducare, verum etiam interdum plures, sicut praecipue videre est in magnis civitatibus, in quibus plures praedicatores simul evangelizant verbum Dei, uno ministrante populo panem epistolae, alio panem Evangelii, alio panem zizaniae vitia reprehendendo, alio panem electi tritici virtutes exaltando, & huiusmodi: hoc autem fit, ut cui non sapit unus panis saltem sapiat alius" (Pepin, *CQ*, 212).

43. Pepin, *CPP*, 451.

44. "Haec enim & his similia sunt declamanda populo rudi & simplici, cui plus debet praedicator condescendere ut proficiat & aedificetur quam doctis & literis viris, qui raro sequuntur verbum Dei" (Ibid.).

45. A. de Poorter, "Un manuel de prédication médiévale," *RNP* 25 (1923): 200.

46. Pepin, *CS*, 180.

47. "Non tamen tenetur nec debet dicere praedicator omni tempore omnem veritatem, sed quae conveniat auditoribus, & quae sit illis utilis.... Hoc autem non sic intelligendum est, quod liceat quandoque docere falsitatem oppositam veritati, sed ut taceatur ipsa veritas non necessaria pro tunc" (Pepin, *CPP*, 246; cf. Lecoy, *La chaire française*, 207).

48. Pepin, *CQ*, 169.

49. "Aliter peccantes ex passione aut humana fragilitate, & aliter obstinati, & ex

certa scientia peccantes. Qui ergo vult bene piscari in praedicatione debet taliter coaptare materiam suam" (Ibid, 498).

50. "Sic & praedicator qui per ipsum orpheus designatur, debet citharizare per suavem monitionem, & invitationem ad poenitentiam" (Pepin, *CPP*, 452).

51. "Secundo praedicatores debent annunciare nomen Domine suaviter, benigne scilicet hortando populum. Si enim fuerit columba melle cibata, tunc solet alias columbas ad columbare Domini sui attrahere, & dulcedine mellis cuius adhuc odorem habet in ore, alias columbas mirabiliter delectare. Ita & praedicator debet habere suavitatem verborum in ore suo, ut alios peccatores attrahat ad Dominum." (Ibid., 451).

52. Ibid., 453–54.

53. Ibid., 452.

54. "Notandum, quod sicut Iohannes obstinatos peccatores, quales erant Pharisaei, & Saducaei, dure increpebat, vocans eos progeniem viperarium, ut dictum est, ita etiam praedicatores moderni debent dure, & aspere increpare obstinatos, & inveteratos peccatores, ut sic saltem perterriti emolliantur ad poenitentiam, qui dulci, & benigna admonitione emollire nolunt." (Pepin, *CS*, 260).

55. Pepin, *DN*, fol. 10.

56. Pepin, *CPP*, 452.

57. Menot, *Paris–1*, 233.

58. "Nunquam equus sub armigero tantum tremuit quando audit vocem tube, quantum populus audiens hanc terribilem vocem debet tremere." (Ibid.).

59. "Credo quod Christus nullum habuit fideliorem servum et militem ipso Paulo" (Ibid., 229).

60. "Dicitur primo, quod in conversione peccatoris duo sunt. Primo, commotio peccatoris ex terrore divinorum iudiciorum & dolore peccatorum. Secundum est sanitas animae, quae est per infusionem gratiae.... Primum potest inducere praedicator, secundum non. Unde Guillelmus Parisiensis: Non est opus praedicatorum conversio peccatorum, sed Dei" (Jean Raulin, *Sermonum quadragesimalium* [*SQ*], [Antwerp: Gasparus Bellerus, 1612], 48).

61. Ibid., 295; cf. LePicart, *Les sermons et instructions chrestiennes, pour tous les iours de caresme, & feries de Pasques* (*Caresme*) (Paris: Nicolas Chesneau, 1566), fol. 26.

62. "Audivi ab ore magistri Huet, in conventu parisiensi predicantis, quod si non alius se obtulisset, virgo Maria tanto zelo amabat redemptionem generis humani, quod propriis manibus filium crucifixisset. Sed capite hoc sane. Cave, o, tu Predicator, ne hoc dicendo scandalizes intellectus simplicem" (Menot, *Paris–2*, 453).

63. Maillard, *Oeuvres*, 14.

64. "Les prescheurs doibvent dire ce qui est dinstruction ès actes de nostre Seigneur pour enflamber les auditeurs à imiter et ambrasser son erudition, principalement celle quil nous a enseignee non seullement de parole mais aussi par oeuvre" (Jean Lansperge, *Sermons*, BN Ms. fr. 2451, fol. 3).

65. "Il fault donner de la doctrine evangelique à un chacum, selon qu'il en est capable, & que son esprit & estomach peult porter & entendre. Qui donneroit de la viande solide à un enfant, elle l'estrangleroit, & pourtant luy fault il du laict.... C'est à dire, qu'à gens qui sont rudes & charnels, il leur fault donner seulement de la doctrine & instruction, selon qu'ils en peuvent porter & entendre: mais à gens spirituels & capables de choses difficiles & ardues il leur faut donner doctrine plus ardue & plus parfaite, selon leur entendement & capacité" (LePicart, *Trinité*, fols. 55–56).

66. LePicart, *Caresme*, fol. 177.

67. "Comme auiourd'huy, si au sermon, on reprend les vitieux, on dira que le predicateur est un mutin, un seditieux" (LePicart, *Trinité*, fol. 91).

68. "Si le monde dit, voyla un bon predicateur: c'est signe que non est, car il dit selon son plaisir" (LePicart, *Avent*, fol. 84).

69. Zawart, *Franciscan Preaching*, 244.

70. James J. Murphy, *Rhetoric in the Middle Ages* (Berkeley: University of California Press, 1974), 298.

71. Harry Caplan, "'Henry of Hesse' on the Art of Preaching," *PMLA* 48 (1933): 348.

72. According to Cruel, there are four methods of homiletic exposition: (1) the regular homily, which explains a verse of scripture; (2) the narrative homily, which uses correlative texts of the gospels for explanation; (3) the incomplete homily or address which only deals very briefly with one or more verses of the pericope; and (4) the composite homily, which discusses part of the epistle, then summarizes or explains the gospel, or follows a freely chosen text. Rudolf Cruel, *Geschichte der deutschen Predigt im Mittelalter* (Darmstadt: Wissenschaftliche Buchgesellschaft, 1966), 3.

73. Murphy, *Rhetoric*, 12.

74. Godin, *Vitrier et Colet*, 31. For examples of Vitrier's sermon style, see Godin, *L'homéliaire*.

75. Roth, *Mittelalterliche Predigttheorie*, 101.

76. Ray Petry (ed.), *No Uncertain Sound: Sermons that Shaped the Pulpit Tradition* (Philadelphia: Westminster Press, 1948), 8.

77. A late medieval tract professing the influence of Saint Thomas Aquinas. Harry Caplan. "The Four Senses of Scriptural Interpretation and the Mediaeval Theory of Preaching," *CP* 28, no. 2 (1933): 282.

78. Caplan, "Henry of Hesse," 349.

79. Marie-Madeleine Davy, *Les sermons universitaires parisiens de 1230–31* (Paris: J. Vrin, 1931), 41.

80. Roth, *Mittelalterliche Predigttheorie*, 60.

81. A homiletic term is any "pure" noun, verb, or participle; consignatives such as "all," "no," "a certain," "some," "any," etc., are excluded. Caplan, "Henry of Hesse," 349–50.

82. A. J. Krailsheimer, *Rabelais and the Franciscans* (Oxford: Clarendon Press, 1963), 61.

83. "Mais jay bonne esperance, que aidant voz bonnes prieres, la grace de dieu enrousera la sterillité de mon entendement." (Jean de Gaigny, *Trois Homélies prêchées en présence de François I* [*Homélies*], BN Ms. fr. [*Colbert*] *1855, fol. 1.*)

84. "In presenti predicatione erunt due partes. In prima, questio theologalis terminabitur. In secunda, expositio thematis proponetur" (Menot, *Tours*, 212).

85. Daniel Lesnick describes the differences between Dominican and Franciscan preaching in the first two centuries of the mendicants' existence: "Abstraction and structuration—favored by the Dominicans in their sermons to the urban laity—present the relation between the individual and external reality as mediated and create a sense of unity in the world. On the other hand, concretion and narrative mode—favored by the Franciscans in their popular preaching—have a greater impact on the emotions and the imagination." Daniel R. Lesnick, *Preaching in Medieval Florence: The Social World of Franciscan and Dominican Spirituality* (Athens: University of Georgia Press, 1989), 95.

86. Ibid., 96, 134.

87. Caplan, "Classical Rhetoric," 86.
88. Etienne Gilson, "Michel Menot et la technique du sermon médiéval," in *Les idées et les lettres* (Paris: J. Vrin, 1932), 128.
89. Gaigny, *Homélies*, fol. 2.
90. Etienne Brulefer, *Opuscula* (Paris: Jehan Petit, 1500), fol. 262.
91. Pepin, *CS*, 9–12.
92. Messier, *QS*, fol. 122.
93. "Vos igitur omnes que frequentastis sermones meos precor studeatis alphabetum. Declaravi vobis viginti litteras alphabeti & quilibet littera significat unum peccatum. A significant adulatoriam; B blasphematoriam; C conspiratoriam; etc." (Maillard, *SA*, fol. 68).
94. "Secundo tenet modum predicatorum in cruce dicens illa septem verba que sunt septem folia pulcherrima contra septem peccata mortalia. Ortus est diligendus propter arbores quando affuerunt bonos fructus" (Maillard, *QO*, fol. 181).
95. Joseph Albert Mosher, *The Exemplum in the Early Religious and Didactic Literature of England* (New York: Columbia University Press, 1911), 1.
96. T. F. Crane, "Mediaeval Sermon-Books and Stories," *Proceedings of the American Philosophical Society*, 21 (1884): 57.
97. Ibid., 55
98. Martin, *Métier*, 487.
99. Schmitt, *Prêcher d'exemples*, 107–20.
100. F. C. Tubach, *Index Exemplorum: A Handbook of Medieval Religious Tales* (Helsinki, 1969); Schmitt, *Prêcher d'exemples*, 11.
101. Schmitt. *Prêcher d'exemples*, 12.
102. "Si non creditis scripture, credatis exemplis" (Menot, *Tours*, 171).
103. Schmitt, *Prêcher d'exemples*, 21.
104. Farinier, *SP*, fol. 23.
105. Alain de Lille warns against their frivolous use: "Praedicatio . . . non debet habere verba scurrilia, vel puerilia, vel rythmorum melodias et consonantias metrorum, quae potius fiunt ad aures demulcendas, quam ad animum instruendum" (Quoted in Roth, *Mittelalterliche Predigttheorie*, 39).
106. "Non ergo praedicabat vana, & curiosa, non fabulas, aut tragoedias, non leges humanas, aut poetas, sicut nonnulli praedicatores moderni, demulcentes aures auditorum" (Pepin, *CQ*, 55–56; cf. Pepin, *CPP*, 450).
107. Lecoy, *La chaire française*, 302–4.
108. "Ubi est . . . Carolus qui in flore iuventutis sue faciebat tremere Italiam? Helas, putrefactus est in terra" (Menot, *Tours*, 37).
109. "[In] Rome erat una mater habens filiam maritatem. Mater vero commisit crimen unde comburi debebat. Filia cum parvulo filio suo genuflexit Imperatori, petens vitam pro matre sua. . . . Imperator autem, considerata mansuetudine illius filie, sententiavit eam mori in carcere, nihil ei ministrando alimentorum. Illa igitur filia obtinuit se nudam demitti in carcerem et foveam et, non erubescens, dixit: Mater, nuda exivi de ventre vestro, et nuda ad vos descendo. Panem afferre, aut victum, non fuit mihi permissum, sed, sicut suxi ubera vestra, ita sugatis mea. Et quotidie sic faciebat. . . . Observata est igitur secrete filia illa ab Imperatore et audit ibi verba dulcia et videt filiam matri ubera sua sugenda prebentem. Filiam igitur trahi de carcere nudam et flentem iussit et, ut vidit charitatem et compassionem filie erga matrem, dixit: Filia mea, do vobis matrem vestram. Ecce qualiter meruit liberationem matris" (Ibid., 86).
110. "Quando mercator ferens multam pecuniam secum adit Romam et, transacta civitate Lugdunensi, incedit per viam plenam latronibus et homicidis, quibus modo

plena est terra, si aliquis prudens vir veniat ad eum: Domine, quo vaditis, quove tenditis? Ponitis vos in evidenti loco mortis vestre; irem ego per aliam viam si essem sicut vos, quia heri in hac via fuerunt expoliati duo magni mercatores; hodie mane, duo excoriati, et nullus hac transit quin relinquat pellem" (Menot, *Paris–1,* 222).

111. "Fabulose potest narrari quod simia videns turpitudinem suam se non posse cooperire, misit nuncium vulpi, petens partem sue caude: cum habeat quandam superfluitatem in cauda. Cui responderunt famuli vulpis: Non certe: dominus non debet aliis caudam dividere quia ipse dominus his scilicet pilis opus habet. Et sic semper mansit simia toute escourtee. Moraliter simia carens cauda, est sacerdos carens beneficio, ideo potest facere longam dictionem quia sine titulo. Vulpes autem abundanter caudata est multipliciter beneficiatus: habens scilicet quattuor vel quinque beneficia: qui non communicat pauperi non habenti: quia dominus his opus habet pro canibus nutriendis, et avibus pascendis, et equis parandis. De talibus dicitur Apocalip. nono. Potestas eorum in cauda eorum" (Messier, *QS,* fol. 128).

112. "Nam si semel fueritis sublimati super alios, tunc patebit imperitia vestra, quae forte nunc latet, & sic eritis in derisum omni populo, quo estis honorati. Da exemplum de simia, quae cum sursum ascendit, tunc ostendit posteriora sua nudata" (Pepin, *CQ,* 121).

113. "Apes enim & formicae, quae sunt animalia prudentissima, sunt circa ventrem valde stricta" (Raulin, *SQ,* 385).

114. Mosher, *Exemplum,* 1.

115. "Nos orabimus deum quod ipse det nobis gratiam in presenti, gloriam in futuro. Amen" (Maillard, *SA,* fol. 105).

116. Dacheux remarks that "he did this, not without malice, in the funeral oration for Albert of Bavaria"; Dacheux, *Un réformateur catholique,* 539.

117. Herminjard, *Corréspondance,* July 6, 1524, 1:222–40.

118. Charles Schmidt, *Gérard Roussel: Prédicateur de la reine Marguerite de Navarre* (Geneva: Slatkine Reprints, 1970), 27.

119. Jean-Pierre Massaut, *Critique et tradition à la veille de la réforme en France* (Paris: J. Vrin, 1974), 40–41, 110–11.

120. Frederick J. McGinness, "Preaching Ideals and Practice in Counter-Reformation Rome," *SCJ* 11, no.2 (1980): 112.

121. Bayley, *Pulpit Oratory,* 49.

122. McGinnis, "Preaching Ideals," 116.

123. Hector Reynaud, *Jean de Monluc, Evêque de Valence et de Die* (Geneva: Slatkine Reprints, 1971), 192.

124. Antoine Degert, "Procès de huit évêques français suspects de calvinisme," *RQH* 76 (1904): 62.

125. Murphy, *Rhetoric,* 276.

126. Augustine, *On Christian Doctrine,* trans. by D. W. Robertson, Jr. (Indianapolis: Bobbs-Merrill, 1958), 142.

127. Murphy, *Rhetoric,* 19.

128. The metaphors from everyday life are explored in great detail by Martin in *Métier,* chap. 11.

129. "Lupanar enim est locus ubi sunt meretrices. Si in domo canonici est meretrix, c'est bordeau. Ubi Rex est, ibi curia est" (Menot, *Tours,* 171).

130. Menot, *Paris-Alia,* 520.

131. Maillard, *Oeuvres,* 52–53.

132. Bayley, *Oratory,* 73.

133. Pepin, *RA,* 262–63.

134. Brulefer, *Opuscula,* fol. 211.

135. "Debent fideles sanctificare nomen dei, opere & facto: insistendo scilicet bonis operationibus & observationi mandatorum dei, & omnia opera bona, elemo-synam, ieiunium, & orationem, ac cetera id genius" (Josse Clichtove, *Sermones* [Paris: Thielmann, 1534], 8).

136. Reynaud, *Jean de Monluc,* 172

137. Étienne Paris, *Homélies suyvant les matières traictees es principales festes & solennitez de l'annee (Homélies)* (Paris: Robineau, 1553), fols. 1–2.

138. Godin, *Vitrier et Colet,* 31.

139. Blench, *Preaching in England,* 41.

140. David Steinmetz, *Luther in Context* (Bloomington: Indiana University Press, 1986), 34.

141. Harry Caplan, "Rhetorical Invention in Some Mediaeval Tractates on Preaching," *Speculum* 2, no.3 (1927): 292.

142. Roth, *Mittelalterliche Predigttheorie,* 158.

143. Henri Estienne, *Apologie pour Hérodote* (The Hague: Scheurleer, 1735), 66.

Chapter 5

1. Paul Kristeller, *Renaissance Thought and Its Sources* (New York: Columbia University Press, 1979), 105.

2. As E. Jane Dempsey Douglass points out, "Another repeatedly expressed warning is that academic disputes should not be aired in the pulpit; their place is in the schools.... Geiler himself readily points out differences of opinion among theologians; but the spirit of his presentations is by no means contentious, and the problems considered are those which are clearly relevant to the thinking of the layman rather than merely speculative questions." (Douglass, *Justification,* 33.)

3. "O popule mi predicare pro salute animarum vestrarum. Et qui voluerit audire predicare philosophiam querat alium et non me" (Illyricus, *SA,* fol. 56).

4. "O quot sunt qui graviora peccatum commiserunt quam adam ex genere... quia Adam non peccavit nisi quia opus erat prohibitum: quia de se erat bonum opus" (Maillard, *QO,* fol. 187).

5. "Nil mirum ergo si primi parentes infecti ceteros sibi succedentes infecerunt. Secundum exemplum: quia lepros: communiter generant leprosos: ita infecti infectos generant" (Raulin, *SA,* fols. 52–53).

6. Pepin, *CQ,* 476.

7. "Quid est inquit homo? Et respondet quod memor es. Ita quod nihil est homo: nisi pro tanto quod est in memoria Dei" (Raulin, *SA,* fol. 43)

8. Menot, *Paris-1,* 223; cf. Raulin, *SA,* fol. 52; Maillard, *QO,* fol. 99.

9. "Id est mundus plenus est peccatis, que avertunt hominem a Deo et a via qua itur ad celum. Nam teste August. peccatum est aversio ab incommutabili bono" (Pepin, *DN,* fol. 2).

10. Oliver Maillard, *Sermones de stipendio peccati (SSP)* (Lyon: Stephen Gueyg-nardi, 1503), fol. 317. A good discussion of the medieval theology of sin can be found in Heiko A. Oberman, *The Harvest of Medieval Theology* (Durham, N.C.: Labyrinth Press, 1983).

11. Menot, *Tours,* 175; cf. Menot, *Paris–1,* 222.

12. Maillard, *SSP,* fol. 317; cf. Pepin, *DN,* fol. 7.

13. Pepin, *DN,* fol. 7; cf. Menot, *Tours,* 211.

14. Pepin, *DN,* fol. 278.

15. Ibid., fols. 200, 278; cf. Pepin, *CDA,* 56; Pepin, *CPP,* 176; Farinier, *SP,* fol. 18.

16. LePicart, *Caresme,* fol. 57.

17. "Peuple, ne criez plus, ne vous tourmentez pas, ne vous desolez plus, esiouyssez vous, & prenez bon courage" (Paris, *Homélies,* fol. 29).

18. Pepin, *CQ,* 112; cf. Paris, *Homélies,* fol. 155; cf. LePicart, *Caresme,* fol. 10.

19. Pepin, *CPP,* 432; cf. Pepin, *CQ,* 307.

20. "O igitur pauper peccator noli desperare de venia, sed considera praesens mysterium, & attende, quia miserationes Domini super omnia opera eius" (Pepin, *CQ,* 441).

21. "Si negasti christum cum petro: si persecutor fuisti cum paulo: si publice peccasti cum magdalena: si convertaris & penitentiam egeris misericordiam obtinebis" (Clerre, *SA,* fol. 28).

22. "Non legitur, quod latro iste aliquid boni prius gesserit, qui tamen finaliter maximam misericordiam apud christum invenit" (Pepin, *CQ,* 441).

23. "Si ergo peccator sum, peccavit etiam & David, peccavit Petrus, peccavit Paulus, peccavit & Magdalena, ac similes, qui tamen per poenitentiam nunc gloriose regnant in coelis" (Pepin, *CDH,* 317).

24. "Si David adulterium commisit: cur non ego?" (Pepin, *DN,* fol. 12).

25. Pepin, *CDA,* 242.

26. Pepin, *DN,* fol. 277.

27. Cleree, *SA,* fol. 36; cf. Tisserand, *SA,* fol. 5; Menot, *Paris-2,* 308.

28. Augustine *De civitate Dei* 5.10, trans. Henry Bettenson (New York: Penguin, 1977), 195.

29. Ibid., 13. 15, 523.

30. "Mulier vidit filium suum capientem malam viam, et dicitur mulieri illi: Estis mala. Et quare? Quia videndo filium malum non eum corrigitis. Ecce videmus populum pati pro principe, patrem pro filius. . . . Dico igitur quod Deus non est causa nec accidentalis, nec permissiva peccatorum commissorum, sed voluntas in ordinata" (Menot, *Tours,* 24).

31. Maillard, *QO,* fol. 108.

32. "Erit in hac villa homo vite pessime, renieur de Dieu. De sero facit bonum vultum: de mane invenitur mortuus. . . . Est sua reprobatio, vel predestinatio? Scotus XLI distinct. primi dicit quod si aliquis sit eternaliter predestinatus, hoc est ex mera Dei gratia. Nullus tamen est a Deo reprobatus, nisi suo exigente demerito" (Menot, *Tours,* 5).

33. Ibid.

34. "Nam debemus nos accusare non excusare neque attribuere deo peccata nostra quia permisit: neque dyabolo quia tentavit. Neque mundo quia inditrit nec constellationi quia inclinavit" (Cleree, *SQ,* fol. 65).

35. Pepin, *DN,* fol. 278.

36. Maillard, *Sermones de sanctis (SS)* (Paris: Jehan Petit, 1504), fol. 2.

37. LePicart, *Caresme,* fol. 4.

38. "Dicitis quod estis Christiani; videatis quomodo servatis legem. Nonne Deus precepit quod diligatur et honoretur; quod serventur festa; quod non blasphemetur nomen eius; quod nullus se periuret in iudicio; quod non frangantur matrimonia; quod non fiant detractiones, luxurie, usure et rapine?" (Menot, *Paris-2,* 429).

39. "Nous achetons l'heritaige de paradis; le vendeur (c'est Dieu le Créateur) nous y met des condicions, ce sont ses commandemens: si nous en laissons ung, le marchié est nul" (Maillard, *Oeuvres,* 10; cf. Maillard, *QO,* fol. 95).

40. Raulin, *SQ*, 587.

41. "Iudaei enim credebant solum actum exteriorem malum esse a Deo prohibitum, utpote furtum, adulterium, homicidium. Non autem actum interiorem, scilicet malam voluntatem" (Pepin, *DN*, fol. 92; cf. Clichtove, *Sermones*, fols. 123–24).

42. "Aussi le vieil testament donné par Moyse qui estoit le serviteur, n'estoit point pour tousiours durer, car il menassoit les gens, & les faisoit servir á Dieu par craincte" (LePicart, *Caresme*, fol. 7).

43. Menot, *Paris-2*, 290; cf. Pepin, *CDH*, 23.

44. Pepin, *DN*, fol. 141.

45. "Vous n'avez pas receu lesperit de servitute en crainte comme devant. Mais lesperit d'adoption des enfantz, pour lequel confidemment et assceurement appellons dieu nostre pere. . . . Aussi ce jour de penthecouste, s'esmeult ung son du ciel, comme ung vehement et puissant vent. Mais d'autre quallite. Car ce qui estoit aux Iuifz terreurs, aux apostres estoit consollation. Pour monstrer que lors estoit loy de craincte et rigueur, maintenant damour et de doulceur" (Gaigny, *Homélies*, fols. 17, 19).

46. LePicart, *Avent*, fol. 195.

47. "Nam hostie veteris legis non erant sufficientes ad pacificandum deum: erant enim hostie mortue" (Messier, *QS*, fol. 63).

48. Lansperge, *Sermons*, fol. 16.

49. "Ce verbe estoit au paravant abscons & celé aux hommes, escript au papier de son pere de lettre si subtile & menue que nul y pouvoit lire. C'estoit sapience mussee, & tresor incongneu, & par le raport des Prophetes, vrayement Dieu caché" (Paris, *Homélies*, fol. 9).

50. Ibid., fol. 2.

51. LePicart, *Caresme*, fol. 62; cf. Maillard, *SS*, fol. 32; Menot, *Tours*, 213.

52. "Christiani christus offert vobis gratiam suam: ponatis penam habendi: & tunc audacter speretis habere paradisum: quia ipsa gratia extinguit desideria inhonesta" (Cleree, *SQ*, fol. 114).

53. "Per nosmetipsos enim non possumus quicquam boni facere, nec etiam minimae tentationi resistere, teste salvatore, ubi ait: Sine me nihil potestis facere" (Pepin, *CPP*, 217; cf. 219).

54. "Si hodie sero essent duo nudi se balneantes in flumine, diceretis: Isti sunt duo magni fatui. Vix possumus califieri in domo et isti sunt nudi in aqua. —O, domina, aliud est. Unus eorum vadit in unam foveam iuxta pontem, ubi submergitur et est in periculo. Dicit ergo persona stans super pontem: Amice, non eatis illuc. Et nihilominus ibit et submergetur. Alius autem vitabit et recedet. Quero utrum existens super pontem fecit eum submergi vel periclitari? Certe non" (Menot, *Tours*, 5).

55. "Si queratis a me: frater quo modo poterimus istam gratiam habere per quam poterimus unum efficium deo? Dico quod si habueritis ista scilicet abundantiam charitatis: promptitudinem voluntatis: & arduitatem operis eritis cum deo" (Maillard, *SA*, fol. 112).

56. Pepin, *CQ*, 454; cf. LePicart, *Trinité*, fol. 110.

57. "Pourquoy donc n'est sauvé tout le monde? C'est pource que tout le monde ne luy obeit pas: tout le monde n'obeit pas à l'Evangile: & à la parole de Nostre Seigneur Iesus Christ: car le fruit & efficace de ceste grace ne viennent pas sinon à ceux qui luy obeissent & gardent ses commandemens" (LePicart, *Caresme*, fol. 104; cf. LePicart, *Avent*, fol. 266).

58. "Sed pro ampliori dilatatione huius sensus moralis est advertendum, quod sunt multa bona semina, quae debet homo seminare in agro suae conscientiae, & hoc cooperando principali seminatori, qui est Deus, & se praeperando, faciendo, quod in

se est, ut ipse Deus infundat in eo virtutes, & ipse homo ex ipsis, sive per ipsas diffundat semen bonorum operarum" (Pepin, *CDH*, 131; cf. LePicart, *Caresme*, fol. 68).

59. "Ecce nunc tempus acceptabile, in quo Deus disposuit dare gratiam omnibus vere penitentibus" (Menot, *Paris-1*, 237).

60. "Si les fleurs ne precedent, leur fruict ne sortira point. Si grace et vertu ne vont devant, glore et beatitude ne suiviront pas" (Gaigny, *Homélies*, fol. 3).

61. "Fides est credere quod non videns" (Maillard, *SS*, fol. 12).

62. Maillard, *QO*, fol. 99.

63. Pepin, *CS*, 349. This metaphor also applies to grace: "Parum denique habemus de lumine divine gratie, multum vero de tenebris culpe" (Pepin, *DN*, fol. 122).

64. "Nisi credideritis, quia ergo sum Dei filius; nisi credideritis, quia ergo sum conditor mundi; nisi credideritis, quia ergo sum formator, & reformator hominis, creator, & recreator, factor, & refactor; nisi haec credideritis, moriemini in peccatis vestris" (Pepin, *CQ*, 104).

65. "Il ne fault poinct demander pourquoy il nest venu plus tost parce que le conseil de Dieu lequel la envoie ne peult estre comprins par lentendement humain" (Claude Despence, *Sermons du premier advenement de nostre Seigneur Iesus Christ*, BN Ms. fr. 454, fol. 9).

66. Pepin, *CS*, 300; cf. Pepin, *CDA*, 52; Pepin, *DN*, fol. 267.

67. "Potissime autem tribus miseriis repletur omnis homo in praesenti, nisi divinitus adiuvetur. Prima miseria est ignorantia unius veri, & summi Dei. Secunda est depressio circa terrena, & inferiora. Tertia est amor sui, quo pervenit homo usque ad contemptum summi boni, quod Deus est. At vero si ipse homo velit cooperari suae saluti, iuvatur a Deo triplici virtute theologica, scilicet fide, spe & charitate, contra praedictam triplicem miseriam. Nam fide illuminatur contra ignorantiam. Spe elevatur contra terrenam depressionem. Charitate inflammatur per contemptum sui, & amorem Dei super omnia" (Pepin, *CDH*, 164).

68. "Aurum enim bonum est fides. Aurum melius est spes, quae sursum animam erigit. Aurum autem optimum est charitas, quae nos coniungit Deo" (Pepin, *CDH*, 170).

69. Clichtove, *Sermones*, fol. 127; cf. Pepin, *CDA*, 188; Pepin, *CPP*, 435; Menot, *Paris-2*, 334.

70. Raulin, *SQ*, 506.

71. "Combien qu'il semble qu'il ne tienne compte de ceste pauvre femme chananée, qui crie apres luy, qu'il luy plaise avoir pitié & misericorde d'elle: si fait, Iesus Christ en fait grande compte, & nous le verrons bien tantost manifestement, quand il parlera à elle publiquement. Mais il fait semblan & simule de la repousser, & de ne la vouloir point ouir, afin de donner á cognoistre sa foy, qu'elle a grande en nostre Seigneur Iesus Christ" (LePicart, *Caresme*, fol. 60).

72. "Nous trouvons en l'escriture que nostre Seigneur Iesus Christ parle d'une petite foy & d'une grande. Il parle de la petite, quand il dit à S. Pierre: Modi ce fidei, quare dubitasti? Et icy à ceste femme, il parle de la grande foy: Magna est fides tua" (Ibid., fol. 62; cf. Raulin *SQ*, 204, 206).

73. Maillard, *Oeuvres*, 30.

74. Menot, *Paris-1*, 262; cf. Pepin, *CPP*, 519.

75. "Persona que in morte se recommendat Deo in merito passionis Christi, secure vadit et lucratur paradisum. Et dico quod si ita essetis sancta sicut Iohannes Baptista, non haberetis paradisum nisi in merito passionis Christ" (Menot, *Tours*, 118–19).

76. "Le Turc gardera fidelité, iustice, & autres vertus, mais pour tout cela il ne

sera plus aggreable à Dieu, car il n'a pas la foy.... L'euvre tout seul, & de soy ne luy est point aggreable. Aussi le Chrestien qui a la foy qui presche & faict miracles & semblables, il n'est pas aggreable à Dieu, s'il n'a charité.... La foy sans charité est morte, mais charité ne peult estre sans la foy" (LePicart, *Avent*, fol. 312).

77. "Ipse autem Deus fidelissimus est in promissis, nec mentiri potest aut fallere ideo quod promittit implebit" (Pepin, *CPP*, 515; cf. Menot, *Paris-1*, 264).

78. Clichtove, *Sermones*, fol. 8; cf. Maillard, *SA*, fol. 15.

79. "Car iamais Dieu ne destitue ny delaisse ceux qui mettent leur cueur & esperance en luy: car il est fidele, & l'a ainsi promis & infailliblement il le fera par sa grace & grande bonté" (LePicart, *Caresme*, fol. 175).

80. Maillard, *SA*, fol. 73; cf. Pepin, *CPP*, 416.

81. "Tu diras: Ouy, mais mon euvre ne sçauroit estre satisfactoire pour mes pechez: Il est vray que ton euvre, comme venant purement de toy, il n'est point satisfactoire: Mais ton euvre appuýe au merite de Iesus Christ, & fondé au merite d'iceluy, alors ton euvre, qui quant est de toy, n'estoit rien.... Le merite de Iesus Christ auquel ton euvre est fondé, faict que ton euvre est satisfactoire pour la remission de tes pechez: & est autant plaisant & aggreable à Dieu, comme si Iesus Christ luy-mesme l'avoit faict" (LePicart, *Caresme*, fol. 65).

82. "Non enim sufficit ad salutem habere fidem in corde: nisi sequantur bona opera tempore, & loco, quia Fides sine operibus mortua est" (Pepin, *CDH*, 192; cf. Pepin, *CDA*, 188; Menot, *Paris-Alia*, 471; Messier, *SQ*, fol. 146).

83. "Nam sicut fructus ostendit qualitatem arboris: sic bona opera conditionem hominis manifestant" (Raulin, *SA*, fol. 52).

84. "Si spiritus sanctus habitat in nobis nos vivificando per gratiam, manifestemus talem vitam interiorem per bona opera exteriora, quae non nisi ab ipso spiritu sancto sunt. Nam bonae operationes sunt signa, quod vivimus spiritualiter & quod Spiritus Sanctus vivat in nobis" (Pepin, *CDA*, 217; cf. Pepin, *CDH*, 166; LePicart, *Avent*, fol. 95).

85. "Femme, tous tes pechez te sont pardonnez.... Nous voyons icy ... que nostre Seigneur Iesus Christ l'attribue à la charité & amour de Dieu, laquelle n'est iamais sans la bonne euvre" (LePicart, *Caresme*, fol. 86).

86. Ibid., fol. 40; cf. Maillard, *SS*, fol. 27.

87. "Nam ex operibus bonis & in gaudio in Spiritu Sancto procedit spes, quae ... est certa expectatio futurae beatitudinis" (Raulin, *SQ*, 244).

88. "Nam bona opera facta spem de dei misericordia generant.... Inter autem omnia bona preterita que iuvat ne homo in desperationem cadat, est elemosyna" (Pepin, *DN*, fol. 282; cf. fol. 276).

89. "Optarent omnes salvari sed pauci sunt qui opera salutis velint facere" (Maillard, *SS*, fol. 19; Cf. Maillard, *SA*, fol. 114.

90. "Et qu'est-ce à dire faire penitence? Premierement c'est muer sa volonté de mal en bien: changer noz mauvais desirs: donner nostre cueur à Dieu, & estre marris de l'avoir offensé" (LePicart, *Caresme*, fol. 64; cf. LePicart, *Avent*, fol. 276).

91. Menot, *Tours*, 201.

92. Pepin, *CDH*, 194.

93. "Non satis est ieiunare vel alia facere opera que sunt de genere bonorum, sed oportet ea facere cum spiritu" (Menot, *Paris-2* 302; cf. 299; Menot, *Tours*, 11).

94. Farinier, *Sermones*, fol. 20; cf. Pepin, *CDH*, 111; Pepin, *CDH*, 89; Pepin, *CDA*, 95; LePicart, *Caresme*, fol. 3; Clichtove, *Sermones*, fol. 8.

95. "Sed prohdolor sunt plerique etiam in omni statu, quorum iustitia est solum verbosa & non operosa. Practica, de multis praelatis, atque praedicatoribus, qui dicunt

multa recta, pulchra, & bona, sed non faciunt" (Pepin, *CDA,* 95; cf. Pepin, *CS,* 519; Raulin, *SQ,* 3, 513).

96. Nicolas Denisse, *Sermones residui a secunda dominica post pascha usque ad aventum* (*SR*) (Rouen: Martin Morin, 1509), fol. 7.

97. "Penitentiam dare possumus, securitatem autem dare non possumus. Nunquid dico: damnabitur. Non. Sed neque dico: salvabitur" (Menot, *Tours,* 200).

98. "Per hoc mare nil aliud intelligitur nisi vita presens et hic mundus periculosus. Nam, sicut persona in [mari] non est in securitate sed semper in periculo, sic est in hac presenti vita" (Menot, *Paris-2,* 291).

99. Pepin, *CDH,* 138; cf. Menot, *Paris-2,* 290.

100. Maillard, *SA,* fol. 71; cf. Menot, *Paris-1,* 258; Cf. Menot, *Paris-2,* 290.

101. Cleree, *SQ,* fol. 26.

102. Menot, *Tours,* 118.

103. Pepin, *CS,* 298; cf. Pepin, *CQ,* 77; Pepin, *CA,* 229.

104. "Si vero interrogetur bonus, & devotus catholicus, quo vadit per mortem, respondere poterit cum fiducia divinae misericordiae: Vado ad patrem meum caelestum cum eo habitaturus in aeternum, & ultra" (Pepin, *CQ,* 101).

105. LePicart, *Avent,* fol. 92.

106. "Quod non est in hoc mundo persona sic iusta que possit notitiam habere de sua electione vel reprobatione. Sed, sicut mors corporalis potest dinosci in infirmo, sic damnatio persone in peccato existentis. Dixi quod quando infirmus non vult capere medicinam neque cibum aliquem et natura est mortificata in eo, et pulsus deficit, signum est quod vadit ad mortem. Sic qui motiones Spiritus sancti posuit sub pedibus, signum est damnationis eterne" (Menot, *Tours,* 110).

107. Raulin, *SQ,* 158; cf. Menot, *Tours,* 10.

108. Menot, *Paris-1,* 236.

109. Pepin, *CDH,* 4; cf. Pepin, *CDH* 292.

110. "Vos estis hodie sani in leticia & gaudio: cras moriemini. Sicut secana non cessat currere: sic vita nostra non est nisi cursus ad mortem: ut dicit Seneca" (Maillard, *QO,* fol. 96; cf. Messier, *QS,* fol. 98).

111. Menot, *Tours,* 36.

112. "Vos voluptuose viventes, invito vos ad servitium et exequias predecessoris vestri qui cras inhumabitur intus." (Menot, *Paris-1,* 248).

113. J. Huizinga, *The Waning of the Middle Ages* (New York: Doubleday, 1954), 30.

114. Jean Delumeau, "Pouvoir, peur et hérésie au début des temps modernes," in Myriam Yardeni (ed.), *Modernité et non-conformisme en France à travers les âges* (Leiden: E. J. Brill, 1983), 24.

115. Delumeau, *Peur,* 15–18ff.

116. Ibid., 218.

117. Martin, *Métier,* 36, 38, 51, 52, 173.

118. Denis Crouzet, "La réprésentation du temps à l'époque de la Ligue," *RH* 270:2 (1983): 320.

119. Delaruelle, *Piété,* 334–36.

120. Chiffoleau, *Comptabilité.* x.

121. Martin, "Ministère," 684, 731.

122. Jacques LeGoff, *The Birth of Purgatory* (Chicago: University of Chicago Press, 1981), 358.

123. Ibid., 3.

124. Chiffoleau, *Comptabilité,* 398.

125. LeGoff, *Purgatory*, 297.

126. "Deus non semper punit maiores peccatores in hoc mundo ut melius puniat eos in alio" (Cleree, *SQ*, fol. 31).

127. LeGoff, *Purgatory*, 158; cf. Maillard, *QO*, fol. 172; Pepin, *CDH*, 84; Menot, *Paris-2*, 279.

128. Pepin, *DN*, fol. 7.

129. "Primae sunt, quae in praesenti aliqua peccata mortalia commiserunt, quae non, nisi in generali confessae sunt, eo quod oblivioni tradita erant. Aliae sunt, quae de mortalibus confessis non plene satisfecerunt. Aliae autem sunt, quae aliqua venalia secum deferunt. Nam etsi mortale peccatum non remittatur, quoad culpam in alio saeculo, bene tamen veniale, & hoc in purgatorio; quia si fuerit iunctum mortali, in inferno nunquam remittetur, eo quod Deus nunquam dat dimidiam veniam. Et est circa hoc notandum, quod primae animae caeteris paribus divitius detinentur in purgatorio, quam secundae, & secundae quam tertiae. Incertum tamen nobis est, quanto tempore una anima pro praecedentibus causis affligatur in purgatoria, sicut incerta est nobis culpae gravitas" (Pepin, *CS*, 505).

130. Pepin, *CQ*, 367.

131. Pepin, *EC*, 59.

132. Ibid., 70.

133. "En purgatoire il y a beaucoup de mal, en sorte que toutes les peines du monde ne sont point à comparer: toutesfois les ames endurent en esperance: car elles sont asseurées d'en estre delivrées" (LePicart, *Avent*, fol. 30).

134. See, e.g., T. Andrus, "The Devil on the Medieval Stage in France" (Ph. D. diss., Syracuse University, 1979); E. DuBruck, "The Devil and Hell in Medieval French Drama," *Romania* 100 (1979): 165–79; Grace Frank, *The Medieval French Drama*, (New York: Oxford University Press, 1954).

135. Philippe Ariès, *The Hour of Our Death* (New York: Alfred A. Knopf, 1981), 462.

136. LeGoff, *Purgatory*, 18–23.

137. Ibid., pp. 25, 28.

138. Ibid., 39.

139. Jeffrey Burton Russell, *Lucifer: The Devil in the Middle Ages* (Ithaca: Cornell University Press, 1984), 71n.

140. LeGoff, *Purgatory*, 193–208.

141. "Ivistis ne ad montes Sabaudie, a la Vaupute, que sunt prope suburbia inferni? Dicitur quod ibi est multitudo sortilegarum mulierum" (Menot, *Paris-2*, 312).

142. "Moraliter sciendum, quod sunt tres provinciae generales, se in generali. Prima superior, quae est coelum. Secunda inferior, quae est infernus. Tertia media, quae est praesens mundus. In prima tantum sunt boni. In secunda tantum mali. In tertio vero boni, & mali sunt simul permixti. Primam provinciam semel tantum purgavit Praeses loci illius, scilicet omnipotens Deus, & hoc cum deiecit ab altitudine coeli in abyssum inferni luciferum cum complicibus suis. . . . Secunda provincia totaliter opposita praecedenti, nunquam purgatur, neque evacuatur malefactoribus. Nam in ea habitant homicidae, sacrilegi, fures, adulteri, blasphemi, luxuriosi, invidi, gulosi, superbi, iracundi, & similes" (Pepin, *CQ*, 40).

143. "Infernus lacus est sine mensura: profundus sine fundo: plenus ardore incorruptibili: fetore intolerabili: plenus dolore inextinguibili et innumerabili.ibi museria.ibi tenebra.ibi ordo nullus.ibi horror eternus.ibi nullus spes boni.nec desperatio mali" (Olivier Maillard, *Sermones dominicales* [*SD*] [Lyon: Stephan Gueygnardi, 1503], fol. 233).

144. "Comme le cadavre est mené au tombeau par quatres porteurs, voici les quatres porteurs qui mèneront l'âme en enfer: le charme de la vie présente,—l'aveuglement de l'esprit,—la présomption sur l'avenir,—la négligence du salut" (Maillard, *Oeuvres,* 126).

145. Menot, *Paris-2,* 309; cf. Raulin, *SQ,* 173.

146. Pepin, *CPP,* 502.

147. "Amica, sicut in carcere descenditur du hault en bas, sic dico quod persona non descendit in infernum tout a ung coup, sed per multos gradus. Primus igitur gradus descendendi in infernum est peccati magnitudo; secundus gradus est peccati multitudo; tertius est peccati turpitudo" (Ibid, 136).

148. "Tunc meretrix cum lenone simul ligabuntur in uno fasce in cibum ignis, quemadmodum simul videmus concatenatos colubros & serpentes" (Raulin, *SQ,* 273).

149. Menot, *Tours,* 8.

150. "Sed quid dicunt nunc multi? O isti predicatores loquuntur nobis de inferno ut inferant nobis timorem" (Maillard, *QO,* fol. 223).

151. "Multi non videntur firmiter credere venturum, quinimo verbo & facto irrident praedicatores de hoc loquentes, dicentes quod illa quae praedicantur de ultimo iudicio, dicuntur de non quia vera sint, sed ut terreantur homines, & ut revocentur a malis" (Pepin, *CA,* 209).

152. Maillard, *SS,* fol. 15.

153. Martin, *Ordres mendiants,* 320.

154. Delumeau, *Peur,* 208.

155. "Proposuit itaque christus in hodierno Evangelio veram historian, & hoc contra derisores avaros, qui derident praedicatores loquentes de poenis inferni, de severitate divini iudicii, aut de operibus pietatis pauperibus exhibendis" (Pepin, *CQ,* 125).

156. "Ut autem sciamus in quam etate christus venit: habetis scire quod sicut septem sunt atetes hominis sic septem sunt etates hominis sic septem sunt etates mundi. Prima etas vocatur infantia. Secunda pueritia. Tertia adolescentia. Quarta iuventus. Quinta virilitas. Sexta senectus. Septima decrepitus.... A principio mundi usque ad finem sunt septem etates. Prima ab Adam ... Secunda a Noe ... Tertia ab Abraam ... Quarta a Moyse ... Quinta a David ... Sexta a transmigratione ... Septima incipit in adventu: et durat usque ad finem mundi" (Maillard, *SA,* fol. 16). The mid-century preacher Louis Peresi also used this schema to draw parallels between human life and saving history (Martin, "Ministère," 691). This schematization is based on Psalm 90 which was widely interpreted in the Middle Ages "meaning that the world would last for six millenia, corresponding to the week in which it had been created; the sixth and last *aetas mundi* was reckoned to have begun with the birth of Christ, a point used to reckon dates from the time of Bede ... onwards" (Horst Fuhrmann, *Germany in the High Middle Ages,* c. 1050–1200, Cambridge: Cambridge University Press, 1986, 3).

157. Norman Cohn, *The Pursuit of the Millenium* (New York: Harper, 1961), 100; Marjorie Reeves, *The Influence of Prophecy in the Later Middle Ages: A Study in Joachimism* (Oxford: Clarendon Press, 1969), 19.

158. Pepin, *CDH,* 318; Menot, *Tours,* 118.

159. "Sic cum est dies finalis et ultimus prelii, toute l'artillerie du diable mittitur. ... Ecce quomodo anima est assaillie in hora mortis" (Menot, *Tours,* 48).

160. "Quod nunc luce clarius apparet, quia romano imperatori nulli aut pauci obediunt: licet tempore apostoli maxime vigeret ipsum imperium.... Secundo post intelligi de discessione ab unitate ecclesie, vel ab obedientia romani pontificis. Et hoc

iam factum est multotiens: et adhuc temporibus nostris. Tertio post intelligi de discessione a fide catholica, non quidem universaliter . . . sed in multis locis. Quod videmus iam factum in Asia & in Africa: que iam defecerunt a christo" (Raulin, *SA*, fol. 26).

161. Tisserand, *Sermones de adventu,* fol. 17.

162. "Sed sufficiunt pro nunc capere signa que ponuntur in evangelio nostri thematis. Cum dicitur: et in terris pressura gentium: quia pressura erit quod gentes se abscondent in cavernis terre. Et hoc pre confusione sonitus maris & fluctuum. Narum elevabit se mare mirabili modo super omnes colles: & iterum in loco cadet. Similiter omnia flumina: & facient sonum mirabilem. . . . Elevaverunt flumina fluctus suos a vocibus aquarum multarum: mirabiles elationes maris: mirabilis in altis dominus. Et tum magnum ictum facient flumina dicit evangelium nostrum: quod homines arescent pre confusione maris et fluctuum" (Ibid.).

163. LeGoff, *Purgatory,* 201

164. Tisserand, *SA,* fol. 19.

165. "Et veniet ignis elementum de celo: cum Christus veniet. . . . Ignis ante ipsum precedet. . . . De operatione ignis: dico quod de eo possumus dicere contra suam naturam veniet virtute divina: quia ignis naturaliter ascendit" (Ibid).

166. "O miserrimi qui pecunias ab hoc & ab hac capitis: ignis vos consumet cum vestra pecunia. . . . Et dico quod purgabit electos: qui iuissent ad purgatorium: quia post iudicium non erit purgatorium. . . . Item post iudicium ignis descendet cum damnatis in inferno: quia aperietur terra: & horror maximus cum damnatis erit. Et cadent simul damnati et ignis: scilicet immundicie: puta sulfur: & similia. Et statim ignis purus post descensum damnatorum: renovabit terram. Et post iudicium ignis elementaris revertetur in sua prima specie" (Ibid, fols. 19–20).

167. Ibid., fol. 27.

168. "Nam in fine saeculi descendet grandis lapis de monte, idest, christus de caelo, & exterminabit minutatem dicta brachia & pectus corporis peccati, quandoquidem deiiciet eos in infernum propter oppressionum pauperum" (Pepis, *CDA,* 89).

169. "Si exterius respicient, videbunt totum mundum ardentem igne conflagrationis" (Pepin, *CDH,* 313).

170. Menot, *Paris-2,* 308.

171. Nicolas Denisse, *Tabula sermonum hyemalium de tempore (TS)* (Strasbourg, 1510), fol. 11.

172. "Hec sedes est thronus imperialis in quo in aere erit Dominus sedens cum omnibus beatis et virgine Maria. Sed tunc terra se aperiet et os inferni erit apertum et inde exient omnes diaboli et miseri damnati facientes magnos rugitus at ululatus et magna suspiria; ponent se super terram prope magnum os inferni, expectantes sententiam divinam super eos faciendam et in illo ore inferni deglutientur in sempiternum et sine fine. Sed beati erunt elevati in aere" (Ibid.).

173. Raulin, *SQ,* 155.

174. Ibid., 255

175. Ibid., 259.

176. LePicart, *Caresme,* fol. 128.

177. "Dies autem iudicii determinate sciri non potest per naturalem rationem, eo quod hoc transcendit humanam investigationem" (Pepin, *CQ,* 42).

178. Menot, *Tours,* 45.

179. "Convertentur ad vesperam [Ps. 58 in the Vulgate], id est, nostris temporibus, in quos fines saeculorum devenerunt" (Raulin, *SQ,* 205; cf. Maillard, *SA,* fol. 2; Pepin *DN,* fol. 265).

180. "S. Paul dit, quand on delaisse la foy de Iesus Christ, & a recognoistre le

Pape, l'eglise Romaine, c'est un signe que le iugement s'approche" (LePicart, *Avent,* fol. 53).

181. Brown, *Pastor,* 169, 254, 256.

182. Quoted in Martin, "Ministère," 653.

183. Ibid., 658.

Chapter 6

1. Bossy, *Christianity,* 11, 13.

2. Martin, "Ministère," 652.

3. Pepin, *DN,* fol. 2; cf. Pepin, *CPP,* 315; LePicart, *Avent,* fol. 216: Menot, *Paris-1,* 270.

4. LePicart, *Caresme,* fol. 129; cf. Farinier, *SP,* fol. 19; cf. Pepin, *CPP,* 181.

5. Pepin, *CS,* 56.

6. Menot, *Tours,* 5; cf. Pepin, *DN,* fol. 45.

7. "Primo igitur piisimus creator Deus, qui non vult mortem peccatoris, sed ut convertatur & vivat: qui etiam neminem vult perire, sed omnes ad viam veritatis pervenire" (Pepin, *CPP,* 329; cf. Menot, *Paris–2,* 301).

8. "Ideo dicit mater Ecclesia: O pauperes filii, revertamini ad Dominum Deum vestrum, qui est tam dulcis, benignus et curialis, qui vos tanto tempore expectat ad penitentiam, nec aliud petit nisi salutem vestram" (Menot, *Paris-1,* 219).

9. Cleree, *SQ,* fol. 30; Pepin, *DN,* fol. 200.

10. "Certe pater familias qui dicitur homo: est deus pater quia habuit similitudinem cum homine. Homo enim est creatura benigna et dulcis inter omnes alias. Sic etiam deus pater est summe benignus. Pater misericordiarum et deus totius consolationis" (Cleree, *SQ,* fol. 58).

11. "Voluit enim Deus post lapsum ad communem hominum pacem nutriendam, & compescendum rebelles, aliquos praeesse" (Pepin, *CS,* 385).

12. Cleree, *SA,* fol. 3.

13. Pepin, *CPP,* 501.

14. LePicart, *Caresme,* fol. 10.

15. "Car si on leur presche tousiours choses plaisantes & delectables, ils ne s'en seront que gaber, & voudront faire des compagnons avec Dieu, & s'en jouer comme d'un homme mortel" (Calvin, *PS,* fol. 446).

16. "Non est mirum si contra eos irascatur, cum non poenitant" (Raulin, *SQ,* 14).

17. "Deus irascitur mittit pestes: mittit guerras et cetera mala que sentimus. Helas pauperes nunc christus opponit se iustitie divine & stat pro nobis dicens patri" (Cleree, *SA,* fol. 13).

18. "Casus est talis, Dame, et capietis faciliter: habetis filium qui habet la gravelle, gallice, vel lapidem. Il le fault tailler. Ploratis, inde; tamen oportet sic fieri et ipsum ponere in periculo mortis et contenter le chirurgien" (Ibid., 23).

19. Pepin, *DN,* fol. 45.

20. "Primo igitur quidam volunt attribuere culpam suam Deo: dicentes quod si Deus vellet, nullus peccaret" (Ibid., fol. 13).

21. "Quod enim oculos non videat lucem solis, non est ex defecto solis, quia quantum est de se, omnibus se offert. Hoc ergo est ex defectu hominis, qui non vult oculos aperire ad receptionem solis" (Ibid.).

22. "Naturali ratione possumus cognoscere, & concludere Deum esse unum. . . .

Videmus enim inter coelos unum esse supremum, quod vocatur primum mobile. Item inter septem planetas solem obtinere primatum. Insuper videmus in politia civili unum esse monarcham supremum, qui caeteris imperat, & praesertim ubi est regimen regale, quod est caeteris regiminibus perfectibus. Idem etiam videmus in politia ecclesiastica, in qua regnat unus solus Pontifex summus. Ex quibus omnibus similitudinibus concludere possumus unitatem Dei" (Pepin, *CDA*, 7).

23. Maillard, *SS*, fol. 17.

24. "Comme le pere considerant en soy soy essence, engendre une congnoissance et intelligence dicelluy. Et ceste intelligence que a le pere de soy, est necessairement autre que le pere. . . . Et touteffois, est autre que le pere ne le filz, en tant que lamour necessairement, est distincte de lamant. Cest amour donc est charité, et la tierce personne, qui pour limbecillite nostre, ne peult estre exprimee suffisamment par ung seul nom" (Gaigny, *Homélies*, fols. 15–16).

25. Ibid., fols. 16–17.

26. Ibid., pp. 17, 19.

27. "Car le Seigneur na voulu tout ce qui estoit necessaire a faire ou croirre, dire a ses apostres, ains en a laisse une partie a disposer a eulx et a leurs successeurs, par la bouche du saint esperit" (Ibid., fol. 20).

28. "Spiritus sanctus venit iuxta cubile tam de die quam de nocte et dicit: Aperi mihi, sponsa mea, soror mea, dando inspirationes" (Menot, *Tours*, 70).

29. "Charissimi igitur sanctus qui est dator gratiarum: est amor procedens a patre & filio. Quicquid agat pater, ut patiatur filius: nihil fit sine spiritu sancto. Scilicet quomodo inspiratur: dico quod per verbum predicatum. Sicut cantatur de incarnatione verbi: per illud ave prolatum: & tuum responsum gratum, est ex te verbum incarnatum: sic per illud verbum predicatum: & consensum datum est in te verbum inspiratum: quo salvantur" (Messier, *QS*, fol. 13).

30. "Econtra autem contemptus divini verbi expellit Spiritum sanctum ab homine" (Pepin, *CS*, 581; cf. Pepin, *CDH*, 356).

31. "Et veritablement bien rarement & atart se debueroit faire sermon auquel ne fust faict memoire ou mention de sa mort & passion & de loeuvre de nostre redemption" (Lansperge, *Sermons*, fol. 3).

32. Menot, *Tours*, 36.

33. Pepin, *SA*, fol. 21; cf. Pepin, *CA*, 107; cf. Pepin, *CPP*, 94.

34. "Ineffabile dei verbum factum est temporaliter caro secundum carnem: preter carnem supra carnem: contra carnem: & propter carnem" (Brulefer, *Opuscula*, fol. 15).

35. Tisserand, *SA*, fol. 2; cf. LePicart, *Caresme*, fol. 153; Menot, *Tours*, 177. Cleree, *SA*, fol. 8; Pepin, *CS*, 534; Paris, *Homélies*, fol. 97.

36. "Et sicut in arbore inserta sunt plures fructus differentes specie ut quando ramus unius arboris inseritur arbori diverse speciei: Ita in unitate persone christi sunt alie proprietates convenientes nature divine, et alie convenientes nature humane" (Illyricus, *SA*, fol. 10).

37. "Iste rex deus pater est qui misit filium suum in utero beate Virginis, quin christus sumpsit humanitatem: & tunc omnes infantes nature humane facti sunt legitimi" (Maillard, *SA*, fol. 104).

38. Here, Maillard was doing verbally what "holy dolls" were supposed to do for women in Italy. "According to Giovanni Dominici, the mother should place representations of child saints before her babies, 'pictures . . . in which your child . . . may take delight . . . Jesus nursing, sleeping in His Mother's lap. . . . So let the child see himself mirrored . . .'" (Christiane Klapisch-Zuber, *Women, Family, and Ritual in Renaissance Italy* [Chicago: University of Chicago Press, 1985], 320).

39. Ibid.; cf. Raulin, *SA,* fol. 125.

40. "Nativitatem habuit humilem, quia in paupercula domo natus est et pauperrimis paramentis adornatus. Paupertatem habuit in vita, quia divitiis et possessionibus terrenis caruit" (Michel Menot, "Carêmes de Paris," Alia Secunda Pars [*Paris-Alia*], 485).

41. LePicart, *Avent,* fol. 148.

42. "Tenete ergo iter et via paradisi quam nos docet Paulus. . . . Imitatores Dei estote" (Menot, *Paris-1,* 241).

43. "Sic nos christum imitantes debemus diligere proximos nostros gratuito amore, & non quia diligunt nos, aut quia benefaciunt nobis, vel quia aluid ab eis speramus" (Pepin, *CDH,* 115; cf. Pepin, *CDA,* 274).

44. Pepin, *CS,* 593.

45. Ibid., 169, 171.

46. Pepin, *CDH,* 57, 199, 201; cf. Pepin, *CS,* 231.

47. "La premiere chose que nostre Seigneur Iesus Christ a presché, quand il est venu en ce monde icy, c'est que nous eussions a faire penitence. . . . Il est impossible que nous soyons sauvez, si nous ne faisons penitence" (LePicart, *Caresme,* fol. 2).

48. Ibid., fol. 40; cf. Pepin, *RA,* 261.

49. "Item si videretis in campis pauperrimas mulieres habentes quinque vel sex pueros laborantes quotidie non comedentes nisi herbas cum sale: & petatur eis: quid cenabitis: cenare Jesu" (Cleree, *SQ,* fol. 6).

50. Pepin, *RA,* 261.

51. Maillard, *QO,* fols. 210, 212; cf. Maillard, *Oeuvres,* 4.

52. "O bone Iesu, quam dulciter cum peccatoribus conversatus estis, a quibus recepistis dura verba, duriora verbera, sed tandem durissima tormenta!" (Menot, *Paris-2,* 428).

53. Lansperge, *Sermons,* fol. 9.

54. "Toute personne doncques, qui desire avoir charité et Dieu aymer, se rende au pié de la Croix, regarde le sang qui decourt, à Dieu le Créateur le presente en pleurant et soupirant, en requerant à Dieu pardon, en demandant sa grace, et sans point de faulte, si elle persevere, elle obtiendra ce qu'elle demande" (Maillard, *Oeuvres,* 5).

55. Maillard, *SS,* fol. 13.

56. "Quando paterfamilias moritur, tota eius familia turbatur et se induit nigris vestimentis. La bonne femme se deult eo quod perdidit bonum maritum suum et quod ipsa manet sola vidua; filii etiam, eo quod sunt orbati patre et orphani et quocumque adiutorio paterno destitui; boni servitores, propter amissionem sui magistri. A fortiori, nos qui sumus in domo christianitatis, in qua christus, verus magister, verus paterfamilias, paratus est ad mortem" (Menot, *Tours,* 177).

57. "La passion de Nostre Seigneur a esté ung merveilleux pelerinaige au quel il s'est reposé six fois. Et pour entrer au mystere d'icelle, nous avons a contempler. . . . Sic etiam quando Dominus noster a eu mis les piedz dedans le jardin, il a eu peur et a esté tout esmeu et tout troublé. . . . Et tunc va lever les yeulx aux cieulx, les deux mains jointes, son povre cueur frappé jusques a la mort, et d'une voix piteuse va crier: O, Pater, si possibile est, O Pere, ceste mort que je doys au jourdhuy souffrir m'est dure et rigoreuse. O Pere, n'y a il remede? Faut il que je meure de telle mort? Je suis vostre seul enfant. Neantmoins, mon Pere, fiat voluntas tua" (Ibid., 179, 181–82).

58. Pilate oyant la parolle de nostre Seigneur congneut que c'estoit ung saige homme et fust estonné de sa responce, tellement qu'il va dire ad Iudeos expectantes

in ostio: Adduxistis hominem, etc. Dico vobis quod nullam invenio in eo causam mortis. Mais je vous diray: Est autem vobis consuetudo, etc. Pilatus voluit ter Christum eripere a morte, sciens ipsum non esse illa dignum" (Ibid., 189).

59. LePicart, *Caresme,* fol. 140.

60. "Ioseph igitur, accersito Pilato, petiit corpus illud et, eo annuente, emit aromata, mixturam myrrhe et aloes quasi libras centum et cum syndone optima venit, et centurio cum scala et estinces, avecques ung marteau, ut illum ex cruce descenderent. Videns beata Maria eos a longe venientes, dixit sociis suis: Helas, on luy va encore faire quelque tourment. —Eisque appropinquantibus, a joinctes mains les va prier de se contenter et quod erat mortuus. Illis autem respondentibus: Ma Dame, nous ne venous pas pour vous desplaire, ni a vostre cher enfant aussi; mais nous venons pour le descendre et inhumer, comme il appartient a sa personne. —Et adonc les va remercier humblement. Apponentes igitur operi manum, ont destaché le premier bras, puys le second et apres, les piedz" (Menot, *Tours,* 194).

61. "Nam per ea, quae christus pertulit in cruce, & praecipue ibi moriendo, confirmavit in nobis veritatem fidei, quae est de sua humanitate. Et similiter per signa tunc ostensa, una etiam cum sua resurrectione a mortuis confirmavit in nobis veritatem fidei, quae est de sua divinitate, ita scilicet, ut credamus eum esse verum Deum, & hominem perfectum" (Pepin, *CS,* 233).

62. LePicart, *Caresme,* fol. 151.

63. Menot, *Tours,* 199.

64. Pepin, *CDH,* 251.

65. Menot, *Tours,* 199.

66. "Mortuus est ut nos redimeret: & nos mortificandos esse spiritualiter erudiret: resurrexit ut spem resurrectionis daret, et nos resurgere a peccatis doceret" (Denisse, *SR,* fol. 26).

67. "Spiritualiter ab eo qui veritas est et potens super omnia promittitur quod tristicia vestra vertetur in gaudium" (Ibid., fol. 16; cf. Pepin, *CPP,* 512).

68. "Il est monté aux cieulx pour continuellement monstrer ses playes à la glorieuse Trinité, pour impetrer remission aux pecheurs. O quelle confiance! quelle espérance! quelle consolation! nostre iuge est nostre advocat et continuel intercesseur" (Maillard, *Oeuvres,* 248; cf. Paris, *Homélies,* fol. 55).

69. Delaruelle, *Piété populaire,* 339; cf. Eire, *War,* 173.

70. John MacQuarrie, *Principles of Christian Theology,* 2d ed. (New York: Charles Scribner's Sons, 1977), 311.

71. Wilhelm Heitmüller, "Hellenistic Christianity before Paul," in *The Writings of St. Paul,* ed. by Wayne A. Meeks (New York: W. W. Norton, 1972), 309.

72. William Wrede, "Paul's Importance in the History of the World," in Thomas Kepler (ed.), *Contemporary Thinking about Paul* (New York: Abingdon-Cokebury Press, 1950), 360.

73. Oberman, *Harvest,* 322.

74. Penny Schine Gold, *The Lady and the Virgin* (Chicago: University of Chicago Press, 1985), 50.

75. Ibid., 61, 64.

76. Hilda Graef, *Mary: A History of Doctrine and Devotion* (New York: Sheed and Ward, 1973), 1:266–67.

77. Ibid., 279–81.

78. "Conceptio christi non potuit aliter esse, quam Sancta, pura & immaculata. Conceptio autem Virginis Mariae nisi divinitus, & ex specialissma Dei gratia fuisset

praeventa, & praeservata, utique fuisset vitiosa, polluta, & maculata, sicut, & conceptiones caeterorum hominum. Et ideo ipsa in recognitionem tanti privilegii ac beneficii" (Pepin, *CS*, 23).

79. "Maria vero tota se infundit plenitudo gratie. Dum enim angelus dixit Marie. Ave gratia plena. In istis verbis denotavit ipsam beatam virginem fuisse sine aliqua macula conceptam, et innocentia originali decoratam" (Illyricus, *SA*, fol. 126).

80. Tisserand, *SA*, fol. 13.

81. Brulefer, *Opuscula*, fol. 259; cf. LePicart, *Caresme*, fol. 165.

82. Massaut, *Critique*, 38.

83. Jaroslav Pelikan, *Jesus through the Centuries* (New Haven: Yale University Press, 1985), 81; cf. Graef, *Mary*, 1, 314–15.

84. Farge, *Orthodoxy*, 163.

85. Maillard, *SS*, fol. 11.

86. "Secundum est quod beata Virgo non fuit concepta solo osculo Joachim & Annae, prout multi simplices fatue credunt, argumentum sumentes ex eo quod vident in ecclesiis & picturis dictos Ioachim & Annam mutuo se osculantes" (Pepin, *Conciones festorum tempore Adventus, loco tertii libri, qui dicitur sanctificationis sacramentalis, illo libro praetermisso pro quolibet de festo* [*CFA*] [Antwerp: Guillelmus Lesteenius & Engelbertus Gymnicus, 1656], 319).

87. "Spiritus sanctus sibi revelavit: Maria non faciatis difficultatem intrandi matrimonium quia ille cum quo debetis coniungi, simile desiderium habet sicut vos et nunquam petet vel rogabit contra vestrum desiderium" (Ibid., 71–72). It is interesting to note that Menot accords Joseph more importance than do most of our preachers, a trend that Gerson had begun early in the fifteenth century (Bossy, *Christianity*, 10). Nève argues that this sermon was one of the earliest dedicated to Joseph (Nève, *Sermons choisis*, 69n.).

88. Pepin, *CS*, 26.

89. LePicart, *Avent*, fol. 147; cf. Gaigny, *Homélies*, fol. 27.

90. Maillard, *SD*, fol. 268.

91. "Les peinctres font & peignent, que la glorieuse Vierge Marie est couchée en son lict, comme si elle eust eu douleur & travail, & qu'elle eust eu besoing de sage femme, c'est abus: car, sans douleur elle a enfanté nostre Seigneur Iesus Christ, & elle seule y a mis la main: l'integrité de son corps a esté gardée" (LePicart, *Avent*, fol. 150).

92. Schine, *Lady*, 71. In *Saints and Society*, 98, Weinstein and Bell argue that "The woman who internalized the ideal of Mary and sought to achieve it was virtually assured of failure, not only because the flesh was weak but because the world demanded marriage and motherhood."

93. "Beata Virgo fuit porta clausa per virginitatem: sed ostium apertum quantum ad intromittendum omnes in coelum per suam charitatem, qua assidue orat pro nobis ad hunc finem . . . sicut sol intrat per vitrum absque illius fractione. Et sicut radius solis induit colorem vitri, per cuius medium transit: sic christus transiens per uterum virginis, qui est vitro mundior, induit carnem immaculatam" (Pepin, *CA*, 55).

94. Illyricus, *SA*, fol. 203.

95. Ibid., fol. 140.

96. Ibid., fol. 136.

97. Ibid., fol. 180.

98. Marina Warner, *Alone of All Her Sex: The Myth and Cult of the Virgin Mary* (New York: Vintage Books, 1983), 338.

99. "Deinde convertens se ad sorores suas flentes, pariter & Magdalenam, &

Iohannem, dicit: Heu heu me succurrite, quia filium meum modo mori video, nec ipsum saltem tangere valeo. . . . Deinde convertens se ad filium suum, iterum dicebat. O fili mi dulcissime quid amodo faciam si supervixero?" (Pepin, *CQ,* 444).

100. Pepin, *CPP,* 386.

101. Raulin, *SA,* fol. 102.

102. Primo ergo dico, quod haec advocatrix sapienter incipit causas nostras coram iudice supremo christo. Nam primo captat benevolentiam iudicis, & iam per Dei gratiam captivavit. . . . Secundo insinuat nostram miseriam. . . . Tertio petit Dei misericordiam pro nobis" (Pepin, *RA,* 116).

103. Illyricus, *SA,* fol. 136.

104. Chrestiens, ie sçay bien, & c'est la verité, que la glorieuse vierge Marie faict & peult faire miracle . . . car Dieu [lui] a donné puissance & vertu de faire miracles, & de faire les euvres que luy-mesme a faict. . . . C'est tres bien faict de se mettre à deux genoux devant l'image de la glorieuse vierge Marie . . . & de prier pour cest enfant" (LePicart, *Caresme,* fol. 69; cf. Menot, *Paris-1,* 219; Paris, *Homélies,* fol. 72).

105. LePicart, *Caresme,* fol. 165.

106. Tisserand, *SA,* fol. 2.

107. Caroline Walker Bynum, *Jesus as Mother: Studies in the Spirituality of the High Middle Ages* (Berkeley: University of California Press, 1982), 110–69.

108. Richard Kieckhefer, *Unquiet Souls: Fourteenth-Century Saints and their Religious Milieu* (Chicago: University of Chicago Press, 1984), 13.

109. Weinstein and Bell, *Saints and Society,* 240.

110. Jean-Claude Schmitt, *Le saint lévrier: Guinefort, guérisseur d'enfants depuis le XIIIe siècle* (Paris: Flammarion, 1979).

111. André Vauchez, *La sainteté en occident aux dernières siècles du Moyen Âge, d'après les procès de canonisation et les documents hagiographiques* (Rome: École française de Rome, 1981).

112. Weinstein and Bell, *Saints and Society,* 162.

113. Lansperge, *Sermons,* fol. 47.

114. Kieckhefer, *Unquiet Souls,* 193–94.

115. "Sed profecto pauci admodum sunt Ambrosii hodie super terram, quinimmo pro uno praesule, qui decedit, duo aut tres, sive plures nituntur sibi succedere. . . . Et ideo paucos videmus hac temptestate, aut nullos Episcopos, qui miracula operentur, sive in vita, sive post mortem" (Pepin, *CS,* 170).

116. "Non enim referunt christi fideles intentionem suam ad ipsas imagines, quasi aliquid numinis in ipsis credentes, sicut idololatrae de idolis suis falso credebant sed fiunt, & ponuntur imagines in Ecclesia, non ut adorentur, sed ad imprimendam efficacius mentibus hominum, & praesertim simpliciter excellentiam, & gloriam sanctorum" (Pepin, *CQ,* 146).

117. Maillard, *SS,* fol. 16.

118. Menot, *Tours,* 213.

119. "Currunt multi ad diversa loca pro visitandis reliquiis sanctorum, et mirantur auditis gestis eorum: ampla edifica templorum inspiciunt, et osculantur sericis et auro involuta sacra ossa ipsorum. Et ecce tu quando presens es in altari deus meus: sanctum sanctorum, creator omnium, et dominus angelorum: modicam tibi exhibent reverentiam. Heu prohdolor: quot et quanta vidi peragrando mundum? In plerisque locis ubi requiescunt alique sanctorum relique: ad honorem ipsarum plures lampades accensas, ac multos cereos tenent: et ad tui preciosissimi corporis honorem vix unam tenent lampadem. . . . O magna hominum dementia. Sepe etiam in reliquiis videndis

est curiositas hominum & novitas invisorum: et modicus reportatur emendationis fructus" (Illyricus, *SA,* fol. 121).

120. Tisserand, *SA,* fol. 23.

121. Paris, *Homélies,* fol. 117.

122. "Ie scay bien qu'il n'y a que Iesuchrist qui nous ait merité salut par sa mort & passion, mais la bonne Dame sa mere, & les saincts & sainctes de paradis, nous impetrent que nous soyons participans de ce merite que nostre Seigneur nous a merité. En telle maniere, ils sont noz moyens & intercesseurs envers Dieu" (LePicart, *Avent,* fol. 361).

123. LePicart, *Caresme,* fol. 59.

124. "Tertio pro dei reverentia orandi sunt sancti ut peccator qui deum offendit. Quasi non audeat deum in propria persona adire. Sed amicorum patrocinium implorare" (Maillard, *SS,* fol. 58; cf. LePicart, *Trinité,* fol. 67).

125. "Quand tu fais ta peregrination en foy & en devotion pour l'amour que tu as en Dieu & aux saincts, pour la grace & vertu que Dieu leur a donnée pour leur merite, & qu'ils ont enduré pour l'honneur de luy: telle euvre & peregrination, si elle est faicte en la grace de Dieu elle est acceptée de vie eternelle. Mais ce qui est bon de soy, aucunesfois que lon abuse, & en tel abus c'est plus irriter l'ire de Dieu, que ce n'est l'appaiser: au moyen de l'irreverence que plusieurs ont en faisans icelle peregrination. . . . Prenons un iour, diras tu, pour aller à sainct Fiacre: il faict si plaisant, si beau temps, pour aller iouer aux champs" (LePicart, *Caresme,* fol. 172).

126. "Angelus est substantia incorporea intellectualis" (Maillard *SS,* fol. 106).

127. Russell, *Lucifer,* 275.

128. Ibid., 275, 209, 259; "Satan was not nearly as horrifying in folk imagery as he was in the minds of most theologians" (Joseph Klaits, *Servants of Satan: The Age of the Witch-Hunts* [Bloomington: Indiana University Press, 1985], 62).

129. "Sathan mauldict, de la guerre inventeur, Et conducteur d'une secte damnée, S'est mys aux champs comme bellicateur, Incitateur de mortelle menée, Et a tyré, par art dyabolique, Tous ses souldarts du gouffre plutonique, Qu'il estimoit hardis, puissans et fors: Et pour monstrer ses perilleux effortz, Tendant avoir victorieuse gloire, Il a cuidé, par armes ou par sors, Prendre à butin, pour luy et ses consors, Le lys croissant en triumphe et victoire" (Maillard, *Oeuvres,* 46).

130. Russell, *Lucifer,* 311.

131. Ibid., 277; Raulin, *SQ,* 226.

132. Menot, *Tours,* 11; cf. Pepin, *CPP,* 161; Pepin, *RA,* 237; Raulin, *SQ,* 152; Denisse, *TS,* fol. 7.

133. Paris, *Homélies,* fol. 51.

134. "Pessima insania nostra cum quotidie videmus draconem contra nos ore aperto paratum ad devorandum: nihilominus dormimus: et lascivimus: et in pigritiis nostris tamquam securi ante eum qui nihil aliud desiderat quam ut nos perdat" (Denisse, *TS,* fol. 9).

135. Raulin, *SQ,* 153.

136. Ibid., 150.

137. Ibid., 255.

138. "Diabolus nunc hic: nunc illuc: nunc agnum: nunc lupum: nunc lucem: nunc tenebras se ostendit. Et singulis quibusque locis et temporibus secundum varias rerum mutationes varias exhibit tentationes" (Denisse, *TS,* fol. 9).

139. Menot, *Paris-2,* 388.

140. Denisse, *TS,* fol. 10.

141. Menot, *Tours*, 52.

142. "Sic & diabolus in extremis hominis collocat milites suos circunquaque, ut non pateat pauperi animae exitus ad coelum, quo non minus rapiatur ab exercitu daemonum illic astantium" (Pepin, *CQ*, 34).

143. Denisse, *TS*, fol. 9; Menot, *Paris-2*, 389; Menot, *Tours*, 48.

144. Pepin, *CPP*, 544; cf. Pepin, *CDA*, 311; Calvin, *PS*, fol. 355.

145. Denisse, *TS*, fol. 7.

146. Menot, *Tours*, 21.

147. Farinier, *SP*, fol. 18.

148. "Haec autem armatura non est aliud, quam virtutes, gratiae, merita, & sancta opera, quae armant hominem contra diabolum" (Pepin, *CDA*, 308).

149. "Ad quod responsum diabolus dedit ei egregiam alapam, dicens: Mentiris, quod diabolus illuc te traxerit. Ego enim sum diabolus, qui tibi apparui in hoc loco, cum illuc ires, & persuasi tibi, ut non illuc te conferres, praedicens tibi periculum tuum. Tu autem noluisti mihi credere, & ecce nunc me inculpas" (Pepin, *EC*, 63).

150. Henry Charles Lea, *A History of the Inquisition of the Middle Ages* (New York: Russell & Russell, 1955), 3, 530–33.

151. "Praeterea prohibitae sunt artes istae magicae sub interminatione mortis, non solum quia in eis daemones adorantur, sed etiam quia fides salubris his artibus quasi sophisticis argumentis impugnatur, quae apparentiam verorum miraculorum gerunt, existentiam vero aut nullam habent, aut falsam, aut si vera sunt, non illam existentiam quae praetendunt, quia a probatione sua deficiunt" (Raulin, *SQ*, 496).

152. Cleree, *SQ*, fol. 54.

153. Pepin, *CS*, 171.

154. Eire, *War*, 11.

155. Weinstein and Bell, *Saints and Society*, 240.

Chapter 7

1. Gordon Leff, "The Apostolic Ideal in Later Medieval Ecclesiology," *JTS*, n. s., 18 (1967), 81.

2. "Sed dico quod nunquam Ecclesia descendit ita basse sicut nunc; nunquam fuerunt ecclesiastici ita indevoti sicut nunc; nunquam religiosi ita imperfecti sicut nunc. Tempore enim beati Francisci erat bene alia perfectio quam sit nunc. . . . Longe enim sumus a primeva institutione" (Menot, *Tours*, 26).

3. "Ecclesia in principio multos filios generabat: puta martyres, confessores. Scilicet nunc cessat" (Messier, *QS*, fol. 123).

4. "Primo igitur christus videns civitatem Ecclesiae flet. . . . Videtur enim hodie Ecclesia militans deserta" (Pepin, *CDA*, 156).

5. "Hunc fructum temporalem primus Constantinus dedit Ecclesie, transferendo imperium ad Ecclesiam. Pontifices sequentes, scilicet Silvestrum, non fuerunt male contenti de hoc, sed approbaverunt factum, ut dicitur capi: Si quis obiecerit, I. quest. III. Quia sicut non potest anima sine corpore vivere, sic nec viri ecclesiastici sine bono temporali. Quicquid sit, legitur quod tunc post illam donationem factam auditus est unus angelus in aere clamans: Hodie venenum effusum est in Ecclesia" (Menot, *Paris-2*, 374).

6. Ibid., 422; cf. LePicart, *Avent*, fol. 219.

7. "Quia quando in sancta die veneris, Ecclesia orat non tantum pro christianis

sed etiam paganis, Iudeis et omnibus generibus, ab oratione sua excludit excommunicatos; illi maledicuntur a Domino" (Menot, *Paris-2*, 423).

8. LePicart, *Avent*, fol. 219.

9. Pepin, *CDA*, 249.

10. "Sunt enim multi simplices infirmi in fide, nescientes articulos fidei, aut qui vacillant circa aliqua credenda, qui tamen parati sunt credere, prout oportet. Tales ergo infirmi in fide sunt supportandi a discretis confessoribus, & benigne instruendi, non autem exprobandi, aut terrendi, prout nonnulli confessores facere solent" (Pepin, *CDA*, 250)

11. Maillard, *SS*, fol. 13.

12. LePicart, *Avent*, fol. 107.

13. "Sed profecto multi iudices ecclesiastici et religionum prelati sunt faciles ad fulminandum sententias & excommunicationes contra subditos, etiam interdum pro levibus causis. Propter quod eque faciliter eorum sentenie contemnuntur, quam faciliter conduntur. Insuper dicti iudices ecclesiastici, quales sunt domini officiales, faciliter absolvunt illos excommunicatos quos forsan propter potentia & tyrannidem timent, aut qui munera tribuunt" (Pepin, *DN*, p. 257; cf. Cleree, *SQ*, fol. 73).

14. LePicart, *Avent*, fol. 109.

15. Pepin, *CDA*, 148; cf. Pepin, *DN*, 255).

16. LePicart, *Avent*, fol. 109.

17. LePicart, *Trinité*, fol. 281.

18. LePicart, *Caresme*, fol. 58.

19. "Nostre Seigneur a donc prins trois de ses disciples & les a menez & faict montez avec luy en la montagne: pour monstre que nul peult venir à Dieu, & à la cognoissance de son salut, s'il ne monte hault sur la montagne" Ibid, fol. 85.

20. "Le prestre les remet, comme ministre, & tenant le lieu de Dieu: & de la puissance & authorité qu'il a receuë de Dieu" (Ibid., fol. 56; cf. Jean Raulin, *Sermones de eucharistia* [*SE*] [Paris: Jehan Petit, 1524], fol. 33; Merlin, *Sermons*, fol. 88).

21. LePicart, *Avent*, fol. 89; cf. LePicart, *Caresme*, fol. 59.

22. "Moy prestre qui suis mauvais, & qui meine mauvaise vie, nonobstant cela ie demeure prestre: car ma dignité & auctorité n'est point fondée en ma bonté ou charité: mais elle est fondée en la parole de Dieu" (LePicart, *Caresme*, fol. 96).

23. LePicart, *Trinité*, fol. 16.

24. Menot, *Tours*, 35; cf. LePicart, *Avent*, fol. 252; LePicart, *Caresme*, fol. 53.

25. "In his autem verbis ostendit Apostolus, quod fideles debent sibi mutuo ministrare, secundum dona sibi a domino collata" (Pepin, *CDH*, 73).

26. "Il est vray, comme nous avons dit, que nous sommes tous religieux, nous sommes tous tenus de garder la religion Chrestienne, les commandemens de Dieu, & de nostre mere saincte Eglise: mais il en y a qui se sont mis en une religion plus estroicte" (LePicart, *Trinité*, fol. 61).

27. LePicart, *Avent*, fol. 88.

28. "L'Eglise ne peut errer ne faillir & mal dire, mais moy ie puis faillir & errer" (LePicart, *Avent*, fol. 255)

29. "L'Eglise estoit devant l'escripture: il fault donc croire à la tradition & interpretation, au sens & intelligence que l'Eglise dirigée par les. Esprit en donne" (LePicart, *Avent*, fol. 250).

30. "Cur ego non credetur prophetis, evangelistis, apostolis, doctoribus et predicatoribus veritatis?" (Pepin, *DN*, fol. 269; cf. LePicart, *Caresme*, fol. 52).

31. "Sed iam videtur etiam quasi decrepita, & ad corruptionem tendere. Cessat

enim nunc devotio in ecclesia, & transivit ad populum, quasi senescat ecclesia" (Raulin, *SQ*, 352).

32. Illyricus, *Libellus de potestate summi pontificus* (*Libellus*) (Tours, 1523), fol. 12.

33. Pepin, *CQ*, 75; cf. Menot, *Paris-2*, 329.

34. Illyricus, *SA*, fol. 185.

35. "Quinto, probatur intentum exemplo de filio aragonie religionem ingresso: de quo legitur quod mortuo patre & universa cognatione sua, papa dispensavit cum eo ut religionem exiret: & matrimonium contraheret pro utilitatem regni. Quod cum fecisset, & heredem procreasset: iterum ad claustrum rediit, dimisso regno filio suo. Erat enim in continuo scrupulo consciencie de eo quod castitatem violasset. Et quod dictum est papam cum eo dispensasse: potest fieri in hoc papa potestatem suam excesserit. In iis enim qui sunt facti: non est inconveniens dicere papam posse errare" (Pepin, *DN*, fol. 144).

36. "O, Frater, vos nescitis verbum bonum, le mot du guet: Dominus Papa dispensavit nos" (Menot, *Paris-2*, 356).

37. Raulin, *SQ*, 398; cf. LePicart, *Caresme*, fol. 172.

38. LePicart, *Trinité*, fol. 314.

39. Alan W. Watts, *Myth and Ritual in Christianity* (Boston: Beacon Press, 1968), 200; cf. Pepin, *DN*, fol. 279.

40. Bossy, *Christianity*, 70.

41. Menot, *Paris-2* 405.

42. "Interior autem cultis magis placere Deo quam exterior, quia cum Deus sit spiritus, oportet eos qui adorant eum, in spiritu & veritate adorare. Exterior vero cultus tantum signum est interioris. Gestus enim & sacrificia signa sunt interioris devotionis. Est ergo signum fallax stante exteriore caerimonia, & non stante interiore affectione, vel devotione actuali. . . . Et quia Deus odit illud signum fallax, & diabolus diligit, ideo accedit domum vacantem affectione, & ornatam caerimoniis, sicut fit in multis religionibus. Dicitur, tamen quod non inde destruendae sunt illae caerimoniae, quia ex eis populus acquirit devotionem" (Raulin, *SQ*, 397–98).

43. "Queritur quare dominus tantum irascitur contra choreizantes? Responsio, quia tales peccant et agunt contra septem sacramenta Ecclesie" (Pepin, *DN*, fol. 119).

44. "Quia sic est ordo effectuum ipsorum. Nam fides precipue est res sacramenti baptisme: & spes confirmationis: et eucharistia est sacramentum amoris: quia baptismus illuminat: confirmatio fortificat: eucharistia incendit" (Raulin, *Sermones de eucharistia* [*SE*] [Paris: Jehan Petit, 1524], fol. 15).

45. "Quando vir vester est infirmus, nonne illico mittitis ad querendum sacerdotem pro confessione? —Non, quia timemus eum contristare et pavorem ei immitere, sed mittimus pro medico corporali et damus ei medicinas ut habeat bonum animum. Sed cum non potest amplius loqui, vadimus cito ad querendum sacerdotem et facimus afferre extreman unctionem, et crucem et aquam benedictam et clamamus: Iesus! bien hault. Quando Christus esset presens cum matre sua et cum omnibus sanctis angelis, dico non esse tempus faciendi penitentiam et te convertendi ad Deum, quia quod prius erat tibi voluntarium, nunc est tibi involuntarium" (Menot, *Tours*, 134).

46. Pepin, *CDH*, 86.

47. "Nos autem sumus serpentes venenosi, qui ex utero matris contrahimus virus peccati originalis, a quo nequimus liberari, nec purgari nisi medio huius cuius virtus operatur in sacramento baptismi remissionem peccatorum" (Pepin, *CA*, 138).

48. Pepin, *CPP*, 536; cf. Tisserand, *SA*, fol. 8.

49. Cleree, *SQ*, fol. 26.

50. "Non fuit satis christo redimere nos: sed voluit aperire cor: & exivit sanguis & aqua miraculose in significatione duorum sacramentorum: scilicet baptismi & eucharistie" (Maillard, *QO,* fol. 212).

51. Pepin, *CDH,* 84.

52. "Et quand l'homme qui est une fois mort par le baptesme, s'il estoit rebaptizé, ce seroit un tesmoignage que Iesus Christ seroit mort encores une fois. Et ce sont les Anabaptistes auiourd'huy qui tiennent cela, qui tiendroit cela c'est erreur." (LePicart, *Avent,* fol. 27).

53. Ozment, *Reformation in the Cities,* 26.

54. Ibid., 50.

55. Thomas Tentler, *Sin and Confession on the Eve of the Reformation* (Princeton: Princeton University Press, 1977), 345–48.

56. Duggan, "Fear and Confession," 165.

57. Ibid., 172.

58. Bossy, *Christianity,* 47.

59. John Bossy, "The Social History of Confession in the Age of the Reformation," *TRHS* 25 (1975): 31.

60. Nicole Lemaître, "Confession privée et confession publique dans les paroisses du XVIe siècle," *RHEF* 69:183 (1983): 206.

61. "Si homo confitetur peccatum suum, lavabitur intus in conscientia, & pulcher fiet in conspectu Domini" (Pepin, *RA,* 254).

62. Pepin, *CDH,* 266.

63. Menot, *Paris-2,* 301.

64. "Car ne la grandeur & magnitude des peches, ne la multitude ou turpitude des delictz, ne la tardite de penitence, scavoir est ne la perseverance en peches ne nous pevent empescher de la perception de remission, pardon, & divine misericorde, moyennant que soyons penitents de nos peches, et que nous veuillons corriger selon la volunte de nostre Seigneur" (Lansperge, *Sermons,* fol. 150).

65. Pepin, *CPP,* 51.

66. "Soyons vrayement contris & faisons penitence & confession au prestre, lieutenant & vicaire de Dieu" (LePicart, *Caresme,* fol. 37; cf; Gaigny, *Homélies,* fol. 6).

67. "Cur confitebor, maxime cum non possim a tali, vel tali a peccato abstinere. Sic enim potius irritatem contra me divinam iram, quam provocarem pro me eius clementiam, & misericordiam. Utpote, iniuriam faciens sacramento confessionis, ad quod nullus accedere debet, qui non proponat morum emendationem" (Pepin, *CDH,* 242).

68. "Item sicut motus maris: sic motus penitentie vomitum provocat in confessione." (Messier, *QS,* fol. 10).

69. Menot, *Paris-2,* 434.

70. "Confessio lavat lachrimis. Contritio vero cum lintheamine tergit et luy met ung beguyn sur la teste gallice" (Maillard, *SA,* fol. 105).

71. Pepin, *CPP,* 271.

72. "Dico quod quantumcunque peccata gravia commisit: si confitearis complete & cum conditionibus requisitis promitto tibi quod non eris damnatus. Pro oppositum: si tu commisisti unum solum peccatum mortale & facias tanta bona sicut est possibile: nisi confitearis nunquam consequeris salutem" (Maillard, *QO,* fol. 139).

73. Menot, *Tours,* 136.

74. Pepin, *CDA,* 208.

75. "Certe nescio oportet confiteri sicut scriptum est in intellectu vestro & vos oportet confiteri clare & nude. Sunt enim alique que non faciunt confessiones sed.

narrationes sicut mes dames les theologiennes qui font ung grant narrabo et hoc ad tegendum peccatam sua grossa. . . . Sed ad quodam presunt ista narrationes ad quattuor mala. Primo ad fragendum caput sacerdos" (Cleree, *SQ*, fol. 56).

76. Fillon, *Speculum*, fol. E.

77. "Probatio. Nam talis confessio non est aliud, quam peccatorem humiliter, & veraciter recognoscere se dominum offendisse, & instanter ab eo veniam petere cum propositio emendandae, atque poenam pro commisso delicto velle portare" (Pepin, *CDA*, 207).

78. Ibid., 213.

79. Pepin, *CPP*, 47.

80. Pepin, *EC*, 36.

81. "Unde mulieri confitenti incestum cum fratre unico non sufficit dicere concubui cum viro, sed habet dicere, concubui cum fratre meo, quamvis per hoc notificetur confessori peccatum alterius hoc tamen intelligi debet, quando non potest habere copiam alterius confessoris" (Ibid., 62).

82. Menot, *Tours*, 169.

83. "Qui enim se excusat super his: aut dicit, non feci: aut feci quidem, et bene feci: aut si male, non tamen multum: aut si multum, non tamen mala intentione" (Pepin, *DN*, fol. 12).

84. "Ita & hodie multi Ninivite, i. peccatores cum confitentur non seipsos, sed vicinos aut alios accusant. Da exemplum de illis qui dicunt quod habent pessimos vicinos, cum quibus impossibile est habere pacem. Item de illis mulieribus que dicunt se habere duros maritos. Item de illis mulieribus que, postquam fuerint adulterate, dicunt quod invite sic egerunt" (Ibid., fol. 14).

85. "Quand on se confesse, il faut dire: Ie me suis courroucé, i'ay batu mon prochain, & semblable: & ne faut pas dire: Il a commencé, car ce seroit diminuer mon peché" (LePicart, *Trinité*, fol. 47).

86. Tisserand, *SA*, fol. 3.

87. "C'est une chose dangereuse & perilleuse de repeter souvent ses pechez à confesse, quand cela vient par inquietude de sa conscience. . . . Vous vous confessez d'une mesme chose deux ou trois fois: & puis vous en estes en plus grande peine: vous repetez pour en avoir remede & tranquilité, & vous en estes plus inquietez. Et donc n'y retournez pas: mais confiez vous & vous appuyez sur nostre Seigneur Iesus Christ, croyez au bon conseil qu'on vous donne. Estimez que Dieu est bon: pensez vous qu'il vous veuille damner si vous faictes vostre devoir au mieux que vous pourrez selon la fragilité humaine? La iustice de Dieu est elle plus cruelle que la iustice des hommes?" (LePicart, *Avent*, fol. 157).

88. Raulin, *SQ*, 123.

89. Pepin, *CDA*, 215.

90. "Ne sentez vous point en vous, apres que vous vous estes confessez, une consolation, un repos & ioye spirituelle en vostre cueur, & un deschargement de vostre conscience?" (LePicart, *Caresme*, fol. 87).

91. "Tertio, devotus catholicus postquam est vere confessus de praeteritis peccatis, debet orare Dominum, ut eum praeservet a futuris malis dicendo corde humili & devoto: O Domine Deus tibi gratias ago, quia cum essem dignus aeterno supplicio, tua misericordia & benignitate remisisti iniquitatem peccati mei, quoniam non possum me a peccato continere, nisi tu ipse dederis, ideo supplex oro dicens cum regio propheta" (Pepin, *CPP*, 283–84).

92. Maillard, *QO*, fols. 139, 159.

93. Cleree, *SQ*, fol. 59; cf. Pepin, *CDA*, 214.

94. Raulin, *SQ*, 123.

95. Pepin, *CDH*, 246.

96. See, e.g., Toussaert, *Le sentiment religieux en Flandre*, 112–13, 117.

97. Tentler, *Sin and Confession*, 78.

98. Douglass, *Justification*, 152.

99. Pepin, *EC*, 32.

100. Pepin, *CDH*, 174; cf. Cleree, *SQ*, fol. 63; cf. Menot, *Paris-2*, 372–73.

101. "Ecce, nonne oportet confiteri. —O, est tempus sufficiens est magnum" (Menot, *Tours*, 100).

102. Fillon, *Speculum*, fol. E.

103. "Pater, confiteor de omnibus peccatis, tam de his etiam que dixi quam de oblitis. —Cur de oblitis?—Pater, hoc anno non fui confessus; sic non possum recordari mediam partem peccatorum meorum. —O magna abusio! Dominus dedit tibi tempus totius anni ad previdendum lectionem tuam, ut legere posses in libro conscientie tue que fecisti" (Menot, *Paris-1*, 257).

104. Menot, *Tours*, 135; cf. Maillard, *SA*, fol. 60.

105. "Et quant vous attendes si tard a vous confesser vous doubtez tousiours & non sans cause vostre confession nest entiere" (Fillon, *Speculum*, fol. E; cf. Menot, *Tours*, 135).

106. Cleree, *SQ*, fol. 56.

107. "Sed dicitis: pater ego non habuit memoriam de uno: aut nesciebam quod esset peccatum: & audio predicare quod est peccatum: utrum fit necesse quod redeam & vadam ad eundem confessorem: aut dicam omnem peccata quod commisi? Dico quod non: si feceris quod in te est" (Maillard, *QO*, fol. 148).

108. "Pater ego fui confessa sepe: sed habeo dubitum: utrum tale quid sit peccatum mortale vel non? Sed dicet ad hec aliqua mulier: Pater ego fui confessa viro doctore & probo iudicio meo: sed adhuc anima mea non est quieta" (Ibid.).

109. Pepin, *DN*, fol. 276.

110. Duggan, "Fear and Confession," 162.

111. "Quarto desperatio, causatur ex abominatione & horrore peccatorum commissorum. . . . Sunt enim nonnulla peccata que postquam commissa sunt, apparent tam horrenda, & abominabilia ut non audeant miseri peccatores illa confiteri: nec credunt deum velle illa remittere: propter quod de illis desperant: cuiusmodi est peccatum contra naturam, sive cum bruto, sive alias" (Pepin, *DN*, fol. 277; cf. Pepin, *CDA*, 184; Pepin, *CDH*, 240; cf. Clichtove, *Sermones*, fol. 38).

112. Pepin, *DN*, fol. 277.

113. LePicart, *Trinité*, fol. 18.

114. "Aliquis magnus usurarius non vult ire ad praedicationem, ac audire veritatem, ne capiatur laqueis docti praedicatoris. Alius non vult confiteri docto, & timorato confessori, ne ostendat sibi peccatorum suorum gravitatem, & sui status periculum" (Pepin, *CQ*, 17; cf. Cleree, *SA*, fol. 44).

115. "Veniet ung gendarmeau, et dicetur ei: Tu non ieiunasti; oportet confiteri. —O, et quid est de se confesser? et quid feci? Ecce incredulitas. Non est timor Dei ante oculos eius" (Menot, *Tours*, 65).

116. Maillard, *QO*, fol. 97.

117. "Quare confitebor? Quid mali facio? Cur portabo pecuniam meam istis sacerdotibus ditioribus me? Per Deum ego citius portarem eam ad tabernam, sive ad aliquam pulchram filiam, quam ad sacerdotes istos" (Pepin, *CQ*, 374).

118. Maillard, *SA*, fol. 70.

119. Brown, *Pastor*, 68–69.

120. Maillard, *QO,* fol. 141.

121. Pepin, *CS,* 124–25.

122. "Quand vous estes malade, & le medecin vous vient voir: vous luy declarez seulement vostre maladie, vostre indigence & necessité, & ne luy dites pas qu'il vous donne telle medecine ne telle, mais delaissez le tout à sa bonne volonté & discretio, & vous obeissez à ce qu'il vous ordonne. Le medecin de vostre ame, c'est nostre Seigneur Iesus Christ. Declarez luy vostre maladie voz pechez, en les disant & confessant au prestre, qui est son lieutenant, auquel il a donné puissance" (LePicart, *Carēsme,* fol. 7; cf. fol. 134).

123. Ibid., fol. 3.

124. Pepin, *EC,* 59; cf. Pepin, *CS,* 73.

125. Pepin, *CDH,* 126.

126. "Quod autem aliqui confessores dicunt: Ego te absolvo ab omnibus peccatis tuis, corde contritis, & ore confessis, male addunt" (Ibid., 375).

127. "[P]resbyter est negligens et n'en demande que la despesche. Tu non queris nisi expedire et dicis: O, ego inveni ung maistre prestre; si voluissem ei ad omnia respondere, non fecissemus adhuc" (Menot, *Tours,* 135).

128. "Et ne bonus confessores vous pas a pasques ouy dea iay mon messire iehan a qui ie garde ung bon teston si me donnera labsolution" (Cleree, *SQ,* fol. 49; cf. Pepin, *EC,* 224).

129. "Praecipue autem mulieres & signanter iuvenes, & formosae debent habere vultum, & oculos demissos in terram. Quibus debet sufficere, quod audiantur a suis confessoribus, & similiter eos audiant, & non quod videant eos, seu videantur ab eis. Et hoc non tam in signum humilitatis quam ad periculum vitandum tentationis carnalis. Tu ergo mulier & tu similiter confessor, tunc averte oculos tuos, ne videant vanitatem. Et ideo discreti confessores plerunque solent manicam suam vel cornetam, vel aliquid simile opponere inter se, & inter faciem mulieris illis confitentis" (Pepin, *EC,* 224).

130. Maillard, *QO,* fol. 141.

131. Pepin, *DN,* fol. 280.

132. "Mais pour bien restituer, il faut sçavoir cincq choses. La première, Propter quid, pourquoy l'on est tenu de restituer. Seigneurs, la raison est bonne: car iustice le veult, charité le requiert, la loi divine le commande. Iustice le veult, car . . . les commandemens de iustice sont telz: honnestement vivre, non bleschier aultruy, et rendre à chascun ce qu'il luy appartient. Charité le requiert, car . . . [il ne faut pas faire] à aultruy ce que tu ne vouldrois que l'on te fist. La loy divine le commande . . . [parce que] se tu veulx offrir ton offrande à Dieu et ton frère, ton proiesme, se plaint de toy, va t'en premier appaisier ton frère, et puis offre ce que tu veulx: aultrement ton offrande ne me sera point agréable" (Maillard, *Oeuvres,* 19–20).

133. Pepin, *CDA,* 184.

134. Pepin, *CQ,* 376.

135. Ibid., 210.

136. Clerval, *Registre,* 232.

137. Maillard, *SA,* fol. 58.

138. "Credo quod capiunt partem suam & sunt omnes fures." (Maillard, *QO,* fol. 110).

139. Messier, *QS,* fol. 25.

140. "Item de illis ruffianis & infamibus, qui vehunt in equis & curribus sacrosanctas sanctorum reliquias, decipientes simplices cum multis mendaciis, & dicentes, quod subtili ingenio extorquendae sunt pecuniae a barbaris" (Pepin, *CA,* 171).

141. "Nolo tamen revocare clavem ecclesie: sed dico quod quando papa & cardinales cognoscunt quod non est aliqua necessitas aut iusta & rationabilis causa: non debent dari indulgentie. In hoc omnes doctores conveniunt. . . . Indulgentie enim date monasteriis pinguibus ubi sunt buffeta & religiosi pleni auro & argento de quibus papa non est sufficienter informatus parum valent. An creditis quod unus magnus usurarius plenis viciis qui habebit mille milia peccatam: dando sex albos trunco habeat remissionem omnium peccatorum suorum? Certe durum est mihi credere & durius predicare" (Maillard, *QO*, fols. 110–11).

142. Pepin, *CA*, 171.

143. Messier, *QS*, fol. 71.

144. Menot, *Paris-1*, 259.

145. Maillard, *QO*, fol. 124.

146. "Annus iubileus est in quo dant remissio peccatorum volentibus ire romam: certe si volumus ambulare viam penitentie per ipsam quadragesimam ipsa sicut duo vel quatuor multiplicata reddunt nobis numerum quadragenarium ita reddet nobis in fine annum iubileum: scilicet diem remissionis omnium peccatorum nostrorum quo ad culpam et magnam partem pene: sed qui non vadit rome non lucratur indulgentias: ita etiam qui non ambulat via penitentie non habebit remissionem peccatorum suorum que via potest comparati vie romane" (Cleree, *SQ*, fol. 15).

147. Maillard, *QO*, fol. 173.

148. There is a very recent study that I did not have the opportunity to examine: Miri Rubin, *Corpus Christi: The Eucharist in Late Medieval Culture* (Cambridge: Cambridge University Press, 1991).

149. LePicart, *Caresme*, fol. 125.

150. "Tertio non debet dari eucharistia pueris ante annos discretionis & devotionis. Nam puer antequam inducetur ad sacram communionem debet habere tris. s. etatem: que attenditur circa undecim vel duodecim annos. Discretionem: ut discernat differentiam inter hoc sacramentum & communem panem. Tertio quod habeat devotionem" (Illyricus, *SA*, fol. 120; cf. Pepin, *CS*, 588; Raulin, *SE*, fol. 37).

151. Illyricus, *SA*, fol. 121.

152. Lansperge, *Sermons*, fols. 14, 20.

153. Clichtove, *Sermones*, fol. 33.

154. Pepin, *CDH*, 247.

155. Lansperge, *Sermons*, fol. 17.

156. Pepin, *CDH*, 247; cf. LePicart, *Caresme*, fol. 6.

157. "Tunc dixit eis [Luc. XXII]: Desiderio desideravi hoc Pascha manducare vobiscum antequam patiar. In hoc [quod] comedit cum eis, nobis ostenditur quod Christus de mensa sua neminem vult expellere. Quantum enim est de se, omnes homines vult salvos fieri" (Menot, *Paris-Alia*, 494).

158. "Or ny a il si miserable ne conclame pecheur, qui n'ait espoir apres sa vie, celebrer ce saint pasque fructifiant, et tous universellement, apres ceste vie, sortir de misere en beatitute" (Gaigny, *Homélies*, fol. 3).

159. LePicart, *Trinité*, fol. 277; cf. Pepin, *CDA*, 110–11.

160. LePicart, *Trinité*, fol. 297.

161. Menot, *Tours*, 106.

162. Illyricus, *SA*, fol. 120.

163. Ibid. The inclusion of jousters in this list reflects continued concern with social disharmony and personal enmity, and was first explicitly condemned by the Fourth Lateran Council in 1215.

164. "Il nayme les indignes & ingratz" (Lansperge, *Sermons*, fol. 19).

165. LePicart, *Trinité,* fol. 320.

166. "Nota quod dixit pro multis et non pro omnibus, quia non omnes fuerunt participes huius sacratissime redemptionis. Sed hic oriter difficultas, si Iude proditori Christus sacramentum suum dederit. Et videtur quod sic, quia Augustinus, super Ioannem, dicit: De uno pane Petrus accepit et Iudas; sed Petrus ad vitam, Iudas vero ad mortem. Sed contra, Christus dicit: Omnes qui ex eo biberint erunt in regno Patris. Sed constat quod Iudas bibit ex eo; igitur. . . . Dico illud intelligendum de illis qui sacramentaliter et spiritualiter sumpserint. Iudas autem sumpsit sacramentaliter tantum et non spiritualiter. Si ergo vis te lavari et purgari per confessionem" (Menot, *Paris-Alia,* 494–95).

167. Maillard, *QO,* fol. 131.

168. "Missa non solum valet virtute meriti personalis sacerdotes offerentis: sed etiam virtute sacrificii & operis operati: vel virtute meriti generalis ecclesie: in cuius persona per ministrum idoneum offertur sacrificium" (Brulefer, *Opuscula,* fol. 212).

169. Ibid., fol. 213.

170. Raulin, *SE,* fols. 33, 42.

171. Cleree, *SQ,* fol. 9.

172. LePicart, *Caresme,* fol. 124; cf. LePicart, *Trinité,* fol. 109; Jean Scoepperus, *Sermon declarant apertement que nous signifient mystiquement plusieurs des ceremonies de l'Eglise Catholique* (Paris: Nicolas Chesneau, 1571), fol. Nii.

173. LePicart, *Trinité,* fol. 110.

174. Pepin, *CDH,* 65.

175. "Le premier qui ayt iamais parlé mal du S. Sacrement de l'Autel, c'est Berengarius. . . . Et depuis par la suasion du diable, sont venus Ioannes Hus: & Ioannes Vuiclef, & autres heretiques du iourd'huy qui ont renouvellé leurs heresies: & sont muables & variables comme le vent" (LePicart, *Caresme,* fol. 52).

176. "Primo igitur quidam scandalizantur de existentia eius in sacramento altaris. Et tales iterum. Sunt in triplici differentia. Primi sunt, qui non reputant possibile, quod sub parva rotunditate specierum sacramentalium contineatur totum christi corpus, & sanguis, reputantes impossibile, quod parva quantitas, contineat in centuplo malorem. Secundi sunt qui reputant inhumanum, & crudele oportere christi fideles manducare christi carnem, & bibere eius sanguinem. . . . Ecce scandalum praedictorum. Tertii sunt, qui reputant impossibile, quod multoties sumatur, tam ab eodem, quam diversis christi corpus in sacramento altaris, nec tamen diminuatur. Sed unicuique praedictorum respondet christus in praesenti Evangelio dicens. Beatus qui non fuerit scandalizatus in me. Primi ergo non debent scandalizari . . . tum quia in utero virgineo tota divinitas. . . . Secundi similiter scandalizari non debent, quia christi corpus non sumitur carnaliter, & visibiliter in hoc sacramento, nec similiter eius sanguis, sed sacramentaliter, & invisibiliter, adeo quod sensus gustus non sentit ibi nisi gustum panis, & vini. . . . Et ideo non relinquitur ibi locus crudelitas, sed potius immensae charitatis. Tertii autem scandalizari non debent, tum quia christi corpus in hoc sacramento non sumitur modo corporali, & ad instar aliorum ciborum, qui diminuuntur ad mensuram qua sumuntur, sed potius modo sacramentali, qui nullum habet alium sumendi modum similem" (Pepin, *CDH,* 39).

177. Raulin, *SE,* fol. 6.

178. LePicart, *Trinité,* fol. 251.

179. Maillard, *QO,* fol. 199.

180. "Car par ce sainct Sacrement, nous participons de la divinité, & sommes tous

transformez en Dieu. Et ainsi qu'un fer qui de sa nature est froid, quand il est mis au feu, il participe du feu, de sorte que ce n'est que feu: aussi l'homme qui reçoit dignement Iesus Christ, ne sent rien de sa nature terrestre, mais est tout deifié, & comme homme divin" (LePicart, *Trinité,* fol. 281).

181. LePicart, *Caresme,* fol. 123.

182. Anonymous, *Sermons,* BN Ms. fr. 1898, fol. 7; cf. Raulin, *SE,* fol. 9.

183. Tisserand, *SA,* fol. 39.

184. "La second merveille est que le corps dJesucrist lequel est contenu soubz lespece du pain nest a mesurer selon les qualites, la couleur, rotundite, ou dimension qui apparoissent & sont veues au pain" (Lansperge, *Sermons,* fol. 18).

185. "Toutesfois on ne peult veoir ne toucher icelluy. Mais les choses qui sont veues, touchees, ou goustees, ou rompues, et le son qui ce faict en la fracture, ce sont les accidens de la chose qui devant la consecration estoit pain" (Ibid., fol. 19).

186. Pepin, *CS,* 535.

187. "O quantum est habere memorationem passionis Christi qui te custodivit a noxiis. Et hoc in sacramento altaris et ideo dicebat Christus: Hec quotiescumque feceritis in mei memoriam, etc. (I Cor. XI), id est mee passionis memoriam facietis. Ideo ut in pluribus hodie sunt figurate aliquo signo passionis Christi, ut facilius recordemur. Ad hoc etiam nos movet id quod facit sacerdos post consecrationem, elevando primo corpus, secundo calicem, sub duabus speciebus, quod nil aliud significat nobis nisi ut memores simus Christi passionis" (Menot, *Paris-Alia,* 483).

188. "Non enim dabit vobis sacerdos calicem, sed tantum hostiam illam salutarem, ad innuendum quod ibi est cibus et potus" (Menot, *Tours,* 102; cf. Illyricus, *SA,* fols. 115–16.

189. LePicart, *Trinité,* fol. 259.

190. "Ideo hereticos studens a se ecclesia separare & tollere ordinavit tam modo laicos qui de facili ad illam falsam credulitatem ducerentur: communicari tam sub una specie. Et si dicatur. Si sub speciebus panis habetur sanguis christi: in vanum sacerdos iterum consecrat calicem: quia frustra habitum est. Item cum sub una specie panis integer esset christus: iam perfectum haberetur sacramentum: & per consequens superlueret calix" (Raulin, *SE,* fol. 40).

191. Ibid., fol. 41.

192. Illyricus, *SA,* fol. 121; cf. Raulin, *SE,* fol. 65.

193. "Nam ibi est verus deus sub speciebus absconditus: ratione cuius in hoc sacramento cessat omnis idolatrie cultus. . . . Primo inducit ad dolorem contritionis. . . . Secundo inducit peccatorem ad pudorem confessionis. . . . Tertio. Inducit peccatores ad laborem satisfactionis. . . . Secundo potus iste sanguinis penitentibus datur in refugium: ne labantur in desperationem" (Raulin, *SE,* fols. 18–20).

194. Virginia Reinburg, "Popular Prayers in Late Medieval and Reformation France" (Ph.D. diss., Princeton University, 1985), 367.

195. Ibid., 221–22.

196. Ibid., 300.

197. "Propterea valde utile est sepe repetere dictam orationem dominicam, pariter et symbolum fidei: Id est credo in Deum" (Pepin, *DN,* fol. 8).

198. Pepin, *CDA,* 168.

199. "Solet tamen communis devotio christi fidelium silentium imponere privatis orationibus, cum legitur Evangelium in missa, & ipsa devota audire. Propter quod nonnulli, & praesertim linguam matinam intelligentes solent tunc propius accedere. Quo lecto redunt ad proprias sedes. Non loquor de illis, qui ita faciunt ut videantur

latini, quamvis etiam non latini hoc possint facere ex speciali devotione, & reverentia ad sanctum Evangelium, maxime cum scriptum sit: Beati, qui audiunt verbum, &c." (Pepin, *EC*, 286).

200. Reinburg, "Popular Prayers," 69.

201. Pepin, *CDA*, 168.

202. Pepin, *CS*, 217; cf. Maillard, *Oeuvres*, 22.

203. "Non enim orationis voces ad Dei aures diriguntur nisi cum animi affectu. Quia melior est quinque Psalmorum cantatio cum devotione, quam totus Psalterii modulatio cum anxietate" (Pepin, *CPP*, 497).

204. Ibid., 534.

205. Robert Mandrou, "Pourquoi se réformer?" in Robert Mandrou, Janine Estèbe, Daniel Ligou, et al. (eds.), *Histoire des Protestants en France* (Toulouse: Privat, 1977), 19.

206. Delumeau, *Christianity*, 167.

207. Keith Thomas, *Religion and the Decline of Magic* (New York: Charles Scribner's Sons, 1971), 48.

208. Brown, *Pastor*, 10, 160.

209. Martin, "Ministère," 667–68.

210. "Unde (secundum Augustinum quarto de Civit. Dei) superstitio dicitur omnis cultus quocumque modo superfluus, sive ex superfluitatibus eorum quae coluntur, sive eorum quae in culta assumuntur, sive ex modo assumendi" (Raulin, *SQ*, 493).

211. Ibid., 496.

212. Maillard, *Oeuvres*, 96–97; cf. Monluc, *Instructions*, fol. 19.

213. Pepin, *CS*, 171.

214. "Hodie apud christianos . . . illi dilatant philacteria sua, qui portant supra se quasdam chartulas, & brevia, in qui. Sunt aliquando figurae, seu nomina ignota, & multa similia ad superstitionem pertinentia, in quibus confidunt, tenentes, & firmiter credentes, quod quamdiu talia habuerint super se, non tanget eos malum, utpote, quod non morientur in bello, sive illuc sint accessuri" (Pepin, *CQ*, 112).

215. Ibid., 379.

216. "Videmus enim frequenter duos, aut plures homines in eadem constellatione, & loco conceptos, & datos. Etiam uterinos, sive geminos diversificari in moribus. Et de hoc extat notissima historia de Iacob, & Esau simul conceptis & natis, quorum tamen unus fuit bonus & electus, alter vero pessimus, & reprobatus. Patet ergo quod sydera mere contingenter, & non necessario influunt appetitum ratione hominis, hinc dicitur, quod vir prudens dominabitur astris. Ex quibus omnibus concluditur, quod peccator non debet sibi assumere excusationem super peccato suo ab influentia syderum" (Pepin, *EC*, 161).

217. Pepin, *CPP*, 161.

218. Raulin, *SQ*, 600.

219. Clichtove, *Sermones*, fol. 62.

220. Menot, *Paris-2*, 301.

Chapter 8

1. Martin, *Métier*, 396, 400.

2. Duggan, "Unresponsiveness," 4.

3. Delumeau, *Catholicism*, 156.

4. Nicole LeMaître, *La Rouergue flamboyante: Clergé et paroisses du diocèse de Rodez, 1417–1563* (Paris: Cerf, 1988).

5. This can clearly be seen in evidence of increasing numbers of Observant monasteries and affiliations with the Windesheim congregation. See, e.g., R. R. Post, "The Windesheimers after c. 1485," in Ozment, *Medieval Perspective,* 157–84; Raymond Darricau, "Quelques aspects de la réforme dominicaine en Provence au XVᵉ siècle," *RHEF* 65, no. 174 (1979): 13–24; Darricau, "La réforme des reguliers en France de la fin du XVᵉ siècle à la fin des guerres de religion," *RHEF* 65, no. 174 (1979): 5–12; Godet, *Congrégation.*

6. Eire, *War,* 171.

7. Raulin, *SQ,* 384.

8. Ibid., 68; cf. Pepin, *CQ,* 10; Farinier, *SP,* fol. 44.

9. "Je vous asseure, tam parum appretiamini predicationem sicut volueritis, sed dico quod nunquam Ecclesia descendit ita basse sicut nunc; nunquam fuerunt ecclesiastici ita indevoti sicut nunc; nunquam religiosi ita imperfecti sicut nunc" (Menot, *Tours,* 26).

10. "Hodie cathedra ecclesie multum debilitatur. . . . Ecce ergo que est cathedra ecclesie: sed hodie videtur quod sit cathedra pestilentie" (Messier, *QS,* fol. 47).

11. "Nous sommes en mauvais temps" (LePicart, *Avent,* fol. 78).

12. "Mais nous sommes si paresseux & negligens à bien faire, que nous sommes pires auiourd'huy que nous n'estions hier" (Ibid., fol. 259; cf. Pepin, *CDH,* 134).

13. Pepin, *CQ,* 223.

14. "Doctores enim nostri qui sunt in Francia sont embaillonez, habent os in ore: ideo non dicunt veritatem et tamen vident quotidie abusus magnos et enormes qui sunt per hoc regnum et qui venerunt de illa curia romana" (Menot, *Paris-2,* 329).

15. "Sed, heu, si vellemus hodie respicere falsos contractus, falsas dispensationes que veniunt de ista curia Romana, que capiuntur directe contra Deum, contra ius, contra ordinationes Ecclesie, in hoc remanet totus pauper intellectus attonitus" (Ibid., 342).

16. "Regnat hodie maximus abusus in Ecclesia: postquam [sunt] episcopi et abbates, Pape, cardinales, oportet quod omnes nepotes sint provisi, . . . oportet quod sint episcopi, abbates et archidiaconi et canonici, dato quod traxerint originem ab uno sartore vel bostillatore feni. . . . Dicitur quod papa Sixtus (IV) nostri ordinis aperuit portam" (Menot, *Paris-2,* 322). The degree of nepotism practice by Sixtus "scandalized even the least sensitive of his contemporaries" (Nicolas Cheetham, *Keepers of the Keys: A History of the Popes from St. Peter to John Paul I* [New York: Charles Scribner's Sons, 1983], 184).

17. "Certe officium cardinalium non solum est asinam.i.animam peccatricem adducere ad christum: sed etiam pape" (Messier, *QS,* fol. 128).

18. Menot, *Paris-1,* 245.

19. Pepin, *DN,* fol. 217.

20. "Quomodo, Frater? Nonne Papa potest nobis remittere penam pro peccatis debitam?" (Menot, *Paris-1,* 258).

21. Pepin, *DN,* fol. 135.

22. Pepin, *CQ,* 37.

23. "Capiatur unus prelatus qui habet centum religiosos sed sunt pauci boni: certe non est honor prelato. Similiter in una civitas in domo episcopi. Et per oppositum dicatur de bonis principibus & prelatis dicit Spiritus sanctus gloria principis est in multitudine populi boni" (Cleree, *SQ,* fol. 31).

24. Menot, *Paris-2,* 307.

25. Pepin, *DN,* fol. 145.

26. "Sunt enim multi praelati pusillanimes, pigri, negligentes, & remissi circa

subditos delinquentes, quinimo multa eis permittunt non permittenda, etiam interdum contra votum paupertatis, sicut nuper audivi, de quodam monasterio olim regularissimo, in quo Abbas concessit fratribus suis, ut possent apud se reservare nummos, usque ad valorem quinque solidorum" (Pepin, *CS*, 447–48).

27. Menot, *Paris-2*, 331–32.

28. Ibid., 374.

29. Menot, *Paris-2*, 322–23.

30. "Hodie pauci, aut nulli Episcopi intrarent coelum, sed committitur suae conscientiae, & discretioni, quid, quantum & quando, & quibus dare debet. Quis si totum velle prodige expendere in mulieribus, & fructibus ventris gravissime peccaret, & cum hoc ad restitutionem, teneretur tanquam defraudator portionis pauperum" (Pepin, *CS*, 146).

31. Messier, *QS*, fol. 48.

32. Illyricus, *SA*, fol. 4.

33. "Si ecclesiasticus retinet ultra victum et vestitum de bonis ab ecclesia perceptis, est latro et non minister seu servitor Dei" (Menot, *Tours*, 94; cf. 116; Maillard, *QO*, fol. 172).

34. Menot, *Tours*, 90.

35. Ibid., 17.

36. Pepin, *CDH*, 237.

37. "Quod si necessitas urgeat religiosum equitem incedere, aut asinum, aut saltem humilem equum sibi assumat in adiutorium. Huius autem contrarium faciunt multi Abbates, & Priores. Nonnulli etiam fratres de ordinibus mendicantium. Mentior, si non vidi religiosum mendicantem, non tamen professionis praedicatorum, qui cum iret ad visitandum quosdam conventus sui ordinis in suo comitatu, non minus, quam 13. equestres habebat, sive fratres suae professionis, sive famulos saeculares" (Pepin, *CS*, 177).

38. Menot, *Paris-1*, 227.

39. Pepin, *CDH*, 220.

40. "Cur castitatem vovistis, si eam observare non vultis?" (Pepin, *DN*, fol. 148; cf. Menot, *Tours*, 80).

41. Farinier, *SP*, fol. 38.

42. "Qui vero concubinas habent: necesse est ut illis similiter provideant, etiam peramplius quam si vere uxores essent. Sunt etiam tales muliercule importune in petendo, infideles in rapiendo, insatiabiles in recipiendo, & tenacissime in detinendo. Cum igitur tam religiosi quam ceteri sacerdotes debeat pre ceteris intendere rebus spiritualibus & divinis: lique aperte quod debent caste vivere" (Pepin, *DN*, fol. 145).

43. Raulin, *SQ*, 457.

44. Maillard, *QO*, fol. 194.

45. Pepin, *DN*, fol. 31.

46. LePicart, *Caresme*, fol. 34.

47. Raulin, *SQ*, 352.

48. LePicart, *Avent*, fol. 257; cf. LePicart, *Trinité*, fol. 245.

49. Messier, *QS*, fol. 47.

50. Menot, *Paris-2*, 321; cf. Pepin, *CQ*, 146; Pepin, *CDA*, 147.

51. "Audiatis domini ecclesiastici: symonia est sacrilegium. Qui sacrilegium comitit: aliena rapit" (Maillard, *QO*, fol. 191).

52. Monluc, *Sermons*, fol. 124.

53. Maillard, *SA*, fol. 60.

54. Raulin, *SQ*, 332.

55. Messier, *QS,* fol. 103.
56. Maillard, *QO,* fol. 156.
57. Menot, *Paris-2,* 323.
58. "Qui enim vult bene gubernare navem oportet quod sit intra: non extra. Multe naves pereunt propter absentiam patroni. Sic & multi ecclesie propter absentiam pastoris. Multi beneficiati sunt similes divitibus habentibus plures naviculas: non ad regendum sed ad locandum & lucrandum. Sic isti locant ecclesias mercenariis: & inde recipiunt lucrum in archa, et damnum in conscientia" (Messier, *QS,* fol. 11).
59. "Habitus non facit monachum" (Menot, *Tours,* 61; cf. Pepin, *DN,* fol. 150; Pepin, *CS,* 488).
60. Maillard, *QO,* fol. 130.
61. "Vos religiosi ite ad conventus reformatos" (Maillard, *SA,* fol. 74).
62. Pepin, *DN,* fol. 135.
63. Menot, *Paris-2,* 321–22.
64. Pepin, *CDA,* 159.
65. Denisse, *SR,* fol. 6.
66. Maillard, *CS,* fol. 31.
67. Martin, *Métier,* 471.
68. Pepin, *CDH,* 7–8.
69. Maillard, *Oeuvres,* 23–24.
70. "Iustitia Regis est neminem iniuste per potentiam opprimere: sine acceptione personarum inter virum et proximum suum iudicare: advenis, pupillis, & viduis defensorem existere: furta cohibere: adulteria punire iniquos non exaltare: impudicos et histriones non nutrire: impios de terra perdere: parricidas et peierantes non sinere vivere: Ecclesias defendere: pauperes elemosynis alere: iustos super negocia regni constituere: senes & sapientes atque sobrios consiliarios habere: superstitionibus non intendere: iracundiam suam differre: patriam fortiter & iuste contra adversarios defendere: per omnia in Deo confidere: prosperitatibus animum non elevare: cuncta adversa patienter ferre: fidem catholicam amplecti defendere: filios suos & familiam non sinere impie agere: certis horis orationibus insistere" (Pepin, *DN,* fols. 60–61).
71. "Debent ergo Reges, & Principes terreni diligere iustitiam reddendo malis poenam, bonis vero, & oppressis defensionem. Vel dic, quod spiritus Sanctus praecipit Regibus, & principibus, qui iudicant terram, id est terrenos, & vitiosos homines vel terram, i. corpora terrena, non autem iudicant animas, ut diligant triplicem iustitiam unam quo ad se sobrie vivendo, aliam quo ad proximum iuste se habendo, aliam ad Deum pie conversando, & nota, quod tales debent primo facere de seipsis, si qua viderint in se corrigenda. Quod cum fecerunt, aptiores erunt ad faciendum iustitiam de aliis. In cuius rei signum Salvator dixit Scribis & Pharisaeis de muliere adultere: Qui sine peccata est, vestrum primus in illam lapidem mittat (Joh. VIII), q.d. puniatur peccatrix, sed non a peccatoribus" (Pepin, *RA,* 282).
72. Maillard, *Oeuvres,* 12.
73. "Fuit tempus in quo non fuerunt reges aut principes: sed unusquisque in libertate sua vivebat. . . . Reges postea venientes et forsan primitus tyrannice principantes et regnantes non poterunt licite aufferre a subditis invitis dominia et possessiones eorum" (Pepin, *DN,* fol. 59).
74. Ibid., fol. 291; cf. Pepin, *CS,* 416.
75. Pepin, *CPP,* 498.
76. LePicart, *Trinité,* fol. 193; cf. LePicart, *Avent,* fol. 241.
77. Pepin, *CDH,* 204.
78. Raulin, *SQ,* 492; cf. Messier, *QS,* fol. 5.

79. Maillard, *QO*, fol. 110.

80. "O sire vous estes le souverain Roy du ciel, & de la terre, mais moy combien que ie sois Roy de France, ie ne suis seulement qu'un petit serviteur aupres de vous. Et que ie sois Roy devant vous, ah non: ie suis seulement vostre serviteur & officier. Le Roy doibt considerer & dire: Ie suis le conducteur du peuple de Dieu: il m'a donné cest office: mais au regard de mon maistre, ie ne suis qu'un chien mort" (LePicart, *Avent*, fol. 235).

81. "En ceste ville de Paris... si le Roy passe, chacun sort hors de sa maison pour le veoir: & quand on porte nostre Seigneur, nous ne diagnons bouger de la maison au moins adorons-le en nostre maison" (LePicart, *Trinité*, fol. 303; cf. Raulin, *SQ*, 197).

82. "Nunquid domini burgenses bonum est obedire regi...? Opus ergo deo obedire" (Maillard, *QO*, fol. 106).

83. "Rex debet habere arma bellica ad defendendum subditos. Scilicet quero si rex poneret le siege gallice in quadam civitate: & vellet facere lassavit: & ibi essent unus capitaneus quando debet intrare civitatem vertit tergum & cum omnibus subditis trahit fugam & vadit ad inimicos. Vos domini de parlemento si veniret ad manus vestras quid faceretis de eo?" (Ibid., fol. 192; cf. Maillard, *SSP*, fol. 331).

84. See, e.g., J. Russell Major, *Representative Institutions in Renaissance France, 1421–1559* (Madison: University of Wisconsin Press, 1960).

85. "Quia enim hodie multi principes vendunt publica officia per multa milia auri & argenti, quod valde periculosum est: ideo tales officiarii se recompensare volentes, multas fraudas committere solet, non contenti propriis stipendiis" (Pepin, *DN*, fol. 169).

86. Maillard, *SA*, fol. 111.

87. "Vos domini officiarii nunquid servatis regnum propter ius iurandum? Estis magis obligati servire regi quam deo?" (Maillard, *QO*, fol. 122).

88. Pepin, *DN*, fol. 64; cf. LePicart, *Avent*, fol. 106.

89. "Et quando est elevatus, tunc neminem cognoscit, est superbus sicut unus magnus diabolus et sepe dedignatur videre suos parentes et forte eos qui sunt in causa quare talia bona habet" (Menot, *Tours*, 59).

90. Ibid., 31.

91. Maillard, *Oeuvres*, 122.

92. "Dicit ibidem Gregorius... qu'il y a aulcuns mestiers grandement prejudiciables et dommageables a la povre ame, inter que ponitur l'estat de la gendarmerie, advocasserie, practique, notaires, marchans de chevalx, courratiers, menteurs, paillardes, intertenentes lupanaria vel domos in quibus se retrahunt seu recipiunt latrones, lusores et estuffes" (Menot, *Tours*, 93).

93. Maillard, *SA*, fol. 18.

94. "Quia alia sunt hominum iudicia et mundi et alia iudicia Dei. Sunt due curie, parlamentum et paradisus, et magna differentia est.... Iudicia enim huius mundi nunquam fiunt tam recte quin sit semper aliquis qui claudicet uno pede; quia aut odium, aut favor, aut defectus prosecutionis, aut ignorantia, faulte de poursuite ou faulte de scavoir, vel nimia prevencio, vel nimia dilatio, vel fraudes, vel acceptio munerum, humana pervertunt iudicia" (Menot, *Paris-2*, 312).

95. Menot, *Tours*, 83; cf. 63, 140.

96. Ibid., 92.

97. Pepin, *DN*, fol. 79

98. "Si velitis solem hodie querere in valle, id est fidelitatem in hominibus modici status, non invenietis" (Menot, *Tours*, 16).

99. Pepin, *EC*, 199.

100. "Mercatores enim prudentes & astuti habent lucrum grossum, & tamen minus laborant, & vivunt delicatius. Pauperes vero portantes onera supra dorsum multo plus laborant, & minus lucrum reportant, immo vix habent quod comedant" (Raulin, *SQ*, 258).

101. Menot, *Tours*, 92.

102. Raulin, *SQ*, 571.

103. "Armigeri in villagia multa faciunt mala pauperibus, comedendo bona eorum et comedendo eorum gallinas" (Menot, *Paris-Alia*, 464).

104. LePicart, *Trinité*, fol. 151.

105. Farinier, *SP*, fol. 26.

106. Pepin, *CQ*, 363.

107. "Cur Dominus voluit in praesenti saeculo aliquos esse divites, & aliquos pauperes. Videtur enim quod melius fecisset si divitias omnibus aequaliter distribuisset. Insuper cum ipse Dominus omnes homines ex parte animae aequaliter dotaverit, saltem in hoc, quod tam magnum, quam parvum fecit ad imaginem, & similitudinem suam. Item homo factus, pro redemptione omnium aequaliter sanguinem suum fudit, consequenter videtur dicendum, quod etiam omnes aequales facere debuerit quantum ad res secundas. Respondeo ex magna Dei ordinatione factum est, & sit usque hodie, ut aliqui abundent divitiis, alii autem deficiant, & hoc, ut singuli habeant materiam merendi regnum Dei. Divites quidem dando eleemosynam pauperibus: Pauperes vero patienter ferendo suam in operam. Insuper & orando pro divitibus eos sustentantibus" (Ibid., 125).

108. "Si ergo regnum coelorum est pauperum, iuxta christi testimonium, consequens est, quod si divites velint illud habere, debet ipsum ab ipsis pauperibus petere, atque ab eis mercari, dando scilicet eis eleemosynam, ut illi dent ipsis regnum caelorum, & hoc suis precibus, aut participatione egestatis eorum: Divites enim non possunt tutius reponere pecuniam suam, quam in manu pauperis" (Pepin, *CQ*, 126; cf. LePicart, *Avent*, fol. 279).

109. "Quis est melioris conditionis simpliciter dives, aut pauper. Certe credo, quod dicitis in cordibus vestris divitem esse melioris conditionis. Et tamen a parte rei non sic est, quinimo pauper est melioris conditionis simpliciter" (Pepin, *CQ*, 126).

110. Menot, *Paris-2*, 359.

111. Menot, *Tours*, 67; cf. Ibid., 60.

112. "O peccatores ac peccatrices vadatis ad cimiterium sanctorum innocentum respiciatis omnia ossa. Nunquid possetis ponere differentiam inter ossa divitum & pauperum? Certe hoc solum inter est inter divites. Per eo quod delicata cibaria comedunt: eorum corpora magis fetent in tumulis quam corpora pauperum" (Maillard, *QO*, fol. 220).

113. Messier, *QS*, fol. 63.

114. "Gregorius, in *Moralibus*, dicit: Signum evidentissimum eterne damnationis est continuus successus in prosperitatibus mundanis. Porcus enim cum est pinguis occiditur" (Menot, *Tours*, 102).

115. Pepin, *RA*, 261; cf. 259.

116. Menot, *Tours*, 82; cf. Pepin, *DN*, 173; LePicart, *Trinité*, fol. 151.

117. "Dico vobis quod sanguis Christi clamat misericordiam pro pauperibus expoliatis et iniuste afflictis et tunica vestra de vobis vindictam, quia est de sanguine pauperculi populi" (Menot *Tours*, 116).

118. Raulin, *SQ*, 343.

119. "Sed hodie videbitis in domibus dominorum, non erit canis, nec catus, nec

gallus aut gallina qui non habeat suum determinatum locum: sed de pauperibus nulla fit mentio" (Menot, *Tours*, 210).

120. "Domina pomposa, Madame la bragarde, habes sex aut septem tunicas in arca tua que vix ter in anno feruntur, non capiunt aerem. . . . [Nescio quam excusationem poterit habere domina que videt pauperem nudum et clamantem per frigore]" (Menot, *Paris-2*, 362; cf. Cleree, *SA*, fol. 27).

121. Pepin, *CDH*, 89.

122. Raulin, *SQ*, 215; cf. Pepin, *EC*, 277.

123. "Habetis multa mala in ista villa? Certe si essent domini & alii loquerer illis. Visitatis ne hospitalia ad videndum si pauperes moriantur fame, & sine confessione? Vaditis ne in propria persona?" (Maillard, *QO*, fol. 130).

124. "Vos affligitis pauperes subditos vestros dupliciter. Primo quidem temporaliter, auferendo ab eis per vim et rapinam pelles eorum.i.bona eorum temporalia, etiam usque ad vestes, que frequenter publice exponuntur venditioni pro solvendis talliis. Secundo vero corporaliter, faciendo eos esurire, & perire fame pro defectu temporalium que aufertis ab eis; vel recludendo eos in carcerem ob defectum solutionis huiusmodi talliarum; sicut fit communiter" (Pepin, *DN*, fol. 60).

125. Pepin, *DN*, fol. 60.

126. Ibid., fol. 182.

127. Ibid., fol. 30; cf. Pepin, *CDH*, 205.

128. Illyricus, *SA*, fol. 81.

129. Menot, *Paris-2*, 349.

130. Menot, *Tours*, 90; cf. Menot, *Paris-1*, 234.

131. Menot, *Tours*, 90.

132. "A ventribus pauperum nunquam fures auferebat, bene ab horreis divitum. Divites quandoque dant pauperibus ut ferant pro se contra demulos falsum testimonium, & pauperes per minas, aut timores, aut suae salutes incuriam, testantur quod volunt divites. Isti bona sua mittunt in ventres, sed ventres pauperum cum eleemosynis mittunt in ignem aeternum. Haec Augustinus" (Raulin, *SQ*, 166).

133. Pepin, *CPP*, 422.

134. "O, domini, quando pauperes clamant in ostiis vestris et ianuis, servi dicunt: Taceatis, vos frangitis aures domini. O, miseri, cum eritis in articulo mortis, petetis misericordiam, et preces vestre non exaudientur, sed eiiciemini extra portam paradisi, sicut eiecistis pauperes de curia vestra" (Menot, *Tours*, 33; cf. Pepin, *CPP*, 63; Messier, *QS*, fol. 119).

135. Menot, *Tours*, 116.

136. Martin, *Métier*, 327.

137. "Olim quidem in Iudeis solum lux ista fulgebat, quia soli habebant fidem veram, spiritualem gratiam et veram doctrinam. Tota autem gentilitas erat in tenebris infidelitas, culpe et ignorantie; sed post Christi resurrectionem, gentilitas est conversa et in ea luxit fides vera, gratia et doctrina" (Menot, *Tours*, 195; cf. Pepin, *RA*, 243).

138. "Patres iudeorum fuerunt ydolatre in deserto: sed moyses extirpavit ydolatriam & fugavit demonem. Nunc vero revertitur ad filios iudeorum incitans eos ad occidendum christum" (Maillard, *QO*, fol. 112).

139. Pepin, *RA*, 243; cf. Pepin, *CDH*, 142–43.

140. Raulin, *SQ*, 279.

141. Maillard, *QO*, fol. 114.

142. Pepin, *CPP*, 455.

143. Pepin, *CDA*, 41.

144. LePicart, *Avent,* fol. 219.

145. "Unde ecclesia generaliter intendit orare pro omnibus viatoribus: non autem pro damnatis: quia viatores sunt adhuc capaces divine gratie et misericordie, non autem damnati. Unde Aug. de verbis domini ser. xi. De nullo inquit desperandum est quamdiu patientia dei ad penitentiam adducit. Paganus est hodie: unde scis utrum futurus sit crastino christianus? Judeus cras sequatur catholicam veritatem? Schismaticus est hodie: quid si cras amplectatur catholicam pacem?" (Pepin, *DN,* fol. 278). The reference is to Augustine *Sermons* 71.21, *De verbis evangelii Matthei* 12.

146. "Quant ce seroit une beste brutte, sy en deveriés vous avoir pityé. Il vous a presché, il vous a resuscité vos mors; il me semble, se il a ne meffaict ne mal parlé de vous aliquo modo, que il en est bien puny. —Sed ipsi maledicti averterunt facies suas dicentes: Crucifige" (Menot, *Tours,* 191; cf. Maillard, *Oeuvres,* 13–14).

147. Tisserand, *SA,* fol. 19.

148. Menot, *Paris-2,* 405; cf. Clichtove, *Sermones,* fols. 123–24.

149. Menot, *Paris-1,* 223.

150. "Unde nota quod in templo Salomonis erant tres partes. Prima vocabatur Sancta sanctorum, in quam Summus sacerdos semel in anno intrabat, et erant ibi tabule Moysi in arca, et ponebantur honorabiliter, sicut apud nos corpus Christi. Secunda pars erat Sanctuarium, et erat locus in quo erant sacerdotes qui pro populo offerebant sacrificia et erat sicut navis Ecclesie. Tertia dicebatur Atrium, et erat quidam locus in principio templi, sicut in aliquibus ecclesiis ante deambulationem et erant ibi Doctores et ibidem populus audiebat verbum Dei et in eodem loco invenit mercatores" (Menot, *Paris-2,* 318).

151. Pepin, *DN,* 160.

152. "Dico quod iudei erant Turonis tempore Ludovici regis octavi: audientes christianos nomen dei blasphemare dixerunt. Vos dicitis quod christus mortuus est pro vobis: miramur nos quod tales sibi in fertis iniurias. Audeo dicere quod plures insolentie fiunt in ecclesia christianorum quam iudeorum" (Maillard, *QO,* fol. 106).

153. Menot, *Paris-2,* 332.

154. Farinier, *SP,* fol. 12.

155. "Fuerunt alias Longobardi et Iudei expulsi a regno Francie, quia totam terram inficiebant usuris; sed nunc permittuntur crassiores diaboli usurarii quam unquam fuerint Longobardi, sive Iudei" (Menot, *Paris-2,* 343).

156. Pepin, *CQ,* 112; cf. LePicart, *Avent,* fol. 173.

157. Menot, *Paris-1,* 263–64.

158. Cleree, *SA,* fols. 33, 44.

159. Cleree, *SQ,* fol. 31.

160. "Et forte hodie apud christianos miracula nulla, aut pauca fiunt propter eandem causam, scilicet propter eorum incredulitatem. Nam hodie multi sunt christiani solo nomine, apud quos etiam fides periit" (Pepin *CQ,* 164).

161. "Multi sunt hodie qui nullum habent ad Deum affectum, non curant de ipso, non eum timent. Considerando bene per omnia vitam quam deducunt, le train qu'ilz mainent, videtur quod credant quod non sit alius paradisus, nec infernus, nec Deus, nec diabolus et quod eis nil nocere possit" (Menot, *Paris-2,* 358).

162. "Il ne fut oncques nation si barbare, ne gent si estrange, & sauvage, qui n'ayt eu en soy par instinct naturel quelque sentement de la divinité" (Paris, *Homélies,* fol. 112).

163. "Auiourd'huy on ne voit point Dieu, il n'est point cogneu" (LePicart, *Caresme,* fol. 121).

164. Guilliaud, *Sermons,* fol. 42.

Chapter 9

1. The seminal article, by Joan Kelly-Gadol ("Did Women Have a Renaissance?" in Renate Bridenthal and Claudia Koonz [eds.], *Becoming Visible: Women in European History,* Boston: Houghton-Mifflin, 1977, 139), argues that "there was no Renaissance for women.... Women as a group ... experienced a contraction of social and personal options." In a study of the early Middle Ages, Suzanne Wemple argues that the cloistered life provided a real alternative for some women, especially as their role in the life of the church became more limited (*Women in Frankish Society: Marriage and the Cloister, 500 to 900,* Philadelphia: University of Pennsylvania Press, 1981). Georgia Harkness feels that the cloister could allow women "security, dignity, and usually a satisfying social life among her peers. Here she could study, learn, and teach, and sometimes have a high order of cultural life.... [C]onventual life ... gave women a status and opportunity for personhood not available elsewhere" (*Women in Church and Society,* Nashville: Abingdon Press, 1972, 81–82). By contrast, in "Women in the Reformation Era," in Bridenthal and Koonz, 167, Sherrin Marshall Wyntjes claims that "because established institutions were being forced to justify their very existence, women had the opportunity to assume different roles from those that were time honored." Eileen Power asserts that for some women, the religious life provided a refuge, "but the refuge merely sealed the degradation of women in general by confining full approbation to those who withdrew themselves from the world" (*Medieval Women,* Cambridge: Cambridge University Press, 1975, 16). Steven Ozment argues that "[f]or Martin Luther and his followers the cloister became the symbol of the age's antifeminism; by suppressing monasteries and nunneries and placing women securely in the home as wives and mothers, the reformers believed they had liberated them from sexual repression, cultural deprivation, and male [clerical] domination" (*When Fathers Ruled: Family Life in Reformation Europe,* Cambridge, Mass.: Harvard University Press, 1983, 1).

2. Caroline Walker Bynum, "... And Women His Humanity?: Female Imagery in the Religious Writing of the Later Middle Ages," in Caroline Walker Bynum, Stevan Harrell, and Paula Richman (eds.), *Gender and Religion: On the Complexity of Symbols* (Boston: Beacon Press, 1986), 257–88; see also Joan Kelly, *Women, History, and Theory* (Chicago: University of Chicago Press, 1984).

3. Bynum, "Female Imagery," 258–59, 279.

4. Krailsheimer, *Rabelais,* 53.

5. Delumeau, *La peur en occident,* 316.

6. Katherine M. Rogers, *The Troublesome Helpmate: A History of Misogyny in Literature* (Seattle: University of Washington Press, 1966), 70, 72.

7. Power, *Medieval Women,* 11.

8. See Romans 5:12 "through one man sin entered the world and with sin death" and Timothy 2:14: "it was not Adam who was deceived by the woman. It was she who was led astray and fell into sin." See also George Tavard, *Woman in Christian Tradition* (Notre Dame: University of Notre Dame Press, 1973), 34.

9. Tavard, *Woman,* 118.

10. Augustine *De sermone Domini in monte,* 1.15 (P.L., 34, 1250), quoted in Tavard, *Woman,* 115.

11. Ambrose *De paradiso* 12.56, quoted in Tavard, *Woman,* 104.

12. Arnold de Liège, *L'alphabet des récits,* quoted in Schmitt, *Prêcher d'exemples,* 112.

13. L. Bourgain, *La chaire française au XIIe siècle* (Paris: Victor Palmé, 1879), 320.

14. Delaruelle, *Piété populaire,* 435.

15. "Mulier autem viri preciosam animam capit" (Farinier, *Sermones,* fol. 44; see also Marie-Thérèse d'Alverny, "Comment les théologiens et les philosophes voient la femme," *CCM* 20 [1977]; 110).

16. Maillard, *SD,* fol. 268; Tisserand, *SA,* fols. 12, 30; Illyricus, *SA,* fol. 127; LePicart *Caresme,* fol. 191.

17. "Manus enim femine nos vulneravit, et manus femine nos sanavit" (Illyricus, *SA,* fol. 26). This clearly refers to Paul's epistle to the Corinthians: "For as woman was made from man, so man is now born of woman" (1 Corinthians 11:12).

18. Tavard, *Woman,* 70.

19. Alverny, "La femme," 110.

20. "Adam enim, post peccatum suam, se excusavit supra mulierem suam, dicens: Mulier quam dedisti mihi, etc. Itaque par ce coste il cuidoit eschapper; mais il fist pis que bien" (Menot, *Paris-2,* 290).

21. Pepin, *CA,* 67.

22. "Insuper erat mirabilis discordia inter viros, & mulieres sibi invicem prævaricationem primorum parentum improperantes, dicentibus viris, mulierum seduxisse virum. Parte ex altera mulieribus dicentibus Adam stulte egisse in hoc, quod voluit plus complacere uxori, quam Deo. Ad pacificanda igitur praedicta bella, venit Christus in hunc mundum tanquam Legatus a latere Dei patris" (Pepin, *CQ,* 342).

23. "Preterea pulchritudo mulierum est magna occasio mali" (Illyricus, *SA,* fol. 138).

24. Ibid., fol. 140.

25. "De rechef doibvent apprendre les filles & adolescentes & femmes de soy voislez, et de cacher les choses qui attirent a amour charnelle" (Lansperge, *Sermons,* fol. 77).

26. "Non potest exire de pulcherrima muliere mundi nisi fetor. . . . O quicquid est in hoc mundo placens, non est nisi fetor" (Menot, *Tours,* 67).

27. "Sed profecto paucae admodum sunt hodie super terram formosae filiae, aut mulieres, quae de pulchritudine sua non glorientur" (Pepin, *CS,* 530).

28. Pepin, *CDA,* 46.

29. "Quando eritis in articulo mortis & videbitis mille diabolos a sinistris vestris qui volent accipere animam vestram: nunquid tunc velletis nunquam duxisse pompas & voluptates quas duxistis? Cavete igitur vobis" (Maillard, *QO,* fol. 216).

30. Meray, *Libres prêcheurs,* 1:65.

31. "Hoc ergo attendant illae mulieres vanae, & curiosae, qui in die festo se ornant & decorant, demum per vicos & plateas cursitant, ut videant, & videantur, in hoc imitantes naturam pavonis, qui in pulchritudine plumarum suarum gloriatur, gaudetque quando secrete ab hominibus inspicitur, & videtur, & exinde superbiens ad rotam faciendum, & caudam dilatandum, & ad ipsum plumarum pulchritudinem ostendendum excitatur" (Pepin, *RA,* 253).

32. "Vos iuvenes mulieres que aperitis pectora vestra ad ostendendum mammillas expediret vobis melius habere unum granum lepre" (Maillard, *SA,* fol. 82).

33. Pepin, *CQ,* 68.

34. "Res mirabilis et abominabilis est quod una mulier hodie, in habitu viri, vadat

ad ludum taxillorum, au mommon, avec une masque, una larva super faciem suam" (Menot, *Paris-2*, 348).

35. Pepin, *CQ*, 195.

36. James Brundage, *Law, Sex, and Christian Society in Medieval Europe* (Chicago: University of Chicago Press, 1987), 536; Bynum, "Female Imagery," 272.

37. Messier, *QS*, fol. 2.

38. Menot, *Tours*, 102.

39. Maillard, *SSP*, fol. 323.

40. "Sed post paululum tot rugas in fronte & vultu contrahet, quod mulier quadraginta annorum reputabitur esse sexaginta vel septuaginta" (Raulin, *SQ*, 29).

41. "Ha mes dames il ne fault plus porter les larges manches ne ung tas de superfluitez. Ha frere on les porte bien sans mal on se peult bien tenir honestement. Certe ego credo sed si sint honeste et bone mulieres postquam dictum est eis deponent. Ha frere dicunt alique nous en voyons porter ad aussi hommes de bien & aussi grans clercs que vous & dicunt quil ny a point de mal. Certe ma dame il ny a clerc qui les puisse porter: & nullus est qui hoc dicat qui non mentiatur" (Cleree, *SQ*, fols. 79–80).

42. "On peindra & fera on les images des benoists saincts & sainctes, autrement qu'on ne doit, & contre verité. On peindra la Magdalene autrement que l'on ne doit, aux pieds de la croix: & elle est penitente. Si ie preschois, qu'elle & la vierge Marie, & aultres, estoient ainsi habilles pompeusement & mondainement comme on les depeint, ie devrois en est reprins, & à bonne cause. Et pourtant, pourquoy permet on faire tels abus? que ne les reprend on?" (LePicart, *Caresme*, fol. 116).

43. Menot *Tours*, 100.

44. D. L. d'Avray and M. Tausche, "Marriage Sermons in *Ad Status* Collections of the Central Middle Ages," *AHDLMA* 47 (1980): 103.

45. "Si c'est avec le prix de la luxure, avec le produit des vols et des contrats malhonnêtes, ces vêtements sont souillés de lèpre, ils doivent être brûlés!" (Maillard, *Oeuvres françaises*, 97).

46. "Proh dolor et in dolore cordis dico: Certe, non est cauda domicellarum nostrarum, que sunt superflue, ex quarum superfluitate, que ad nihil deserviunt nisi ad mundanum plateam, bene haberent vestem pauperes orphani, vidue et egeni qui moriuntur frigore" (Menot, *Paris-1*, 226–27).

47. "Et vos mulieres quae facitis signa amorosa amatoribus vestris dicendo horas vestras" (Maillard, *SA*, fol. 51).

48. "Non poinct comme vont tas de meschans gens, qui viennent aulx sermons, plus tost pour voir les belles femmes que pour y prouffcter" (Merlin, *Sermons*, fol. 61). Brundage found a statute from Perugia that actually forbade men between the ages of fifteen and forty from standing around churches to look at women. The same statutes reveal numerous instances of "illicit copulation" in churches and cemeteries (Brundage, *Law*, 491, 493).

49. "Huius generis sunt multae mulieres incontinentes, gyrovagae, & inconstantes, quae vagantur per Ecclesias, & loca sacra, ut videant, & videantur. Et tales polluunt templum sanctum Domini, saltem in cordibus suis. Quarti veniunt in templum, in spiritu ebrietatis, & crapulae, ut sunt multi rurales, qui observant quasdam confraternitates, ob quarum honorem, ut dicunt, certis diebus anni in unum conveniunt & convivia sua celebrant intra Ecclesiam, eo forte, quod non habent domos adeo spatiosas, quae valeant eos in unum recipere: Et ita suis crapulis, & ebrietatis, spurcitiis, & clamoribus prophanant, atque polluunt sanctuarium Dei" (Pepin, *CS*, 114).

50. "Non enim habent communiter caput forte ad portandum vinum sicut viri" (Pepin, *DN,* fol. 103; cf. Farinier, *SP,* fol. 35).

51. "Non certe talis mulier point se supra me in ecclesia: et tamen ego sum de meliori domo quam ipsa sit" (Cleree, *SQ,* fol. 117).

52. Maillard, *QO,* fol. 97.

53. Cleree, *SQ,* fol. 74.

54. "Cum enim semel praedicaret in quodam loco, & hirundines, quae multae ibi erant, suo garritu impedirent assistentes, ne libere praedicationem suam audire possent, ait illis. Sorores meae hirundines iam tempus est, ut loquar; quia vos quidem satis, usque nunc locutae estis" (Pepin, *CS,* 457).

55. Lecoy, *La chaire française,* 429.

56. "Speciale enim dei donum est quod vir & mulier diversorum parentum, & forsan regionum, atque fortassis contrariorum morum et complexionum, se mutuo diligant in domino postquam sunt in unum matrimonialiter coniuncti" (Pepin, *DN,* fol. 205).

57. "Significat enim aliquid excellentissimus, dignissimus, atque altissimus, scilicet coniunctionem christi cum ecclesia" (Ibid., fol. 142; cf. Cleree, *SQ,* fol. 84).

58. Raulin, *SQ,* 618.

59. Clichtove, *Sermones,* fol. 52.

60. Maillard, *SA,* fol. 68.

61. Ibid., fols. 31, 53.

62. "In opere ergo matrimoniali quaeretur principaliter finis matrimonii, qui est procreatio prolis ad Dei honorem, & naturae humanae multiplicationem, atque caelestium mansionum repletionem, & reparationem" (Pepin, *CDH,* 189).

63. "Similes ferme assuero sunt multi moderni nobiles, qui tarde intrant matrimonium, & suam iuventutem dedicant multis lubricitatibus, qui postquam stupraverunt aliquas puellas tandem eas tradunt nubendas suis famulis vel subditis, ut sic forte earum copiam possint facilius habere cum liberavit. Alii vero sunt, qui & si debito tempore intrent nuptias, nihilominus post mortem uxorem suarum eligunt vidui remanere, ne scilicet intrantes secundas nuptias suscitent novam prolem in diminutionem haereditatis priorum. Qui cum dicant se non posse continere, impudicam ducentes vitam abundant bastardis & huiusmodi" (Pepin, *CPP,* 131).

64. Cleree, *SQ,* fol. 114.

65. "Non est semper tempus canendi et accipiendi son plaisir in matrimonio: Oportet habere frenum" (Menot, *Tours,* 215–16).

66. Maillard, *SA,* fol. 68.

67. "Mulieres sunt multe insane et faciunt vota multa de non reddendo debitum" (Cleree, *SQ,* fol. 128).

68. See Tentler, *Sin and Confession,* 186–223.

69. "Est honestum matrimonium, sed sub hoc pallio multa feda, inhonesta et execrabilia perpetrantur, que bestie et bruta erubescerent.... Et multi viri et multe uxores damnabuntur propter inhonestatem in matrimonio habitam, citius quam adultere et meretrices fuissent" (Menot, *Paris-2,* 353).

70. "Sed Frater, quid faciemus? Dominus meus hoc mihi precepit. Vivo stipendius suis; nisi fecero, me a domo expellet et forte cum duobus magnis ictibus baculi, avecques deux grans coups de bastons" (Ibid.).

71. Alverny, "La femme," 118.

72. Maillard, *SA,* fol. 68; cf. Avray and Tausche, "Marriage Sermons," 106.

73. Pepin, *DN,* fol. 136.

74. Raulin, *SQ*, 503.

75. Cleree, *SQ*, fol. 128.

76. "Mulieres dominus vocat vos ad statum matrimonii unde vox ordinetis omnia que facitis in te si vos eritis parrochiane christi et unde ubi solvitis decimas" (Ibid., fol. 56).

77. Ibid., fol. 132.

78. The fifteenth century Italian preacher Bernardino of Siena exhorted his female listeners: "O, woman! In the morning when thou comest to the fount of life and of the teaching of God, to the sermon, leave not your husband abed, or your son, or your brother, but see to it that you wake him out of his sleep, & see to it that he also cometh to hear that which if he be dead will restore him to life" (quoted in Petry, *No Uncertain Sound*, 271).

79. "Salvatus est homo malus per mulierem bonam" (Menot, *Tours*, 71).

80. "Mulier potest esse advocata in spiritualibus, & in his quae concernunt animarum salutem" (Pepin, *RA*, 116).

81. "Maintenant [les maris] les appellent viles catins, meretrices; les mordent, les frappent sans raison et quelquefois les tuent. Maris et femmes sont aujourd'hui chiens et chats" (Méray, *Libres prêcheurs*, 2:142–43).

82. "Quomodo haberet quis pacem in domo sua, ubi est mala uxor, & quinque filii garrulosi, qui nunquam satiantur?" (Raulin, *SQ*, 537).

83. "[Uxoribus] ... plus honorantes canem, quam maritum. Nam si maritus redierit de foris cum cane, utroque domum intrante, quandoque uxor facit festum cani, & applaudit illi, & faciem a viro suo avertit" (Pepin, *RA*, 127).

84. "Dico enim vobis quod sepe quando uxores vident viros suos ita miseros et tam infelicis regiminis et quod nulli sunt eis precio, tunc etiam ille de alia parte sunt dedite luxurie et infamie, et sic sepe vir est causa malorum que uxor facit, que tamen non deberet facere pro toto mundo" (Menot, *Paris-2*, 414).

85. Pepin, *CQ*, 205.

86. "Quod enim non licet mulieribus, etiam non licet viris" (Pepin, *DN*, fol. 211; cf. Menot. *Paris-2*, 413).

87. See James A. Brundage, "Carnal Delight: Canonistic Theories of Sexuality," in Stephan Kuttner and Kenneth Pennington (eds.), *Proceedings of the Fifth International Congress of Medieval Canon Law* (Vatican City, 1980), 376; Brundage, *Law*, 492; Klaits, *Servants of Satan*, 67; Alverny, "La femme," 124; Otis, *Prostitution*, 104.

88. This is also a common theme among the preachers, and has its roots in Thomas Aquinas, *Summa Theologica*, trans. by Fathers of the English Dominican Province (New York: Benziger Brothers, 1947), 3 suppl.:2802.

89. Pepin, *DN*, fol. 210.

90. "Si mulier quelibet ex adulterio habet filium, sine comparatione plus peccat quam vir, quia tunc hunc facit heredem et alios privat hereditate pro parte, admittendo cum eis illum quem scit spurium" (Menot, *Paris-2*, 414).

91. Ibid., 415.

92. Ibid., 373.

93. Menot, *Tours*, fol. 143.

94. Pepin, *DN*, fol. 212.

95. "Dicet mihi una iuvenis domina noviter uxorata, que per suam infamem vitam commisit adulterium sepissime, ad damnationem sue paupercule anime et ad confusionem totius sue cognationis, et Dei offensam, et iniuriam et confusionem sui mariti: O, Pater, ego sum infelicior mulier totius terre; vellem nunquam fuisse nata; utinam

terra nunc absorberet et deglutiret me, quia nimis enormiter offendi virum meum et scio quod pessime egi. —O, Amica mea, non desperetis, quia nullum est malum quod per penitentiam non remittatur. . . . Redeatis ad maritum et humiliter ei petatis veniam. . . . —O, Pater, libenter facerem quid dicitis, sed ipse est rudis et severus, nec me recipiet ad misericordiam. —Audi, Filia, illud Hieremie III: Tu fornicata es cum amatoribus multis; tamen revertere ad me et ego suscipiam te. —O, Pater, dato quod me recipiet, tamen non habebit curam mei, eroque cum eo ut ancilla et ut coqua, non dignabitur me respicere. —Non, Filia mea, non erit ita. . . . —O, Pater, verum est, sed percutiet me et torquebit usque ad mortem. —Non, faciet, quia dicitur, Ezechielis XVIII(XXXIII): Nolo mortem peccatoris, sed ut magis convertatur et vivat. —O, Pater, relinquet me solam et non manebit mecum. —Non, non, Filia. Zacharie I: Convertimini ad me et ego convertar ad vos, dicit Dominus. Nulla unquam certe tam dulciter et amorose osculata est mater parvulum suum qui in terram cecidit, levando eum et amplectendo, sicut facit Dominus animam peccatricem que per penitentiam ad eum revertitur" (Menot, *Paris-1,* 224; cf. Pepin, *CPP,* 11–12).

96. P. P. A. Biller, "Birth Control in the West in the Thirteenth and Early Fourteenth Centuries," *PP* 94 (1982): 25–26.

97. Pepin, *CA,* 26; cf. Raulin, *SQ,* 79.

98. See, e.g., Richard T. Vann, "Toward a New Lifestyle: Women in Preindustrial Capitalism," in Bridenthal and Koonz, *Becoming Visible,* 197.

99. LePicart, *Trinité,* fol. 153.

100. Maillard, *SSP,* fol. 339.

101. Maillard, *SA,* fol. 99.

102. "De hoc tamen sobrie inquendum est ad populum ne detur occasio mulieribus praegnantibus minus soletur se & foetum suum custodiendi. False ergo praedicant nonnulli illustrati viri, dogmatizantes tales parvulos expetere vindictam a domino de matribus suis. Nolo excusare universaliter matres a culpa, sed volo cum sacris doctoribus praedictos parvulos excludere generaliter ab omni tristitia & poena sensitiva perpetua" (Pepin, *CPP,* 403).

103. Augustine *De civitate Dei* 22. 13; trans. Henry Betterson (New York: Penguin, 1977), 1054.

104. A. M. Jacquin, "La prédestination d'après St. Augustin," *Miscellanea Agostiniana* 2 (1931): 868.

105. Raulin, *SQ,* 80.

106. Pepin, *DN,* fol. 230.

107. Farinier, *SP,* fol. 20.

108. Pepin, *CQ,* 92.

109. "Sunt enim multe fatue matres que non possunt tolerare correctionem filiorum suorum" (Pepin, *DN,* fol. 151).

110. Lawrence Stone, *The Family, Sex, and Marriage in England, 1500 to 1800* (New York: Harper and Row, 1979). An effective refutation of Stone's position can be found in David Herlihy, *Medieval Households* (Cambridge: Harvard University Press, 1985), 120–30; Weinstein and Bell, *Saints and Society,* 45, 68, 246.

111. "Mulieres que habetis filias quae incipiunt respicere infra bursas vestras et filios octo annorum certe nisi removeatis ab eis consuetudinem a iuventute quando erunt magni scient bene per sanguinem" (Cleree, *SQ,* fol. 38).

112. Clichtove, *Sermones,* fol. 66; cf. Pepin, *DN,* fol. 150.

113. Clichtove, *Sermones,* fol. 66.

114. Pepin, *DN,* fols. 150–51.

115. "Qu'y apprendront elles? Et vostre fils avec ce monsieur & Evesque, est-ce pour y chercher Iesus Christ? C'est pour l'y oublier, & quelque bonne doctrine qu'il ait, il l'y perdra incontinant" (LePicart, *Avent,* fol. 239).

116. "Mes dames estis ne imitatrices istius mulieris quin vos datis filias vestras nuptui respicitis si datis eam uni grosso predoni usurario certe est nobis idem nec de anima cogitatis dummodo corpus bene stet quod detur homini tenenti statum grandem" (Cleree, *SQ,* fol. 51).

117. Maillard, *SSP,* fol. 337.

118. Elizabeth Clark and Herbert Richardson, *Women and Religion* (New York: Harper and Row, 1977), 5.

119. "Longe perfectior et salubrior est status viduitatis bene observatus, quam status matrimonii bene comprobatus" (Menot, *Tours,* 111–12).

120. Ibid., 114.

121. "Habui virum boni nominis; ipse obiit. Venit quidam iuvenis satis bonus, cum quo bene essem. Quero vobis vestram opinionem. —Si videatur vobis, Amica, hoc bonum esse, ponatis vos cum eo. Ita, dicet, Pater, sed timeo ne capiat conditiones malas. —Si timeas, non ponas te cum eo" (Ibid., 112).

122. Pepin, *CS,* 322.

123. "Nulli magis contemnuntur [quam vidue]" (Menot, *Tours,* 113).

124. "Mulier que nupta est, sollicita est circa ea que mundi sunt et quomodo placeat viro. Non auderet testamentari, dare de bono suo, loqui confessori quotiens vellet. Habet maritum qui est ung diable enchainé, qui tota die manet in taberna et in sero verberat illam, et oportet quod illa patiatur hec omnia" (Ibid.).

125. "Tum quia mulier non transiens ad secunda nuptias, sed in viduitate permanens in maiori libertate constituitur. Est enim domina sui ipsius, familiae, & domus, quae redeundo ad secundas nuptias sub viri potestate constituitur, nec postea ad libitum disponere, sive de se, sive de bonis suis, nisi forte de paraphernalibus" (Pepin, *CQ,* 200).

126. Merry E. Wiesner, "Women's Defense of Their Public Role," in Mary Beth Rose (ed.), *Women in the Middle Ages and Renaissance: Literary and Historical Perspectives* (Syracuse: Syracuse University Press, 1986), 5.

127. "Tunc illa bona domina se videns ita perplexam, ingemuit et valde fuit attonita" (Menot, *Paris,* 262).

128. "[D]ucitis mulieres in matrimonio de nocte sine solennitate ecclesie" (Maillard, *QO,* fol. 192).

129. Ibid., fol. 163.

130. "Lubrici viri satagunt decipere pudicas virgines sponsalium provisione. Multi nempe nobiles ac divites, partier ut ecclesiastici beneficiati promittunt plerumque puellis ac virginibus quod alte maritabunt eas cum multis bonis, nunquam quoque illis deficient, dummodo velint consentire voluntati eorum" (Pepin, *DN,* fol. 223).

131. "Que tu ne prennes accoinctance d'ung jeune calamistratus, souffleurs de plume, qui nihil aliud faciunt nisi abuser femmes" (Menot, *Tours,* 114).

132. Menot, "Carêmes de Paris, Alia Secunda Pars," 474; see also Jacques Rossiaud, *Medieval Prostitution* (New York: Basil Blackwell, 1988), 12–26, 77, 110.

133. "Ecce, mulier vidua est sola. Si habeat processum, nullus defendit eam. Venit ad advocatum ut habeat tres literas scripture. Si velit habere, oportet quod corpus suum maneat pour gaige. C'est piteux mesaige mittere iuvenem mulierem ad multos et hodie mille deceptiones se y font" (Menot, *Tours,* 112; cf. 56).

134. "Unus ecclesiasticus, vel advocatus, sub specie eundi ad bibendum vel ien-

tandum, luxuriam suam sequetur, quia ibi in taberna inveniet lupanar. Ponis filiam in taberna, ad serviedum. Melius esset mittere ad elemosynam, quia efficietur ibi une meretrix" (Ibid.; cf. Pepin, *RA*, 181). The role of the tavern as a meeting place for prostitutes and their clients is well documented. Jacques Rossiaud, "Prostitution, jeunesse et société dans les villes du Sud-est au XVᵉ siècle," *Annales: E.S.C.* 31 (1976): 290–91. Rossiaud also discusses the double victimization of rape in the fifteenth century: "Ainsi la violence précède souvent l'action du proxénétisme ou du macquerellage, et la lutte autour de l'ordre matrimoniale alimente naturellement la prostitution" (301; see also Martin, *Métier*, 374).

135. "Ego inquit infelix fui muliercula in domo patris mei: garrula: vaga: cantatrix: & in omni petulanti: licet virgo: exposita tandem instinctu diabolico pater meus me defloravit: & nobis perseverantibus in hoc peccato noticiam de hoc habens mater mea acriter me increpavit. Sed ego nolens dimittere adii maleficam te accepi ab ea cibum venenarum quem tradidi matri et mortua est. Et sic nullo arguente liberius peccavi cum patre: qui post aliquos annos cognoscens suum peccatum renuit perseverare: sed dolens vilitatem peccati et magnitudinem ostendit mihi: quod mihi displicuit. Et rediens ad maleficam feci patri sicut et matri. Ego feci hec: sed si est locus penitentie parata sum sustinere quicquid potest ex cogitari" (Farinier, *SP,* fol. 19).

136. "Tunc vocato populo. Audistis inquit confessionem istius peccatricis: scitote quia si penituerit interius sicut ostendit exterius confido in deo quod remissum est ei peccatum suum. Sed quia valde difficule est ut pro tanto flagitio non sequatur pena magna oremus omnes ad dominicam ut penam debitam dimittere, aut certe alleviare ei dignetur" (Ibid.).

137. "O Predicator noli orare pro ea: sed rogate eam ut oret pro vobis: quia iam cum deo est. Si proniam non egerimus incidemus in manus domini et non in manus hominum" (Ibid.).

138. Menot, *Tours,* 137–38.

139. Ibid., 136.

140. Farinier *SP,* fol. 43.

141. Margaret Wade LaBarge, *A Small Sound of the Trumpet: Women in Medieval Life.* (Boston: Beacon Press, 1986), 26.

142. "Iuxta Lugdunum erat unus de ses gallans des quatres pilliers de taverne. Et uxor dixit predicatori: Amore Dei, audiatis virum meum de confessione. Mirum est de lamentandum de eius vita. Vadit ad tabernam; verberat me de sero, frangit omnia" (Menot, *Tours,* 201; cf. Maillard, *SA,* fol. 75; cf. Avray and Tausche, "Marriage Sermons," 106).

143. Cleree, *SQ,* fol. 97.

144. Maillard, *SA,* fol. 75.

145. "C'est une chose trop indecente de battre sa femme. Quelle consolation est-ce aux enfans de veoir leur pere & mere estre en noises & debats?" (LePicart, *Avent,* fol. 262).

146. On the law and society's acceptance of wife-beating, see LaBarge, *A Small Sound,* 26 and 204. For a discussion of popular thinking about rape, see Ibid., 26 and 202.

147. The best discussion can be found in Otis, *Prostitution,* 25–39.

148. Vern L. Bullough, "The Prostitute in the Middle Ages," *Studies in Medieval Culture* 10 (1977): 10.

149. Farinier, *SP,* fol. 43.

150. "Nihil est periculosius viro quam mulier, & mulieri quam vir" (Pepin, *DN,* fol. 230).

151. "Quare enim vult garsio te tangere, nisi ut de te faciat une paillarde?" (Menot, *Tours,* 216).

152. "Quando sponsi ante nuptias veniunt ad vos, nolite promittere quod faciant illas truphas quas communiter faciunt: quam post nuptias improperabunt vobis & dicunt quod similiter potestis facere cum uno alio" (Maillard, *SA,* fol. 99).

153. "Domine hospitisse, non habetis hodie in domibus vestris ancillas que dantur in istis tabernis ad serviendum, bone et honeste filie, et sub umbra huius servitii, statim destruuntur et tandem egrediuntur meretrices" (Menot, *Paris-1,* 251).

154. Menot, *Tours,* 160.

155. "Sunt ne hic matres que ducunt filias suas ad loca dominorum introducunt in cameram et claudent ostium super eas" (Maillard, *SSP,* fol. 321). In Dijon, one-quarter of all prostitutes had been led into the life by their families (Brundage, *Law,* 522).

156. Menot, *Tours,* 147.

157. Bullough, "Prostitute," 14.

158. "Sed hodie quis vicos non abundet meretricibus?" (Maillard, *QO,* fol. 128).

159. "Quid enim est causa quod sunt tot mulieres uxorate & virgines Parisius deflorate? Certe sunt macquerelles, & vos non punitis eas" (Ibid., fol. 200).

160. Otis, *Prostitution,* 113; LaBarge, *A Small Sound,* 202; Rossiaud, *Medieval Prostitution,* 36.

161. "Les paillardes se sont converties in predicatione" (Menot, *Tours,* 56).

162. Sessevalle, *Histoire générale,* 2:130.

163. Zawart, *Franciscan Preaching,* 304. This was so successful that a number of poor Parisian women set themselves up as prostitutes in order to qualify for admission; Brundage, *Law,* 529–30.

164. Rossiaud, "Prostitution," 310.

165. It is likely that this refers to Thomas Illyricus, who spent the summer of 1518 in Saint-Maximin (Provence) venerating the relics of Mary Magdalene, while en route to the shrine of Santiago de Compostella in Spain.

166. "[Il y a] . . . difficulté de nourrir et d'abriter ces nouvelles repenties" (Archives Communales de Lyon, BB36).

167. "Pourquoy m'amenderay—ie? tousiours on me monstrera au doigt, escoutez: la Magdaleine estoit une femme publique, qu'on monstroit au doigt. Nonobstant Dieu luy a pardonné" (LePicart, *Avent,* fol. 114).

168. Rossiaud, "Prostitution," 310.

169. "Celui qui fait célébrer la messe par un prêtre tenant avec lui une femme suspecte, pèche mortellement" (Paul Demeuldre, "Frère Jean Angeli: Episode des conflits entre le clergé seculier et le clergé regulier à Tournai [1482–1493], *Bulletin de l'Academie Royale des Sciences, des Lettres et des Beaux Arts de Belgique,* 5th ser., 8 [1898]: 323).

170. LePicart, *Avent,* fol. 43; cf. Menot, *Paris-2,* 300.

171. See Beatrice Gottlieb, "The Problem of Feminism in the Fifteenth Century," in Julius Kirshner and Suzanne Wemple (eds.), *Women of the Medieval World* (New York: Basil Blackwell, 1985), 361.

172. Maillard, *QO,* fols. 144–45.

173. "Patet ergo ex istis historiis, quod mulieres naturaliter compatiuntur infirmis & aegrotis, etiam plus quam viri, quia talia non leguntur de viris. Et propter hoc plerumque in magnis hospitalibus statuuntur mulieres religiosae ad ministrandum & humanitatis obsequia infirmis quibuscunque praestandum, sicut patet in domum Dei apud Parisiensis. Item in Magdalene apud Rothomagum" (Pepin, *RA,* 352; cf. Raulin,

SQ, 351). An excellent discussion of medieval women's roles as healers appears in LaBarge, *A Small Sound,* 173–94.

174. Menot, *Paris-Alia,* 470.

175. Pepin, *CS,* 296.

176. Pepin, *CQ,* 434.

177. "Mulieres facilius alliciuntur ad fidem & morum emendationem, quam viri. Unde videmus saepe gravissimas peccatrices compungi ad verba praedicatorum. Viros autem sceleratos raro, & tarde videmus inde emendari. Et huius ratio in parte est, eo quod viri praesumunt, & confidunt in proprio sensu. Non sic autem mulieres. Unde, & illae sunt communiter devotiores viris" (Ibid., 517).

178. "Et non est modernum quod mulieres sequuntur sermones: quam tempore christi multe sequebantur" (Maillard, *SSP,* fol. 337).

179. "Regina saba, quae venit a finibus terrae audire sapientiam Salomonis, significat, quod mulieres, ut in pluribus sunt avidiores ad audiendum verbum Dei, quam viri. Viri confidunt in suo sensu, & ideo parum curant frequentare sermones" (Pepin, *CQ,* 60; cf. Maillard, *SD,* fol. 278).

180. Herminjard, *Corréspondance,* April 1, 1534, 3:161.

181. This phenomenon was apparently not confined to France. In England, Bishop Brunton of Rochester stated that the churches were filled with women, men being only in a minority. Owst, *Preaching in Medieval England,* 173.

182. Pepin, *RA,* 352.

183. Menot, *Paris-2,* 409–10.

184. "Entre nous gens d'Eglise, nous parlons mal d'une femme, laquelle y va tous les dimenches, & disons que ce n'est pas affair à une femme d'y aller si souvent. Cela c'est mal parlé, & ie conseille à ceux qui le pourront faire d'y aller tous les iours, s'ils peuvent" (LePicart, *Trinité,* fol. 296).

185. Pepin, *CDA,* 277.

186. "Sed dicet aliqua proba mulier: pater ego habeo remorsum in conscientia de aliquo ego feci in matrimonio: sed confessor nunquam me interrogavit. Nescio si illud sit mortale vel veniale" (Maillard, *QO,* fol. 148).

187. Ibid.

188. "Sunt enim mulieres ut in pluribus viris devotiores sive orando sive loca sacra frequentando, sive etiam sacramenta suscipiendo. Multae enim saepe confitentur, & communicant praesertim in praecipuis solennitatibus, & festis, ubi pauci admodum viri quod faciunt" (Pepin, *RA,* 352).

189. Maillard, *QO,* fol. 111.

190. See Caroline Walker Bynum, *Holy Feast and Holy Fast: The Religious Significance of Food to Medieval Women* (Berkeley: University of California Press, 1987); Rudolph Bell, *Holy Anorexia,* (Chicago: University of Chicago Press 1985).

191. "Sunt tamen nonnullae quae credentes magnum famulatam exhibere filio, & matri, volunt cessare ab omni opere manuali in die Sabbati, & praesertim ab hora meridiana, & deinceps, iudicantes illos peccare quos tunc vident operari. . . . Contra igitur huiusmodi indiscretam & pernitiosam devotionem talium muliercularum constanter latrare debent singuli praedicatores, pariter & ecclesiae pastores, ne sub praetextu devotioni introducatur superstitio & haereses" (Ibid., 353; cf. Pepin, *RA,* 352–53).

192. Pepin, *EC,* 358.

193. Dahmus, "Preaching to the Laity," 59.

194. Dacheux, *Un réformateur catholique,* 22.

195. Kelley, *Beginning of Ideology,* 107.

196. Brown *Pastor,* 219.

197. "Nunquid studetis in theologia? Utinam essetis bone theologiane & bene diligeretis deum" (Maillard, *QO,* fol. 120).

198. In a discussion of corporal punishment, Cleree remarks: "Helas scitem libenter comment on se acquite in ista parrochia sunt ne aliqui ingrati habetis ne multos infantes puta scolasticos: pueros: filia tua vadit ne ad scolas cum aliis? et magistra est ne une femme de bien?" (*SQ,* fol. 76).

199. "Sunt & quaedam mulieres quae ad ecclesiam deferunt, seu deferri ad tergum faciunt libros devotionales, quos horas appellant, illos aperientes revolvunt diversas historias de auratas ibi depictas, quas osculantur sine magna devotione, sed ut a circumstantibus videantur, quod non fit absque nota superbiae, aut hypocrisis" (Pepin, *CPP,* 531). Reinburg finds that "those who actually prayed from their books were probably a minority among owners" (Reinburg, "Popular Prayers," 77).

200. Maillard, *QO,* fol. 194.

201. "Domine burgenses habetis ne bibliam in gallico thalamus proprie est venter?" (Maillard, *SA,* fol. 72).

202. "Domine, mes Dames, habetis ne Bibliam in gallico et les romans? Invenietis ne aliquem perseverantem in suis pompis, sicut vos, qui vel que sint in paradiso" (Menot, *Tours,* 199–200).

203. Chrisman, *Lay Culture, Learned Culture,* 114.

204. Krailsheimer, *Rabelais,* 31.

205. Margaret Deanesley, *The Lollard Bible and Other Medieval Biblical Versions.* (Cambridge: Cambridge University Press, 1920; repr. 1966), 109.

206. Susan Groag Bell, "Medieval Women Book Owners: Arbiters of Lay Piety and Ambassadors of Culture," *Signs* 7:4 (1982). 759. Mahaut, countess of Artois, commissioned two different copies of the Bible in French between 1316 and 1328 (Ibid., 750).

207. "Sed aliquis posset querere quare Christus primus apparuit Marie Magdalene quam Petro et aliis discipulos. Resurrectio christi viris per feminam nunciata est: ut contraria arte serpens vinceretur: quia enim ille mortem primo homini per feminam nunciavit: ita & viris vita per feminam nunciata est" (Illyricus, *SA,* fol. 84).

208. "Tu ante apostolos iesum vides & iesum alloqueris. . . . Tu nomine tuo a christo vocaris. Tu in mysterium resurrectionis ut primus testis eligeris" (Ibid.).

209. Messier, *QS,* fol. 153.

210. Maillard, *QO,* fol. 213.

211. "Plures mulieres flebant. . . . Et en montant la montaigne, va regarder deça et dela s'il y avoit point de ses disciples. Helas, non" (Menot, *Tours,* 192).

212. "Probatur, quod mulieres sint devotiores viris, & hoc exemplaritate, id est, exemplo illarum scientiarum mulierum quae christo fuerunt devotissimae. Quamquam enim christus quosdam dum hic viveret viros gratos invenerit, nunquam tamen tam constantem, & tam perseverantem devotionem in Apostolis suis invenit, quantam in mulieribus sibi devotis. Hae sunt enim qua ipsum per patrias praedicantem sequebantur ministrantes ei de facultatibus suis. Item hae sunt quae eum pendentem in cruce fugientibus discipulis comitabantur. Similiter hae sunt quae mortuo corpori sepulto unguenta aromatica paraverunt. Caeterum hae sunt quae nec tenebrosae noctis caligine, nec militum armatorum saevitia terrebantur. . . . Et ideo prae viris omnibus christus huic sexu; primam suae resurrectionis nunciavit triumphum, sciens quoniam super omnem gratiam est gratia mulieris" (Pepin, *RA,* 353; cf. Pepin, *CQ,* 434).

213. Pepin, *CDH,* 258.

214. Bynum, "Female Imagery," 268.

215. "Vous avez bien entendu la cause pour laquelle il a voulu premierement declarer & manifester sa resurrection aux femmes. . . . Quand nostre Seigneur a voulu faire de grandes choses, il a tousiours prins des gens idiots, pauvres pecheurs. Et en telle maniere il a voulu premierement manifester sa resurrection aux femmes, qui sont de sexe fragile, & de petite vertu" (LePicart, *Caresme,* fol. 159).

216. "Elle le vouloit tenir & embrasser, afin qu'elle ne le perdist plus. Elle faisoit cela par imbecillité" (Ibid., fol. 171).

217. Calvin, *PS,* 270–81.

218. Lecoy de la Marche, *La chaire française,* 32n.

219. Zawart, *Franciscan Preaching,* 266.

220. LaBarge, *A Small Sound,* 32.

221. Weinstein and Bell, *Saints and Society,* 34, 107.

222. Quoted in Martin, "Ministère," 672.

223. M. D. Lambert, *Medieval Heresy: Popular Movements from Bogomil to Hus* (London: Arnold, 1977), 76, 170–71.

224. Lucas Wadding, *Scriptores ordinis minorum* (Florence: Quarachi, 1933), 2:382.

225. "Prima est defectus sensus: de quo non presumitur in muliere tantum sicut in viro. Secunda est conditio subiectionis, quae inflicta est ei. . . . Tertia est, quia si praedicaret, aspectu suo provocaret ad luxuriam. . . . Quarta, in memoriam stultiae primae mulieres" (Humbert of Romans, *De eruditione praedicatorum* [Sebastian a Cormelias, 1607], 31).

226. Raulin, *SQ,* 507.

227. Pepin, *CDH,* 66–67.

228. "Et si quis obiiciat praedicationis officium mulieri non esse committendum, cum hoc prohibeat Apostolus, dicens: Docere muliere non permitto, conceditur regulariter, & de communi lege. Secus autem in casu, & maxime cum hoc sit ex speciali instinctu Spiritus Sancti, cuiusmodi creditur factum fecisse in proposito" (Pepin, *CQ,* 309).

229. See Victor Saxer, *Le culte de Marie Madeleine des origines à la fin du Moyen Age.* (Paris: Clavreuil, 1959), 6.

230. "Tum illum in civitate Marsiliae, & deinde in civitate Aquensi annunciando, & populum ad fidem sua praedicatione attrahendo. Et si dicatur, quod mulier non debet palam praedicare, cum hoc prohibeat Apostolus dicens, I ad Thimotheum 2. Docere muliere, supple, sed esse in silentio. Respondetur hoc verum esse regulariter. Deus tamen, qui nullus alligatur legibus, potest mulieres, sicut & viros ad praedicationis officium assumere" (Pepin, *CS,* 292; cf. Clichtove, *Sermones,* fol. 195).

231. "[Elle] . . . est allee en la cité annoncer à tous ce que Iesus Christ luy avoit dit, disant a par elle: Nunquid ipse est Christus? N'est-ce pas le fils de Dieu, le vray Messias promis en la loy? Il m'a dit & declaré tout ce que i'avois fait par toute ma vie. Par ce lieu icy les Lutheriens ont voulu dire qu'il appartient, aux femmes de prescher & que la Samaritaine a presché. La Samaritaine n'a point icy parlé par maniere de predication, mais par une admiration qu'elle avoit de ce que Nostre Seigneur luy avoit declaré toute sa vie" (LePicart, *Caresme,* fol. 172).

232. "Il est defendu aux femmes de prescher & enseigner en lieu public: mais privément la mere peut enseigner ses enfans, & ceux de sa maison, comme serviteurs & autres. L'abesse peut bien enseigner & remonstrer à ses nonnains. Mais en public & pleine congregation, il ne compte pas aux femmes d'enseigner: & leur

repugne de prescher. Et la raison est que prescher c'est avoir authorité. Et le naturel, & la propre condition des femmes, c'est qu'elles doivent este subiectes" (Ibid., fol. 173).

233. "[L] a doctrine publique n'appartient qu'au sexe parfaict, qui a plus solide raison, iugement plus entier, plus grand erudition. Leur charge ne porte prescher en public, car ainsi seroient authorisees dessus les hommes auditeurs en subversion de l'ordre de nature, qui ne consent femme dominer a homme" (Paris, *Homélies,* fol. 65).

234. Bynum, "Female Imagery," 279.

235. In Strasbourg, the late fifteenth century preacher Geiler von Kaysersberg went so far as to invoke a variation on the Lord's prayer: "Our Mother, who art in heaven, give us this day our daily bread" (E. Jane Dempsey Douglass, *Justification in Late Medieval Preaching: A Study of John Geiler of Keisersberg* [Leiden: E. J. Brill, 1966], 191–92). This view can be traced to the Pseudo-Albertus Magnus, Richard of Saint Laurent (died after 1245), who said: "Our Mother, who art in heaven, give us our daily bread," and "Mary so loved the world that she gave her only begotten son for the salvation of the world" (Graef, *Mary,* 1:266). Similarly, Julian of Norwich could address herself as follows to her Lord: "Thus, our Lady is our mother, in whom we are entirely enclosed and of whom we are born in Christ. For she who is the mother of our savior is the mother of all who are saved in our savior. And our savior is our true mother; in him we are endlessly born, and we shall never come out of him" (Julian of Norwich, *Revelations of Divine Love,* New York: Image, 1977, 186). See also Caroline Walker Bynum, "The Body of Christ in the Later Middle Ages: A Reply to Leo Steinberg," *RQ* 39:3 (1986): 399–439).

236. Herlihy, *Medieval Households,* 113.

237. A good example was Margery Kempe, although her emulation of Saint Bridget and others did not always have happy consequences. Clarissa Atkinson, *Mystic and Pilgrim: Margery Kempe* (Ithaca: Cornell University Press, 1983).

238. Eire, *War,* 315.

239. Weinstein and Bell, *Saints and Society,* 221.

Chapter 10

1. Excellent discussions of the Waldensian heresy and preaching can be found in Gabriel Audisio, *Le barbe et l'inquisiteur: Procès du barbe Pierre Griot par l'inquisiteur Jean de Roma (Apt, 1532)* (Aix: Edisud, 1979); Cameron, *Reformation of the Heretics;* and Giuliano Procacci, "La Provence à la veille des guerres de religion: Une période décisive: 1535–45," *RHMC* 5 (1958): 249–50. The Bibliothèque Municipale of Dijon has in its collection a Waldensian sermon (*Recueil Vaudois,* Ms. 234 [195–1], fols. 72–77).

2. Cameron, *Reformation of the Heretics,* 57.

3. Bossy, *Christianity,* 83.

4. Lambert, *Medieval Heresy,* xii.

5. Gordon Leff, *Heresy in the Later Middle Ages: The Relation of Heterodoxy to Dissent, c. 1250–1450* (New York: Barnes & Noble, 1967), 1:2.

6. Edward Peters (ed.), *Heresy and Authority in Medieval Europe* (Philadelphia: University of Pennsylvania Press, 1980), 3.

7. Ibid., 21–22.

8. Lambert, *Medieval Heresy,* 4

9. Martin, "Prédications déviantes," 254.

10. Ibid.

11. Godin, *L'homéliaire*, 9.

12. Charles Duplessis d'Argentré, *Collectio judiciorum de novis erroribus* (Paris: Cailleau, 1728), 1:340–41.

13. Godin, *L'homéliaire*, 9–10.

14. Robert Mandrou, "Hérétiques méconnus du XVIe siècle européen," in Myriam Yardeni (ed.), *Modernité et nonconformisme en France à travers les âges* (Leiden: E. J. Brill, 1983), 32; Godin, *L'homéliaire*, 13.

15. Demeuldre, "Angeli," 319.

16. This was an opinion commonly objected to; see Bossy, *Christianity*, 56.

17. Demeuldre, "Angeli," 320–25.

18. Ibid., 326–27, 336.

19. Clerval, *Registre*, 199–203.

20. Ibid., 207, 209.

21. Godet, *Montaigu*, 18.

22. Duplessis d'Angentré, *Collectio judiciorum*, 308.

23. Ibid.

24. Ibid., 309.

25. Martin, "Prédication déviantes," 255.

26. Duplessis d'Argentré, *Collectio judiciorum*, 313, 317.

27. Ibid., 257.

28. Clerval, *Registre*, 32.

29. Eire, *War*, 21.

30. "At ergo, sacerdos ille qui non querit nisi expeditionem et pecuniam, expedit te immediate hore; dat tibi absolutionem et dicit tibi: O, Amice, vade. —Et quo ibit cum tale absolutione? Ad omnes diabolos" (Menot, *Paris-1*, 257; cf. Maillard, *SA*, fol. 66; Pepin, *CS*, 41).

31. "Puta quia ex devotione accedit ad ecclesias mendicantium vel aliorum: tamen sacramenta non debent parochiani alibi recipere sine licentia sacerdotis proprii excepto sacramento penitentie quod possunt recipere a mendicantibus" (Maillard, *QO*, fol. 131).

32. "Dico quod lex ligat et ille qui est ligatus, il n'est pas a sa voulenté, nec en sa liberté" (Menot, *Tours*, 134).

33. Farge, *Biographical Register*, 293.

34. Massaut, *Critique*, 95.

35. "Secunda apparitio factu tribus Mariis in unum congregatis designat, quod Dominus apparet per gratiam omnibus recte credentibus Deum esse trinum & unum" (Pepin, *CDH*, 268).

36. See Homily 23 of Jean Vitrier, which Godin thinks closely resembles the sermon from which the propositions were taken; Godin, *L'homéliaire*, 214–16.

Chapter 11

1. Edmond Grin, "Deux sermons de Pierre Viret, leurs thèmes théologiques et leur actualité," *TZ* 18:2 (1962): 116–32.

2. An example was Martial Mazurier's "Homélie sur la salutation évangélique." Farge, *Biographical Register*, 322.

3. Ibid., 14.

4. Some of the most comprehensive and/or provocative studies of the French Reformation include Mark Greengrass, *The French Reformation* (Oxford: Basil Black-

well, 1987); Imbart de la Tour, *Origines,* vols. 3 and 4; Kelley, *Beginning of Ideology;* Lucien Febvre, "Une question mal posée: Les origines de la réforme française et le problème général des causes de la réforme," *RH* 161 (1929): 1–73; and the many articles of Nathanaël Weiss in the *BSHPF.*

5. Eire, *War,* 173.

6. See Robert Kingdon, *Geneva and the Coming of the Wars of Religion in France, 1555–1563* (Geneva: Droz, 1956).

7. Eugène Arnaud, *Histoire des Protestants du Vivarais et du Velay: Pays de Languedoc de la réforme à la révolution* (Geneva: Slatkine Reprints, 1979), 19–20.

8. Ibid., 29.

9. Gabriel Loirette, "Catholiques et Protestants en Languedoc à la veille des guerres civiles (1560)," *RHEF* 23 (1937): 514.

10. Samuel Mours, *Le Protestantisme en France au XVIe siècle* (Paris: Librairie Protestante, 1959), 148.

11. Kingdon, *Geneva,* 31.

12. Between 1555 and 1562, the Company of Pastors dispatched only eighty-eight pastors to France. Greengrass, *French Reformation,* 40.

13. Venard, "L'église d'Avignon," 1:456.

14. Robert Linder, *The Political Ideas of Pierre Viret* (Geneva: Droz, 1964), 20–21.

15. Eugene Arnaud, *Histoire des Protestants du Dauphiné aux XVIe, XVIIe et XVIIIe siècles* (Geneva: Slatkine Reprints, 1970), 1:32.

16. Herminjard, *Corréspondance,* June 18, 1531 (2:343).

17. Ibid., December 15, 1529 (2:218).

18. Nathanaël Weiss, "Une mission à la foire de Guibray: Lettre d'un ministère Normand à Calvin, août 1561," *BSHPF* 20 (1879): 461.

19. Haton, *Mémoires,* 1:49–50.

20. This painting can be seen in the Musée de la Réformation in Geneva, Switzerland.

21. Herminjard, *Correspondance,* December, 1525, 1:406–7.

22. Glaumeau, *Journal,* 78.

23. Beza, *Histoire ecclésiastique,* 1:75.

24. Glaumeau, *Journal,* 104.

25. Haton, *Mémoires,* 12, 14, 20.

26. Weiss, "Mission," 458.

27. Haton, *Mémoires,* 51; Weiss. "Mission," 459.

28. Kelley, *Beginning,* 115–16.

29. Mours, *Protestantisme,* 142.

30. Leriche, *Journal,* 79.

31. Kelley, *Beginning,* 117.

32. Haton, *Mémoires,* 12.

33. "Apres on verra beaucoup de stupides, qui ne sont esmeus nullement, & ne peuvent estre touchez non plus que des pierres" (Calvin, *PS,* fol. 507).

34. Beza, *Histoire ecclésiastique,* 1:74.

35. Henri Tribout de Morembert, *La réforme à Metz: Le lutheranisme. 1519–1522* (Nancy: Annales de l'Est, 1969), 1:55.

36. Jean Crespin, *Histoire des martyrs,* ed. Daniel Benoît (Toulouse: Société des livres religieux, 1885), 306.

37. Haton, *Mémoires,* 1:7.

38. Ibid., 41–42.

39. Nancy L. Roelker, "The Appeal of Calvinism to French Noblewomen in the Sixteenth Century," *JIH* 2 (1972): 400.

40. Loirette, "Catholiques et Protestantes," 519.

41. Beza, *Histoire ecclésiastique,* 1:74–75.

42. Weiss, "Bourges," 347.

43. Herminjard, *Corréspondance,* August 20, 1524, (1:268–69).

44. Farge, *Biographical Register,* 109.

45. Kelley, *Beginning,* 116.

46. Henri Hauser, "The French Reformation and the French People in the Sixteenth Century," *AHR* 4 (1899): 225.

47. Ibid., 97.

48. Victor Carrière, "Guillaume Farel: Propagandiste de la réformation," *RHEF* 20 (1934): 67.

49. Leriche, *Journal,* 80.

50. J.-P. Hugues, *Histoire de l'église réformée d'Anduze depuis son origine jusqu'à la révolution* (Paris: Privat, 1864), 53–54.

51. Haton, *Mémoires,* 22.

52. Beza, *Histoire ecclésiastique,* 1:75.

53. Herminjard, *Corréspondance,* June 28, 1529 (2:181–82).

54. Archives Communales d'Amiens, BB32, fol. 33.

55. Loirette, "Catholiques et Protestants," 514.

56. Herminjard, *Corréspondance,* 1534 (2:241).

57. Schmidt, *Gérard Roussel,* 164

58. Stanley D. Schneider, "Luther, Preaching and the Reformation," in *Interpreting Luther's Legacy,* ed. by Fred W. Meuser and Stanley D. Schneider (Minneapolis: Augsburg Publishing House, 1969), 126.

59. Harold J. Grimm. "The Human Element in Luther's Sermons," *ARG* 49 (1957): 50–60, especially 52.

60. James McCue, "Luther and the Problem of Popular Preaching," *SCJ* 16 (1983): 42.

61. Bayley, *Pulpit Oratory,* 61.

62. Richard Stauffer, "Un Calvin méconnu: le prédicateur de Genève," *BSHPF* 123 (1977): 188.

63. "Aujourd'huy . . . les bestes sauvages, les loups ravissans et les tirans sont bandez contre la povre Eglise de Dieu" (Pierre Viret, *Quatres sermons sur Esaie 65 [mars 1559],* ed. by Henri Meylan [Lausanne: Librairie Payot, 1961], 33).

64. Robert Scribner, *For the Sake of Simple Folk: Popular Propaganda for the German Reformation* (Cambridge: Cambridge University Press, 1981), 76.

65. See Linder, *Political Ideas,* 34; Stauffer, "Calvin," 192–93.

66. Personal communication from James Smither.

67. Duplessis d'Argentré, *Collectio judiciorum,* 26.

68. Farge, *Biographical Register,* 40.

69. Duplessis d'Argentré, *Collectio judiciorum,* 46.

70. Ibid., 97.

71. Clerval, *Registre,* 368–69.

72. Ibid., 343.

73. Duplessis d'Argentré, *Collectio judiciorum,* 30–34.

74. Quoted in Carrière, "Farel," 47–48.

75. Eire, *War,* 168.

76. Ibid., 67.

77. Herminjard, *Corréspondance*. 2:23–25.

78. Versoris, *Livre de raison*, 33–34.

79. Beza, *Histoire ecclésiastique*, 1:77; Crespin, *Martyrs*, 264.

80. Farge, *Biographical Register*, 292.

81. Ibid., 296.

82. Imbart de la Tour, *Origines*, 3:191.

83. Nathanaël Weiss, "Le réformateur Aimé Meigret," *BSHPF* 39 (1890): 245–69.

84. Henri Hours, "Procès d'hérésie contre Aimé Meigret," *BHR* 19 (1857): 14–43.

85. Guy, "Sermon," 182.

86. Hours, "Procès," 26–27.

87. Ibid., 40.

88. "Par plusieurs manières et diverses sentences le Prophète et Roy David, inspiré de la grace du Sainct Esprit, nous a manifesté la gloire de Dieu pour nous donner a cognoistre que toute bonté et perfection de luy procède, et n'est cause d'aulcun mal" (Meigret, "Sermon," 194).

89. Psalm 13:2–3; Meigret, "Sermon," 195.

90. Meigret, "Sermon," 195.

91. Psalm 14:1; Meigret, "Sermon," 195.

92. "Laquelle sentence, fichée dedans le cueur humain, le fait tresbuscher de mal en pis, de vice en plus grand vice, de fragilité en iniquité, d'ignorance en malice, d'inconstance en obstination, de pechez remissibles en pechez execrables" (Meigret, "Sermon," 195–96.

93. Psalm 14:3; Meigret, "Sermon," 196.

94. Guy, "Sermon," 182.

95. "Qui a esté (a vostre advis) la cause que, par si long temps, les humains (un seul peuple judaïque excepté) ont esté en si grandes tenèbres, de sens reprouvez, d'entendement alienez, faisantz (comme dict Sainct Paul) oeuvres non convenable, mais contraire a leur nature? N'est ce pas pource qu'ils ont dict: Non est Deus?" (Meigret, "Sermon," 196).

96. Ibid., 197.

97. "Dont viennent (dira quelcun) tant de maladies, soubdaines morts, saccagements de villes, perils sur mer, guerres sur la terre, pestilences, oppressions de pauvres gens et aultres maulx inhumains et deraisonnables?" (Ibid.).

98. Ibid., 198.

99. "Je ne veulx avec Jeremie disputer contre Dieu, mais contre toy et tes semblables, quiconques estes de Dieu calomninateurs, plus prompts a l'accuser pour les maulx lesquels tresjustment pour vos pechez endurez, que a le louer pour les biens, lesquels de sa seule bonté vous sont distribuez" (Ibid.).

100. James 1:5–6; Meigret, "Sermon," 199.

101. "En recognoissance que tout nostre bien vient de divine grace, celebrons les festes des Saincts, affin que tout premierement soit Dieu loué et honoré pour les graces qu'il luy a pleu leur faire plus que aux aultres; et, secondement, affin que soyons incitez a les ensuyvre pour estre a Dieu de plus en plus aggreables" (Meigret, "Sermon," 199).

102. "Qui luy a faict la grace de si grand humilité que (comme dit sainct Jerosme) il se coupa le poulce, soy estimant indigne de prestrise et ecclesiastique prelature, sinon celuy de qui seul tout bien procède" (Ibid., 200).

103. "Non par contraincte, non par necessité de nature, non esmeu par nos merites, mais par la seule grace nous a engendrez et donné vie" (Ibid., 201).

104. Ibid., 202.

105. "Le cueur d'un Roy est en la main de Dieu, qui du tout en peult faire a son plaisir" (Ibid., Meigret's translation of Proverbs 21:1).

106. "Et en un aultre lieu commanda nostre Seigneur aux enfans d'Israël user de la passion de Ire contre les Madianites, par telles paroles nous endoctrinant nous servir de la passion de Ire comme d'armes invasives. Pourtant Moyse, qui (tesmoing l'Escripture) estoit le plus doulx homme qui fut sur la terre, pour punir l'idolatrie de son peuple feit armer les Levites contre leur propre lignage" (Ibid., 203).

107. "Par ces histoires voyez que Ire et raisonnable fureur souvent est ministre de bonnes et justes oeuvres" (Ibid., 204).

108. Ibid.

109. "De peccato quidem: quia non credierunt in me" (Ibid.).

110. Ibid.

111. "Qu'est ce que croire en Jesus Christ? Est ce croire qu'il est Dieu et homme, crucifié et mort pour nous, descendu ès enfers, monté ès cieulx, assis a la dextre de Dieu, qui viendra juger tout le monde? Je dis (suyvant la sentence de sainct Jaques) que non. Quelle donc doibt estre nostre foy? La foy que tu doibs avoir, est croire fermement et esperer certainement que, pource que le fils de Dieu s'est faict homme, toy qui es pure et pauvre creature, de nulle estime comparée a Dieu, communiqueras ès divines perfections. Pource que Jesus Christ a souffert douloureuse mort, tes pechez te seront pardonnez. Pour ce qu'il est descendu ès enfers, le diable n'aura puissance sur toy. Pource qu'il est resuscité, un jour le ferons comme luy, communiquans et participans a son immortalité, clarté, impassibilité et semblables privilèges. Pource qu'il est monté ès cieulx, nous est ouvert Paradis, et y entrerons après luy. Bref, la foy de Jesus Christ est croire que rien n'aurons jamais en Paradis que par la vertu de la foy ou confiance (c'est tout un) que avons en luy" (Ibid., 205–6).

112. Menot, *Tours,* 118–19.

113. Meigret, "Sermon," 206.

114. "Telle est la doctrine qu'avez accoustumé d'ouïr d'entre nous preschers et docteurs academiques, qui manifestement mettons la charrue devant les boeufs" (Ibid.).

115. "Si justification procède de la vertu de nos oeuvres, inutile est la mort de Jesus Christ" (Ibid.).

116. "Bien sçay que ceste doctrine nous est nouvelle et a d'aulcuns d'entre vous fascheuse et peu aggreable. Et que voulez vous que je face pour vous contenter? . . . A telle misère sommes venus que qui vous presche et declaire l'Evangile est heretique ou Lutherien; qui magnifie les humaines traditions et inventions (a vostre jugement) est prescheur evangelique. Or, si ce sermon, qui est le premier par moy en vostre presence presché, vous est desplaisant, content suis qu'il soit le dernier. Desja vous voy-je murmurer et en vousmesmes disputer et dire que, si la foy est suffisante pour nous saulver, nous n'avons que faire de bonnes oeuvres" (Ibid., 206–7).

117. Ibid., 207.

118. "Par la foy sommes justifiez. Les bonnes oeuvres et a Dieu aggreables sont le fruict de nostre justification" (Ibid., 208).

119. "Parquoy fut la loy nostre pedagogue, qui nous conduisoit a la foy de Jesus Christ pour estre justifiez" (Ibid., 209).

120. Ibid.

121. "Soyent les loix de sainct François, sainct Benoist, sainct Dominique et aultres tant raisonnables que vouldrez, instructives et bien nous addressantes au chemin de Paradis, si elles sont contrainctives, elles sont pedagogiques. Et quand elles ne seroyent coërcives, si elles ne sont justificatives, elles sont pedagogiques. Voulez vous que je donne plus grande dignité a une loy par les hommes inventée que a celle de Dieu? a la reigle sainct François ou sainct Augustin que a la loy donnée a Moyse? Je ne veux maintenant reprouver ne dire que ce soit mal faict d'estre vestu d'une longue robbe grise, porter une corde en lieu de ceincture, un blanchet en lieu d'une chemise, avoir les souliers descoupez, le chaperon cousu, la teste rase et point d'argent en bourse. Je ne dy que ce soit peché porter une robbe blanche et, pour parfaire la livrée, une chappe noire dessus, un scapulaire pendant dessoubs, ne manger point de chair, ne boire qu'a deux mains, et innumerables aultres telles ceremonies exterieures. Mais je dy que celuy qui a cela t'oblige, usant de puissance coërcive, te commandant telles choses observer sur peine d'eternelle damnation (ou, comme vous dictes, sur peine deue a peché mortel) et aultres peines temporelles ou spirituelles, il te met soubs le pedagogue" (Ibid., 209–10).

122. "Qu'avons nous affaire des petits magistrorum, lesquels le plus souvent ne sçavent euxmesmes gouverner." (Ibid., 211).

123. Ibid.

124. Ibid.

125. "Quia vado ad Patrem, et jam non videbitis me" (Ibid.).

126. John 16:7; Meigret, "Sermon," 212.

127. Meigret, "Sermon," 213.

128. Ibid.

129. Ibid., 213–14.

130. "Mais si nous perseverons et avons en Dieu bonne confiance, il nous dira comme aux Apostres: Tristitia vestra vertetur in gaudium" (Ibid., 215).

131. "Maintenant est le jugement du monde; maintenant sera le prince de ce monde hors de sa seigneurie chassé. Par lesquelles parolles assez entendez que, par nostre Seigneur, a este ostée la puissance que le diable avoit sur nous. Et pource que le monde a remis Satan en sa première authorité, le constituant son prince et se mettant en sa subjection, par le Saint Esprit sera redargué de judicio: quia princeps hujus mundi jam judicatus est" (Ibid., 216).

132. "Et quelles loix diaboliques (dira quelqu'un) a le monde approuvé comme bonnes? Quels statuts sont par les Chrestiens observez comme necessaires pour faire leur salut, qui soyent par le diable inventez et baillez? Est il possible que aultres soyent les commandemens de Satan que droictement contraires aux commandemens de Dieu. . . . Pourtant nous fault cercher des loix qui ayent apparence de bonté et justice, telles que dit sainct Paul, ayants espèce de sapience en observance de religion et humilité, et toutesfois soyent diaboliques" (Ibid., 216–17).

133. Ibid., 217.

134. Ibid., 218.

135. "Et ne considèrent pas l'humaine fragilité, que tant plus l'oeuvre est excellente, moins de gens suffiront a l'accomplir, plus sera le commandement difficile et importable. Ne voyant ces commandeurs que (tesmoing sainct Paul) multiplication de loix est occasion de multiplication de pechez. . . . Innumerables Chrestiens sont allez a perdition, qui seroyent en Paradis, n'eussent esté les commandemens des jeusnes et aultres telles ceremonies et abstinences" (Ibid., 219–20).

136. Ibid., 220.

137. Ibid., 221.

138. "L'oeuvre est juste et louable; le commandement inique et diabolique" (Ibid).

139. Ibid., 222.

140. "Atque utinam verbum Dei, qui ignis est ad consummationem usque extenuans, ita rubiginem omnem a Delphinatu expurgasset atque emundasset, ut nihil erroris, nihil satanicarum legum, nihil hypocriticarum ceremoniarum, nihil denique indoctarum et anilium fabularum apud vos remaneant!" (Meigret, "Epistre," 186).

141. Ibid., 186–87.

142. Meigret had almost certainly read Luther's *Babylonian Captivity of the Church* (1520). Such phrases of Luther's as "But listen to our distinguished distinguisher of 'kinds,' to whom the decision of the church and the command of Christ are the same thing," and "in sacred things I am opposed to the invention of human fictions" seem to have influenced Meigret. Martin Luther, *Three Treatises,* trans. Charles M. Jacobs (Philadelphia: Fortress Press, 1978).

143. Ibid., 188.

144. "Haec est sententia Joannis a Gersono, viri celebratissimi et cui hodie Parisienses primas in divinis literis tribuunt; quae facile, si divina illis testimonia non satis sunt . . . dictis sanctorum Augustini, Ambrosii et aliorum ostendi potest" (Ibid., 189).

145. Ibid., 190.

146. "Lupos, inquam, qui, cum se pastores dicant, nulla sollicitudine, nulla diligentia ovibus provident; nec quod infirmatum est confortant; et quod male habuit non corroborant; quod contribulatum est non consolidant; quod erravit non revocant; quod periit non inquirunt. Quin vero gregem Domini deglubunt, mactant, perdunt" (Ibid., 192).

147. Duplessis d'Argentré, *Collectio judiciorum,* 15–17.

148. Ibid., 12–14.

149. Hours, "Procès," 31.

150. Ibid., 32, 36, 39–41.

151. Ibid., 37–38, 42–43.

152. Farge, *Biographical Register,* 293.

153. Hours, *Procès,* 24–25.

154. Bourgeois, *Journal,* 183.

155. Farge, *Biographical Register,* 295.

156. Weiss, "Meigret," 269.

157. Greengrass, *French Reformation,* 36.

Chapter 12

1. David Nicholls, "Inertia and Reform in the Pre-Tridentine French Church: The Response to Protestantism in the Diocese of Rouen, 1520–1540," *JEH* 32:2 (1981): 196.

2. Ibid., 191.

3. Hoffman, *Church and Community,* 36.

4. Venard, "L'église d'Avignon," 1:441.

5. Eisenstein, *Printing Press,* 72.

6. Hirsch, *Printing,* 95.

7. Farge, *Orthodoxy,* 215.

8. Duplessis d'Argentré, *Collectio judiciorum,* 2:ix.

9. Clerval, *Registre,* 335.

10. Farge, *Biographical Register,* 327–28.

11. Ibid., 386–87.

12. "Non invenio quod propter temporalia debeant fulminationes et excommunicationes fieri" (Menot, *Tours,* 139).

13. Ibid., 208.

14. Venard, *L'église d'Avignon,* 1:457.

15. Bourgeois, *Journal,* 245.

16. Hilarion de Coste, *Le parfait ecclésiastique,* 143.

17. "Et ses disciples sont encore plus meschans que luy: car plusieurs d'entre-eux ont dit & soustenu que ce n'est rien du sacrement de l'autel, & plusieurs ont esté bruslez pour soustenir leur meschanceté & damnable heresie & opinion: & moy-mesme l'ay veu" (LePicart, *Trinité,* 257).

18. Crespin, *Histoire des martyrs,* 518.

19. Ibid., 286.

20. Farge, *Biographical Register,* 45.

21. Ibid., 214.

22. Peters, *Heresy and Authority,* 7.

23. "Sed heu prohdolor. Non coniecturis utebatur, sed certissima vaticinatione, qua preteritis coniectens presentia: causasque rerum, et principa recordans, velut oculis videre videbatur. Nescio quod futuram per grandem tempestatem. Ea autem ut videmus quotidie increscunt, ut in ea opinione confirmet. Erant lapsis temporibus in orthodoxa fide reges, principes, presules, quorum viribus freta ecclesia, se tuebatur adversus impugnantes. Nunc quasi omnes amici eius spreverunt eam: et facti sunt ei inimici" (Illyricus, *SA,* note at end of volume, unpaginated).

24. See, e.g., "Feria Quarta Cinerum," *Paris-2,* 277–79.

25. See "Sabbato Post Feriam Quartam Cinerum," Ibid., 289–97.

26. Pepin, *DN,* fol. 82.

27. "Nuperrime autem dictus inimicus homo per nefandum organum unius discipulorum suorum, cui nomen Lutherus, Alemanus sive Germanus natione: cui tanquam Jude melius esset si natus non fuisset: non tantum novas suscitavit hereses: quantum antiquas & prius condemnatas visus est renovasse, quibus totam ferme Germaniam cum adiacentibus regnis et provinciis corrupit, infecit, & maculavit: ita ut suum pestiferum venenum effuderit usque ad nostram Galliam, in cuius laudem olim placuit dicere barbato illi Hieronymo, quod sola Gallia monstris caret i. hereticis" (Ibid., fols. 263–64).

28. "Deus enim neminem cogit ad recte credendum in vera fide: Sed unumquemque relinquit in arbitrio suo. . . . Fides enim est primum fundamentum totius spiritualis edificii; et precipue inter tres virtutes theologicas: que sunt fides, spes, charitas" (Ibid., fol. 267).

29. Ibid., 266.

30. "Et istud est contra Lutherianos: qui dicunt quod sancti non sunt a nobis rogandi ut orent pro nobis" (Ibid., 278).

31. "Nam adeo falsa est quod non potest tanquam vera probari auctoritate sacre scripture" (Ibid., fol. 271).

32. Ibid., fols. 273–74.

33. "At vero hac tempestate a nonnullis Senioribus iudicibus qui videntur regere populum, sive in temporalibus sive in spiritualibus, egreditur iniquitas.i.heresis, que est maxima iniquitas. Multi enim nobiles et potentes, multi ecclesiastici, multi qui docti estimantur, multi post denique promiscui sexus homines in damnationem animarum suarum, & signanter tot censura ecclesiastica que nuper emanaverunt a sede apostolica, non timent nec erubescunt favere, fovere, tueri et defendere, nunc palam,

nunc occulte, pestiferos errores quos de mortuis suscitavit filius ille perditionis, quem Lutherem vocant." (Ibid., fol. 264).

34. Ibid.

35. "Ita etiam Germania frigida natio est: et hoc propter distantiam a sole. Nolo tamen simpliciter maculam ponere in gloria dicte regionis: sciens olim et huius que eam gloriosos viros genuisse, et maiestatem imperialem per multa annorum curricula promeruisse: sed improbo sceleratissimus illum Lutherum cum complicibus suis: quem utinam nunquam Germanua genuisset" (Ibid., fol. 270).

36. "Queritur cur dominus permittit dictos hereticos tanto tempore prolongare iniquitatem suam? Videtur enim aliquibus devotis catholicis quod deberet illos cito exterminare. Unde nuperrime audivi de quodam magno & generoso principe huius regni Francie, quod cum quadam die haberetur verbum de lutherianis coram eo, cepit cum fervore spiritus et zelo fidei accensus dicere: Libenter vellem manu propria tradere in mortem omnes lutherianos, & esse tortor eorum" (Ibid., fol. 266).

37. Ibid., fol. 272.

38. "Hec est igitur pena temporalis heresis, quod omnis hereticis perdit officium, beneficium, omnem que dignitatem, & si qua talia habet: omnem quoque temporalem substantiam, si quam habet. Omnia nempe bona ipsorum hereticorum ipso iure sunt confiscata" (Ibid.).

39. "Si enim (inquit) heretici sepe reciperentur ut conservarentur in vita & aliis temporalibus bonis: istud posset esse in preiudicium salutis aliorum: tum quia si relaberentur, possent de facili multos bonos catholicos inficere: tum etiam quia si fine pena evaderent, alii securius in heresim relaberentur" (Ibid., fol. 273).

40. "Tertio heresis procurat penam corporalem, non qualemcunque, sed penam mortis. . . . Multo gravius est corrumpere fidem, per quam falsare pecuniam, per quam tantum subvenitur vite temporali. Sed falsarii pecunie et alii malefactores statim per seculares principes morti traduntur. Ergo a fortiori heretici statim ex quo de heresi convincuntur, possent non solum excoriari, verumetiam iuste occidi. At tamen ecclesia utitur erga eos magna misericordia. Non enim pro primo lapsu in heresim tradit eos statim brachio seculari exterminandos per mortem, sed expectat primam correptionem: postquam si voluerit redire ad fidem, et abiurare omnem heresim: iniungitur quidem illi penitentia: sed tamen parcitur sibi a morte. Quod si postea relabatur: ulterius sibi non parcitur, sed traditur brachio seculari per mortem puniendus" (Ibid.).

41. "Quarto heresis procurat penam eternalem: sicut & cetera peccata mortalia, etiam multo graviorem quam multa alia peccata, pro quanto est gravioris culpe" (Ibid.).

42. "O quantum igitur stupebant miseri Lutheriani cum post hanc vitam viderint se vitari a confortio electorum, & detrudi confusibiliter ad societatem demonum, et omnium damnatorum" (Ibid.).

43. Pepin, *CDA,* 287.

44. "Nam sepenumero propter hereses insurgentes insurrexerunt pariter bella, discordie, et dissensiones inter catholicos & hereticos: et ubi prevaluerunt heretici, maxima damna intulerunt catholicis" (Pepin, *DN,* fol. 264).

45. Ibid.

46. "Advertendum est autem circa hanc materiam de permissione heresum atque hereticorum, quod duplices sunt heretici. Primi quidem occulti: secundi autem manifesti. Primo non sunt statim eradicandi ab ecclesie, nisi forsan per publicas predicationes. Et huius ratio est: quia ecclesia non iudicat de occultis, sed tantum de manifestis. Item quia tales possunt adhuc redire ad gremium matris ecclesie, et boni

atque devoti catholici fieri. Secundi autem sunt quantocius eradicandi, extirpandi, atque interficiendi: presertim ubi sunt omnino incorrigibiles, convicti, obstinati, et pertinaces" (Ibid., fol. 266).

47. Pepin, *CS,* 171.

48. "Quoties oves invaduntur ab haereticis, tenentur pastores eas personaliter tueri & defendere, non obstante mortis periculo. Probatur si haec veritas praelati, & praesertim episcopi obligant se in suscipiendo curam pastoralem ad exequendum officium pastorale propter subditorum salutem. Ergo quoties salus subditorum exigit praesentiam realem pastoris, non debet personaliter suum gregem deferere, nec propter aliquod personale periculum imminens, maxime cum bonus pastor debeat animam suam pro ovibus suis ponere. Sic est autem, quod salus subditorum exigit, ut persona pastoris sit praesens cum suis ovibus, quoties invaduntur ab haereticis, ut eos repellat, tum devota oratione, tum sancte praedicatione, tum sana doctrina, & disputatione" (Pepin, *CDH,* 278).

49. Clichtove, *Sermones,* fol. 71.

50. Ibid., fol. 127.

51. "Sic ipsi miscent melli & vino venenum, ut non percipiatur toxicum" (Ibid., fol. 126).

52. "Tant que en France demeurera lintegrité de ceste foy, nous naurons occasions de craindre noz ennemis. Mais il ne se fault arrester en la foy seullement. Il fault venir en la montaine dolivet, et de l'eminente vertu de charité. . . . Il fault avoir les oeuvres, et charité de dieu et son prochain, avec la foy" (Gaigny, *Homélies,* fol. 7).

53. "Capite nobis vulpes quod demoliuntur vineas. Nam vulpes habet os acutum. Sic noster Leutheros os acutum habet: scilicet in eloquentia: in rhetorica. Vulpes pilum habet pulchrum: id est scientia eius videtur esse pulchra: scilicet quod sacerdotes possunt ducere uxorem: et similia: sed hec scientia nihil valet. Vulpes habet caudam bien tofue. Sic sunt multi heretici illum insequentes. Vulpes anhelit um habet fetidum: sic tota scientia illius fetet et nil valet" (Messier, *QS,* fol. 58).

54. "Scilicet heretici: qui suis falsis expositionibus & doctrinis nituntur extinguere veritatem scripture" (Ibid., fol. 80).

55. "Qui erraret in materia fidei putans ecclesiam sic credere, paratus corrigi & emendari cum audierit veritatem, non censetur hereticus" (Illyricus, *Libellus,* end of volume, unpaginated).

56. "Quia summus pontifex atque etiam collegium cardinalium posset a gratia cadere & a fide deviare" (Ibid.).

57. Ibid.

58. Paul Broutin, *L'évêque dans la tradition pastorale du XVIᵉ siècle* (Mechelen: Desclée de Brouwer, 1953), 79. Another such reformer was Cardinal Georges d'Armagnac, bishop of Rodez, who continued and accelerated work already begun before the Reformation. He regulated ordination and preaching, published manuals and statutes, and held synods. The idea was not merely to counter Protestantism, but to improve Catholicism.

59. Farge, *Biographical Register,* 265–66.

60. Brother Ivollé, referred to in Chapter 2, may have been more typical. His *Dix Sermons de la saincte messe et ceremonies d'icelle* were published together with Simon Vigor's *Sermons et predications chrestiennes et catholiques du S. Sacrement de l'Autel, accommodées pour tous les jours des octaves de la feste Dieu,* ed. Jean Christi (Paris: Nicolas Chesneau, 1577). These sermons respond to the Protestants insofar as they defend the mass, but they were written in 1558 and do not directly attack the Huguenots. In the fourth sermon (pp. 423–83), Ivollé suggests that heretics are dead

members of the church and should be cut off. He defends the pope in the same sermon. The Vigor sermons date from the 1560s (probably before 1567, but definitely after the Colloquy of Poissy in 1561) and direct theological arguments against Calvin, Beza, Luther, Zwingli, and Oecolampadius. While some of these sermons are not all that virulent and do not differ greatly from those of LePicart, Vigor's *Sermons Catholiques, pour tous les jours de Caresme et Feries de Pasques, faites en l'Eglise S. Estienne du Mont à Paris, par feu de bonne memoire maistre Simon Vigor, Docteur en Theologie, nagueres Archevesque de Narbonne et Predicateur du Roy*, ed. Jean Christi (Paris: Gabriel Buon, 1588), dating from 1568, a time of war, are more stridently anti-Huguenot, and are the best examples of Catholic preaching during the religious wars.

61. Farge, *Orthodoxy*, 202. One of LePicart's colleagues, Jacques Merlin, *penitencier* of Paris, had been jailed and exiled to Nantes from 1527 to 1529 for criticizing Louise of Savoy. Farge, *Biographical Register*, 328.

62. Venard, "L'église d'Avignon," 2:568.

63. "Et monsieur sainct Ierome louoit ce pays de France, parce qu'en son temps il n'y avoit point eu de monstres, c'est à dire, d'heretiques. Et auiourd'huy il en y a infinis, il ne faut point aller loing qu'en ceste ville de Paris" (LePicart, *Trinité*, fol. 41).

64. Ibid., fol. 256.

65. "Et depuis leur temps on n'a point mal parlé du sainct sacrement de l'autel, sinon depuis trente ans en ça, ou environ que ce meschant & malheureux Luther, pire que le diable, a recommencé & renouvellé l'heresie de ces deux maudits Anglois [Wyclif et Hus], lequel a plus de disciples que n'eut iamais Mohammet, & tous les iours pululent, & croissent en tel sorte, qu'à grand peine peult on trouver trois personnages l'un, qui n'en soit infecté & envenimé. Et ses disciples sont encores plus meschans que luy" (Ibid., fol. 257).

66. "Et au contraire, l'esprit des heretiques, ce n'est que tout orgueil. Ils appellent le Pape Antechrist, cela ne sent pas l'esprit de mansuetude ny d'humilité" (Ibid., fol. 105).

67. "Doncques celuy qui faict, dit, ou sent autrement que l'Eglise n'a dit & determiné, il est heretique: car il n'ignore pas: c'est pertinacité qui est en luy" (LePicart, *Avent*, fol. 261).

68. "Mais ces gens icy, ces heretiques, ils ne disent rien publiquement, mais tout occultement, & ne parleront iamais à deux personnages, qui soient ensemble, s'ils ne sont de leurs sectes: mais seulement à un, encores le feront ils iurer de ne nommer celuy qui luy a dit" (LePicart, *Trinité*, fol. 295).

69. Ibid. fol. 84.

70. "L'heretique fera de grandes aumosnes, comme auiourd'huy on voit par experience, il semble par apparence qu'il y ait entre eux plus grande charité, qu'entre les catholiques.... Ils sont plus gens de bien que nous, & semble que leur maniere de vivre soit meilleure que la nostre.... Vous voyez que les heretiques donnent tant aux pauvres, tout cela ne leur prouffite de rien.... Ils ont une apparence de religion" (LePicart, *Avent*, fols. 112–13).

71. "Ils ont tousiours Iesus Christ en la bouche: mais ils ne l'ont pas au cueur & à l'affection" (LePicart, *Caresme*, fol. 133).

72. "Ils ont une parole doulce & simulée, qui semble bonne" (LePicart, *Trinité*, fol. 103).

73. "Aucunesfois il vous semblera qu'ils disent bien à leur predication: mais ceux qui ont accoustumé de les hanter, les entendent bien, & leurs mots secrets, qu'ils ont entre eux" (Ibid., fol. 283).

74. "Car combien que les heretiques disent aucunes fois la verité, c'est contre leur intervention. Ils parlent pour decevoir & pour bailler leur venin soubs couleur de verité. L'heretique pour pallier la verité & couvrir sa faulseté, il prend l'escriture. . . . Toute la fin de l'heretique n'est que pour decevoir autruy, & le divertir du vray sens de l'escriture: & voudroit que les autres l'entendissent ainsi mal comme luy. Il est comme le loup, qui ne cherche sinon à tuer & destruire" (LePicart, *Caresme,* fol. 24).

75. Clichtove, *Determinatio theologice facultatis Parisiensis super doctrina Lutheriana hactenus per eam visa* (Paris, 1521).

76. "Et quand Dieu permet qu'un heretique en son obstination aille ioyeusement à la mort, en sorte qu'il semble qu'il soit constant, c'est une tentation que Dieu vous donne, pour voir si vous l'aymez de tout vostre cueur, & si vous luy estes fideles & fermes en la foy. Ouy, mais vous voyez la constance de cestuy-là. Il n'a pas peur de mourir. Ah! Chrestien, ce n'est pas constance que cela, mais dureté & obstination. Il est des martyrs du diable" (LePicart, *Avent,* fol. 361).

77. "Notez par cela, que l'Eglise des heretiques, n'est pas veritable, car il n'y a point d'union, ny de concorde. Vous voyez que leurs opinions sont contraires" (Ibid., fol. 111).

78. Ibid., fol. 234.

79. "Il y a plusieurs heretiques & schismatiques qui s'en separent. A cause de quoy, Dieu permet que pour noz fautes & demerites le Turc & les infideles prennent pied, ruinent & gastent la chrestienté" (LePicart, *Caresme,* fol. 136).

80. "Et neantmoins, nous voyons quasi en tous lieux, en toutes places, tant de divers prescheurs, qui preschent & disent tout autrement que n'a fait l'Eglise Romaine. . . . Et neantmoins, on les endure & ne les punit on point, qui est tres mal fait" (Ibid.).

81. "Encores, ces meschans gens Lutheriens & heretiques, pour flatter les princes, disent & confessent bien qu'il leur fault obeïr, à la puissance seculiere, & non pas à la puissance de l'Eglise, aux superieurs d'icelle, comme au Pape, à mon Evesque, à mon curé" (LePicart, *Trinité,* fol. 36).

82. "Et neantmoins, c'est horreur de ce que l'heretique dit auiourd'huy qu'un Chrestien n'est point subiect à personne, mais qu'il doit vivre en liberté, sans obeissance ne subiection de personne: pource que par le baptesme, il est fait enfant de Dieu, & que puis qu'il est enfant de Dieu, il est mis en liberté, & ne doit point estre subiect. . . . Et neantmoins, noz Lutheriens osteroit volontiers le Royaume & l'Empire s'ils pouvoient, ils feroient tous esgal, ils veulent reduire l'ordre en confusion" (Ibid., fols. 35–36).

83. LePicart, *Caresme,* fol. 40.

84. LePicart, *Avent,* fol. 313.

85. "Ils disent que l'homme ne peult faire un bon euvre aggreable à Dieu, mais plustost luy desplaist" (Ibid., fol. 105).

86. LePicart, *Caresme,* fol. 86.

87. "Le lutherien ne veult point ouyr parler d'aller à confesse. . . . Un lutherien dit: Ie me repens, ie suis un grand pecheur, &c. Sans declarer rien en particulier" (LePicart, *Avent,* fol. 331).

88. Ibid., fol. 347; cf. LePicart, *Trinité,* fol. 114.

89. "Et les heretiques disent qu'il ne fault rien croire s'il n'est expressement escript en la saincte escriture" (LePicart, *Avent,* fol. 360).

90. LePicart, *Caresme,* fol. 25.

91. LePicart, *Trinité,* fol. 207.

92. LePicart, *Caresme,* fol. 73.

93. "Les heretiques disent qu'ils la faut dire en françoit, ce qu'il ne faut faire: & quand on la diroit en françois, & tu ne l'entendois, elle ne te prouffiteroit non plus, que si on la disoit en Hebreu, ou en Espagnol, ou en autre language qui t'est incogneu" (LePicart, *Trinité*, fol. 227).

94. "Aussi ceux qui veulent traitter la saincte escriture, & ne l'entendent pas, comme sont les simples gens, n'ont ils pas esté bruslez pour leur erreur & mauvaise intelligence? Venez au sermon & retenez ce que vous voyez. Mirez vous au sermon & pratiquez ce que vous avez ouy" (LePicart, *Avent*, fol. 253).

95. "Pourquoy un homme seculier entreprend il l'office d'un prestre, d'un curé? C'est exceder les limites de la grace que Dieu vous a donnée" (Ibid., fol. 247).

96. LePicart, *Trinité*, fol. 56.

97. LePicart, *Avent*, fol. 53.

98. "Il ne suffit pas de croire, que le precieux corps de Iesus Christ soit au S. Sacrement de l'Autel: car combien que Luther soit heretique, il croit bien cela. Mais il faut que nostre foy soit pleine & entiere" (LePicart, *Trinité*, fol. 278).

99. "Et comme nous avons dit, il y a aucuns des disciples de Martin Luther qui disent & font pis que luy: car luy mesme dit & confesse, que veritablement nostre Seigneur Iesus Christ est au sainct sacrement de l'autel: mais il fault & erre en ce qu'il dit, que le pain & le vin au S. sacrement de l'autel, demeurent en leur substance & nature" (Ibid., fol. 258).

100. "Vous voyez qu'en la multitude des Lutheriens, auiourd'huy ils sont divisez, ils ne sont point d'accord, ny en une mesme opinion. S'il est question de parler du sainct sacrement de l'autel, il y a cinq ou six opinions diverses. L'un dit que ce n'est que pain, l'autre dit que Iesus Christ y est mais que la substance du pain y demeure, & n'est pas transsubstantié. Un autre dit, que ce n'est que le corps de nostre Seigneur, & non pas un sacrifice & oblation. Un autre dit, que ce sacrifice ne prouffite sinon à celuy qui le reçoit, & non pas aux vivans & trespassez. Un autre dit qu'il faut bailler ce sainct sacrifice aux gens lays, sous les deux especes de pain & du vin. La division & varieté d'opinions qu'ils ont entre eux, c'est un vray argument & signe evident qu'ils n'ont pas le sainct esprit, mais ils parlent par l'esprit de Satan, & du diable" (Ibid., fols. 87–88).

101. LePicart, *Caresme*, fol. 162.

102. "Et puis, toy heretique tu dis que Dieu ne se soucie point de noz euvres, ny que nous ieusnions: que nous oyons la saincte messe" (Ibid., fol. 53).

103. Ibid., fol. 5.

104. "Le lutherien appelle les ymages ydoles. Nous trouvons par S. Paul que ydolum nihil est (I Cor. 8). Les images des saincts ne sont pas ydoles: car elles representent quelque chose" (LePicart, *Avent*, fol. 347).

105. LePicart, *Caresme*, fol. 148.

106. "Il y a grand danger qu'en cuidans suyvre l'Evangile, de fil à fil, que nous ne facions contre l'Evangile: quand nous ne voulons croire sinon ce qui est escrit en l'Evangile. Où trouverez vous en l'Evangile que la glorieuse vierge Marie, mere de Dieu, soit demeurée perpetuellement vierge: qu'elle ayt esté conceuë sans peché originel?" (Ibid., fol. 148).

107. LePicart, *Trinité*, fol. 203.

108. LePicart, *Caresme*, fol. 127.

109. Ibid., fol. 22.

110. Ibid., fol. 163.

111. "Si ie vous preschois icy quelque erreur . . . il ne fauldroit pas attendre de le me dire & me reprendre apres le sermon: car ceux qui m'oyent prescher tel erreur,

ne seront pas par-aventure tous presens apres le sermon, mais s'en iront ainsi scandalizsez & mal enseignez de moy. Et pource, on me doit reprendre publiquement & en la chaire, & me dire mon erreur" (Ibid., fol. 147).

112. "Fuyez les heretiques & Lutheriens, plus que ne feriez un homme qui auroit mille pestes, ne conversez avec eux, & ne les oyez aucunement, car le venin de leur doctrine donne la mort corporelle & spirituelle" (LePicart, *Trinité,* fol. 82).

113. LePicart, *Avent,* fol. 178.

114. "On faict plusieurs bons livres mais les heretiques ne seront pas surmontez par là, car ils produisent & alleguent les abbus qui sont aux estats, mais si nous vivions bien, nous les confondrions par là, & le fondement de leur erreur sera osté, & s'en ira comme fumée. Mais quand ie regarde tant d'abbus, ie suis quasi au desespoir que les heresies cessent" (LePicart, *Trinité,* fol. 90).

115. LePicart, *Caresme,* fols. 21–22

116. LePicart, *Avent,* fol. 153.

117. LePicart, *Caresme,* fols. 80–81.

118. "Le dereiglement & mauvaise vie de plusieurs de religion, qui ne gardent pas bien les reigles & ordonnances d'icelles, est occasion aux heretiques de mal parler, & mal sentir des religions, combien que pour cela, il ne fault pas oster ny abolir les religions: mais il fault oster les abbus, & desordres qu'on y comment, & les tres bien reformer par bonnes euvres & ordonnances" (LePicart, *Trinité,* fol. 245).

119. LePicart, *Avent,* fols. 269–70.

120. "Dieu vueille que Martin Luther soit mort en vray repentance & contrition de son cueur: car s'il est mort obstiné, il en a tout son saoul: & pour tous ceux qui on esté & seront damnez par son erreur, sa peine accidentale luy en sera augmentée" (LePicart, *Caresme,* fol. 111).

121. LePicart, *Trinité,* fol. 80.

122. "Aussi ces meschans heretiques ne dureront gueres mais bien tost seront annichilez & abolis" (Ibid., fol. 206).

123. "Aussi comme Lutheriens, & gens que soubz quelque liberté charnelle, pour eulx preschée, tendoient a faire tout commun, commençans a soy respandre par tout, a la similitude des Gotz, Gepides, Vuandalles, Allains, Ostrogotz, & autres Barbares, pour ruiner l'Universelle Chrestienté" (Claude Guilliaud, *L'oraison funebre declarative des gestes, meurs, vie & trespas du tresillustre prince, Claude de Lorraine, duc de Guyse & d'Aumalle, pair de France, gouverner & lieutenant general pour le roy en ses pays de Bourgongne* [Paris: Iehan Dallier, 1550], fol. 21).

124. Lansperge, *Sermons,* fol. 17.

125. "Celuy crache en la face de Jesuscrist, qui condempne son superieur ou prelat, qui luy resiste en la face, ou qui se mocque des parolles & admonitions de la saincte escripture" (Ibid., fol. 72).

126. "Parquoy il convient persuader a tous chretiens que sans aulcune disputation ou curiosite de investiguer, ilz croyent en ce sacrement estre le vray corps & sang de Jesuscrist, et quilz chassent & reiectent de leur cueur toutes doubtes & difficultes qui leur pevent venir en la foy, et quilz les laissent sans discution: car la vie presente en laquelle nous sommes est de foy et non pas de congnoissance. . . . Mais de ceci cest asses." (Ibid., fol. 17).

127. "En telle compagnie assiste le sainct Esprit, non à ceulx qui sont singuliers & parciaulx en leurs affections & intentions, qui s'esloignent de la commune doctrine des saincts Peres, reprouvent la commune sentence de l'Eglise, se separent de la commune religion, voulant par leur opiniastreries, singuliers apparoistre. Ceste singularité est fille aisnee d'orgueil, plus mal apprise que sa mere, rameau plus pestilent

que sa racine, engendrant pertinacité, qui est la mere d'heresie." (Paris, *Homélies,* fol. 71).

128. "Le bon Roy en telle preuve de sa foy, & religion, à l'edification de toute l'Eglise de France, a aigrement despité Satan, & ses satellites, par lesquels comme antechrist opere ia son iniquité, qui ne peut gouster la veneration des saincts, mais au contraire, ignorans & malings, legiers & volages, comme guirouettes, qui s'esbranlent à tous vents, mesprisent leurs suffrages, reiettent leurs invocations, ont tollu des Eglises leurs images, & remembrances: & pour le comble de leur forcennerie, ont en certains lieux brisé & bruslé leur saincts os, cuidant par telles tyrannies & enrageries du tout effacer la memoire d'iceulx, tant ardemment ils zelent, & ialousent la gloire de Dieu." (Ibid., fol. 116).

129. Haton, *Mémoires,* 138.
130. Ibid., 140.
131. Archives Communales d'Amiens, BB34, fol. 83.
132. Ibid., BB35.

Chapter 13

1. Eire, *War,* 11.
2. Greengrass, *French Reformation,* 62.
3. Martin, *Métier,* 268.
4. Estienne, *Apologie,* 40.
5. Eire, *War,* 316.
6. Ibid., 173.
7. Hirsch, *Printing,* 7.

Bibliography

Primary Sources

Archival Records

Archives communales d'Agen
BB25
CC292
GG182

Archives communales d'Amiens
BB5–BB15
BB17–BB21
BB24–BB26
BB28
BB30
BB32–BB35
BB37

*Archives communales de
Boulogne-sur-Mer*
1, fol. 3b
4, fol. 6b

Archives communales de Dijon
D13

Archives communales de Grenoble
BB3
BB5–BB6
BB9
BB12
BB18
BB20
CC580
CC592
CC600

CC629
CC1406

Archives communales de Lyon
BB8
BB23
BB36
BB65

Archives communales de Nantes
CC99

Archives départementales du Gard
G586–G587
G1330

Archives départementales de la Gironde
G497
G505

*Archives départementales de la
Seine-Maritime*
G226–G232
G234
G236
G238
G242
G244–G248

Archives départementales de la Vienne
G505

327

Manuscript Sermons

Bibliothèque Nationale, Paris
Ms. fr. 1898. Anonymous sermons.
Ms. fr. 454. Despence, Claude, "Sermons du premier advenement de nostre Seigneur Iesus Christ."
Ms. fr. (Colbert) 1855. Gaigny, Jean de, "Trois homélies prechees en presence de François I."
Ms. fr. 2451. Lansperge, Jean, "Sermons."
Ms. fr. 13319. Merlin, Jacques, "Sermons."

Bibliothèque municipale de Dijon
Ms. 234 (195–1), fols. 72–77. "Recueil Vaudois."

Printed Sermons

Anonymous. *Ung notable sermon contenant l'excellence et saincteté du pur et saint vierge ioseph espoux a la tres digne mere de Dieu la viergé honoree.* Rouen: Martin Morin, n.d.
Brulefer, Étienne. *Opuscula.* Paris: Jehan Petit, 1500.
Calvin, John. *Plusieurs Sermons.* Geneva: Conrad Badius, 1558.
Cleree, Jean. *Sermones quadragesimales declamati Parisius apud sanctum Severinum.* Paris: Engleberto Marnesio, n.d.
———. *Precordialissimi ac impecciabiles de adventu Domini sermones.* Paris: Engleberto Marnesio, 1526.
Clichtove, Josse. *Sermones.* Paris: Thielmann, 1534.
Denisse, Nicolas. *Sermones residui a secunda dominica post pascha usque ad adventum.* Rouen: Martin Morin, 1509.
———. *Tabula sermonum hyemalium de tempore.* Strasbourg, 1510.
Farinier, Antoine. *Sermones viginti & unus de peccatis.* Paris, 1519.
Fillon, Artus. *Speculum curatorum una cum confessionale ac tractatu de misterio misse & his que concernunt eum de videlicet: de sacramenti altaris dignitate: utilitate: & processione. Necnon de sacerdotalibus vestimentis ad dei laudem statusque ecclesiastici decorem.* Paris, 1503.
Guilliaud, Claude. *L'oraison funèbre déclarative des gestes, meurs, vie & trespas de tresillustre prince, Claude de Lorraine, duc de Guyse & d'Aumalle.* Paris: Jehan Dallier, 1550
Illyricus, Thomas. *Sermones aurei ac excellentissimi.* Toulouse, 1521.
———, *Libellus de potestate summi pontificus.* Tours, 1523.
Ivollé, Brother. *Dix sermons de la saincte messe et ceremonies d'icelle.* In Simon Vigor, *Sermons et predications chrestiennes et catholiques du S. Sacrement de l'Autel, accommodées pour tous les jours des octaves de la feste Dieu,* ed Jean Christi. Paris: Nicolas Chesneau, 1577.
LePicart, Francois. *Les sermons et instructions chrestiennes, pour tous les iours de caresme, & feries de Pasques.* Paris: Nicolas Chesneau, 1566.
———. *Les sermons et instructions chrestiennes, pour tous les iours de l'Avent, iusques à Noel: & de tous les Dimenches & Festes, depuis Noel iusques à Caresme.* Paris: Nicolas Chesneau, 1566.
———. *Les sermons et instructions chrestiennes pour tous les dimenches & toutes les*

festes des saincts, depuis Pasques iusques à la Trinité. Paris: Nicolas Chesneau, 1566.

Maillard, Olivier. *Sermones de sanctis.* Paris: Jehan Petit, 1504.

——. *Quadragesimale opus Parisius predicatum.* Lyon: Stephan Gueygnardi, 1503.

——. *Sermones dominicales.* Lyon: Stephan Gueygnardi, 1503.

——. *Sermones de adventu.* Paris: Jehan Petit, 1506.

——. *Sermones de stipendio peccati.* Lyon: Stephan Gueygnardi, 1503.

——. *Oeuvres françaises d'Olivier Maillard,* ed. by Arthur Laborderie. Geneva: Slatkine Reprints, 1968.

Meigret, Aimé. *Sermon.* In Henry Guy ed., "Le sermon d'Aimé Meigret." *Annales de l'Université de Grenoble* 15 (1928): 181–212.

Messier, Robert. *Super epistola et evangelia totius quadragesime sermones.* Paris: Jehan Petit, 1531.

Monluc, Jean de. *Deux instructions et deux epistres faictes, & envoyees au clergé & peuple de Valence, & de Dye, par leur Evesque.* Paris: Vascosan, 1557.

——. *Sermons de l'Evesque de Valence, sur certains poincts de la religion, recueillis fidelement, ainsi qu'ilz ont esté prononcez.* Paris: Vascosan, 1558.

Nève, Joseph (ed.). *Sermons choisis de Michel Menot.* Paris: Honoré Champion, 1924.

Paris, Etienne. *Homélies suyvant les matieres traictees ès principales festes & solennitez de l'annee.* Paris: Robineau, 1553.

Pepin, Guillaume. *Sermones quadraginta de destructione Ninive.* Paris: Claude Chevallon, 1527.

——. *Rosareum aurem B. Mariae virginis.* Antwerp: Guillelmus Lesteenius and Engelbertus Gymnicus, 1656.

——. *Conciones sub numero septenario intitulatae salutate Mariam.* Antwerp: Guillelmus Lesteenius and Engelbertus Gymnicus, 1656.

——. *Conciones in septem Psalmos poenitentiales.* Antwerp: Guillelmus Lesteenius and Engelbertus Gymnicus, 1656.

——. *Conciones festorum tempore adventus, loco tertii libri, qui dicitur sanctificationis sacramentalis, illo libro praetermisso pro quolibet de festo.* Antwerp: Guillelmus Lesteenius and Engelbertus Gymnicus, 1656.

——. *Concionum dominicalium ex epistolis et evangeliis totius anni, pars hiemalis.* Antwerp: Guillelmus Lesteenius and Engelbertus Gymnicus, 1656.

——. *Concionum dominicalium ex epistolis et evangeliis totius anni, pars aestivalis.* Antwerp: Guillelmus Lesteenius and Engelbertus Gymnicus, 1656.

——. *Elucidationem in Confiteor.* Antwerp: Guillelmus Lesteenius and Engelbertus Gymnicus, 1656.

——. *Conciones de adventu Domini.* Antwerp: Guillelmus Lesteenius and Engelbertus Gymnicus, 1656.

——. *Conciones quadragesimales ad sacros evangeliorum sensus pro feriis quadragesimae mystice et moraliter explicandos.* Antwerp: Guillelmus Lesteenius and Engelbertus Gymnicus, 1656.

——. *Conciones de sanctis sive de imitatione sanctorum.* Antwerp: Guillelmus Lesteenius and Engelbertus Gymnicus, 1656.

Raulin, Jean. *Sermonum quadragesimalium.* Antwerp: Gasparus Bellerus, 1612.

——. *Sermones de eucharistia.* Paris: Jehan Petit, 1524.

——. *Opus sermonum de adventu.* Paris: Jehan Petit, 1516.

Rodier, Esprit. *Praeconium ac defensio quadragesime; cui pluribus requirentibus, ad-*

junctus est sermo de ratione institutionis divinissimi Eucharistiae sacramenti. Toulouse: Boudeville, 1552.

Scoepperus, Jean. *Sermon declarant apertement que nous signifient mystiquement plusieurs des ceremonies de l'eglise Catholique.* Paris: Nicolas Chesneau, 1571.

Tisserand, Jean. *Sermones de adventu.* Paris, 1517.

Viret, Pierre. *Quatre sermons français sur Esaie 65 (mars 1559),* ed. Henri Meylan. Lausanne: Librairie Payot, 1961.

Other Sources

Aquinas, Thomas. *Summa Theologica,* trans. Fathers of the English Dominican Province. New York: Benziger Brothers, 1947.

Augustine. *The City of God,* trans. Henry Bettenson. New York: Penguin, 1977.

———. *On Christian Doctrine,* trans. D. W. Robertson, Jr. Indianapolis: Bobbs-Merrill, 1958.

Auger, Emond. *La manière d'ouïr messe avec dévotion and fruict spirituel.* Paris: Nicolas Chesneau, 1571.

Auton, Jean d'. *Chroniques de Louis XII.* Paris: Renouard, 1893.

Barrillon, Jean. *Journal de Jean Barrillon,* ed. Pierre de Vaissière. Paris: Renouard, 1897.

Beauxamis, Thomas. *Resolution des principaux points de la religion catholique apostolique and Romaine, mis en controverse par les heretiques de nostre temps & publiez en leurs escrits.* Paris: Guillaume Cavellat, 1596.

Bernard of Clairvaux. *Sermons choisis de S. Bernard,* ed. M. de Villefore. Paris: Desprez, 1737.

Beza, Theodore. *The Life of John Calvin.* Philadelphia: J. Whetham, 1836.

———. *Histoire écclésiastique,* ed. G. Baum. Vol. 1. Paris: Fischbacher, 1883.

Bourgeois de Paris. *Le journal d'un Bourgeois de Paris sous le règne de François Ier (1515–1536),* ed. V. L. Bourrilly. Paris: Alphonše Picard, 1910.

Calvin, John. *Commentaries de Jean Calvin sur l'Ancien Testament, Tome Premier: Le Livre de la Genèse.* Geneva: Laboré et Fides, 1961.

Clichtove, Josse. *Determinatio theologice facultatis Parisiensis super doctrina Lutheriana hactenus per eam visa.* Paris, 1521.

Coyecque, Ernest. *Recueils d'actes notariés relatifs à l'histoire de Paris et de ses environs 1532–55.* Paris: Imprimérie nationale, 1924.

Crespin, Jean. *Histoire des martyrs,* ed. Daniel Bénoit. Toulouse: Société des livres religieux, 1885.

Du Bellay, Jean. *Corréspondence du Cardinal Jean du Bellay,* ed. Rémy Scheurer. Vol. 1. Paris: Klincksieck, 1969.

Duplessis d'Argentré, Charles. *Collectio judiciorum de novis erroribus.* Paris: Cailleau, 1728.

Estienne, Henri. *Apologie pour Hérodote.* The Hague: Scheurleer, 1735.

Illyricus, Thomas. *Epistola ad milites sub rege Francorum.* Toulouse: Jean, 1519.

———. *Epistola pro defensione nominis Ihesu directa ad sacrum Senatum Tholosarum.* Toulouse: Jean Favre, 1519.

———. *Epistola de ordine servando in matrimonio: ac de laudibus matrimonii ad omnes Christi fideles directa.* Toulouse: Jean Favre, 1519.

———. *Modus confidenti.* Toulouse: Jean Favre, 1523.

———. *Regule et laudes matrimonii cum invectivus feminarum in viros et viros in feminas ac remedio contra concubinas.* Toulouse: Jean Favre, 1519.

Glaumeau, Jehan. *Journal de Jehan Glaumeau, Bourges, 1541–62.* Paris: Aubry, 1867–1868.

Gouberville, sire de. *Le journal du Sire de Gouberville,* ed. Eugène Robillard de Beaurepaire. Caen: Henri de Lesques, 1892.

Haton, Claude. *Mémoirs de Claude Haton,* ed. Felix Bourquélot. Vol. 1. Paris: Imprimérie impériale, 1857.

Herminjard, A. L., *Corréspondance des réformateurs dans les pays de langue française.* Paris: Levy, 1870.

Hours, Henri. "Procès d'hérésie contre Aimé Meigret," *BHR* 19 (1857): 14–43.

Humbert de Romans. *De eruditione praedicatorum.* Rome: Sebastian à Cormelias, 1607.

Julian of Norwich. *Revelations of Divine Love.* New York: Image, 1977.

LeRiche, Guillaume, and Michel LeRiche. *Journal de Guillaume et de Michel LeRiche (de 1534 à 1586),* ed. A. D. de la Fantonelle-Mandoré. Saint-Maixent: Reversé. 1846.

Luther, Martin. *Three Treatises,* ed. Charles M. Jacobs. Philadelphia: Fortress Press, 1978.

——. *Sermons de Luther,* ed. A. Vincent. Paris: Librairie prostestante, n.d.

Maillard, Olivier. *L'épitaphe du frère Olivier Maillard.* Lyon, 1502.

Marguerite d'Angoulême. *Lettres de Marguerite d'Angoulême,* ed. F. Génin. Paris: Renouard, 1841.

Pepin, Guillaume. *De imitatione sanctorum.* Paris: Claude Chevallon, 1528.

——. *Decretales moralizate.* Caen: Angier, 1523.

——. *Expositio in Genesim.* Paris: Claude Chevallon, 1528.

——. *Expositio in Exodum.* Paris: Claude Chevallon, 1534.

——. *Expositio evangeliorum quadragesimalium.* Paris: A. Girault, 1540.

Raulin, Jean. *Doctrinale mortis.* Caen: Laurent Hostingue, 1521.

Roye, Jean de. *Journal de Jean de Roye connu sous le nom de chronique scandaleuse, 1460–83,* ed. Bernard de Mandrot. Paris: Renouard, 1896.

Versoris, Nicolas de. *Livre de raison.* Paris: G. Fagnier, 1885.

Rodier, Esprit, *Contras astrologos et divinatricem astrologiam.* Toulouse: Boudeville, 1549.

Secondary Sources

Althaus, Paul. *The Theology of Martin Luther.* Philadelphia: Fortress Press, 1966.

Alverny, Marie-Thérèse d'. "Comment les théologiens et les philosophes voient la femme." *CCM* 20 (1977): 105–29.

Andrus, T. "The Devil on the Medieval Stage in France." Ph.D. diss., Syracuse University, 1979.

Ariès, Philippe. *The Hour of Our Death.* New York: Alfred A. Knopf, 1981.

Arnaud, Eugène. *Histoire des Protestants du Dauphiné aux XVIᵉ· XVIIᵉ et XVIIIᵉ siècles.* Vol. 1: 1522–98. Geneva: Slatkine Reprints, 1970.

——. *Histoire des protestants du Vivarais et du Velay: Pays de Languedoc de la réforme à la révolution.* Geneva: Slatkine Reprints, 1979.

——. *Histoire des protestants de Provence, du Comtat Venaissin et de la principauté d'Orange.* Paris: Grassart, 1884.

Atkinson, Clarissa. *Mystic and Pilgrim: Margery Kempe.* Ithaca: Cornell University Press, 1983.

Audisio, Gabriel. *Le barbe et l'inquisiteur: Procès du barbe Pierre Griot par l'inquisiteur Jean de Roma (Apt, 1532)*. Aix: Edisud, 1979.

Avray, D. L. d'. *The Preaching of the Friars: Sermons Diffused from Paris before 1300*. Oxford: Clarendon Press, 1985.

Avray, D. L. d', and M., Tausche. "Marriage Sermons in *Ad Status* Collections of the Central Middle Ages." *AHDLMA* 47 (1980): 71–119.

Baudrier, J. *Bibliographie lyonnaise*. Reprint. Paris: F. de Noble, 1964.

Bayley, Peter. *French Pulpit Oratory, 1598–1650*. Cambridge: Cambridge University Press, 1980.

Beaurepaire, Charles de, ed. "Quittance d'un prédicāteur envoyé par Louis XI en Normandie." *Précis analytique des travaux de l'Académie des sciences, belles-lettres et arts de Rouen* (1897–98): 199–200.

Bell, Rudolph. *Holy Anorexia*. Chicago: University of Chicago Press, 1985.

Bell, Susan Groag. "Medieval Women Book Owners," *Signs* 7 (1982): 742–68.

Bennett, R. F. *The Early Dominicans: Studies in 13th Century Dominican History*. New York: Russell and Russell, 1971.

Berthoud, Gabrielle. *Antoine Marcourt*. Geneva: Droz, 1973.

Biller, P. P. A. "Birth Control in the West in the Thirteenth and Early Fourteenth Centuries." *PP* 94 (1982): 3–26.

Blaisdell, Charmarie Jenkins. "Calvin's Letters to Women: The Courting of Ladies in High Places." *SCJ* 13:3 (1982): 67–84.

Blench, J. W. *Preaching in England in the Late Fifteenth and Sixteenth Centuries: A Study of English Sermons, 1450–c. 1600*. New York: Barnes and Noble, 1964.

Bornkamm, Günther. *Paul*. New York: Harper and Row, 1969.

Bossy, John. *Christianity in the West, 1400–1700*. Oxford: Oxford University Press, 1987.

———. "The Social History of Confession in the Age of the Reformation." *TRHS* 25 (1975): 21–38.

Bourgain, L. *La chaire française au XIIᵉ siècle*. Paris: Victor Palmé, 1879.

Bourrilly, V.-L. "François Iᵉʳ et les Protestants: Les essais de concorde en 1535." *BSHPF* 49 (1900): 337–65, 477–95.

Boutruche, Robert. *Bordeaux de 1453 à 1715*. Bordeaux, 1966.

Bower, H. M. *The Fourteen of Meaux*. London: Longmans, Green, 1894.

Bratt, John. "The Role and Status of Women in the Writings of John Calvin." In Peter de Klerk, ed., *Renaissance, Reformation, Resurgence*. Grand Rapids: Calvin Theological Seminary, 1976.

Bridenthal, Renate, and Claudia Koonz, eds. *Becoming Visible: Women in European History*. Boston: Houghton Mifflin, 1977.

Brooks, Peter, ed. *Reformation Principle and Practice: Essays in Honour of Arthur Geoffrey Dickens*. London: Scolar Press, 1980.

Broutin, Paul. *L'évêque dans la tradition du XVIᵉ siècle*. Mechelen: Desclée de Brouwer, 1953.

Brown, D. Catherine. *Pastor and Laity in the Theology of Jean Gerson*. Cambridge: Cambridge University Press, 1987.

Brundage, James A. "Carnal Delight: Canonistic Theories of Sexuality," in Stephan Kuttner and Kenneth Pennington, eds., *Proceedings of the Fifth International Congress of Medieval Canon Law*. Vatican City, 1980. Pages 361–85.

———. *Law, Sex and Medieval Society*. Philadelphia: University of Pennsylvania Press, 1987.

Bullough, Vern. "The Prostitute in the Middle Ages." *Studies in Medieval Culture* 10 (1977): 9–17.

Bynum, Caroline Walker. ". . . And Women His Humanity?: Female Imagery in the Religious Writings of the Later Middle Ages." In Caroline Walker Bynum, Steven Harnell, and Paula Richman, eds., *Gender and Religion: On the Complexity of Symbols*. Boston: Beacon Press, 1986. Pages 257–88.

Bynum, Caroline Walker. *Holy Feast & Holy Fast: The Religious Significance of Food to Medieval Women*. Berkeley: University of California Press, 1987.

———. "The Body of Christ in the Later Middle Ages: A Reply to Leo Steinberg." *RQ* 39 (1986): 399–439.

———. *Jesus as Mother: Studies in the Spirituality of the High Middle Ages*. Berkeley: University of California Press, 1982.

Cameron, Euan. *The Reformation of the Heretics*. Oxford: Clarendon Press, 1984.

Caplan, Harry. "Classical Rhetoric and the Mediaeval Theory of Preaching." *CP* 28 (1933): 73–96.

———. "The Four Senses of Scriptural Interpretation and the Mediaeval Theory of Preaching." *CP* 28 (1933): 282–90.

———. "'Henry of Hesse' on the Art of Preaching." *PMLA* 48 (1933): 340–61.

———. "Rhetorical Invention in Some Mediaeval Tractates on Preaching." *Speculum* (1927): 284–95.

Carrière, Victor. "Guillaume Farel: Propagandiste de la réformation." *RHEF* 20 (1934): 37–78.

Chapotin, Marie-Dominique. "Le couvent royal de Saint-Louis d'Évreux." In *Etudes historiques sur la province dominicaine de France*. Paris: Lecoffre, 1890. Pages 1–102.

Cheetham, Nicolas. *Keepers of the Keys: A History of the Popes from St. Peter to John Paul I*. New York: Charles Scribner's Sons, 1983.

Chevalier, Bernard. "Olivier Maillard et la réforme des Cordeliers (1482–1502)." *RHEF* 65:174 (1979): 25–39.

Chevalier, Bernard, and Robert Sauzet, eds. *Les réformes enracinement socio-culturel. XXVᵉ colloque intérnational de Tours*. Paris: Editions de la Maisnie, 1982.

Chevalier, Pierre. *Henri III*. Paris: Fayard, 1985.

Chiffoleau, Jacques. *La comptabilité de l'au-delà*. Rome: Farnese, 1980.

Chrisman, Miriam. *Lay Culture, Learned Culture: Books and Social Change in Strasbourg, 1480–1599*. New Haven: Yale University Press, 1982.

———. *Strasbourg and the Reform: A Study in the Process of Change*. New Haven: Yale University Press, 1967.

———. "Women and the Reformation in Strasbourg 1490–1530," *ARG* 63 (1972): 143–67.

Clark, Elizabeth, and Herbert, Richardson. *Women and Religion*. New York: Harper and Row, 1977.

Clerval, J.-A. *Régistre des procès verbaux de la faculté de théologie de Paris*. Paris: Lecoffre, 1917.

———. *De Judoci Clichtovei: Vita et operibus, 1472–1543*. Paris: Picard, 1894.

Cohn, Norman. *The Pursuit of the Millenium*. New York: Harper, 1961.

Congar, Yves. *Luther, sa foi, sa réforme*. Paris: Cerf, 1983.

Contrasty, J. "Les prédicateurs du XVIᵉ siècle à Sainte-Marie-de-la-Dalbade à Toulouse." *RHT* 34:114 (1947): 1–102.

Cox, Charles. *Pulpits, Lecterns, and Organs in English Churches*. London: Oxford University Press, 1915.

Crane, T. F. "Medieval Sermon Books and Stories." *Proceedings of the American Philosophical Society* 21 (1884): 49–78.

Crouzet, Denis. "La représentation du temps à l'époque de la Ligue." *RH* 270 (1983): 297–388.

Cruel, Rudolf. *Geschichte der deutschen Predigt im Mittelalter.* Darmstadt: Wissenschaftliche Buchgesellschaft, 1966.

Dacheux, L. *Un réformateur catholique à la fin du XVᵉ siècle: Jean Geiler de Kaisersberg.* Paris: Charles de la Grave, 1876.

Dahmus, John. "Preaching to the Laity in Fifteenth Century Germany: Johannes Nider's 'Harps.'" *JEH* 12 (1982): 55–68.

Dahmus, Joseph. *Dictionary of Medieval Civilization.* New York: Macmillan, 1984.

Dargan, Edward Charles. *A History of Preaching from the Apostolic Fathers to the Great Reformers, A.D. 70–1572.* New York: Burt Franklin, 1968.

Darricau, Raymond. "Quelques aspects de la réforme dominicaine en Provence au XVᵉ siècle." *RHEF* 65:174 (1979): 13–24.

———. "La réforme des reguliers en France de la fin du XVᵉ siècle à la fin des guerres de religion." *RHEF* 65:174 (1979): 5–12.

Davis, Natalie Zemon. "City Women and Religious Change." In *Society and Culture in Early Modern France.* Stanford, CA: Stanford Press, 1975.

Davy, Marie-Madeleine. *Les sermons universitaires parisiens de 1230–31.* Paris: J. Vrin, 1931.

Deanesley, Margaret. *The Lollard Bible and Other Medieval Biblical Versions.* Cambridge: Cambridge University Press, 1920. Reprint, 1966.

Degert, Antoine. "Procès de huit évêques français suspects de calvinisme." *RQH* 76 (1904): 61–108.

Delaruelle, Étienne. *La piété populaire au moyen âge.* Turin: Bottega d'Erasmo, 1975.

Delcorno, Carlo. *Giordano da Pisa e l'antica predicazione volgare.* Florence: Biblioteca delle lettere italiane, 1975.

———. *La predicazione nell'eta comunale.* Florence, 1974.

Delorme, Ferdinand. "Olivier Maillard et le Bx Duns Scot à Toulouse." *La France franciscaine* 2d ser., 17 (1934): 347–65.

Delumeau, Jean. *Catholicism between Luther and Voltaire.* London: Burns and Oates, 1977.

———. *La peur en occident, XIVᵉ–XVIIIᵉ siècles.* Paris: Fayard, 1978.

———. "Pouvoir, peur et hérésie au début des temps moderne." In Myriam Yardeni, ed., *Modernité et nonconformisme en France à travers les âges.* Leiden: E. J. Brill, 1983.

Demeuldre, Paul. "Frère Jean Angeli: Episode des conflits entre le clergé séculier et le clergé régulier à Tournai (1482–1483)." *Bulletin de l'Academie Royale des sciences, des lettres et des beaux arts de Belgique* 5th ser., 8 (1898): 313–68.

Derville, Alain. "Jean Vitrier et les religieuses de Sainte-Marguerite." *RN* 42 (1960): 207–39.

Desgraves, Louis. *Répertoire bibliographique des livres imprimés en France au seizième siècle.* Bordeaux: Heitz, 1968–1980.

Diefendorf, Barbara. "Prologue to a Massacre: Popular Unrest in Paris, 1557–1572." *AHR* 90 (1985): 1067–91.

———. "Simon Vigor: A Radical Preacher in Sixteenth-Century France." *SCJ* 18 (1987): 399–410.

Dodd, C. H. *The Apostolic Preaching and Its Development: Three Lectures.* New York: Harper and Bros., 1936.

Dolan, Claire. *Entre tours et clochers: Les gens d'église à Aix-en-Provence au XVI* *siècle.* Sherbrooke, Que.: Centre d'études de la Renaissance, 1981.

Douglass, E. Jane Dempsey. *Justification in Late Medieval Preaching: A Study of John Geiler of Keisersberg.* Leiden: E. J. Brill, 1966.

――――. "Women and the Continental Reformation." In Rosemary Ruether, ed., *Religion and Sexism:* Images of Women in the Jewish and Christian Traditions. New York: Simon and Schuster, 1974; 292–318.

DuBruck, E. "The Devil and Hell in Medieval French Drama." *Romania* 100 (1979): 165–79.

Duggan, Lawrence. "The Unresponsiveness of the Late Medieval Church: A Reconsideration." *SCJ* 9 (1978): 3–26.

Eire, Carlos M. N. *War against the Idols: The Reformation of Worship from Erasmus to Calvin.* Cambridge: Cambridge University Press, 1986.

Eisenstein, Elizabeth L. *The Printing Press as an Agent of Change.* Cambridge: Cambridge University Press, 1979.

Emery, Richard W. *The Friars in Medieval France.* New York: Columbia, 1962.

Farge, James. *Biographical Register of Paris Doctors of Theology, 1500–1536.* Toronto: Pontifical Institute of Medieval Studies, 1980.

――――. *Orthodoxy and Reform in Early Reformation France.* Leiden: E. J. Brill, 1985.

Farrar, Frederic W. *A History of Interpretation: Eight Lectures.* New York: E. P. Dutton, 1886.

Febvre, Lucien. "Une question mal posée: Les origines de la réforme française et le problème général des causes de la réforme." *RH* 161 (1929): 1–73.

Febvre, Lucien, and Henri-Jean Martin. *The Coming of the Book: The Impact of Printing, 1450–1800.* London: NLD, 1976.

Feret, H. M. *La faculté de théologie et ses docteurs les plus célèbres: Moyen âge et époque moderne.* Paris: Picard, 1896.

――――. "Vie intellectuelle et vie scolaire dans l'ordre des prêcheurs." *AHD* 53 (1945): 5–37.

Fiot, Robert. "Saint François de Paule et la réforme des réguliers (Plessis-les-Tours, 1483–1507)." *RHEF* 65 (1979): 56–74.

Fossier, Robert. *Histoire de la Picardie.* Toulouse: Privat, 1974.

France, Peter. "Les protestants à Grenoble au XVI⁰ siècle." *CH* 7 (1962): 319–31.

Frank, G. *The Medieval French Drama.* New York: Oxford University Press, 1954.

Fromenthal, Jacques. *La réforme en Bourgogne aux XVI* *et XVII* *siècles.* Paris: Société des Belles Lettres, 1968.

Fuhrmann, Horst. *Germany in the High Middle Ages, c. 1050–1200.* Cambridge: Cambridge University Press, 1986.

Gadol, Joan Kelly. *Women, History, and Theory.* Chicago: University of Chicago Press, 1984.

Galpern, A. N., *The Religions of the People in Sixteenth-Century Champagne.* Cambridge: Harvard University Press, 1976.

Garrisson-Estèbe, Janine. *Protestants du Midi, 1559–1598.* Toulouse: Privat, 1977.

Gillot, A., and Charles Boëll. *Supplément au catalogue des livres de la bibliothèque d'un chanoine d'Autun: Claude Guilliaud, 1493–1551.* Autun: Mémoires de la société Eduenne, new ser., 1890.

Gilson, Etienne. "De quelques raisonnements scripturaires usités au moyen âge." In *Les idées et les lettres.* Paris: J. Vrin, 1932. Pages 155–69.

————. "Michel Menot et la technique du sermon médiévale." *In Les idées et les lettres*. Paris: J. Vrin, 1932. Pages 93–154.

Godet, Marc. *La congrégation de Montaigu (1490–1580)*. Paris: Champion, 1912.

Godet, Marcel. "Consultation de Tours pour la réforme de l'église de France (12 novembre 1493)." *RHEF* 2 (1911): 175–96, 333–48.

Godfroy, Marie-France. "La prédicateur franciscain Thomas Illyricus à Toulouse (novembre 1518–mai 1519)." *AM* 97 (1985): 101–14.

Godin, André. *Érasme: Vies de Jean Vitrier et de John Colet*. Angers: Editions Moreana, 1982.

————. *L'homéliaire de Jean Vitrier*. Geneva: Droz, 1971.

Godineau, G. "Statuts synodaux inédits du diocèse de Bourges promulgués par Jean Coeur en 1451." *RHEF* 72 (1986): 49–66.

Gold, Penny Schine. *The Lady and the Virgin: Image, Attitude, and Experience in Twelfth-Century France*. Chicago: University of Chicago Press, 1985.

Gottlieb, Beatrice. "The Problem of Feminism in the Fifteenth Century." In Julius Kirschner and Suzanne Wemple, eds. *Women of the Medieval World*. New York: Basil Blackwell, 1985. Pages 337–64.

Graef, Hilda. *Mary: A History of Doctrine and Devotion*. New York: Sheed and Ward, 1973.

Greengrass, Mark. *The French Reformation*. Oxford: Basil Blackwell, 1987.

Grimm, Harold J. "The Human Element in Luther's Sermons." *ARG* 49 (1957): 50–60.

Grin, Edmond. "Deux sermons de Pierre Viret, leurs thèmes théologiques et leur actualité." *TZ* 18 (1962): 116–32.

Harding, Robert. "Revolution and Reform in the Holy League: Angers, Rennes, Nantes," *JMH* 53 (1981): 379–416.

Harkness, Georgia. *Women in Church and Society*. Nashville: Abingdon Press, 1972.

Haureau, B. *Histoire littéraire de la France*, vol. 26. Paris: Imprimérie Nationale, 1973.

Hauser, H. *Études sur la réforme française*. Paris: Picard, 1909.

————. "The French Reformation and the French People in the Sixteenth Century." *ARH* 4 (1899): 217–27.

Havette, R. "La notation des sermons à l'audition et la sténographie." *RB* (1903): 321–39.

Heitmüller, Wilhem. "Hellenistic Christianity before Paul." *In The Writings of St. Paul*, ed. Wayne A. Meeks. New York: W. W. Norton, 1972.

Heller, Henry. "Famine, Revolt and Heresy at Meaux: 1521–1525." *ARG* 68 (1977): 133–57.

————. "Nicolas of Cusa and Early French Evangelism." *ARG* 63 (1972): 6–21.

Hempsall, David. "The Languedoc 1520–1540: A Study of Pre-Calvinist Heresy in France." *ARG* 62 (1971): 225–44.

Hengel, Martin. *Between Jesus and Paul*. Philadelphia: Fortress Press, 1983.

Herlihy, David. *Medieval Households*. Cambridge, MA: Harvard University Press, 1985.

Higman, Francis. "Le levain et l'évangile." In *Histoire de l'édition française*. Paris: Promodis, 1982.

Hilarion de Coste, F. *Le parfait écclésiastique ou l'histoire de la vie et de la mort de François LePicart, seigneur d'Attily & de Villeron, docteur en théologie de Paris & doyen de Saint-Germain l'Auxerrois*. Paris: Sebastien Cramoisy, 1658.

Hinnebusch, William A. *The Early English Friars Preacher*. Vatican City: Institutum Historicum FF. Praedicatorum, 1951.

————. *The History of the Dominican Order: Intellectual and Cultural Life to 1500.* New York: Alba House, 1973.

Hirsch, Rudolf. *Printing, Selling, and Reading, 1450–1550.* Wiesbaden: Harrassowitz, 1967.

————. "Surgant's List of Recommended Books for Preachers." *RQ* 20 (1967): 199–210.

Hoffman, Philip T. *Church and Community in the Diocese of Lyon, 1500–1789.* New Haven, CT: Yale University Press, 1984.

Hugues, J.-P. *Histoire de l'église réformée d'Anduze depuis son origine jusqu'à la révolution française.* Paris: Privat, 1864.

Huizinga, J. *The Waning of the Middle Ages.* New York: Doubleday, 1954.

Imbart de la Tour, P. *Les origines de la réforme.* Paris: Hachette, 1909.

Jacquin, A. M. "La prédestination d'après St. Augustin." *Miscellanea agostiniana* 2 (1931): 853–78.

Jervell, Jacob. *The Unknown Paul.* Minneapolis: Augsburg, 1984.

Jungmann, Joseph A. *The Mass of the Roman Rite: Its Origins and Development.* New York: Benziger Brothers, 1951.

Kelley, Donald. *The Beginning of Ideology: Consciousness and Society in the French Reformation.* Cambridge: Cambridge University Press, 1981.

Kendall, Paul. *Louis XI.* New York: W. W. Norton, 1971.

Kepler, Thomas. *Contemporary Thinking about Paul.* New York: Abingdon-Cokesbury Press, 1950.

Kieckhefer, Richard. *Uniquiet Souls: Fourteenth-Century Saints and Their Religious Milieu.* Chicago: University of Chicago Press, 1984.

Kiessling, Elmer Carl. *The Early Sermons of Luther and their Relation to the Pre-Reformation Sermon.* Grand Rapids, MI: Zondervan, 1935.

Kingdon, Robert. *Geneva and the Coming of the Wars of Religion in France, 1555–1563.* Geneva: Droz, 1956.

Klaits, Joseph. *Servants of Satan: The Age of the Witch-Hunts.* Bloomington: Indiana University Press, 1985.

Klapisch-Zuber, Christiane. *Women, Family, and Ritual in Renaissance Italy,* Chicago: University of Chicago Press, 1985.

Knecht, R. J. *Francis I.* Cambridge: Cambridge University Press, 1982.

Knowles, David. *The Evolution of Medieval Thought.* New York: Vintage Press, 1962.

Krailsheimer, A. J. *Rabelais and the Franciscans.* Oxford: Clarendon Press, 1963.

Kristeller, Paul. *Renaissance Thought and Its Sources.* New York: Columbia, 1979.

LaBarge, Margaret Wade. *A Small Sound of the Trumpet: Women in Medieval Life.* Boston: Beacon Press, 1986.

Labitte, Charles. *De la démocratie chez les prédicateurs de la Ligue.* Paris: Joubert, 1841.

Lambert, M. D. *Medieval Heresy: Popular Movements from Bogomil to Hus.* London: Arnold, 1977.

Langlois, C.-V. "L'éloquence sacrée au moyen âge." *Revue des deux mondes* 115 (1893): 170–201.

Larroque, Philippe Tamizey de. *Notes et documents inédits pour servir à la biographie de Jean de Monluc, évêque de Valence.* Paris: Auguste Aubry, 1868.

Lawrence, C. H. *Medieval Monasticism: Forms of Religious Life in Western Europe in the Middle Ages.* London: Longman, 1984.

Lea, Henry Charles. *A History of the Inquisition of the Middle Ages,* vol. 3. New York: Russell and Russell, 1953.

Le Bras, Gabriel. *Études de sociologie religieuse.* Paris: Presses universitaires de France, 1955–1956.

———. *Sociologie et religion.* Paris: Fayard, 1958.

Lecoy de la Marche, Albert. *La chaire française au Moyen Age.* Geneva: Slatkine Reprints, 1974.

Leff, Gordon. "The Apostolic Ideal in Later Medieval Ecclesiology." *JTS,* new ser., 18 (1967): 58–82.

———. *The Dissolution of the Medieval Outlook.* New York: New York University Press, 1976.

———. *Hersey in the Later Middle Ages: The Relation of Heterodoxy to Dissent, c. 1250–c.1450.* New York: Barnes and Noble, 1967.

———. *Paris and Oxford Universities in the Thirteenth and Fourteenth Centuries: An Institutional and Intellectual History.* New York: John Wiley, 1968.

LeGoff, Jacques. *The Birth of Purgatory.* Chicago: University of Chicago Press, 1981.

Lemaître, Nicole. "Confession privée et confession publique dans les paroisses du XVIᵉ siècle." *RHEF* 69 (1983): 189–208.

———. *Le Rouergue flamboyant: Clergé et paroisses du diocèse de Rodez, 1417–1563.* Paris: Cerf, 1988.

Lengwiler, Eduard. *Die vorreformatorischen Prädikaturen der deutschen Schweiz von ihrer Entstehung bis 1530.* Freiburg: Kanisius, 1955.

Lesnick, Daniel. *Preaching in Medieval Florence: The Social World of Franciscan and Dominican Spirituality.* Athens: University of Georgia Press, 1989.

Lièvre, Auguste. *Histoire des protestants et des églises réformées du Poitou.* Paris: Grassart, 1856.

Linder, Robert. *The Political Ideas of Pierre Viret.* Geneva: Droz, 1964.

Lippens, Hugolin. "Jean Glapion, Défenseur de la réforme de l'Observance." *AFH* 44 (1951): 3–70.

Loirette, Gabriel. "Catholiques et Protestants en Languedoc à la veille des guerres civiles (1560)." *RHEF* 23 (1937): 503–25.

Longère, Jean. *La prédication médiévale.* Paris: Études augustiniennes, 1983.

Mabille de Poncheville, Andrée. *Bienheureux Oliver Maillard.* Paris: Éditions franciscaines, 1946.

Macquarrie, John. *Principles of Christian Theology.* New York: Charles Scribner's Sons, 1977.

Major, J. Russell. "Noble Income, Inflation, and the Wars of Religion in France." *AHR* 86 (1981): 21–48.

———. *Representative Institutions in Renaissance France, 1421–1559.* Madison: University of Wisconsin Press, 1960.

Mandrou, Robert. "Hérétiques méconnus du XVIᵉ siècle européen" In Myriam Yardeni, ed., *Modernité et nonconformisme en France à travers les âges.* Leiden: E. J. Brill, 1983.

———. "Pourquoi se réformer?" In Robert Mandrou, Janine Estèbe, Daniel Ligou, et al., eds., *Histoire des Protestants en France.* Toulouse: Privat, 1977.

Martin, Hervé. *Le métier du prédicateur à la fin du Moyen Age, 1350–1520.* Paris: Cerf, 1988.

———. "La ministère de la parole en France septentrionale de la peste noire à la réforme." Dissertation for the doctorat d'état, Université de Paris IV/Sorbonne, 1986.

————. *Les ordres mendiants en Bretagne, vers 1230–vers 1530: Pauvreté volontaire et prédication à la fin du moyen-âge.* Rennes: Institut armoricain de recherches historiques, 1975.

————. "Les prédications déviantes, du début du XVe siècle au début du XVe siècle, dans les provinces septentrionales de la France." In Bernard Chevalier and Robert Sauzet, eds., *Les réformes enracinement socio-culturel: XXe* colloque de Tours. Paris: Editions de la Maisnie, 1985. Pages 251–65.

Massaut, Jean-Pierre. *Critique et tradition à la veille de la réforme en France.* Paris: J. Vrin, 1974.

Mauriac, R.M. "Un réformateur catholique: Thomas Illyricus, frère mineur de l'Observance." *Études franciscaines* 23: (1934): 329–47; 24 (1935): 58–71.

McCue, James. "Luther and the Problem of Popular Preaching." *SCJ* 16 (1985): 33–43.

McGinniss, Fredrick J. "Preaching Ideals and Practice in Counter-Reformation Rome." *SCJ* 11 (1980): 109–27.

McIntyre, Olivia Holloway. "The Celestines of Paris: Monastic Life and Thought in the Sixteenth Century." Ph.D. thesis, Stanford University, 1984.

Meeks, Wayne A., ed. *The Writings of Saint Paul.* New York: W. W. Norton, 1972.

Méray, Antony. *La vie au temps des libres prêcheurs,* 2 vols. Paris: Claudin, 1878.

Meyer, Albert de. *La congrégation d'Hollande ou la réforme dominicaine en territoire bourguignonne, 1465–1515.* Liège: Soledi, 1946.

Moeller, Bernd. "Piety in Germany around 1500." In Steven Ozment, ed., *The Reformation in Medieval Perspective.* Chicago, Quadrangle, 1971. Pages 50–75.

Moore, W.G. "Historical Revision: The Early French Reformation." *History* 25 (1940): 48–53.

Moorman, John. *A History of the Franciscan Order from Its Origins to the Year 1517.* Oxford: Clarendon Press, 1968.

Moreau, Gerard. *Histoire du protestantisme à Tournai jusqu'à la veille de la révolution des Pays-Bas.* Paris: Les Belles Lettres, 1962.

Mosher, Joseph Albert. *The Exemplum in the Early Religious and Didactic Literature of England.* New York: Columbia University Press, 1911.

Mours, Samuel. *La Protestantisme en France au XVIe siècle.* Paris: Librairie protestante, 1959.

Mousseaux, M. *Aux sources françaises de la réforme: La Brie protestante.* Paris: Librairie protestante, n.d.

Murphy, James. *Rhetoric in the Middle Ages.* Berkeley: University of California Press, 1974.

Nicholls, David. "Inertia and Reform in the Pre-Tridentine French Church: The Response to Protestantism in the Diocese of Rouen." *JEH* 32 (1981): 185–97.

————. "Social Change and Early Protestantism in France: Normandy, 1520–62." *European Studies Review* 10 (1980); 279–308.

Oakley, Francis. *The Western Church in the Later Middle Ages.* Ithaca, NY: Cornell University Press, 1979.

Oberman, Heiko A. *Forerunners of the Reformation: The Shape of Late Medieval Thought.* Philadelphia: Fortress Press, 1981.

————. *The Harvest of Medieval Theology.* Durham, N.C.: Labyrinth Press, 1983.

Olin. John C. *The Catholic Reformation: Savonarola to Ignatius Loyola, Reform in the Church, 1495–1540.* New York: Harper and Row, 1969.

O'Malley, John. *Praise and Blame in Renaissance Rome*. Durham, NC: Duke University Press, 1979.

Otis. Leah L. *Prostitution in Medieval Society*. Chicago: University of Chicago Press, 1985.

Oursel, C. *Notes pour servir à l'histoire de la réforme en Normandie au temps de François Ier*. Caen: Henri Deslesques, 1913.

Owst, G. R. *Preaching in Medieval England: An Introduction to Sermon Manuscripts of the Period, 1350–1450*. Cambridge University Press, 1926.

Ozment, Steven. *The Reformation: A Guide to Research*. St. Louis: Center for Reformation Research, 1982.

———. *The Reformation in the Cities: The Appeal of Protestantism to Sixteenth-Century Germany and Switzerland*. New Haven: Yale University Press, 1975.

———. *When Fathers Ruled: Family Life in Reformation Europe*. Cambridge: Harvard University Press, 1983.

Pelikan, Jaroslav. *The Christian Tradition: A History of the Development of Doctrine: Reformation of Church and Dogma (1300—1700)*. Chicago: University of Chicago Press, 1984.

———. *Jesus through the Centuries*. New Haven: Yale University Press, 1985.

Pellechet, Marie. *Catalogue des livres de la bibliothèque d'un chanoine d'Autun: Claude Guilliaud, 1493–1551*. Autun: Mémoires de la société Eduenne, new ser., 1890.

Petit de Julleville, L. *Histoire de la langue et de la littérature française: Moyen âge*. Paris: Armand Colin, 1896.

Petry, Ray, ed. *No Uncertain Sound: Sermons that Shaped the Pulpit Tradition*. Philadelphia: Westminister Press, 1948.

Picot, Émile. *Artus Fillon: Chanoine d'Evreux et de Rouen, puis évêque de Senlis*. Evreux: Herissey, 1911.

Piton, M. "L'idéal épiscopal selon les prédicateurs français de la fin du XVe siècle et du début du XVIe." *RHE* (1966): 77–118, 393–423.

Poorter, A. de. "Un manuel de prédication médiévale." *RNP* 25 (1923): 192–209.

Poton, Didier. "Aux origines du protestantisme en Basses Cevennes." *BSHPF* (1982): 469–88.

Power, Eileen. *Medieval Women*. Cambridge: Cambridge University Press, 1975.

Procacci, Giuliano. "La Provence à la veille des guerres de religion: Une période décisive: 1535–45." *RHMC* 5 (1958): 249–50.

Prudhomme, A. *Simples notes sur Pierre de Sebiville*. Bourgoin: Vauvillez, 1884.

Quétif, J., and J. Echard. *Scriptores ordinis praedicatorum*. New York: Franklin, 1959.

Raynal, Louis. *Histoire du Berry*. Bourges: Vermeil, 1844.

Recordon, C.-L. B. *Le protestantisme en Champagne*. Paris: Librairie françaises et étrangères, 1863.

Reeves, Marjorie. *The Influence of Prophecy in the Later Middle Ages: A Study in Joachimism*. Oxford: Clarendon Press, 1969.

Reinburg, Virginia. "Popular Prayers in Late Medieval and Reformation France." Ph.D. diss., Princeton University, 1985.

Renaudet, A. *Préréforme et humanisme à Paris pendant les premières guerres d'Italie*. Paris: Honoré Champion, 1916.

Renouard, Philippe. *Imprimeurs et libraires Parisiens du XVIe siècle*. Paris: Baaleu-Banville, 1969.

Reynaud, Hector. *Jean de Monluc, évêque de Valence et de Die*. Geneva: Slatkine Reprints, 1969.

Roelker, Nancy Lyman. "The Appeal of Calvinism to French Noblewomen in the Sixteenth Century." *JIH* 2 (1972): 391–418.

———. "The Role of Noblewomen in the French Reformation." *ARG* 63 (1972): 168–95.

Rogers, Katharine M. *The Troublesome Helpmate: A History of Misogyny in Literature*. Seattle: University of Washington Press, 1966.

Rossiaud, Jacques. *Medieval Prostitution*. New York: Basil Blackwell, 1988.

———. "Prostitution, jeunesse et société dans les villes du sudest au XVIᵉ siècle." *Annales: E.S.C.* 31 (1976): 289–320.

Roth, Dorothea, *Die mittelalterliche Predigttheorie und das Manuale curatorum des Johann Ulrich Surgant*. Basel and Stuttgart: Helbing and Lichtenhahn, 1956.

Rubin, Miri. *Corpus Christi: The Eucharist in Late Medieval Culture*. Cambridge: Cambridge University Press, 1991.

Russell, Jeffrey Burton. *The Devil in the Middle Ages*. Ithaca, NY: Cornell University Press, 1984.

Samouillan, Alexandre. *Olivier Maillard: Sa prédication et son temps*. Toulouse: Edouard, 1891.

Saxer, Victor. *Le culte de Marie Madeleine des origines à la fin du Moyen Age*. Paris: Clavreuil, 1959.

Schmidt, Charles. *Gerard Roussel: Prédicateur de la reine Marguerite de Navarre*. Geneva: Slatkine Reprints, 1970.

Schmitt, Jean-Claude. *Prêcher d'exemples*. Paris: Stock, 1985.

———. *Le saint lévrier: Guinefort, guérisseur d'enfants depuis le XIIIᵉ siècle*. Paris: Flammarion, 1979.

Schneider, Stanley. "Luther, Preaching, and the Reformation." In Fred W. Meuser and Stanley D. Schneider, eds., *Interpreting Luther's Legacy*. Minneapolis: Augsburg Publishing House, 1969. Pages 120–35.

Schoeps, H. J. *Paul: The Theology of the Apostle in the Light of Jewish History*. Philadelphia: Westminster Press, 1961.

Scott, Ernest. "Difficulties in Paul's Religion." In Thomas Kepler, ed., *Contemporary Thinking about Paul*. New York: Abingdon-Cokesbury Press, 1950.

Scribner, Robert. *For the Sake of Simple Folk: Popular Propaganda for the German Reformation*. Cambridge: Cambridge University Press, 1981.

Serent, Antoine de. *Les frères mineurs français en face du protestantisme au XVIᵉ siècle*. Paris: Société et librairie St. François d'Assise, 1930.

Sessevalle, François de. *Histoire générale de l'ordre de Saint François: Le moyen âge (1209–1517)*, vol. 2. LePuy-en-Velay: La Haute-Loire, 1937.

Siggins, Ian. *Luther and His Mother*. Philadelphia: Fortress Press, 1981.

Stauffer, Richard. "Un Calvin méconnu: Le prédicateur de Genève." *BSHPF* 123 (1977): 184–203.

Steinmetz, David. *Luther in Context*. Bloomington: Indiana University Press, 1986.

Stock, Brian. *The Implications of Literacy: Written Language and Models of Interpretation in the Eleventh and Twelfth Centuries*. Princeton: Princeton University Press, 1983.

Stone, Lawrence. *The Family, Sex, and Marriage in England, 1500 to 1800*. New York: Harper and Row, 1979.

Strohl, Henri. "La théorie et la pratique de quatres ministères de Strasbourg avant l'arrivée de Calvin." *BSHPF* 84 (1935): 184–203.

Sypher, G. Wylie. "Faisant ce qu'il leur vient à plaisir: Images of Protestantism in

French Catholic Polemic on the Eve of the Religious Wars." *SCJ* 11 (1980): 59–84.

Tavard, George. *Woman in Christian Tradition*. Notre Dame, IN: University of Notre Dame Press, 1973.

Tentler, Thomas. *Sin and Confession on the Eve of the Reformation*. Princeton: Princeton University Press, 1977.

Thomas, Keith. *Religion and the Decline of Magic*. New York: Charles Scribner's Sons, 1971.

Toussaert, Jacques. *Le sentiment religieuse en Flandre à la fin du Moyen Âge*. Paris: Plon, 1963.

Tribout de Morembert, Henri. *La réforme à Metz: Le luthéranisme, 1519–1552,* vol. 1. Nancy: Annales de l'est, 1969.

Trinkaus, Charles, ed. *The Pursuit of Holiness in Late Medieval and Renaissance Religion*. Leiden: E. J. Brill, 1974.

Tubach, F. C. *Index Exemplorum: A Handbook of Medieval Religious Tales*. Helsinki: Suomalainen Tiedeakatemia, 1969.

Vacant, A., E. Mangenot, and E. Amman, eds. *Dictionnaire de théologie catholique*. Paris: Letouzey et Ané, 1899–1950.

Vann, Richard T. "Toward a New Lifestyle: Women in Preindustrial Capitalism." In Renate Bridenthal and Claudia Koonz, eds. *Becoming Visible: Women in European History*. Boston: Houghton Mifflin, 1977.

Vauchez, André. *La sainteté en occident aux dernières siècles du Moyen Age d'après les procès de canonisation et les documents hagiographiques*. Rome: École française de Rome, 1981.

Veissière, Michel. "Le groupe évangélique de Meaux à la lumière de quelques travaux récents." *Bullétin de la Société d'histoire et d'art du diocèse de Meaux* 24 (1973): 1–9.

Venard, Marc. "L'église d'Avignon au XVIème siècle." Dissertation, l'Université de Paris IV, 1977.

Vienot, John. *Histoire de la réforme française des origines à l'édit de Nantes*. Paris: Fischbacher, 1926.

Vogler, Bernard. *Le clergé protestant rhénan au siècle de la réforme (1555–1619)*. Paris: Ophrys, 1976.

Vuilleumier, H. *Histoire de l'église réformée du pays de Vaud*. Lausanne: Éditions la Concorde, 1927.

Wadding, Lucas. *Scriptores ordinis minorum*. Florence: Quaracchi, 1933.

Warner, Marina. *Alone of All Her Sex: The Myth and Cult of the Virgin Mary*. New York: Alfred A. Knopf, 1976.

Watts, Alan W. *Myth and Ritual in Christianity*. Boston: Beacon Press, 1968.

Weinstein, Donald. *Savonarola and Florence: Prophecy and Patriotism in the Renaissance*. Princeton: Princeton University Press, 1970.

Weinstein, Donald, and Rudolph Bell. *Saints and Society: The Two Worlds of Western Christendom, 1000–1700*. Chicago: University of Chicago Press, 1982.

Weiss, Nathanaël. "Documents inédits pour servir à l'histoire de la réforme sous François I$^{\text{er.}}$" *BSHPF* 34 (1885): 164–77.

———. "L'hérésie dans le Maine en 1535." *BSHPF* 36 (1887): 58–61.

———. "Une mission à la foire de Guibray: Lettre d'un ministre Normand à Calvin, août 1561." *BSHPF* 20 (1879): 455–64.

———. "Les premières professions de foi des protestants français, 1532–47." *BSHPF* 43 (1894): 57–74.

————. "La réformateur Aimé Meigret." *BSHPF* 39 (1890): 245–69.

————. "La réforme à Bourges au XVIᵉ siècle." *BSHPF* 53 (1904): 307–478.

————. "La réforme à Metz et à Thionville en 1524." *BSHPF* 36 (1887): 453–58.

Wemple, Suzanne. *Women in Frankish Society: Marriage and the Cloister, 500 to 900.* Philadelphia: University of Pennsylvania Press, 1981.

Wiesner, Merry. "Women's Defense of their Public Role." In Mary Beth Rose, ed., *Women in the Middle Ages and Renaissance: Literary and Historical Perspectives.* Syracuse: Syracuse: Syracuse University Press, 1986.

Winters, R. *Francis Lambert of Avignon.* Philadelphia: United Lutheran Publishing House, 1938.

Wolfe, Martin. *The Fiscal System of Renaissance France.* New Haven: Yale University Press, 1972.

Wrede, William. "Paul's Importance in the History of the World." In Thomas Kepler, ed., *Contemporary Thinking about Paul.* New York: Abingdon-Cokesbury Press, 1950.

Zawart, Anscar. *The History of Franciscan Preaching and of Franciscan Preachers (1209–1927).* New York: Wagner, 1928.

Zink, Michael. *La prédication en langue romane avant 1300.* Paris: Honoré Champion, 1976.

Index

Index